THE BEST PLAYS OF 1982–1983

THE
BURNS MANTLE
YEARBOOK

THE
BEST PLAYS
OF 1982-1983

EDITED BY OTIS L. GUERNSEY JR.

*Illustrated with photographs and
with drawings by* HIRSCHFELD

○○○○○○

DODD, MEAD & COMPANY
NEW YORK

EDITOR'S NOTE

DURING the past year, Dodd, Mead & Company, publisher of this series of *Best Plays* theater yearbooks since it began with the season of 1919–20, became a part of the larger corporate entity of Thomas Nelson Publishers. This has not changed the shape or direction of the series started by the late Burns Mantle and carried forward under the editorship of John Chapman, Louis Kronenberger, Henry Hewes and the incumbent. *The Best Plays of 1982–83* has the same devoted contributors in its various departments, the same diligent assistance by the editor's wife in striving for accuracy, the same careful supervision by Jonathan Dodd of Dodd, Mead, with the aim of putting out a superlatively informative and inspirited record of a year of American theater activity.

This 64th volume in the series contains complete factual details of every production on the professional New York stage in our listings of 1982–83 productions on and off Broadway, plus the most broadly comprehensive collection of program information about off off Broadway by Camille Croce and about regional theater transcontinentally acquired by Ella A. Malin. Rue Canvin keeps our record of necrology and publications; Stanley Green records the year's major cast replacements in New York shows at home, on tour and abroad; Henry Hewes provides details of the New York Drama Critics Circle voting, and William Schelble does the same for the Tonys. Additional and indispensable assistance with the facts is generously provided by scores of members of the theater's public relations departments, while others who have helped us keep the record broad and straight include Hobe Morrison of *Variety*, Ralph Newman of the Drama Book Shop, Robert Nahas of Theater Arts Book Shop, Alan Hewitt, Thomas T. Foose and Alfred Simon.

Significant developments for better or for worse within this wealth of data about 1982–83 are pointed out by the editor in his report on The Season in New York, while Mel Gussow, distinguished New York *Times* drama critic, does the same for the off-off-Broadway year. Al Hirschfeld's incomparable drawings enhance these pages as they do the pages of the *Times* during the season, and we are proud of his long and continuing participation in our project. On behalf of our readers, we extend our gratitude for the stage design sketches illustrative of the year's best work in this field (provided for us by Patricia Zipprodt, John Napier and Rita Ryack), as well as for the expressive photos which freeze the "look" of our theater in New York and across the country in the excellent work of Martha Swope, Bert Andrews, Mark Avery, Robert Burroughs, Jack Buxbaum, William B. Carter, Peter Cunningham, Zoë Dominic, Kenn Duncan, Anita Feldman-Shevett, Richard Feldman, David Friedman, Gerry Goodstein, Henry Grossman, James Hamilton, Andy Hanson, Barry Holniker, David Jiranek, Kenneth Kauffman, Joan Marcus, Mike Martin, Inge Morath, Lanny Nagler, Bill Pierce, Charles Rafshoon, Carol Rosegg, Jeff A. Slotnick, Ron M. Stone, Jay Thompson, Sandy Underwood and VMT Photo.

The inspirited part of our coverage annually reaches its climax in the synopses of New York's ten Best Plays and of the outstanding cross-country script. The former are selected solely by the editor, the latter by a committee of the American Theater Critics Association, headed by Ann Holmes of the Houston *Chronicle,* for inclusion in the *Best Plays* volume as an introduction to our section on The Theater Around the United States (together with brief reviews by critics around the country of other outstanding works nominated in this process, providing a panoramic view of the peaks of 1982–83 theater in the U.S.). These synopses of the Best Plays, prepared by the editor and two contemporary playwrights— Jeffrey Sweet and Sally Dixon Wiener—are like reflections on the wall of Plato's cave, as close an approximation of the real thing as possible within the limits of the medium. At the very least, they document the existence and personality of that reality: a vibrantly expressive theater, long predating Plato and long to outlast our reflective homage, capably tended by a large group of modern drama- tists which, like our *Best Plays* yearbook, refreshes and renews itself year after year.

OTIS L. GUERNSEY Jr.

July 1, 1983

CONTENTS

Drawings by HIRSCHFELD

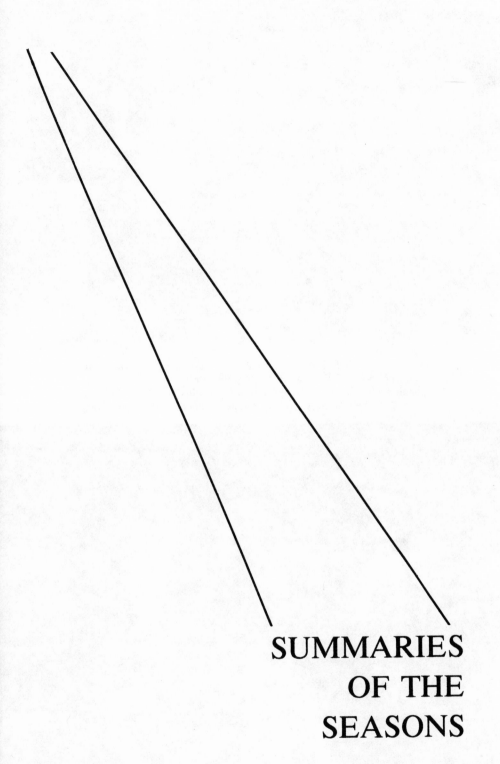

SUMMARIES
OF THE
SEASONS

MUSICAL HIGHLIGHTS OF 1982–83—*Above,* Twiggy *(center)* with aqua chorus (Jill Cook, Susan Hartley, Niki Harris, Nana Visitor, Stephanie Eley, Karen Tamburrelli) in *My One and Only; below,* a scene from *Cats* with René Ceballos, Bonnie Simmons and Donna King

THE SEASON IN NEW YORK

By Otis L. Guernsey Jr.

FOR the second season in a row, British playwrights dominated the New York stages. In 1981–82 they did it by standing especially tall with the towering, multi-award-winning *The Life & Adventures of Nicholas Nickleby*. In 1982–83 they did it with the force of numbers, pervading every production area with new scripts of major distinction.

The Best Plays list for 1982–83 records this transatlantic triumph with five of the ten from British dramatists: the musical *Cats* and the plays *Good* and *Foxfire* on Broadway, *Quartermaine's Terms* off Broadway and *Plenty* both off and on. And behind these loomed a backup contingent of strong 1982–83 British offerings in all shapes and sizes: *Slab Boys*, *Top Girls*, *Passion*, *Whodunnit*, *Steaming*, *Skirmishes*, plus the Royal Shakespeare Company's production of *All's Well That Ends Well*, in a humbling display of energy and virtuosity.

It's some consolation that the season's best-of-bests was the stark *'night, Mother*, Marsha Norman's piteously detailed study of suicidal despair; and that the American musical stage finally—*finally*—provided *My One and Only* to share the limelight with *Cats*, but it took a Gershwin score, Peter Stone co-authorship of the book and Tommy Tune dances to do it. Other American dramatists who made this year's Best Plays list were William Mastrosimone, in whose *Extremities* a victim of an attempted rape turns on her attacker; Patrick Meyers with his implacably cliff-hanging *K2*; and Lanford Wilson exposing various strong-minded individuals to a possible nuclear accident in *Angels Fall*.

So our American authors managed at last to occupy half the places on the Best Plays list. The other five were preempted by their British counterparts, as noted above: Andrew Lloyd Webber, Trevor Nunn and the late Anglicized American T.S. Eliot with their celebration of felinity in *Cats*; Susan Cooper and the Americanized Canadian Hume Cronyn with their Blue Ridge ballad, *Foxfire*; the late C.P. Taylor with a terrifying outline of creeping Nazism in *Good*; David Hare with a despairing view of what his Britain may have become in *Plenty*; and Simon Gray with still another closeup of self-destructive alienation in *Quartermaine's Terms* (and John Byrne's abrasive comedy of industrial underdogs, *Slab Boys*, came very close to making the list).

Two musicals and eight plays; six Broadway productions (*Cats*, *Good*, *Foxfire*; *'night, Mother*; *My One and Only*, *K2*), two off Broadway (*Extremities*, *Quartermaine's Terms*) and two transferred from off to on (*Plenty*, *Angels Fall*); four from London (*Cats*, *Good*, *Quartermaine's Terms*, *Plenty*), four from previous exposure in regional theater (*Foxfire*; *'night, Mother*; *Extremities*, *K2*), one produced directly for Broadway via Boston tryout (*My One and*

3

Only) and one directly for off Broadway (*Angels Fall*), with only one of the ten (as far as we know) ever having used OOB as a stepping stone along the way (*Extremities*); two professional playwriting debuts (Susan Cooper and Timothy S. Mayer, co-author of *My One and Only*) four repeat Best Play authors (Marsha Norman, Simon Gray, Peter Stone and Lanford Wilson), six if we count T.S. Eliot and the Gershwins—such was the composition of the 1982–83 Best Plays list.

Other best-challenging 1982–83 American works were, on Broadway, *Twice Around the Park* by Murray Schisgal; and, off Broadway, *Talking With* by "Jane Martin," the pseudonymous author of last season's ATCA selection brought to New York by Manhattan Theater Club; *Edmond* by David Mamet; *The Middle Ages* by A.R. Gurney Jr., and the musical *Little Shop of Horrors* by Howard Ashman and Alan Menken, which won this year's Critics Award for best musical. On the other side of the coin, our theater's need for a continuous supply of new authorship is strongly suggested by the unhappy 1982–83 showing of such "established" dramatists as Edward Albee, William Gibson, Betty Comden and Adolph Green, Jay Presson Allen, Alan Jay Lerner, Beth Henley and even Neil Simon, whose latest work *Brighton Beach Memoirs* fell far below his usual, unrivaled comic standard, the Critics Award for best-of-bests to the contrary notwithstanding.

A funny thing happened to the Broadway theater on the way to seemingly infinite riches: the price of a ticket was rising steadily toward the impossible dream of $50, with the $45 musical becoming a commonplace and *Cats* determined to go higher at the turn of the year, when the whole hydraulically inflationary process ran out of power. *Cats* never did make it to $50, at least not as of the end of the 1982–83 theater season on May 31. According to *Variety* estimate, the *average* paid Broadway admission had risen during the twelve months to $27.69 from $23.08 (which it had reached from $19.72 the year before); even so, the total overall Broadway gross fell off, failing to establish a new record for the first time in many seasons. It fell from $221 million last year to $203,126,127 in 1982–83, while the road receipts dropped from a record $249 million to $184,-321,475. These were still the second-highest New York and third-highest road grosses in theater history; but with production costs finding it possible to reach $4 million for a full-scale musical and $1 million for a straight play, these receding totals put the Broadway theater right in the middle of the 1980s recession along with everything else. Its most vital statistic—total paid attendance—fell off from about 10.7 million in 1981–82 to 8,102,262 in 1982–83, or about 73 per cent of capacity on the average, a level at which few Broadway productions could even hold their own, let alone ever make it into the black. This may account for the fact that of the 1982–83 Broadway offerings, only *Plenty* had paid off its investment as of the end of the season, according to *Variety*.

Now for the good news: production activity held up pretty well during the past year, both on and off Broadway. Not counting specialties, Broadway housed 49 new productions as compared with only 45 in 1981–82, 51 the year before that and 58 at a 1979–80 peak. This year's 49 included 14 revivals, so that the total number of new Broadway plays, musicals and revues amounted to 35, two more than last year, including three transfers and a return engagement. Musicals held

BRITISH COMEDIES—*Above,* Bob
Gunton, Cathryn Damon, E. Kather-
ine Kerr and Frank Langella in Peter
Nichols's *Passion; at right,* Sean Penn,
Kevin Bacon and Jackie Earle Haley
in John Byrne's *Slab Boys*

their level of ten new shows (plus three important, full-scale revival productions), and while new American plays fell off a bit, British imports took up the slack. The bad activity news was the continuing drop in Broadway playing weeks (if ten shows play ten weeks, that's 100 playing weeks) from the record 1,545 in 1980–81 to 1,461 in 1981–82 to 1,259 in 1982–83.

Off Broadway, the production of new plays and musicals (routinely at a $14–16 top but rising above $20 on occasion) also held steady, reaching 59 in 1982–83 after 60 last year. The pinch was felt most strongly off Broadway in the demise of the Phoenix Theater, which called it quits after 30 years of distinguished contribution to the New York stage; and in the wavering of some groups moving their productions up and down across the boundary between off and off off Broadway, with their differing commitments, at the mercy of the ebb and flow of financial tides. Only Manhattan Theater Club and Circle Repertory Company seemed to strengthen in 1982–83, the former bringing all of its Upstage offerings (previously OOB) up to off-Broadway status equal to its Downstage productions, and the latter mounting a remarkable parade of new scripts by American dramatists.

Financial data on individual shows didn't seem to be disseminated as freely as in past seasons, but there were inklings of both triumph and disaster in what few press reports were available. In these random *Variety* citations of recent figures on a series of hit musicals, note the rising production costs: *Company* (1970), $245,000 profit on an original investment of $530,000; *Nine* (1982), $546,000 profit on $2,750,000; *A Doll's Life* (1982), a clean loss at $4 million; *My One and Only* (1983), capitalized at $2,750,000 but reported to have cost over $4 million. And the March 1983 West Coast production of *Dreamgirls* cost almost as much to put on ($3 million) as the original 1981 Broadway version ($3.6 million)—but *Dreamgirls* paid off its huge nut in 34 weeks, by August 1982, something of a modern record.

Under such conditions, it can come as a surprise to few that producing shows in the New York theater of 1982–83 has evolved from an impresario to a team effort, with numbers that rival a baseball aggregation, the bench included (i.e., it took nine producers to put on the musical *Nine* a year ago, and five *organizations* plus four producers for *All's Well That Ends Well* this season). As a corollary, an active producing unit was apt to make the team of a goodly number of shows (gone were the days when one impresario laid one egg, golden or otherwise, or nursed one chicken to maturity). By our count—and it's possible that we've overlooked one or more at bats—Kennedy Center and/or Roger L. Stevens were most active, participating in ten (*Ghosts, Twice Around the Park, Monday After the Miracle, Angels Fall, On Your Toes, Dance a Little Closer, Show Boat, The Caine Mutiny Court-Martial* and the two Broadway-bound plays that closed out of town, *Outrage* and *Make and Break*). Slightly less active but even more conspicuous was The Shubert Organization with eight, four of them Best Plays (*Cats, Good, Angels Fall;* '*night, Mother; Marcel Marceau* and *All's Well That Ends Well* on Broadway and *The Middle Ages* and *Little Shop of Horrors* off). James M. Nederlander got into the game with six (*Ghosts, A Doll's Life, Merlin, Dance a Little Closer, Teaneck Tanzi: The Venus Flytrap* and *Show Boat*), two of them very costly and very short-lived musicals.

Claire Nichtern's Warner Theater Productions also backed six (*A Doll's Life*, *Good*, *Foxfire*, *The Wake of Jamey Foster*, *A Little Family Business* and *Twice Around the Park*), two of them Best Plays. David Geffen's name was on *Cats*, *Good* and *Little Shop of Horrors*—two Best Plays and a Critics Award winner. Elizabeth I. McCann and Nelle Nugent continued their class act with *Good* and *All's Well That Ends Well* but suffered a setback with *Total Abandon*. Paramount Theater Productions covered itself with the glory of *My One and Only* and *Slab Boys*; CBS Broadcast Group put its money on *Ghosts*; Radio City put on *Porgy and Bess* and then went outside the Music Hall and put its toe in the water of *Brighton Beach Memoirs*; Columbia Pictures Stage Productions gave us *Merlin*, while ABC and M-G-M participated in *All's Well That Ends Well*.

The year's most flamboyant direction was Trevor Nunn's of *Cats*, for which he won the best-musical-direction Tony; and he also staged the visiting *All's Well That Ends Well* and was nominated for the best-play-direction Tony. The most beguiling was Tommy Tune's and Thommie Walsh's of *My One and Only*. Robert Allan Ackerman had an outstanding season with the Best Play *Extremities* and *Slab Boys*, as did Marshall W. Mason with the Best Play *Angels Fall* and *Passion*, not forgetting David Trainer (*Foxfire*), Terry Schreiber (*K2*), Tom Moore ('*night, Mother*), Howard Davies (*Good*), Arvin Brown (*A View From the Bridge*) and nonagenarian George Abbott revitalizing his own musical *On Your Toes*. Other authors who staged their own work this season with either marked success or marked absence of it were Howard Ashman (*Little Shop of Horrors*), James Roose-Evans (*84 Charing Cross Road*), Eva Le Gallienne (*Alice in Wonderland*), Edward Albee (*The Man Who Had Three Arms*), David Hare (*Plenty*) and Alan Jay Lerner (*Dance a Little Closer*).

Design achievement, like beauty, is very much in the eye of the beholder, and Ming Cho Lee certainly knocked it out with his representation of a Himalayan 20,000-footer in *K2*. So did John Napier with set and Tony-winning costumes of *Cats*. John Lee Beatty had a phenomenally prolific and effective season of set design with *The Middle Ages*, *Monday After the Miracle*, *Alice in Wonderland*, *Angels Fall*, *What I Did Last Summer* and *Passion*. Other shows that in the eye of this beholder seemed unusually well served by their scenery were *Foxfire* (David Mitchell, who also did *Brighton Beach Memoirs*, *Dance a Little Closer* and *Private Lives*), *Steaming* (Marjorie Bradley Kellogg, who also did *Extremities*, *Wild Life*, *Present Laughter*, *The Misanthrope* and the short-lived *Moose Murders*), *My One and Only* (Adrianne Lobel), *Slab Boys* (by its author, John Byrne), *84 Charing Cross Road* (Oliver Smith) and *Whodunnit* (Andrew Jackness), the latter play enjoying the standout costume designs of Patricia Zipprodt, who also costumed *Alice in Wonderland* (after the Tenniel drawings), *Brighton Beach Memoirs* and *Don Juan*.

Busiest this season among the costume creators was Theoni V. Aldredge with *Ghosts*, *A Little Family Business*, *Merlin*, *Hamlet*, *Private Lives* and *Buried Inside Extra*. Jennifer Von Mayrhauser costumed *The Wake of Jamey Foster*, *Steaming*, *Angels Fall*, *What I Did Last Summer* and *Passion*. And John Byrne's costumes for his own *Slab Boys*, Pearl Somner's for *84 Charing Cross Road*, Jane Greenwood's for *Plenty* and Rita Ryack's for *My One and Only*

Pictured *above* are examples of Patricia Zipprodt's costume design sketches for Anthony Shaffer's comedy thriller *Whodunnit,* for the characters Lady Tremurrain (A Dotty Aristocrat) at *left* and Lavinia Hargreaves (A Sweet Young Thing) at *right*

seemed particularly well adapted to the mood and content of their productions.

Annually, the saddest tale we have to tell is of gifted actors and actresses left stranded in the glare of public attention by the collapse of flimsy vehicles. In 1982–83, this bitter experience was shared by the likes of Jane Alexander, Leslie Uggams, Angela Lansbury, John McMartin, Robert Drivas, Kevin O'Connor, Richard Dreyfuss, Georgia Engel, George Rose, Peter Falk and Len Cariou. In heavy counterbalance, there were the major 1982–83 achievements of the New York acting community: Jessica Tandy with Hume Cronyn in *Foxfire* and Kathy Bates with Anne Pitoniak in *'night, Mother* . . . Alan Howard becoming a Nazi in *Good* . . . Tommy Tune as a tall, bashful, 1920s aviator who can also tap-dance up a storm in *My One and Only*, in partnership with the soulful Twiggy . . . Jeffrey De Munn clinging to the ice wall in *K2* . . . Susan Sarandon hoisting James Russo on his own petard in *Extremities* . . . The calculated repulsiveness of Nicol Williamson in *The Entertainer*, John Malkovich in *True West* and Kate Nelligan in *Plenty* . . . The subtle magnetism of Joseph Maher and Ellen Burstyn in *84 Charing Cross Road* and of Remak Ramsay in *Quartermaine's Terms* . . . The special star quality of Sean Penn in *Slab Boys*, Judith Ivey in *Steaming*, George C. Scott in *Present Laughter*, Tony Lo Bianco in *A View From the Bridge*, Matthew Broderick in *Brighton Beach Memoirs* and Harvey Fierstein repeating his *Torch Song Trilogy* for Broadway audiences . . . The comic personae of Eli Wallach and Anne Jackson in *Twice Around the Park*, and of Frank Langella and Bob Gunton in pursuit of Roxanne

Hart in *Passion* . . . Jason Robards at the head of a star-studded cast in the latest return of *You Can't Take It With You* . . . Betty Buckley, Timothy Scott and company in *Cats* . . . The ensembles of *Talking With* and *Top Girls* (both British and American casts). Such were the 1982–83 performance impressions foremost in memory and likely to be the last to fade from it.

The ultimate insignia of New York professional theater achievement (we insist) are the Best Plays citations in these volumes, designations which are 16 years older than the Critics Awards and only three years younger than the Pulitzer Prizes. Each Best Play selection is now made with the script itself as the first consideration, for the reason (as we've stated in previous volumes) that the script is the spirit of the theater's physical manifestation. It is not only the quintessence of the present, it is most of what endures into the future. So the Best Plays are the best scripts, with as little weight as humanly possible given to comparative production values. The choice is made without any regard whatever to a play's type—musical, comedy or drama—or origin on or off Broadway, or popularity at the box office, or lack of same.

We don't take the scripts of other eras into consideration for Best Play citation in this one, whatever their technical status as American or New York "premieres" which didn't happen to have a previous production of record. We draw the line between adaptations and revivals, the former eligible for Best Play selection but the latter not, on a case-by-case basis. We likewise consider the eligibility of borderline examples of limited-engagement and showcase production case by case, ascertaining whether they're probably "frozen" in final script version and no longer works-in-progress before considering them for Best Play citation (and in the case of a late-season arrival the determination may not be possible until the following year).

If a script influences the very character of a season, or by some function of consensus wins the Critics, Pulitzer or Tony Awards, we take into account its future historical as well as present esthetic importance. This is the only special consideration we give, and we don't always tilt in its direction, as the record shows.

The ten Best Plays of 1982–83 are listed here for visual convenience in the order in which they opened in New York (a plus sign + with the performance number signifies that the play was still running after May 31, 1983).

Cats
  (Broadway; 270+ perfs.)

Extremities
  (Off Broadway; 182+ perfs.)

Good
  (Broadway; 125 perfs.)

Quartermaine's Terms
  (Off Broadway; 111+ perfs.)

Angels Fall
  (Off 65; Broadway 64 perfs.)

K2
  (Broadway; 71+ perfs.)

Plenty
  (Off 45; Broadway 92 perfs.)

'night, Mother
  (Broadway; 70+ perfs.)

Foxfire
  (Broadway; 213 perfs.)

My One and Only
  (Broadway; 33+ perfs.)

BRIGHTON BEACH MEMOIRS—Mandy Ingber, Matthew Broderick, Elizabeth Franz, Joyce Van Patten and Jodi Thelen in a scene from the Critics Award-winning comedy by Neil Simon

Broadway

In the vanguard of this season's British parade was the vivacious and imaginative *Cats*, in which Andrew Lloyd Webber set portions of T.S. Eliot's *Old Possum's Book of Practical Cats* to music, with additional material based on Eliot works adapted by Trevor Nunn and Richard Stilgoe (the exact etymology of this show's libretto is described in Nunn's *Playbill* footnote, quoted in the *Cats* portion of the Best Plays section of this volume). To begin with, Eliot's verses are irresistible. The cast acted them out in high spirits, tails up and costumed by John Napier to appear uniformly feline in vividly individualistic ways (see the *Cats* photos in the Best Plays section of this volume); and Napier's deliberately overblown set represented a cat-scale garbage dump—that is, the simulated trash on the Winter Garden's stage was enlarged so that the size of strewn objects was in the same proportion to the human actors as those in a real dump would be to real cats. A whispered suggestion of "plot" was superimposed on the Eliot sketches: an aged puss named Grizabella (Betty Buckley), mourning past possibilities in her hapless present with the haunting ballad "Memory," is magically endowed with new life by sage Old Deuteronomy (Ken Page) in another sphere beyond the Heaviside Layer. But the main business of this theme musical was to fill its theater with essence of Cat with a capital C (the word is always capitalized in the Eliot poems) in the many personalities of the agile ensemble featuring such as Timothy Scott (Mistoffolees), Terrence V. Mann (Rum Tum Tugger), Stephen Hanan (Growltiger) and Bonnie Simmons (Jellylorum). Under Nunn's direction, *Cats* was a live wire crackling with cat-fur electricity of humor and style.

The *Cats* company barely had time to read its notices before the arrival from London of another British Best Play: the late C.P. Taylor's *Good* in the Royal Shakespeare Company's production, starring Alan Howard under the direction of Howard Davies in the role of a German university professor, a veteran of World War I, who temporizes little by little the Nazi encroachment upon his life and ideals, until finally he out-Himmlers Himmler. As the playwright saw it, the act of becoming a Nazi was a bitterly comedic act, however ghastly its effect. The professor has a mother who is succumbing to senility in a nursing home, which she detests; he writes a book in which the case for euthanasia is considered; he is recruited by Eichmann to make reports in this field; then, inadvertently but inevitably, he loses himself forever in the smoke of burning books, the sound of breaking glass, the smell of escaping gas. The professor's one clear obsession is music, and Taylor used snatches of songs, symphonies, etc. to set the mood for each sequence of *Good* (a title making reference to "good" Germans), which was itself like a musical composition of briefly experienced notes of character (Hitler, Goebbels, etc.), some recurring and some not. All these notes found their place in a scheme which brought Howard's portrayal of intellectual-turned-viper to its climax: a black-uniformed SS officer with pinched features under the peaked cap, pulling on his leather gloves preparatory to going to see how he can improve efficiency at Auschwitz. In Howard's memorable performance, he is the principal victim of his own venomous progress, the clownish point of a horror story.

Still another 1982–83 British Best Play came to Broadway the long way round, from London's National Theater to Chicago to New York Shakespeare Festival downtown, and finally under the same auspices uptown. *Plenty* was the star of Joseph Papp's season, and Kate Nelligan was the dark star of *Plenty* in the role of an English Anywoman who, after rising to the demanding occasion of World War II, disintegrates in parallel with what she sees as her country's decay in the post-war period into crass commercial, political and social expediency. Hers is a slow-motion tantrum of selfishness, with Miss Nelligan turning herself and her character into a thoroughly reprehensible person, and with Edward Herrmann as her diplomat-husband trying to cope with his wife's mental and emotional disintegration, symbolizing that of her country. Written and directed by David Hare, *Plenty* was not so much a requiem for the England that was, as a head-on confrontation of what England might become, in a play that was both arresting and repellent.

The inimitable *Foxfire* must also be credited to this category of foreign plays, though it doesn't comfortably fit there. Its authors, though U.S. residents, are British (Susan Cooper) and Canadian (Hume Cronyn). Its subject—the life and times of a hardscrabble Georgia hillbilly farm couple—is as American as its production here on Broadway (but it *did* have its first production in Toronto). One thing is perfectly clear, however: it belongs on the 1982–83 Best Plays list

with a script, adapted from material on Appalachia edited by Eliot Wigginton, that captures and gently celebrates the rough-hewn, indomitable character
of these mountain folk. Yes, there were shining performances: Jessica Tandy as
an aging farm widow clinging to her mountain home and her memories of her
ornery husband (Hume Cronyn), while trying to understand her guitar-playing
son (Keith Carradine). David Trainer's direction maintained the clarity of scenes
which shifted through the present in reality, the present in imagination and
various points of past time, and David Mitchell's mountain-view set was most
appealing. Intercraft and international collaboration was the open secret of
Foxfire's success, with writing, performances, direction and design serving each
other with conspicuously heartwarming results.

Foxfire and *Good* and probably even *Plenty* are comedies in the broadest sense
of that term. In the simple dimension of laughter, however, nothing this season
exceeded *Slab Boys*, another foreign visitor traveling the long way from Edinburgh, London, regional theater and off off Broadway to a small house in the West
Forties. The boys of this John Byrne script's title are wage slaves mixing pigments
in the battered back room of a studio for designers of carpets and wall paper.
Social and educational discards, they are out of reach of even the bottom rung
of any ladder, but they have developed a style of their own and the imagination
to relieve the drudgery and monotony by splashing their walls with color and
their lives with an irrepressible comic spirit expressed in arrogance toward their
superiors and an infinite variety of pranks played on each other. Under Robert
Allan Ackerman's open-throttle direction, in a paint-spattered set designed by the
play's author, the back-room types—bully, gaffer, victim, tea lady, even sex object
—were led through their energetic paces by Sean Penn as the head boy looking
as though he had been born working at his slab. The comedic form was familiar
and the message obvious (youth against the demeaning world), but the laughter
was plentiful in this Scottish version of the tale.

Peter Nichols's *Passion* (known in London as *Passion Play*) also concentrated on
the winsome notes at the lighter end of the scale, exploring comic possibilities of
love among characters who are not only of two minds but in some cases also of two
embodiments. In this play by the author of *Joe Egg*, husband and wife have been
virtually faithful to each other in long and respectable wedlock. The wife has had
one minor fling but is now ready to settle for home and husband, at precisely the
moment that the husband, who has never strayed, is ready to surrender to the
charms of a cheerful young blonde (Roxanne Hart) swinging a tantalizing mini-
skirt. Husband and wife were each played by two performers dressed alike and
working in tandem but not in unison, representing different aspects of each
personality in each circumstance. Bob Gunton and Cathryn Damon were the
long-married couple keeping up appearances, while Frank Langella and E. Katherine Kerr moved about more freely as the adventurous side of their natures, acting
out impulses which the sedate pair might never even dare express in words.
Inevitably, *Passion* ran down into sitcom after a while; but certainly in its first half
it was subtly and amusingly insightful into some of the ways of affection.

Other British imports to Broadway represented the London stage in an even
more frivolous mood. Nell Dunn's *Steaming* featured a group of women skinny-
dipping in an onstage swimming pool; but it was more remarkable for the engag-

The 1982–83 Season on Broadway

PLAYS (15)

Torch Song Trilogy (transfer)
The Wake of Jamey Foster
Twice Around the Park
84 Charing Cross Road
Monday After the Miracle
A Little Family Business
Almost an Eagle
ANGELS FALL (transfer)
Moose Murders
Brighton Beach Memoirs
K2
'NIGHT, MOTHER
The Man Who Had Three Arms
Total Abandon
Breakfast With Les and Bess

MUSICALS (10)

Blues in the Night
Cleavage
Play Me a Country Song
Seven Brides for Seven Brothers
Your Arms Too Short to Box With God (return engagement)
A Doll's Life
CATS
Merlin
MY ONE AND ONLY
Dance a Little Closer

FOREIGN PLAYS IN ENGLISH (8)

GOOD
FOXFIRE
Steaming
Whodunnit
PLENTY
Slab Boys
Teaneck Tanzi: The Venus Flytrap
Passion

REVUES (2)

Rock 'n Roll: The First 5,000 Years
The Flying Karamazov Brothers

REVIVALS (14)

Circle in the Square: Present Laughter
The Queen and the Rebels
The Misanthrope
The Caine Mutiny Court-Martial
Ghosts
Alice in Wonderland
A View From the Bridge
On Your Toes
You Can't Take It With You
Porgy and Bess
All's Well That Ends Well
Show Boat
The Ritz
Private Lives

SPECIALTIES (3)

Herman van Veen: All of Him
Marcel Marceau on Broadway
Aznavour

HOLDOVERS WHICH BECAME HITS IN 1982–83

Dreamgirls
Nine

Categorized above are all the new productions listed in the Plays Produced on Broadway section of this volume.
Plays listed in CAPITAL LETTERS have been designated Best Plays of 1982–83.
Plays listed in *italics* were still running after May 31, 1983.
Plays listed in **bold face type** were classified as hits in *Variety*'s annual estimate published June 1, 1983.

TWICE AROUND THE PARK—Anne Jackson and Eli Wallach as wife and husband in the "A Need for Less Expertise" segment of Murray Schisgal's two-part comedy

ing performance of Judith Ivey as an open-hearted, man-loving Cockney lass than for its dialogue about sex and sexism. Anthony Shaffer's *Whodunnit* (previously seen in London as *The Case of the Oily Levantine*) was a takeoff of the country-house murder mystery, with a gloomily paneled set by Andrew Jackness and deceitful costumes by Patricia Zipprodt for a set of duplicitous Agatha-Christie-type characters confronting one another with chicanery and menace. The caricature was almost too perfect—right down to the identity of the killer—for *Whodunnit* to achieve the full maturity as a work of theater reached by the author's previous *Sleuth*. As for a third comic entry from Britain, *Teaneck Tanzi: The Venus Flytrap* (staging the battle of the sexes as a wrestling match with its theater, the Nederlander, temporarily converted into a wrestling arena), it visited

Broadway for only a single performance, the only foreign play so short-lived this season (American authors suffered the same fate with two plays—*Moose Murders* and *Total Abandon*—one revival—*The Ritz*—and three musicals—*Cleavage*, *Play Me a Country Song* and *Dance a Little Closer*).

American playwrights kept part of this season's franchise by dominating the drama category both on and off Broadway, most notably with the Pulitzer Prize-winning (on the basis of its Boston production) Best Play (in Broadway production) '*night, Mother* by Marsha Norman, a closeup of a suicide—not the act itself, but its motivation. A clock on the wall of an appropriately nondescript living-room-kitchen set (the work of Heidi Landesman) marked time running out without intermission or faltering of purpose for a daughter (Kathy Bates) who informs her mother (Anne Pitoniak) that she has made all the necessary arrangements for her carefully considered and planned suicide, which she intends to effect by pistol shot this very evening. After the older woman's reflexive "No!" came the pleading "Why?", the question which lay at the heart of this play's paralyzing matter. Is the intended suicide agonized by disease? (No, but she has had epilepsy, now under control.) Is she suffering unrequited love? (No, but her husband has long since left her, and so has her son, a flagrant delinquent.) Is she a lonely outcast? (No, but she is not "good company" either.) Is she insane? (No, it is her very inward-probing intelligence which has brought her to this brink.) She is simply an unremarkable human being who, perhaps through little fault of her own, was unable to realize any of her modest dreams and now finds her existence devoid of any pleasure, opportunity or meaning, or the prospect of any. Her life is empty, and she says "No" to hope. Inside, there remains to her the resolve to be master of her fate and to make an efficient exit. She asks herself "Why not?", and the terror of this play took the form of gradually dawning awareness that all the mother's arguments (and all the reassurances that came most quickly to mind as we listened to the daughter's conclusions) would be inadequate to deflect her inexorable purpose. Miss Bates's starring performance was excruciatingly matter-of-fact in contrast to the subject, while Miss Pitoniak's encompassed both fear and pity with scarcely a trace of love. Tom Moore's direction earned its share of applause, maintaining an even texture and total concentration on Miss Norman's moving, disturbing, perplexing theme, in a play which was certainly the best-of-bests of this 1982–83 New York season.

The standard of drama was also held high by Patrick Meyers in *K2*, a literally cliff-hanging adventure of two climbers whose place in history has been assured because they have just scaled the Himalayas' second-highest peak, but whose lives are in extreme jeopardy because of an accident that has taken place on the way back, exacerbated by a careless omission in preparing for the expedition. The two men are trapped on a ledge indenting the sheer ice wall. The team leader (Jeffrey De Munn), a macho district attorney in civilian life, has neglected to include in his pack the spare length of rope essential for lowering his teammate (Jay Patterson), a physicist and liberal humanist, who cannot climb down because he has broken his leg in a fall to this ledge. The former will have to climb back up to retrieve discarded rope, if they are both to survive. Ming Cho Lee designed a shockingly bleak and forbidding mountain soaring out of sight above the rim of the proscenium. De Munn (and director Terry Schreiber) devised agile means

STEAMING—Linda Thorson, Margaret Whitton and Judith Ivey in the comedy by Nell Dunn

of climbing it that created a compelling illusion within the compact, intermissionless running time. An ongoing right-vs.-left discussion between the two men established an emotional context for their adventure in this Best Play, which was just about as theatrical as the theater can get.

Lanford Wilson turned his attention from the Talley family (*Fifth of July*, *Talley's Folly*, *A Tale Told*) to the more pressing question of 20th-century reaction to the ever-present possibility of nuclear holocaust. Wilson's Best Play *Angels Fall* (transferred to Broadway after its premiere at Circle Repertory) imagines a nuclear emergency in New Mexico, with the Army hovering overhead in helicopters, sounding the alarm and sending people in the area to shelter. A random assortment of folks take cover in a mission: a renegade professor (Fritz Weaver), his supportive wife (Nancy Snyder), a patroness of art (Tanya Berezin) and her tennis-champ consort (Brian Tarantina), an aggressively promising young Indian doctor (Danton Stone) and a jocular mission priest (Barnard Hughes) maintaining Catholicism in the desert, even if it means conducting the Mass in Navaho. On the whole, their individual convictions (the professor's that his own teaching has lacked validity, the doctor's to become a researcher instead of a local M.D., the priest's faith in God and man) hold up under the weight of the emergency. No major detonation takes place, of course (New Mexico is still there, even in imagination), but there were plenty of bursts of irony and provocation among the characters, whose development in this dramatic process was given sharp outlines in Wilson's writing and Marshall W. Mason's direction.

In a lighter vein of domestic playwriting was Murray Schisgal's *Twice Around the Park*, a pair of one-act two-character comedies written, acted (by the Wallachs, Eli and Anne Jackson) and directed (by Arthur Storch) as episodes in the ongoing identity clash between men and women, so painful to experience, so amusing to observe. In the first, he was an actor and she was a female cop who lives upstairs and comes down to give him a summons for disturbing the peace with his noisy rehearsing—but the lady is distracted by his romantic ploys. In the second, they were a modern middle-aged couple trying to juice up their drab marriage with a tape-recording of instructions by a cultist sex guru. Masterfully constructed and executed, Schisgal's concept resembled those which Neil Simon has handled so very adroitly in the past, but which eluded Simon's grasp in this season's *Brighton Beach Memoirs*, a series of crayon-colored caricatures of puberty and other matters in a Brooklyn boyhood, reputedly based somewhat on the author's own, received by many theatergoers with laughtrack enthusiasm but leaving others cold. Its major asset was the ingenious performance of the youth by Matthew Broderick, who appeared off Broadway last season as the teen-ager in the final segment of Harvey Fierstein's *Torch Song Trilogy*. In early June 1982, Fierstein transferred this 1981–82 Best Play (on the basis of its off-Broadway showing) and his own outstanding performance as the drag queen in it to Broadway, flavoring the uptown season with its bittersweet comedy and collecting the 1983 Tonys for both best play and best performance. Young Broderick, who won the 1983 featured-actor Tony for his performance in Simon's play, had long since left the cast of Fierstein's.

A real charmer was *84 Charing Cross Road*, the true story of pen-pal affection blossoming between a book-loving New Yorker and the manager of a London second-hand-book store supplying her literary needs by mail over a period of 32 years, adapted and directed by James Roose-Evans from Helene Hanff's book. Joseph Maher's restrained, sensitive portrayal of the London bookman, opposite Ellen Burstyn as Miss Hanff, was one of the season's acting gems. In the play as in reality, the two never met; by the time she was able to travel to England, her bookdealer friend had died. For all its virtues, *84 Charing Cross Road* suffered from its determination to remain true to the original, so that an obligatory scene—a face-to-face meeting, at last, between the two transatlantic friends—was missing.

William Gibson took another look at his *The Miracle Worker* pair in a 16-years-after sequel, *Monday After the Miracle*, with the relationship between now world-famous Helen Keller (Karen Allen) and her mentor Annie Sullivan (Jane Alexander) disturbed by the presence and personality of a man (William Converse-Roberts) who arrives on the scene as a literary advisor for Helen and stays to marry Annie. This emotionally searching play, directed by Arthur Penn who also did *Miracle Worker*, was abruptly withdrawn after only 7 performances but inspired minority partisanship and looks like making a place for itself on the international theater scene. A less promising future might be predicted for Edward Albee's 1983 effort *The Man Who Had Three Arms*, a diatribe about celebrity delivered in lecture form by Robert Drivas as "Himself" under the author's own direction. Beth Henley followed her prizewinning *Crimes of the Heart* with *The Wake of Jamey Foster*, about another small-town family in crisis but lacking the deadly aim of her previous work. Jay Presson Allen entered the lists again with the adaptation of a French comedy by Pierre Barillet and Jean-Pierre Gredy, *A Little Family Business*, with Angela Lansbury as a wife taking over her ailing husband's affairs, this time without the success of the collaborators' previous *Forty Carats*. Lee Kalcheim's *Breakfast With Les and Bess* brought

the tribulations of a radio talk show couple all the way from OOB to a Broadway production. Another entry, *Almost an Eagle*, sputtered briefly with Boy Scout adventures, while *Moose Murders* attempted a spoof of murder mysteries for only a single performance, a fate shared by *Total Abandon*, with Richard Dreyfuss as a divorced father who violently abuses his infant son.

If a disastrous musical season can be redeemed at the 11th hour by a single show, then 1982–83 on Broadway can be said to have achieved success through the arrival in May of *My One and Only*—but except for the borrowed finery of *Cats*, magicianship and revivals, it was a disaster on all other counts. Full-scale musical productions folded one after another, on occasion after only 1 performance lambasted by the reviewers, with single-show losses estimated in the millions.

Three modest theme-musical pot pourris started things off inauspiciously in June: *Blues in the Night*, a compendium of 24 mostly blues numbers by various authors; plus *Cleavage* and *Play Me a Country Song*, haplessly folding after only 1 performance each. Next came the disappointing full-scale production of a stage version of the M-G-M musical *Seven Brides for Seven Brothers* for a mere 5 performances. A limited return engagement of Vinnette Carroll's inspiring *Your Arms Too Short to Box With God* lifted spirits which were destined soon to be dashed by another disappointing major musical effort, *A Doll's Life* by Betty Comden, Adolph Green and Larry Grossman, which imagined Nora's struggle

CATS COSTUMES—Pictured here are examples of John Napier's Tony Award-winning costume designs for the British musical, as follows: *far left,* on opposite page, the design for the character Skimbleshanks; *left,* for Bombalurina; *right,* for Growltiger. Photos of the actors portraying these characters and wearing these costumes in the show appear in the frontispiece to this section and in the *Cats* coverage in the Best Plays section

to survive on her own in the male chauvinistic 19th century after she walked out on her husband and slammed the door in Ibsen's play *A Doll's House*. Co-produced and directed by Harold Prince, this show was a smoothly crafted failure of expertise, dismally skillful, vanishing into the mists after only 5 performances despite its gilt-edged credentials.

The distinguished visitor *Cats* then lit the lights in the New York musical theater in October and kept them burning and beckoning. Except for some handsome revivals, the only response was *Merlin*, a Doug Henning magic show in a musical wrapper, with Henning's spectacular illusions coming off far more believably than his efforts to portray King Arthur's wizard as a young man in a book and score crammed into the interstices between his magic tricks.

Then in May, to nearly everyone's delighted astonishment, there arrived what could rationally be labeled a "new" Gershwin musical, *My One and Only*, taking its place beside *Cats* on our list of 1982–83 Best Plays on the basis of its charming book by Peter Stone and Timothy S. Mayer (parenthetically, the Tony eligibility committee declared both musicals eligible for nomination in all "new" categories, excepting only the Gershwin score of *My One and Only* because it had been previously used in shows, but not excepting the Eliot verses of *Cats* because they hadn't). The musical's joyful presence was all the more uplifting because it was so unexpected. When *My One and Only* began its tryout engagement in Boston in February, it was billed as "a new production of George and Ira Gershwin's *Funny Face*," with a new book and appropriate numbers from other shows augmenting the *Funny Face* score. Initial reaction was mixed, but instead of saying die the participants went to work to develop their show. The supremely accomplished librettist Peter Stone came in to work on the book about the romance between a boyish 1920s aviator (who is going to fly the Atlantic non-stop solo in what looks like a Ryan monoplane) and a wide-eyed flapper celebrated for having swum the English Channel. The star and co-choreographer Tommy Tune, whose current credits include no less than the direction of the long-run hits *Nine* and *Cloud 9*, took over the staging with his colleague Thommie Walsh, and other show business friends-in-need like Mike Nichols were said to have been helpful.

Thirteen weeks and an estimated $4.5 million later, *My One and Only* opened on Broadway—a spectacular surprise hit, remarkable not only in that each and every department was worthy of the exhilarating Gershwin tunes, but also that the many individual contributions had been brought together into a seamlessly unified whole. As the gangling aviator, Tommy Tune was an engaging presence, and of course an absolutely superb dancer. Twiggy showed herself capable of playing Ginger Rogers to his Astaire in both song and dance, with a twinkle in her eye that would have excused much, had there been anything to excuse. The Stone-Mayer book was a musical comedy masterpiece—not a developed theme, or a "play with music," or an opera manqué, but a *musical comedy* honoring its glorious form like *42nd Street*, stylishly warm and lighthearted, unselfconscious except in the service of wit, tongue sometimes inimitably in cheek but taking pains to avoid pastiche, all in fun and quite a trick if you can make it work. The Tune-Walsh dances, showing off Tune's limber limbs and the close-order work of a lively chorus, were also masterful. The attractive cardboard-cutout scenery by Adrianne Lobel and flapper-era costumes of Rita Ryack contributed to the merriment, as did the supporting performances in every instance, particularly those of Charles "Honi" Coles matching wits and taps with Tommy Tune, Denny Dillon as a slangy but cherubic grease monkey, Bruce McGill as a deep-dyed villain, the New Rhythm Boys (David Jackson, Ken Leigh Rogers and Ronald Dennis) setting the show's pace and the Ritz Quartette echoing its spirit with sweet harmonies. Tommy Tune's entire cohort put *My One and Only* right up there alongside other memorable Gershwin musical comedies, and they looked for all the world as though they were having fun doing it.

But before the month of May and the season ended, Broadway was to suffer still another major musical disappointment. Much was expected of *Dance a Little Closer*, an updated musical version of Robert E. Sherwood's *Idiot's Delight*, with book, lyrics and direction by Alan Jay Lerner. The Charles Strouse score seemed perfectly adequate, and Len Cariou played Harry, the American hoofer, as though he were testing the tensile strength of the character, but the show around him could not find its feet or settle on an approach to its tale of the international set awaiting the beginning of a new World War in a luxury Austrian resort hotel. At any rate, *Dance a Little Closer* closed after only 1 performance, an expensive (in wasted talent as well as cost) debacle.

The revue form made its appearance twice this season on Broadway, in *Rock 'n Roll: The First 5,000 Years*, a show which promoted that musical genre with

ON YOUR TOES—Lara Teeter and Natalia Makarova in the "Slaughter on Tenth Avenue" ballet in the Tony Award-winning revival of the Rodgers and Hart musical, directed by co-author George Abbott

60—count 'em, 60—musical numbers; and *The Flying Karamazov Brothers*, a variety show of juggling, comedy and other displays at the Ritz Theater, newly refurbished for legitimate stage use. Broadway theaters also housed a number of one-man concert-style shows during the year, among them those of Barry Manilow, the pop singer; Charles Aznavour, the French balladeer; and Herman van Veen, the Dutch comedian. And internationally renowned Marcel Marceau paid Broadway a visit with a program which included half a dozen new pantomimes among the Bip and other characterizations in his famed repertory.

Here's where we list the *Best Plays* choices for the top individual achievements of the season on and off Broadway. In the acting categories, clear distinction among "starring," "featured" or "supporting" players can't be made on the basis of official billing, which is as much a matter of contracts as of esthetics. Here in these volumes we divide acting into "primary" and "secondary" roles, a primary role being one which might some day cause a star to inspire a revival in order to appear in that character. All others, be they vivid as Mercutio, are classed as secondary. And we have an example this season of how fine even this line must sometimes be drawn. Kathy Bates and Anne Pitoniak are equally challenged and equally achieve in the two roles of *'night, Mother*; but, being convinced that no one would revive this outstanding play in order to appear in the latter's role, we have categorized it as secondary to the other's primary. In any event, both superbly gifted actresses appear among our best selections below.

Furthermore, our list of individual bests makes room for more than a single choice when appropriate. We believe that no useful purpose is served by forcing ourselves into an arbitrary selection of a single best when we come upon multiple examples of comparable quality. In that case we include them all in our list.

Here, then, are the Best Plays best of 1982–83:

PLAYS

BEST PLAY: *'night, Mother* by Marsha Norman

BEST FOREIGN PLAY: *Foxfire* by Susan Cooper and Hume Cronyn

BEST REVIVAL: *A View From the Bridge* by Arthur Miller, directed by Arvin Brown

BEST ACTOR IN A PRIMARY ROLE: Hume Cronyn as Hector Nations in *Foxfire*; Alan Howard as Halder in *Good*

BEST ACTRESS IN A PRIMARY ROLE: Kathy Bates as Jessie Cates in *'night, Mother*; Jessica Tandy as Annie Nations in *Foxfire*

BEST ACTOR IN A SECONDARY ROLE: Barnard Hughes as Father William Doherty in *Angels Fall*; James Russo as Raul in *Extremities*

BEST ACTRESS IN A SECONDARY ROLE: Anne Pitoniak as Thelma Cates in *'night, Mother* and in the "Lamps" segment of *Talking With*

BEST DIRECTOR: Robert Allan Ackerman for *Extremities* and *Slab Boys*

BEST SCENERY: Ming Cho Lee for *K2*

BEST COSTUMES: Patricia Zipprodt for *Alice in Wonderland* and *Whodunnit*

MUSICALS

BEST MUSICAL: *My One and Only*

BEST BOOK: *My One and Only* by Peter Stone and Timothy S. Mayer

BEST MUSIC: Andrew Lloyd Webber for *Cats*

BEST LYRICS: Trevor Nunn (adaptor) for *Cats*

BEST REVIVAL: *On Your Toes* by George Abbott, Richard Rodgers and Lorenz Hart, directed by George Abbott

BEST ACTOR IN A PRIMARY ROLE: Tommy Tune as Capt. Billy Buck Chandler in *My One and Only*

BEST ACTRESS IN A PRIMARY ROLE: Twiggy as Edith Herbert in *My One and Only*

BEST ACTOR IN A SECONDARY ROLE: Charles "Honi" Coles as Mr. Magix in *My One and Only*

BEST ACTRESS IN A SECONDARY ROLE: Betty Buckley as Grizabella in *Cats*; Denny Dillon as Mickey in *My One and Only*

BEST DIRECTOR AND CHOREOGRAPHER: Thommie Walsh and Tommy Tune for *My One and Only*

BEST SCENERY: Adrianne Lobel for *My One and Only*

BEST COSTUMES: John Napier for *Cats;* Rita Ryack for *My One and Only*

LITTLE SHOP OF HORRORS—Ellen Greene *(right)* as Audrey, in the presence of her namesake, the man-eating plant Audrey II *(left),* in the Critics Award-winning musical

Off Broadway

It's a good thing that Joseph Papp and his New York Shakespeare Festival took part in welcoming the British visitors to the smaller New York playhouses, because it resulted in his having a lion's share—what else—of the off-Broadway year's major achievements. First he brought in David Hare's *Plenty* (described in the previous section of this report) which had been produced at London's National Theater and went on to Broadway after its Public Theater engagement. He then made an exchange agreement with the Royal Court Theater which brought over their production of Caryl Churchill's *Top Girls* and sent over New York Shakespeare's subsequent production of a new Thomas Babe play. Miss Churchill is the author of the long-running Best Play *Cloud 9,* a comedy of sexual sleight-of-hand, and it's clear in her subsequent *Top Girls* that she is a player of games onstage. The game in the first act of this new one is an all-female dinner party brimming with philosophical observations among guests including famous women of history like Pope Joan and Dull Gret. But the name of the game in her second act is Theater with a capital T in a confrontation between two sisters, one of whom has risen to high-gloss success as the head of an employment agency in London, the other remaining a country drudge cleaning other people's houses for a living. These women are electrifyingly symbolic of major social currents, with neither given an edge by the author. The ambitious sister has earned her success and has a right to it, but the drudge and the admittedly unpromising child she is raising are also human beings—and as in the case of Willy Loman, some attention must be paid. An American cast replaced the Royal Court cast in *Top Girls* in mid-season, without loss of momentum. Once past its forgettable dinner party, this Churchill script rivaled anything in *Plenty* and the other off-Broadway British Best Play, Simon Gray's independently-produced *Quartermaine's Terms* (described in detail in the Best Plays section of this volume). Furthermore, Joseph Papp punctuated his season in late May by bringing over the London production of Miss Churchill's *Fen*, another play of strong imagination and socioeconomic convictions, telling of the hard lives of rural folk in an outlying district and conferring on its author the very rare, if not unique, distinction of having three off-Broadway productions running simultaneously.

We must take pains to explain what we mean by "off Broadway." Its border lines are smudging at both the Broadway and off-off-Broadway ends, as most other publications including *Variety* and the New York *Times* apply the term loosely, sometimes to plays that are clearly OOB (weekend or Wednesday-to-Saturday performances only, reduced ticket prices, Equity concessions) and frequently to "mini-contract" OOB productions (Equity concessions and closed-end engagements). We cannot draw indelible lines, but we must try to distinguish between professional and experimental categories; between what is probably a work-in-progress which may itself evolve as it rises to a higher level of commitment, and what is probably a "frozen" script facing the world for better or for worse as a completed work in production or publication. Only the latter is regularly considered for Best Play designation, for obvious reasons. Full off-Broadway plays and musicals are thus eligible for Best Play designation on the same terms as those classified under the Broadway heading, whereas works-in-progress are not.

By the lights of these *Best Plays* volumes, an off-Broadway production is one a) with an Equity cast b) giving 8 performances a week c) in an off-Broadway theater d) after inviting comment by reviewers on opening nights. And according to Paul Libin, president of the League of Off-Broadway Theaters, an off-Broadway theater is a house seating 499 or fewer and situated in Manhattan *outside* the area bounded by Fifth and Ninth Avenues between 34th and 56th Streets, and by Fifth Avenue and the Hudson River between 56th and 72nd Streets.

Obviously, we make exceptions to each of these rules; no dimension of "off" or "off off" can be applied exactly. In each *Best Plays* volume we stretch them somewhat in the direction of inclusion—never of exclusion. The point is, off Broadway isn't an exact location either geographically or esthetically, it's a state of the art, a level of expertise and professional commitment. In these *Best Plays* volumes we'll continue to categorize it, however, as accurately as we can, as long as it seems useful for the record, while reminding those who read these lines that distinctions are no longer as clear as they once were—and elsewhere in this volume we publish the most comprehensive list of 1982–83 off-off-Broadway

The 1982–83 Season Off Broadway

PLAYS (39)

Booth
Looking-Glass
Divine Hysteria
Jane Avril
Negro Ensemble:
Abercrombie Apocalypse
Sons and Fathers of Sons
About Heaven and Earth
Manhattan Made Me
Circle Repertory:
A Think Piece
ANGELS FALL
Black Angel
What I Did Last Summer
Domestic Issues
Young Playwrights Festival
Fool for Love
Herringbone
The Fox
Inserts
Manhattan Theater Club:
Talking With
Standing on My Knees
Triple Feature
Elba
Early Warnings
The Price of Genius

Baseball Wives
Greater Tuna
Edmond
Some Men Need Help
Penelope
EXTREMITIES
Balloon
Hannah
Goodnight, Grandpa
Buck
The Middle Ages
Win/Lose/Draw
Wild Life
Buried Inside Extra
Out of the Night

REVUES (5)

Forbidden Broadway (transfer)
R.S.V.P.
Upstairs at O'Neals'
A Bundle of Nerves
It's Better With a Band

MUSICALS (7)

A Drifter, the Grifter & Heather McBride
Life Is Not a Doris Day Movie
Broken Toys
The Death of Von Richtofen as Witnessed From Earth
Little Shop of Horrors
Charlotte Sweet
Snoopy

FOREIGN PLAYS IN ENGLISH (13)

Manhattan Theater Club:
The Singular Life of Albert Nobbs
Skirmishes
Summer
Lennon
N.Y. Shakespeare:
PLENTY
Top Girls
Fen
Two Fish in the Sky
Nurse Jane Goes to Hawaii
Poppie Nongena

QUARTERMAINE'S TERMS
The Other Side of the Swamp
Welcome Home Jacko

REVIVALS (36)

Roundabout:
The Learned Ladies
The Holly and the Ivy
The Entertainer
Duet for One
Winners & How He Lied to Her Husband
Delacorte:
Don Juan
A Midsummer Night's Dream
Three Sisters
True West
CSC:
Faust Part One
Faust Part Two
Ghost Sonata
Wild Oats
Danton's Death

LOOM:
H.M.S. Pinafore
The Gondoliers
Rose Marie
(12 operettas in running repertory)
Hamlet
Acting Company:
Pericles
Tartuffe
Play and Other Plays
My Astonishing Self
The Cradle Will Rock
Jacques Brel Is Alive and Well and Living in Paris

SPECIALTIES (8)

With Love and Laughter
Johnny Got His Gun
a/k/a/ Tennessee
Anthem for Doomed Youth
Do Lord Remember Me
A Christmas Carol
Egyptology: My Head Was a Sledgehammer
Jeeves Takes Charge

Categorized above are all the new productions listed in the Plays Produced Off Broadway section of this volume. Plays listed in CAPITAL LETTERS have been designated Best Plays of 1982–83. Plays listed in *italics* were still running off Broadway after May 31, 1983.

OFF-BROADWAY DUOS

Below, Joe Sears and Jaston Williams as two of the many characters they portray in *Greater Tuna,* comedy about a small Texas town

Above, Jeffrey Keller and Mara Beckerman in a scene from the musical *Charlotte Sweet*

productions anywhere, compiled by Camille Croce, plus a review of the season OOB by the incomparably well qualified Mel Gussow.

This said, let us record that 1982–83 production of new scripts off Broadway continued at about last year's level (see the one-page summary of the off-Broadway season accompanying this report). There were 59 as compared with 58 and 2 return engagements in 1981–82. The 1982–83 contingent comprised 39 American straight-play programs, 7 musicals and 13 foreign plays, as compared with 45-9-7, 33-14-8, 39-7-12 in the past three seasons and the peak 38-15-12 of 1979. In addition to the 59 abovementioned, there were 5 revues, 36 revivals and 8 specialties, making a grand total of 108 programs presented off Broadway during the past twelve months.

The standard-bearer for domestic playwriting was William Mastrosimone's Best Play *Extremities*, with Susan Sarandon as a winsome blonde who manages to overpower a would-be rapist (James Russo), trusses him up and coolly considers torturing and destroying him. Tautly directed by Robert Allan Ackerman, Mastrosimone's second New York production (his first was *The Woolgatherers*) raised provocative questions within the melodrama, questions about the failure of the intended victim's friends to offer appropriate support and sympathy, distrust of the law's ability to dish out punishment, fear of letting the attacker go, unwarranted shame and warranted fury at being demeaned as a woman and as a human being.

Extremities stood taller than other American scripts off Broadway this season, but it did not stand alone. David Mamet's *Edmond* examined in even more varied detail the dark side of human nature, in the decline and fall of a middle-class family man who wilfully immolates himself in the nighttime evils of Manhattan streets, participating finally in brutal murder and sodomy. Also in independent production, John Ford Noonan's *Some Men Need Help* described an attachment between two ill-matched men (as the women were ill-matched in the author's previous *A Coupla White Chicks Sitting Around Talking*), with the older (Philip Bosco) helping the younger (Treat Williams) fight alcoholism. On the lighter side, A.R. Gurney Jr.'s *The Middle Ages* reviewed the past few decades of WASP high life in a country club setting through the antics of a black sheep (Jack Gilpin) getting his kicks from disrupting family rituals. And the tour de force *Greater Tuna* by Jaston Williams, Joe Sears and Ed Howard took an affectionate view of a small Texas town with a host of local characters all played by the Messrs. Williams and Sears.

Among off Broadway's producing organizations, Circle Repertory Company turned its season into an opportunity for some of the contemporary theater's clearest voices to be heard. Jules Feiffer's *A Think Piece*, about a family's subsurface stresses, played the Circle in June and July; then in October a new cycle of plays began with Lanford Wilson's Best Play *Angels Fall* (described in the previous section of this report) which later moved uptown for further acclaim including a Tony nomination. The cycle continued with Michael Cristofer's *Black Angel*, a probe of Nazi war guilt; A.R. Gurney Jr.'s *What I Did Last Summer*, about a youth constrained by his WASP environment; Corinne Jacker's *Domestic Issues*, taking another look at the 1960s radicals in today's light; and Sam Shepard's *Fool for Love*, an abrasively comic lovers' meeting that was more of a collision than an embrace. And Circle Rep articulated the works not only of these veteran American playwrights but also of the young people's one-actors chosen by the Dramatists Guild Foundation in its second annual Young Playwrights Festival, a contest which brings to light and encourages writing talent among teens and sub-teens. This Circle Rep-Dramatists Guild program received a special citation from the New York Drama Critics Circle in the annual voting for the season's bests.

Manhattan Theater Club's recent concentration on the works of foreign authors lapped over from last season with the presentation in June of Simone Benmussa's *The Singular Life of Albert Nobbs*, based on a George Moore tale of a woman posing as a man in order to make something of herself in the sexually restrictive Ireland of the 1860s. There followed at MTC a season weighted with American playwrights, beginning with a script selected by the American Theater Critics Association as an outstanding cross-country accomplishment, featured in the 1981–82 *Best Plays* volume: *Talking With*, a collection of striking character monologues written under the nom de plume "Jane Martin," with a truly remarkable ensemble of actresses (including Anne Pitoniak) repeating the roles they created in the original Actors Theater of Louisville production. MTC continued with a new Jean-Claude van Itallie version of Chekhov's *Three Sisters* and later a showcase of van Itallie one-acters, *Early Warnings*; Vaughn McBride's *Elba*, about the plight of the elderly; John Olive's *Standing on My Knees*, telling of a

THE MIDDLE AGES—Jack Gilpin, Jo Henderson, Andre Gregory and Ann McDonough in the comedy by A.R. Gurney Jr.

poet's schizophrenia; and three one-act showcases for playwrights and directors, *Triple Feature*. Also embedded in the MTC schedule were the British plays *Summer*, Edward Bond's reflections on the Nazi occupation of the Balkans, and Catherine Hayes's *Skirmishes*, a stark conflict between two sisters quarreling over their duty to their dying mother. This season the MTC raised its Upstage presentations from off-off-Broadway to off-Broadway status equal to those in its Downstage facility, thereby considerably increasing the scope of its major activities.

In the wake of its memorable 1981–82 Best Play and Critics and Pulitzer Prizewinning *A Soldier's Play*, The Negro Ensemble Company busied itself with a one-act play program, *About Heaven and Earth*, staged by the group's artistic director, Douglas Turner Ward, and including a work of Ward's own, *Redeemer*, in which an assortment of individuals prepares for Judgment Day, each in his or her own fashion. The NEC schedule also took in Paul Carter Harrison's *Abercrombie Apocalypse*, pitting the black caretaker of a vacated mansion against the son of its late owner, an allegory of evil; and Ray Aranha's *Sons and Fathers of Sons*, about the travails of student, professor and sharecropper's son in a small Mississippi town from 1943 to 1960. NEC peaked in May with Gus Edwards's *Manhattan Made Me*, the adventures of an out-of-work art director (played by Eugene Lee) in the Big Apple, directed by Ward and viewed through a comic lens.

Playwrights Horizons, which last season came up with three outstanding off-Broadway offerings including a Best Play, barely got into the game this year with Tom Cone's *Herringbone* (a play with songs, with David Rounds playing all ten roles), the co-production of Ronald Ribman's *Buck* (with Priscilla Lopez in an indictment of cable TV as an exploiter of violence) and a William Finn musical that didn't get past its previews.

In July, as a sort of afterthought to 1981–82, Joseph Papp presented the interesting Des McAnuff musical *The Death of Von Richtofen as Witnessed From Earth*, the Red Baron's life and times presaging the yearning for a larger-than-life-sized leader. Besides the aforementioned British entries, Papp's eclectic schedule also took in a revival of *Hamlet* with an actress, Diane Venora, in the title role, and the new Thomas Babe comedy—*Buried Inside Extra*—with an all-star cast under Papp's direction playing newsroom types in the twilight of their paper, the show which was exported to the Royal Court in London for six weeks in exchange for *Top Girls*.

Aside from its cabaret and Women's Project programs (see their listing in the Plays Produced Off Off Broadway section of this volume), American Place made the scene this season only with the co-production of *Buck*, plus James De-Jongh's *Do Lord Remember Me*, whose cast headed by Frances Foster repeated a 1930s Federal Theater project recording first-hand memories of slavery in the United States. T. Edward Hambleton's Phoenix Theater, alas, made a final exit, cutting short its projected three-play season—and ceasing to function altogether —after the short run of *Two Fish in the Sky*, a British play about a wily Jamaican thwarting the authorities' efforts to deport him from England.

Among highlights in independent off-Broadway production were *Baseball Wives* by Grubb Graebner, looking at the tribulations of three wives of baseball superstars from opening day through the World Series; and *Poppie Nongena*, with an imported cast interpreting a Sandra Kotze-Elsa Joubert play with songs based on the latter's book about a South African girl progressing with dignity from age 13 to age 36 through the pitfalls of apartheid. An English play with music, *Lennon*, celebrated the person and accomplishments of that widely admired member of the Beatles, while Canadian sources contributed a farce about a female author of romantic novels, *Nurse Jane Goes to Hawaii*. Other subjects under scrutiny on the off-Broadway circuit this season included the Booth brothers and the Lincoln assasination (*Booth*), the life of Lewis Carroll (*Looking-Glass*), doomsday in New York (*Divine Hysteria*), Toulouse-Lautrec and friends (*Jane Avril*), a D.H. Lawrence novella, adapted by Allan Miller, about a young man's impact on the lives of two women (*The Fox*, presented on the Roundabout's schedule), blue movies (*Inserts*), a 17th century Mexican playwright-poet (*The*

EDMOND—Laura Innes and Colin Stinton, a knife gleaming
faintly in his hand, in a scene from David Mamet's drama

Price of Genius), Benjamin Franklin (in Karen Sunde's *Balloon* on CSC's schedule), a 1930s stage star (*Penelope*), the actual heroics of a Jewish woman battling
the Nazis (*Hannah*), a centenarian (played by Milton Berle in *Goodnight,
Grandpa*), Communist disillusionment (*Out of the Night*), a sendup of big-time
TV (in Shel Silverstein's *Wild Life*, a program of one-acts whose centerpiece, *The
Lady or the Tiger Show*, reenacted that timeless cliff-hanger as a Houston Astrodome spectacular with full TV coverage); and, again from London, homosex-
ual men in love (Royce Ryton's *The Other Side of the Swamp*) and the club life
of London's black youths (Mustapha Matura's *Welcome Home Jacko* in the
Quaigh Theater's imported Black Theater Cooperative production).

Off Broadway enjoyed a substantial musical season. *Little Shop of Horrors*
opened early, stayed on and carried off the Critics Award for best musical, the
first such they have voted in three years in their exotic system of proportional
consensus. With book and lyrics by Howard Ashman and music by Alan
Menken, this show was based on a Roger Corman horror film about a flytrap-type
plant which grows so formidably large that it's finally able to ingest a whole
human being. The score and performances (led by Lee Wilkof as the florist's
assistant who grows the monstrous plant) were amiable in definite contrast, under
Ashman's direction, to the plant itself, "Audrey II," the bloodthirsty star of this
outrageous tale. Audrey II was designed (we presume) and manipulated by
puppeteer Martin P. Robinson to gobble up everything that comes near it, including the inoffensive heroine of the piece (Ellen Greene), the "Audrey" after whom

this fatal foliage is named. *Little Shop of Horrors* was a very good thing in a small package, snapping up the Critics Award like Audrey II devouring a juicy dentist, under the very noses of the two large-package musicals uptown.

A heartwarming echo of the music hall in turn-of-the-century England also found a place on the off-Broadway musical scene in *Charlotte Sweet* (book and lyrics by Michael Colby, music by Gerald Jay Markoe). *Snoopy*, a musical with Charles M. Schulz's "Peanuts" comic strip characters, a score by Larry Grossman and Hal Hackady and David Garrison playing Charley Brown's quixotic pet, charmed audiences all season long, though not with the irresistible force of its Clark Gesner predecessor and Best Play *You're a Good Man Charlie Brown*. And as previously mentioned, *The Death of Von Richtofen as Witnessed From Earth* was a stimulating musical fantasy. Three other 1982–83 off-Broadway musicals—*A Drifter, the Grifter & Heather McBride* (a romantic triangle), *Life Is Not a Doris Day Movie* (performers seeking that first big break) and *Broken Toys* (love brings a toy soldier to life)—failed to make the grade. But four out of seven wasn't bad, especially when you added in Martin Charnin's hit cabaret musical *Upstairs at O'Neals'*, a grab bag of witty and acerbic musical comments written by a multitude of contributors and performed by an energetically talented cast; plus the cabaret musical *Forbidden Broadway* at Palsson's, a send-up of past and present pretensions in the big theaters, which opened as an OOB offering last year but soon raised its status and settled in for a long off-Broadway run.

The specialty programs, always an important element of an off-Broadway season, ranged through an evening of recitation by Celeste Holm, Wesley Addy and Gordon Connell of excerpts from the works of stage authors (*With Love and Laughter*); Jeff Daniels as the quadriplegic in an adaptation of Dalton Trumbo's famous *Johnny Got His Gun*; a one-man portrait gallery by Edward Duke of Bertie Wooster, his gentleman's gentleman and ten other P.G. Wodehouse characters in *Jeeves Takes Charge*; Tennessee Williams excerpts (*a/k/a Tennessee*) and Wilfrid Owen excerpts (*Anthem for Doomed Youth*). It included the sublime (Orson Bean's adaptation of *A Christmas Carol*) and ended with the absurd (in a non-pejorative sense) in another of Richard Foreman's assemblage of stage effects—dramatic, comic and musical—in this case expressing some of his ideas about different cultures, as boisterous as its title *Egyptology: My Head Was a Sledgehammer*.

Viewed in twelve-month perspective, the 1982–83 off-Broadway season was eminently rewarding. There was no dog-wagging in the smaller playhouses as in some previous seasons, but the tail end of the professional New York theater was in continuous and vigorous action, resulting in four Best Plays—*Plenty*, *Extremities*, *Angels Fall* and *Quartermaine's Terms*—and the clever *Little Shop of Horrors*. For good measure, there were *Top Girls*, *Edmond*, *Talking With*, *The Middle Ages*, *Greater Tuna*, *Upstairs at O'Neals'* and Circle Rep's barrage of American scripts—a measure in which entertainment was mixed generously with accomplishment.

A VIEW FROM THE BRIDGE—Tony Lo Bianco, Rose Gregorio, Saundra Santiago, James Hayden and Alan Feinstein in a scene from the Broadway revival of Arthur Miller's play

Revivals on and off Broadway

Arthur Miller, George Abbott, Richard Rodgers and Lorenz Hart, George and Ira Gershwin, Noel Coward, George S. Kaufman and Moss Hart, Oscar Hammerstein II and Jerome Kern—these were some of the authors featured prominently on the marquees around New York this season, together with—of course —William Shakespeare, Molière, Ibsen, Chekhov and Gilbert and Sullivan. In the protracted 1982–83 scarcity of new musical get-up-and-go, Abbott himself directed a spirited reincarnation of his and Rodgers and Hart's *On Your Toes*, a Tony Award-winning revival starring Tony Award-winning Natalia Makarova as the prima ballerina in that show's choreography by the late, great George Balanchine, including the famous "Slaughter on Tenth Avenue." This outstanding show, whose company included George S. Irving and Dina Merrill, overrode an unfavorable New York *Times* review, demonstrating that it could be done, and went on to fame and fortune at a $40 top. Abbott is in his middle 90s with at least 110 shows on his list of author's and director's credits (and this year he received Kennedy Center Honors for "lifetime achievement in the theater," which is putting it mildly). Here he enjoyed the help of younger men like 88-year-old Hans Spialek, who recreated his original orchestrations and arrangements. This ebullient *On Your Toes* was indeed a multifaceted triumph.

The Gershwins also made Broadway this season—thrice, each time in a big way. Their immortal *Porgy and Bess* came to Radio City Music Hall in its uncut version, in a production so impressively suited to the dimensions of the Music Hall stage that it may have been bigger (it was observed) than the real Catfish Row locale for this folk opera. With a host of gifted performers sharing the responsibilities of the leading roles in a huge cast, this *Porgy and Bess* was a resounding Gershwin spectacle, followed a month later by the musical phenomenon *My One and Only*, the "new" Gershwin musical described in a previous section of this report. Its Gershwin score was assembled from *Funny Face* and other stage and screen productions, and a listing of these sources appears with the synopsis of *My One and Only* in the Best Plays section of this volume.

The Gershwins also provided the theme music for the 1983 Tony Awards ceremonies, at which they received an additional fanfare with the changing of the name of Broadway's vast Uris Theater, home of the Theater Hall of Fame, henceforth to be called the Gershwin Theater. At the time of its renaming, Jerome Kern and Oscar Hammerstein II were also being honored within the Gershwin Theater's walls with a lavish production of their own renowned *Show Boat*, revived full-scale under the direction of Michael Kahn in the Houston Grand Opera production imported to Broadway, with Donald O'Connor presiding as Cap'n Andy. The sweetest of memories was awakened with such songs as "Only Make Believe," "Why Do I Love You," "Bill" (with its P.G. Wodehouse lyric) and the organ timbre of "Ol' Man River" sung by Bruce Hubbard.

On the straight-play side of the revival season, Arthur Miller's *A View From the Bridge* regenerated its power in an Arvin Brown-staged Long Wharf Theater production brought to Broadway with Tony Lo Bianco in a dynamic portrayal of the Brooklyn longshoreman passionately obsessed by the niece he and his wife have raised like a child of their own. This Miller work appeared originally in September 1955 as a one-acter and Best Play of its season, then was expanded to full length to be produced first by Peter Brook in London the following year and then by Ulu Grosbard off Broadway with Robert Duvall in January 1965 for 780 performances. This season's *A View From the Bridge* was billed in some of its promotion as "a new play," and in some ways indeed it was: new to Broadway, staged and acted with new insights, yielding not merely a reproduction but new values of compressed emotion.

Herman Wouk's *The Caine Mutiny Court-Martial* also rekindled its dramatic fires in revival under Arthur Sherman's direction at Circle in the Square, with Michael Moriarty as the arrogant, crumbling Lt. Cmdr. Queeg so indelibly branded in memory by Lloyd Nolan, who created the role onstage, and Humphrey Bogart, who took it to the screen. Perhaps there was little that Moriarty could add to their portrayals, but he did not disappoint, nor did John Rubinstein in the Henry Fonda role of attorney for the defense.

The Broadway revival schedule for 1982–83 also included, on the drama side, a new Arthur Kopit adaptation of Ibsen's *Ghosts*, starring Liv Ullmann. On the

NOEL COWARD
REVISITED—
Above, George C. Scott
in *Present Laughter;*
right, Elizabeth Tay-
lor and Richard Bur-
ton in *Private Lives*

lighter end of the scale, Noel Coward won one and lost one this season. George C. Scott's interpretation, both as actor and director, of the life and loves of a matinee idol in a Circle in the Square revival of *Present Laughter* was one of the year's major assets, opening in July and so tenaciously popular that it forced the Circle to open its fall season at the Plymouth while its own house was so pleasantly occupied. On the other hand, the widely-promoted revival of *Private Lives*, starring those two vividly public-lived personalities Richard Burton and Elizabeth Taylor, was unable to get into step with the style and mood of this brilliant Coward duologue, though as a kind of romp it attracted star-struck, curiosity-seeking customers at a $45 top.

Kaufman and Hart were much better served by a high-spirited, star-studded reproduction of *You Can't Take It With You* directed by Ellis Rabb (who did the same for the 1965 hit revival of this play), with Jason Robards at the head of an exceptionally gifted company in the many individualistic roles of this engaging, stimulating and durable comedy. Shakespeare was also exceptionally well served by his home-town devotees, the Royal Shakespeare Company of Stratford-on-Avon and London, in a highly developed and polished production of *All's Well That Ends Well*, presented as though the action of this 1603 comedy were taking place in the Edwardian era, and staged by Trevor Nunn, Royal Shakespeare's joint artistic director, whose *Cats* was already a bright fixture of the season. Molière too found a place on the sunny side of Broadway with Circle in the Square's *The Misanthrope* with Brian Bedford, Carole Shelley and Mary Beth Hurt under Stephen Porter's direction. Elsewhere, Broadway revival production took in Ugo Betti's *The Queen and the Rebels*, with Colleen Dewhurst, about a group of travellers detained by a revolution in a small country; and the Eva Le Gallienne-Florida Friebus 1932 *Alice in Wonderland* with Miss Le Gallienne directing and playing the White Queen, and with John Lee Beatty's scenery and Patricia Zipprodt's Tony-nominated costumes recreating the Tenniel-drawing "look." And a restaging of Terrence McNally's Turkish-bath farce *The Ritz* survived for only one performance as an adjunct of the disco Xenon, formerly Henry Miller's Theater.

The revival-producing organizations, which year after year make off Broadway a treasure trove of the theatrical past, hardly broke stride along the rocky financial paths of 1982–83. "The high point of the 1982–83 season as to stage history," theater historian Thomas T. Foose informs us, "was in the summer of 1982 when one found playing concurrently fully professional productions of two rare plays by Molière. At the Delacorte was the Public Theater production of *Don Juan* (or as purists have it, *Dom Juan*). At about the same time, the Roundabout was offering *The Learned Ladies* (*Les Femmes Savantes*). Richard Wilbur's 1977 translation as *The Learned Ladies* sparked interest in a Molière play long neglected in English. Wilbur's translation has been offered in Cleveland, Costa Mesa, Denver, Kansas City and last summer in New York. In the United States, stagings of *Les Femmes Savantes* prior to 1977 have been very few.

"As to United States stagings of the Molière *Don Juan*, the most important prior to the Delacorte production was that at the Guthrie Theater in Minneapolis in June of 1981, from which stemmed the Delacorte staging just one year later. The Donald M. Frame translation, the Richard Foreman direction and settings and the Patricia Zipprodt costumes were all the same, with modifications, of course, for the out-of-doors."

Furthermore, John Seitz as Don Juan and Roy Brocksmith as Sganarelle repeated their Guthrie Theater performances in the Central Park cast. Thus, even in the area of revivals our cross-country theater plays its vital part, having previously scaled both peaks of New York's "high point of the 1982–83 season as to stage history."

Gene Feist's hardy Roundabout Theater Company maintained its customary high standards, following up *The Learned Ladies* with a series of works of 20th century theater, beginning with Wynyard Browne's *The Holly and the Ivy* (the American premiere of the 1948 London play about a village minister's troubled family) directed by Lindsay Anderson. Nicol Williamson colored with his own brush the Laurence Olivier role of the British music hall comedian in John Osborne's *The Entertainer*. And the Roundabout did Brian Friel's 1968 *Winners* about a loving but ill-fated young Irish couple, and Tom Kempinski's two-character *Duet for One* with Eva Marie Saint in the role of the concert violinist crippled by disease, played on Broadway only last season by Anne Bancroft. Roundabout Producing Director Feist's former colleague, Michael Fried, left the group this season, and Todd Haimes joined it as managing director.

The classic mode was well represented on other stages around town. Joseph Papp's season included *A Midsummer Night's Dream* in Central Park and *Hamlet* at the Public Theater, while Manhattan Theater Club inserted a *Three Sisters* in its schedule. Christopher Martin's Classic Stage Company (CSC) distinguished itself and its artistic director with Goethe's complete *Faust* (reputedly the American premiere of *Faust* unabridged) translated by Philip Wayne and directed and designed by Martin in two parts, each of which was presented as a

NOTABLE REVIVALS—*Above,* Noble Shropshire as Mephisto and Christopher Martin in the title role of Goethe's *Faust; below,* John Malkovich and Gary Sinise in *True West,* the 1980 play by Sam Shepard

full-length play. Strindberg (*Ghost Sonata*), O'Keeffe (*Wild Oats*) and Buechner (*Danton's Death*) were also honored in CSC production.

William Mount-Burke's Light Opera of Manhattan (LOOM) provided its uptown patrons with new productions of *H.M.S. Pinafore*, *The Gondoliers* and Rudolf Friml's *Rose Marie*, meanwhile keeping up its 12-month schedule of Gilbert and Sullivan, Victor Herbert and other operettas. And this year's Acting Company repertory included *Tartuffe* along with Shakespeare's seldom-seen *Pericles, Prince of Tyre*, plus Samuel Beckett's *Come and Go* on a one-act program with his *Play* and *Krapp's Last Tape*. As an extra added attraction, the Acting Company assembled a group of its alumni for a special production of Marc Blitzstein's *The Cradle Will Rock* under the direction of John Houseman, the group's producing artistic director, who also took center stage to deliver a short introductory talk at each performance, detailing the colorful origins of this musical satire on the labor movement which he himself co-produced at the Mercury Theater in 1938.

Independent production of revivals off-Broadway virtually ground to a halt this season. A repeat of Donal Donnelly's one-man portrait of George Bernard Shaw in *My Astonishing Self*, the 15th anniversary revival of the Jacques Brel revue at First City and Sam Shepard's *True West* were the only ones offered outside organizational shelter—and Shepard's play was in one sense more of a premiere than a revival. Its first production at the Public Theater in January 1981 was repudiated by its author, who is said to have considered this 1982–83 one the authentic representation of his script about a loathesome desert rat (repellently personified by John Malkovich) moving in on his respectable screenwriting brother (Gary Sinise, who also directed this version) and forcing him into an exchange of personalities. Like other Shepard plays, it managed powerfully ironic and emotional moments within a showoff kind of theater which thumbs (and in this case picked) its nose at the audience with a jumble of shock effects and harsh words.

Anyhow, the off-Broadway revival season provided Shepard, one of our most prolific and generally admired contemporary dramatists, with a second hearing for a problematical work, as it has in the past for Tennessee Williams, Arthur Miller and many others. This is a hugely important asset, nearly equal in long-term value to the celebration of the recognized historical glories of Shakespeare, Molière, Chekhov, Ibsen and company. Fortunately, our revival stages remained alert to both these functions in the season of 1982–83.

Offstage

An atmosphere of hard economic times pervaded all areas of the theater in 1982–83. The rumbles of distant financial thunder persisted in news reports of the drying-up of support from economizing government, foundation and private sources; of the curtailing of festival and other production schedules at home and abroad; of the growing scarcity of middle-income backers; of regional theater shrinkage and the Guthrie Theater's first deficit ($632,000) in 13 years; of the disappointing audience response to pay-TV's first-ever live broadcast Nov. 5 of a Broadway show, *Sophisticated Ladies*, which attracted a mere 60,000 viewers at $15 apiece from a pool potentially more than ten times that size.

Closer to home and more specifically damaging to the New York theater, T. Edward Hambleton's noted Phoenix Theater called it quits after 30 years and more than 100 productions which enlarged the scope of the contemporary stage in all dimensions. The Phoenix had been a major presence in the not-for-profit theater with its schedules of mind-expanding imports and important revivals, sprinkled with new scripts by American dramatists, including Marsha Norman's first play, *Getting Out*. The Phoenix production of Tolstoi's massive *War and Peace* on a tiny uptown stage was a feat of imagination to match Shakespeare's Battle of Agincourt at the old Globe, as unforgettable as such other Phoenix highlights as Ionesco's *Exit the King*, Mary Rodgers's *Once Upon a Mattress*, Arthur Kopit's *Oh, Dad, Poor Dad*, etc., Daniel Berrigan's *The Trial of the Catonsville Nine*, Conor Cruise O'Brien's *Murderous Angels* and David Berry's *G.R. Point*, not to mention eloquent homage to Shakespeare, Shaw, Eliot, Brecht, Chekhov, Ibsen, Marlowe, Molière, even Boucicault, Goldsmith and Richard Brinsley Sheridan. The Phoenix was a casualty of general economic conditions: cuts in its funding from all sectors had stripped it to the bone, when a seemingly unrelated Wall Street problem caused the cancellation of an expected corporate grant, a last straw which broke its three-decades-long spine of production. After only one offering, the Phoenix's 1982–83 season was cancelled with a finality that included the dissolving of its charter, so that no ashes remained from which it could rise. Its passing leaves a distressingly empty space on the New York stage.

As we were going to press with last year's *Best Plays* volume, a reported rift between producers and authors widened into a chasm of lawsuits unbridged by season-long efforts to negotiate the differences, still yawning as we sent this volume to the printer. The men and women who write the plays and musicals, most of them members of the Dramatists Guild, *lease* their work for a percentage of the box office gross laid down in a Minimum Basic Agreement drawn up in the 1920s: for plays, 5 per cent of the first $5,000, 7.5 per cent of the next $2,000 and 10 per cent thereafter; and for musicals, 6 per cent divided among the authors. Ownership of the work remains in the hands of the dramatist (unlike that, say, of the screen writer, who sells his work to the producer outright), who may continue to lease it again and again for other productions in other places and circumstances.

For several years in the recent past, representatives of the League of New York

Theaters and Producers (the producers' organization) and the Dramatists Guild have explored the possibility of modernizing the old agreement in line with changed conditions of the contemporary theater; but, according to *Variety,* their discussions ended in an impasse and were broken off in the fall of 1981. Then, on July 7, 1982, the League filed an anti-trust suit against the Dramatists Guild in the Federal Court in New York, seeking "injunctive relief to enable producers to negotiate freely with authors, and to prohibit the Guild from requiring the use of contracts containing minimum terms and conditions, or involving itself in any way, directly or indirectly, in negotiations between an author and a producer concerning the terms and conditions for the rights to produce any author's works." The suit was filed in the name of Richard Barr, president of the League, and in *Variety's* estimation "is expected to be prolonged over a number of years."

The Dramatists Guild "vigorously denied" allegations of anti-trust practises; and then, in October, League and Guild representatives resumed the discussions broken off a year earlier, in a new effort to settle their differences, with *Variety* reporting that "Many producers and playwrights are unhappy with the lawsuit, which is seen as a divisive and costly development at a time when existing economic conditions in legit are heading out of control." These talks broke off again in February, with no agreement reached and the League suit being pressed. And then on April 29 the Dramatists Guild's answering volley came: a counter-suit charging anti-trust violations, filed in Federal Court in New York, naming as defendants the League, The Shubert Organization, the Shubert Foundation, the Nederlander Organization and, as individuals, Gerald Schoenfeld and Bernard B. Jacobs (Shubert officers) and James M. Nederlander (but not Richard Barr, in whose name the League suit had been filed). This counterclaim stated that the Shubert group (owners of 16½ Broadway theaters) and the Nederlander group (owners of 12 Broadway theaters, two of them in process of renovation) "have control of every facet of theatrical production, and are able to dictate the positions which the League takes with the Guild in dealing with playwrights" and have tried to force dramatists to accept "artificially low and non-competitive levels" of payment for the use of their scripts. A New York *Times* article reported that "The Guild, in its counterclaim, takes the position that . . . it is in fact the League and the Shubert and Nederlander organizations who are guilty of anti-trust violations because they have been bargaining with the Guild for years." At season's end, this cloud of internecine dissension seemed at its darkest, hovering low over the New York theater and showing no signs of disappearing any time soon.

Among the theater's other organizations, the Society of Stage Directors and Choreographers reached an agreement with the League which runs through October 1984, granting a small rise in minimum fees to $6,800 for directors and $5,500 for choreographers, plus non-returnable advances against royalties of $4,700 and $4,000. Local One of IATSE (the stagehands) negotiated 5, 6 and 7 per cent raises over a period of three years, with weekly wages topping out at $475.43 to $621.63 for department heads. Actors' Equity Association negotiated a 21.4 per cent raise in the performers' minimum salaries over a three-year period, bringing actors' base pay from $575 to $610 weekly in the first year of the new

SEVEN BRIDES FOR SEVEN BROTHERS—A scene from the short-lived musical

contract, with a corresponding rise in the $385 weekly living expense allotment for those on tour.

At the Theater Development Fund, which oversees the half-price TKTS booths, $29-million-a-year important to the theater's finances, Hugh Southern resigned his executive directorship to become deputy chief of the National Endowment and was replaced by Henry Guettel. Drama Desk, an organization of reporters and editors in the theater field, named *Variety's* John Madden its president.

1982–83 was a year of abrasive controversies involving the critics, beginning with last summer's angry reaction of the *Seven Brides for Seven Brothers* cast to Frank Rich's sharply unfavorable review of that short-lived musical, with the laid-off actors picketing the *Times* for "killing family entertainment." In March, however, Rich turned thumbs down on the revival of *On Your Toes* staged by George Abbott, but this show turned the tables on him, developing into a solid, Tony-winning hit over the dead body of his unfavorable review (we hasten to add that we are describing events here, not pointing the finger; the minority position is an honorable one, in which every critic ought to find him/herself from time to time, as we ourselves do this season in the case of Neil Simon's *Brighton Beach Memoirs*).

The *Times* itself was the subject of some criticism for its decision to have Rich review the musical *Merlin* on Jan. 31 while that show was still in the development stage in a long series of preview performances (the *Daily News* covered *Merlin* along with the *Times,* but the *Post* held off until the show's formal announcement of its premiere Feb. 13). *Merlin* seemed certainly to have still been in work on Jan. 31, having recently cancelled four midweek matinees to make time for introducing new material. But the *Times* contended that the advertising and ticket price scale of *Merlin* suggested that it had gone public, and "Our responsibility is to our readers. When a show becomes a public event, a good newspaper ought to cover it." Clive Barnes of the *Post* took a contrary view: "I personally deplore the acts of my colleagues. I don't think reviewing a show is the same as covering a fire." And one of the *Merlin* producers argued, "We should be allowed to be reviewed when we think we're ready and not before." This controversy flared into a meeting of more than 100 producers, managers and press agents for discussion and protest, without material result.

Taking a last long look over our shoulder at the 1982–83 season in New York, we are left with the impression that it was a year of growing fiscal concern over such developments as declining attendance, the $45 Broadway and $22 off-Broadway ticket, the $4 million musical, the confrontation of authors and producers over the distribution of box office receipts. It's sometimes hard to remember that what we call "theater" in one word doesn't stand or fall, suffer or enjoy, as a unit. We must continuously remind ourselves that even "Broadway" isn't a single big business with a lot of branch offices, it is an assembly of separate parts whose individual condition is of greater importance to the well-being of what we call "theater" than the sum total of achievement or average condition of the whole.

As we look back on 1982–83, we can see clearly that *Cats* and *Torch Song Trilogy* and *My One and Only* and *'night, Mother* have joined the dance with *Amadeus* and *42nd Street* and *Nine*, while off Broadway *Extremities* and *Little Shop of Horrors* and *Quartermaine's Terms* have come into step with *Cloud 9* and *The Dining Room*—at least for a goodly part of a season, and not forgetting *The Fantasticks* way, way out there at the head of the cotillion. We conclude that, whatever its shortcomings and continuing problems, 1982–83 succeeded in bringing forth for the audience's enjoyment and stimulation a number of impressive shows—and there's little in "theater" of greater value than that.

OFF OFF BROADWAY

By Mel Gussow

Off off Broadway is an amorphous alternative theater extending throughout New York City. Increasingly its effect has been national and international, with a network of theaters, exchanging plays and information with those in New York. Through the encouragement of such companies as Ellen Stewart's LaMama and such organizations as the International Theater Institute, American companies travel to foreign cities and festivals; and we are visited by troupes from Europe, Africa, South America and the Far East. Typical of this season's international exchange, Fernando Arrabal, the Spanish exile playwright living in Paris, came to New York to direct the American premiere of his play *Inquisition* for the Puerto Rican Travelling Theater, one of New York's many Hispanic companies.

Companies representing a specific ethnicity or culture are playing a more significant role in the life of the New York theater—Hispanic, black, Greek, Irish, Jewish, and, most importantly in the past few years, Asian American. One of the outstanding non-profit off-off-Broadway companies is the Pan Asian Repertory Theater, under the artistic direction of its founder, Tisa Chang. The Pan Asian company has presented plays by Americans of Chinese, Japanese and Filipino descent and has nurtured an ensemble of actors, directors and designers. A highlight of the 1982–83 season was the Pan Asian production of *Yellow Fever*, a captivating spoof of private-eye mysteries, written by a young Canadian author, R. A. Shiomi. In all respects, this was one of the Pan Asian's best productions, and in June the comedy reopened with its original cast for an extended off-Broadway run. Pan Asian followed *Yellow Fever* with a lavish production of Lao She's *Teahouse*, a socio-historical chronicle of modern China, and a bilingual production of *A Midsummer Night's Dream*.

Every year there are new companies off off Broadway; and at the same time other companies, discouraged by economics, decide to curtail operation. To survive, the theaters need achievement and courage as well as enterprise. Among the noteworthy long-running companies are the following:

The Ensemble Studio Theater—Along with its regular season of new full-length plays by member playwrights, this year including Eduardo Machado's chronicle of Cuba, *The Modern Ladies of Guanabacoa*, the Ensemble Studio presents an annual marathon of one-act plays. The 1983 festival was highlighted by James G. Richardson's *Eulogy*, Percy Granger's *The Dolphin Position*, Wendy Kesselman's *I Love You, I Love You Not*, Peter Maloney's *Pastoral* and Willie Reale's *Fast Women*. Under the artistic direction of Curt Dempster, the Ensemble Studio also maintains a West Coast branch.

The WPA Theater—This has become a major nurturing ground for new plays and musicals, having sent *Little Shop of Horrors*, *Key Exchange* and *Nuts*, among others, into the commercial theater. This season, the WPA introduced *Asian Shade*, the latest work by one of its favorite writers, Larry Ketron. This was a

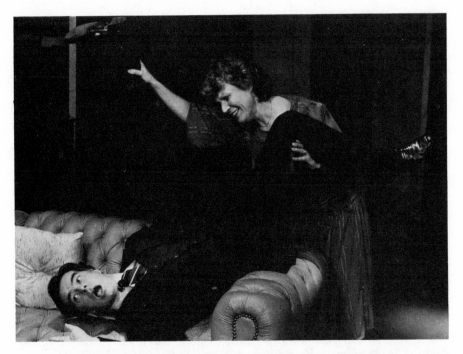

NEW FEDERAL THEATER—William Mooney and Marilyn Chris
in a scene from *The Upper Depths* by David Steven Rappoport

wistful study of two young recruits coming home before being shipped to Vietnam. Varying its repertory, the WPA revived *Vieux Carré,* elevating that play's stature among the later works of Tennessee Williams.

The Second Stage—Under the direction of Carole Rothman and Robyn Goodman, this company is dedicated to rediscovering works of the recent past, giving a second production to plays that may have failed in their first attempt. The group also puts on worthy new plays, including, this season, Tina Howe's *Painting Churches,* a sensitive contemplation of a daughter's role as an artist within an artistic family. Donald Moffat, Frances Conroy and Marian Seldes were the ensemble cast. The Second Stage also gave a first New York platform to Adele Edling Shank, a California playwright of "hyper-real" theater, as represented by *Winterplay.*

The Mabou Mines—This group is a collaborative company of artists, writers, designers and actors, who interact among the disciplines and studiously avoid any single artistic leadership. This year various Mabou Mines members created *Cold Harbor,* an informative multi-linear exploration of the life and history of Ulysses S. Grant (featuring the co-author, Bill Raymond, as Grant); a stage version of Samuel Beckett's story, *Company*; and *Hajj,* an abstract synthesis of live theater and television.

The Ridiculous Theatrical Company—Founded and directed by Charles Ludlam, who is also the resident playwright and chief clown, the company ended the season with one of its funniest shows, *Le Bourgeois Avant-Garde,* which put

Molière on his avant-garde. Mr. Ludlam wrote and directed the play and also acted the leading role as a scion of supermarkets who has dreams of being the Medici of minimalism. As author, he was faithful both to his source and to his own sense of the Ridiculous.

LaMama Experimental Theater Club (ETC)—For more than 20 years, Ellen Stewart's LaMama has been a cornerstone of off off Broadway and of the international theater, this year welcoming a diverse array of companies from France, Japan, Italy and South America. Among the home-grown productions were Jean-Claude van Itallie's *The Tibetan Book of the Dead*, with an international company of actors; Elizabeth Swados's *Three Travels of Aladdin With the Magic Lamp*; Ping Chong's striking *Anna Into Nightlight*; George Ferencz's slashing version of Sam Shepard's *The Tooth of Crime*; and *Andrea's Got Two Boy-Friends*, a touching, collaborative vignette about retardation.

The Performing Garage—This is a way station for experimental companies of varying coloration, including the resident Wooster Group as well as visitors from California. Bi-coastal talent included Chris Hardman with his environmental maze, *Artery*; Laura Farabough's quizzical *Obedience School* and Alan and Bean Finneran's elliptical double bill *Voodoo Automatic* and *Red Rain*. Spalding Gray, a Performing Garage faithful, offered an eight-play retrospective of his engaging life-is-a-monologue performances.

The Music-Theater Group/Lenox Arts Center—This organization was in residence at St. Clement's with a revival of Virgil Thomson's opera *The Mother of Us All*; Wendy Kesselman's ballad based on the Grimm fairy tale *The Juniper Tree*; and Welcome Msomi's spirited African jamboree *The Day, the Night*.

On weekends at 11 P.M., the Dance Theater Workshop becomes the Economy Tires Theater, with performance events under the direction of David White. The group presented *The Flying Karamazov Brothers*, a troupe of zany jugglers and clowns, at the Brooklyn Academy of Music (later the Brothers moved to Broadway). In its home theater, Economy Tires premiered *Foolsfire*, an uproarious and artistic evening of clowning and juggling by Bob Berky, Fred Garbo and Michael Moschen, and also welcomed Daniel Stein's stylized mime tableau *Inclined to Agree*.

Among the other events of note was a New York appearance by the San Francisco Mime Troupe with a scathing musical satire of American policies in Central America, *Americans, or Last Tango in Huahuatenango*. Nicholas Kazan's chilling modern Gothic, *Blood Moon*, was at the Production Company, along with a late-night collage of the beatnik era called *Jazz Poets at the Grotto*. Robert Kalfin's Chelsea Theater Center briefly reappeared, in a co-production with Woodie King Jr.'s New Federal Theater, of Steven Rappoport's nihilistic family comedy *The Upper Depths*.

The Manhattan Punch Line specializes in comedies from the past, including works by George S. Kaufman. This season it presented the New York premiere of Terrence McNally's *It's Only a Play*, a devastating spoof of make-or-break Broadway that had originally been intended for Broadway. The off-off-Broadway season ended with laughter—the First New York Festival of Clown-Theater, five weeks of first-class tomfoolery.

THE SEASON
AROUND THE UNITED STATES

with

A DIRECTORY OF PROFESSIONAL
REGIONAL THEATER

Including casts and credits of new plays

and

OUTSTANDING NEW PLAYS
CITED BY
AMERICAN THEATER CRITICS
ASSOCIATION

THE American Theater Critics Association (ATCA) is the organization of more than 250 leading drama critics of all media in all sections of the United States. One of this group's stated purposes is "To increase public awareness of the theater as a *national* resource" (italics ours). To this end, ATCA has cited a number of outstanding new plays produced this season across the country, to be listed and briefly described in this volume; and has designated one of them for us to offer as an introduction to our coverage of "The Season Around the United States" in the form of a synopsis with excerpts, in much the same manner as Best Plays of the New York season.

The critics made their citations, including their principal one of *Closely Related* by Bruce MacDonald in the following manner: member critics everywhere were asked to call the attention of an ATCA committee to outstanding new work in their areas. The 1982–83 committee was chaired by Ann Holmes of the Houston *Chronicle* and comprised William Gale of the Providence *Journal,* Julius Novick of the *Village Voice,* Damien Jacques of the Milwaukee *Journal,* Sylvie Drake of the Los Angeles *Times* and Bernard Weiner of the San Francisco *Chronicle.* These committee members studied scripts of the nominated plays and made their choices on the basis of script rather than production, thus placing very much the same emphasis as the editor of this volume gives to the script in making his New York Best Plays selections. There were no eligibility requirements (such as Equity cast or formal resident-theater status) except that a nominee be the first full professional production of a new work outside New York City within this volume's time frame of June 1, 1982 to May 31, 1983.

It should be noted that Marsha Norman's *'night, Mother*, Sam Shepard's *Fool for Love* and *Yellow Fever* by R. A. Shiomi were nominated but became ineligible for synopsis here when they opened in New York during this season.

The list of other 1982–83 plays nominated by members of ATCA as outstanding presentations in their areas, with descriptions written by the critics who saw and nominated them, follows the synopsis of *Closely Related*, which was prepared by the *Best Plays* editor.

*Cited by American Theater Critics
as an Outstanding New Play
of 1982–83*

CLOSELY RELATED

A Play in Two Acts

BY BRUCE MacDONALD

Cast and credits appear on page 81

*BRUCE MacDONALD was born in 1951 in Bryn Mawr, Pa., where his father
was a dentist. He graduated from Williams College in 1973 and received his
M.A. in dramatic arts from the University of California at Berkeley in 1976. He
moved into teaching in the Boston area—English at Northeastern, theater at
Salem State College—until, in 1979, John Sayles cast him as a performer in the
movie* Return of the Secaucus 7. *In pursuit of an acting career, his inevitable
periods of unemployment gave him the time, which he'd never had before, to try
writing scripts. His first two he showed to no one, but his third,* Closely Related,
*aroused the interest of the New American Playwrights Program at South Coast
Repertory in Costa Mesa, Calif., which helped him to develop it. This group
produced a later draft on March 3, 1983, on the basis of which it was nominated
and chosen by the ATCA committee for synopsis here as an outstanding new
1982–83 script in cross-country theater.*

*MacDonald lives in Cambridge, Mass. and continues to support his writing time
with acting jobs. He has another script,* Getting Off, *in revision and a third in work.
He is married, with two daughters.*

ACT I

Scene 1

SYNOPSIS: Melissa Gifford, *"almost 15 years old,"* is standing alone, lit as though in a dream, saying, "A couple years after he died I started having these dreams. I was maybe nine. They were never the same. But usually I was chasing him, like a race or something, and then a car would come, like from nowhere, and run him over. And I'd keep on running until I woke up. *(Pause.)* Once I asked my mother, after I had one of the dreams, if that's what happened, and she got angry. She said, dreams are not real, you don't remember."

As the lighting changes from dream to reality, Melissa's monologue continues: "I have this thing where I can tell if somebody's lying." When she began to notice her parents communicating to each other in ways which she wasn't supposed to understand—signs, whispering, spelling out words—she turned herself into a sort of spy, making a game of eavesdropping and prying. In this way, she learned that both her parents were involved in extramarital attachments with persons named Myrna and Tim. Her father took Melissa to see Myrna in a play and then pretended—transparently—that he was meeting her for the first time when they went backstage after the show. "It was worse acting than the play," Melissa comments, "Really, he just wanted her to meet me, or she wanted to see what I looked like, or something."

After this incident, Melissa watched outside Myrna's apartment from time to time and learned that Myrna has a son about Melissa's age. His name is Christian, and "He was real restless looking, wouldn't stand still, he always looked like he was about to run off somewhere. I think he thought it was tough looking, you know, don't bother me." One day Melissa walked right up to him and declared, "Your mother and my father are having an affair." Christian was speechless, so Melissa gave him a piece of paper with her phone number on it and walked away. "That was definitely the coolest thing I've ever done," she remembers.

Scene 2

Alan Gifford (a neurosurgeon) and his wife Alison, Melissa's parents, are talking casually, almost without paying attention to one another, in their living room. He is going over the check book, she is reading the paper.

ALAN: Is Melissa here or is she out walking?

ALISON: She's walking, she and her binoculars.

ALAN *(after brief pause)*: Did I tell you a boy called the other day?

ALISON *(looks up)*: A boy? Why?

ALAN *(back to the checks)*: Well, Alison, she's almost fifteen, it's mating season, and I imagine he wanted to talk to her.

ALISON: What did he want?

ALAN: I didn't listen in.

     Pause. Alison lets the paper drop.

ALISON: A boy? She's never been interested in boys. Did you ask her what he wanted?

Penelope Windust as Alison and Lycia Naff as Melissa in a scene
from *Closely Related* at South Coast Repertory, Costa Mesa, Calif.

ALAN: It's none of my business what he wanted. Alison, there is going to be
the first boy, prepare yourself.

ALISON: *You* know what they are at this age, Alan. Walking erections. Little
walking erections.

ALAN: Well, as long as they're little.

> *Pause. Alan finds a check that makes him stop. He holds it up.*

Here's one to Timothy Lord, speaking of erections. Sixty-eight fifty.

ALISON: Did I add something wrong?

ALAN: No, it's just the first time I've seen a check to him.

> *He turns the check over, examines the signature.*

ALISON: Well, he's so good I really feel I have to express my appreciation, and
on that particular day I didn't have any cash. We made love twelve times that
afternoon. I think it was twelve.

ALAN: I suppose that's reasonable. What, six bucks a shot?

ALISON: You know, he has a sliding scale.

ALAN: Ahh.

> *Pause.*

ALISON: Why, what does she get?

ALAN: Oh, it varies.

ALISON: Mmmhmm?

ALAN: Depends on what's involved. Whips and chains are extra.

The phone rings. Alison goes to answer it and pretends it's Myrna calling, which gives Alan a start. Actually it's Alan's mother, and as he takes the phone to talk to her, Melissa enters *"dressed in her spy outfit: French beret, shoulder sack, binoculars around her neck"* and soon senses the tension in the room. While Alan is trying to end his phone conversation with his mother, Melissa informs Alison that she knows who Myrna is and has been watching her. Alan hangs up the phone, and Alison calls him over to hear what Melissa has to say. She repeats that she has been watching Myrna through her binoculars.

ALAN: Who?
ALISON: *Myrna.*
ALAN: Ahhh. Myrna.
MELISSA: I know who she is, Dad. I've known for a while.
ALAN: You know who she is? (*Melissa nods.*) What are you doing, spying on people?
MELISSA: Sort of.
ALAN: I don't understand, you've been watching . . . this woman? For what purpose?
MELISSA: I was curious. I wanted to know who she was.

Now she knows, and she's glad to bring it all out in the open. And this is not all she knows.

MELISSA: I know about Tim, too.
ALISON: *Tim?* You know what about Tim, Melissa?
MELISSA: That you're lovers, like Dad and Myrna.
        Alison and Alan regard each other; pause.
We don't have to talk about it any more if you don't want to. I wanted you to know that I knew.
ALISON: Yes.
MELISSA: I figured it was time. (*Alison nods her head.*) And since it's just the three of us, like, why can't we all be cool about what's going on?

It's obvious to Melissa that Alan and Alison mean to stay together, so why not just take these matters in stride? Alan apologizes, but Melissa leaves the room commenting, "It's no big deal," leaving her parents—Alan in particular—feeling a bit foolish.

Scene 3

In a park, Christian and Melissa have arranged to meet and are talking. Christian explains that his father, like his mother Myrna, is a performer but is away working most of the time in Los Angeles, separated but not divorced from his mother. Melissa tells Christian that she has seen and admired his mother on the stage as Lady Macbeth and has met her offstage. And she has spied out the fact that her father and Christian's mother are lovers. They meet sometimes at a hotel, but mostly at Myrna's house.

To demonstrate her prowess as an observer, Melissa tells Christian what she has found out about him.

MELISSA (*recites*): Sixteen years old, sophomore at Kennedy, above average student, could do better . . .
CHRISTIAN: What?
MELISSA: Runs track, mostly sprints, likes hot pastrami sandwiches with mustard, which you had one day at Armando's deli, rides a tenspeed European something . . . let's see, what else? Pretty much of a loner. (*Pause.*) And has at least one girlfriend. N'est-ce pas? Right?
CHRISTIAN: I'm fifteen. (*Shrugs.*) But some people think I look older. (*Pause.*) How old are you?
MELISSA: Fifteen (*Slight pause.*) In a couple weeks. (*Pause.*) So? How'd I do?
CHRISTIAN: What do you mean, a loner?
MELISSA: You walk like you want to be alone, like this.
     Melissa imitates his walk, slightly exaggerated, a thug.
CHRISTIAN (*laughs a little*): I don't walk like that, you look like an idiot. (*Pause.*) And what's this about a girlfriend?
MELISSA: You don't have a girlfriend?
CHRISTIAN: Unh uh, why'd you think that?
MELISSA: That was the one thing I wasn't positive about, that and your age. (*Pause.*) Can't be perfect.

Scene 4

Tim's pottery studio and Myrna's apartment are simultaneously visible on the stage. Tim is moving unfired objects out of the room, while Alison works on a bowl. Myrna, dressed in her bathrobe and alone, is smoking a cigarette, looking at the clock, waiting. When the buzzer on her intercom sounds, she ascertains that it is Alan and presses the downstairs buzzer to admit him.
     In the studio, Alison tells Tim she believes that she's been flunking life lately. She's certain, at at least, that she's not doing a satisfactory job with her piece of pottery.
     Alan enters Myrna's apartment. He's tired and drained after a seven-hour operation to remove a brain tumor from a little boy, whose unnatural stillness on the operating table brought back memories: "I know how death looks, there are no surprises, you acquire this *distance.* But today brought it back, seeing my own son on the table and thinking . . . what *is* this, this stillness? (*Pause.*) When you lose the distance, you're lost."
     Myrna is worried because Christian has been asking her questions and seems to have guessed, somehow, that she is carrying on an affair with a married man, a brain surgeon. Myrna doesn't want Christian to think of his mother as "a sleazy slut of a marriage breaker," she tells Alan as they exit into the bedroom.
     In the studio, Alison throws her despised bit of pottery into the air and lets it smash itself to pieces on the floor. She confesses to Tim that she is somewhat fearful of what Melissa thinks about her parents; she and Alan have pretended, since their son Ned's death, that Ned never existed, and Alison fears that maybe

Melissa believes it and believes her mother and father's relationship is closer than it really is. Tim assures Alison that Melissa will work out her own destiny. Tim massages her shoulders and temples to relax her.

TIM: How does it work with Alan?
ALISON: What?
TIM: Do you make love?
ALISON (*pause*): Not for a long time.
TIM (*pause*): Why?
ALISON: Because it makes me too sad.
    He massages her for a few more moments, then stops.
TIM (*resting his hands on her shoulders*): There.
    Pause. Then reaching for one of his hands, Alison swivels around on the stool.
ALISON: Will you kiss me?
    Pause.
TIM (*looks at her*): Alison . . .
ALISON: Just once.
    He leans in and kisses her, lightly, but for a long moment. Then, slowly, they pull away. Her eyes are closed, and finally she opens them, sees him watching her. Pause.
Thank you.
TIM: You could be a star lover. A real star.
ALISON: You think so?
TIM: Positively star material.
ALISON: I think I was once, actually.

In the apartment, Christian comes in and calls out for Myrna. There are panicky sounds from the bedroom, then Myrna appears in her bathrobe. Christian has come home early because he has quit the track team—the coach is "a Nazi idiot." Myrna persuades him to go out and get them some Chinese food for dinner, and Christian exits.

Alan enters, pulling on his trousers, taking the whole thing as a joke.

ALAN: Myrna, what would it matter if he knew? Melissa survived.
MYRNA: We won't defile her home with our filthy adulterous bodies. (*Pause.*) Did you hear he quit the track team?
ALAN: So?
MYRNA: So there go our afternoons, Alan.
ALAN: Ahhh. Well, there's always the. . . . . Inn.
    Pause. She moves away, angry.
Myrna? *Myrna.* Love will find a way.
MYRNA: We'll just see what happens?
ALAN: What do you want me to do, call the coach? That Nazi?
    She collapses in a chair. He goes to her.
Myrna love, what can I do, what do you want?
MYRNA: We're not allowed to talk about what I want.
ALAN: Oh. (*Pause.*) A yacht on the Mediterranean.

MYRNA: The question is whether you know what *you* want. (*Pause.*) I'm sorry. (*She gets up, goes to him.*) I *am* sorry, I didn't mean that. (*She embraces him.*) I'm very happy.

Scene 5

Melissa and Christian are sitting on a park bench, she scanning the area with her binoculars. She persuades Christian to kneel and look her closely in the eye —either one. She points out that he can see himself reflected there.

Scene 6

At the breakfast table, Alison is troubled because Melissa is seeing Christian every day—she's even given up spying. Alan feels this is a normal part of the growing-up process. Alison accuses him of being a "hip" parent encouraging Melissa to become a "hip" daughter, against Alison's better judgment. Before Alan can find out exactly what Alison means by "hip," Melissa enters and takes a bit of breakfast on the wing as she heads for school. She is planning to meet Christian this afternoon after they finish at their separate schools, and Alan half-heartedly cautions her against seeing too much of him.

In the course of the conversation Alison asks for the friend's name, and without thinking Melissa replies "Christian." Alan freezes. Melissa having let the cat this far out of the bag, decides to open it all the way and adds, "He's Myrna's kid. It's . . . something that happened." Melissa goes off to school, leaving her parents hardly knowing what to say to each other.

Scene 7

Christian and Melissa come in to Myrna's apartment and find a note from Myrna apoligizing for not being there to make Melissa's acquaintance, as planned, today—a friend has an emergency, and Myrna will be out all evening.

The young people are both a bit selfconscious. Christian tries to light a ciga- rette, and Melissa tries to stop him. A roughhouse soon develops, with Melissa doubling him over with a punch in the solar plexus and (the cigarette abandoned) with Christian getting her down, sitting on her, making as though to kiss her but not doing it.

When they calm down, Christian massages a sore spot on Melissa's back. At the same time, he wonders about Melissa's father: being a doctor, he must sometimes see his patients die. This thought disturbs Melissa, but she rises above it, moving around the room, picking up and studying a framed picture of Chris- tian as a young child.

MELISSA: Look at you, Christian.
　　　He moves a little closer behind her.
You were beautiful.
CHRISTIAN (*a little embarrassed laugh*): Beautiful?
MELISSA: Tres gentil. (*Pause.*) You still are. (*Pause.*) Sometimes . . . sometimes you can see from pictures what people are going to be . . . what you're going to . . .

*She stops, seized by an emotion the picture has awakened. But she bat-
tles it, and very deliberately, mechanically, she places the frame back
on the table. She then places her palms on the table, supports herself.*
CHRISTIAN (*takes a step toward her*): Melissa?

*We see that she is crying, quietly, all to herself, trying to hold it in.
Christian moves to her, unsure, puts his hands on her shoulders. Melissa
lets her head fall back against him, and he holds her, tentatively. After
a moment she turns to him, looks at him. She touches his face with her
hand, and he doesn't move. Slowly, she pulls him to her and she kisses
him, lightly. She pulls away, then she kisses him again. When this kiss
is broken, she pulls away—and she laughs—a soft, astonished sound
of joy and release. Christian is lost in her.*

*What follows is like a dance, a series of movements that have ele-
ments of game and ritual, a dance of love and a prelude to lovemaking.
Moments of breaking away, coming together, twirling, teasing, pursu-
ing, yielding.*

*At the end they come together a last time. Whatever the final actions
become, we have an implicit understanding that they are about to make
love. Lights fade to black. Curtain.*

ACT II

Scene 8

The dual playing areas in this scene are the Gifford living room and Myrna's
apartment. In the latter, Christian is sitting alone, reading a letter. In the former,
Melissa has just told her parents that she is pregnant. Alison is taking it calmly,
but Alan is agitated, asking "Why?" and again "Why?" Melissa replies evenly,
"There isn't an answer for everything, Dad."

Myrna joins Christian, who has just finished reading a letter from his father
in Los Angeles. Christian doesn't want to go out there this summer as he cus-
tomarily does; he'd prefer to get a job and stay here.

Alison is trying to get things organized: Alan can set things up at his hospital
so that Melissa will have complete privacy. But Melissa doesn't want this—she
wants Christian to escort her to some other hospital to have herself taken care
of. She exits before her parents can comment.

At Myrna's, Christian's mother is assuring him that if he spends the summer
with his father, Melissa will still be here when he comes home, and there are
plenty of girls out there. Christian tries to convince Myrna that his fondness for
Melissa is not trivial.

CHRISTIAN: . . . . . I think it's *real.*
MYRNA: Of course you do, honey, you always think it's real, and sometimes
it *is* real. (*Pause.*) What do you mean, real?
CHRISTIAN: I mean . . . *love* real.
MYRNA: Oh. *Oh.* (*Pause.*) You're both *fifteen,* honey.

CHRISTIAN: What about your thing, is that love real? Even though he's married and all that?

MYRNA: Well . . . I think we love each other *despite* things like that, Christian, you have to try to forget the things you need to forget. (*Slight pause.*) So there's no reason not to go to California, you can write letters.

CHRISTIAN: You can just forget all that stuff?

MYRNA: You *try*, Christian. No, you can't forget, but you get to a point where you say, "If I think about that it's going to drive me crazy," so . . . That's what love is sometimes, honey, you take what you get and you say, all *right*, maybe it's not everything you ever . . . And . . . (*She sees his puzzled face, stops; exhales it.*) Oh Christ.

In the Gifford living room, Alison puts her arms around Alan (a rarity these days, which they both find pleasant) and reassures him that things will work out. But Alan is troubled when Alison tells him gently that she will now probably have to meet Myrna some time to find out what kind of person she is.

ALAN: Why don't you invite Timothy, too. We can have a sleep-over.
    Pause.

ALISON (*very matter-of-fact*): Timothy and I are not lovers, Alan, I think you should know that.

ALAN (*pause; then*): What?

ALISON: I . . . pretended. The funny thing was, I think I actually started to believe it. Have you ever done that? Make something up for long enough that you forgot you made it up?

ALAN: No, Alison, I find that hard to accept, actually.

ALISON: Timothy and I work together, Alan, that's it. Does that disappoint you? (*She looks at him.*) It does, doesn't it?

ALAN (*thinking*): Disappoint me? No, I . . . What do you want me to say, Alison? (*Pause.*) Why would you want to make me believe you were . . . ?

ALISON: To make it easier for you? To feel even with you? I don't know. Can you believe I did that?
    Pause. He makes a gesture of incomprehension.
Well. When this is all over, I want to figure out what we're up against, find out if it's worth it.

ALAN (*small, facetious laugh*): What, make a . . . determination? Thumbs up or thumbs down, like some Roman emperor?

ALISON (*smiles, nods*): Something like that.

Scene 9

Melissa visits Tim in his studio, knowing that her mother will not be there. She has come here, she says, just to "hang out" for a while and gets Tim to promise not to tell anyone else she was here. Tim shows her the shelves of his and Alison's latest pottery, quite obviously differing in style; as Melissa observes, "Hers are all kinda crazy, and yours all look like eggshells or something."

Tim explains that in making pottery you have to let yourself go, let your instincts and the clay take over, fire it and hope for the best. Melissa sees in this something of an analogy of her own present creative feelings.

Scene 10

Outdoors, Christian and Melissa are discussing the immediate future. Christian is determined to stay here in town this summer. His mother has a good part in an Ibsen play, so he and Melissa will have her apartment to themselves most evenings if the show is a success.

Christian hopes Melissa will want to make love with him again soon. Shyly, they discuss the previous time. Melissa declares she could feel herself become pregnant. Then she confesses to Christian that she has decided not to take any measures to terminate the pregnancy, as he had thought she would.

MELISSA: . . . . . I'm going to have the baby.
CHRISTIAN: You didn't . . . ?
> *He half squints at her, tries to see if she's serious. Looks away, then back at her. He can't speak.*
MELISSA (*nods slowly, softly*): I'm going to.
> *He sinks back a little, helpless.*
Christian . . . I couldn't tell you. It was something I had to decide myself. (*Pause.*) But really I didn't have to decide, I just knew.
> *Pause.*
CHRISTIAN (*softly imploring*): You don't want to have a *baby*, Melissa. *Do* you?
MELISSA (*looks away, then back to him*): Christian, I . . . I *had* to. (*She tries to say something else, can't, shakes her head; then, very simple.*) I can't explain it.
CHRISTIAN: Uh huh.
MELISSA: You don't have to do anything you don't want to do, Christian, ever, I mean, if you want you can just visit sometimes . . . I take all the responsibility, all of it.
> *Pause.*
CHRISTIAN: Did you tell anybody?
MELISSA (*shakes her head*): They don't have anything to do with it.
> *Pause.*
CHRISTIAN: What am *I* supposed to do?
MELISSA: Nothing. If you can, just try to understand, even if you don't.
CHRISTIAN: Yeah.
> *Pause. She reaches for him, he lowers his head, and she gently embraces him.*

Scene 11

At the Giffords', Alan and Alison are preparing to receive Myrna and Christian for the first time. Melissa joins them. Nervously, Alan prepares drinks for himself and Alison.

The doorbell rings, and Alan answers it—it's Myrna, alone. It seems that Christian is unexpectedly busy because his old coach has persuaded him to take part in a track meet. The necessary introduction takes place, then Melissa decides to go for a walk, as Alan fixes Myrna a drink. Awkwardly, the grownups try to find polite things to say to each other, until Alan can bear it no longer and departs, leaving the women to cope with each other.

Alison and Myrna explore various subjects including Tim (of whom Myrna has heard) and Myrna's lapsing marriage. As Alison makes them another drink, Myrna remarks that from what she knows about it she has imagined that the Giffords have an ongoing successful marriage, reasonably content, each with a lover. Alison replies, "Well, yes, I suppose it was, has been, despite everything. You do what you do, you chat, you eat dinner, you sleep, you get up, your life is going along and you never really worry too hard about where it's going."

On her side, Alison has always imagined Myrna as 32 (she is 37), and content, though in fact she is not—she lacks a husband.

ALISON: But you have mine.
    Pause.
MYRNA: So, we've come to it.
ALISON: No, I want you to understand, I don't blame you. You did nothing but fill a void, you filled a void in Alan's life, and I welcomed you. I *welcomed* you. (*Pause.*) When my son died, part of me . . . left Alan. It just happened. Alan stayed at the hospital, I took long walks, and we slept apart . . . for a long time.
MYRNA: You don't have to tell me this.
ALISON: When Alan found you I was *glad*. I want you to understand that I never resented you for that. I was grateful.
MYRNA: And *you* had your potter friend.
ALISON: Yes, I had pottery. Which did for me what you did for Alan. It brought me out of mourning.

The two women discover that they each requested Alan to arrange for her to meet the other—Myrna because she felt sorry for Alison when she heard about Melissa. And now the Melissa-Christian friendship seems to be winding down, with Christian back on the track team.

Alison comments, "Melissa said that he, that Christian was wonderful when . . . she went for the abortion." Myrna, in surprise, declares, "Christian said you took her." "Some sort of confusion," Alison concludes.

Scene 12

Melissa, alone, says to herself, "Sometimes when I was little I'd lie in bed and . . . there were these things in the air. (*Pause.*) I'd watch these, like . . . these shadows, kind of move across the ceiling . . . like little spirits. Sometimes I'd talk to 'em in my head, you know, it was like they knew how to read my mind. (*Pause.*) I still think about them."

Scene 13

Two areas are visible: Tim's studio and a sidewalk cafe. In the studio, Tim and Alison are working diligently, while in the cafe Alan and Myrna are talking about a tour Myrna has been offered, which will take her out of town—and away from

Alan—for a couple of months. Myrna thinks of herself as Alan's back-up system, but Alan swears that he loves her. Myrna has sometimes dreamed that Alison would leave Alan free by running off with Tim; nevertheless, she has decided to accept the offer of the tour, though Alan clearly wants her to stay. Myrna now knows that Melissa is having the baby, which will be "equally a part of *me,* and I intend to do everything I can to make it know that, Alan, to love it." That's what matters most to Myrna now. As she gets up to go, she advises Alan, "Distance yourself. You're usually good at it."

In the studio, Alison has just mixed the clay for a new piece, as the scene ends.

Scene 14

Christian and Melissa meet in the park and talk about school. Her friends are beginning to notice that she is gaining weight. He won the 220-yard dash in the recent meet. Christian refers sarcastically to Melissa's reluctance to repeat the lovemaking with him, implying that there might be others in line ahead of him. He means this as a joke, but Melissa is nevertheless offended by his attitude and declares, "I would never make love with anybody else. *Ever"* unless and until she heard that Christian had been unfaithful.

Finally Christian informs Melissa that he has decided to spend the summer in Los Angeles with his father, after all.

MELISSA: Sounds like a good idea, Christian.
CHRISTIAN: It does?
MELISSA: You have to do what you have to do.
CHRISTIAN (*nods slowly*): Right.
MELISSA: You *have* to.
CHRISTIAN: Well, I am. That's what I'm gonna do.
      Pause. Melissa stands on the bench, holds up her binoculars, looks out.
      After a moment, Christian stands, unsure. She senses he's leaving.
MELISSA (*with the glasses to her eyes, looking away from him*): See you later, Christian.
CHRISTIAN: (*looks at her, puzzled; then*): Yeah.
      He turns and moves away, slowly; looks back once before he exits. Melissa drops the glasses, looks off where he went. Then she cries, silently, painfully. It overtakes her.

Scene 15

In the middle of the night in the Giffords' living room, Alan assures Alison that he has no plans to try to join Myrna in some far-off city: "I'm not *going* anywhere." Alison sums up her first impression of Myrna: "I thought, 'What a lovely woman.' No fangs. No skin under her nails. I saw the attraction. I'm sure she'll be a good grandmother."

Alan wants to go on with their marriage as they are, and Alison accuses him of avoiding the realities of his life year after year. Alan asserts that he has lived: "When you were off wallowing in yourself, I *was* alive, working, feeling, loving." Why didn't he leave her? Alison wonders. "Because there was nowhere to go . . . . .And I didn't want to."

Alison recalls the night they came home from the hospital after the accident. Alan wondered how it had happened.

ALAN (*pleading*): *Please* . . .

ALISON: No, Alan, I have to do this. And I told you? That I was still in the store, paying for some presents and . . . and I let him get out of my sight?

> *Pause. Alan is still looking away.*

And you said . . . you let him get out of your sight? You *let* him get out of your sight? (*Pause.*) You made me mourn alone, Alan.

ALAN (*turning*): I also mourned.

ALISON: Alone! You made me mourn alone. (*Pause.*) I waited and waited and waited. For seven years, since the moment he was killed, Alan, I've waited for you to forgive me.

ALAN (*shaking*): You forget what it was like, Alison. You gave up, you gave me up.

ALISON: And then Myrna came along and claimed you?

ALAN: She made me *like* myself better.

ALISON (*crying out*): That's my job! You let her do it instead to punish me, Alan, and you're still punishing me. (*Pause.*) Well. We're going to have another child in our house. And before that happens, Alan, before that happens, I have to know.

ALAN (*looks at her, he's struggling not to cry*): I couldn't then, I couldn't.

ALISON (*softly*): I know. (*Pause.*) And now, Alan? Can you forgive me now?

ALAN: I *want* to, Alison, I . . .

ALISON (*raises a hand, cutting him off*): Please. Don't say any more. That's enough.

Scene 16

Melissa is alone in dream lighting similar to that in the first scene. She remembers a dream long ago, when she was 7 years old, with a ride in an ambulance and a lot of screaming and whispering in it.

MELISSA: . . . . . It was Christmastime. We came out of the store, and we're going down this sidewalk, Ned and me, and I see a Santa Claus on the next block. And I say to Ned, race you to Santa! And I give him a head start, cause, you know, he's only four, it wouldn't be fair. (*Pause.*) And we run, and he's ahead. And when he gets to the curb he can't stop. And then the taxi comes.

> *Pause. A change in the lights.*

I named her Aimee, A-I-M-E-E, like the French spell it.

> *Pause.*

Ned used to tell me that he could see himself in my eye, it was like a game we played. He would stare in my eye and look real hard, like he was trying to find out a secret I had. I'm sure he never thought of it like a secret, he was just looking for his reflection.

> *Pause.*

Lots of times with Aimee I hold her and stare in her eyes the same way. And I sing her songs in French, I talk to her about Christian. I tell her she is my

lovechild, mon Aimee. Sometimes I can't get her to look straight at me, she moves all around, looking in different directions. But sometimes, when she looks right at me, I can see my reflection. And sometimes, sometimes I see Ned. I believe in . . . spirits.
>   *Pause.*
Some day, Aimee and I are going to go and live in France. And Christian too, if he wants.
>   *Lights fade to black. Curtain.*

Other Outstanding New Plays Cited
By American Theater Critics Association Members

E/R Emergency Room, company-developed (Chicago: Organic Theater)—*E/R Emergency Room* is a comedy about life and death in an emergency room in a small Chicago hospital. The patients and their problems are often grotesque and incredible, but *E/R* is firmly anchored in the reality of emergency medicine. And while comedy dominates, the play also pays respect to the fragile human lives that begin and end in emergency rooms.

Like time-lapse photography, *E/R* records all that occurs during one shift in the emergency room at Lincoln Memorial Hospital. We see the boss, Dr. Sherman, a young physician whose specialty is emergency medicine and whose personality is wry macho. The good doctor relishes overruling his staff and practising his science with an urgent bravado. We see an earth-motherly nurse who has seen it all and can handle it all; another physician who works double shifts to overcome the financial ruin caused by a divorce; and a wall-flowerish receptionist who becomes tough as a drill sergeant when chaos threatens to engulf the emergency room.

But most of all, *E/R* shows us funny sketches of real, believable people. There is the well-dressed man who arrives complaining of an earache. His actual problem is a light bulb that is lodged in the mostly unlikely and sensitive area imaginable—far from his ear. How did it get there? He doesn't know. A teen-age girl arrives, complaining of constipation; her constipation quickly becomes a baby. After the delivery, she defiantly shouts to her mother, "I didn't have no baby." And there is the elderly hypochondriac, desperate for someone to find something physically wrong with her. At one point she declares that she is suffering from "fireballs of the Eucharist."

E/R has found some of the basic elements of comedy and tragedy in American urban life and reflected them accurately.

> DAMIEN JACQUES
> Milwaukee *Journal*

Fool for Love by Sam Shepard (San Francisco: Magic Theater)—Thrilling theater can come from such basic formulas as: X wants to stay in the room and Y wants to get him out. In *Fool for Love*, May is X, determined not to be coaxed out of

MILWAUKEE REPERTORY THEATER—Alan Brooks and
William Leach in a scene from *The Foreigner* by Larry Shue

her motel room in order to live with that damn fool, Eddie, who always dumps
her the minute he gets her back; and Eddie is Y, determined to reclaim his woman
—he hasn't driven his horse-trailer 2,480 miles for zip.

Who's that whiskered geezer in the rocking chair? That's May's and Eddie's
father. It seems they're half-brother and sister, as well as ex-lovers. Maybe that's
why they're so good at fighting. Is the father really there? In their minds, anyhow.
What about this Countess that May accuses Eddie of cheating with? She may be
a figment, too. But something's prowling around out there in the American dark.
And it's for sure that May's got a date for the movies.

This is a fine, taut play, full of real behavior, with a mystery in the corner that
won't be solved and that we don't particularly want solved. No need, given
characters as vivid as May and Eddie, who come at each other like Kate and
Petruchio. But no one's going to get tamed here. It's an equal match, whoever
gets the last fall.

The play gives us Shepard's love for women who can hold their own, also his
love for unrepentant rummies and banged-up stunt-riders, also his love for the
conjectural past—the truth of the tall story.

DAN SULLIVAN
Los Angeles *Times*

The Foreigner by Larry Shue (Milwaukee Repertory Theater)—Larry Shue,
an actor in the Milwaukee Repertory Theater company, deals with communication in his *The Foreigner*. He contends that a person unable to speak or
understand the language of his surroundings places himself in something of
a place of honor where he will be taken care of and loved. It also puts

him in the embarrassing position of overhearing much more than he wants to.

A British visitor to a family inn in America's South wanting to avoid entangling intercourse pretends to speak a nonsense language. His unavoidable eavesdropping moves him to drop his pretense in order to combat the cruel domination over the family's slow-witted son, to thwart the fortune-hunting courtship of a hypocritical preacher and to bring down the tyranny of a vicious sheriff.

Before the hero accomplishes his ends in a farcical finale of whirlwind proportions, Shue has subtly demonstrated the value of loving tolerance and the folly of brutal bigotry.

The Foreigner contains sly slaps at the illogical nature of the English language, tender praise for human nature and devastating criticism of ignorant oppression.

JAY JOSLYN
Milwaukee *Sentinel*

Gandhiji by Rose Leiman Goldemberg (Los Angeles: Los Angeles Actors' Theater)—As Shaw noted in *St. Joan*, the world doesn't welcome its saints. But is this always the world's fault? What if you, reader, had to share your life with a "selfless" man who was absolutely convinced that he was doing God's work? To live with a saint takes the patience of one.

This is the theme of *Gandhiji*, a far less reverential look at Mohandas Gandhi than the recent film. There we saw Gandhi the ikon. Here we see Gandhi the man—a great and holy man, Goldemberg has no doubt. But his greatness had a price. And his loved ones, particularly the women, paid a good deal of it.

The play transpires in Gandhi's mind a split-second before an assassin's bullet darkens it forever. He and a troupe of imaginary strolling players act out his life for his and our judgement. We see his painful uphill fight to master his nerves and his lusts and to reach the calm of truth. Less admirably, we see the enormous demands he routinely made on those around him, as if their basic purpose on earth was to help him achieve a higher spiritual plane.

If Gandhi was a saint, says the play, he was also a bit of an exploiter. If he was selfless, he was also a typical Indian husband who expected to be obeyed, married to a woman with no taste for obedience. (This leads to some pungent domestic comedy.) *Gandhiji* is a skeptical study of a difficult man. Interesting how much closer one feels to him than to the figure in the film.

DAN SULLIVAN
Los Angeles *Times*

Going to See the Elephant by Karen Hensel and Elana Kent, based on an idea by Patti Johns (Pasadena: Los Angeles Repertory Theater)—*Going to See the Elephant* deals with four women on the Kansas frontier in 1870.

Sarah, a young wife and mother, is struggling to make a home on the bleak prairie for her husband and young children—who are away, at the time of the play, on a several-days' journey to bring supplies from the settlement.

She is aided by Ma, her mother-in-law, who plans to stay only long enough to help get the family settled. Then she is going to move on farther west, perhaps to nurse soldiers in Colorado. She is not, despite her age, going to settle down and take root. She wants to "see the elephant"—to see what's over the next hill.

Mrs. Nichols, who came out with her husband and young son hoping to find an idealistic, Thoreau-like life and instead found only tragedy—the death of their son—and despair, is ready to give up and return to the East. She has stopped off with Sarah and Ma because of the illness of her husband—Ma having a reputation for healing powers.

Etta, a young neighbor, has walked the more than ten miles from her farm at the word that there are strangers, new faces, to be seen. While taking in the splendor of Mrs. Nichols and her Eastern clothes, she discusses with Sarah her plans for marriage to a young Army officer who was one of the company who rescued her from captivity with the Indians.

The four women discuss their situations, they fight off an attack of wolves on the livestock, and at the end Mrs. Nichols leaves to continue her retreat to the East, leaving her husband in Ma's care. Sarah and Etta resolve to continue to make the best of the hard frontier life, and Ma remains determined to see as much of the world—of "the elephant"—as she can while she still has the strength.

T.E. FOREMAN
Riverside *Press-Enterprise*

Letters From Prison by Jack Henry Abbott (Providence: Trinity Square Repertory Company)—When Jack Henry Abbott began a correspondence with Norman Mailer he was a furious man, his anger springing from a life lived in a trash bin, a life in which his parents gave up early and saw him spend all but 18 months of his adult life behind bars.

His edited letters became *In the Belly of the Beast*, a critically successful book adapted for the stage by Providence's Trinity Square Repertory Company. The theater was excited by Abbott's whip-sharp prose and his vivid view of life on the inside.

The book was no anecdotal memoir. It was a scream in the night, a kaleidoscope of black holes and beatings around a center concerning the fear and power gained in the act of killing another man with a knife. *In the Belly of the Beast* was unrelentingly discomfiting, but it shone with hard truth and provided a perhaps unique view of the other-than-John-Wayne reality of that American icon, the man alone.

Adapted and directed by Adrian Hall, with a set by Eugene Lee and with Richard Jenkins giving an elastic and subtle performance as Jack Abbott, Trinity's production was a stunning piece of work. The play—changed considerably just before the opening—ranged from isolation cells where Abbott survived on cockroaches to his last moments of freedom when he knifed another victim in New York.

The staged work asked how our society could produce a man as deranged as Jack Abbott. By its very nature the play was also dangerously close to an apology for the man. But in the end it was one of those works that help us to re-think, those with still open minds, what seemed a closed situation.

In the end, *Letters From Prison* offered no answers but was that rare commodity, a play that let us see with new eyes.

WILLIAM K. GALE
Providence *Journal-Bulletin*

The Man Who Could See Through Time by Terri Wagener (Houston: Stages)—
The atmosphere in the tranquil attic where the physicist Prof. Mordecai Bates
works is broken by the startling and at first resented arrival of a young woman,
Ellen Brock, formerly his student and now a sculptor with the promise of the big
time.

She's there to do a sculptured bust of the important scientist, commissioned
by his sister who owns the house where he lives and works. The play becomes
a collision of personalities at critical moments in both their lives. She, as a woman,
represents a new freedom and, being younger, still has the promise of tomorrow.
He, past his prime, once yearned for the Nobel Prize and suffers a growing lack
of confidence, loneliness and the possibility of narrow vision.

As Ellen returns to work on the sculpture, the tense relationship takes unexpected turns. Ellen, it is revealed, had been the lover of Tom Fielder, Bates's
treasured young colleague, a brilliant former student who had gone on to develop
the acclaimed Fielder lens. "That mechanism, when used in conjunction with
mathematics, seems by all experimentation so far to distinguish relative motion
from pure motion," Bates explains. "The physics world is on its collective ear
. . . . . Tom has gifted the scientific world with, quite literally, the ability to see
through time. Time travel should be next, Miss Brock," Bates says to his young
visitor.

But Fielder, who could have been another Einstein in Bates's belief, has died,
victim of a bleeding disease. The painful irony, as Bates puts it, is "that a group
of so-called medical geniuses whose job it is to replace hearts and repair brains
could not save a brilliant young man." Further irony develops as Ellen breaks
the news to the professor that Fielder has been awarded the Nobel Prize, and that
she will be the recipient of the funds that accompany it—at Fielder's request.
Ellen and Bates move subtly into adversary positions, and their exchange becomes
in part a debate on the respective virtues of art and science.

Wagener has structured her play for two characters so that Bates appears
frequently before his class (actually the audience) to lecture on such subjects as
Einstein's Unified Field theory; the atmosphere of Venus; the abacus and the rose;
the echo of the Big Bang. At one of these, Ellen rises and challenges the professor.

Wagener has done her research admirably and further has nimbly laced it into
these lectures so that they are not as formidable as they sound, and one may
actually have a sense of understanding. The scholarly tangents that these lectures
provide don't detract from the play's main thrust: the delicacy of the relationship.
There is a moment when the two experience a warm moment, but they veer off.
There's a frustration in the sense that Bates and Ellen could get together but don't
or can't. That's a strength of the play, however. Less satisfying is Ellen's approach
to her calling. As a sculptor of high promise, she is unprofessional in her emotional response when the sculpture is given a violent blow by the angered professor. Any true artist would know that the work could be restored; the question
is: does she have the desire?

Nevertheless the play is a bright exploration of the passing association of two
individuals, like comets, affected by the pull of a number of universal forces.

ANN HOLMES
Houston *Chronicle*

On the Money by John Kostmayer (Burbank: Victory Theater)—This is an exceptionally powerful, ably constructed, naturalistic play about the evils of money—or the lack of money—in the Violent Society, that starts out with deceptively light humor and ends in a bloodbath as stark and unrelenting as reality itself.

Three overworked and underpaid employees of Candy Solomon's Black River Cafe, a basement restaurant and bar in New York City, devise a Sunday night holdup that might give each of them a relatively harmless way out of serious financial dilemmas. It's the almost perfect setup, and a weekend's take is a drop in the bucket for their ungenerous employer. But it might give Jack, the debt-ridden bartender with a working wife and three kids, a chance to pay off the loan shark; it might enable Nancy, the waitress, to settle huge doctor bills and put her kid in a school where she won't get beaten up; it might give the gambling waiter Benny (who dreams up the idea) a desperately needed chance to pay back money borrowed from dangerous characters and lost on the horses. But the plan misfires, ending in Benny's death and a harrowing confrontation between Jack and an unhinged gunman.

Kostmayer's primary skill, after carefully building his house of cards, is in persuasively demonstrating that each individual—loan shark, criminal, psychopath and miserly boss—is ultimately a victim of social conditioning. The catapulting events of Act II brilliantly reinforce that proposition. This is a stark, startling piece of high-powered action-drama that carries with it unexpected philosophical resonances, reaching deep into our collective conscience for an honest assessment of the principles on which our society is founded.

SYLVIE DRAKE
Los Angeles *Times*

Sand Castles by Adele Edling Shank (San Francisco: Magic Theater; Actors Theater of Louisville)—Adele Edling Shank, author of *Sunset/Sunrise* and *Winterplay*, continues her exploration of America's suburban lost in this comedy-drama set on a California beach. Several characters overlap from her previous play *Stuck*, an examination of business types; here, they, along with friends and family, are confronting their thwarted dreams and hopes, coming to new sexual and social arrangements, taking care of business—all on a hyper-realistically designed beach setting. It's a kind of Chekhovian tragicomedy in modern dress, one that walks a fine line between soap opera and acute social analysis. As in Shank's other plays, there is a technological twist: in this case, walkie-talkies utilized by a prostitute and her daughter as a business tool/security check. There is also an interesting theatrical device of switching from foreground on the beach to background on the boardwalk. The result is a quintessentially American play that compels attention.

BERNARD WEINER
San Francisco *Chronicle*

She Also Dances by Kenneth Arnold (Costa Mesa: South Coast Repertory)—This play is so meticulously conceived that its elements come together like music. Arnold has set himself a number of unusual obstacles, one of which is to write interestingly of a hard-to-capture period, one's teens to early 20s; another of which is to make one of the principals handicapped during a time when it seems that an entire wing of the American theater is being converted into a hospital for the suicidal, cancer-ridden, or otherwise terminally afflicted; and yet another of which is to work his action in a non-naturalistic mode. If that isn't enough, one of the two characters in *She Also Dances* must have gymnastic skills, since he has to perform on a high bar throughout.

Lucy is the handicapped daughter of wealthy Newport (California) parents who hires Ted, an aspiring dancer and gymnast, to push her wheelchair around campus. She can't move; he's all movement, a nervous reaction to her caustic wit and probing intelligence. Arnold is especially skilled at suggesting the thorny labyrinths Lucy surrounds herself with in order to spare herself disappointment. Lucy's smart, somewhat bitter dialogue is a bit hard for the gentler, ostensibly good-humored (but privately fearful) Ted to handle. In time they (and we) learn a great deal about their lives; their tentative emotional pas de deux is elevated into an informal dance as a central guiding metaphor. "People don't know the dances they do," Ted tells her. "They don't notice what happens when two people touch." They hold their palms up to each other, and we see what he means: body language works in a continuous relation with the surrounding world.

At one point Ted dumps her out of the chair onto the floor. It's a shocking, seemingly crude gesture, but it serves its purpose—it gets her out of her metal fortress. He picks her up and twirls her around his body, gently but exuberantly, and she discovers what he means: life is movement. When they become lovers, we don't think "How great it is that handicapped girl can make it with young stud." Instead, it becomes a powerfully unselfconscious expression here of what sex would be: a confluence of physical, emotional and spiritual movement.

Arnold is a poet, which means he has an eye and ear for the rightness of details, and he's added an onstage clarinet accompanist to help with mood and tone. When done well, as it was at the South Coast Rep (Jules Aaron directed Patti Johns and Marc Vahanian), the ending of *She Also Dances* seems to have a palpable ping.

LAWRENCE CHRISTON
Los Angeles *Times*

The Value of Names by Jeffrey Sweet (Actors Theater of Louisville)—How long is long enough to remember the wrongs that have been done against us? Jeffrey Sweet's *The Value of Names* explores that question as it relates to a blacklisted actor, his actress daughter and the director who named him before the House Un-American Activities Committee. Benny was a successful actor until his good friend Leo gave his name to HUAC in order to save Leo's then-promising directorial career. As a result, Benny could not work for six years. Though Benny has recently attained fame in a TV situation comedy, he remains bitter towards Leo. And this bitterness is the cause of the main conflict in Sweet's play; for, when Norma, his daughter, lands a choice role in a play whose director is fired, the replacement director is the now-famous Leo. Should Norma give up her opportunity in support of her father, by refusing to work with Leo? Has enough time passed to enable Benny to forgive Leo when he comes asking for Benny's renewed friendship? With humor and compassion, Sweet has his characters grapple with these problems until they reach their individual—and probably inevitable—conclusions.

DEBBI WASSERMAN
Westchester

A Weekend Near Madison by Kathleen Tolan (Actors Theater of Louisville)— In the *Fifth of July* mode, Kathleen Tolan's sensitive new play brings a group of old friends together for a weekend of reckoning. They had been passionate liberals together in a commune during the 1970s. Now their lives are on an emotional roller coaster, as the three women exercise their options (lesbianism, abortion, feminism), and the two men (brothers) founder in emotional confusion and uncertainty.

A Weekend Near Madison is not in the least a polemic for feminism or anything else. It's an amusing and touching exploration of the emotional havoc alternative lifestyles can wreak, particularly when the biological urge to have a child makes its demand.

The five friends assemble in the home of David, a kind and accepting psychiatrist, and his wife Doe, who has been despondent since she had an abortion. David's brother Jim once loved Vanessa, who has deserted him for Samantha, her lesbian lover and sister-in-song (they're singers) in the feminist movement. Vanessa and Samantha are happy together, but they want a child to make their union complete. Could Jim possibly oblige?

What could have been sitcom comedy/pathos in lesser hands becomes three-dimensional and moving in Tolan's grasp. There is much good writing in the script and an abundance of compassion. But there's also far too much pop talk of the "Wow!" variety, a favored expression of Vanessa's, which makes her seem silly, when she isn't. Only in this instance does Tolan do a disservice to her characters.

HELEN C. SMITH
Atlanta *Journal*-Atlanta *Constitution*

Yellow Fever by R.A. Shiomi (San Francisco: Asian American Theater Company)—Using the form of a Sam Spade-type detective thriller, playwright R. A. Shiomi takes the audience entertainingly behind the scenes of the Japanese-American community, revealing both the internal politics and widely varying points of view, as well as trenchantly pointing up the racist society that surrounds, and attempts to define and thus control, it. That description may sound heavy, but in practise, it's anything but, as the *Maltese Falcon*-like comic plot unfolds.

BERNARD WEINER
San Francisco *Chronicle*

A DIRECTORY OF PROFESSIONAL REGIONAL THEATER

Compiled by Ella A. Malin

Professional 1982–83 programs and repertory productions by leading resident companies around the United States, plus major Shakespeare festivals, are grouped in alphabetical order of their locations and listed in date order from May, 1982 to June, 1983. This list generally does not include Broadway, off-Broadway or touring New York shows (unless the local company took some special part), summer theaters, single productions by commercial producers or college or other nonprofessional productions. The Directory was compiled by Ella A. Malin for *The Best Plays of 1982–83* from information provided by the resident producing organizations at Miss Malin's request. First productions of new plays—American or world premieres—in regional theaters are listed with full cast and credits, as available. Figures in parentheses following title give number of performances and date given is opening date, included whenever a record of these facts was obtainable from the producing managements. Guest productions listed in the Directory were not included in this summary, unless the host theater was directly involved in the production or was the first point of origin. Producing organizations continued community outreach programs for special audiences, and many theaters have installed special facilities, and sometimes performances, for the physically handicapped.

ABINGDON, VA.

Barter Theater

(Producing director, Rex Partington; founder, Robert Porterfield)

YOU CAN'T TAKE IT WITH YOU (23). By George S. Kaufman and Moss Hart. June 9, 1982. Director, Thomas Gruenewald. With Cleo Holladay, Arlene Lencioni, Diane Reynolds, Ken Costigan, Harry Ellerbe.

HEDDA GABLER (23). By Henrik Ibsen; adapted by John Osborne. June 30, 1982. Director, Paul Berman. With Dorothy Holland, George Hosmer, Paula Mann, Ross Bickell, Edward Gero.

THE MATCHMAKER (23). By Thornton Wilder. July 21, 1982. Director, Rex Partington. With Rex Partington, George Hosmer, Ross Bickell, Cleo Holladay, Gerry Goodman, Kate Kelly.

TINTYPES (23). By Mary Kyte, with Mel Marvin and Gary Pearle. August 11, 1982. Director-choreographer, Pamela Hunt; musical director, Marvin Jones. With Don Bradford, Randy Brenner, Audrey Heffernan, Barbara Niles, Vanessa Shaw.

I OUGHT TO BE IN PICTURES (28). By Neil Simon. September 1, 1982. Director, Ken Costigan. With Cleo Holladay, Catherine Coray, Ross Bickell.

THE MOUSETRAP (39). By Agatha Christie. September 29, 1982. Director, Dorothy Marie Robinson. With Cynthia Barnett, Drew Keil, Michael P. O'Brien, Cleo Holladay, Ian Stuart, Alexandra O'Karma, Sherman Lloyd, Jason Culp.

Designers: scenery, Daniel H. Ettinger, Bennet Averyt, John C. Larrance, Lynn Pecktal; lighting, Christopher J. Shaw, Charles Beatty, Tony Partington; costumes, Judianna Makovsky, Georgia Baker, Sigrid Insull, Barbara Forbes, Albert Oxter.

Note: Barter Theater presented the following productions, 12 performances each, at George Mason University in Fairfax, Va., between November and March: *Hedda Gabler, The Matchmaker, The Mousetrap, Hay Fever, Tintypes.* At the end of the winter season, the Barter Players took *The Mousetrap* to more than 25 cities and towns in five states, returning to the home theater in Abingdon in April, opening the spring season.

ANCHORAGE, ALASKA

Alaska Repertory Theater: Sydney Laurence Auditorium

(Artistic director, Robert J. Farley; associate artistic directors, Walton Jones, John Going)

NIGHTINGALE (23). By Charles Strouse; adapted from the fairy tale. December 23, 1982. Director, Meridee Stein. With The First All Children's Theater of New York company.

MAJOR BARBARA (23). By George Bernard Shaw. January 27, 1983. Director, John Going. With Emery Battis, Ivar Brogger, Elizabeth McGovern, Gary McGurk, Elizabeth Parrish.

AIN'T MISBEHAVIN' (23). Songs by Fats Waller; based on an idea by Murray Horowitz and Richard Maltby Jr. March 3, 1983. Director, Murray Horowitz; arranger-orchestrator, Luther Henderson; choreographer, Connie Gould; conductor, J. Leonard Oxley. With Debra Byrd, Andre De Shields, Adriane Lenoz, Ken Primus, Roz Ryan.

Designers: scenery, William Schroder, Ron Placzek; lighting, Spencer Mosse, Pat Collins; costumes, Kurt Wilhelm, Randy Barcelo.

Note: *Ain't Misbehavin'* and *Diamond Studs* were presented in Fairbanks in spring 1983. In the fall of 1982, Alaska Repertory Theater presented Tukak Teatret (the professional Eskimo theater) in a production of *Inuit* throughout the state.

ASHLAND, ORE.

Oregon Shakespearean Festival: Elizabethan Stage

(Founder, Angus L. Bowmer; artistic director, Jerry Turner; executive director, William W. Patton; general manager, Paul Nicholson)

THE COMEDY OF ERRORS (34). By William Shakespeare. June 15, 1982. Director, Julian Lopez-Morillas. With James Carpenter, Daniel Mayes, Joyce Harris, Gloria Biegler, Sam Pond, Lawrence Paulsen.

ROMEO AND JULIET (34). By William Shakespeare. June 16, 1982. Director, Dennis

Bigelow. With Kyle MacLachlan, Gloria Biegler, Wayne Ballantyne, James Carpenter, Daniel Mayes.

HENRY V (34). By William Shakespeare. June 17, 1982. Director, Pat Patton. With Bruce Gooch, Cal Winn, Tina Marie Goff, Barry Kraft, William Keeler.

Oregon Shakeapearean Festival: Angus Bowmer Theater

JULIUS CAESAR (43). By William Shakespeare. June 2, 1982. Director, Jerry Turner. With Cal Winn, Barry Kraft, Philip Davidson, Joan Stuart-Morris, Shirley Patton, Joyce Harris.

SPOKESONG (54). By Stewart Parker and Jimmy Kennedy. June 3, 1982. Director, Denis

Arndt. With James Finnegan, Richard Poe, Gayle Bellows.

BLITHE SPIRIT (34). By Noel Coward. June 4, 1982. Director, Pat Patton. With Joan Stuart-Morris, Richard Elmore, Priscilla Hake Lauris, JoAnn Johnson Patton.

ALLIANCE THEATER COMPANY, ATLANTA—Mary Nell Santacroce, Stephen Hamilton and Jim Peck in *Immorality Play* by James Yaffe

THE FATHER (54). By August Strindberg; translated by Jerry Turner. July 15, 1982. With Denis Arndt, Mary Turner, Gloria Biegler, Lawrence Paulsen.

THE MATCHMAKER (43). By Thornton Wilder. August 27, 1982. Director, Rod Alexander. With Margaret Rubin, Michael Kevin, Mark Murphey, Jeanne Paulsen, Lawrence Paulsen, Tina Marie Goff/Amy Potozkin, Richard Elmore, Priscilla Hake Lauris.

INHERIT THE WIND (16). By Jerome Lawrence and Robert E. Lee. September 11, 1982. Director, Dennis Bigelow. With Wayne Bal-

lantyne, Philip Davidson, Phyllis Courtney, Sam Pond, Stefan Fischer, Gayle Bellows.

HAMLET (23). By William Shakespeare. February 25, 1983. Director, Robert Benedetti. With Mark Murphey, Denis Arndt, Megan Cole, Gayle Bellows, Bruce Gooch, Allen Nause.

MAN AND SUPERMAN (23). By George Bernard Shaw. February 26, 1983. Director, James Moll. With Joan Stuart-Morris, Joe Vincent, Michael Kevin, Allen Nause, Gayle Bellows, Daniel Mayes, Robert Sicular, Shirley Patton.

AH, WILDERNESS! (24). By Eugene O'-Neill. February 27, 1983. Director, Jerry

Turner. With Philip Davidson, Mary Turner, Craig Rovere, William Keeler, Priscilla Hake Lauris, Robert Sicular, Jill Jones, William McKereghan.

WHAT THE BUTLER SAW (11). By Joe Orton. April 29, 1983. Director, Pat Patton. With Philip Davidson, Priscilla Hake Lauris, Richard Elmore, Amy Potozkin, Daniel Mayes, Paul Vincent O'Connor.

Oregon Shakespearean Festival: Black Swan

HOLD ME! (23). By Jules Feiffer. June 3, 1982. Director, Paul Barnes. With Joan Stuart-Morris, Cal Winn, Sam Pond, Tina Marie Goff, JoAnn Johnson Patton.

WINGS (13). By Arthur Kopit. June 4, 1982. Director, James Moll. With Karen Norris, Jeanne Paulsen, Daniel Mayes.

THE ENTERTAINER (40). By John Osborne. February 25, 1983. Director, Dennis Bigelow. With Denis Arndt, Zoaunne LeRoy, William McKereghan, Helen Machin-Smith, Bruce Gooch.

DON JUAN IN HELL (36). By George Bernard Shaw. February 27, 1983. Director, James Moll. With Joe Vincent, Joan Stuart-Morris, Wayne Ballantyne, Michael Kevin.

Designers: scenery, William Bloodgood, Karen Gjelsteen, Richard L. Hay; lighting, Robert Peterson, Peter Allen, James Sale, Richard Ridell; costumes, Jeannie Davidson, Candace Cain, Carole Wheeldon, Mariann Verhagen, Deborah Dryden, Martha Burke, Warren Travis, Claudia Everett.

ATLANTA

Alliance Theater Company: Mainstage

(Managing director, Bernard Havard; artistic director, Fred Chappell)

ANOTHER PART OF THE FOREST (33). By Lillian Hellman. September 8, 1982. Director, Fred Chappell. With Michele Farr, Mary Nell Santacroce, Eddie Lee, Gary Reineke, Larry Larson.

CHEKHOV IN YALTA (32). By John Driver and Jeffrey Haddow. October 20, 1982. Director, Fred Chappell. With Alan Mixon, Al Hamacher, Judy Langford, Eddie Lee, Gary Reineke, Yetta Levitt.

MAME (33). Book by Jerome Lawrence and Robert E. Lee; music and lyrics by Jerry Herman. December 1, 1982. Director, Russell Treyz; musical director, Michael Fauss; choreographer, Mary Jane Houdina. With Judy Langford, Benji Wilhoite, Stanton Cunningham, Jan Maris, Ginny Parker.

FIFTH OF JULY (33). By Lanford Wilson. January 12, 1983. Director, Kent Stephens. With Betty Leighton, Eric Conger, Don Spaulding, Linda Stephens, Suzanne Calvert.

A LITTLE NIGHT MUSIC (33). Music and lyrics by Stephen Sondheim; book by Hugh Wheeler; based on Ingamar Bergman's film *Smiles of a Summer Night.* February 23, 1983. Director, Fred Chappell; music director, Michael Fauss; choreographer, Lee Harper. With Betty Leighton, Linda Stephens, Jeff Richards, Suzanne Sloan, Larry Solowitz, Roy Alan Wilson, Lynn Fitzpatrick.

TWELFTH NIGHT (33). By William Shakespeare. April 6, 1983. Director, Kent Stephens. With Michele Farr, Fran McDormand, Lane Davies, Skip Foster, Eddie Lee, Brooks Baldwin, Marianne Hammock.

Alliance Theater Company: Studio Theater

MY SISTER IN THIS HOUSE (11). By Wendy Kesselman. January 5, 1983. Director, Bob Wright. With Chondra Wolle, Cathy Larson, Muriel Moore, Kathryn Caden.

IMMORALITY PLAY (11). By James Yaffe. February 16, 1983 (world premiere). Director, David McKenna.
Harry Lowenthal................ Jim Peck
Polly Lowenthal ...... Mary Nell Santacroce

Edith Wilshire . . . . Bea Swanson
Melvin McMullan . . . . Stephen Hamilton
Dave DeVito . . . . Larry Larson.

HOME (11). By Samm-Art Williams. March 30, 1983. Director, Walter Dallas. With Bill Nunn, Sharlene Ross, Iris Little Roberts.

EDUCATING RITA (17). By Ntozake Shangé; adapted from the play by Willy Russell. May 11, 1983 (world premiere). Director, Fred Chappell.
Rita . . . . Lynne Thigpen
Frank . . . . David Canary

Alliance Theater Company: Atlanta Children's Theater

COTTON PATCH GOSPEL. Book by Tom Key and Russell Treyz; music and lyrics by Harry Chapin; based on Clarence Jordan's book *The Cotton Patch Version of Matthew and John.* Director, Russell Treyz; musical director-arranger, Tom Chapin. With Tom Key, the Cotton Pickers.

THE EMPEROR'S NEW CLOTHES. By Larry

Shue; based on the story by Hans Christian Andersen. October 4, 1982. Director, Kent Stephens; musical director-arranger, David Smadbeck.

THE PIRATES OF PENZANCE by W.S. Gilbert and Arthur Sullivan; adapted by Charles Abbott. Director, Kent Stephens; choreographer, Patrick McCann.

Designers: scenery, Mark Morton, Angie Riserbato, Lynne Spencer, Tony Loadholt, John Falabella; lighting, William B. Duncan, Paul Valoris, Michael Stauffer, Pete Shim, Paul Ackerman, Kevin Myrick, Dudley Voll; costumes, Thom Coates, Susan Hirshfeld, Fannie Shubert, Linda Acetta, Joyce Andrulot, John Falaballa.

Note: Alliance Theater Company presented the following readings during the 1982–83 season: *The Reeve's Tale,* directed by Bob Wright; *The Swooning Virgin* by Joel E. Green, directed by Billings La Pierre; *Tennessee Waltz* by Michael Russell, directed by Skip Foster; *A Woman's Place* by Lezley Havard, directed by Kent Stephens.

BALTIMORE

Center Stage: Mainstage

(Artistic director, Stan Wojewodski Jr.; managing director, Peter W. Culman)

LAST LOOKS (42). By Grace McKeaney. September 27, 1982 (world premiere). Director, Jackson Phippin.
Ray Morrow . . . . Emery Battis
Delia Morrow . . . . Gloria Cromwell
Val . . . . Chris Weatherhead
Guy . . . . Graham Beckel
Clair . . . . Lucinda Jenney
Mercedes . . . . Sarah Chodoff
Joey . . . . Josh MacFarland
Howard Benson . . . . John Procaccino
      Time: Saturday, August 25. Place: Day's End, the Morrow family home on the Eastern shore of the Chesapeake. Two intermissions.

THE MISER (43). By Molière; adapted by Miles Malleson. November 5, 1982. Director, Stan Wojewodski Jr. With Bill McCutcheon, James McDonnell, Patricia Kalember, Tony Soper, Jeff Natter, Tana Hicken.

DIVISION STREET (42). By Steve Tesich. December 17, 1982. Director, Stan Wojewodski

Jr. With Keith Langsdale, Paulene Myers, Victor Argo, Carolyn Hurlburt, Billy Padgett.

WINGS (42). By Arthur Kopit. January 28, 1983. Director, Stan Wojewodski Jr. With Bette Henritze, Phyllis Somerville, Daniel Szelag.

THE WOMAN (42). By Edward Bond. March 11, 1983 (American premiere). Director, Jackson Phippin.
The Greeks:
  Heros . . . . Peter Burnell
  Ismene . . . . Jennifer Harmon
  Nestor . . . . Emery Battis
  Thersites; Temi . . . . Anderson Matthews
  Ajax . . . . Tony Soper
  High Priest; Artos . . . . J. S. Johnson
  Captain . . . . Wil Love
  Callis . . . . Timothy Boisvert
  Lakis . . . . Lance Newman
The Trojans:
  Hecuba . . . . Beatrice Manley
  Son . . . . Rodney W. Clark

Cassandra .... Tania Myren
Astynax .... Lisa Ellen Abrams
High Priest .... Daniel Szelag
Shallios .... Vivienne Shub
Porpoise............. Rosemary Knower
Dark Man................ Tom Kopache
Princesses, Plague Women: Susan Beverly,
Shirley Harris, Joanne Manley, Kate Phelan,
Lorraine Toussaint.
Act I: Ilium, action alternates between the

Greek encampment and the Trojan palace environs. Act II: Twelve years later, an island fishing village, early spring through late fall.

LOVE'S LABOUR'S LOST (43). By William Shakespeare. April 22, 1983. Director, Stan Wojewodski Jr. With Peter Burnell, Boyd Gaines, Anderson Matthews, Lorraine Toussaint, Emery Battis.

Designers: scenery, Hugh Landwehr, Richard R. Goodwin, Ed Wittstein; lighting, Judy Rasmuson, Craig Miller, Bonnie Ann Brown, Ann C. Wrightson, Arden Fingerhut; costumes, Linda Fisher, Don Granata, Del W. Risberg, Walter Pickette, Robert Wojewodski.

Center Stage: First Stage

Reading of workshop premieres, 1 performance each, Mondays

SISTERS by Patricia Montley; director, Stan Wojewodski Jr.
THE SLEEP OF REASON by Antonio Buero Vallejo; translated by Marion Peter Holt; director Travis Preston.
ASIAN SHADE by Larry Ketron; director, Stan Wojewodski Jr.

HITCHIN' by Lewis Black; director, Mark Linn-Baker.
THE MANDRAKE by Rosalyn Drexler; music by Lance Malcahy; adapted from Machievelli's *La Mandragola*; director, Edward Stone.
NATIVE SPEECH by Eric Overmyer; director, Paul Berman.

Note: The Young People's Theater of Center Stage toured Baltimore and through Maryland, Feb. 7-April 29, with *Yes, I Can!*, written and directed by Edward Stone.

BERKELEY, CALIF.

Berkeley Repertory Theater: Mainstage

(Producing director, Michael Leibert; general manager, Mitzi Sales)

In rotating repertory:

TONIGHT AT 8:30 (72) By Noel Coward. WE WERE DANCING and WAYS AND MEANS, June 22, 1982; FAMILY ALBUM and BRIEF ENCOUNTER, June 25, 1982; SHADOW PLAY and RED PEPPERS, June 29, 1982. Director, Alex Kinney; musical director, Richard Koldewyn; choreographer, Larry Berthelot. With Charles Dean, Stephen J. Godwin, Irving Israel, Kimberly King, Michael Leibert, Judith Marx.

HAPPY END (32). By Bertolt Brecht and Kurt Weill; adapted by Michael Feingold. September 28, 1982. Director, Michael Leibert; musical director, John Geist. With Kimberly King, Stephen J. Godwin, Judith Marx, William McKereghan, Sally Smythe, Ina Wittich.

CHEKHOV IN YALTA (32). By John Driver and Jeffrey Haddow. November 2, 1982. Director, Albert Takazaukas. With Brian

Thompson, Tony Amendola, Sally Smythe, Charles Dean, Richard Rossi.

THE GLASS MENAGERIE (40). By Tennessee Williams. December 7, 1982. Director, Michael Leibert. With Joy Carlin, Charles Dean, Kimberly King, Tony Amendola.

THE SHOW-OFF (32). By George Kelly. January 18, 1983. Director, John R. Freimann. With David Booth, Barbara Oliver, Judith Marx.

BEYOND THERAPY (32). By Christopher Durang. February 22, 1983. Director, Joy Carlin. With Shirley Jac Wagner, Judith Marx, Charles Dean, Brian Thompson, David Booth.

U.S.A. (32). By John Dos Passos; adapted by Paul Shyre. May 3, 1983. Director, Gregory Boyd. With Stephen J. Godwin.

CENTER STAGE, BALTIMORE—Lucinda Jenney and Graham Beckel in a scene from *Last Looks* by Grace McKeaney

Berkeley Repertory Theater: Playworks

Staged readings of new plays

THE AUTHENTIC LIFE OF BILLY THE KID by Lee Blessing, directed by David Booth, December 16, 1982.

THE MARGARET GHOST by Carole Braverman, directed by Terrence P. O'Brien, January 27, 1983.

FRIENDS by Lee Kalcheim, directed by Tena Achen, February, 10, 1983.

IN FLIGHT by Robert Gordon, directed by Barbara Oliver, March 10, 1983.

EINSTEIN IN IXTLAN by Scott Christopher Wren, directed by Hope Alexander-Willis, April 7, 1983.

CAROLYN by Toni Press, directed by Tony Amendola, June, 1983.

Designers: scenery, Henry May, Richard Norgard, Bernard J. Vyzga, Tom Rasmussen; lighting, Tom Ruzika, Greg Sullivan, Barbara Du Bois, Larry French; costumes, Deborah Brothers-Lowry, Jeannie Davidson, Deborah Dryden, Tom Rasmussen.

BOSTON

The Huntington Theater Company at Boston University

(Producing director, Peter Altman; managing director, Michael Maso; artistic advisor, Zelda Fichandler)

NIGHT AND DAY (26). By Tom Stoppard. October 23, 1982. Director, Toby Robertson. With Caroline Lagerfelt, Jack Ryland, Edmond Genest, Milledge Mosley, William Cain.

THE DINING ROOM (26). By A.R. Gurney Jr. November 27, 1982. Director, Thomas

Gruenewald. With Denise Bessette, Lynn Bowman, Peter Davies, Douglas Jones, Tanny McDonald, Robert Stattel.

TRANSLATIONS (26). By Brian Friel. Director, Jacques Cartier. January 8, 1983. With Jack Aranson, Ray Dooley, Raymond Hardie, Linda

Kozlowski, Richard Seer, Eric Tull.

TIME AND THE CONWAYS (25). By J.B. Priestley. April 23, 1983. Director, Elinor Renfield. With Pauline Flanagan, Margaret Whitton, Ralph Byers, Pamela Lewis, Karen Sederholm.

THE TAMING OF THE SHREW (26). By William Shakespeare. May 28, 1983. Director, Toby Robertson. With Margot Dionne, David Purdham, Anna Levine, George Hall, Richard Poe.

Designers: scenery, Franco Colavecchia, James Leonard Joy, Richard Isackes, Hugh Landwehr; lighting, William Mintzer, Jeff Davis, Roger Meeker; costumes, Rachel Kurland, Mariann Verheyen, Ann Wallace, Michaele Hite.

BUFFALO

Studio Arena Theater

(Artistic director, David Frank; managing director, Michael P. Pitek III)

SHE STOOPS TO CONQUER (29). By Oliver Goldsmith. September 24, 1982. Director, David Frank. With Lenka Peterson, Clement Fowler, Sam Tsoutsouvas, Wanda Simson, Ellen Fiske, James Maxwell, Warren David Keith.

TRUE WEST (29). By Sam Shepard. October 29, 1982. Director, Kathryn Long. With Beeson Carroll, Helen Harrelson, James Maxwell, Timothy Meyers.

WITNESS FOR THE PROSECUTION (29). By Agatha Christie. December 3, 1982. Director, David Frank. With Holly Baron, Walter Barrett, Kate Olena, John Clarkson, David Frederick.

A RAISIN IN THE SUN (29). By Lorraine Hansbury. January 7, 1983. Director, Harold Scott. With Herb Downer, Theresa Merritt, Kim Yancey, L. Scott Caldwell, Keith Mixon.

WEAPONS OF HAPPINESS (29). By Howard Brenton. February 11, 1983 (American premiere). Director, Geoffrey Sherman.
Josef Frank . . . . Robert Burr
Ralph Makepeace;
   Russian Adviser . . . . Carl Schurr
Billy . . . . Evan Handler
Ken. . . . . David Bottrell
Stacky. . . . . Brett Porter
Janice . . . . Tara Loewenstern
Liz . . . . Nona Waldeck
Alf. . . . . Dermot McNamara
Sylvia Makepeace . . . . Diana Van Fossen
Mr. Stanley . . . . John Rainer
Inspector Miller; Doubek;
   Interrogator. . . . . Doug Stender
Hicks; Kohoutek;
   Interrogator. . . . . Robert Spencer

Clementis . . . . Earle Edgerton
Stalin; Commentator . . . . Brian LaTulip
Waiter. . . . . Brian DeMarco
Act I, Scene 1: Outside the Makepeace Crisp Factory, South London, night, the present. Scene 2: The factory yard, lunch break. Scene 3: The factory office. Scene 4: A Czechoslovakian interrogation room, 1952. Scene 5: The factory office. Scene 6: A London street, early evening. Scene 7: A Moscow street, night, 1947. Scene 8: A London street, evening. Scene 9: London dockland, night. Scene 10: The factory yard, morning. Act II, Scene 1: A Czech prison yard and the Makepeace factory. Scene 2: The factory yard, night. Scene 3: The factory by the drain, night. Scene 4: The factory by the drain, later. Scene 5: A snow covered field in Wales, some time later.

IN THE SWEET BYE AND BYE (29). By Donald Driver. March 18, 1983 (world premiere). Director, John Henry Davis.
Hagen . . . . Addison Powell
Jessie. . . . . Mary Carver
Neva . . . . Scotty Bloch
Carmel . . . . Alma Cuervo
Bill Leland . . . . Carl Schurr
Lamar Shooler. . . . . Robert Spencer
Dale Shooler . . . . Gerald Halter
Act I, Scene 1: A kitchen in an Oregon farmhouse, a Wednesday in the present. Act II, Scene 1: Wednesday, one week later. Scene 2: Evening, several hours later. Scene 3: Wednesday morning, one week later.

ABSURD PERSON SINGULAR (29). By Alan Ayckbourn. April 22, 1983. Director, David Frank. With Cynthia Carle, le Clanche du Rand, Carl Schurr, John Rainer, Nancy Mette, Robert Spencer.

Designers: scenery, Robert Morgan, Gary C. Eckhart, J. Robin Modereger, Tom Cariello, Paul Wonsek, Grady Larkins; lighting, Robert Jared, Robby Monk, Michael Orris Watson, Shirley Prendergast, Rich Menke, Brett Thomas; costumes, Robert Morgan, Donna Langham, Judy Dearing, Catherine B. Reich, Janice I. Lines.

CAMBRIDGE, MASS.

American Repertory Theater: Loeb Drama Center

(Artistic director, Robert Brustein; managing director, Robert J. Orchard).

THREE SISTERS (21). By Anton Chekhov; translated and adapted by Jean-Claude van Itallie. December 1, 1982. Director, Andrei Serban. With Marianne Owen, Cherry Jones, Cheryl Giannini, Jeremy Geidt, Alvin Epstein, Thomas Darrah, Karen MacDonald.

G'NIGHT MOTHER (19). By Marsha Norman. December 15, 1982. Director, Tom Moore.
Mother .... Anne Pitoniak
Jessie, her daughter .... Kathy Bates
1983 Pulitzer Prize winner, later titled 'night, Mother. No intermission.

WAITING FOR GODOT (23). By Samuel Beckett. January 19, 1983. Director, Andrei Belgrader. With John Bottoms, Mark Linn-Baker, Tony Shalhoub, Richard Spore, Seth Goldstein.

THE BOYS FROM SYRACUSE (23). Music by Richard Rodgers; lyrics by Lorenz Hart; book by George Abbott. February 23, 1983. Director, Alvin Epstein; musical director-arranger, Paul Schierhorn; choreographer, Kathryn Posin. With Thomas Darrah, Stephen Rose, Harry Murphy, Susan Larson, Jeremy Geidt, Marianne Owen.

THE SCHOOL FOR SCANDAL (30). By Richard Brinsley Sheridan. May 13, 1983. Director, Jonathan Miller. With Alvin Epstein, Cherry Jones, Karen MacDonald, Stephen Rowe, Shirley Wilber.

American Repertory Theater: Hasty Pudding Theater

BABY WITH THE BATHWATER (14). By Christopher Durang. April 1983 (world premiere). Director, Mark Linn-Baker. With Cherry Jones, Karen MacDonald, Marianne Owen, Stephen Rose.

HUGHIE by Eugene O'Neill, directed by Bill Foeller; FOOTFALLS and ROCKABY by Samuel Beckett, directed by John Grant-Phillips. (14). April 7, 1983. With John Bottoms, Richard Spore, Karen MacDonald, Marianne Owen.

Designers: scenery, Beni Montresor, Heidi Landesman, Tom Lynch, Patrick Robinson, Don Soule; lighting Beni Montresor, James F. Ingalls, Jennifer Tipton, Thom Palm; costumes, Beni Montresor, Heidi Landesman, Nancy Thun, Rosemary Vercoe, Liz Pearlman.

CHICAGO

Goodman Theater: Mainstage

(Artistic director, Gregory Mosher; managing director, Roche Schuler)

THE MAN WHO HAD THREE ARMS (29). Written and directed by Edward Albee. October 4, 1982. With Robert Drivas, Wyman Pendleton, Patricia Kilgarriff.

A CHRISTMAS CAROL (38). By Charles Dickens; adapted by Barbara Field. November 29, 1982. Director, Tony Mockus. With William J. Norris, Robert Thompson, Jamie Wild, Roger Mueller, Del Close.

THE COMEDY OF ERRORS (37). By William Shakespeare. January 24, 1983. Director, Robert Woodruff. With the Flying Karamazov Brothers (Timothy Furst, Paul Magid, Randy Nelson, Howard Patterson, Sam Williams), Sophie Schwab, Gina Leishman.

THE DINING ROOM (29). By A. R. Gurney Jr. March 14, 1983. Director, Michael Maggio. With Joseph Guzaldo, Cordis Heard, B. J. Jones, Linda Kimbrough, Pamela Nyberg, Rob Riley.

RED RIVER (30). By Pierre Laville; translated by David Mamet. May 2, 1983 (American premiere). Director, Robert Woodruff; composer-conducter, William Harper; choreographer, Charlie Vernon.

Vladimir Mayakovsky... Christopher McCann
Ludmilla Priakhina........... Jane MacIver
Mikhail Bulgakov............ John Spencer
Helena Bulgakov.............. Caryn West
Woland................... Roy Brocksmith
Hella................... Mary McDonnell
Ermolinsky............... Mike Nussbaum

Goodman Theater: Studio

OHIO IMPROMPTU; EH, JOE; A PIECE OF MONOLOGUE (12). Program of one-act plays by Samuel Beckett. January 18, 1983. Directors, Alan Schneider, Rick Cluchey, David Warrilow, Rocky Greenberg. With David Warrilow, Rick Cluchey, Helen Gary Bishop.

MONOLOGUES (12) Written and performed by Spalding Gray. February 1, 1983.

JUNGLE COUP (18). By Richard Nelson. February 28, 1983 (world premiere). Director, David Chambers.
Hopper....................... Seth Allen
Mott....................... Jack Wallace
Bellows.................. Mike Nussbaum

Behemoth............. Lionel Mark Smith
President; Kayenstsev;
  Matthieu Levi............. D. W. Moffett
Adolescent; Actress.......... Rebecca Cole
Actor; Student................. Allan Ruck
  Time and Place: Post-Revolutionary Russia.

A SOLDIER'S PLAY (50). By Charles Fuller. June 13, 1983. The Negro Ensemble Company's original production, directed by Douglas Turner Ward.

GARDENIA (34). By John Guare. April 25, 1983. Director, Gregory Mosher. With Elizabeth Perkins, Gary Cole, William L. Petersen, Richard Seer/David Perry, Jack Wallace.

HOT LINE by Elaine May; THE DISAPPEARENCE OF THE JEWS by David Mamet; GORILLA by Shel Silverstein (18). June 14, 1983 (world premieres of one-act plays).
  Hot Line directed by Art Wolf; with Elaine May, Peter Falk, Del Close.
  The Disappearance of the Jews directed by Gregory Mosher; with Norman Parker, Joe Mantegna.
  Gorilla directed by Shel Silverstein; with Ron Silver, Paul Guilfoyle.

Designers: scenery, John Jensen, Joseph Nieminski, David Gropman, Karen Schulz, Rocky Greenberg, Kevin Rigdon, David Emmons, Franne Lee; lighting, F. Mitchell Dana, Robert Christen, Paul Gallo, Jennifer Tipton; costumes, Barbara A. Bell, James Edmund Brady, Susan Hilferty, Marsha Kowal, Teresita Garcia Suro, Nan Cibula, Franne Lee.

Note: Burr Tilstrom's Kukla and Ollie Live! returned for its 4th annual holiday presentation, December 17, 1982. The Goodman also presented Writers in Performance, the prose and poetry of South African, American and Caribbean authors now writing in the U.S., February 21, 1983, with Dennis Brutus, Leon Forrest, James Allen McPherson and Derek Walcott reading from their own works. On April 4, 1983 the series continued with poets and contemporary composers (Kathleen Lombardo, Richard Wilbur, Lucian Stryk).

CINCINNATI

Cincinnati Playhouse in the Park: Robert S. Marx Theater

(Producing director, Michael Murray; managing director, Baylor Landrum)

INHERIT THE WIND (36). By Jerome Lawrence and Robert E. Lee. September 28, 1982. Director, John Going. With Paul C. Thomas, David O. Petersen, Donna Adams, John Wylie, Nancy Boykin, James Hillgartner, Jane Welch.

THE WIZARD OF OZ (45). By L. Frank Baum; adapted by Frank Gabrielson; music and

lyrics by Harold Arlen and E.Y. Harburg. November 16, 1982. Director and additional music and lyrics by Worth Gardner. With Diane Della Piazza, Jack Hoffmann, Tony Hoty, Peter Moran, Tom Flagg.

THE DRESSER (36). By Ronald Harwood. January 4, 1983. Director, Josephine Abady. With Jon Polito, John Wylie, Angela Thornton.

CINCINNATI PLAYHOUSE IN THE PARK—Thomas Calabro
and Cecile Callan in a scene from *Sweet Basil* by Lloyd Gold

MEDEA (36). By Euripides. February 22, 1983. Director, Amy Saltz; chorus director, Theodore Pappas. With Mary Lou Rosato, John Hertzler, Jay Devlin, Marge Kotlisky.

THE PRICE (36). By Arthur Miller. April 12, 1983. Director, Michael Hankins. With William

Kiehl, Nada Rowand, Stefan Schnabel, Brian Smiar.

THE IMPORTANCE OF BEING EARNEST (36). By Oscar Wilde. May 31, 1983. Director, Michael Murray. With Robert Black, Ray Dooley, Rachel Gurney, Jessie K. Jones, Diana Van Fossen.

Cincinnati Playhouse in the Park: Thompson Shelterhouse Theater

MASS APPEAL (24). By Bill C. Davis. October 28, 1982. Director, Tom Toner. With Paul C. Thomas, Charles Shaw-Robinson.

FIFTH OF JULY (24). By Lanford Wilson. February 3, 1983. Director, Leonard Mozzi. With Charles Shaw-Robinson, Mark McConnell, Lynn Ritchie, Dori Arnold, Anne Shropshire.

SWEET BASIL (18). By Lloyd Gold; suggested by a Boccaccio tale. March 29, 1983 (world pre-

miere). Director, Michael Murray.

Belle Mooney	Cecile Callan
Naomi Boyle	Anne Shropshire
Jimmy Mooney	John P. Connolly
Tim Fogarty	Timothy Phillips
Enzo Basile	Thomas Calabro

Time: The present. Place: New Orleans. One intermission.

STRANGE SNOW (24). Written and directed by Stephen Metcalfe. May 12, 1983. With Dave Florek, Margo Martindale, Buck Schirner.

Designers: scenery, John Jensen, Paul R. Shortt, David Potts, Alison Ford, David Ariosa; lighting, William Mintzer, Jeff Davis, Barry Arnold, F. Mitchell Dana, Jay Depenbrock; costumes, James Berton Harris, Paul R. Shortt, Caley Summers, Kurt Wilhelm, Rebecca Senske, William Schroder, Ann Firestone.

Note: Cincinnati Playhouse presented *The Arkansaw Bear* (4) by Aurand Harris, December 11 and 18, directed by Wendy Liscow, with the Playhouse Intern company.

CLEVELAND

The Cleveland Play House: Drury Theater

(Director, Richard Oberlin; managing director, Janet Wade)

APPEAR AND SHOW CAUSE (31). By Stephen Taylor; adapted from a story by Leon H. Gilpin and Stephen Taylor. October 8, 1982 (world premiere). Director, Woodie King Jr.
Frank Harrow .... Ray Aranha
Noah Lincoln Keyes .... Graham Brown
Joshua Harrow .... Marcus Naylor
Maj. Evans Chandler .... Morgan Lund
Sgt. Andrew "L.C." Smith.. Paul A. Floriano
Sgt. Hugh Connor............. Allan Byrne
Lt. Peter Carlsen........ William Roudebush
Col. Harlan Philips........ James P. Kisicki
Colonel; Brigadier General; President
   of Board of Inquiry ..... Allen Leatherman

BLACK COFFEE (36). By Agatha Christie. November 19, 1982. Director, Paul Lee. With Richard Halverson, Paul Lee, Thomas S. Oleniacz, Anthony Kitrell, Lisa Kitrell, Alden Redgrave, Cassandra Wolfe.

TOMFOOLERY (36). Words and music by Tom Lehrer; adapted by Cameron Mackintosh and Robin Ray. January 14, 1983. Director, William Roudebush. With Cliff Bemis, Paul A. Floriano, Jill Hayman, Robert D. Phillips.

KEY EXCHANGE (36). By Kevin Wade. March 4, 1983. Director, Dennis Zacek. With Anthony Kitrell, Lisa Kitrell, William Roudebush.

THE ROBBER BRIDEGROOM (33). Book and lyrics by Alfred Uhry; music by Robert Waldman; based on Eudora Welty's novella. April 8, 1983. Director, Michael Maggio; musical director, David Gooding. With Cliff Bemis, Theresa Piteo, Richard Halverson, Evie McElroy.

The Cleveland Play House: Euclid-77th Street Theater

FIFTH OF JULY (26). By Lanford Wilson. October 22, 1982. Director, Michael Maggio. With Evie McElroy, William Rhys, Gregory M. Del Torto, Catherine Albers, Jill Hayman.

A TALE OF TWO CITIES (26). By Charles Dickens; adapted by Mark Fitzgibbons; music by David Gooding. January 28, 1983. Director, William Rhys. With Si Osborne, John Buck Jr., Morgan Lund, Tracee Patterson and members of the company.

TEN TIMES TABLE (36). By Alan Ayckbourn. March 25, 1983. (American professional premiere). Director, Paul Lee.
Ray Dixon .... Morgan Lund
Helen .... Carolyn Reed
Donald Evans .... James P. Kisicki
Audrey Evans .... Alden Redgrave
Lawrence Adamson....... Allen Leatherman
Sophie................... Sharon Bicknell
Tim................... Thomas S. Oleniacz
Eric........................ Si Osborne
Philippa .... Tracee Patterson

The Cleveland Play House: Brooks Theater

THE MIDDLE AGES (40). By A. R. Gurney Jr. October 15, 1982 (reopened at the Drury, May 11, 1983). Director, Harper Jane McAdoo. With Wayne S. Turney, Richard Halverson, Sharon Bicknell, Carolyn Reed.

SEA MARKS (18). By Gardner McKay. January 21, 1983. Director, Thomas Riccio. With Thomas S. Oleniacz, Catherine Albers.

THE POTSDAM QUARTET (18). By David Pinner. April 15, 1983. Director, William Roudebush. With Paul Lee, John Buck Jr., Ron Newell, Kelly C. Morgan.

Designers: scenery and lighting, Richard Gould, James Irwin; costumes, Estelle Painter, Frances Blau, Richard Gould, Jeff Smart, Kim A. Trotter.

Note: *The Middle Ages* was presented for a limited engagement June 1–19 in Columbus, Ohio. Youtheater, the Cleveland Play House young people's acting school, presented an original musical, *Billie And Her Hillbilly Barnyard Band* (4) by Cassandra Wolfe and Robert Noll, with music by David Pogue, at the Drury Theater April 22. Directors, Kerro Knox III, Elizabeth Farwell; musical director-orchestrater, David Wolfson, with Youtheater students making up the cast.

Great Lakes Shakespeare Festival: Ohio Theater

(Producing director, Vincent Dowling)

AS YOU LIKE IT (12). By William Shakespeare. July 9, 1982. Director, Thomas Gruenewald. With Clive Rosengren, Maggie Thatcher, Madylon Branstetter, Michael Haney, Tom Blair, Robert Elliott.

THE PLAYBOY OF THE WESTERN WORLD (15). By John Millington Synge. July 16, 1982. Director, Vincent Dowling. With Frank Grimes, Larry Gates, Clive Rosengren, Barbre Dowling, Aideen O'Kelly.

PIAF: LA VIE L'AMOUR (13). Written and performed by Gay Marshall, with Lane Bateman. August 5, 1982. Director, Vincent Dowling with Marcia Rock; musical arranger-conductor, Robert Ashens.

THE LIFE & ADVENTURES OF NICHOLAS NICKLEBY (46). By Charles Dickens; adapted by David Edgar; music and lyrics by Stephen Oliver. Part I, August 26, 1982; Part II, August 27, 1982. Directors, Robert Lanchester and Edward Stern. With David Purdham, Maggie Thatcher, Bob Breuler, Sara Woods.

A CHILD'S CHRISTMAS IN WALES (23). By Dylan Thomas; adapted by Jeremy Brooks and Adrian Mitchell December 1983. Director, Clifford Williams; musical director, Daniel Hathaway. With Neal Jones, Nesbitt Blaisdell, Margaret Hilton, Edith Owen, Malachy McCourt, Sylvia Gassell.

Designers: scenery, John Ezell; lighting, Roger Morgan, Kirk Bookman, Toni Golden, Natasha Katz; costumes, Gene Lakin, Paul Costelloe, Mary-Anne Aston, Lewis D. Rampino.

COCONUT GROVE, FLA.

Players State Theater

(Artistic advisor, José Ferrer; managing director, G. David Black)

THE DRESSER (29). By Ronald Harwood. November 5, 1982. Director, Douglas Seale. With José Ferrer, Michael Tolaydo, Brenda Curtis.

FIFTH OF JULY (29) By Lanford Wilson. December 3, 1982. Director, Kent Stephens. With Eric Conger, Linda Stephens, Betty Leighton, Suzanne Calvert, Don Spaulding.

A COUPLA WHITE CHICKS SITTING AROUND TALKING (29). By John Ford Noonan. January 7, 1983. Director, James Riley. With Megan McTavish, Annie Stafford.

FALLEN ANGELS (29). By Noel Coward. February 4, 1983. Director, Frith Banbury. With Tudi Wiggins, Peggy Cosgrove, Ronald Shelley, Peter Haig, Alfredo Alvarez-Calderon.

A DESTINY WITH HALF MOON STREET (29). By Paul Zindel. March 4, 1983 (world premiere). Director, José Ferrer.

Harold Farley	Rafael Ferrer
Floyd DiPardi	Danny Aiello
Mrs. DePardi	Sondra Barrett
Richie; Hospital Attendant No. 1	Lenny Pass
Leroy; Hospital Attendant No. 2	Martin Patrick Tobin
Nurse Helen Boyd	Anne Meacham
Chris Boyd	Brian Backer
Joey	Douglas Weiser

Other boys: Randy Bass, Alan Curelap, Scott Stuart.

Time: 1955. Place: The DiPardi home, Prince's Street, Staten Island. Act I, Scene 1: Morning. Scene 2: Afternoon, the following day.

Scene 3: A little later. Scene 4: That evening. Act II, Scene 1: The next morning. Scene 2: Later that afternoon. Scene 3: That evening. Scene 4: Later, the same night. One intermission.

WITNESS FOR THE PROSECUTION (45). By Agatha Christie. April 1, 1983. Director, Douglas Seale. With Daren Kelly, James Valentine, Richard Liberty, Jennifer Sternberg.

Designers: scenery, David Trimble, Kenneth N. Kurtz, H. Paul Mazer, Marsha Hardy; lighting, David Goodman, Kenneth N. Kurtz, Pat Simmons, Stephen Welsh; costumes, Claire Gatrell, Ellis Tillman, Steve Lambert, David Trimble, Barbara Forbes.

Note: Players State Theater officially became the Coconut Grove Playhouse in April 1983. It toured two children's theater productions: *The Sleeping Prince* (24), adapted and directed by David Robert Kanter from the African folktale *Fenda Maria,* toured Dade County parks July 12–30, 1982. During the winter of 1983, the touring production was *Pepperpot* (54) by Susan Westfall; music and lyrics by Roberto Lozan; director, Tony Wagner.

COSTA MESA, CALIF.

South Coast Repertory: Mainstage

(Producing artistic director, David Emmes; artistic director, Martin Benson)

ALL IN FAVOUR SAID NO! (39). By Bernard Farrell. September 14, 1982 (American premiere). Director, David Emmes.

Gilbert Donnelly	Tom Rosqui
Christy Metcalf	Paul Rudd
Dave	Steven Breese
Liam	Jeffrey Combs
Miss Temple	Patricia Fraser
Sally	Mary Beth Evans
Mike Reynolds	Hal Landon Jr.
Dee Kavanaugh	Kendall McLean
Eddie Malone	Richard Doyle
Una	Kristen Lowman
Joan	Anni Long
Ronnie Partridge	John-David Keller

Time: The present. Place: The offices of Donnycarney Metal Works. One intermission.

THE DIVINERS (39). By Jim Leonard Jr. October 26, 1982. Director, Martin Benson. With Don Tuche, John Walcutt, Jeffrey Combs, Joe McNeely, Rita René Stevens, Emily Heebner, Thomas R. Oglesby, Wayne Grace, Martha McFarland, Sylvia Meredith, Patti Johns.

A CHRISTMAS CAROL (22). By Charles Dickens; adapted by Jerry Patch. December 8,

1982. Director, John-David Keller. With Hal Landon Jr., John Ellington, Charlie Cummins, Don Tuche.

BOY MEETS GIRL (39). By Bella and Samuel Spewack. January 11, 1983. Director, Lee Shallat. With Kristoffer Tabori, Hal Landon Jr., William Bogert, Diane dePriest, Wayne Alexander.

BETRAYAL (38). By Harold Pinter. February 22, 1983. Director, David Emmes. With Thomas R. Oglesby, Cecelia Riddett, Dan Kern, Art Koustik.

THE IMAGINARY INVALID (39). By Molière. April 12, 1983. Director, Richard Russell Ramos. With Raye Birk, Kristen Lowman, Irene Roseen, Wayne Alexander, Robert Machray, John-David Keller, Ron Bousson, Michelle Wallen.

MAJOR BARBARA (39). By George Bernard Shaw. May 24, 1983. Director, Martin Benson. With Kathleen Lloyd, John Ellington, Reid Shelton, Paul Rudd, Richard Doyle, Patricia Fraser.

South Coast Repertory: Second Stage

BROTHERS (21). By George Sibbald. November 3, 1982 (world premiere). Director, Lee Sankowich. With George Murdock, Joe Pantoliano, Jonathan Terry, Dennis Franz, David Ralph.

SHE ALSO DANCES (21) By Kenneth Ar-

nold. January 19, 1983 (world premiere). With Patti Johns, Marc Vahanian. (See synopsis in the introduction to this section.)

CLOSELY RELATED (21). By Bruce Mac-Donald. March 2, 1983 (world premiere). Director, Lee Shallat.

Melissa . . . . Lycia Naff
Alan . . . . Stephen Keep
Alison . . . . Penelope Windust
Tim . . . . Kaz Garas
Christian . . . . Brad Cowgill
Myrna . . . . Laura Campbell.
   Time: The present. Place: In and about a large
American city. One intermission. (See synopsis
in the introduction to this section.)

GOODBYE FREDDY (21). By Elizabeth
Diggs. April 20, 1983 (world premiere). Direc-
tor, Jules Aaron. With Andrew Prine, Pamela
Dunlap, Charles Parks, Joan Welles, Timothy
Shelton, Susan Barnes.

APRIL SNOW (21). By Romulus Linney. June
1, 1983 (world premiere). Director, David
Emmes. With Jordan Charney, Scott Hylands,
K. Callan, Rhonda Aldrich, Brad Cowgill.

Designers: scenery, Michael Devine, Susan Tuohy, Cliff Faulkner, Mark Donnelley, Thomas A.
Walsh, John Ivo Gilles; lighting, Cameron Harvey, Tom Ruzika, Donna Ruzika, Paulie Jenkins, Greg
Sullivan, Richard Devin; costumes, Tom Rasmussen, Merrily Murray-Walsh, Dwight Richard
Odle, Carol Brolaski, Skipper Skeoch, Kim Simmons, Barbara Cox.

Note: In the 1982–83 season, South Coast Repertory presented new play readings: *The Sea Lion* by
Robert Potter, *Diane* by Gregory Gorelick, *Goodbye Freddy* by Elizabeth Diggs and *She Also
Dances* by Kenneth Arnold.

DALLAS

Dallas Theater Center: Kalita Humphreys Theater

(Artistic director, Mary Sue Jones; general manager, Albert Milano; founder, Paul Baker)

THE GIN GAME (46). By D.L. Coburn. July
6, 1982. Director, Karl Guttmann, with Felix
Guttman. With Patricia Fraser, Warren
Frost.

THE THREE MUSKETEERS (46). By Peter
Raby; adapted from Alexandre Dumas's novel.
October 12, 1982. Director, David Pursley. With
Richard Raether, Cliff Stephens, Royal Brant-
ley, Lee Lowrimore, Norma Moore.

A MURDER IS ANNOUNCED (46). By Agatha Christie; adapted by Leslie Darbon. December 7, 1982. Director, Robyn Flatt. With Jeff
Kinghorn, Jeanne Cairns, Judith Davis.

A LESSON FROM ALOES (46). By Athol
Fugard. February 8, 1983. Director, Judith
Davis. With James Hurdle, Jenny Pichanick,
Paul Winfield.

THE THREEPENNY OPERA (46). book and
lyrics by Bertolt Brecht; music by Kurt Weill;
English adaptation by Marc Blitzstein. March
29, 1983. Director, Ivan Rider; musical director,
Raymond Allen. With Christopher Councill,
Candy Buckley, Gary Moody, Sandy Rowe,
Marcee Smith, Ronald Wilcox, Lou Williford.

THE DRESSER (46). By Ronald Harwood.
May 24, 1983. Director, Mary Sue Jones. With
Jack Gwillim, Randy Moore, Synthia Rogers.

Dallas Theater Center: Down Center Stage

EMBARCADERO FUGUE (22). By Thomas
Strelich. November 2, 1982. Director, Kaki
Hopkins. With Andrew Way, Anna Heins, Bar-
bara Enlow, Andrew Christopher Gauff.

TOPEKA SCUFFLE (22). By Paul Munger.
January 11, 1983 (world premiere). Director,
Dennis Vincent.
Johnny Jarrod . . . . Michael Dendy
Steve Miles . . . . Geoffrey Ward
Billy Mimms . . . . Russell Henderson
Tony . . . . Karl Schaeffer.
   Place: A janitorial storage room of a large,
old municipal coliseum in Topeka. One intermis-
sion.

THE PRIDE OF THE BRITTONS (22). By
Kenneth Robbins. March 1, 1983 (professional
premiere). Director, Randy Bonifay.
Louisa Britton . . . . Eleanor Lindsay
Old Man Britton . . . . Barry Nash
Mrs. Britton . . . . Lynn Trammell
Solomon Mears . . . . T. R. Green
Jonathan Nye . . . . Lee Lowrimore
Cristy McMann . . . . David Edwards
Ida Mosely . . . . Susan McDaniel Hill
   Time: 1864. Place: Central South Carolina.
One intermission.

ANGEL AND DRAGON (22). By Sally Netzel. April 19, 1983 (world premiere). Director,

DALLAS THEATER CENTER—Virginia McKinney, Kaki Dowling Hopkins *(seated)* and Jillian Raye in *Angel and Dragon* by Sally Netzel

B. Jack Jones.
Maggie Irving .... Kaki Dowling Hopkins
Model .... Virginia McKinney
Anna Forbish. .... Jillian Raye

Act I, Scene 1: New York City, 1945. Scene 2: Paris, 1890. Scene 3: Paris, 1895. Scene 4: Paris, 1900. Act II, Scene 1: Paris 1917. Scene 2: Paris, 1925. Scene 3: New York City, 1945.

Dallas Theater Center: Brookhaven Community College Theater Center

A CHRISTMAS CAROL (13). By Charles Dickens; adapted by John Figlmiller and Sally Netzel. December 10, 1982. Director, Candy Buckley. With Randy Moore, Harl Asoff, Arthur Olaisen, John Figlmiller, Lynne Moon.

Dallas Theater Center: Magic Turtle Children's Theater

THE LION, THE WITCH AND THE WARDROBE (8). By C. S. Lewis. October 23, 1982. Director, Eleanor Lindsay.

JANE EYRE (8). By Charlotte Bronte; adapted by John Logan. January 8, 1983. Director, Mary Lou Hoyle. With Susan G. Neely, Art Moss.

STEP ON A CRACK (9). By Susan Zeder. February 19, 1983. Director, Kenneth Hill.

OZ, LAND OF MAGIC (9). Book and lyrics by Jim Marvin; music by Randolph Tallman and Joe Cox; based on the Oz books by L. Frank Baum. April 9, 1983. Director, Paul Munger; musical director, Merlaine Angwall; choreography, Gary Whitehead, Daniel Stephens, Lynne Moon.

Dallas Theater Center: Eugene McKinney New Play Readings

UNCOMMON DENOMINATORS by Mark Donald. October 25, 1982.
WIDOW'S WATCH by Jeffrey Kinghorn; director, Peter Lynch. November 15, 1982.
THE DREAM MACHINE by Deborah A. Kinghorn; director, Eleanor Lindsay. January 24, 1983.
MEN WITH TATTOOS AND LADIES WHO WORK IN LAUNDERIES by Annabelle Weenick; director, Hanna Cusick. February 21, 1983.
MAN TIME AT THE RIVER PLACE by Thomas W. Stephens. March 14, 1983.
TAP DANCING ACROSS THE UNIVERSE by William Borden; director, Octavio Solis. April 18, 1983.
THE IS NOT by William Kirk; director, Merlaine Angwall. May 2, 1983.
FAMILY HONOR AND OTHER ILLUSIONS by Smith Oliver. May 9, 1983.

Designers: scenery, Peter Lynch, Robert Duffy, Zak Herring, Virgil Beavers, Stella McCord, Sally Askins, Irene Corey, John H. Landon; lighting, Randy Bonifay, Robyn Flatt, Ken Hudson, Robert Duffy, Randy Moore, John Vigna, Terrie Clark, Barbara Sanderson, Linda Blase, John H. Landon; costumes, Tim Haynes, Stella McCord, Sally Askins, Deborah Kinghorn, Lynne Moon, Russell Henderson, Ann Stephens, Irene Corey, Felicia Denney, Carol Miles, John Vigna.

EVANSTON, ILL.

North Light Repertory: Mainstage.

(Artistic director, Michael Maggio; managing director, Jeffrey Bentley)

WHO'S AFRAID OF VIRGINIA WOOLF? (47). By Edward Albee. September 11, 1982. Director, Eric Steiner. With Jack McLaughlin-Gray, Megan McTavish, Laurie Metcalf, Rick Snyder.

FILTHY RICH (43). By George F. Walker. November 6, 1982. Director, Robert Woodruff. With Ron Parady, P.J. Barry, Diane D'Aquila, Brooks Gardner, Michael Grodenchik, Maria Ricossa.

DUET FOR ONE (48). By Tom Kempinski.

January 5, 1983. Director, Jeffrey Haden. With Eva Marie Saint, Milton Selzer.

CHILDREN (47). By A. R. Gurney Jr.; based on a story by John Cheever. March 12, 1983. Director, Mary F. Monroe. With Allison Giglio, Fern Persons, Elizabeth Smith, Peter Syversten.

THE IMPROMPTU OF OUTREMONT (40). By Michel Tremblay; translated by John Van Burek. May 7, 1983. Director, Eric Steiner. With Pauline Brailsford, Laurel Cronin, Diane D'Aquila, Allison Giglio.

North Light Repertory: Satellite Season

THE EARLY MALE YEARS (6). By John McNamara. October 27, 1982. Director, Mary F. Monroe. With Debra Engle, Pam Gay, Johnny Heller, Edward Henzel, James W. Sudik.

DOUGLAS (7). A dramatic portrait of William O. Douglas by Robert Litz. March 2, 1983 (world premiere). Director, David Rotenberg. With Glenn Mazen.
    Time: An hour or so before noon, Wednesday, Nov. 12, 1975. Place: Suite 108, the Supreme Court Building, Justice Douglas's Chambers. One intermission.

DEMOLITION JOB (6). By Gordon Graham. April 27, 1983 (American premiere). Director, Edward Stern.
Kelvin . . . . Jeff Ginsberg
Roy . . . . Joe D. Lauck
Quentin . . . . Robert Browning
    Time: The present. Place: A derelict schoolroom. One intermission.

Designers: scenery, Nels Anderson, Michael Merritt, David Emmons, Bob Barnett, Shawn Kerwin, Nan Zabriskie; lighting, Dawn Hollingsworth, Robert Shook; costumes, Kate Bergh, Jordan Ross, Jessica Hahn, Nan Zabriskie.

Note: Emlyn Williams appeared in *Dylan Thomas Growing Up* (14) from Dec. 12 to Jan. 2.

HARTFORD

Hartford Stage: John W. Huntington Theater

(Artistic director, Mark Lamos; managing director, William Stewart)

ON BORROWED TIME (44). By Paul Osborn. September 24, 1982. Director, Tony Giordano. With C. B. Barnes, William Swetland, Leora Dana, Sloane Shelton, Maurice Copeland.

THE GREAT MAGOO (46). By Ben Hecht and Gene Fowler. November 12, 1982. Director, Mark Lamos. With Robert Blumenfeld, Robert Machray, Michael O'Hare.

THE PORTAGE OF SAN CRISTOBAL OF A. H. (44). Adapted by Christopher Hampton; from the novel by George Steiner. December 31, 1982 (American premiere). Director, Mark Lamos.
Emmanuel Lieber . . . . Robert Blumenfeld
Simeon . . . . Alan Mixon
Gideon Benasseraf . . . . Mark Zeller
John Asher . . . . Ian Stuart
Elie Barach . . . . Mordecai Lawner
Isaac Amsel . . . . Dennis Bacigalupi
Guard #1; an Indian;
  Reporter . . . . Mark Wayne Nelson
Guard #2, Teku . . . . Talbott Dowst
A. H. . . . . John Cullum
Prof. Ryder; Grusdev;
  Dr. Röthling; Josquin . . . . Robert Blackburn
Col. Shepilov; Luckyer . . . . . . Thomas Carson
Hoving; Hanfmann;
  Reporter . . . . Jerry Allan Jones
Kulken; Reporter . . . . Robert Machray
Indian Woman; Reporter . . . . Carla Dean

Marvin Crownbacker;
  Reporter . . . . Michael O'Hare
Anna Röthling;
  Reporter . . . . Ann-Sara Matthews
  Time: May 1970. Places: Tel Aviv, the jungle, Oxford, Moscow, Orosso, Köln, Paris, Washington. One intermission.

DOG EAT DOG (44). By Mary Gallagher. February 18, 1983 (world premiere). Director, Mary B. Robinson.
Marina Foley . . . . Susan Pellegrino
Al Foley . . . . Lewis Arlt
Charlie Flynn . . . . Peter Boyden
Fred Talbot . . . . Robert Nichols
Colleen Flynn . . . . Jeanne Michels
Woman . . . . Lynn Cohen
Edith Talbot . . . . Jane Connell
Dell Brown . . . . Vic Polizos
  Flynn children: Denise Desimone, Justin McGlamery, Kayden Will.
  One intermission.

THE MISANTHROPE (48). By Molière. April 5, 1983. Director, Mark Lamos. With Nicholas Woodeson, Tandy Cronyn, Pamela Payton-Wright, Will Lyman, Ivar Brogger.

THE GLASS MENAGERIE (44). By Tennessee Williams. May 27, 1983. Director, George Keathley. With Jan Miner, Eric Roberts, Laura Hughes, Kevin Geer.

Designers: scenery, Karen Schulz, Tony Straiges, John Conklin, Andrew Jackness, Kevin Rupnik, Santo Loquasto, Paul Gallo, Arden Fingerhut, Pat Collins; Robert Jared, James F. Ingalls; costumes, David Murin, Linda Fisher, Merrily Murray-Walsh, Nan Cibula, Dunya Ramicova, Santo Loquasto.

HOUSTON

The Nina Vance Alley Theater: Large Stage

(Artistic director, Pat Brown; associate artistic director, George Anderson; managing director, Tom Spray)

THE UNEXPECTED GUEST (16). By Agatha Christie. July 15, 1982. Director, John Vreeke.

With Andrew Smoot, Robin Moseley, Michael LaGue, Bob Burrus, Patricia Kilgarriff.

HARTFORD STAGE—Lewis Arlt and Susan Pellegrino in a scene from *Dog Eat Dog* by Mary Gallagher

HOME (16). By Samm-Art Williams. August 31, 1982. Director, Horacena J. Taylor. With the Negro Ensemble Company.

CLOSE TIES (38). By Elizabeth Diggs. October 14, 1982. Director, Pat Brown. With Ruth Nelson, Lillian Evans, James E. Brodhead.

THE RIVALS (44). By Richard Brinsley Sheridan. November 25, 1982. Director, John Going. With Daydrie Hague, Jeannette Clift, John Cagan, Glynis Bell, Dan LaRocque, Jim McQueen, Robert Graham.

NUTS (38). By Tom Topor. January 13, 1983. Director, Charles Abbott. With Robin Moseley, Jean Proctor, Bob Burrus, Dale Helward, Jim McQueen, Rutherford Craven.

THE VISIT (38). By Friedrich Duerrenmatt; translated by Maurice Valency. February 24, 1983. Director, Beth Sanford. With Ruth Ford, Bruce Hall, Dale Helward, Robert Graham, Philip Fisher.

THE DINING ROOM (38). By A.R. Gurney Jr. April 14, 1983. Director, Beth Sanford. With Laurie Daniels, Lillian Evans, Bettye Fitzpatrick, Robert Graham, Dan LaRocque, Jim McQueen.

TAKING STEPS (38). By Alan Ayckbourn. May 25, 1983. Director, Robert Graham. With Holly Villaire, Jim Bernhard, Marry Barry, John Cagan.

The Nina Vance Alley Theater: Arena Stage

GREATER TUNA (32). Written and performed by Jaston Williams and Joe Sears. July 29, 1982.

FIFTH OF JULY (42). By Lanford Wilson. December 9, 1982. Director, Neil Havens. With John Woodson, Bettye Fitzpatrick, William Johnson, Dede Lowe, Cynthia Lammel.

FAMILY BUSINESS (28). By Dick Goldberg. January 14, 1983. Director, George Anderson. With Timothy Arrington, John Wood-

son, James Belcher, Michael LaGue, Dan LaRocque, Larry Schneider.

HOW I GOT THAT STORY (28). By Amlin Gray. March 10, 1983. Director, Pat Brown. With John Woodson, Michael LaGue.

HOLY GHOSTS (16). Written and directed by Romulus Linney. April 28, 1983. With Bob Burrus, Cynthia Lammel, Blue Deckert, Brandon Smith.

Lunchtime Theater: Arena

SCENES FROM AMERICAN LIFE by A.R. Gurney Jr. directed by Beth Sanford; PVT WARS by James McLure, directed by Michael LaGue (14). September 30, 1982.

THE AMERICAN DREAM (18). By Edward Albee. March 17, 1983. Director, John Vreeke.

Monday Night Live: Staged readings

A LAND BREEZE by Jean Lenox Toddie, directed by Beth Sanford, November 8, 1982. FAN DANCE by Monty Philip Holamon, directed by John Vreeke, December 13, 1982. THE BUNKHOUSE by Terrence Ortwein, directed by George Anderson, March 2, 1983.

NOTHING IMMEDIATE by Shirley Lauro, directed by George Anderson; BLANKO by Sam Havens, directed by John Vreeke; HOMER by Thomas Gibbons, directed by Beth Sanford. May 9, 1983.

Designers: scenery, Michael Olich, Felix E. Cochren, Michael Miller, John Jensen, William Bloodgood, John Carver Sullivan, Robert Blackman, Keith Belli, James F. Franklin, Keith Hein; lighting, Jonathan Duff, William H. Grant III, James Sale, Gregory Sullivan, Sean Murphy, Penny Remsen; costumes, Tom McKenley, Alvin B. Perry, Mariann Verheyen, Tom Rasmussen, Ainslie Bruneau, Robert Blackman, John Carver Sullivan, Rosemary Ingham.

Note: Nina Vance Alley Theater presented the following plays for young people during the 1982–83 season: *The Prince and the Pauper*, adapted by Charlotte B. Chorpenning; *Pinocchio* by Carlos Collodi; and *Yellow Brick Road*.

INDIANAPOLIS

Indiana Repertory Theater: Mainstage

(Artistic director, Tom Haas; managing director, Len Alexander)

A MIDSUMMER NIGHT'S DREAM (23). By William Shakespeare. October 15, 1982. Director, Tom Haas. With James Tasse, Jennifer Dunegan, Craig Fuller, Karen Nelson, Dallas Greer. Scott Wentworth, Henry J. Jordan, Priscilla Lindsay.

BILLY BISHOP GOES TO WAR (48). By John Gray with Eric Peterson. November 11, 1982. Director, Ben Cameron. With Christopher McCann, Steven A. Freeman.

TARTUFFE (23). By Molière; translated by Richard Wilbur. January 7, 1983. Director, David Rotenberg. With Henry J. Jordan, Lowry Miller, Bella Jarrett, Priscilla Lindsay, Jennifer Dunegan, Scott Wentworth, Craig Fuller.

YOU CAN'T TAKE IT WITH YOU (23). By George S. Kaufman and Moss Hart. February 11, 1983. Director, Ben Cameron. With Bella Jarrett, Priscilla Lindsay, Avery Sommers, Barry McGuire, Frank Raiter.

DESIRE UNDER THE ELMS (23). By Eugene O'Neill. March 18, 1983. Director, Tom Haas. With Tana Hicken, Scott Wentworth, Craig Fuller, Terry Moore, Marco St. John.

PAL JOEY (23). Book by John O'Hara, music by Richard Rodgers, lyrics by Lorenz Hart. April 22, 1983. Director, Tom Haas; choreographer, Peter Anastos; musical director; James Kowal. With Scott Wentworth, Bernadette Galanti, Beverley Boseman, Bernard Kates.

Indiana Repertory Theater: Upper Stage

A CHRISTMAS CAROL (39). By Charles Dickens; adapted by Tom Haas. November 19, 1982. Director, Scott Wentworth. With Frank

Raiter, Craig Fuller, Demian Hostetter, Bella Jarrett, Doug Johnson, Stephen Preusse.

Designers: scenery, Steven Rubin, Bob Barnett, Douglas Stein, Russell Metheny, Ming Cho Lee, Michael Yeargan, Karen Schulz; lighting, Craig Miller, Stuart Duke, William Armstrong,

Rachel Budin; costumes, Bill Walker, Michael Yeuell, Gene K. Lakin, Judianna Makovsky, Swan Hilfery, Martha Kelly.

Note: IRT's Cabaret Theater presented original material by Tom Haas (directed by Ben Cameron, with musical direction by staff members), as well as guest artists and productions.

KANSAS CITY, MO.

Missouri Repertory Theater: Helen F. Spencer Theater

(Producing director, Patricia McIlrath)

ANTHONY AND CLEOPATRA (20). By William Shakespeare. July 8, 1982. Director, Eric Vos. With Claude Woolman, Juliet Randall, Richard Gustin, Robert Lewis Karlin, Ken Latimer.

HAY FEVER (18). By Noel Coward. July 15, 1982. Director, Francis Cullinan. With Peg Small, Jim Birdsall, Rob Knepper, Sarah Nall.

THE MAGNIFICENT YANKEE (17). By Emmet Lavery. July 29, 1982. Director, Albert Pertalion. With Robert Lewis Karlin, Robin Humphrey, Tom Small, Ken Latimer, Geoffrey Beauchamp, Claude Woolman.

TERRA NOVA (18). By Ted Tally. September 9, 1982. Director, James Assad. With Jack Aranson, Ronald Wendschuh, Sarah Nall, Martin Marinaro, Jim Birdsall, Rob Knepper, Ken Latimer.

A CHRISTMAS CAROL (30). By Charles Dickens, adapted by Barbara Field. December 1, 1982. Director, James Assad. With Jim Birdsall, Peter Umbras, David Schuster, Piper Carter, Becca Ross.

THE INNOCENTS (19). By William Archibald, based on Henry James's The Turn of the Screw. January 27, 1983. Director, Cedric Messina. With Peg Small, Sarah Nall, Melissa Judd/Laura Schaefer, Aleksander Peterson/Chris Koeberl, Randy Messersmith.

TRANSLATIONS (18) By Brian Friel. February 3, 1983. Director, Vincent Dowling. With Gary Neal Johnson, Becca Ross, Mark Robbins, Richard Gustin, Margaret Humphreys, Robert Lewis Karlin, Cynthia M. Rendlen, Jim Birdsall.

NICHOLAS NICKLEBY (17). By Charles Dickens, adapted by David Edgar. March 18 (Part I) and March 19, 1983 (Part II). Directors, Leon Rubin, James Assad. With Jeffrey Hayenga, Peg Small, Sarah Nall, David Barron, Company.

Designers: scenery, John Ezell, Tom Schenk, Wray Steven Graham, Harry Feiner, David Potts; lighting, Joseph Appelt, Ruth E. Ludwick, Keri Muir, Robert Jared; costumes, Baker S. Smith, Tom Schenk, John Carver Sullivan, Vincent Scassallati, Judith Dolan.

LOS ANGELES

Center Theater Group: Ahmanson Theater

(Artistic director, Robert Fryer)

A LITTLE FAMILY BUSINESS (51). Adapted by Jay Presson Allen from a play by Barillet and Gredy. October 8, 1982 (American premiere). Director, Vivian Matalon; production supervisor, Martin Charnin.
Lillian . . . . Angela Lansbury
Ben . . . . John McMartin
Nadine . . . . Joanna Gleason
Scott . . . . Anthony Shaw
Connie . . . . Ann Risley
Sal . . . . Theodore Sorel
Edward . . . . Tony Cummings

Aerobic Dance Instructor . . . . Lisa Carroll
Television News
Commentator . . . . Tony Cummings
    Act I, Scene 1: A May morning. Scene 2: The following morning. Scene 3: A few hours later. Act II, Scene 1: Three months later. Scene 2: Two weeks later. One intermission.

BRIGHTON BEACH MEMOIRS (59). By Neil Simon. December 10, 1982 (world premiere). Director, Gene Saks.
Eugene . . . . Matthew Broderick

Blanche................. Joyce Van Patten
Kate .... Elizabeth Franz
Laurie.................... Mandy Ingber
Nora....................... Jodi Thelen
Stanley .... Zeljko Ivanek
Jack................. Peter Michael Goetz
Time: September, 1937. Place: Brighton Beach, Brooklyn, New York. Act I: 6:30 P.M. Act II: Wednesday, a week later, about 6:45 in the evening.

HAY FEVER (59). By Noel Coward. February 12, 1983. Director, Tom Moore. With Celeste Holm, Michael Allison, Laurie Kennedy, Courtney Burr, Patricia Elliott.

CRIMES OF THE HEART (51). By Beth Henley. April 4, 1983. Director, Melvin Bernhardt. With Mia Dillon, Mary Beth Hurt, Lizbeth Mackay, Peter MacNicol, Raymond Baker. Sharon Ullrick.

Designers: scenery, David Gropman, David Mitchell, Richard Seger, John Lee Beatty; lighting, Richard Nelson, Tharon Musser, Martin Aronstein, Dennis Parichy; costumes, Theoni V. Aldredge, Patricia Zipprodt, Robert Blackman, Patricia McGourty.

Center Theater Group: Mark Taper Forum—Mainstage

(Artistic director, Gordon Davidson; acting artistic director, Kenneth Brecher; managing director, William P. Wingate)

A SOLDIER'S PLAY (52). By Charles Fuller. August 19, 1982. With David Ackroyd, Denzel Washington, Charles Weldon, Earl Billings, Robert Hooks, Philip Reeves.

METAMORPHOSIS (52). By Franz Kafka; adapted and directed by Steven Berkoff. October 21, 1982 (American premiere).
Gregor .... Brad Davis
Mr. Samsa .... Pat McNamara
Greta .... Annabella Price
Mrs. Samsa .... Priscilla Smith
Chief Clerk; Lodger .... Ebbe Roe Smith
Musician.................. Gregg Johnson

ACCIDENTAL DEATH OF AN ANARCHIST (52). By Dario Fo; adapted by John Lahr. January 20, 1983 (American premiere). Director, Mel Shapiro.
Detective Bertozzo .... John Carpenter
Patrolman.................... Tony Azito
Fool .... Ned Beatty

Inspector Pissani.......... Paul E. Richards
Massimo.................. Andrew Bloch
Chief....................... Tom Toner
Maria Feletti .... Sue Kiel
Time: The present. Place: A police station in Milan. One intermission.

GROWN UPS (52). By Jules Feiffer. March 24, 1983. Director, John Madden. With Nan Martin, Harold Gould, Mimi Kennedy, Bob Dishy, Cheryl Giannini, Jennie Dundas.

In repertory May 29–July 24:
A MONTH IN THE COUNTRY by Ivan Turgenev; adapted by Willis Bell. May 29, 1983. Director, Tom Moore. With Irene Tedrow, Paul Shenar, Michael Learned, Rene Auberjonois, Lawrence Pressman.
RICHARD III by William Shakespeare. May 30, 1983. Director, Diana Maddox. With Rene Auberjonois, Sally Kemp, James R. Winker, Gary Dontzig, Lawrence Pressman.

Center Theater Group: Mark Taper Forum Lab

VALESA (13). By Jerzy Tymicki; translated and adapted by Maya Haddow and Jeffrey Haddow. December 8, 1982. Director, Ben Levit.

ESTONIA YOU FALL (13). By Martin Weetman; director, John Frank Levey. February 11, 1983.

47 BEDS, INTERVIEWING THE AUDIENCE, A PERSONAL HISTORY OF THE AMERICAN THEATER (12). Written and performed by Spalding Gray. March 8, 1983.

SCHOOL TALK (3). By Peter C. Brosius and the ITP Company; director, Peter C. Brosius; composer, Jeff Hull; musical director, Elizabeth Meyers; choreographer, Michele Summers. March 31, 1983.

THE LIFE AND TIMES OF ALBERT EINSTEIN (12). By Kres Mersky; director, Edward Parone. May 19, 1983.

Designers: scenery, Michael Devine, Thomas A. Walsh, David Jenkins, Tom Lynch, Ralph Funicello, Lisette Thomas, Martyn Bookwalter, John Gilles; lighting, Martin Aronstein, Marilyn

MARK TAPER FORUM, LOS ANGELES—Tony Azito, Paul E. Richards, Tom Toner and Ned Beatty in John Lahr's adaptation of Dario Fo's
Italian farce *Accidental Death of an Anarchist*

Rennagel, Paul Gallo, Paulie Jenkins, Brian Gale, Elizabeth Stillwell; costumes, Judy Dearing,
Terence Tom Soon, Marianna Elliott, Dunya Ramicova, Robert Blackman, Peter Hall, Lisette
Thomas, Marilyn Fusich, Tina Haatainen.

Note: Mark Taper Forum presented some special programs developed at the theater including *August
6, 1945* adapted and songs composed by Dory Previn; additional music by Brad Fiedel; a work-in-
progress based on work by Dr. Helen Caldicott. In addition, company members performed and
directed poems, stories, and other writings at a literary cabaret, Sundays between Sept. 12 and June
26.

LOUISVILLE

Actors Theater of Louisville: Pamela Brown Auditorium

(Producing director, Jon Jory)

ARABIAN NIGHTS (18). Translated by Richard F. Burton. July 8, 1982. Director, Jon
Jory.

JULIUS CAESAR (36). By William Shakes-
peare. September 30, 1982. Director, Norris
Houghton. With Ray Fry, Dierk Torsek, John C.
Vennema, Mary Diveny, Jessie K. Jones.

COUP and CLUCKS (11). By Jane Martin. November 14, 1982 (world premiere). Director, Jon Jory.

Coup

Miz Zifty	Jen Jones
Don	William Mesnik
Beaulah	Beatrice Winde
Brenda Lee	Dawn Didawick
Tooth	Dierk Torsek
Essie	Jessie K. Jones
Bobby Joe	Daniel Jenkins
Dr. Kennedy	Reuben Green

Time: 4th of July, noon. Place: Miz Zifty's living room in the small town of Brine, Ala.

Clucks

Travis	Murphy Guyer
Tooth	Dierk Torsek
Bobby Joe	Daniel Jenkins
Pritchard	Ray Fry
Ryman	William Mesnik
Zits	John Short
Dr. Kennedy	Reuben Green
Essie	Jessie K. Jones

Time: 4th of July, evening. Place: Outside Dr. Kennedy's home. One intermission.

MINE (7). By David Epstein, directed by Frazier W. Marsh; NICE PEOPLE DANCING TO GOOD COUNTRY MUSIC by Lee Blessing, directed by Larry Deckel. November 6, 1982 (world premiere).

Mine

Rita-Jean Morgan	Mary Diveny
Bonnie Morgan	Kerstin Kilgo
Lynda Butcher	Dawn Didawick
Patti-Faye Howard	Nancy Mette
Frank Morgan	Vaughn McBride
Men	William Mesnik, Murphy Guyer

Time: Winter. Place: A mining camp.

Nice People Dancing to Good Country Music

Catherine Empanger	Kerstin Kilgo
Eve Wilfong	Kirtan Coan
Jason Wilfong	Daniel Jenkins
Roy Manual	William Mesnik
Jim Stools	Murphy Guyer

Time: A late September afternoon. Place: On an outside deck above a Houston Bar.

THE ART OF SELF-DEFENSE (8). By Trish Johnson (8). November 9, 1982 (world premiere). Director, Larry Deckel.

Ruth	Mary Diveny
Frannie	Kirtan Coan
Elizabeth	Nancy Mette
Jan	Dawn Didawick
C.Y.	Dale Soules
Male Voice	John Short

Place: In and around a downtown health club.

A CHRISTMAS CAROL (29). By Charles Dickens; adapted by Barbara Field. December 2, 1982. Director, Ray Fry. With John C. Vennema, Dierk Torsek, Chris Wilhite, William Mesnik.

MURDER AT THE VICARAGE (34). By Agatha Christie; adapted by Moie Charles and Barbara Toy. December 30, 1982. Director, Larry Deckel. With Adale O'Brien, Andy Backer, Cynthia Carle, Daniel Jenkins.

MASS APPEAL (27).By Bill C. Davis. February 3, 1983. Director, Russell Treyz. With Ray Fry, Dan Butler.

SAND CASTLES (12). By Adele Edling Shank. March 3, 1983 (professional premiere). Director, Theodore Shank.

Iris; Pregnant Woman;	
Sailor	Mary Seward-McKeon
Stephen	John C. Vennema
Carol	Connor Steffens
Aussie; Fast Floyd; Photographer;	
Bookworm	William Mesnik
Kim; Biker Chick	Stephanie Saft
Andy; Fritz; Policeman; Texan;	
Condo John's Voice	Scott Phelps.
Glen; Retired Man;	
Andy's father	Frederic Major
Ginger;	
Retired Woman	Carol Shoup-Sanders
Linda Blue; Aussie's Woman	Becky Mayo
Anemone; Jogger	Sally Faye Reit

Time: The following summer. Place: A southern California beach. One intermission. (See synopsis in the introduction to this section.)

THANKSGIVING (13). By James McLure. March 6, 1983 (world premiere). Director, Jon Jory.

Kate	Dawn Didawick
Winston	Murphy Guyer
Rob	Fred Saners
Eileen	Margo Martindale
James	Dierk Torsek
Vanessa	Susan Kingsley

Time: The present. Place: A suburban home in New Jersey. One intermission.

IN A NORTHERN LANDSCAPE (10). By Timothy Mason March 10, 1983 (world premiere). Director, Frazier W. Marsh.

Charlotte Bredahl	Peggy Cowles
Matthew Bredehl	Frederic Major
Emma Bredal	Laura Innes
Samuel Bredahl	Reed Birney
Anders Thorson	George Kimmel
Per Olafsson	Shawn Dougherty

Fritz Thatcher . . . . Mark Loftis
Mikkel Guntner . . . . Clint Allen
Nils Ogdahl . . . . George Sutton
Time: Back and forth between 1926 and 1928.
Place: Rural Minnesota. One intermission.

THE HABITUAL ACCEPTANCE by Kent
Broadhurst, directed by Adale O'Brien;
PARTNERS by Dave Higgins, directed by Robert Spera; BARTOK AS DOG by Patrick Tovatt, directed by Frazier W. Marsh. March 18,
1983 (world premieres).

THE HASTY HEART (28). By John Patrick.
April 7, 1983. Director, Adale O'Brien. With
Dennis Dixie, Ellen Fiske, Ray Fry, Bruce
Kuhn, William Mesnik, Robert Moran, Fritz
Sperberg, Dierk Torsek, John Anthony
Weaver.

WUTHERING HEIGHTS (36). By Emily
Bronte, adapted by Randolph Carter. May 5,
1983. Director, Jon Jory. With Gordana Rashovich, Ben Gotlieb, Marco Barricelli, Johanna
Leister.

Actors Theater of Louisville: Victor Jory Theater

World premieres

HAPPY WORKER by Stephen Feinberg, directed by Dierk Torsek; PARTNERS by Dave
Higgins, directed by Robert Spera; GOOD OLD
BOYS written and directed by Vaughn
McBride. (6) November 3, 1982.
A TANTALIZING by William Mastrosimone and THE VALUE OF NAMES by Jeffrey
Sweet (7) (See synopsis in the introduction to this
section). November 5, 1982. Director, Emily
Mann.
FLIGHT LINES by Barbara Schneider, directed
by Vaughn McBride; I WANT TO BE AN
INDIAN by William Borden; THE HABITUAL ACCEPTANCE OF THE NEAR
ENOUGH by Kent Broadhurst, directed by
Adale O'Brien. (6). November 7, 1982.
THE CAMEO by Ray Fry; IN THE BAG by
Lezley Havard; I LOVE YOU, I LOVE YOU
NOT by Wendy Kesselman; BARTOK AS
DOG by Patrick Tovatt. November 19, 1982.
Director, Frazier W. Marsh.

THE GIFT OF THE MAGI (37). By O.
Henry; adapted by Peter Eckstrom. December 1,
1982. Director, James Kramer. With Patricia
Arnell, Robert Stoeckle.

MISALLIANCE (19). By George Bernard
Shaw. January 12, 1983. Director, Thomas
Bullard. With Gilbert Cole, Ray Fry, Patricia
Hodges, K. Lype O'Dell, Joyce Krempel.

EDEN COURT (13). By Murphy Guyer. February 23, 1983 (world premiere). Director, Ken
Jenkins. With Murphy Guyer, Dawn Didawick, Holly Hunter, Steve Rankin.

NEUTRAL COUNTRIES (10). By Barbara
Fields. February 26, 1983 (world premiere). Director, Robert Falls. With Andy Backer, Kent
Broadhurst, Laura Hughes, Daniel Jenkins,
Adale O'Brien.

A WEEKEND NEAR MADISON (7). By
Kathleen Tolan. March 11, 1983 (world premiere). With Robin Groves, Holly Hunter, Randle Mell, William Mesnik. (See synopsis in the
introduction to this section.)

KEY EXCHANGE (18). By Kevin Wade. April
6, 1983. Director, Larry Deckel. With Steve
Rankin, Sally Faye Reit, Fred Sanders.

Designers: scenery, Paul Owen, Joseph A. Varga; lighting, Jeff Hill, Paul Owen, Karl Haas;
costumes, Karen Gerson, Kurt Wilhelm.

Note: Actors Theater of Louisville presented the following plays at the Lunchtime Theater: *Casting* by Andy Backer; *The Stickup* by Jon Huffman, *Cervelles au Beurre Noir* by John Jory, *HiTech* by Carol Mack, *French Fries* by Jane Martin, April 26–May 28, 1983.

MADISON, N.J.

New Jersey Shakespeare Festival: Drew University

(Artistic director, Paul Barry; producing director, Ellen Barry)

TWELFTH NIGHT (30). By William Shakespeare. June 22, 1982. Director, Paul Barry. With
Robin Leary, John Barrett, Dane Knell, Bertina

Johnson, Gary Sloan, Annie Stafford, Ron
Steelman, Zeke Zaccaro.

TIMON OF ATHENS (24). By William Shakespeare. July 6, 1982. Director, Paul Barry. With Paul Barry, Don Perkins, J. C. Hoyt.

WILD OATS (25). By John O'Keeffe. August 3, 1982. Director, Christopher Martin. With Gary Sloan, Tom Spackman, J. C. Hoyt, Patrick Husted, Bertina Johnson, Don Perkins, Ron Steelman.

OUR TOWN (25). By Thornton Wilder. September 21, 1982. Director, Paul Barry. With Don Perkins, Geddeth Smith, Cornelia Evans, John Pietrowski.

CAT ON A HOT TIN ROOF (25). By Tennessee Williams. October 19, 1982. Director, Paul Barry. With Ellen Barry, John Abajian, Graham Pollock, Lynn Cohen, J. C. Hoyt, Margery Shaw.

FIFTH OF JULY (24). By Lanford Wilson. November 16, 1982. Director, Paul Barry. With Peter Burnell, Virginia Matis, Nila Novy.

Designers: scenery, Ann E. Gumpper; lighting, Richard Dorfman; costumes, Heidi Hollmann, Alice S. Hughes.

Note: New Jersey Shakespeare Festival presented a variety of Monday night special events including music, dance, mime and theater.

MILWAUKEE

Milwaukee Repertory Theater: Todd Wehr Theater—Mainstage

(Artistic director, John Dillon; managing director, Sara O'Connor)

MISS LULU BETT (45). By Zona Gale. September 10, 1982. Director, John Dillon. With Rose Pickering, Victor Raider-Wexler, James Pickering, Darrie Lawrence.

BURIED CHILD (45). By Sam Shepard. October 22, 1982. Director, Sharon Ott. With Maury Cooper, Rosemary Prinz, James Pickering, Ellen Lauren, Eric Hill, Larry Shue, Victor Raider-Wexler.

THE GLASS MENAGERIE (45). By Tennessee Williams. December 3, 1982. Director, John Dillon. With Rosemary Prinz, James Pickering, Ellen Lauren, Eric Hill.

THE FOREIGNER (45). By Larry Shue. January 14, 1983 (world premiere). Director, Nick Faust.
Froggy . . . . Kenneth Albers
Charlie . . . . Alan Brooks
Betty . . . . Bonnie Horan
David . . . . Laurence Ballard

Catherine . . . . Ellen Lauren
Owen . . . . William Leach
Ellard . . . . Peter Rybolt
    Time: The spring. Place: Betty Meeks's lakeside resort, Tilghman, Ga. One intermission. (See synopsis in the introduction to this section.)

UNCLE VANYA (45). By Anton Chekhov; translated and directed by Richard Cottrell. February 25, 1983. With James Pickering, Albert Corbin, Peggity Price, Daniel Mooney, Rose Pickering.

THE GOVERNMENT MAN (45). By Felipe Santander; translated by Joe Rosenberg. April 8, 1983 (English language premiere).
Cruz . . . . Jose Santana
Conconero . . . . Raoul Breton
Benito . . . . Abel Franco
Maximo . . . . Daniel Mooney
    Others: Millie Vega, William Ontiveros and members of MRT Company.
    Place: A poor Mexican village.

Milwaukee Repertory Theater: Pabst Theater

A CHRISTMAS CAROL (31). By Charles Dickens; adapted by Nagle Jackson. December 1, 1982. Director, Nick Faust. With Maury Cooper, Laurence Ballard, Rose Pickering, Daniel R. Poppert.

Milwaukee Repertory Theater: Court Street Theater

THE PENTECOST (17). By William Stancil. March 3, 1983 (world premiere). Director, Robert E. Goodman.
Flora Spincks . . . . Edith Elliott

Lula Sprowl . . . . Julia Follansbee
Hattie Crims . . . . Jeanne Schlegel
Ada Fincher. . . . . Mimi Honce
Jared Sprowl . . . . Kenneth Albers
Dr. Fenton Underwood Jr... Laurence Ballard
Time, 1948. Place: Etowah City, Ga. Act I,
Scene 1: The afternoon of Friday, May 20. Scene
2: Later that evening. Act II, Scene 1: Morning
of Saturday, May 21. Scene 2: Morning of Sunday, May 22.

THE EIGHTIES, OR LAST LOVE (17). By
Tom Cole. March 24, 1983 (world premiere).
Director, Sharon Ott.
He . . . . Emmett O'Sullivan-Moore
She . . . . Megan Hunt.
Time: Early in the 1980s.

THE FUEHRER IS STILL ALIVE (12). By
Tsuneari Fukuda; translated by Thomas
Rimer. April 14, 1983 (American premiere). Director, Tetsuo Arakawa.
Fujii Yumeko. . . . . Virginia Wing
Misui Hikoichi. . . . . Keone Young
Adolf Bormann . . . . Kenneth Albers
Helga Neidinger . . . . Katherine Udall
Kada Hitomi . . . . Kiya Ann Joyce
Tanouchi Heisuke . . . . Michael Paul Chan
Kada Hiroshi. . . . . Ernest Harada
Hishiyama Hajime. . . . . Fredric Mao
Hermann Schmidt . . . . Larry Shue
    Time: 1970. Place: In the living room of Fujii
Yumeko and Adolf Bormann, Japan.

Designers: scenery, Hugh Landwehr, Tim Thomas, Laura Maurer, Bil Mikulewicz, David Jenkins; lighting, Spencer Mosse, Rachel Budin, Dawn Chiang, Daniel Kotlowitz, Dan Brovarney; costumes, Kurt Wilhelm, Colleen Muscha, Patricia Risser, Elizabeth Covey, Sam Fleming, Katherine E. Duckert, Gayle M. Strege, Mary Piering.

Note: MRT's productions of *The Glass Menagerie* and *Buried Child* toured Japan and South Korea, May-June 1983, as part of a continuing theater exchange program between the U. S. and Japan.

MINNEAPOLIS

The Guthrie Theater

(Artistic director, Liviu Ciulei; managing director, Donald Schoenbaum; associate artistic director, Garland Wright)

In rotating repertory, June 5-November 21:

SUMMER VACATION MADNESS by Carlo
Goldoni. June 5, 1982. Director, Garland
Wright. With Seth Allen, Caitlin Clarke, Munson Hicks, Kristine Nielsen.

REQUIEM FOR A NUN by William
Faulkner. June 24, 1982. Director, Liviu Ciulei. With Richard Frank, Linda Kazlowski, Isabell Monk, Bill Moor.

THE MARRIAGE OF FIGARO by Beaumarchais, adapted by Richard Nelson. July 15,
1982. Director, Andrei Serban. With Richard
Dorfman, Cristine Rose, Jana Schneider, David
Warrilow.

ROOM SERVICE by John Murray and Allen
Boretz. August 19, 1982. Director, Harold
Stone. With Ken Ruta, Seth Allen, Warren
Pincus.

HEARTBREAK HOUSE by George Bernard
Shaw. October 14, 1982. Director, Christopher
Markle. With Robert Pastene, Kristine

Nielsen, Dillon Evans, Delphi Harrington,
Annie Murray.

A CHRISTMAS CAROL (45). By Charles
Dickens; adapted by Barbara Field. November
25, 1982. Director, Christopher Markle.

ENTERTAINING MR. SLOANE (28). By Joe
Orton. January 6, 1983. Director, Gary Gisselman. With Richard Sale, Yolanda Childress,
James Harper, Dillon Evans.

PEER GYNT (50). By Henrik Ibsen; translated
by Rolf Fjelde. February 12, 1983. Director,
Liviu Ciulei. With Greg Martyn, Jossie de
Guzman, Gerry Bamman, Gail Grate, Gloria
Foster. Music by Fiorenza Carpi and Paul
Goldstaub; choreography, Maria Cheng.

MASTER HAROLD . . . AND THE BOYS
(36). Written and directed by Athol Fugard. May
3, 1983. With James Earl Jones, Delroy
Lindo, Charles Michael Wright.

Designers: scenery, Adrianne Lobel, Santo Loquasto, Jack Barkla, Michael Yeargan, Beni Montresor; lighting, Craig Miller, Jennifer Tipton, Paul Scharfenberger, William Armstrong, Duane Schuler; costumes, Anne Hould-Ward, Santo Loquasto, Jack Edwards, Lawrence Casey, Beni Montresor, Jared Aswegan.

NEW HAVEN

Long Wharf Theater: Mainstage

(Artistic director, Arvin Brown; executive director, M. Edgar Rosenblum)

OPEN ADMISSIONS (47). By Shirley Lauro. October 14, 1982 (world premiere). Director, Arvin Brown.

Peter	Paul Gleason
Ginny	Roberta Maxwell
Salina	Mary Alice
Calvin	Calvin Levels
Cathy	Wendy Ann Finnegan
Georgia	Pamela Potillo
Heidi Horowitz	Paula Fritz
Nick Rizzoli	Thomas Calabro
Juan Rivera	Even H. Miranda
Punkin	Ntombi Peters/Tarah Roberts

Act I, Scene 1: Calvin's and Ginny's apartments in Manhattan, morning, the present. Scene 2: The City College, immediately thereafter, during the morning and afternoon of the same day. Act II, Scene 1: Calvin's and Ginny's apartments, immediately thereafter, early evening of the same day. Scene 2: The City College, immediately thereafter, that night. One intermission.

HOLIDAY (47). By Philip Barry. November 26, 1982. Director, John Pasquin. With Richard Jenkins, Jill Eikenberry, Joanne Camp, William Swetland.

ANOTHER COUNTRY (47). By Julian Mitchell. January 6, 1983 (American premiere). Director, John Tillinger.

Guy Bennett	Peter Gallagher
Tommy Judd	Peter MacNicol
Donald Devenish	Tait Ruppert
Jim Menzies	Albert Macklin
Fowler	Owen Thompson
Sanderson	Tyrone Power
Barclay	Mark Moses

Delahay	Rob Gomes
Wharton	Robert Byron Allen
Vaughan Cunningham	Edmond Genest

Time: Summer, in the early 1930s. Place: An English Public School. Act I, Scene 1: The fourth year library, Gascoigne's House. Scene 2: Barclay's study, that evening. Scene 3: Dormitory, that night. Scene 4: Library, night, a week later. Act II, Scene 1: Study, morning, a few days later. Scene 2: Library, that night. Scene 4: Study, the following evening. Scene 5: Cricket field, the next day. Scene 6: Library, that evening. One intermission.

THE GUARDSMAN (47). By Ferenc Molnar. February 17, 1983. Director, Harris Yulin. With Richard Jordan, Maria Tucci, Paul Benedict, Jane Cronin.

PAL JOEY (47). Music by Richard Rodgers, lyrics by Lorenz Hart, book by John O'Hara based on his stories. March 31, 1983. Director, Kenneth Frankel; music director, Thomas Fay; choreographer, Dan Siretta. With Philip Casnoff, Joyce Ebert, Betsy Joslyn, Louisa Flaningam, Bill McIntyre, D'Jamin Bartlett.

THE CHERRY ORCHARD (47). By Anton Chekhov; translated by Jean-Claude van Itallie. May 12, 1983. Director, Arvin Brown. With Joyce Ebert, John Tillinger, Tom Atkins, Fran Brill, Stephanie Zimbalist, Mark Blum, Pippa Scott, Morris Carnovsky.

MOLLY (32). By Simon Gray. July 7, 1983. Director, Stephen Hollis. With Tammy Grimes, David Huddleston, Thomas Hulce, Barbara Bryne, Roger Forbes.

Long Wharf Theater: Stage Two

ELEGY FOR A LADY and SOME KIND OF LOVE STORY (48). Written and directed by Arthur Miller. October 26, 1982 (world premiere).

Elegy For A Lady

Man	Charles Cioffi
Proprietress	Christine Lahti.

Time: the present. Place: A boutique in an American city.

LONG WHARF THEATER, NEW HAVEN—*Above,* William Swetland
and Phyllis Thaxter in *Free and Clear* by Robert Anderson; *below,* Charles
Cioffi in the Arthur Miller one-acter *Elegy for a Lady*

Some Kind of Love Story
Angela .... Christine Lahti
Tom .... Charles Cioffi
Time: The present. Place: Angela's bedroom in an American city.

QUARTERMAINE'S TERMS (48). By Simon Gray. December 14, 1983 (American premiere). Director, Kenneth Frankel.
St. John Quartermaine ...... Remak Ramsay
Anita Manchip .... Caroline Lagerfelt
Mark Sackling .... Kelsey Grammer
Eddie Loomis.................... Roy Poole
Derek Meadle .... Anthony Heald
Henry Windscape .... John Cunningham
Melanie Garth.................. Dana Ivey
Time: Over a period of three years in the early 1960s. Place: The staff room of the Cull-Loomis School of English for Foreigners, Cambridge, England. Act I, Scene 1: Springtime, Monday, 9:30 in the morning. Scene 2: Some weeks later, Friday afternoon, a few minutes before 5. Act II, Scene 1: The following year, towards summer, Monday morning, about 9:30. Scene 2: A Friday evening, some months later.

Scene 3: 18 months later, around Christmas, evening.

THE LADY AND THE CLARINET (48). By Michael Cristofer. February 1, 1983. Director, Gordon Davidson. With Stockard Channing, Kevin Geer, Michael Brandon, Josef Sommer, David Singer.

FREE AND CLEAR (48). By Robert Anderson. March 22, 1983 (world premiere). Director, Arvin Brown.
Jack....................... James Naughton
Larry .... David Marshall Grant
John .... William Swetland
Sarah...................... Phyllis Thaxter
Act I, Scene 1: Side porch of the Morrisons' large, old family home in Westchester County, New York, 3 in the morning on a hot, early summer's day in 1940. Scene 2: Outside the same house, later in the morning. Scene 3: Inside the house, still later that morning. Act II, Scene 1: On the porch, that evening. Scene 2: On the porch, near dawn the next morning.

Designers: scenery, Marjorie Bradley Kellogg, Steven Rubin, John Conklin, John Jensen, Andrew Jackness, Hugh Landwehr, David Jenkins, Michael Yeargan, Karl Eigsti; lighting, Ronald Wallace, Pat Collins, Jamie Gallagher, Judy Rasmuson, Paul Gallo; costumes, Ann Roth/Gary Jones, Bill Walker, Jane Greenwood, Robert Wojewodski.

Yale Repertory Theater

(Artistic director, Lloyd Richards; managing director, Benjamin Mordecai)

A DOLL'S HOUSE (20). By Henrik Ibsen; translated by Rolf Fjelde. October 5, 1982. Director, Lloyd Richards. With Dianne Wiest, Richard Jenkins, Lisa Banes, Earle Hyman, John Glover.

HELLO AND GOODBYE (20). By Athol Fugard. November 2, 1982. Director, Tony Giordano. With Warren Manzi, Jenny O'-Hara.

THE PHILANDERER (20). By George Bernard Shaw. November 30, 1982. Director, David Hammond. With Christopher Walken, Tandy Cronyn, Brooke Adams, Addison Powell, Dann Florek.

In rotating repertory, Jan. 17-Feb. 26:
ASTAPOVO (14). By Leon Katz. January 17, 1983. Director, Lawrence Kornfeld.
Sergeyenko .... Charles S. Dutton
Sergey....................... Reno Roop
Ozolin....................... Joel Rooks

Chertkov................. Andreas Katsulas
Sasha.................... Jocelyn Johnson
Dushan................... David Margulies
Tanya .... Lauren Klein
Andrey .... Rick Grove
Sonya .... Jan Miner
Elizaveta................ Marilyn Sommer
Railroad Worker .... John Turturro
Meyer...................... William Kux
Father Varsonofy....... Christian Clemenson
Time: November, 1910. Place: A railroad siding in Astapovo, Russia. Act I: November 2. Act II: November 7.

COYOTE UGLY (14). By Lynn Siefert. January 18, 1983. Director, Christian Angermann.
Scarlet Pewsy............ Sallyanne Tackus
Andreas Pewsy .... Dorothy Holland
Red Pewsy .... Edward Seamon
Dowd Pewsy .... Mark Metcalf
Penny Pewsy .... Barbara Somerville
Time: The present. Place: Arizona.

PLAYING IN LOCAL BANDS (14). By Nancy Fales Garrett. January 19, 1983. Director, William Ludel.
Shanti . . . . Lauren Klein
Roger . . . . John Harnagel
Monique . . . . Seret Scott
James Donne . . . . Michael Murphy
Kendra Wilson . . . . Julie Boyd
    Time: The present. Place: New York City.

MUCH ADO ABOUT NOTHING (20). By William Shakespeare. March 8, 1983. Director, Walton Jones. With Roxanne Hart, Mia Dillon, Marshall Bordon, Jon DeVries, Patrick James Clarke, Marcell Rosenblatt.

ABOUT FACE (20). By Dario Fo; English version by Dale McAdoo and Charles Mann. April 5, 1983 (English language premiere). Director, Andrei Belgrader.

Antonio/Agnelli . . . . Andreas Katsulas
Lucia . . . . Patricia Richardson
Rose . . . . Karen Shallo
D.A. . . . . William Duell
Doctor . . . . Warren Keith
Sergeant . . . . Joe Grifasi
Squadron Chief . . . . Keith Reddin
Squadron Leader; Waiter . . . . Dylan Baker
Waiter; Orderly . . . . Patterson Skipper
Policeman; Orderly . . . . David Thornton
    Time: The present. Place: Milan, Italy. Act I, Scene 1: An auto junkyard. Scene 2: A hospital. Scene 3: The same. Act II, Scene 1: Rosa's house, some months later. Scene 2: The same.

A TOUCH OF THE POET (20). By Eugene O'Neill. May 21, 1983. Director, Lloyd Richards. With George Grizzard, Julie Fulton, Barbara Caruso, Katharine Houghton, Rex Everhart.

Designers: scenery, G. W. Mercier, Philipp Jung, Christopher H. Barreca, Michael Yeargan, Robert M. Wierzel, Joel Fontaine, Ricardo Morin, Wing Lee; lighting, William B. Warfel, Robert M. Wierzel, Stephen Strawbridge, Andrew Carter, Laurence F. Schwartz, Peter Maradudin, Jennifer Tipton; costumes, Dunya Ramicova, Donna Zakowski, Connie Singer, Catherine Zuber, Richard Mays, Ricardo Morin, G. W. Mercier, Philipp Jung.

Note: During the 1982–83 season, the Yale School of Drama presented *Fanshen* by David Hare, directed by Bob Barron; *The Bewitched* by Peter Barnes, directed by Christian Angermann; *The Lower Depths* by Maxim Gorky in a translation by Alex Szogi; *The House of York,* chronicling the Wars of the Roses, adapted from materials compiled by Royston Coppenger, directed by David Hammond.

PHILADELPHIA

Philadelphia Drama Guild: Zellerbach Theater—Annenberg Center

(Managing director, Gregory Poggi)

THE DIARY OF ANNE FRANK (24). By Frances Goodrich and Albert Hackett. November 25, 1982. Director, William Woodman. With Jan Leslie Harding, Barbara Caruso, John Dukakis, Conrad L. Osborne, Marilyn Sokol.

THE KEEPER (22). By Karolyn Nelke. October 14, 1982 (professional premiere). Director, Steven Schachter.
William Fletcher . . . . Stuart Germain
John Cam Hobhouse . . . . Richard Frank
Mr. Neems . . . . I.M. Hobson
Lady Byron . . . . Valerie Mahaffey
Lord Byron . . . . Dwight Schultz
Mary Ann Clermont . . . . Eunice Anderson

Augusta Mary Leigh . . . . Patricia Elliott
    Time: November 1815 through April 1816. Place: London. One intermission.

TALLEY'S FOLLY (22). By Lanford Wilson. January 6, 1983. Director, Charles I. Karchmer. With Jerry Zaks, Robin Groves.

DAUGHTERS (22). By John Morgan Evans. March 10, 1983. Director, Tony Giordano. With Jenny O'Hara, Vera Lockwood, Kathleen Doyle, Yudie Bank, Roxann Caballero.

ALL MY SONS (22). By Arthur Miller. April 21, 1983. Director, William Woodman. With Dan Frazer, Court Miller, Morgan Land/Judd Serotta, Lenka Peterson, Adrian Sparks.

PHILADELPHIA DRAMA GUILD—Dwight Schultz and I.M. Hobson in
a scene from *The Keeper* by Karolyn Nelke

Designers: scenery, Eldon Elder, Roger Mooney, John Falabella, Karen Schulz, John Jensen;
lighting, William Armstrong, Dennis Parichy, Ann Wrightson; costumes, Jess Goldstein, John David
Ridge, Frankie Fehr, David Murin.

Philadelphia Playrights' Project: Studio Theater

(Project coordinator, Steven Schachter)

Staged readings, 2 performances each
THE CHILD by Anthony Giardina, director
William Woodman. October 25, 1982.
CIRCLES by Joseph M. Orazi; director, Steven
Schachter.December 6, 1982.
THE INNER STATION by David Ives; direc-
tor, Kay Matschullat. January 31, 1983.

PITTSBURGH

Pittsburgh Public Theater: Hazlett Theater in the Alleghany Center

(Artistic director, Larry Arrick; managing director, Dennis A. Babcock)

TOM JONES (48). Adapted and directed by Larry Arrick; music and songs by Barbara Damashek; based on Henry Fielding's novel. September 9, 1982. With Rosalyn Farinella, Keith David, Don Howard, Ann Kerry, Derek Meader, Jill O'Hara.

A STREETCAR NAMED DESIRE (48). By Tennessee Williams. October 28, 1982. Director, Larry Arrick. With April Shawhan. Stephen Lang, Ann Kerry, William Verderber.

QUILTERS (48 and 38). By Molly Newman and Barbara Damashek; music, lyrics and direction by Barbara Damashek. December 16, 1982 (reopened June 30, 1983). With Evalyn Baron, Lenka Peterson, Lynn Lovvan, Kate Lohman, Rosemary McNamara, Barbara Sieck Taylor, Catherine Way.

ALMS FOR THE MIDDLE CLASS (48). By Stuart Hample. February 3, 1983 (world premiere). Director, Larry Arrick.

Ken Gaines	Marcus Diamond
Sarah	Bethany Faye Decof
Marshall Gaines	Richard Greene
Doris Gaines	Evalyn Baron
Keith	Timothy Donoghue

Time: Various times. Place: Vermont and New York. One intermission.

WHO'S AFRAID OF VIRGINIA WOOLF? (48). By Edward Albee. March 24, 1983. Director, Larry Arrick. With Timothy Donoghue, Melissa Hurst, Alan Mixon, April Shawhan.

THE PRICE (48). By Arthur Miller. May 12, 1983. Director, Gene Lesser. With Harold Gary, William Hardy, Alan Mixon, Marilyn Rockafellow.

Designers: scenery, Ursula Belden, John Jensen, Thomas A. Walsh; lighting, Allen Lee Hughes, Dennis Parichy, Kristine Bick, Robert Jared; costumes, Elizabeth P. Palmer, Jess Goldstein, Flozanne A. John.

PORTLAND, ME.

Portland Stage Company

(Producing director, Barbara Rosoff; general manager, Patricia Egan)

GETTING OUT (30). By Marsha Norman. October 21, 1982. Director, Barbara Rosoff. With Rebecca Nelson, Cynthia Mace, Anna Minot, William Hall Jr., J. D. Swain.

THE DINING ROOM (30). By A. R. Gurney Jr. November 25, 1982. Director, Lynn Polan. With Mona Stiles, James Selby, James Seymour, Shaw Purnell, Cynthia Barnett, Richard Maynard.

GARDENIA (30). By John Guare. December 30, 1982. Director, Barbara Rosoff. With Keliher Walsh, Michael Landrum, Richard Maynard, Thomas A. Stewart.

A LESSON FROM ALOES (30). By Athol Fugard. January 27, 1983. Director, Arden Fingerhut. With Tad Ingram, Susan Stevens, William Hall Jr.

HOW I GOT THAT STORY (30). By Amlin Gray. February 24, 1983. Director, Louis Rackoff. With Stanley Flood, Stephen C. Bradbury.

ECCO! (30). By Gerry Bamman. March 24, 1983 (world premiere). Director, Barbara Rosoff.

Richard	Robert Burns
Harry	Conan McCarty
Suzanne	Sofia Landon
Nicholas	Dexter Witherell
Irene	Susan Botti
Tom	Paul Walker
Angela	Etain O'Malley
Peter	Peter Dane
Pauline	Sandra T. Colby
John	Stephen C. Bradbury
Bernardo	Michael Hughes

Place: Terrace and garden of a summer home on Cape Cod. Act I: August 1920. Act II, Scene 1: July 1921, late afternoon. Scene 2: That evening. Act III: June 1922. Two intermissions.

Designers: scenery, John Döepp, Leslie Taylor, Patricia Woodbridge, Marjorie Bradley Kellogg; lighting, Ann Wrightson, Arden Fingerhut; costumes, Eren Ozker, Heidi Hollmann, Rachel Kurland, Robert Wojewodski, Leslie Taylor, Marie Ann Chiment.

Portland Stage Company: New Play Readings

AMENDS by Marsha Sheiness, November 14, 1982. Director, Barbara Rossoff.
NATIONAL ANTHEMS by Dennis McIntyre. January 16, 1983. Director, Lynn Polan.

STEEPLE JACK by Dennis Reardon. February 13, 1983. Director, Lynn Polan.
VERA WITH KATE by Toni Press. April 10, 1983. Director, Lynn Polan.

PORTSMOUTH, N. H.

Theater by the Sea

(Producing director, Jon Kimball)

SWING SHIFT (32). Music by Michael Dansicker; lyrics by Sarah Schlesinger; conceived and directed by Jack Allison. September 24, 1982 (world premiere). Musical director, Bruce W. Coyle; choreographer-associate director, Helen Butleroff.
Vera .... Catherine Cox
Dot .... Louisa Flaningam
Maisie .... Ann-Ngaire Martin
    Time: 1942. Place: An aircraft assembly plant.

ARMS AND THE MAN (32). By George Bernard Shaw. October 29, 1982. Director, Larry Carpenter. With Cecile Callan, Marian Baer, Samuel Maupin, Jerry Gershman, Tom Celli.

THE BUTTERFINGERS ANGEL (32). By William Gibson. December 3, 1982. Director, Tom Celli, With Cecile Callan, J. Scott Williams, Roger Curtis, Scott Weintraub, Maxine Taylor-Morris.

DEATHTRAP (32). By Ira Levin. January 7, 1983. Director, Peter Bennett. With Tom Celli, Victoria Boothby, Jeff McCarthy, Stephanie Voss, Dick Sabol.

CHILDREN OF A LESSER GOD (32). By Mark Medoff. February 16, 1983. Director, Edmund Waterstreet. With Linda Bove, David Fitzsimmons.

MASS APPEAL (32). By Bill C. Davis. March 23, 1983. Director, Tom Celli. With Charles Welch, Jeff McCarthy.

PIPPIN (32). Book by Roger O. Hirson; music and lyrics by Stephen Schwartz. April 28, 1983. Director, Loyd Sannes. With Billy Hester, George Emch, Ginger Prince.

Theater by the Sea: Prescott Park Arts Festival

CAROUSEL (23). Music by Richard Rodgers; book and lyrics by Oscar Hammerstein II; based on Ferenc Molnar's Liliom. July 1, 1982. Director, Jon Kimbell; musical director, Bruce W. Coyle; choreographer, Jayne Persch. With Mark McGrath, Faith Prince, Vicki Lewis, Loyd Sannes, Marilyn Hudgins.

    Designers: scenery, Richard Chambers, Kathie Iannicelli, Mark Pirolo, John Döepp, Edward Cesaitis; lighting, Bruce K. Morriss, Sid Bennett; costumes, Kathie Iannicelli.

PRINCETON, N.J.

McCarter Theater Company: Mainstage

(Artistic director, Nagle Jackson; managing director, Alison Harris)

BLITHE SPIRIT (16). By Noel Coward. October 1, 1982. Director, William Woodman. With Marion Lines, Paul Shenar, Anna Russell, Christine Baranski.

HAMLET (17). By William Shakespeare. October 29, 1982. Director, Nagle Jackson. With Harry Hamlin, Stacy Ray, Neil Vipond, Jill Tanner, Jay Doyle, Gary Roberts.

A CHRISTMAS CAROL (14). By Charles Dickens; adapted and directed by Nagle Jackson. November 27, 1982. With Herb Foster, Gerald Lancaster, Robin Chadwick, Penelope Reed, Lawrence Holofcener, Jonathan Holub.

THE DAY THEY SHOT JOHN LENNON (16). By James McLure. January 21, 1983 (world premiere). Director, Robert Lanchester.
Fran .... Mercedes Ruehl
Sally .... Ann Adams
Kevin .... Greg Thornton
Mike .... Clifford Fetters
Larry .... Damien Leake
Morris....................... Karl Light
Silvio..................... Tony Campisi

Gately.................... Gregory Grove
Brian...................... Gary Roberts
    Place: In front of the Dakota, New York City. Time: December 9, 1980. No intermission.

THREE SISTERS (16). By Anton Chekhov; translated by Randall Jarrell. March 4, 1983. Director, Nagle Jackson. With Penelope Reed, Stacy Ray, Mercedes Ruehl, Jay Doyle, David O'Brien, Robert Lanchester, Leslie Geraci.

A DELICATE BALANCE (17). By Edward Albee. April 1, 1983. Director, Paul Weidner. With Nancy Marchand, Paul Sparer, Barbara Cason, Myra Carter, Karl Light, Elaine Bromka.

McCarter Theater Company: Stage Two

AT THIS EVENING'S PERFORMANCE (13). Written and directed by Nagle Jackson. January 30, 1983. With Stacy Ray, Robin

Chadwick, Stephen Oates Smith, Raye Birk, Penelope Reed, Steven Moses, Jay Doyle.

McCarter Theater Company: Playwrights-at-McCarter

New play readings, 1 performance each
PUBLIC LIVES by Julia Cameron. March 14, 1983. Director, Rosary O'Neill.
THE KINDNESS OF STRANGERS by Maura Swanson. March 28, 1983. Director, Robert Lanchester.
MEMPHIS IS GONE by Richard Hobson. April 4, 1983. Director, Robert Lanchester.
AMERICAN BEAUTY by Richard Brennan

Camp. April 25, 1983. Director, Robert Lanchester.
FIERCE DREAMS by Jack Maeby and Carol Tanzman. May 9, 1983. Director, Carol Tanzman.
DEBUT by Bruce E. Rodgers. May 16, 1983. Director, Richard Russell Ramos.

Designers: Scenery, Daniel Boylen, Brian Martin, Elizabeth Fischer; lighting, Richard Moore; costumes, Susan Rheume, Elizabeth Covey, M.L. Holmes.

PROVIDENCE, R.I.

Trinity Square Repertory Company: Downstairs Theater

(Director, Adrian Hall)

TINTYPES (24). By Mary Kyte, with Mel Marvin and Gary Pearle. June 8, 1982. Director, Sharon Jenkins. With Richard Ferrone, Rose Weaver, Bonnie Strickman, Anne Scurria, Keith Jochim.

THE CRUCIFER OF BLOOD (29). By Paul Giovanni. July 16, 1982. Director, Philip Minor. With Dan Butler, Richard Kneel, Keith Jochim, Timothy Crowe, Lori Cardille.

13 RUE DE L'AMOUR (36). By Georges Feydeau; adapted by Mawby Green and Ed Feilbert. August 13, 1982. Director, David

Wheeler. With Margo Skinner, Peter Gerety, Keith Jochim, Barbara Meek.

THE WEB (50). By Martha Boesing. October 5, 1982 (world premiere). Director, Adrian Hall.
Abigail Sater .... Margo Skinner
Abby as a Girl................ Becca Lish
Eleanor Sater................ Betty Moore
Carol Sater................ Thomas Deedy
Tobias Sater............ Richard Kavanaugh
Hester Sater................ Ann Hamilton
Gloria Sater................ Bonnie Black
Jesse Trace.................. Robert Black
    Time: Now. Place: The mind, memory

and imagination of Abigail Sater. One intermission.

THE DRESSER (58). By Ronald Harwood. November 30, 1982. Director, David Wheeler. With Richard Kneeland, Ford Rainey, Barbara Orson.

TRANSLATIONS (52). By Brian Friel. February 15, 1983. Director, Henry Velez. With David

C. Jones, Timothy Crowe, Anne Scurria, David Kennett, Pat Thomas.

LETTERS FROM PRISON (58). By Jack Henry Abbott. April 16, 1983 (world premiere). Director, Adrian Hall. With Richard Jenkins, Timothy Crowe, David Kennett. (See synopsis in the introduction to this section.)

Trinity Square Repertory Company: Upstairs Theater

A CHRISTMAS CAROL (39). By Charles Dickens; adapted by Adrian Hall and Richard Cumming. December 3, 1982. Director, Peter Gerety. With Ed Hall, Keith Jochim, Richard Kavanaugh, Sean Reilly/Neil Handwerger.

THE FRONT PAGE (37). By Ben Hecht and Charles MacArthur. February 1, 1983. Director, Philip Minor. With Richard Kneeland, Peter Gerety, Barbara Orson, Lura Bane Howes.

THE TEMPEST (37). By William Shakespeare. March 11, 1983. Director, Adrian Hall. With Richard Kneeland, Amy Van Nostrand, Richard Ferrone, Richard Kavanaugh.

PYGMALION (36). By George Bernard Shaw. April 22, 1983. Director, Philip Minor. With Jean Marsh, Richard Kavanaugh, Ed Hall, Anne Gerety, Keith Jochim.

Composer-musical director, Richard Cumming. Designers: scenery, Eugene Lee, Robert D. Soule; lighting, Eugene Lee, John F. Custer; costumes, William Lane.

Note: Trinity Square continued to present special performances for students of the regularly scheduled plays, as part of their curriculum.

RICHMOND

Virginia Museum Theater: Mainstage

(Artistic director, Tom Markus; managing director, Ira Schlosser)

THE PLAY'S THE THING (26). By Ferenc Molnar; translated by P. G. Wodehouse. October 8, 1982. Director, Tom Markus. With Carole Monferdini, James Braden, Humbert Astredo, Eric Swemer, Dan Bedard, William Denis, Robert Foley.

THE HIDING PLACE (27). Written and directed by Alfred Drake. November 19, 1982 (world premiere).

Katherine Ruyker . . . . Kim Beaty
Lawrence Pasten . . . . Rudolph Willrich
Edgell Carpenter . . . . Dana Mills
Duncan Ruyker . . . . Lucien Douglas
Hendryk Ruyker . . . . Tom McDermott
Alexander Baillie . . . . Norman Barrs
Peter Dean . . . . Alfred Drake
Marta Muratian . . . . Marion Lines
Thomas Ruyker Jr . . . . Charles Baxter
Charles Kendall . . . . Charles Brown
James Felton . . . . Andrew Umberger
  Place: The tower room in a Scottish castle above the Hudson River. Act I, Scene 1: Friday,

9 P.M. in early May. Scene 2: Saturday, 3 A.M. Act II, Scene 1: Saturday, 5 P.M. Scene 2: Saturday, 9 P.M.

A CHRISTMAS CAROL (26). By Charles Dickens; adapted by Tom Markus. December 17, 1982. Director, Terry Burgler. With Don Christopher, Ben Appleton, Adrian Rieder, Robert Foley.

THE LION IN WINTER (26). By James Goldman. January 7, 1983. Director, Tom Markus. With Robert Gerringer, Patricia Falkenhain, Terry Burgler, Maury Erickson, Todd Tayler, Eric Zwemer, Sherry Skinker.

THE GIN GAME (26). By D.L. Coburn. February 18, 1983. Director, Terry Burgler. With Robert Gerringer, Patricia Falkenhain.

HAVEN'T A CLUE (26). By Douglas Watson. March 18, 1983. Director, Tom Markus. With Eric Christmas, Laura Copland, Henson Keys, Ian Stuart, Randolph Walker.

VIRGINIA MUSEUM THEATER, RICHMOND—Charles Brown, Norman Barrs, Kim Beaty, Marion Lines *(foreground),* Dana Mills, Tom McDermott, Alfred Drake (the author of this play) and Lucien Douglas in a scene from *The Hiding Place*

DAMES AT SEA (26). Book and lyrics by George Haimson and Robin Miller; music by Jim Wise. April 29, 1983. Director, Darwin Knight. With Todd Taylor, Lora Jeanne Martens, Barbara Walsh, Kim Morgan, N.A. Klein, Tim Barber.

Virginia Museum Theater: Studio Theater

HOME (12). By Samm-Art Williams. November 5, 1982. Director, Woodie King Jr. With Elizabeth Van Dyke, Nadyne Cassandra Spratt, Samm-Art Williams.

A STRETCH OF THE IMAGINATION (12). By Jack Hibberd. February 3, 1983 (American premiere). Director, Tom Markus. With William Dennis.

BILLY BISHOP GOES TO WAR (12). By John Gray and Eric Peterson. April 15, 1983. Director, Terry Burgler. With Dan Hamilton, Manford Abrahamson.

Designers: scenery, Charles Caldwell, Joseph A. Varga, Neil Bierbower, Susan Senita; lighting, Richard Devin, Kevin Rigdon, Richard Moore, Lynne M. Hartman, F. Mitchell Dana, Jane Epperson; costumes, Susan Tsu, Bronwyn Jones Caldwell, Julie D. Keen, Rebecca Senske.

ROCHESTER, MICH.

Oakland University Professional Theater Program: Meadow Brook Theater

(General director, Terence Kilburn)

MACBETH (29). By William Shakespeare. October 7, 1982. Director, Arif Hasnain. With David Regal, Lisa McMillan, Richard Hilger, Linda Gehringer, Philip Locker.

THE ROYAL FAMILY (29). By George S. Kaufman and Edna Ferber. November 4, 1982. Director, Terence Kilburn. With Marian Primont, Jane Lowry, William Le Massena, Eric Tavaris, Sara Morrison.

A CHRISTMAS CAROL (29). By Charles Dickens; adapted by Charles Nolte. December 2, 1982. Director, Carl Schurr. With Booth Colman, Thom Haneline, Wil Love, Graham Pollock, Kevin Skiles, Grace Aiello.

TALLEY'S FOLLY (29). By Lanford Wilson. December 30, 1982. Director, Charles Nolte. With Deanna Dunagan, David Regal.

THE CHILDREN'S HOUR (29). By Lillian Hellman. January 27, 1983. Director, Terence Kilburn. With Bethany Carpenter, Linda Gehringer, Anne-Catherine O'Connell, Katherine Thorpe, Philip Locker.

MORNING'S AT SEVEN (29). By Paul Osborn. February 24, 1983. Director, Terence Kilburn. With Roslyn Alexander, Jeanne Arnold, Mary Benson, Maureen Steindler, Harry Ellerbe, Philip Pruneau.

THE UNEXPECTED GUEST (29). By Agatha Christie. March 24, 1983. Director, Terence Kilburn. With Barbara Barringer, Richard Blumenfeld, Peter Brandon, George Gitto, Philip Locker, Tom Mahard.

THE FANTASTICKS (29). Book and lyrics by Tom Jones, music by Harvey Schmidt; suggested by Edmond Rostand's *Les Romantiques*. April 21, 1983. Director-choreographer, Judith Haskell: musical director, Robert McNamee. With Keith David, Tamara Tunie, Jaison Walker, Hugh L. Hurd, Norman Matlock.

Designers: scenery, Peter W. Hicks, Barry Griffith; lighting, Reid G. Johnson, Barry Griffith, Deatra Smith; costumes, Mary Lynn Crum.

ROCHESTER, N.Y.

GeVa Theater

(Producing director, Howard J. Millman)

A HISTORY OF THE AMERICAN FILM (23). By Christopher Durang; music by Mel Marvin. October 30, 1982. Director, Howard J. Millman; musical director, Mark Goodman; choreographer, Jim Hoskins. With Monique Morgan, William Pitts, Alison Fraser, Matthew Kimbrough, Barbara Redmond.

THE GIN GAME (23). By D. L. Coburn. November 27, 1982. Director, Stephen Rothman. With Arthur Peterson, Norma Ransom.

TARTUFFE: ALIAS "THE PREACHER" (23). By Molière; translated and adapted by Eberle Thomas and Robert Strane. December 31, 1982. Director, Eberle Thomas. With John Sterling Arnold, Jay Bell, Kathleen Klein, Saylor Cressell, Philip LeStrange, Monique Morgan.

MASS APPEAL (23). By Bill C. Davis. January 29, 1983. Director, Gus Kaikkonen. With Gerald Richards, Todd Waring.

ALMS FOR THE MIDDLE CLASS (23). By Stuart Hample. February 26, 1983. Director, William Ludel. With Robert Downey, Laura Esterman, Steven Gilborn, Kerstin Kilgo, Fritz Sperberg.

AH, WILDERNESS! (23). By Eugene O'Neill. March 26, 1983. Director, Thomas Gruenewald. With John Peakes, Carmen Decker, Bill Pullman, Gerald Richards, Valerie von Volz, Daniel Tamm, Denise Bessette.

Designers: scenery, David Emmons, Bennet Averyt, Rick Pike, Bob Barnett, John Kasarda, William Barclay: lighting, Walter R. Uhrman, William Armstrong, Bennet Averyt, Jeffrey Beecroft, Phil Monat; costumes, Pamela Scofield, Mary-Anne Aston, Henri Ewaskio.

ST. LOUIS

The Repertory Theater of St. Louis: Mainstage

(Artistic director, Wallace Chappell; managing director, Steven Woolf)

TARTUFFE (35). By Molière; adapted by Miles Malleson. September 8, 1982. Director, Philip Kerr. With John Christopher Jones, Patrick Farrelly, Joan Croydon, Sarah-Jane Gwillim, Chris Limber, Susan Saunders, Joneal Joplin, Arthur Hanket.

A TALE OF TWO CITIES (40). By Charles Dickens; adapted and directed by Wallace Chappell. October 20, 1982. With Philip Kerr, Craig Dudley, Judith Roberts, Susan Leigh, Brendan Burke.

A CHRISTMAS TAPESTRY (35). By Anton Chekhov; adapted and directed by Jan Eliasberg. December 1, 1982. With Skip Foster, Jeff Ginsberg, Bradley Mott, Jim Reardon, Richard Wharton.

PRESENT LAUGHTER (35). By Noel Coward. January 5, 1983. Director, Philip Kerr. With Philip Kerr, Sarah-Jane Gwillim, John Christopher Jones, James Paul, Sharon Laughlin.

HEDDA GABLER (35). By Henrik Ibsen; translated by Rolf Fjelde. February 9, 1983. Director, Jan Eliasberg. With Katherine Borowitz, John Christopher Jones, Martin Donegan, Donna Snow, Richard Wharton.

UNDER THE ILEX TREE (35). By Clyde Talmage. March 16, 1983 (world premiere). Director, Charles Nelson Reilly.

Dora de Houghton
Carrington Partridge .... Julie Harris
Giles Lytton Strachey .... Leonard Frey
Time: Dawn, March 11, 1932. Place: Ham Spray House, Hungerford, England. Two intermissions.

The Repertory Theater of St. Louis: Studio Theater

SORE THROATS (17). By Howard Brenton. April 1, 1983 (American premiere). Director, Jan Eliasberg.
Judy .... Joan MacIntosh

Jack........................ David Little
Sally .... Denise Stephenson
Place: A bare flat in South London. One intermission.

Designers: scenery, John Carver Sullivan, Carolyn L. Ross, John Roslevich Jr., Marjorie Bradley Kellogg, Tim Jozwick; lighting, Glenn Dunn, Peter E. Sargent, Max De Volder; costumes, John Carver Sullivan, Dorothy L. Marshall, Carolyn L. Ross, Noel Taylor.

Note: Play readings (2 performances each) were presented by the company at the First Street Forum: *Dual Heads* by Shelley Berc, *The Brides* by Harry Kondoleon and *Female Parts* by Dario Fo, March 11–20, 1983. The Imaginary Theater Company toured Missouri mid-January to April, 1983, playing 107 performances of *Not so Grimm* and *A Wealth of Poe,* adapted by Kim Bozark, director, Wayne Salomon.

ST. PAUL

Actors Theater of St. Paul: Foley Theater

(Artistic director, Michael Andrew Miner)

THE SEAGULL (30). By Anton Chekhov. October 29, 1982. Director, Michael Andrew Miner. With Louise Goetz, Barbara Kingsley, David M. Kwiat, D. Scott Glasser.

FALLEN ANGELS (30). By Noel Coward. December 3, 1982. Director, David Parrish. With Barbara Kingsley, David Lenthall, Sally Wingert, James Cada.

SEA MARKS (30). By Gardner McKay. January 7, 1983. Director, Michael Andrew Miner. With Barbara Kingsley, D. Scott Glasser.

DISABILITY: A COMEDY (30). By Ron Whyte. February 4, 1983. Directors, David Ira Goldstein, Michael Andrew Miner. With David M. Kwiat, Sally Wingert, Louise Goetz, David Lenthall.

ANGEL STREET (30). By Patrick Hamilton. February 25, 1983. Director, James Cada. With David M. Kwiat, Louise Goetz, David Lenthall, Barbara Kingsley, Sally Wingert.

PANTOMIME (30). By Derek Walcott. March 25, 1983. With James Cada, Wilbert Holder.

HAVE YOU ANYTHING TO DECLARE? (30). By Maurice Hennequin and Pierre Veber; translated and adapted by Cogo-Fawcett and Braham Murray. April 22, 1983. Director, Sharon Ott. With Dianne Benjamin Hill, James Lawless.

Designers: scenery, James Guenther, Chris Johnson, Dick Leerhoff, Arthur Ridley; lighting, Chris Johnson, Paul Scharfenberg; costumes, Arthur Ridley, Chris Johnson, Nayna Raymey.

SAN DIEGO

Old Globe Theater: Edison Center—Festival Stage

(Executive producer, Craig Noel; artistic director, Jack O'Brien; managing director, Thomas R. Hall)

THE MISER (47). By Molière; adapted by Miles Malleson. June 10, 1982. Director, Joseph Hardy. With Paxton Whitehead, Victor Garber, Deborah Fallender, Gary Dontzig, Bill Geisslinger.

THE TAMING OF THE SHREW (40). By William Shakespeare. July 22, 1982. Director, Joseph Hardy. With Tony Musante, Amanda McBroom, Robert Strane, Deborah Fallender, Francisco Lagueruela.

Old Globe Theater: Edison Center

THE TEMPEST (51). By William Shakespeare. June 12, 1982. Director, Jack O'Brien. With Ellis Rabb, Monique Fowler, J. Kenneth Campbell, Christopher Brown.

THE IMPORTANCE OF BEING EARNEST (53). By Oscar Wilde. July 24, 1982. Director, Tom Moore. With Harry Groener/Donald Corren, Victor Garber, Ellis Rabb, Barbara Dirickson, Kate Wilkinson, Sands Hall.

THE SKIN OF OUR TEETH (36). By Thornton Wilder. January 13, 1983. Director, Jack O'Brien. With Blair Brown, Sada Thompson, Harold Gould, Monique Fowler, Jeffrey Combs.

TERRA NOVA (36). By Ted Tally. March 3, 1983. Director, Gerald Gutierrez. With Benja-

min Henrickson, Michael MacRae, Christine Healy, James Coyle, Larry Drake, Jonathan McMurtry, Mark Harelik.

CLAP YOUR HANDS (36). By Ellis Rabb with Nicholas Martin. April 21, 1983 (world premiere). Director, Ellis Rabb.
Mr.Darling..................... G. Wood
Wendy .... Patricia Conolly
Peter..................... Ralph Williams
    Time: The fall of the year at the present. Place: The second-story library of a home built during the Victorian era. Act I, Scene 1: Very late one evening. Scene 2: Only moments later. Scene 3: Too early the next morning. Act II, Scene 4: At least a day later. Scene 5: Enough time later, near dawn.

Old Globe Theater: Cassius Carter Center Stage

BILLY BISHOP GOES TO WAR (48). By John Gray, with Eric Peterson. June 17, 1982. Director, Craig Noel. With Harry Groener/Donald Ogden Stiers, David Colacci.

THE GIN GAME (50). By D.L. Coburn. July 29, 1982. Director, Jack O'Brien. With Eve Roberts, G. Wood.

MASS APPEAL (37). By Bill C. Davis. January 19, 1983. Director, David McClendon. With

Mark Dolson, Andrew Stevens.

WINGS (37). By Arthur Kopit. March 9, 1983. Director, Eve Roberts. With Teresa Wright, Tamu Gray, Robert Ellenstein, G. Wood.

THE DINING ROOM (37). By A.R. Gurney Jr. April 27, 1983. Director, Craig Noel. With Jonathan McMurtry, Kandis Chappell, Michael Byers, Deborah Taylor, Jay Bell, Caroline Smith.

OLD GLOBE THEATER, SAN DIEGO—Patricia Conolly and
G. Wood in *Clap Your Hands,* written and directed by Ellis Rabb

Designers: scenery, Steven Rubin, Douglas W. Schmidt, Richard Seger, Douglas Stein, Kent Dorsey, Robert Morgan, Mark Donnelley, Alan Okazaki; lighting, Kent Dorsey, David F. Segal, Gilbert V. Hemsley Jr, Robert Peterson, Steve Peterson; costumes, Steven Rubin, Sam Kirkpatrick, Robert Morgan, Ann Emonts, Dianne Holly, Mary Gibson, Sally Cleveland.

Old Globe Theater: Play Discovery Project

(Supervisor, Andrew J. Traister).

Staged readings, 1 performance each

THE DAY THEY SHOT JOHN LENNON by James McClure; director, Ann Graham. January 24, 1983.
NORMAL DOESN'T MEAN PERFECT by Don Gordon; director, Andrew J. Traister. February 28, 1983.

STILL LIFE by Emily Mann; director David Hay. April 25, 1983.
CHILD'S PLAY by William Parker; director, James Bush. May 9, 1983.
STRANGE SNOW by Steve Metcalfe; director, David McClendon. May 30, 1983.

Note: Old Globe presented two educational tours: *Actors, Lovers and Fools,* a Shakespeare Mosaic (56) Oct. 16-Dec. 13; and *The Story of Macbeth* by William Shakespeare as told by Charles and Mary Lamb (58), Feb. 10 to April 16, director, David Hay.

SAN FRANCISCO

American Conservatory Theater: Geary Theater

(General director, William Ball)

THE DINING ROOM (48). By A. R. Gurney Jr. August 4, 1982. Director, David Trainer. With Barry Nelson, Cathryn Damon, Richard Backus, Nicholas Hormann, Jeanne Ruskin, Mary Catherine Wright.

THE GIN GAME (27). By D.L. Coburn. September 28, 1982. Director, James Edmondson. With Marrian Walters, William Paterson.

DEAR LIAR (30). By Jerome Kilty, based on correspondence between George Bernard Shaw and Mrs. Patrick Campbell. October 19, 1982. Director, James Edmondson. With DeAnn Mears, Dakin Matthews.

THE CHALK GARDEN (33) by Enid Bagnold. November 9, 1982. Director, Dakin Matthews. With Barbara Dirickson, Marrian Walters, Annette Bening, Ray Reinhardt, Sydney Walker.

A CHRISTMAS CAROL (26). By Charles Dickens, adapted by Laird Williamson and Dennis Powers. December 2, 1982. Director, Eugene Barcone. With William Paterson/Sydney Walker, Lawrence Hecht/Dakin Matthews, Jeremy Roberts, Tom Parker.

UNCLE VANYA (28). By Anton Chekhov, translated by Pam Gems. January 18, 1983. Directors, Helen Burns, Michael Langham, with Eugene Barcone. With Dakin Matthews, Peter Donat, Deborah May, Barbara Dirickson, William Paterson.

LOOT (30). By Joe Orton. February 1, 1983. Director, Ken Ruta. With Sydney Walker, Ray Reinhardt, Sally Smythe, Bruce Williams.

MORNING'S AT SEVEN (30). By Paul Osborn. March 15, 1983. Director, Allen Fletcher. With Anne Lawder, DeAnn Mears, Carol Teitel, Marrian Walters, Ray Reinhardt, William Paterson, Sydney Walker.

THE HOLDUP (31) By Marsha Norman. April 12, 1983. Director, Edward Hastings. With Peter Donat, Barbara Dirickson, Tom O'Brien, Lawrence Hecht.

Designers: scenery, Richard Seger, Robert Blackman, Ralph Funicello; lighting, Greg Sullivan, Joseph Appelt, Dirk Epperson, James Sale, Duane Schuler, Robert Peterson; costumes, Michael Casey, Robert Morgan.

American Conservatory Theater: Plays-in-Progress—The Playroom

A QUEEN FOR A DAY (13). By Allis Davidson. February 8, 1983. director, Anne McNaughton.

THE DOLLY (13). By Robert Locke. March 1, 1983. Director, Lawrence Hecht.
DEAD LETTERS (13). By Howard Koch. March 16, 1983. Director, Janice Hutchins.

Note: ACT gave 26 special student matinees and interpreted six plays in sign language for the hearing impaired. *The Gin Game, Dear Liar* and *The Holdup* toured northern California. *Uncle Vanya* played two weeks at the Huntington Hartford Theater and *The Chalk Garden* and *Morning's at Seven* toured Hawaii, ACT's 11th annual tour there. In September 1982, as part of a cultural exchange with China, four Chinese theater specialists spent three weeks with ACT; and on April 28, 1983, William Ball and three other company members went to China to observe theater in Shanghai, Beijin, Souzhou and Xian.

SARASOTA

Asolo State Theater Company: Ringling Museums' Court Playhouse

(Artistic director, John Ulmer; managing director, David S. Levinson; executive director/founder, Richard G. Fallon)

CHARLEY'S AUNT (37). By Brandon Thomas. June 24, 1982. Director, Stuart Vaughan. With Joseph Culliton, John FitzGibbon, Isa Thomas, Vicki March, Carol McCann.

THE MALE ANIMAL (33). By James Thurber and Elliott Nugent. July 2, 1982. Director, Jonathan Bolt. With Robert Murch, Mary Francina Golden, Kenneth Kay, Dion Chesse, Bette Oliver.

THE GIRL OF THE GOLDEN WEST (33). By David Belasco. July 9, 1982. Director, Stuart Vaughan. With Mary Francina Golden, Kenneth Kay, Robert Murch, Karl Redcoff, David S. Howard.

THE DINING ROOM (44). By A.R. Gurney Jr. February 17, 1983. Director, Isa Thomas. With Stephen Daley, Richard Hoyt-Miller, Gretchen Lord, Innes-Fergus McDade, Victor Slezak, Colleen Smith Wallnau.

A VIEW FROM THE BRIDGE (39). By Arthur Miller. February 25, 1983. Director, John Ulmer. With Stephen Daley, Karl Redcoff, Colleen Smith Wallnau, Gretchen Lord, Victor Slezak, Rory Kelly.

MISALLIANCE (38). By George Bernard Shaw. March 4, 1983. Director, Norris Houghton. With Bradford Wallace, Bette Oliver, Richard Hoyt-Miller, Cynthia Dozier, Karl Redcoff.

MAN WITH A LOAD OF MISCHIEF (35). Book by Ben Tarver; music by John Clifton; lyrics by John Clifton and Ben Tarver. May 20, 1983. Director, Jim Hoskins; musical director-conductor, David Brunetti. With Peter Blaxill, Suzanne Grodner, Nancy Johnston, Maggie Task, Roy Alan Wilson, Mark Zimmerman.

Designers: scenery, Gordon Micunis, John Ezell, John Döepp; lighting, Martin Petlock; costumes, Catherine King, Vicki S. Holden; Sally Kos Harrison.

Note: During the 1982–83 season, Asolo Touring Theater presented two companies in plays for young people throughout Florida and the Southeast. The repertory included *Peter and the Hungry Wolf* (kindergarten through 3d grade); *Hercules and Friends* by Eric Tull (4th to 8th grades); and *Six Canterbury Tales* by Eberle Thomas (grades 9 to 12 and adults).

SEATTLE

A Contemporary Theater

(Founder/director, Gregory A. Falls)

FRIDAYS (23). By Andrew John. June 3, 1982. Director, Clayton Corzatte. With Andrew John, John Gilbert, R. A. Farrell, Kathryn Mesney, Ursula Meyer, Allen Nause, Lyn Tyrell.

WAITING FOR THE PARADE (23). By John Murrell. July 1, 1982. Director, Richard Edwards. With Suzy Hunt, Kathryn Mesmey, Ursula Meyer, Mara Scott-Wood, Lyn Tyrell.

THE GIN GAME (23). By D.L. Coburn. July 29, 1982. Director, Joy Carlin. With Ben Tone, Julia Follansbee.

THE GREEKS: THE WAR (24) and THE GODS (24). By John Barton and Kenneth Cavander. September 11, 1982. Director, Gregory A. Falls, with Anne-Denise Ford; music by David Hunter Koch and Andrew Buchman. With John Aylward, Katherine Ferrand, Christine Healy, R. A. Farrell and the ACT Company.

A CHRISTMAS CAROL (45). By Charles Dickens; adapted by Gregory A. Falls. December 3, 1982. Director, Eileen MacRae Murphy. With John Gilbert/David Pickette, R. A. Farrell, Noah Marks.

THE DRESSER (22). By Ronald Harwood. May 5, 1983. Director, Jay Broad. With Donald Ewer, Robert Blumenfeld.

Designers: scenery, Thomas M. Fichter, Bill Forrester, Scott Weldin, Shelley Henze Schermer; lighting, Jody Briggs, Phil Schermer, Donna Grout; costumes, Shay Cunliffe, Sally Richardson, Marian Cottrell, Shelley Henze Schermer, Susan Min.

Note: ACT presented the Flying Karamazov Brothers on the mainstage Nov. 3–27. The Young ACT Company, the professional touring company for young audiences, presented *Aladdin and the Magic Lamp* (10) adapted by Gregory A. Falls, directed by Anne-Denise Ford, in the home theater and then in nearby schools in the community, as well as on a three-week tour of Alaska.

Seattle Repertory Theater: Seattle Center Playhouse: Mainstage

(Artistic director, Daniel Sullivan; producing director, Peter Donnelley; associate director, Robert Egan)

ROMEO AND JULIET (33). By William Shakespeare. October 20, 1982. Director, Daniel Sullivan. With Tuck Milligan, Amy Irving, Lance Davis, Jeffrey Hutchinson, Florence Stanley, Clayton Corzatte.

THE FRONT PAGE (32). By Ben Hecht and Charles MacArthur. November 24, 1982. Director, Daniel Sullivan. With Denis Arndt, Tom Toner, Katherine Ferrand, Lori Larsen, Jeffrey Hutchinson.

DEATH OF A SALESMAN (33). By Arthur Miller. December 29, 1982. Director, Allen Fletcher. With Edward Binns, Mary Doyle, Mark Jenkins, John Procaccino, Robert Ellenstein, Gibby Brand.

TAKING STEPS (29). By Alan Ayckbourn. February 2, 1983. Director, Daniel Sullivan. With Ted D'Arms, Brenda Wehle, Shaun Austin-Olsen, Susan Cash, Brad O'Hare, Michael Santo.

TRANSLATIONS (30). By Brian Friel. March 9, 1983. Director, Robert Egan. With Anthony Mockus, Sean Griffin, Josh Clark, Peter Webster, Marek Johnson, Ted D'Arms.

THE VINEGAR TREE (30). By Paul Osborn. April 13, 1983. Director, Daniel Sullivan. With Ludi Claire, David White, Woody Eney, Lori Larsen, Eve Bennett-Gordon, Nathan Haas.

Seattle Repertory Theater: New Plays in Progress

(Director, Robert Egan)

Workshop premieres, 3 performances each

CROSSFIRE by Theodore Gross. January 10, 1983. Director, Roberta Levitow.
THE BALLAD OF SOAPY SMITH by Michael Weller. January 24, 1983. Director, Robert Egan.

MY UNCLE SAM by Len Jenkin. February 7, 1983. Director, Len Jenkin.
SHIVAREE by William Mastrosimone. February 21, 1983. Director, Daniel Sullivan.

Designers: scenery, Robert LaVigne, Edie Whitsett, Robert Dahlstrom, Ralph Funicello, Scott Weldin, Kate Edmunds, Hugh Landwehr, Tom Fichter, Keith Brumley; lighting, Robert Dahlstrom, James F. Ingalls, James Sale, James Verery, Christopher Beardsley; costumes, Robert Blackman, Robert Wojewodski, Sally Richardson, Kurt Wilhelm, Julie James, Lisa Cervany.

STAMFORD, CONN.

The Hartman Theater

(Producing artistic director, Edwin Sherin; executive director, Harris Goldman)

A STREETCAR NAMED DESIRE (28). By Tennessee Williams. October 8, 1982. Director, Edwin Sherin. With Shirley Knight, Fran Brill, Peter Weller, Stephen Mendillo.

STEAMING (28). By Nell Dunn. November 5, 1982. Director, Roger Smith. With Pauline Flanagan, Judith Ivey, John Messenger, Lisa Jane Persky, Polly Rowles, Linda Thorson, Margaret Whitton.

A CHRISTMAS CAROL (28). By Charles Dickens; musical adaptation, book and lyrics by Sheldon Harnick; music by Michel LeGrand. December 10, 1982. Director-choreographer, Charles Abbott; musical director, Ada Janik; musical arrangements and additional music,

Steven Margoshes; assistant choreographer, William Rohrig. With Woody Romoff, Dan Strickler, Gordon Connell, Mary Ellen Ashley, R. D. Robb.

THE CAINE MUTINY COURT-MARTIAL (28). By Herman Wouk; based on his novel. January 7, 1983. Director, Arthur Sherman. With Michael Moriarty, John Rubinstein, Geoffrey Horne.

ACTORS AND ACTRESSES (28). By Neil Simon. February 18, 1983 (world premiere). Director, Glenn Jordan.
Nicholas Cassell . . . . Jack Warden
Harmon Andrews . . . . Tom Aldredge
Vince Barbosa . . . . Jay O. Sanders

HARTMAN THEATER, STAMFORD—Jack Warden and Michael Learned in *Actors and Actresses,* a new play by Neil Simon

Polly Devore .... Polly Draper
Cara Heywood .... Michael Learned
Waiter .... Garrett M. Brown
Tom Pryor .... Steven Culp
Place: A motel in Gary, Ind. Act I: About 9:30 A.M. Act II: The same evening about 11:15 P.M. One intermission.

THE THREE MUSKETEERS (28). A musical based on the novel by Alexandre Dumas; music by Rudolf Friml; lyrics by P. G. Wodehouse and Clifford Grey; original play by William Anthony McGuire; adapted and directed by Mark Bramble. March 18, 1983. Choreographer, Onna White; musical director-arranger, Glen Roven; orchestrations, Larry Wilcox; dance arrangements, Donald York. With Lynne Clifton Allen, Clent Bowers, George Dvorsky, David Garrison, Patrick Quinn, Jeffrey Reynolds.

Designers: scenery, John Falabella, Marjorie Bradley Kellogg, Victor Capecce, Nancy Winters; lighting, Marcia Madeira, Pat Collins, Andrea Wilson, Marilyn Rennegal; costumes, David Murin, Jennifer Von Mayrhauser, Allen E. Munch, Freddy Wittop.

STRATFORD, CONN.

American Shakespeare Festival

(Artistic director, Peter Coe)

HENRY IV, PART 1 (32). By William Shakespeare. July 6, 1982. Director, Peter Coe. With Chris Sarandon, Michael Allinson, Roy Dotrice, Mary Wickes.

HAMLET (40). By William Shakespeare. August 3, 1982. Director, Peter Coe. With Christopher Walken, Anne Baxter, Fred Gwynne.

Designers: scenery and costumes, David Chapman; lighting, Marc B. Weiss.

SYRACUSE, N. Y.

Syracuse Stage: John D. Archbold Theater—Mainstage

(Producing director, Arthur Storch; managing director, James A. Clark)

CAT ON A HOT TIN ROOF (28). By Tennessee Williams. October 22, 1982. Director, John Going. With Kate Mulgrew, Robert Gentry, Margaret Phillips, Walter Flanagan.

WE WON'T PAY! WE WON'T PAY! (28). By Dario Fo; North American version by R.G. Davis. November 26, 1982. Director, Jerome Guardino. With Judy Scarpone, Valery Daemke, Frank Biancamano, Robert DeFrank, Vic Polizos.

DEATH OF A SALESMAN (28). By Arthur Miller. December 31, 1982. Director, Steven Schachter. With John Carpenter, Sylvia Gassell, Richard Cottrell, Stephen Lang, Jeff Natter, Philip Pruneau.

THE IMPROMPTU OF OUTREMONT (28). By Michel Tremblay; translated by John Van Burek. February 4, 1983. Director, Arthur Storch. With le Clanche du Rand, Mary Jay, Delphi Lawrence, Margaret Warncke.

DEATHTRAP (28). By Ira Levin. March 11, 1983. Director, Edward Stern. With Rudolph Willrich, Carole Lockwood, John Abajian, Jill Tanner, John Perkins.

THE TOOTH OF CRIME (28) By Sam Shepard. April 15, 1983. Director, George Ferencz; musical director-arranger, Bob Jewett. With Ray Wise, Jodi Long, Richard Allen, John Nesci, Peter Jay Fernandez, Raul Aranas, Stephen Mellor, Benmio Easterling.

Syracuse Stage: Landmark Theater

A CHRISTMAS CAROL (8). By Charles Dickens; adapted by Stephen Willems. December 15, 1982. Director, Arthur Storch. With John Carpenter, Gerard Moses, John P. Connolly, Beverly Bluem, Scott A. Norton.

Designers: scenery, William Schroder, Kristine Haugen, Patricia Woodbridge, Hal Tiné, Charles Cosler, Bob Davidson, Bill Stabile; lighting, Spencer Mosse, Paul Mathiesen, Marc B. Weiss, Judy Rasmuson, William T. Paton; costumes, William Schroder, Kristine Haugen, John David Ridge, Nanzi Adzuma, Maria Marrero, Sally Lesser.

Note: Syracuse Stage presented a reading of *November* by Charles Primerano, January 9, 1983, directed by Amy Dohrmann. *Flashback* (5), a children's theater production, directed by William S. Morris, toured New York State during 1982–83.

TUCSON

Arizona Theater Company: Tucson Community Center Theater

(Artistic director, Gary Gisselman; managing director, David Hawkanson)

WHAT THE BUTLER SAW (28). By Joe Orton. November 6, 1982. Director, Gary Gisselman. With Tony DeBruno, Liz Georges, Arnie Krauss, Benjamin Stewart, Lillian Garrett, Oliver Cliff.

A CHRISTMAS CAROL (28). By Charles Dickens; adapted by Frederick Gaines. December 4, 1982. Director, Jon Cranney. With Benjamin Stewart, Henry Kendrick, Tony DeBruno, Danny Taylor.

JOURNEY'S END (28). By R. C. Sherriff. January 1, 1983. Director, Jon Cranney. With Henry Kendrick, John-Frederick Jones, Douglas Anderson, Cameron Smith, John Jellison, Troy Evans, Michael Ellison, Benjamin Stewart, Oliver Cliff.

MASS APPEAL (28). By Bill C. Davis. February 5, 1983. Director, Jay Broad. With Charles White, Casey Biggs.

UNCLE VANYA (28). By Anton Chekhov. March 5, 1983. Director, Gary Gisselman. With Benjamin Stewart, Ken Ruta, Paul Ballantyne, Katherine Ferrand.

THE DINING ROOM (28). April 2, 1983. Director, Jon Cranney. With J. Patrick Martin,

Glenda Young, Richard Howard, Carol Kuy-kendall, Judy Leavell, Guy Paul.

A FUNNY THING HAPPENED ON THE WAY TO THE FORUM (28). Book by Burt Shevelove and Larry Gelbart; music and lyrics by Stephen Sondheim. May 25, 1983. Director, Gary Gisselman. With Oliver Cliff, Ruth Kobart, Cameron Smith, Michael Ellison, Benjamin Stewart, Kitty Carroll.

Designers: scenery, Peter Davis, Jack Barkla, Don Yunker; lighting, Kent Dorsey, Don Darnutzer, Michael Vannerstram; costumes, Sally Cleveland, Gene Davis Buck, David Kay Mickelsen, Bobbi Culbert, Jared Aswegan.

Note: *Mass Appeal, What the Butler Saw, Uncle Vanya, The Dining Room, A Funny Thing Happened on the Way to the Forum* were presented at Phoenix College Theater for 12 days each from January 12, 1983 through May 10, 1983.

WASHINGTON, D.C.

Arena Stage: Arena Theater

(Producing director, Zelda Fichandler; executive director, Thomas C. Fichandler; associate director, Douglas C. Wager)

ON THE RAZZLE (39). By Tom Stoppard; adapted from Johann Nestroy's *Einen Jux Will Er Sich Machen.* October 15, 1982 (American premiere). Director, Douglas C. Wager.

Weinberl	Stanley Anderson
Christopher	Christina Moore
Sonders	Kevin Donovan
Marie	Yeardley Smith
Zangler	Mark Hammer
Gertrud	Franchelle Stewart Dorn
Belgian Foreigner	Joe Palmieri
Melchior	Charles Janasz
Hupfer; Waiter	Henry Strozier
Philippine	Cary Anne Spear
Mme. Knorr	Barbara Sohmers
Mrs. Fisher	Halo Wines
Coachman	Terrence Currier
Waiter	J. Fred Shiffman
German Man	Michael T. Skinner
German Woman	Jenny Brown
Scots Man	Michael Heintzman
Scots Woman	Katherine Leask
Constable	David Toney
Piper	Andrew Dodge/Douglas Nelson
Lisette	Deborah Offner
Miss Blumenblatt	Dorothea Hammond
Ragamuffin	John Edward Mueller/ Seth Resnik

Time: Mid-19th Century. Place: A small town on the outskirts of Vienna. One intermission.

CYMBELINE (39). By William Shakespeare. December 3, 1982. Director, David Chambers; musical director-composer, Mel Marvin. With Mark Hammer, Halo Wines, Caris Corfman, Philip Casnoff, Robert Burr.

SCREENPLAY (39). By Istvan Orkeny; adapted by Gitta Honegger with Zelda Fichandler; from a literal translation by Eniko Molnar Basa. February 4, 1983. (American premiere). Director, Zelda Fichandler.

Stella	Joan MacIntosh
Misi	Frank Maraden
Adam Barabas	Stanley Anderson
Novotni	Terrence Currier
Marosi	Mark Hammer
Piri	Laura Hicks
Mrs. Litke	Regina David
Maestro	John Seitz
Mrs. Barabas	Frances Chaney
Soldier; Musician	Skip LaPlante

Soldiers: Britt Burr, Hand Bachmann, Michael Govan.

Time: September 22, 1949. Place: The great circus of the capital, Budapest. One intermission.

GENIUSES (30). By Jonathan Reynolds. March 25, 1983. Director, Gary Pearle. With Charles Janasz, Dan Strickler, Linda Lee Johnson, Joe Palmieri, Dan Desmond, Joey Ginza.

CANDIDE (39+) Music by Leonard Bernstein; book by Hugh Wheeler; lyrics by Richard Wilbur, Stephen Sondheim, John Latouche. May 13, 1983. Director, Douglas C. Wager; music director-conductor, Robert Fisher; choreographer, Theodore Pappas. With Paul Binotto, Marilyn Caskey/Julie Osborn, Richard Bauer.

Arena Stage: Kreeger Theater

HOME (39). By Samm-Art Williams. October 22, 1982. Director, Horacena J. Taylor. With Samuel L. Jackson, Elain Graham, S. Epatha Merkerson.

THE IMAGINARY INVALID (39). By Molière. January 21, 1983. Director, Garland Wright. With Richard Bauer, Christina Moore, Marilyn Caskey, Charles Janasz, Henry Strozier, Halo Wines.

BURIED CHILD (39). By Sam Shepard. April 15, 1983. Director, Gilbert Moses. With Stanley Anderson, Halo Wines, Kevin Donovan, Kevin Tighe, Christopher McHale, Christina Moore, Henry Strozier.

Arena Stage: Play Lab

(Douglas C. Wager, James Nicola, co-directors)

New play readings, workshop premieres

FILIAL PIETIES by George Freek, January 30, 1983.

STREGA, OR THE WITCH by Anna Cascio. February 6, 1983.

HITCHIN' by Lewis Black. February 13, 1983.

MAN WITH A RAINCOAT by William Wise. February 20, 1983.

Designers: scenery, Tony Straiges, Ming Cho Lee, Karl Eigsti, Zack Brown, John Arnone; lighting, Allen Lee Hughes, Frances Aronson, Arden Fingerhut, William Mintzer, Hugh Lester; costumes, Marjorie Slaiman, Anne Hould-Ward, Mary Ann Powell.

Folger Theater Group

(Artistic director, John Neville-Andrews)

THE MERCHANT OF VENICE (56). By William Shakespeare. September 28, 1982. Director, John Neville-Andrews. With Richard Bauer, Mikel Lambert, Jim Beard, Floyd King.

A MEDIEVAL CHRISTMAS PAGEANT (35) December 6, 1982. Director, Ross Allen. With Jim Beard, Thomas Schall, Floyd King, Chris Casaday.

SHE STOOPS TO CONQUER (35). By Oliver Goldsmith. January 24, 1983. Director, Davey Marlin-Jones. With Thomas Schall, Jim Beard, John Neville-Andrews, Chris Casaday, John Wojda, Lucinda Hitchcock Cone.

MARRIAGE A LA MODE (36). By John Dryden; adapted and directed by Giles Havergal. March 7, 1983.

ALL'S WELL THAT ENDS WELL (38). By William Shakespeare. May 2, 1983. Director, John Neville-Andrews. With Peter Webster, Gwendolyn Lewis, Floyd King, John Wylie, Mikel Lambert.

Designers: scenery, Russell Metheny, Hugh McKay, Lewis Folden; lighting, Richard Winkler, Hugh Lester; costumes, Barry Allen Odom.

WATERFORD, CONN.

Eugene O'Neill Theater Center: National Playwright's Conference

(President, George C. White; artistic director, Lloyd Richards)

New works in progress; 2 performances each, July 11–Aug. 8

PROUD FLESH by James Nicholson; director, William Ludel.

FIRST DRAFT by Yale Udoff; director, Dennis Scott.

MA RAINEY'S BLACK BOTTOM by August Wilson; director, William Partlan.

THE FURTHER ADVENTURES OF SALLY by Russell Davis; director, Tony Giordano.

AWOL by Carol Williams; director, Amy Saltz.

THE BUNKHOUSE by Terrence Ortwein; director, John Pasquin.

ARENA STAGE, WASHINGTON, D.C.—Christina Moore and Stanley
Anderson in the American premiere of Tom Stoppard's *On the Razzle*

STITCHERS AND STARLIGHT TALK-
ERS by Kathleen Betsko; director, Amy
Saltz.
A KNIFE IN THE HEART by Susan Yanko-
witz; director, Dennis Scott.
THEATER IN THE TIME OF NERO AND
SENECA by Edvard Radzinsky; translated by
Alma H. Law; director, Dennis Scott.
SOME RAIN by James Edward Luczak; direc-
tor, William Partlan.
PLAYING IN LOCAL BANDS by Nancy
Fales Garrett; director, William Ludel.
COYOTE UGLY by Lynn Siefert; director,
Tony Giordano.

Company: Angela Bassett, Kathy Bates, Julie Boyd, John Braden, Joel Brooks, Rosanna
Carter, Veronica Castang, Dominic Chianese, Bryan Clark, Anita Dangler, Polly Draper, John
Dukakis, Charles S. Dutton, Roo Dutton, Christine Estabrook, Kevin Geer, Jack Gilpin, David
Marshall Grant, Jo Henderson, Kevin Kane, Kevin Kline, Leonard Jackson, Richard Jenkins, Robert
Judd, Paul Meacham, Paul McCrane, Alexandra Paxton, Pippa Pearthree, Vic Polizos, Barry
Primus, James Ray, Willie Reale, Scott Richards, Marc Routh, Robert Schenkkan, Jamie
Schmitt, Seret Scott, Joe Seneca, Sloane Shelton, David Strathairn, Michael Tucker, Scott
Waara, Ken Welsh.

Designers: C. Russell Christian, Jeff Goodman, Fred Voelpel, Ann Wrightson, Michael Yeargan.

Dramaturgs: Martin Esslin, Michael Feingold, Edith Oliver.

WEST SPRINGFIELD, MASS.

StageWest

(Producing director, Stephen E. Hays)

THE CRUCIFER OF BLOOD (23). By Paul
Giovanni. October 21, 1982. Director, Ted
Weiant. With Gregory Salata, John Doolittle,
Kimberly Farr, Richard Abernethy.
MASS APPEAL (23). By Bill C. Davis. Novem-
ber 18, 1982. Director, Gregory Abels. With
Larry Keith, Steven Culp.

SIDE BY SIDE BY SONDHEIM (23). Music and lyrics by Stephen Sondheim, additional music by Leonard Bernstein, Mary Rodgers, Richard Rodgers, Jule Styne; continuity by Ned Sherin. December 16, 1982. Director, Wayne Bryan; musical director, J.T. Smith. With Anna Marie Gutierrez, Michael Magnusen, Henrietta Valor, Stephen E. Hays, J. T. Smith.

THE BELLE OF AMHERST (23). By William Luce; compiled by Timothy Helgeson. January 13, 1983. Director, Donald Hicken. With Tana Hicken.

HOME (23). By Samm-Art Williams. February 10, 1983. Director, Woodie King Jr. With Elizabeth Van Dyke, Nadyne Cassandra, Samm-Art Williams.

A STREETCAR NAMED DESIRE (23). By Tennessee Williams. March 10, 1983. Director, Timothy Near. With Erika Petersen, John Homa, Elizabeth Hess, Matthew Kimbrough.

CHAPTER TWO (24). By Neil Simon, April 7, 1983. Director, Stephen E. Hays. With Rudy Hornish, John LaGioia, Jody Catlin, Annette Miller.

Designers: scenery, Patricia Woodbridge, Joseph W. Long, Jeffrey Struckman, Jeffrey A. Fiala, Paul Wonsek; lighting, Ned Halleck, Paul J. Horton, Margaret Lee, Paul Wonsek; costumes, John Carver Sullivan, Georgia Carney, Jeffrey Struckman, Jan Morrison, Rebecca Senske.

Note: StageWest hosted a series of guest productions for children, including *Maggie Magalita* by Wendy Kesselman, May 10–14, 1983. New Play readings in the 1982–83 season included *Brass Birds Don't Sing* by Samm-Art Williams and *Other Work* by Steve Carter.

CANADA

HALIFAX, NOVA SCOTIA

Neptune Theater: Mainstage

(Artistic director, John Neville)

JUNO AND THE PAYCOCK (25). By Sean O'Casey. November 12, 1982. Director, Tom Kerr. With Joan Orenstein, Owen Foran, Sean Mulcahy, Aaron Fry, Cathy O'Connell.

THE WIZARD OF OZ (32). Adapted by Alfred Bradley from L. Frank Baum's book. December 10, 1982. Director, Ronald Ulrich. With Sherry Thomson, Stuart Nemtin, Donald Burda, Garrison Chrisjohn, Bill Carr.

SPECIAL OCCASIONS (25). By Bernard Slade. December 17, 1982. With John Neville, Susan Wright.

FILTHY RICH (25). By George F. Walker. February 4, 1983. Director, Peter Froelich. With Donald Davis, Susan Hogan, Kate Lynch, Tony Nardi, George Merner, Victor Ertmanis.

THE APPLE CART (25). By George Bernard Shaw. March 11, 1983. Directors, John Neville, Tom Kerr. With John Neville, Lenora Zann, Sean Mulcahy, George Merner, David Renton, Paddy English.

COMEBACK (25). By Ron Chudley. April 15, 1983. Director, Paddy English. With Charles Kerr, Jill Frappier, Don Allison, Laura Press.

Neptune Theater: Lunchtime Theater

THE GREEN GROW (7). By Sean Mulcahy. November 23, 1982. Director, Paddy English. With Joan Gregson, David Renton, Caitlyn Colquahon, Barrie Dunn, Sean Mulcahy.

REUNION (14). By David Mamet. February 15, 1983. Director, John Neville. With Cathy O'-

Connell, John Dunsworth.

THE PROPOSAL (12). By Anton Chekhov. March 29, 1983. Director, David Schurmann. With George Merner, Cathy O'Connell, Aaron Fry.

Designers: scenery and costumes, Arthur Penson, Ray Robitschek, Andrew Murray; lighting, Gary K. Clarke, Ray Robitschek.

Note: *Special Occasions* toured Nova Scotia, New Brunswick and Prince Edward Island April 5–17, with David Brown and Nonnie Griffin.

MONTREAL, QUE.

The Centaur Theater Company

(Artistic and executive director, Maurice Podbrey)

BREW (BROUE) (48). By Claude Meunier, Jean-Pierre Plante, Francine Ruel, Louis Saïa, Michel Cote, Marcel Gauthier, Marc Messier; translated by Michel Fremont-Cote, David McDonald. October 7, 1982 (English language premiere). With Michel Cote, Marcel Gauthier, Marc Messier.

DUET FOR ONE (48). By Tom Kempinski. November 6, 1982. Director, Scott Swan. With Maurice Podbrey, Fiona Reid.

TRANSLATIONS (48). By Brian Friel. January 6, 1983. Director, Elsa Bolam. With Marcy Cohen, Geraint Wyn Davies, William Dunlop, Michael Egan, Terence Kelly, Sean McCann, Nancy Palk.

MOVING (48) By David Fennario. February 3, 1983 (world premiere). Director, Simon Malbogat.

Betty Ann	Diana Belshaw
Pa Wilson	Griffith Brewer
Francine	Myriam Cyr
Janet	Jennifer Dean
Jimmy Wilson	Robert King
Ronnie	Roger A. McKeen
Richard	Dennis O'Connor

Ma Wilson . . . . Jennifer Phipps
    Act I: A day in May. Act II, Scene 1: July. Scene 2: August. Scene 3: September. Scene 4: February.

QUIET IN THE LAND (48). By Anne Chislett. March 17, 1983. Director, James Ray. With Kenneth Welsh, John Aylward, Daniel Nalback, Diane Gordon, Arthur Janzen, Stephanie Morgenstern, Florence Paterson, John O'Krancy, Dan Lett, Karen Woolridge.

EMPRESS EUGENIE (48). By Jason Lindsey. April 14, 1983 (North American premiere). Director, Marianne MacNaghten. With Viola Léger, Griffith Brewer.

PLAYING THE FOOL (48). By Alun Hibbert. May 26, 1983 (world premiere). Director, Gary Reineke.

John	Gillie Fenwick
Harry	Sean Sullivan
Ben	Ken James
Sheila	Nicola Lipman
Tonelli	Vincent Ierfino
Ambulance Man	Gilles Tordjman

    Time: 1979. Place: Montreal. One intermission.

Designers: scenery, Denis Rousseau, Barbra Matis, Michael Joy, Marcel Dauphinais, Guido Tondino; lighting, Claude Accolas, Alexander Gazale, Freddie Grimwood, Steven Hawkins; costumes, Francois LaPlante, Barbra Matis, Michael Joy, Francois Barbeau.

Note: Centaur opened the season with *The Main* (7), a collective creation celebrating the history of Montreal. September 22, 1982. Directors, Damir Andrei, Rene-Daniel Dubois; music by Domenic Cuzzocrea. With Sonia Benezra, John Blackwood, Domenic Cuzzocrea, Michael Rudder, Maria Vacratsis, Renato Trujillo. Centaur operates two theaters, upstairs and downstairs.

STRATFORD, ONT.

Stratford Festival: Festival Stage

(Artistic director, John Hirsch; executive producer, John Hayes; founder, Tom Patterson)

In repertory:

JULIUS CAESAR by William Shakespeare. June 6, 1982. Director, Derek Goldby. With Jack Medley, R. H. Thomson, Len Cariou, Nicholas Pennell.
THE MERRY WIVES OF WINDSOR by Wil-

liam Shakespeare. June 8, 1982. Director, Robert Beard. With Douglas Campbell, Nicholas Pennell, Graeme Campbell, Pat Galloway, Susan Wright, Amelia Hall.
THE TEMPEST by William Shakespeare. June

9, 1982. Director, John Hirsch. With Len
Cariou, Sharry Flett, Ian Deakin, Miles Pot-
ter, Jim Mezon.
ARMS AND THE MAN by George Bernard

Shaw. August 5, 1982. Director, Michael
Langham. With Helen Carey, Carole Shelley,
Susan Wright, Douglas Campbell, Brian Bed-
ford.

Stratford Festival: Avon Stage

THE MIKADO by W. S. Gilbert and Arthur
Sullivan. June 7, 1982. Director-choreographer,
Brian Macdonald; musical director, Berthold
Carriere. With Gidon Saks, Henry Ingram, Eric
Donkin, Christina James, Marie Baron.

TRANSLATIONS by Brian Friel. July 17, 1982.
Director, Guy Sprung. With Biff McGuire,
Lewis Gordon, John Jarvis, Kate Trotter, Mary
Haney.

MARY STUART by Friedrich Schiller; translated and adapted by Joe McClinton with Michal Schonberg. August 6, 1982. Director, John
Hirsch. With Margot Dionne, Pat Galloway,
William Needles, Amelia Hall, Jack Medley.

BLITHE SPIRIT by Noel Coward. September
10, 1982. Director, Brian Bedford. With Karen
Wood, Helen Carey, Brian Bedford, Tammy
Grimes, Carole Shelley.

Stratford Festival: Third Stage

A MIDSUMMER NIGHT'S DREAM by Wil-
liam Shakespeare. July 16, 1982. Director, Peter
Froehlich. Cheryl Swarts, David Huband, Diego
Matamoros, Seana McKenna, Eric Keenley-
side, Nicky Guadagni.

ALL'S WELL THAT ENDS WELL by William

Shakespeare. July 17, 1982. Director, Richard
Cottrell. With Fiona Reid, Charmion King, John
Novak, Diego Matamoros.

DAMIEN by Aldyth Morris. August 4, 1982.
Director, Guy Sprung. With Lewis Gordon.

Designers: scenery, John Pennoyer, Desmond Heeley, Susan Benson, Douglas McLean, Philip
Silver, Ming Cho Lee, David Walker, Patrick Clark, Christina Poddubiuk, Barbara Matis; lighting,
Michael J. Whitfield, Harry Frehner, Beverly Emmons, Steven Hawkins; costumes, Susan Ben-
son, Patrick Clark, Debra Hanson, Tanya Moiseiwitsch, David Walker.

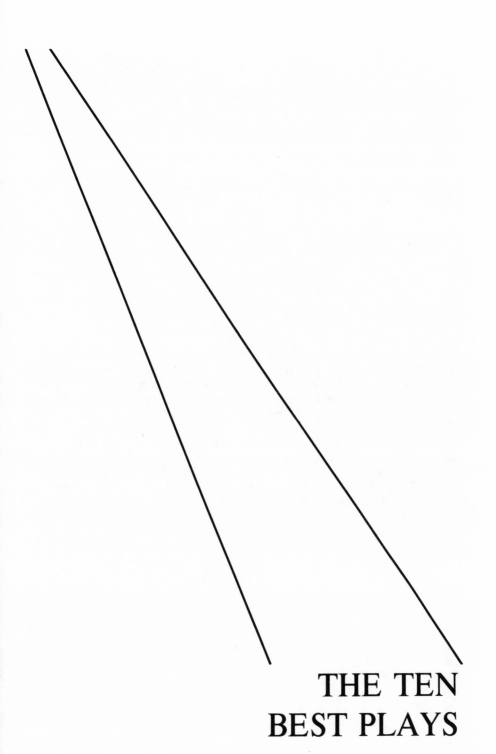

THE TEN
BEST PLAYS

Here are details of 1982–83's Best Plays—synopses, biographical sketches of authors and other material. By permission of the publishing companies which own the exclusive rights to publish these scripts in full in the United States, most of our continuities include substantial quotations from crucial/pivotal scenes in order to provide a permanent reference to style and quality as well as theme, structure and story line.

In the case of such quotations, scenes and lines of dialogue, stage directions and descriptions appear *exactly* as in the stage version or published script unless (in a very few instances, for technical reasons) an abridgement is indicated by five dots (. . . . .). The appearance of the three dots (. . .) is the script's own punctuation to denote the timing of a spoken line.

GOOD

A Play With Music in Two Acts

BY C.P. TAYLOR

Cast and credits appear on page 341

CECIL (C.P.) TAYLOR was born in Glasgow Nov. 6, 1929, the son of a salesman and part-time journalist. He died Dec. 9, 1981, about two months after his play Good *was first presented by the Royal Shakespeare Company at The Warehouse but before its subsequent presentations at the Aldwych Theater in April 1982 and in New York in October. Taylor began writing plays at 30 and completed at least 70 works produced in the West End, throughout England and on television before his death at 52. He wrote most frequently for the highly-regarded Live Theater Company at Newcastle, where he was resident dramatist. He also served as literary adviser to the Northumberland Youth Theater Association (1967–79), Tyneside Theater Trust (1971–74), Everyman Theater in Liverpool (1971–73) and Traverse Theater (1971–74). He was known for his work with mentally and physically handicapped and other deprived persons, applying drama therapy at the Northgate Hospital Arts Center, which he helped to establish, and in many other places and instances.*

The highlights of Taylor's playwriting career have included Bread and Butter *(1969),* Black and White Minstrels *(1972),* Bandits *(produced by RSC in 1977 and off off Broadway at the Labor Theater April 19, 1979 for 12 performances),* A Nightingale Sang *(1980) and* Schippel *(1981).* Good, *his only major American production and Best Play, opened on Broadway Oct. 13, 1982 for a 125-performance run. Taylor was twice married, with four children. At the time of his death he lived at Long Horsley near Newcastle.*

Time: The 1930s

Place: Germany

ACT I

SYNOPSIS: The locales throughout the play are symbolized by typical objects or furnishings—a bed, a piano, a chair, etc.—rather than represented by fully realized sets. Many of the mood and scene changes are keyed to music which rises in the mind of the leading character, Halder, and is played by musicians or sung by persons visible on stage. The scenes often shift abruptly from place to place and even back and forth in time.

A 1930s dance band ensemble is playing "I'm Always Chasing Rainbows," Halder, a young teacher at the university in Frankfurt, Germany, explains to the audience: "The bands came in 1933. So you can't say they came with the rise of the Nazis, exactly. The Nazis were on the rise long before that. To some extent, it was a device that was with me from childhood. Bringing music into the dramatic moments of my life. But from '33, they became an addiction. Jazz bands . . . Cafe bands . . . Tenors . . . Crooners . . . Symphony orchestras . . . depending on the particular situation and my mood. A strategy for survival? Turning the reality into fantasy?. . . . ."

A Sister calls out to Halder that he can now see his mother, who is brought in in a wheelchair. Halder's mother is being treated for senility in a Hamburg facility. She is losing touch with reality—she thinks that Halder's wife Helen has also come to visit and is in the room (she isn't), and she imagines that her son is a Marxist (he isn't) who is about to be put in prison by Hitler.

MOTHER: Listen . . . I'm going out of my mind . . . Johnnie, I've got to go home.

HALDER: You can't *see,* mother.

MOTHER: What about your house?

HALDER: With the children and Helen . . . I couldn't cope with you, mother. *I* would . . . but how can I ask the children and Helen . . .

MOTHER: Listen. Is that my imagination too? This place, it's a *front.* Men come up here to go with the women . . . that Sister, there . . .

HALDER: This hospital's a front for a brothel?

MOTHER: Is it not? . . . Johnnie, this is a bad business . . . I'm going out of my mind.

HALDER: I could cope with you for a *week,* mother . . . We'd *like* to have you for a week or so . . . But you know what Helen's like. She can't even organize the house with just *us* in it . . . You couldn't be happy . . . You never are there . . .

MOTHER: The best thing is to take twenty or thirty of my pills and finish myself off once and for all . . .

HALDER: You could do that. It's against the law, but . . .

BEFORE AND AFTER IN *GOOD*—Alan Howard
as a university professor (*above*, with Felicity Dean)
gradually remodeled into a member of the Nazi SS
(*left*)

MOTHER: What have I got to live for? I can't see. My eyes are finished. Nobody wants me . . . I'm better out of it . . . What have I got to live for, for God's sake!

HALDER: (*looks round . . . lost . . .*): A difficult question, that.

The scene shifts to a government office building where Halder is looking for Over-Leader Philip Bouller and his newly-formed Committee for Research. Halder has an appointment and is impressed with these handsome quarters in what was once a luxurious private dwelling.

The scene shifts again, abruptly, to a consultation between Halder and his closest friend, Maurice, a doctor. Halder is suffering from what Maurice calls "a bad attack of bands."

HALDER: Not very big bands . . . Music, generally. Odd times, the Berlin Philharmonic . . . Last Senate meeting it was the Phil . . . playing the storm movement of the Pastoral . . .

MAURICE: What's he saying to me? I don't understand what you're saying to me . . . You've made a decision to try and throw off this neurosis you've been living with all your life to give your work and family relationships a more healthy basis . . . What does *that* mean, Johnny? That's just words. We don't work like that, for Christ's sake . . . You and me.

HALDER: I want to *try* . . . All my work so far has been based on this bloody anxiety neurosis . . . I do . . . I want to see what work I can do, free of it . . .

MAURICE: People don't go to analysts to streamline their lives . . . They go to free themselves from agony . . . Just now, my agony . . . my neurotic track . . . that wakes me up at four o'clock in the morning in a panic . . . I'll tell you about it . . . Give you insights into yours . . . I can see . . . objectively . . . Intellectually . . . The Nazis . . . That's just flag-waving to get hold of the masses . . . This anti-Jewish hysteria . . . Now it's got them where they wanted to go . . .

HALDER: I can't get lost, you see. I can't *lose* myself in people or situations. Everything's acted out against this bloody musical background. I mean, could it be some subconscious comment on my loose grip of reality? The whole of my life's a performance. Is that too glib, do you think, Maurice?

MAURICE: If you knew the unconscious like I do . . . nothing's too glib for that bastard. . . . .

A clerk at the government building comes to tell Halder that Over-Leader Bouller will see him shortly.

Then back to Maurice, who has no simple way of ridding Halder of his music neurosis. As for his own nightmare, "I know how much Germany depends on Jewish brains . . . Jewish business . . . Hitler's got all the power he needs now. They're bound to drop all that racial shit they had to throw around to get their votes . . . They can't afford *not* to . . . I *know* that . . . But I can't believe it."

Halder agrees, but Maurice goes on about his feelings—Jewish or not, he is a German first and intensely proud of his beautiful city of Frankfurt, his home.

Meanwhile Halder is talking to himself about Maurice: "He's a nice man. I love him. But I cannot get involved with his problems. So in the next few months they might kick in his teeth. But just now, he's all right. What's he worried about? I bet you *he* has no problems in bed with his wife." Halder's problems are immediate.

Maurice, recalling that Goethe once ignored a desperate appeal from Beethoven for money, declares, "Hitler has perverted the whole nature of our relationship," placing Maurice in danger while Halder is free to pursue his promising academic career, untroubled. Halder tries to reassure his friend: "They've got to drop the anti-Jew program . . . In the long run . . . for the survival of the bloody state."

A cafe trio is playing "Star of Eve" from *Tannhauser* as Halder makes his way through the messy clutter of his house. His wife Helen is lying in front of the fire, reading, waiting for Halder to cook the children's supper. Husband and wife converse in recitative, to the music. Helen is appalled at her own slovenliness and can't think why Halder should love her—but he does.

In the government office building, Over-Leader Bouller will finally see Halder. The two men "Heil Hitler" at each other and proceed to discuss a matter which Bouller characterizes as top secret. Bouller's superiors have recommended Halder as "a person of total loyalty to the state and National Socialism." Halder goes so far as to admit, "I am committed to use whatever abilities and talents I might have for the betterment of the lives of the people round me."

In his latest novel—about life in a home for the aged—Halder has apparently dealt with matters of morality in such a way as to attract the attention of the Nazi leadership as "a comrade who we can trust and who is, at the same time, something of a figure in the academic world." Now they want Halder to look at a letter from the father of a deformed child—and not a word about it to anyone, not even his wife.

Back in his home, Helen calls to Halder. He assures her he doesn't mind that the house is a mess.

HALDER: . . . . . It's all right. The children are used to it.

HELEN: You come back from a hard day at work, and I overwhelm you with self pity . . .

HALDER: Yes.

HELEN: You shouldn't stand this. Me turning your house into a shithouse, Johnnie.

HALDER: Tell you what. After tea, we'll clean it up.

HELEN (*with a pastry*): I wish you wouldn't buy pastries any more. It's just indulging my greed and making me fat . . .

HALDER: Don't eat them.

HELEN: For Christ's sake, why do you love me?

HALDER: I don't know why I love you. Have you got to?

HELEN: I can't even look after your bloody kids. . . . .

Helen's father phoned today to suggest that Halder join the National Socialist Party in order to insure his future at the university (Goebbels has read and admires Halder's *Faust and Goethe in Weimar*). Halder assures Helen that she and the children mean everything to him, and he tells her again that he loves her.

In a moment, Halder is again with Maurice telling the doctor of a young female student's visit to his office. A tenor enters singing "You Are My Heart's Delight" (which Halder heard during the visit) as the student, Anne, describes to her professor her inability to relate literature to life, the everyday facts of which seem more important to her than the great visions of Goethe. Halder, aroused by Anne, suggests they continue to explore this subject in an appointment that evening. Anne agrees. Halder tells Maurice, "Listen . . . What could it be . . . Is nothing I touch real . . . Is it? My whole life is like that . . . I do everything, more or less, that everybody else does . . . But I don't *feel* it's real. Like other people."

Marlene Dietrich is heard singing "Falling in Love Again," as Halder thinks out his situation aloud, concentrating on problems he might face if he left Helen for Anne. When Helen wakes up, Halder tells her of the student asleep on the couch downstairs, and that he's decided to join the Nazi Party "because I love you . . . You know that. If it was just myself, I'd take a chance. I'm not one hundred per cent sure about Hitler . . . You understand that . . . I love you and the children . . ." Helen must never leave him, she's the best wife in the world, and he loves her.

In the Over-Leader's office, Bouller reveals that Goebbels himself admired Halder's novel. Halder admits to the audience, "They got me at a bad time," and adds, "With my mother in the state she got herself in . . . and the state I got in at her state, I had to write all the guilt out in a pro-euthanasia novel." But Halder can't help feeling a thrill of pride when he learns that Hitler himself has looked over the "pro-euthanasia" work and commented, "Written from the heart!"

Halder hears a Bavarian Mountain trio singing and playing while he imagines himself living in the forest with Anne. She comes in wearing Halder's dressing gown, and she senses that Halder is now fighting the fondness for her he expressed the night before, even though the feeling is clearly mutual. Halder tries to explain that in spite of everything he is devoted to his children and could never leave them, but Anne comments, "John . . . you're drowning . . . I'm not saying that because I love you and I need you . . . You're drowning . . ."

Helen enters in her dressing gown, apologizing to Anne for the mess the house seems to be in. Helen is struck by Anne's youthful appearance (Anne is nearly 20), though she herself has come to terms with her own age, which is 30.

A street musician strikes up a few bars of a Yiddish wedding song, of which Maurice sings a few bars as Adolf Hitler strikes a pose and is soon addressing the world on such subjects as the makeup of a human being ("a complex electrical and chemical network"), the human condition ("man, you are born to uncertainty"), manhood ("for the first time in my life I am breaking free from the emotional umbilical cords that tied me to my mother"), etc. Maurice labels much of this "Charlie Chaplin," and Halder tries to explain that Hitler exists because the Nazis gave the workers what the Social Democrats promised but failed to deliver.

HITLER (*to the world*): Breaking through to manhood. Completing myself as a human being . . . Establishing new emotional and physical umbilical strands with a woman I have chosen in my manhood. (*To Maurice.*) Yes. I'm being pretentious and heavily profound. But it does happen. From time to time, you are confronted by profundities . . . (*To himself.*) I have got to get out of this . . . apologizing for any profound universal statement that comes to me . . . watching my thoughts and language so that they're continually muted, tied to the earth . . . when you fly, you fly . . . when you walk on the earth you walk on the earth.

MAURICE (*to Halder*): You see . . . my fellow Jews. I can't stand them. My best friends are gentiles and Nazis.

HITLER: (*to the world*): What is the objective reality? The objective reality is, there is no objective reality. I don't know. Who knows? Where am I? I don't know where I am. I don't know what I'm doing. I don't know I don't know what I'm doing. Is that possible?

MAURICE: I'm telling you, you're right. Johnny, tell him he's right.

HITLER: How do I bring about a balance between the electrical and chemical forces in my body to make for something like the optimum functioning of myself as an organism?

HALDER: By joining the Nazis?

HITLER: But now I am moving to a soul union.

MAURICE: Huh!

HITLER: What the fuck else is it, for Christ's sake? That's what it is. That's what I'm looking for. A soul union. . . . . (*To the world.*) Now I am moving to a soul union.

HALDER and HITLER: Joining the Nazis is no longer a simple case of my own electrical and chemical state.

HITLER: It is *hers* too.

HALDER (*to Hitler*): That's what I'm telling you. I have to see Anne, first. Before I can make a definite decision.

HITLER: (*to himself*): Yes. *Now,* I understand *why* I have to see her.

HALDER: Do I?

MAURICE: John. This is a classic neurotic relationship. My best loved friend is a Nazi.

Halder consults Anne about joining the Nazis. Anne hates their anti-Jewish policies (Halder agrees that a Germany without Jews would be unreal) but to her, the important thing is to survive independently in one's own family corner, hurting others as little as possible. Halder concludes, "It's not only survival, is it? Joining the Nazis. If people like us join them . . . instead of keeping away from them, being purist. . . . .and pushed them a bit towards humanity . . . is that kidding yourself?"

Anne is afraid that maybe the Nazis might push them instead. If so, Halder assures her, "I'd get out . . . no question about it. . . . . We'd get out of the country." Nevertheless, Anne is afraid for Halder.

In Bouller's office, the Over-Leader hands Halder a letter, explaining that it is one of many requests received at the Chancellery from relatives of incompetent persons requesting that they be put to mercy death—an example of citizens of the new Germany coming to terms with reality. Halder tries to argue that such an attitude "does not always lead to humanity and compassion," but Bouller continues on his own track.

BOULLER: Halder, we want a paper from you. Arguing along the same lines as you do in your novel, the necessity for such an approach to mercy killings of the incurable and hopelessly insane, on the grounds of humanity and compassion.

HALDER: The novel came out of a direct experience . . . my mother's senile dementia.

BOULLER: Exactly. This is what makes your analysis so potent. As the Leader says, "From the heart" . . . And I would add, from the mind. I take it the opinions so clearly expressed in your book, Halder, are firm personal convictions . . .

HALDER: Below a certain level of the quality of human life . . . yes . . . I can't see it worth preserving. From the individual sufferer's point of view and his family's . . . yes . . .

BOULLER: Look here, Professor . . . let me be open and frank with you . . . I could rest much easier in my bed, with your participation in this project . . . You and I know how these things can get out of hand . . . There are certain elements in the party . . . And aside from that aspect . . . the inhumanities that can happen in hospitals and other medical institutions . . . If we have you with us. You follow me? This would be for me, a guarantee that the whole question of humanity in the carrying out of this project would never be lost from the initial stages of planning, to the final implementation of the scheme.

HALDER: I'll draft out a paper for you, Over-Leader . . . in the next week . . .

Bouller joins a group of SS men waving tankards of beer and singing "The Drinking Song" from *The Student Prince.* The atmosphere of camaraderie here in the marble halls of the National Socialist Office lifts Halder's spirits. An SS major, Freddie, comes forward to join him in reminiscence of their service with the army in 1916. Joining the Nazi party reminds Halder of the thrill of wearing his army uniform for the first time. The Major suggests that an old soldier and intellectual like Halder should aim for membership in the SS, an elite corps comparable to the onetime Kaiser's Imperial Guard. Freddie and his SS troop seem so friendly that Halder can't help liking them.

HALDER (*to audience*): He was such a nice, open man . . . His father was a school teacher . . . So was his wife's father . . . He wasn't a cliche Nazi ex-jailbird thug . . . And he told me what Hitler had said to him . . .

FREDDIE: I can hear his voice, now. That Austrian accent. Pleasant, quiet, concerned. He was so concerned about us.

HALDER and HITLER: I should like to make you two pledges. I will never give a command to march against the lawful government of Germany—that is, I will never attempt a second time to come to power by force.

FREDDIE: We all looked at him. Everybody was surprised. This is 1932 I am talking about. The terrible conditions. Inflation. Unemployment. Children in the streets in winter without shoes . . .

HALDER and HITLER: And I promise you, I will never give you an order which goes against your conscience.

The chorus swells—"Drink, drink drink. . . . .Let every true comrade salute the true flag. . . . ." *Curtain.*

ACT II

Maurice begs Halder to get him tickets to Switzerland. Halder assures "my only bloody friend" that he would if he could, and he promises himself that if Maurice is caught in a roundup he'll join him in prison. As Maurice continues to beg Halder for help to get away, Halder's mind skips to a time when his mother was beginning to realize that her mind was going and she could no longer manage without help, even in her own home.

A burst of flame signals the existence of a bonfire where Halder is helping an assistant named Bok to screen books for the burning, while a jazz trio plays Bach's fugue in D major and/or a jazz version of "Hold That Tiger." Proust's *Remembrance of Things Past* goes into the flames ("Don't want to waste any time on the past, do we?") as the SS Major, Freddie, enters, followed by his wife Elisabeth and Anne. Elisabeth is pleading with her husband to find Halder and Anne a place to live. "We'll organize that. Don't worry about it," Freddie assures his wife.

Halder is visiting a hospital, inspecting it, and explaining to a doctor: "I think Berlin sees me as some kind of humanity expert . . . My role is to look round, assess the arrangements and make some recommendations on general humane grounds."

To show that he trusts his friend Halder, Freddie lets him in on the secret of his private vice: he collects jazz records, which are considered by the party to be "decadent Negroid swamp jungle music"—and he knows for a fact that Hitler enjoys watching the movies of Charlie Chaplin, who is a Jew. Freddie is behaving in this more than ordinarily friendly fashion toward Halder because he has a difficult order to transmit to him. Freddie hands the paper to Halder, who reads it and discovers he is directed to organize a book-burning ceremony at the university. Halder is relieved: "It's just *books.*" Apparently he feared it might be something worse.

Halder tells himself there is "a positive aspect" to the consigning of works of Thomas Mann, Remarque and Freud to the bonfire: "One of the basic defects of university life is learning from *books.* Not from *experience.* . . . .The burning is symbolic of a new, healthy approach to university learning." Halder means to keep his own copies, however, just as Freddie has his illicit "jungle music" collection.

A lieder, Schubert's "Standchen," is the music background as Halder, who is planning to leave Helen for Anne, is trying to teach his wife a recipe for goulash because it is especially easy to prepare. His mother calls to him from upstairs that she has to use the toilet. Halder goes to assist her, and she proceeds awkwardly through this embarassingly physical process.

MOTHER: . . . . .Where's the toilet paper? . . . My God. I can't find it. This miserable house . . . They don't even have any toilet paper . . . I knew it was an unlucky house the first time I stepped through the door . . .

HALDER: There's the toilet paper, for God's sake. Mother—why the hell did you have to tell Helen about Anne?

MOTHER: Where's the wash-hand basin? I need to wash my hands . . .

HALDER: Follow the wall . . . Use your imagination . . . You'll never be able to bloody live on your own if you don't give yourself a shake . . .

MOTHER: I'm sorry, son . . . I can't perform for you . . . I can't take it in . . . and be independent, so you can run off with your prostitute and leave me on my own without feeling guilty . . . Where's the bloody tap . . .

HALDER: Use your imagination . . .

MOTHER: I can't wash my hands with imagination, son. Maybe you can. God in heaven . . . The women you pick . . . I told you from the beginning . . . Your father did . . . That woman is no good to you . . . Didn't we plead with you . . . the night before your wedding, to call it off . . . Where are you taking me now?

HALDER: I'm taking you back to the bedroom.

MOTHER: I've been stuck up there all day. I want to go downstairs . . . What are you going to do about the children?

HALDER: They'll be all right . . . I'll look after them.

MOTHER: That woman. Dear God, she can't even make a cup of coffee. She gave me bread and butter this morning . . . The bread was cut like doorsteps . . . I want to go *downstairs* . . .

HALDER: Sit in your room a minute . . .

MOTHER: Will you take me downstairs . . . What do you think you're doing . . . Torturing me here . . . Locking me up like a prisoner with not a soul coming to see me all day . . . If that is what you wanted to do . . . Giving me a holiday with you . . . You should never have taken me out of the hospital . . .

Halder is showing Helen how to prepare a detail of the goulash, while she tells him she began falling in love with him long after they were married, only a few months ago, so that his loving someone else hurts her deeply. Halder tells Helen he won't leave her (and doesn't himself know whether he means it). Halder's mother is calling him from upstairs to go to the toilet again, while Helen goes on about her total dependency on Halder, even for friendship—he is her only friend as well as her husband.

Abruptly, Halder is talking to a doctor in the facility he was visiting and inspecting.

DOCTOR: When you come to this level . . . Is this *human* life? She has no control over her bladder or her bowels . . . The dimmest awareness of her environment and what is happening round her.

HALDER: We can take the arguments as read I think, Doctor. What we have to make sure of is that the procedure is carried out humanely . . . Their last hour must be absolutely free from any trace of anxiety.

DOCTOR: Absolutely . . . of course . . .

HALDER: This room is adequate . . . But it needs to be made more ordinary and reassuring . . . Could it be made to look like a bathroom, perhaps? . . . So that the patients are reassured and believe they are being taken for a bath . . .

DOCTOR: Yes. So they come in here . . . Ostensibly for a bath . . . a normal daily routine.

The manner in which the families will be informed of the decease of their loved ones is an important detail ("The families have had enough pain as it is, looking *after* poor souls"), and Halder plans to hold a conference to discuss it.

Then Halder is meeting his friend Maurice in a park—under the circumstances, neither can be seen going to the other's house. Even more desperately than before, Maurice needs five tickets to Switzerland for himself and family; but even though he is now an SS officer, Halder can't just go up to the window and buy them. He advises Maurice not to panic. He is inwardly torn ("I love Jews . . . I'm attracted to their whole culture . . . Their existence is a joy to me . . . Why has it got to be a bloody problem to everybody . . ."). Maurice is afraid that the Nazis "want to crucify me" and will soon go so far as to pass laws "against men without any foreskins." Halder reassures his friend that Hitler can't last more than a year or so, until the capitalist system starts working again, with "everybody moving in the one direction."

Maurice offers to give Halder his cottage, where Halder and Anne can live in privacy, in exchange for tickets to Switzerland, but Halder fears that the railroad station is watched. Maurice has brought Halder some cheesecake, purchased from a man named Epstein, commenting as he hands it to Halder, "I can't *stand* Jews. I spent thirty-five marks there in one go. They didn't even look at me. You're right. There is something seriously wrong with the Jews. I can see Hitler's point."

HALDER (*to himself*): Thirty-five marks. For a *grocery order!*

MAURICE: What kind of neurotic am I . . . I've been through analysis . . . Nazis I buy cheesecake for, while they're passing laws to ruin my whole life. Jews, in the same boat as me, who haven't done me any harm, except they don't wish me "Good afternoon," I can't stand . . .

HALDER: Another word for the human being Maurice, neurotic.

MAURICE: Yes—from the moment you're born into the world . . .

HALDER: Maurice, stop panicking, for God's sake. It'll be all right, I'm telling you.

MAURICE: Yes, for you it'll be all right, for Nazi cunts it's going to be a beautiful world.

HALDER: Maurice, you are in a panic state. It is pointless trying to reason with you just now. We'll talk about it when you are calmer.

MAURICE: Yes, when I'm lying in the fucking ground raked with Nazi cunt machine gun bullets.

HALDER: That's right, Maurice, we'll talk about it then.

Halder is discussing with the Doctor the problem of the families of euthanasia patients. They should be told that their loved ones are being taken for a new kind of treatment, which should always seem like normal procedure to the patient. But "once the decision has been reached to terminate," there should be no delay in implementing it.

The flames of the bonfire leap up to the music of a fugue, as Anne and Halder discuss the possibility of using the summer house belonging to Freddie. The book-burning frightens Anne, and she and Halder cling to each other as the flames flare up.

A crooner is providing the musical background, singing "My Blue Heaven," as Freddie brings a load of logs into the house where Halder and Anne are now living (not the summer house, but a full-fledged establishment) and where they have invited Freddie and his wife Elisabeth for dinner. Freddie confides to Halder that he and Elisabeth can't have children (the defect is his), which will earn him the disapproval of the Nazis and bar him from any further promotion.

A blond young man arrives on a motorbike with a despatch for Freddie: a Polish Jew has shot a German diplomat, Von Rath, in the Paris embassy, and Freddie is ordered to come to headquarters at once. He speculates that it might be prudent to have someone like the young despatch rider produce a child with his wife Elisabeth. Anyhow, Freddie has to leave the dinner party and go on duty "to burn down a few synagogues and arrest some Jews." A "spontaneous demonstration of the indignation of the people of Germany" will be carefully planned and arranged for the next night.

Abruptly, Halder is being interviewed by Over-Leader Eichmann, who tells him, "I think we can work well together." Eichmann has noticed that Halder has never written specifically on the Jewish question (his field, after all, is German literature), but he has made some important comment on the "corrupting" influence of the Jews on Western literature. And Eichmann has noted that Halder has a Jewish friend, one Maurice Gluckstein. Halder comments that it is "mainly a professional relationship," patient and doctor.

Halder launches into a monologue as though lecturing to students, addressing the audience, then himself, then Maurice. He tells his class that Jewish literature ignored the social character and needs of man in favor of the individual. He tells the audience that the "Jew operation" known as the Night of the Broken Glass weighed on his mind and upset his digestion. He tells himself that he is happy and successful. He tells Maurice (with a Mendelsohn violin concerto in the background) that even the violent excesses of anti-Jewish action must be viewed in historical perspective.

HALDER: . . . . .I am not deluding myself . . am I? Maurice? This is a regime in its childhood . . . It's social experiment in its earliest stages . . . You know what a child is like . . . Self discipline isn't formed, yet a large element of unpredictability . . . It *could* be . . . if the Jews stayed here much longer . . . You see what I'm getting at? . . . Some of the extreme elements in the regime, could get out of hand . . . Christ knows *what* they would do to the Jews next . . . I see tonight . . . As a basically humane action . . . It's going to shock the Jews into the *reality* of their situation in Nazi Germany . . . Tomorrow morning . . . they'll be running for their lives out of the country . . . A sharp, sudden shock . . . that is going to make those who still delude themselves they can stay here in peace to face reality . . . and . . .

Music stops.
Keep out of it . . . as much as possible . . . You can do fuck all about it. Tonight
. . . what can I do about it? All over the country they'll be marching against the
Jews. It's a bad thing. No question about it. . . . .

But bad as it is, on Halder's "anxiety scale" it ranks below his own death or
imprisonment or the possibility that Anne would leave him for another man.

Bok arrives bringing orders for Halder. Nobody cares much about the individual who was shot in Paris, Von Rath, it's the idea of a Jew shooting a German
that is going to trigger the major event that has caused everyone to stop work
to prepare themselves with torches and banners. Halder is ordered to "move into
action" at 3 P.M. He challenges Bok: would it really make him happy to live in
a world entirely without Jews? Bok replies that Hitler knew what he was talking
about, blaming the Jews for economic difficulties which are now being alleviated
as the Jews are being suppressed: "Herr Professor . . . *You* didn't like living in
a Jew Germany . . . Did you? Now . . . you walk about in the streets. And you
feel it . . . You know. This is *our* place now . . . Don't you? He's got us back our
own country. . . . ."

Again, Halder tells himself that he has every reason to be happy (but his mother
intrudes on his thoughts; the Sister has reported that she climbs out of her bed
at night in an effort to find her way home).

Eichmann tells Halder that they want his "usual, clear objective reports" on
the general situation at the camps. Halder is concerned about an order to resettle
all Jews by the end of the year—he fears such a program will put too much of
a strain on Germany's resources, now that they are in a two-front war.

EICHMANN: Russia, we'll soon finish off. . . . .That'll be one front less . . . In
any case . . . that's our orders.

HALDER: I was curious about the need for such urgency . . .

EICHMANN: Your point about fighting the war on so many fronts . . . All the
more reason to keep the enemy within under tight control . . . You can see that,
can't you? . . . From the question of security alone . . . You'll make the arrangements, then . . . You'll need to base yourself in Berlin during your assignment
with me . . .

HALDER: I'll make arrangements . . . Yes . . .

EICHMANN: The leadership, of course, have ordered me that on no account are
you to cut yourself totally off from your university. . . . .

With Anne, Halder is suffering qualms about Germany being turned into "one
great prison" and even considers the possibility of running away. Bok's visit has
left him in a state of panic and guilt. Anne reassures him (as she helps him on
with his SS uniform) that she loves him, and that he is involved only in a perfectly
legitimate police action, not to shoot Jews but to keep things under control. And
she adds, "In any case, for God's sake . . . If I was Jewish I'd have got out of
here *years* back . . . The first year Hitler was in power . . . Any Jew with sense
is out by now. The ones that are left must be utterly stupid or desperate to hang
on to their property." Halder admires her logic, and Anne admires his looks in

his uniform. Halder straps on his loaded revolver as Anne tells him, "No prisons or yawning chasms in front of you."

Eichmann consults Halder about what to do with the sick and the diseased, "the volume of Jews and antisocials flooding into the camps." Yes, the sick and the highly infectiously diseased could be a problem, Halder admits, while Eichmann keeps adding the "antisocials" and the "unfit" to his roster of concern. The order to deal with them has been issued. Eichmann wants Halder to go and look over the possibilities in Silesia, consider them in his characteristic "human, without sentimentality approach" and report back directly and secretly to Eichmann alone.

Halder's friend Maurice had disappeared many months before, but he comes to Halder's thoughts during that night of violence, in the smoke of burning buildings, to the musical accompaniment of the Frankfurt Jewish Choral Society singing "Jesu Joy of Man's Desiring." Halder tries to tell Maurice that they have oversimplified the situation with stock responses of victim vs. persecutor, and that this "Jewish, moralistic, humanistic, Marxist total fuck up" is the fault of the Jews. The Jews certainly bear its effects, Maurice agrees, of murder, mutilation and rape. "No," Maurice concludes, "I take that back . . . most of them couldn't rape a sparrow."

Maybe they're suffering a sort of national nervous breakdown, Halder decides. The way things are going, people won't be inhabiting the planet much longer; it'll be left to hardy plants which are managing to grow up through the cracks in the concrete.

Anne helps Halder on with his greatcoat—he is bound on Eichmann's errand for a place Anne has never heard of: Auschwitz, in Upper Silesia.

ANNE: Are you all right, now, love?

HALDER: I'm fine . . .

ANNE: John . . . Listen to me . . . Whatever happens round us . . . however we get pushed . . . I know we're good people . . . both of us . . . It just isn't what's happened . . . You destroyed me . . . pulled me down . . . It isn't . . . It's the other way round . . . You've pulled me up . . . I've done the same for you . . . from the first time we came together . . .

HALDER: Yes . . . We probably are . . . *good* . . . Yes . . . whatever that means.

ANNE: You know what it means.

HALDER: Yes.

ANNE: *Remember* it then.

HALDER (*to audience*): I got into Auschwitz early in the morning. It was an ordinary dirty industrial town. Big station. Munition trains . . . Sparrows on the platform poking at microscopic crumbs on the concrete. People going about their work. Like a normal town. I was sitting on the platform, feeling insecure like I always feel away from home . . . Absolutely longing for Anne and the children . . . the comfort of her hand in mine. I'd taken out a book, while I was waiting for a car from the camp to pick me up. A German translation of Don Quixote . . . I could only read escapist literature like that in these days . . .

ANNE: Remember it, then. And remember that I love you. And you love me . . . And we'll always love one another . . . Will you remember that . . .

HALDER (*kissing her eyelids*): I'll remember that.
> *Up Schubert march.*

(*To audience.*) When we arrived at the camp, Hoess, the commandant, was waiting at the gate for me. (*Hoess comes forward. To audience, as he shakes hands with Hoess.*) Funny man . . . Poor soul . . . Something *wrong* with him. I was trying to work out what exactly it was, all the time he was welcoming me . . . He showed no emotion. That was it. Might have been some mental condition. On the other hand, just stress . . . The poor bastard had a hell of a job . . . he did make a supreme effort and *smiled.* The funny thing was . . . I could hear this band. Playing a Schubert march. "Oh . . ." I registered to myself. "We're having Schubert, now" . . . Then I became aware that there was in fact a group of prisoners . . . Maybe in my honor, I'm not sure . . . The important thing was . . . the significant thing: the band was *REAL.*

> *Up band . . . Halder watching them.*

. . . The band was *REAL!*

> *Up music. Curtain.*

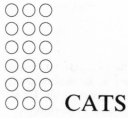

CATS

A Musical in Two Acts

WORDS BY T.S. ELIOT

MUSIC BY ANDREW LLOYD WEBBER

ADDITIONAL LYRICS BY TREVOR NUNN

Cast and credits appear on page 340

THOMAS STEARNS (T.S.) ELIOT (words), the Nobel Prize-winning poet, was born in St. Louis, Mo. on Sept. 26, 1888 and died in London in January 1965. During his world-renowned career he wrote a number of works for the theater, the first of which was the verse drama Murder in the Cathedral *which had the first of many productions March 20, 1936 for 38 performances on Broadway. His* The Family Reunion *appeared off Broadway in the 1947–48 season and on Broadway Oct. 20, 1958 for 32 performances. His* The Cocktail Party *proved to be one of the most important plays of the modern theater in Broadway production Jan. 21, 1950 for 409 performances, designated a Best Play of that season and winning the Critics Award. His short* Sweeney Agonistes *appeared off Broadway on a program with works by Pablo Picasso and Gertrude Stein in the 1951–52 season. Two years later, again on Broadway, a new Eliot play,* The Confidential Clerk, *appeared Feb. 11, 1954 for 117 performances and was named a Best Play. Three decades later, not a season goes by without revival of his plays and programs of excerpts from his poetry in New York and regional theaters.*

Eliot's slender volume of poems Old Possum's Book of Practical Cats *("Pos-*

sum" was one of his nicknames among close friends) was published in October 1939. An off-off-Broadway version adapted by Jonathan Foster appeared at Soho Rep in the spring of 1980. The full-scale musical created by Andrew Lloyd Webber and Trevor Nunn from this material opened in London May 11, 1981 and then was produced for Broadway October 7, 1982, Eliot's third Best Play.

ANDREW LLOYD WEBBER (music) was born in London, England March 22, 1948. He attended Westminster School as a Queen's Scholar and went on to Magdalen College, Oxford and the Royal College of Music. His early work includes a suite for his toy theater at age 9 and, in 1965, the as yet unproduced musical The Likes of Us *with lyrics by Tim Rice. The Webber-Rice collaboration flared forth on an international scale with* Joseph and the Amazing Technicolor Dreamcoat *(1967, off Broadway 1976 and 1981, Broadway 1982 in Tony-nominated revival),* Jesus Christ Superstar *(1970, Broadway 1971 with Tony-nominated score) and* Evita *(1976, Broadway 1979 in Tony-winning production, with Tony-winning book and score, and awarded the Drama Critics citation as best musical). Other West End productions composed by Webber were* Jeeves *(1975, lyrics by Alan Ayckbourn),* Tell Me on a Sunday *(lyrics by Don Black),* Cats *(1981) and the current* Song and Dance *which includes material from his gold record album entitled* Variations. *He is married, with two children.*

TREVOR NUNN (additional lyrics) was the director as well as a co-author of Cats. *He was born in Ipswich, England, Jan. 14, 1940 and was educated at Cambridge, where he directed a number of productions. In 1962 he won an ABC television trainee director's scholarship to the Belgrade Theater Company in Coventry and by 1963 became its resident director. In 1965 he joined the Royal Shakespeare Company as an associate director, becoming its artistic director in 1968. He has staged a number of its outstanding productions in Stratford and at the Aldwych in London over the years, including last season's phenomenal* The Life & Adventures of Nicholas Nickleby *and this year's* Henry IV, Parts 1 and 2, *which opened RSC's new London home at the Barbican Theater, and* All's Well That Ends Well, *which visited Broadway in the spring.*

For Cats, *Nunn added lyric material (in collaboration with Richard Stilgoe) to the prologue "Jellicle Songs for Jellicle Cats," and he wrote the lyrics to the song "Memory" based on Eliot poems. "Eight lines have been added to the song of the Jellicles," Nunn stated in a program note to the Broadway production and continued, "Some of our lyrics, notably 'The Marching Song of the Pollicle Dogs' and the story of Grizabella were discovered among the unpublished writings of Eliot. The prologue is based on ideas and incorporates lines from another unpublished poem entitled 'Pollicle Dogs and Jellicle Cats.' Growltiger's aria is taken from an Italian translation of* Old Possum's Book of Practical Cats. *'Memory' includes lines from and is suggested by 'Rhapsody on a Windy Night' and other poems of the* Prufrock *period. All other words in the show are taken from the Collected Poems."*

Cats is a unique theatrical concept which it would not be useful to synopsize in the manner of most other Best Plays in these pages. Instead, we illustrate how the show interpreted visually T.S. Eliot's written imagery, with the excellent photos by Martha Swope picturing each of the musical numbers, many of them captioned with excerpts from the corresponding Eliot material which served as a lyric for that number.

The photographs depict the succession of scenes in Cats *as produced by Cameron Mackintosh, The Really Useful Company, Ltd., David Geffen and The Shubert Organization and as directed by Trevor Nunn, with Gillian Lynne serving as associate director and choreographer, with scenery and costumes by John Napier and lighting by David Hersey. Our special thanks are tendered to the producers and their press representatives, Fred Nathan & Associates, Eileen McMahon and Anne S. Abrams, for making available these selections from Martha Swope's photographs of* Cats.

CATS

PART ONE

"WHEN CATS ARE MADDENED BY THE MIDNIGHT DANCE"

Prologue: Jellicle Songs for Jellicle Cats—Company

Jellicle Cats come out tonight
Jellicle Cats come one come all
The Jellicle Moon is shining bright—
Jellicles come to the Jellicle ball.

Jellicle Cats are black and white,
Jellicle Cats are rather small,

Jellicle Cats are merry and bright,
And pleasant to hear
           when they caterwaul.
Jellicle Cats have cheerful faces.
Jellicle Cats have bright black eyes;
They like to practise their airs and graces
And wait for the Jellicle Moon to rise.

Scene 1: The Naming of Cats—Company (above)

When you notice a Cat
      in profound meditation,
The reason, I tell you,
      is always the same:
His mind is engaged
      in a rapt contemplation
Of the thought, of the thought,
      of the thought of his name.

*Scene 2: The Invitation to the
       Jellicle Ball—Cynthia
       Onrubia (right)*

Scene 3: The Old Gumbie Cat—Anna McNeely (below, right)

All day she sits upon the stair or on the steps or on the mat:
She sits and sits and sits and sits—and that's what makes a Gumbie Cat!

But when the day's hustle and bustle is done,
Then the Gumbie Cat's work is but hardly begun.
And when all the family's in bed and asleep,
She slips down the stairs to the basement to creep.
She is deeply concerned with the ways of the mice—
Their behavior's not good and their manners not nice;
So when she has got them lined up on the matting,
She teaches them music, crocheting and tatting.

Scene 4: The Rum Tum Tugger—Terrence V. Mann and Company (above)

Yes the Rum Tum Tugger
                 is a Curious Cat—
And there isn't any call for me to shout it:
For he will do
As he will do
And there's no doing anything about it!

*Scene 5: Grizabella, the Glamour Cat—
Betty Buckley (right) as the
Tabby way past her prime*

Scene 6: Bustopher Jones—
Stephen Hanen

He's the Cat we all greet
    as he walks down the street
In his coat of fastidious black:
No commonplace mousers
        have such well-cut trousers
Or such an impeccable back.
In the whole of St. James's
        the smartest of names is
The name of
        this Brummell of Cats;
And we're all of us proud to
        be nodded or bowed to
By Bustopher Jones in white spats!

Scene 7: Mungojerrie and Rumpleteazer—Timothy Scott (below, center)

Mungojerrie and Rumpleteazer had a wonderful way of working together.
And some of the time you would say it was luck,
                and some of the time you would say it was weather.
They would go through the house like a hurricane,
                and no sober person could take his oath
Was it Mungojerrie—or Rumpleteazer? or could you have sworn
                that it mightn't be both?

Scene 8: Old Deuteronomy—Ken Page (center) and Company

Old Deuteronomy's lived a long time;
He's a Cat who has lived many lives in succession.
He was famous in proverb and famous in rhyme
A long while before Queen Victoria's accession.

*Scene 9: The Awefull Battle of the Pekes and Pollicles together
with The Marching Songs of the Pollicle Dogs (above)*

Scene 10: The Jellicle Ball—Company

Scene 11: Memory—Betty Buckley (left)

Midnight, not a sound from the pavement.
Has the moon lost her memory?
She is smiling alone.
In the lamp light the withered leaves
                        collect at my feet
And the wind begins to moan.

Memory. All alone in the moonlight
I can smile at the old days.
I was beautiful then.
I remember the time
            I knew what happiness was,
Let the memory live again. . . . .

Daylight. I must wait for the sunrise
I must think of a new life
And I mustn't give in.
When the dawn comes
            tonight will be a memory, too
And a new day will begin. . . . .

Touch me. It's so easy to leave me
All alone with the memory
Of my days in the sun.
If you touch me you'll understand
                        what happiness is.
Look, a new day has begun.

PART TWO

"WHY WILL THE SUMMER DAY DELAY—WHEN WILL TIME FLOW AWAY"

Scene 12: The Moments of Happiness—Ken Page (at top, left) and Company

Scene 13: Gus: The Theater Cat—Stephen Hanan with Bonnie Simmons (above)

> He isn't the Cat that he was in his prime;
> Though his name was quite famous, he says, in its time. . . .
> For he once was a star of the highest degree—
> He has acted with Irving, he's acted with Tree.
> And he likes to relate his success on the Halls,
> Where the Gallery once gave him seven cat-calls.

*Scene 14 (left, on opposite page): "Growltiger's Last Stand"—Stephen
    Hanan (center, as Gus the Theater Cat playing "Growltiger,"
    a seafarer ambushed by a horde of Siamese) and Company*

Growltiger had no eye or ear for aught but Griddlebone,
And the Lady seemed enraptured by his manly baritone,
Disposed to relaxation, and awaiting no surprise—
But the moonlight shone reflected from a hundred bright blue eyes.

You may say that by and large
     it is Skimble who's in charge
Of the Sleeping Car Express.
From the driver and the guards
     to the bagmen playing cards
He will supervise them all,
             more or less. . . . .
You can play no pranks
          with Skimbleshanks!
He's a Cat that cannot be ignored;
So nothing goes wrong
         on the Northern Mail
When Skimbleshanks is aboard.

Scene 16: Macavity—Kenneth Ard and Harry Groener (below)

Macavity, Macavity,
     there's no one like Macavity,
There never was a Cat of such
         deceitfulness and suavity.
He always has an alibi,
         and one or two to spare:
At whatever time
        the deed took place—
MACAVITY WASN'T THERE!

Scene 17: Mr. Mistoffelees—
*   Timothy Scott (right)*

At prestidigitation
And at legerdemain
He'll defy examination
And deceive you again.
The greatest magicians
            have something to learn
From Mr. Mistoffelees'
            Conjuring Turn. . . . .
And not so long ago
            this phenomenal Cat
Produced *seven kittens*
            right out of a hat!

Scenes 18 & 19: Memory (Reprise) and The Journey to the Heaviside Layer
*   (below) in which Old Deuteronomy (Ken Page, arms raised)*
*   transports Grizabella over the rainbow to magical rebirth*

Scene 20: The Ad-dressing of Cats—Company

With Cats, some say, one rule is true:
Don't speak till you are spoken to.
Myself, I do not hold with that—
I say, you should ad-dress a Cat.
But always keep in mind that he
Resents familiarity.
I bow, and taking off my hat,
Address him in this form: O CAT!

ANGELS FALL

A Play in Two Acts

BY LANFORD WILSON

Cast and credits appear on page 349 & 386

LANFORD WILSON was born in Lebanon, Mo. April 13, 1937 and was raised in Ozark, Mo. He was educated at San Diego State College and the University of Chicago, where he started writing plays. Arriving in New York in 1963, he gravitated to the Caffe Cino, one of the first of the off-off-Broadway situations. He made his New York playwriting debut there with So Long at the Fair, *followed by* Home Free *and* The Madness of Lady Bright, *which latter claims an OOB long-run record of 250 performances. In 1965 his first full-length play,* Balm in Gilead, *was produced at Cafe La Mama and directed by Marshall W. Mason, who has figured importantly in Wilson's later career. That same year the prolific author's* Ludlow Fair *and* This Is the Rill Speaking *were presented at Caffe Cino.*

Wilson's off-Broadway debut took place with the appearance of Home Free *on a New Playwrights Series program for 23 performances at the Cherry Lane Theater in February 1965.* Ludlow Fair *and* The Madness of Lady Bright *appeared off Broadway and in London in 1966.* The Rimers of Eldritch *(a development of* This Is the Rill Speaking*) won its author a Vernon Rice Award off Broadway in 1967. In 1968 his* Wandering *was part of the off-Broadway program* Collision Course, *and he tried out an untitled work with Al Carmines at Judson Poets' Theater.*

In 1969 Wilson moved uptown to Broadway for the first time with the short-lived but favorably-remembered The Gingham Dog, *following its production a year*

153

earlier at the Washington, D.C. Theater Club. Almost equally short-lived but even more favorably received (in subsequent productions) was his Lemon Sky *(1970). The following year he wrote the libretto for Lee Hoiby's opera version of Tennessee Williams's* Summer and Smoke, *which premiered in St. Paul, Minn. and was presented by New York City Opera in 1972. He also collaborated with Williams on the film script* The Migrants, *which was produced by CBS and won an Emmy nomination and a Christopher Award.*

Wilson was a founding member of Marshall W. Mason's Circle Theater (now Circle Repertory Company) and is one of its 21 playwrights-in-residence. His scripts produced at this home base have included Sextet (Yes) *in 1971 and* The Great Nebula in Orion, The Family Continues *and* Ikke, Ikke, Nye, Nye, Nye *during the 1972 season. They were directed by Mason, as was Wilson's* The Hot l Baltimore, *which premiered OOB at the Circle Jan. 27, 1973, moved to an off-Broadway theater March 22, 1973 where it ran for 1,166 performances (a new record for an American straight play), was named a Best Play of its season, won the Critics (best American play), Obie and Outer Circle Awards and was adapted into a TV series.*

In 1975, Wilson's The Mound Builders *was produced at the Circle under Mason's direction, won an Obie and was filmed for the Theater in America series on WNET-TV. In the season of 1975–76, the well-established group crossed the boundary between OOB and off Broadway; and Wilson's* Serenading Louie *was produced there for 33 performances, becoming its author's second Best Play (it had been written between* Lemon Sky *and* The Hot l Baltimore *and was rewritten for this production).*

In 1977–78, the Circle produced Wilson's one-acter Brontosaurus *as well as his third Best Play, the full-length* The 5th of July, *which opened its 159-performance run April 27, 1978. In it, a member of the Talley family, Aunt Sally, is visiting the Talley homestead in Missouri in order to inter her late husband's ashes. The second play in Wilson's Missouri trilogy,* Talley's Folly, *concerned itself with the courtship of Aunt Sally and her Matt on a July 4 evening 33 years before the events of* The 5th of July. Talley's Folly *opened at the Circle under Mason's direction May 1, 1979 and played 44 performances before moving uptown to Broadway Feb. 20, 1980 for 277 more performances, winning Wilson's third Best Play citation, plus the Pulitzer Prize and the Critics Award for best-of-bests.*

The first play of the trilogy was then remounted for Broadway in November 1980 as Fifth of July, *playing 239 performances, and the third,* A Tale Told, *appeared at the Circle June 11, 1981 for 30 performances. This season, Wilson returned to matters other than the Talley family with his fourth Best Play,* Angels Fall, *which opened under Mason's direction at the Circle Oct. 17 for 65 performances and then moved to Broadway Jan. 22 for 64 more performances.*

Wilson has been the recipient of the Brandeis University Creative Arts Award, the Institute of Arts and Letters Award, plus Rockefeller, Guggenheim and ABC Yale fellowships. He is a bachelor and lives in Sag Harbor, N.Y.

The following synopsis of Angels Fall *was prepared by Sally Dixon Wiener.*

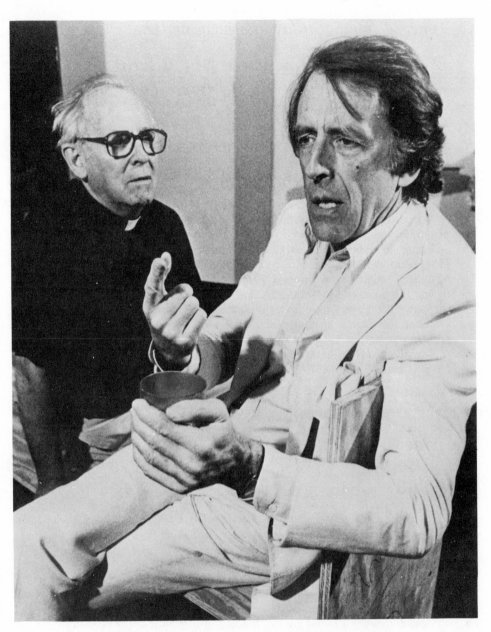

Barnard Hughes as Father William Doherty and Fritz
Weaver as Niles Harris in Lanford Wilson's *Angels Fall*

Time: A late Saturday afternoon in June

Place: A mission in northwest New Mexico

ACT I

SYNOPSIS: In the interior of a simple adobe church, the altar, with its faded blue and yellow paint, is upstage; and upstage left, to one side of the altar, is a door to the living quarters. There is a Madonna painting, primitive, on a barrel top, and backless wooden benches. Stage right are the front doors that lead to a sandy parking lot and a pay telephone. A bell hangs just outside the front doors. Stage left, opposite the front doors, are doors leading to a sandy garden. Strong sunlight penetrates the dark coolness of the church from deep-set narrow windows.

Sitting alone staring at the wall is Don Tabaha, *"mid-20s, half-Indian, intense."* He gets up and exits through the door into the residence area. We hear voices offstage of people coming toward the front doors from the parking area. Relieved to find the doors not locked, Niles and Vita Harris enter, and the light coming through the doorway illuminates the church. Niles is *"56, an art historian and professor. He is tall, elegant, and disheveled."* Vita is *"30, his wife, thin and strikingly attractive."*

Vita suggests Niles sit down while she goes off to see if the telephone is working. He is anxious to get back on the road.

> . . . . . *Niles moves to the window, looks out after her. He takes a prescription bottle from his pocket, has difficulty opening it, peers into the bottle, dumps the only pill onto his hand.*

NILES: Sanctuary.

> *He looks into the empty bottle, carefully breaks the pill in half, and returns half to the bottle.*

Well, half a sanctuary.

> *He looks around the church. There is water in the font; he decides against that and moves to the garden doors. As they open, the interior grows lighter. Niles sees what he is looking for and goes out the door. The church is empty for a moment.*

VITA (*entering*): Niles? Are you all right?

NILES: (*offstage*): Just a minute.

VITA (*notices the pill bottle, picks it up, smiling at the half pill; calling*): Where have you got to? (*Puts the bottle in her purse.*)

NILES (*offstage*): I found a water faucet I'm sure hasn't been opened in twenty years. I'll die of typhoid, but I'll die refreshed. (*He re-enters, wiping his face with a damp handkerchief.*) I must have half of New Mexico on my face.

VITA: You were beginning to look a little like a cinnamon doughnut, yes.

NILES: Sixty miles on a dirt road with nothing to look at except sagebrush, only to be turned back by the highway patrol and have to look at the same sagebrush all over again from the other side. You told Dr. Singer we'll be a day late?

VITA: He's in a meeting. His secretary has gone to the bank.

NILES: At twelve hundred dollars a day per shrunken head, you'd think Singer's institute would own the bank by now.

VITA: I left the number of the pay phone out there.

NILES: Darling, I'm not going to stand in a church in the middle of the wilderness waiting for some secretary to return our call.

VITA: If we don't hear in ten minutes, I'll try again. (*Niles notices the pill bottle is gone.*) I've got it.

NILES: Good. I may need it. (*Looks at his watch.*) We'll give her five minutes . . .

Niles, as they wait, is preoccupied with how it will be in Phoenix for Vita, "living down the road from the asylum," but admits that he will be appreciative of her being nearby. Don comes back onstage and gives them a very cold reception. Vita explains that they just stopped to use the telephone. Don says the phone is only for medical emergencies. He continues to rebuff her efforts to be friendly, until an offstage voice distracts him and he goes out to the parking lot, where "*a motorcycle starts up and drives off.*" Vita concludes that the Honda was the inhospitable young man's.

The voice offstage was that of Marion Clay, "*early 40s, a gallery owner, handsome, well turned out*" and she enters now, complaining mightily to her companion Salvatore (Zappy) Zappala, "*21, almost skinny, quite energetic, a professional tennis player,*" who is standing in the doorway. The newcomers greet Niles and Vita and explain that they're trying to make a plane. Marion, with change, heads for the phone and sends Zap back for her purse. "What do you suppose is the nature of that relationship?" Vita asks Niles, as they realize the telephone is tied up for now.

While Niles is wondering if he dares smoke, Father William Doherty, "*65, the parish priest,*" enters from the garden. " 'And the road was a ribbon of moonlight, over the purple moor' " he is quoting to himself, when he sees Niles and Vita—"Oh, dear goodness." He jumps to the conclusion that he is late for an appointment with them. Assured that he is wrong, he's convinced he's forgotten some other reason why they would be there, and Vita explains they are waiting for a telephone call. Doherty assumes they are lost. Vita says they were turned back at the fork, that there's a bridge out.

DOHERTY: No, no, no, no. There couldn't be a bridge out. There's no bridge. I've never heard of the road being impassable in June. We'll be in for the light rains soon, if they come; the "she-rains" they call them, isn't that lovely? There's no bridge out. It's some problem with the nuclear thing again. The radio was saying something about it. I never listen, but it's good company when you're driving along. I'm not really so rushed, I'm just like this. I'll learn to relax one day. (*Singsong.*) Learn to relax, learn to relax. Now. Maybe I can interest you in the fifty-cent tour.

NILES: Some problem with the nuclear thing again?

DOHERTY: There usually is, and they usually say something coy like the bridge is out. We don't pay much attention any more. Don didn't come through here, did he? Short, dark, surly . . . ?

VITA: In and out.

DOHERTY: In from where and out to where?

VITA: In from there and out on a Honda in a cloud of dust.

DOHERTY (*sitting*): Oh, no. Oh, dear.

VITA: Is there something wrong?

DOHERTY (*gets up, goes out the front door; pleasantly*): Yes, of course, anything you like.

NILES: He's not really rushed, he's just like that.

VITA: You are going to be nice.

NILES: I am not. I have every intention of being inordinately difficult.

Father Doherty enters again, ho-ho-ho-ing to himself about Don, who is down at the intersection having an argument with the highway patrolman. Doherty off-handedly tells the others the "nuclear thing" is nothing to get alarmed about. He rambles on about "a wonderful fright three years ago"—radioactive clouds, but apparently no one thought they were worth evacuating. The next day, men in jeeps with bleepers, shouting above the sound: "No problem. Nothing to be alarmed about. Minor levels, minor levels." Pressed by Niles about these emergencies, Doherty says they're attempting to install a dump to the south of the mission; to the west are about seven mines and mills; to the east the Rio Puerco is awash with some kind of waste periodically; and there is the Los Alamos reactor, the White Sands missile base, and things seeping into the water: ". . . All the Perils of Pauline, but I just get into trouble every time I say anything about it. We aren't supposed to notice . . ." He explains that the phone outside is the only public one in the village, so it sometimes becomes "the hot corner."

Zap and Marion re-enter. They can't get through to anybody on the phone— the airport, the highway patrol or the weather station. All busy. But on the car radio they've heard that something happened when a plane was being loaded at the Chin Rock Mine—no cause for alarm, but traffic's been stopped for a hundred miles as a precaution. Marion tells Zap to stay inside, that there's no point in him wearing himself out. He has a tennis match tomorrow in San Diego.

"*The noise of a helicopter approaches, growing deafeningly loud.*" It is flying very low and is announcing with loud speakers that the roads are closed and to please stay indoors. The last time they said that, Marion remembers, traffic was rerouted for four days around the area. Zap, who has gone out to get a thermos and his zinc pill, reports that the radio says it was not a plane crash, it was a truck.

Meanwhile, Doherty has another parish problem to deal with—Mrs. Valdez has stopped eating: "Says she's going to die . . . She said she'd lived to be ninety, and that's all she'd planned on."

MARION: What are you doing here? I didn't expect to see you.

DOHERTY: I've changed my schedule. Our little genius is running away. You've settled the estate?

MARION: What with the sale and the transfer of the paintings, I've signed my name in the last two days more than most rock stars.

DOHERTY: Are you all right? You're not, of course, neither am I. I have to ask, and you have to say "I'm fine."

MARION: I'm fine.

DOHERTY: As bad as that?

MARION: I'm fine.

DOHERTY (*looking out the door*): He's turned around. The little ingrate. Those choppers must have done the trick. He's coming back. Not a word.

VITA: It looks as if we're detained for a few minutes. Is it all right if we wait here?

DOHERTY: Oh, yes. Maria will be very happy. Happy, happy. She always makes refreshments when she sees a car stop, so we'll have a little treat. She loves people, but she's terrified of them. Wouldn't go near one. But this sort of thing makes her day.

MARION: Lucky for her that it happens all the time.

DOHERTY: Marion can tell you. No alarm, no alarm.

Doherty goes into the residence. Vita says that she's going to bring in the hamper because Niles hasn't eaten a bite. He hasn't been hungry, he doesn't know why. Zap, with a thermos in one hand and his pill in the other, complains that he can't take a pill with gin: "This ain't cocoa"—it's a thermos of martinis. He's a little weird about pills; the way he grew up, a pill was taken with one full glass of water. Marion's laughter makes him remark to her that sportswriters all over the country every day "eat me for breakfast; I don't need it from my old lady, you know?" "Old lady" is too close to home to suit her. He finally takes the pill with a drink from the martini thermos and goes out to garden. He's a total child, Marion says, but a good tennis player who could use better luck on the first-round draw.

Don Tabaha comes back in, wondering what Marion knows about the situation. He can't get Chin Rock on the phone. The telephone rings; it's for Vita, and Don doesn't want her to tie up the line. While Vita goes to the phone it comes out in the conversation that Niles is a teacher on a sabbatical during which he was planning to write his next book but will now "conform to the ancient Israelite sabbatical in which every seventh year the field was left untilled." He tells Marion that his field was art history. "And art history sells," she says. She knows. She owns the Clay Gallery in Chicago. She is Marion Branch, the famous artist Ernest Branch's widow.

Vita comes back in carrying a picnic basket. Niles wants to know about the call from Phoenix—it was from the secretary, and the doctor will call Niles back (he says he will not speak with the doctor; Vita says she will). Doherty is backing in with a tray of lemonade and sugar, apparently trying to get Maria to make an appearance, which she won't. Doherty tells Don not to look so surprised to see him, he rearranged his schedule to see Don off. Don didn't see Doherty's car because Doherty parked it around back. "Aren't I cunning?" he asks Don. He is aware that Don has packed his knapsack and has his motorbike working again "for his getaway."

Doherty passes the glasses of lemonade around, suggesting that maybe they should drink to Don's "newfound fortune." Don says to skip it, and Doherty changes it to "new found opportunity." Don says if he didn't know better, he'd think Doherty had arranged the roadblock. Marion wonders if Maria has the newspaper—the draw was this morning for the tennis matches—and Don volunteers to get it. While Don is offstage, Doherty explains that he is Maria's nephew, that his mother abandoned him, father unknown, and that the church has been his playroom. Don always wanted to be a doctor. He went to medical school, on full scholarship and is interning now. The big city has worked its wiles, but Doherty is sure "we can set him straight."

Vita, urging Niles not to pace about, grows concerned about him and feels his forehead. It's burning up, she says, and he admits that he's perspiring heavily. To Marion's question as to when he will go back to the college, he answers that he's burned his bridges and won't be going back. He's experienced a crisis of faith, a "disturbance in my willful suspension of disbelief that allowed me to see what I had done for what it was." He made the mistake of rereading his books; and to every didactic, authoritative sentence he had written he could say, "Yes, of course, and exactly the opposite could be as true." He asked himself what he'd been doing for 30 years and suspected he'd been bought, or worse.

VITA: Three weeks before the term final, he burst into his classroom—
NILES: Certainly not. I walked majestically and deliberately to my desk and did not sit down.
VITA: And announced to his class that the course was useless.
NILES: I said it was something akin to buffalo chips.
VITA:—took his three published books from his briefcase and ripped them in half.
NILES: And flung them in the air. I was exalted. *The Imagination of Ancient Greece.* (*Rips in half.*) There! to *The Imagination of Ancient Greece.* I know nothing about it, and neither does anyone else. Oh, it was wonderful.
VITA: And in his exaltation he had mislaid his glasses, so on his way to class he drove the car straight across the iris bed at the entrance to the college.
NILES: I was fired with the message of truth.
VITA: And coming back he drove the shortest route to the street, which was directly across the badminton court.
NILES: *Nolo contendere.*

As a result of this, some of the reactionary students' parents are suing the college. (Vita says that her class would have applauded enthusiastically. It seems she was an A-minus student who had the nerve to come to him to complain about the minus; that's how they met.) Niles was completely exonerated by his colleagues, but the Board of Governors "was not quite so obliging". It was sick behavior, Niles acknowledges. Doherty is concerned that Niles experienced a disturbance in his willful suspension of disbelief. Doherty says he thinks this would be very troubling. Niles agrees, but says better now "than on . . . say . . . one's deathbed."

Don enters with the newspaper and goes out again. Marion mentions that Ernie painted Don. It's the only picture she's sure she's going to keep. Don pretended to hate Ernest, but didn't really, and that's what Ernie painted. "The smugness, the fear, the belligerence, the uncertainty, the superiority, the distrust of the painter, the love. All staring right out at you."

Zap is wearing earphones, listening to the radio report of the catastrophe. When Don comes back and asks Zap what's going on, he tells Don a man has already died, an Indian, but they won't release the name until the family is notified.

ZAP: What's yellow cake?

DOHERTY: Where was this?

ZAP: Up at the Chin Rock Mine. It's a mess. This truck was supposed to be being loaded and instead it backed up over the containers and they busted, and the wind blew all this yellow cake stuff all over the guys that were loading it. Those helicopters were coming to take the guys who are still alive to the hospital in Los Alamos.

MARION: Up from White Sands. Wouldn't you know they'd get into the act.

VITA: Yellow cake is pure uranium, refined at the mill. That's from my protesting days.

ZAP: How far away is that Chin Rock Mine?

DOHERTY: Twenty miles? Thirty miles?

MARION: Twenty miles as the buzzard flies.

ZAP: What really gripes you, though—what they're saying is, anybody not in the immediate area won't get sick for about twelve years.

DOHERTY: Minor levels, minor levels.

NILES: Don't panic the populus.

ZAP: You get the picture, twelve years from now you're walking down the street, you're feeling great, all of a sudden you're a spot on the sidewalk.

> Pause. They look to Doherty, who has his fingers pressed to his forehead, his eyes closed. His lips are moving. He prays silently. After a moment he crosses himself, looks up, smiles. Vita moves to a window, looking out.

VITA: I keep envisioning us all being slowly covered with Chin Rock ash. Like the people of Pompeii. A thousand years from now this will be an archaeological site with markers saying: This is a professor, this is his wife, this is a hopeful tennis player, with his rackets.

ZAP: Come on.

DOHERTY: No, no, it sounds very minor. We're not that close. People all over the country are going to be terribly disappointed. They'd rather have a big gaudy cataclysm. They've been preparing themselves for years.

VITA: Look at it. It looks so clean and immutable.

DOHERTY: No, no, quite mutable. Mute, mute, mute. Those solid-looking mountains, if you tried to climb them, would mute right out from under your foot.

In spite of this, Vita envies anyone who owns a place here. You love it or hate it, Marion tells her. She's sold their place. She couldn't hack it—rattlesnakes, scorpions. But she did spend a month here in the summer and a month in the winter.

"They'd have to blast me out," Doherty says. They sent him all the way from

Worcester, Mass., but they'd have to drag him away. He misses Ernie, however, he misses their Sunday afternoons when they would steal an hour under Maria's arbor out back. "He'd drink wine and I'd drink tea, and we both got drunk," Doherty reminisces. "I miss all that. I don't sit there any more . . . . . Sunday afternoons."

Marion puts the paper aside, saying there's nothing in it, of course, and she's going to call San Diego and get the information about the tennis draw over the phone. When she exits, Zap tells Doherty it wasn't easy on Marion coming back here. He says he'll ask her to marry him again. "I ask her every coupla days. She always gets a good laugh outta that."

Vita asks Don when he's going to finish his internship, but Doherty says Don has decided he doesn't want to be a doctor any more, so he doesn't have to finish. Don tells Vita that Dr. Lindermann has asked him to join his cancer research team at Berkeley. The last year or so he's been interested in gene structure, protein production, cellular experiments. Don seems to understand the complicated machinery and equipment that's involved better than some people. Marion, having come back, remarks that she thought he had turned the offer down, but Doherty says that was a previous offer from a lab in Pittsburgh. Doherty describes Dr. Lindermann, a charismatic person interviewed on television, now returning, after three months at the college, to his research, trying to take his brightest star with him with an offer of a high salary and a glamor job.

DON (*very angry*): If I were interested in being glamorous and making money, I could stay right here and be glamorous as hell and rake it in by the kilo. What do you think, Marion? Maybe I should hang up my shingle as the half-breed podiatrist. All those seven-foot Texans in Santa Fe walking around in their pointy boots. Their toes must be killing them.

MARION: Mine too, but I'm not sure I'd put my feet in your hands.

DOHERTY: Neither would they.

DON: And with this sun they'll need a dermatologist.

DOHERTY (*to Don*): Tell us about the respiratory disease among the Navaho mine workers.

DON: And a handsome young endocrinologist could make a killing.

DOHERTY (*rather heated*): Talk to us about the rate of birth defects on the reservation.

DON: And there's a pretty penny here for a proctologist.

DOHERTY: I've never seen a pretty penny.

DON: And the entire desert is weeping for an anaesthesiologist. I know I am.

DOHERTY: I know I am.

MARION: Wasn't that fun. Only now you're both hyperventilating.

DON: Not me.

VITA: Why would there be a higher rate of birth defects on the reservation than there would be in the rest of the area?

MARION: They live right in the middle of the uranium mines.

DOHERTY: Most of the men work there.

DON (*still quite angry*): Congenital anomalies, lung cancer, tuberculosis, chromosomal aberrations, sperm morphological distortion—begins to get scary, doesn't it?

VITA: I can see why Father Doherty doesn't want to lose you.

DON: I'm just getting started, honey. Kidney disease, glaucoma, and there's no time for one person in a hundred years to begin to correct a millennium of genetic neglect.

VITA: So you just wave goodbye to it.

DON: In abject humiliation, yes.

VITA: You think that's all just romantic folly now?

DON: No, darlin', I think that is a deep and abiding tragedy.

Niles get into a discussion with Don and takes umbrage when Don repeatedly calls him "Doctor" instead of "Professor." Niles is not himself, and whoever he is, he seems to be losing control. Marion suggests a Valium, but Vita thinks Dr. Singer doesn't believe in tranquillizers. Singer's name clears it all up for Don: Niles is on his way to a sanatarium to be shock-treated or warm-bathed. Niles explains that he's only going to Singer's because the Board of Governors of the college thinks it will mollify the parents if they can say that he's had a complete collapse. He's humoring them, but he admits that, since the arrangement was made, he's been preparing himself by becoming a basket case.

Doherty points out that Niles is running away, and Don is running away too. Don says *he* isn't, but that he thinks it's commendable of Niles to be taking a tour through the real world on the way to Singer's and hopes he learns a lot. Most of Singer's patrons fly from penthouses to the padded cells without touching down. Niles begs to differ—the real world has come slouching into his room hourly for 30 years, and he would expect youth today to see the way things are more clearly.

VITA: Don't get upset.

NILES: I am not upset. I am strident and overbearing.

VITA: And a touch irrational—

NILES: This young person is justifiably sickened by the effete performance of professors of my ilk—

VITA: No one is quite like you, I'm sure.

NILES: Oh, let us hope. No, people are snowflakes; there's none quite like any. I'm sure there is no comparison to the deprivation you have lived with and are running from, but the fact is that the ivory tower is a bloody shambles. How can you be in school and not know that? The fact of the graceless routine of my life in academe is being awakened at three in the morning, called to the village morgue to identify the mutilated and alcohol-sodden corpse of the victim of a car crash. The fact is—let go of me—is having the brightest light of my fraudulent teaching career quench itself by jumping off the bridge into the bay because in your enlightened age of sexual permissiveness, he was afraid he was sexually deviant. (*Mumbles.*) Ivory tower . . . There have been, in fact, seven suicides in the past ten years; in fact, one third of my class each year, and of yours, I'm sure, if you had bothered to look around you, burn themselves out on drugs and overwork and exposure to the pressures of academic life, and are unable to return, probably to their everlasting benefit, if they knew it. Dear God, how can anyone with eyes (*Vita touches his arm*)—stop that, please—think that we are out of touch with the real world. If that's the real world, I beg to plead very familiar with the real world, thank you. The calumny, Lord! (*Vita takes hold of his arm.*) Stop touching me, please! What are you trying to do? Make it better? It will not be better, thank you! I won't embarrass you again. You won't have to endure that again. I wish in God's name the door to this building weren't so heavy, so I could slam it. (*He strides out the front door.*)

VITA: Niles, don't go out there! I'd better—well, I'd better not, is what I'd better. He'll walk around. He's been getting very—lately—irrational. (*To Don.*) Still, it was unnecessary for you to goad him like that. He's unwell physically as well as—I'm sorry.

The helicopters are overhead again, and Doherty assumes they are taking the injured mine workers to the hospital. He's sure the racket must be frightening Maria, who is also frightened of the telephone, though she did call him this morning to say that he must come at once, that "our doctor is running away." Again Doherty takes a dig at Don about Dr. Lindermann, and Don exits to the parking lot, but not to his bike. Doherty throws some keys to Zap and says to hide them and not to tell Doherty where. Zap exits to the garden, while Marion tells Doherty he should be ashamed. Doherty says he isn't—"Not a bit." Vita admits that she's at the end of her tether, but, no, she doesn't want to talk to Doherty. Marion exits to call San Diego again. Doherty goes off into the residence.

> *Vita folds Niles's jacket, holding it on her arm. She turns to the front door, to the garden. A second helicopter goes over, higher, the sound farther away. She looks up and then slowly turns to look at the altar. She stands facing the altar, her back to us. Curtain.*

ACT II

A half hour later, Father Doherty is kneeling at the altar. Zap, on the floor, is listening to his headset. When Vita comes in, from the garden, Doherty rises. *"He might speak a little less brightly in this act."* Zap reports that Interstate 40 is now definitely moving, everything under control, and what he's listening to is the Moody Blues. "They're good company, very cheering," Doherty says of the Moody Blues. "I hear all those in the car," as he drives to his missions 30 or 40 miles apart.

Vita looks out and sees Don Tabaha sitting on his bike, head down, looking into the dust, looking like the painting "End of the Trail." "Tabaha" means "by the river" in Navaho, Doherty tells Vita. Doherty has been listening to Zap's headset and says that the miner who died at Chin Rock was 23 and his wife is eight months pregnant. Four others are ill. Occupational hazard is what they're calling it.

VITA: What time is Mass?
DOHERTY: Eight.
VITA: If we're still here, I'd like to see the service.
DOHERTY: No, no, nothing to see. I'm afraid there isn't anything to watch. Not

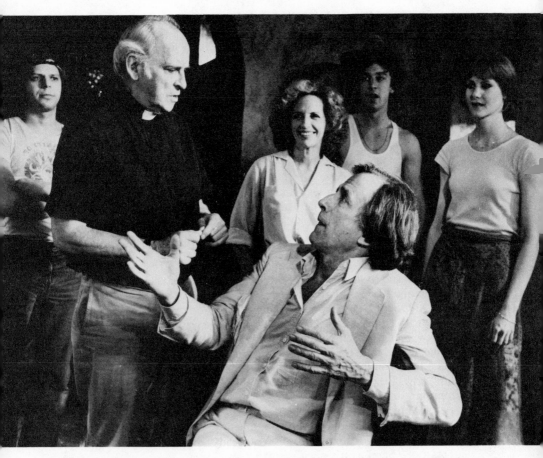

In background, Nancy Snyder, Brian Tarantina, Tanya Berezin and Danton Stone with *(foreground)* Fritz Weaver and Barnard Hughes in a scene from *Angels Fall*

even picturesque, I don't imagine. Twelve, fifteen stoic Navahos shuffle in, kneel, I mumble sincerely, and they shuffle out. Nothing to see. Nothing on their faces, probably nothing on mine. In and out. Shuffle—shuffle.

VITA: It must mean something to them, though. And to you.

DOHERTY: Oh, it's what we live for, but there's nothing to see. You're welcome to stay, but you'll be on the road. They'll get all this cleared up, they'll have a good cover-up story by tomorrow. Bad publicity for the mines if they don't, and the mines are already complaining that the price of uranium has dropped thirty percent in the last ten years. Must be the only price that has. No, you'll be on the road. On the trail by then. Living your life.

Marion comes in. She called for a plane, and it will be ready when she and Zap are. She's broken every nail showing Indian carpenters how to crate paintings. The pots are going to a museum in Albuquerque, the furniture was sold with the buildings. The women agree that moving, breaking up households, is hard. Marion expected it to be morbid, looking over the paintings, readying them for a retrospective, but it was very exciting. The show is going to be important, she tells Vita, not at her gallery, but at the Art Institute of Chicago.

MARION: . . . . . He always wanted that. The bastards had to wait for him to kick off before they gave it to him.

VITA: I imagine he knew it would happen eventually.

MARION: On good days. Then go from Chicago to Denver, then Los Angeles, Dallas, probably not New York. Maybe a few other places. They're all designated for different museums after that. That'll be the hard part, seeing the collection broken up. But it's what he wanted.

She is trying not to cry.

VITA: I'll have to see it.

MARION: Try to catch it.

Moving to the window.

The radio said soon, you said? I think the professor has cooled down a bit. Looks like he might be wandering this way.

VITA: Good. Did Zappy know him?

MARION: Ernie? Yeah. They got along. Ernie was working rather furiously the last few years. He felt better if I had a project. They got along. It's been good for me, it was good for Ernie. Maybe it hasn't been completely fair to Zappy. He gets a little confused. Father Doherty thinks we should "sanctify our relationship" now. I think not. I'll be there 'til he needs something else. So we do learn from our—Zappy, are you hearing this?

ZAP: Sure.

MARION: I forgot you were there, creep.

ZAP: Yeah, I got that problem. You ready to hit the road?

MARION: Soon as it's open.

ZAP: You are getting so weepy, you know? The last week you can't talk about me, you can't talk about Ernie, she can't talk about tumbleweed without the faucet. Yesterday she was crying over the damn sunset.

MARION: Shut up.

ZAP: I can't wait to get you out of here. Get you bossing everybody around again.

Niles enters, full of apologies. When Don enters, Niles tells him his attack was nothing personal. Don claims that Father Doherty stirs everybody up with his "Don't you think, Don?" and "Wouldn't you agree, Professor?" He adds that it is interesting to see someone freak out for a change.

Niles has never felt so twitchy, and besides knowing he's exposing himself to terminal radiation poisoning, he thinks huge ants and spiders are going to come up over the hill. Doherty tells Niles, in answer to Niles's apologies, that he was struck by what Niles did because teachers with concern are rare. "By your age," he says to Niles, "too many teachers have become cynical. Teachers and preachers."

Don saw a lot of that, Doherty elaborates. He was at the top of his class—one of the chosen. "Many are called but only two are chosen:" Dr. Indian Don and

Dr. Alice, a bright young woman intern. Don has to be in Santa Fe tonight to meet the Great Man and the woman intern, then the three of them are off to San Francisco.

All this is none of Doherty's business, Don insists, and he storms out only to re-enter to ask about the keys for his bike. He's sure Doherty knows where they are, but Doherty says he doesn't know exactly where they are. Don says he is not going to do what Doherty thinks he should, but Doherty has every confidence Don will do what Don thinks he should.

Marion enters with a memo pad. She's got Zap's whole schedule. He plays at eleven in the morning. Zap pauses and tells Marion she better read it to him, and then he asks to see her note.

ZAP: . . . . . "Zappala-Evans, Baley-Syse, Bouton-Tryne, Carey-Luff." I can take Evans in straight sets—6-1, 6-1 if he lucks out. Baley-Syse is like a matching from the tadpole pool. Tryne gets mad, Carey is a fairy, and Luff—with all due respect to my fellow players, Luff is a cream puff. Evans, Baley, Syse, Bouton, Tryne, Carey, Luff. Woooo! Son-of-a—— Woooo! I mean, I don't want to disparage true professionals who will, I'm sure, play up to their ability and with great heart, but this is a list of the seven most candy-ass tennis players I've ever seen. This is the Skeeter League. If I couldn't make the final eight in a—Where's Rose? Where's Charley Tick is the question. They got all those guys together on the other leg? What kind of a lopsided draw— Tryne does not possess a serve. None. Carey is, in all humility, probably the worst professional sportsman I've ever seen. What Paul Carey most needs is vocational guidance. Syse I have personally beaten four times without him winning one game. 6-zip, 6-zip Zap! You candy-asses. Woooo! I gotta walk, I gotta walk. You charter the plane?
    Exits.
MARION: He's waiting on the runway.
NILES: Is it really that easy a field?
MARION: Luff could be a problem, but I don't think so. It's so much luckier than any draw he's had—nothing's sure, but it's very fair.
    Enormous yell offstage. Everybody gets up, looks out.
No, it's just Zappy. He's okay. What do you know. What do you know. Son-of-a-gun.

Zap comes back in, furious now: "Is that what they think of me?" Okay, he says, he must not get overconfident and not get a big head. His biggest problem is to not fall asleep facing Charley Baley across the net.

Don wants to know if Zap has his bike keys. Zap says he doesn't (but he doesn't mind lying like a priest would). Don moves toward Zap, but Zap dodges him and exits.

Doherty begins goading Don again. He doesn't know why Don should think any of them are opposed to his success: "Could you see a motive for anything but rejoicing, Professor?" Niles admits he doesn't see the point in badgering the boy, that it's his decision.

Don wants to know how Doherty found out about the research opportunity. Doherty admits that Dr. Lindermann called him for a reference. Doherty was surprised to discover Don had visited there: "Your Great Man said he'd been impressed with the way you presented yourself. Thought you'd be useful eventually in an administrative position." Doherty can see Don now making a grant proposal. Don says it's the best-endowed place in the country, that Doherty doesn't know anything about it.

Niles, who is holding his hand up to his head, argues with Doherty that it isn't up to them to judge what is right, but Doherty holds that teachers and preachers are here to elucidate matters. Vita is worried about Niles again, but he says it's probably too much sun, and he's anxious to get under way. He wants Vita to pack up their things and put them in the car. Vita takes the car keys from him. He mumbles and is supporting himself against the wall, then gets himself onto the bench.

Medically concerned, Don inquires whether Niles has been eating. Vita admits that he hasn't been hungry (no, he doesn't have diabetes as far as she knows). They have stretched Niles out flat, and Don assures himself that Niles can feel and move his arms and legs. He tells Marion to put a lot of sugar in a glass of lemonade. Don doesn't know what's the matter, but Niles's pulse is "exceeding the speed limit," and Don makes Niles drink the lemonade. Niles is in-and-out of it, but expresses confidence in Don, though he doesn't know why. Don's opinion is that any of about ten things could be the matter. He asks Vita if Niles's flying off the handle is usual. She replies in the negative. The not eating is not usual, either. Even though he hasn't been going to doctors, he's been careful of his health.

"Until he made his dramatic denouncement to his class?" Doherty asks, and Vita says yes. Doherty surmises that must have surprised Vita. She saw his point, though, and they were in agreement that it was the only thing he could do. Doherty wonders what their plans are after Dr. Singer's. She doesn't know if they have any.

Don checks—Niles's pulse is down some. Niles hopes his condition has nothing to do with radiation poisoning. Don thinks it could be the heat, a slight stroke, stress, nerves, a hypoglycemic attack. The last Niles resents, it's too much "the thing to have." Don tells him it's not fun if you do, but there's no way to know without tests. Niles feels like an imbecile, coming apart at the seams, everything coming unglued all at once.

Niles finishes a second lemonade, and Don urges a third on him. It's amazing stuff, Niles concedes, but won't concede that his histrionics are due to low blood sugar. More complicated than that, Don replies. He gives Niles a note scribbled on a pad to take to Singer's. Doherty expounds on the subject of what Niles calls his "ivory tower."

DOHERTY: . . . . . You experienced a—what did you call it? I liked that so much. You experienced a disturbance in your willful suspension of disbelief. Wonderfully articulate, those poets. It took me fifteen minutes to figure out what that could possibly mean. All those negatives. Disbelief. What a thing to require. But disbelief is rampant nowadays. People are running about disbelieving all over the place. But a willful suspension of disbelief is believing, isn't it? So a disturbance in one's willful suspension of disbelief is right in my wheelhouse.

NILES: Oh, dear.

DON: Comes with the territory.

NILES: When I started teaching I was a renegade, believed nothing, investigated everything. And subtly over thirty years I became absolutely dogmatic. This is true, that is false. *A* is better than *B. B* is superior to *C.* Look for *A* about you. Anyone today not able to accomplish *A* is no kind of artist at all. All very neat and formulated. And they copy it in their workbooks slavishly. . . . . They don't even realize they're being brainwashed. They don't care. The thing they most often ask is, "Is this going to be on the test?" Once in a thousand students, someone says, "How do you know that?" "Why, good Lord, man, when you've looked at the art of the Renaissance for as long as I have, with utterly blind eyes, you'll know that too."

DOHERTY: So you blew the whistle on yourself; took yourself right out of the game.

NILES: The sporting move when I discovered I was useless.

DOHERTY: Then, like a silly, you stopped eating and made yourself sick. You threw it all away and looked up and saw yourself standing at a crossroads, and you looked down the wrong road at the wrong future and you saw nothing, of course, there's nothing down that road. But you can't do nothing, man. You have a young wife, the possibility of a family, I would think. What manner of person ought we to be? I'm afraid I'm not going to be able to refrain from preaching a little sermon tonight. The only good thing that can come from these silly emergencies, these rehearsals for the end of the world, is that it makes us get our act together.

Niles tells Doherty that he isn't in any state to follow him to the end of the world. As Doherty looks through the Bible he's taken from the altar, he remarks that he would not have been able to resist saying "And I quit" when he stormed out of the classroom in a rage. Niles still has that to look forward to, but Doherty points out that he could go back for the next term. Niles can't, the one thing he's sure of is that teaching is harmful. Doherty remarks that anyone as clever as Niles could teach "Heresy 101. . . . . like St. Peter meeting the early Christians in the catacombs outside Rome."

NILES: If there was a way to survey my subject without comment, without comparisons. "This is a painting. What does it say to you? There will be no test, make friends where you like." Oh, dear. Given today's students, begging for structure, half the class would have breakdowns within a week.

DOHERTY *(with a Bible):* Ah ha!

VITA: What?

DOHERTY: This is the end of the world. *(Reading.)* "The day of the Lord will come as a thief in the night; in which the heavens shall pass away with a great noise, and the elements shall melt with fervent heat. The earth also and the works that are therein shall be burned up. Seeing then that all these things shall be dissolved, what manner of persons ought ye to be in all holy conversation and godliness?" It seems appropriate tonight to remind ourselves of that. And you are a teacher. So you simply have to find a way to teach. One of those professions,

I've always thought, one is called to. As an artist is called, or as a priest is called, or as a doctor is called.

Zappy relates to this—that "call," the magic that happens when you know who you are, like a doctor or a teacher; like Marion (she demurs) who told him she wanted to show artists' work; like when he found out he was a tennis player and went to church and lit a candle. Giving thanks for the light, Doherty comments.

ZAP: Really. I said my novenas, man, 'cause it had been like a—not a miracle that anyone would know except just me—but it had been like when those girls saw Our Lady of Fatima up on that hill. It was really weird. I was like in the fifth grade and I was watching these two hamburgers on some practise court, and they took a break and one of them hands me his racket. So I threw up a toss like I'd seen them do and zap! Three inches over the net, two inches inside the line. There wasn't nobody over there, but that was an ace, man. . . . . . So this guy shows me a backhand grip and he hits one to me and zap! You mother! Backhand! Right down the line. And the thing is, that's where I wanted it. I saw the ball come at me, and I said I'm gonna backhand this sucker right down the line, and I did. . . . . . But that was it. I hit that first ball and I said, "This is me. This is what I do. What I do is tennis." And once you know, then there's no way out. You've been showed something. Even if it's just tennis, you can't turn around and say you wasn't showed that. So I went to church and said a novena for those meatballs, 'cause they didn't know all the butterflies that was in my stomach, that they'd been my angels. But, man, on the way home, anybody had asked me what I did, right there I'd have said, "I play tennis." Didn't know love from lob, didn't matter. That's what I am. 'Cause once you know what you are, the rest is just work.

The helicopters are overhead again, and the loud speakers are blaring—the road is clear. They've given us "our monthly dose of fear" Doherty says, shaming them. The microphones blare again that the road is clear. Doherty has gone out and yelled at them; he gets so angry. "Look at how foolish I am," he says, coming back inside and dusting off his shirt. He claims that they worship energy and that things have regressed back to the days of the cavemen who were astonished by fire.

An astronomer said to him on a radio show that the universe had started with a Big Bang, and Doherty had told him that he knew who pushed the button. It was a local talk panel, he tells Marion, and his superiors aren't happy about his being on it. They'd send him someplace else, but there's no place left. Not that he'd go, anyway. Someone must stay, he insists, or "the vultures will pick the Indians clean." The Indians have inadequate medical facilities, and Don's departure will mean they will have even less help.

Niles notes that Doherty is drifting back to the subject of Don again. Doherty says that Niles left the college because he thought he'd been bought, and he's sure to recognize the purchase of someone else. Don has been a doctor since he was five years old, Doherty goes on, and the need of the Indians is something Niles can't comprehend. But Niles doesn't believe need is the question.

DOHERTY *(to Don):* Weren't you called to be a physician? Didn't you kneel here at this altar with me and pray after you told me you had been called to help your people?

DON: I was eleven years old.

DOHERTY: Have you been called now to alter your course?

DON: Shut up, Father.

DOHERTY: Have you, have you? Did you hear a voice saying to you: "Leave your people and leave your land and go with this great television personality?" Did you?

DON: I discovered I have a very special talent for research; if that's hearing a call, then I've been called.

DOHERTY: No, you just decided you can't turn down this opportunity for a better personal life. . . . . . You know what manner of person you ought to be.

DON: You are tearing me apart!

NILES *(to Doherty):* You don't care a damn what he does for *him.*

VITA: What do you care?

DOHERTY: Your brightest star jumped in/the bay. What would you have done if you had the chance? This is my brightest star. Ten seconds from now he'll be in midair over the water. What would you do?

NILES: You cannot hold power over another man; even for his own good. This is your foster child. You see your reflection in him. I've seen it with teachers a dozen times. I've done it myself.

VITA: Not now.

NILES: You want that for you. You may be right as rain, but you're doing it for yourself. I don't know if that's Christian, but it's certainly not kosher.

Doherty goes to the window and looks out of it for a moment. There are tears in his eyes when he turns back and admits that, if it matters, Niles is right. He was thinking of himself. The helicopters said the road is clear, but he believes they were more truthful when they said the bridge was out.

Vita reminds Zap he has a plane to catch. She thanks Doherty—a good friend to all. Doherty acknowledges this by saying that he takes more than he gives.

In the midst of the parting remarks, Zap asks Doherty if he would bless him, not so that he will win, but so he won't fall over his feet and make Marion look foolish. Doherty does so. After Zap (not forgetting to give Don his motorcycle keys) and Marion leave, Doherty confesses that he cheated and said "Make him win."

Doherty pauses to remark on the fact that somebody is pumping water outside. It's Mrs. Valdez, the old woman who wouldn't eat. She's changed her mind because Doherty made a pact with her granddaughter, who is pretending to be deathly ill, so that Mrs. Valdez got up to care for her.

Vita comments on how beautiful it is here. Niles says he can imagine living here as well as he can imagine living anywhere, but Doherty says Niles is going to get a good rest and then go back to work and raise Cain. Like Peter outside the gates of Rome who was crucified upside down, Niles remarks. "But in a good cause," Doherty says.

Doherty remembers that he asked Vita to stay on for Mass and that she accepted. It was her idea, Vita says, but she thinks she's forgotten the responses. Doherty believes they'll come back, like riding a bicycle. He'll be speaking Navaho, the congregation will reply in Navaho, and a little broken Latin will work in. He goes into the residence and returns with the Mass kit.

> *Doherty spreads the two cloths on the table that serves as an altar. Vita and Niles look at Don a moment, then exit into garden. Doherty sets out two little vials—wine and holy oil, then two candlesticks and two candles.*

DON (*after a long pause*): I'm glad I saw you.

DOHERTY (*sets out two goblets and covers one*): Me, too. Don By-the-River.

DON: Tabaha.

DOHERTY (*sets up cross*): No, no, By-the-River. Don By-the-River. Like the song. (*Sings lightly.*) "Don-by-the-riverside." Dr. Don. I've been too fond, young man. Too fond.

DON: Me, too, Father.

DOHERTY: Yes, yes . . . well . . . (*He goes to the altar, lighting the two candles.*) *Don is crying. He looks around the church, picks up his duffel bag, and leaves. Doherty turns from the altar and moves to the window. The motorcycle starts up. The sound fades away. Doherty turns back, looking to the altar. After a moment he checks his watch and walks slowly outside and begins ringing the bell to call the congregation to Mass as the lights fade. Curtain.*

PLENTY

A Play in Two Acts

BY DAVID HARE

Cast and credits appear on page 348 & 388

DAVID HARE was born at St. Leonards in Sussex, England on June 5, 1947 and was educated at school there and at Lancing College and then for three years at Cambridge. He has been writing plays since the age of 22. His first full-length work, Slag, was produced in London at the Royal Court before appearing in his American debut production at New York Shakespeare Festival Public Theater, first in an experimental staging at the Other Stage and finally as a full-fledged off-Broadway offering at the Florence S. Anspacher Theater February 21, 1971 for 37 performances, at which time its author received an Obie nomination for most promising playwright. The list of Hare's plays produced on this side of the Atlantic includes Knuckle as a Phoenix Theater Side Show in 1975 and off off Broadway at the Hudson Guild in 1981; Fanshen in Milwaukee Repertory March 18, 1976 and in other regional productions and off off Broadway in 1977; and Teeth 'n' Smiles at Folger Theater Group in Washington, D.C. October 17, 1977.

Hare's first Best Play, Plenty, was produced in 1978 by the National Theater in London prior to its American premiere at the Arena stage in Washington, D.C. April 4, 1980 and subsequent staging in March 1981 at the Goodman Theater in Chicago. Its New York debut took place October 21, 1982 off Broadway at New York Shakespeare Festival for 45 performances, after which it was moved by Joseph Papp to Broadway for an extended run of 92 performances and was named the season's best foreign play by the New York Drama Critics Circle.

The newest Hare play, A Map of the World, *was presented in London by the National Theater this season under its author's direction (and Hare has directed other new scripts at both the National and the Royal Court). His TV films have included* Licking Hitler, Dreams of Living *and the forthcoming* Saigon, *about the final days of the U.S. presence in Vietnam. His works have been honored in his own country by the Evening Standard Drama Award, the John Llewellyn Rhys Prize and the British Acadeny of Films and Television Arts Award for the best play of the year. He lives in London, near Notting Hill Gate.*

The following synopsis of Plenty *was prepared by Jeffrey Sweet.*

Time: Various times from 1943 to 1962

Place: France, Brussels and various locations in England

ACT I

Scene 1

SYNOPSIS: The time is Easter 1962. The spacious room of a house in Knightsbridge has been methodically stripped bare of its fancy furnishings. As Susan Traherne's husband, Raymond Brock, lies on the floor sleeping off the effects of nembutal, scotch and a fight with her the night before, Susan, a *"well presented"* woman in her mid-30s, finishes telling her *"slightly younger"* friend Alice Park what she needs to know in order to take over the house. Susan is giving Alice the house to be used as a home for unwed mothers. Having finished the instructions, Susan exits, leaving Alice with the task of having to explain to Brock (when he regains consciousness) that his wife has walked out on him, taking with her nothing that is his.

Scene 2

A British agent, codenamed Lazar, parachutes into the darkness of occupied France in November 1943 and is met by Susan, in this scene in her late teens. She has been waiting for a drop of supplies. Because of an emergency, Lazar has taken advantage of her signal and has landed some 80 miles off course. Susan gives him tips on how to avoid being picked up. She has been in the field a year, and the sustained fear has taken its toll on her.

The expected supplies are now dropped. From out of the shadows, a French resistance fighter tries to grab them, but Susan intercepts him. They quarrel in French over the supplies until Lazar chases the Frenchman away with a gun.

"Bloody Gaullists," says Lazar, "I mean what do they have for brains?"

"They just expect the British to die. They sit and watch us spitting blood in the streets," is Susan's bitter response. And then her attempt at self-possession cracks. She's not even an agent, she tells him, just a courier. She came out for this drop because nobody else of her circuit is left. The wireless operator she

Edward Herrmann and Kate Nelligan in a scene from *Plenty*

worked with was caught by the Gestapo and taken to Buchenwald. She embraces Lazar, crying, "I don't want to die. I don't want to die like that."

Lazar comforts her as best he can. Having calmed her, he helps her collect the supplies. As they disappear into the night, she realizes she doesn't know the real name of the man she has just embraced.

Scene 3

The time is June 1947, and we are in the Brussels office of Sir Leonard Darwin, the British ambassador. Darwin, in his late 40s, is working behind his desk as the third secretary, Brock (in his late 20s) enters to tell him that a Mrs. Radley is waiting to see him. Her British husband has died during their holiday together, and she has come by for assistance from the embassy. "It should be quite easy," says Brock, "she's taking it well." And now Brock ushers in Susan.

With Susan's encouragement, Brock describes the macabre details of the embalming process. Brock's black humor does not sit well with Darwin, who takes the earliest opportunity to leave to attend to the details of flying the body back to England.

Alone now with Susan, Brock cheerfully acknowledges his contempt for Darwin's Blimpishness and his own disappointment at not having a more interesting assignment. Susan in turn acknowledges that she was not married to the late Mr. Radley, a fact which doesn't take Brock by surprise. She further explains that she and Tony Radley had worked together behind the lines in France. He recently had called out of the blue to suggest a holiday together, and, even though she hadn't known him well, she had accepted the invitation because of the bond of experience between them.

SUSAN: . . . . . Those of us who went through this kind of war, I think we do have something in common. It's a kind of impatience, we're rather intolerant, we don't suffer fools. And so we get rather restless back in England, the people who stayed behind seem childish and a little silly. I think that's why Tony needed to get away. If you haven't suffered . . . well. And so driving through Europe with Tony I knew that at least I'd be able to act as I pleased for a while. That's all. (*Pause.*) It's kind of you not to have told the ambassador.

BROCK: Perhaps I will. (*He smiles.*) May I ask a question?

SUSAN: Yes.

BROCK: If you're not his wife, did he have one?

SUSAN: Yes. . . . . She believes that Tony was travelling alone. He'd told her he needed two weeks by himself. That's what I was hoping you could do for me.

BROCK: Ah.

SUSAN: Phone her. I've written the number down. I'm afraid I did it before I came.

Susan opens her handbag and hands across a card. Brock takes it.

BROCK: And lie?

SUSAN: Yes. I'd prefer it if you lied. But it's up to you.

She looks at Brock. He makes a nervous half-laugh.

All right doesn't matter . . .

BROCK: That's not what I said.

SUSAN: Please, it doesn't matter.

> *Pause.*

BROCK: When did you choose me?

SUSAN: What?

BROCK: For the job. You didn't choose Darwin.

SUSAN: I might have done.

> *Pause.*

BROCK: You don't think it's just a little bit previous—coming in here and asking me to lie. Of course I know it must mean nothing to you. This smart club of people you belong to who had a very bad war . . .

SUSAN: All right.

BROCK: I mean I know it must have put you on a different level from the rest of us . . .

SUSAN: You won't shame me, you know. There's no point.

> *Pause.*

It was an innocent relationship. That doesn't mean unphysical. Unphysical isn't innocent. Unphysical in my view is repressed. It just means there was no guilt. I wasn't particularly fond of Tony, he was rather slow-moving and egg-stained, if you know what I mean, but we'd known some sorrow together and I came with him. And so it seemed a shocking injustice when he fell in the lobby, unjust for him of course, but also unjust for me, alone, a long way from home, and worst of all for his wife, bitterly unfair if she had to have the news from me. Unfair for life. And so I approached the embassy.

> *Pause.*

Obviously I shouldn't even have mentioned the war. Tony used to say don't talk about it. He had a dread of being trapped in small rooms with large Jewish women. I know exactly what he meant. I should have just come here this evening and sat with my legs apart, pretended to be a scarlet woman, then at least you would have been able to place me. It makes no difference. Lie or don't lie. It's a matter of indifference.

> *Brock gets up and moves uncertainly around the room. Susan stays where she is.*

BROCK: Would you . . . perhaps I could ask you to dinner? Just so we could talk . . .

SUSAN: No. I refuse to tell you anything now. If I told you anything about myself you would just think I was pleading, that I was trying to get round you. So I tell you nothing. I just say look at me—don't creep round the furniture—look at me and make a judgement.   ∤

Darwin returns with the news that all is arranged. Brock leaves and, for a brief moment, Darwin opens up a bit. He was previously posted in Djakarta. Now, here in Brussels, he sees the work as a challenge. "Marvellous time to be alive in Europe," he says. "No end of it. Roads to be built. People to be educated. Land to be tilled. Lots to get on with. . . . . The diplomat's eye is the clearest in the world. Seen from Djakarta, this continent looks so old, so beautiful. We don't realize what we have in our hands."

Brock returns with a summons for Darwin from Mrs. Darwin for dinner. Darwin leaves "Mrs. Radley" to Brock's charge. Alone again, Brock tells her that he's decided to go along with her on the lie.

Scene 4

Late at night in a small flat in Pimlico in September 1947, Brock has fallen asleep in his suit. Susan's friend Alice (18 in this scene) is on the floor smoking a hookah. She tells Susan that she's making a systematic tour of degradation so as to have material for a novel. The idea of getting a job in an office has no appeal. "How are you going to live?" Susan asks. "Off you mostly," Alice replies with a smile.

Susan speaks wryly of the work she barely tolerates in the office of an import-export firm, and of a Mr. Mendlicott's sexual overtures. "Alice, I must get out . . . . . I'd like to change everything but I don't know how." So saying, she *"starts to oil and clean her gun."*

Alice suggests that Susan drop Brock for somebody younger. Alice has a number of candidates. "I'm sure," says Susan. "I've only known you three weeks, but I've got the idea. Your flair for agonized young men. I think you get them in bulk from the tuberculosis wards . . ."

Brock wakes. He's not feeling terribly well. Susan goes off to make him something to eat. Alice remarks on Brock's habit of bringing parcels over for Susan when he makes his quick trips from Brussels.

BROCK: I certainly try to bring a gift if I can.

ALICE: You must have lots of money.

BROCK: Well, I suppose. I find it immoderately easy to acquire. I seem to have a sort of mathematical gift. The stock exchange. Money sticks to my fingers, I find. I triple my income. What can I do?

ALICE: It must be very tiresome.

BROCK: Oh . . . I'm acclimatizing you know. (*Smiles.*) I think everyone's going to be rich very soon. Once we've got over the effects of the war. It's going to be coming out of everyone's ears.

ALICE: Is that what you think?

BROCK: I'm absolutely sure. (*Pause.*) I do enjoy these weekends, you know. Susan leads such an interesting life. Books. Conversation. People like you. The Foreign Office can make you feel pretty isolated, also, to be honest, makes you feel pretty small, as if you're living on sufferance, you can imagine . . .

ALICE: Yes.

BROCK: Till I met Susan. The very day I met her, she showed me you must always do what you want. If you want something you must get it. I think that's a wonderful way to live don't you?

ALICE: I do. . . . .

As Susan returns, Alice complains about the quality of dope. Susan jokingly suggests that Brock might be posted to Morocco and bring back good stuff in the diplomatic pouch. Susan goes on to observe that those she has met in the diplomatic corps would probably be too dim to notice. Over Brock's protests, she tells Alice some of the rude things Brock has said about Darwin. Sensing his irritation, Susan reminds him that it was he himself who called Darwin a buffoon, a joke. "He's a joke between us," Brock replies sternly. "He's not a joke to the entire world." At Susan's suggestion, Alice goes to another room.

Brock is not too happy with the idea of Alice living with Susan. "I like her," Susan replies. "She makes me laugh." End of topic. A moment's quiet, and Brock tries to repair the damage.

BROCK: I'm sorry, I was awful, I apologize. But the work I do is not entirely contemptible. Of course our people are dull, they're stuffy, they're death. But what other world do I have?
　　Pause.
SUSAN: I think of France more than I tell you. I was seventeen and I was thrown into the war. I often think of it.
BROCK: I'm sure.
SUSAN: The most unlikely people. People I met only for an hour or two. Astonishing kindness. Bravery. The fact you could meet someone for an hour or two and see the very best of them and then move on. Can you understand?
　　Pause. Brock does not move.
For instance, there was a man in France. His code name was Lazar. I'd been there a year, I suppose, and one night I had to see him on his way. He just dropped out of the sky. An agent. He was lost. I was trying to be blasé, trying to be tough, all the usual stuff—and then suddenly I began to cry. Onto the shoulder of a man I'd never met before. But not a day goes by without my wondering where he is. . . . .
BROCK: Susan.
SUSAN: I think we should try a winter apart. I really do. I think it's all a bit easy this way. These weekends. Nothing is tested. I think a test would be good. And what better test than a winter apart?
BROCK: A winter together.
　　Pause. They smile.
SUSAN: I would love to come to Brussels, you know that. I would love to come if it weren't for my job. But the shipping office is very important to me. I do find it fulfilling. And I just couldn't let Mr. Mendlicott down.
　　Pause.
You must say what you think.
　　Brock looks at Susan hard, then shrugs and smiles.
I know you've been dreading the winter crossings, high seas . . .
BROCK: Don't patronize me, Susan.
SUSAN: Anyway, perhaps it would be really nice to meet in the spring . . .
BROCK: Please don't insult my intelligence. I know you better than you think. I recognize the signs. When you talk lovingly about the war . . . some deception usually follows.
　　Brock kisses Susan.
Goodbye.

Brock leaves. Alice returns to the room. As she and Susan prepare to go to sleep, they talk idly of prospects for amusement. Finally Alice quotes Brock on his belief that they will all be rich. "Oh really?" says Susan. "Peace and plenty," Alice responds.

Scene 5

Susan has asked Mick, a young man in his 30s, to meet her here on the Embankment across from where fireworks will be shot off as part of the May 1951 Festival of Britain. Susan works for the Festival now. She knows Mick slightly, both through his job as a food utensils supplier and as a casual friend of Alice. As they munch on the food she's lifted from the Festival's opening night dinner, she tells him why she wanted to see him: she wants him to father a child for her.

He's flattered, but he wonders why she doesn't look for someone from her own circles. She explains that she doesn't want to marry any of the people she knows.

SUSAN: I'm afraid I'm rather strong-minded as you know, and so with them I usually feel I'm holding myself in for fear of literally blowing them out the room. They are kind, they are able, but I don't see . . . why I should have to compromise, why I should have to make some sad and decorous marriage just to have a child. I don't see why any woman should have to do that.

MICK: But you don't have to marry . . .

SUSAN: Ah well . . .

MICK: Just go off with them.

SUSAN: But that's really the problem. These same men, these kind and likeable men, they do have another side to their nature and that is that they are very limited in their ideas, they are frightened of the unknown, they want a quiet life where sex is either sport or duty but absolutely nothing in between, and they simply would not agree to sleep with me if they knew it was a child I was after.

MICK: But you wouldn't have to tell them . . .

SUSAN: I did think that. But then I thought it would be dishonest. And so I had the idea of asking a person whom I barely knew.
    Pause.
MICK: What about the kid?

SUSAN: What?

MICK: Doesn't sound a very good deal. Never to see his dad . . .

SUSAN: It's not . . .

MICK: I take it that is what you mean.

SUSAN: I think it's what I mean.

MICK: Well?

SUSAN: The child will manage.

MICK: How do you know?

SUSAN: Being a bastard won't always be so bad . . .

MICK: I wouldn't bet on it.

SUSAN: England can't be like this forever.

Mick wants to know how he happened to be elected. She explains that it's the very fact that they don't live near each other and that, because of class differences, they would be unlikely to encounter each other much afterwards that makes him attractive for her purposes. Also, she rather likes him.

He says that this arrangement can't be what she really wants. No, she replies, "Deep down I'd do the whole damn thing by myself. But there we are. You're second best."

He agrees to her proposition, at the same time making a side-deal with her on some cheese graters for the Festival, and they stay to watch the fireworks. Something about this sky reminds her of the sky in France. Mick, of course, doesn't understand the reference.

Scene 6

We're back in the bed-sitting room we saw in Scene 4. It's been transformed for Susan and Alice's work purposes. At the moment, Alice is painting a design onto the naked body of a young girl named Louise. The design is an entry for an artists' party later that night which will usher in the new year—1953. Meanwhile, Susan is agonizing over the advertising job she does well and finds repellent. Alice wryly talks about the social disease she (Alice) choses to believe she's gotten as a gift once removed from the wife of a man she's been seeing.

Mick appears at the door. Louise excuses herself from the room to dress, leaving Mick alone with Susan and Alice. Susan is furious. He's gone back on their promise not to meet again. Susan angrily explains to Alice that for 18 months she and Mick met in attempts to make her pregnant. The attempts failed and, having reached the "point of decency at which the experiment should stop," Susan indeed called an end to what might technically be called their relationship. Mick complains that he feels he has been used. Susan replies that the experience has been no kind of pleasure for her, and in fact she's given up her plan, saying, "the whole exploit has broken my heart."

Mick asks if she thinks it's his fault. Susan tells him the whole object of her plan was never to have to go through this kind of scene. Now, she really must attend to the wretched advertising copy she's working on.

But Mick won't leave. He accuses Susan and Alice of being "cruel and dangerous." "You fuck people up," he tells Susan. "This little tart and her string of married men, all fucked up, all fucking ruined by this tart. And you . . . and you . . ."

Susan leaves the room and returns with her revolver which she fires over his head. *"He falls to the ground. She fires three more times."*

Scene 7

An evening in October 1956, the spacious Knightsbridge room from Scene 1 is fully furnished, being the residence of the Brocks. At rise, Brock and a Burmese gentleman named Aung, both dressed in dinner jackets, are engaged in after-dinner conversation. They are joined by Sir Leonard Darwin, who was Brock's superior in Scene 3. Darwin has missed the dinner but has come by because "there seemed nothing left to do." After introducing Darwin to Aung, Brock goes to tell

Susan of Darwin's arrival. Alone, Darwin shows good grace as Aung is almost offensively obsequious.

Susan now bursts into the room followed by her husband. Radiating forced cheer, she tells Darwin that he has found a haven in their house. She assures him nobody will breathe a word of the diplomatic catastrophe called Suez in his presence. She is quite deliberate in making this point several times. She herds Aung out of the room so that Brock and Darwin may speak alone.

During the next sequence, we get caught up on the intervening years. Brock married Susan after she suffered a breakdown. He is trying "to help her back up." Darwin assures Brock that having a wife who's a bit potty can actually be an asset in diplomatic circles. Darwin shudders when he hears that Madame Aung is in the house, too. He's never met her, but he knows the type—the cultural pretensions of such women are particularly grating. Darwin confesses he's near the end of his rope regarding his diplomatic career. "One more Aung and I throw in the can." And now Suez does indeed come up.

DARWIN: . . . . . We have been betrayed. We claim to be intervening as a neutral party in a dispute between Israel and Egypt. Last Monday the Israelis launched their attack. On Tuesday we issued our ultimatum saying both sides must withdraw to either side of the Canal. But Raymond, the Israelis, the aggressors, they were nowhere near the Canal. They'd have had to advance a hundred miles to make the retreat.

BROCK: Who told you that?

DARWIN: Last week the Foreign Secretary went abroad. I was not briefed. We believe he met with the French and the Israelis, urged the Israelis to attack. I believe our ultimatum was written in France last week, hence the mistake in the wording. The Israelis had reckoned to reach the Canal, but met with unexpectedly heavy resistance. I think the entire war is a fraud cooked up by the British as an excuse for seizing the Canal. And we, we who have to execute this policy, even we were not told.

   Pause.

BROCK: Well . . . what difference does it make?

DARWIN: My dear boy.

BROCK: I mean it . . .

DARWIN: Raymond.

BROCK: It makes no difference.

DARWIN: I was lied to.

BROCK: Yes but you were against it from the start.

DARWIN: I . . .

BROCK: Oh come on, we all were, the Foreign Office hated the operation from the first mention so what difference does it make now . . .

DARWIN: All the difference in the world.

BROCK: None at all.

DARWIN: The government lied to me.

BROCK: If the policy was wrong, if it was wrong to begin with . . .

DARWIN: They are not in good faith.

BROCK: I see, I see, so what you're saying is, the British may do anything, doesn't matter how murderous, doesn't matter how silly, just so long as we do it in good faith.

DARWIN: Yes. I would have defended it, I wouldn't have minded how damn stupid it was. I would have defended it had it been honestly done. But this time we are cowboys, and when the English are the cowboys, then in truth I fear for the future of the globe.

A pause. Darwin walks to the curtained window and stares out. Brock, left sitting, doesn't turn as he speaks.

BROCK: Eden is weak. For years he has been weak. For years people have taunted him, why aren't you strong? Like Churchill? He goes round, begins to think "I must find somebody to be strong on." He finds Nasser. Now he'll show them. He does it to impress. He does it badly. No one is impressed.

Darwin turns to look at Brock.

Mostly what we do is what we think people expect of us. Mostly it's wrong.

Susan, Alice, Aung and Madame Aung enter the room, Madame Aung talking about the wonderful new film by that Norwegian director, Ingmar Bergman. Susan jabs away at Darwin and her husband about Suez, obviously unaware of Darwin's true feelings about the matter. She shifts into demeaning comments about her marriage. Brock and Alice try to calm her down, but it is to no avail. Susan's stream of sarcasm now takes a peculiar turn into sympathy for the parachutists involved in the Suez operation.

SUSAN: . . . . . I do know how they feel. Even now. Cities. Fields. Trees. Farms. Dark spaces. Lights. The parachute opens. We descend.

Pause.

Of course we were comparatively welcome, not always ecstatic, not the Gaullists of course, but by and large we did make it our business to land in countries where we were welcome. Certainly the men were. I mean, some of the relationships, I can't tell you. I remember a colleague of mine telling me of the heat, of the smell of a particular young girl, the hot wet smell he said. Nothing since. Nothing since then. I can't see the Egyptian girls somehow . . . no. Not in Egypt now. I mean there were broken hearts when we left. I mean, there are girls today who mourn Englishmen who died in Dachau, died naked in Dachau, men with whom they had spent a single night. Well.

Pause. The tears are pouring down Susan's face, she can barely speak.

But then . . . even for myself I do like to make a point of sleeping with men I don't know. I do find once you get to know them you usually don't want to sleep with them any more . . .

Brock gets up and shouts at the top of his voice across the room.

BROCK: Please can you stop, can you stop fucking talking for five fucking minutes on end?

SUSAN: I would stop, I would stop, I would stop fucking talking if I ever heard anyone say anything worth fucking stopping talking for.

Pause. Then Darwin moves.

DARWIN: I'm sorry. I apologize. I really must go. (*Crossing the room.*) M. Aung. Farewell.

Kate Nelligan as Susan Traherne in *Plenty*

AUNG: We are behind you, sir. There is wisdom in your expedition.
DARWIN: Thank you.
AUNG: May I say sir, these gyps need whipping and you are the man to do it?
DARWIN: Thank you very much. Mme. Aung.
MME. AUNG: We never really met.
DARWIN: No. No. We never met, that is true. But perhaps before I go, I may nevertheless set you right on a point of fact. Ingmar Bergman is not a bloody Norwegian, he is a bloody Swede. (*He nods slightly.*) Good night everyone.
      Darwin goes out. . . . .
BROCK: He's going to resign.
      Pause.
SUSAN: Isn't this an exciting week? Don't you think? Isn't this thrilling? Don't you think? Everything is up for grabs. At last. We will see some changes. Thank the Lord. Now, there was dinner. I made some more dinner for Leonard. A little ham. And chicken. And some pickles and tomato. And lettuce. And there are a couple of pheasants in the fridge. And I can get twelve bottles of claret from the cellar. Why not? . . . There is plenty . . . Shall we eat again? (*Curtain.*)

ACT II

Scene 8

At the Brocks' home in Knightsbridge again, in July 1961, Brock enters the room, the furniture of which is covered in white dust sheets. He is followed by Alice and a 17-year-old girl named Dorcas. They have just returned from Darwin's funeral. Dorcas, one of Alice's history students, did not know Darwin and was brought along for the ride. Alice explains to Brock that she is now teaching in a school "for the daughters of the rich and the congenitally stupid," of whom Dorcas is almost proud to number herself one.

Susan has entered during Alice's explanation, and she now sends her husband out of the room to make tea. She tells Alice that she and Brock are supposed to leave soon to catch a plane for Iran, where her husband has been in a diplomatic post for the past three years. They had only come over for a quick visit to attend the funeral. Apparently, they were among the few present for the service. Darwin had lost a lot of his old friends by speaking out publicly on Suez. Dorcas has never heard of Suez. Alice and Susan speak affectionately of Darwin's obsession with protocol, joking about how properly and discreetly he would endeavor to conduct himself were he to come to in his coffin and find it necessary to rise from his grave.

And now to the purpose of Alice bringing Dorcas here—the girl is pregnant by a friend of Alice's and needs to borrow some money. Alice has suggested that Susan might help. Dorcas is very casual about the idea of an abortion. Susan quietly says that she is good for the money. "Kill a child. That's easy. No problem at all." Dorcas is oblivious to the way Alice and Susan stare at each other during this exchange.

Brock returns with the tea and the news that he and Susan really must leave immediately to make their flight. As Susan writes the check for Dorcas, Brock speaks of how happy they've been in Iran. The phrases he uses rather recall some of Darwin's enthusiasm for the challenge of post-war Europe in Scene 3. Susan hands Dorcas a check for the money, explaining to Brock she's lending it for an operation that will enable Dorcas to play an instrument again.

Brock asks Dorcas for help in hauling some stuff down to the car. Alone with Alice, Susan says, "I knew if I came over I would never return." She now pulls the sheets off the furniture and turns on all the lights. "I've missed you," she tells Alice. Brock appears now to ask if Susan is ready to leave.

Scene 9

In the dark, we hear an excerpt from a BBC radio interview with Susan. She talks of the faith she had in the organization that sent her to work in France during the war and, moreover, expresses her opinion that these undercover activities were one part of the effort "from which the British emerge with the greatest possible valor and distinction." No, she tells the interviewer, she never talks about the old days with her former colleagues. "We aren't clubbable."

The lights come up on a waiting room in the Foreign Office in January 1962. An aide to Sir Andrew Charleson introduces Susan to him and leaves them alone. Charleson, in his early 50s, is head of personnel. Susan has come to him behind her husband's back because she suspects that Brock is being penalized profession-ally for not returning to his post in Iran. Susan is quick to explain the fault was hers, and Charleson has a ready supply of sympathy to offer. Still, Susan presses. Is Brock's career suffering on her account?

CHARLESON: Mrs. Brock, believe me I recognize your tone. Women have come in here and used it before . . . I also have read the stories in your file, so nothing in your manner is likely to amaze. I do know exactly the kind of person you are. When you have chosen a particular course . . . (*He pauses.*) When there is something which you very badly want . . . (*He pauses again.*) But in this matter I must tell you, Mrs. Brock, it is more than likely you have met your match.

(The two of them stare straight at each other.)

We are talking of achievement at the highest level. Brock cannot expect to be cossetted through. It's not enough to be clever, everyone here is clever, everyone is gifted, everyone is diligent. These are merely the minimum skills. Far more important is an attitude of mind. Along the corridor I boast a colleague who in 1945 drafted a memorandum to the government advising them not to accept the Volkswagen works as war reparation, because the Volkswagen plainly had no commercial future. I must tell you, unlikely as it may seem, that man has risen to the very, very top. All sorts of diplomatic virtues he displays. He has forbearance. He is gracious. He is sociable. Perhaps you begin to understand . . .

SUSAN: You are saying . . .

CHARLESON: I am saying that certain qualities are valued here above a simple gift of being right or wrong. Qualities sometimes hard to define . . .

SUSAN: What you are saying is that nobody may speak, nobody may question . . .

CHARLESON: Certainly tact is valued very highly.

Pause.

SUSAN (*very low*): Tell me, Sir Andrew, do you never find it in yourself to despise a job in which nobody may speak his mind?

CHARLESON: That is the nature of the service, Mrs. Brock. It is called diplomacy. And in its practise the English lead the world. (*He smiles.*) The irony is this: we had an empire to administer, there were six hundred of us in this place. Now it's to be dismantled and there are six thousand. As your power declines, the fight among us for access to that power becomes a little more urgent, a little uglier perhaps. As our influence wanes, as our empire collapses, there is little to believe in. Behavior is all.

Pause.

This is a lesson which you both most learn.

A moment, then Susan picks up her handbag to go.

SUSAN: Sir Andrew, I must thank you for your frankness . . .

CHARLESON: Not at all.

SUSAN: I must, however, warn you of my plan. If Brock is not promoted in the next six days, I am intending to shoot myself.

Charleson calls Begley, his assistant, and they try to persuade her to go to the surgery. She has no intention of doing so, she explains in progressively agitated tones. She has a function to attend at which she is expected to be rude, and she wouldn't dream of disappointing.

CHARLESON: I think it would be better if you . . .

SUSAN (*starts to shout*): Please.

Charleson and Begley stop. Susan is hysterical. She waits a moment.

I can't . . . always manage with people.

Pause.
I think you have destroyed my husband, you see.

Scene 10

At the Brocks' home again, Easter 1962, some hours before the time of Scene 1, Brock sits figuring the finances while Alice puts leaflets into envelopes. Brock talks of the need to move to a smaller place. He is hopeful about the effect of the move. "I can't help feeling it will be better, I'm sure. Too much money. I think that's what went wrong. Something about it corrupts the will to live. Too many years spent sploshing around." We begin to get the idea that Brock and Alice trade off keeping an eye on Susan. Alice speaks ironically of some of her former friends, conveying something of the distance she has put between herself and them. Brock is an an ironic mood as well.

BROCK: Looking back, I seem to have been eating all the time. My years in the Foreign Service I mean. I don't think I missed a single canape. Not one. The silver tray flashed and bang, I was there.
ALICE: Do you miss it?
BROCK: Almost all the time. There's not much glamor in insurance, you know.
　　　He smiles.
Something in the Foreign Office suited my style. At least they were hypocrites, I do value that now. Hypocrisy does keep things pleasant for at least part of the time. Whereas down in the City they don't even try.
ALICE: You chose it.
BROCK: That's right. That isn't so strange. The strange bit is always . . . why I remain.
　　　He stands staring a moment.
Still, it gives her something new to despise. The sad thing is this time . . . I despise it as well.
　　　Alice reaches for a typed list of names, pushes aside the pile of envelopes.
ALICE: Eight hundred addresses, eight hundred names . . .
　　　Brock turns and looks at her.
BROCK: You were never attracted? A regular job?
ALICE: I never had time. Too busy relating to various young men. Falling in and out of love, turns out to be like any other career.
　　　She looks up.
I had an idea that lust . . . that lust was very good. And could be made simple. And cheering. And light. Perhaps I was simply out of my time.
BROCK: You speak as if it's over . . . . .
ALICE: That's why I feel it may be time to do good.

Susan enters in an edgy state, asking them to give her a short time alone. Brock is suspicious of a bit of blood he sees on her. Just a fingernail, she insists. Brock asks Alice to get some nembutal out of a drawer.
Susan now says she thinks that, rather than sell the house, she and Brock

should give it to Alice's charity for unmarried mothers. They should put down mattresses and thereby help rid themselves of the corruption of the money they have had. In this spirit, she has already tossed out of the window many of their expensive and fragile *objects d'art*. Susan disappears, then reappears with a couple of packing cases. The sound of the props of gracious living rattles inside. She rants about their lack of true meaning. "What is this shit? What are these godforsaken bloody awful things?" Brock confronts her.

BROCK: Which is the braver? To live as I do? Or never, ever to face life like you?

> *He holds up the small card he has found.*

This is the doctor's number, my dear. With my permission he can put you inside. I am quite capable of doing it tonight. So why don't you start to put all those things back?

> *A pause. Susan looks at him, then to Alice.*

SUSAN: Alice, would your women value my clothing?

ALICE: Well, I . . .

SUSAN: It sounds fairly silly, I have thirteen evening dresses though.

BROCK: Susan.

SUSAN: Not much use as they are. But possibly they could be re-cut. Re-sewn?

> *She reaches out and with one hand picks up an ornament from the mantelpiece which she throws with a crash into the crate. A pause.*

BROCK: Your life is selfish, self-interested gain. That's the most charitable interpretation to hand. You claim to be protecting some personal ideal, always at a cost of almost infinite pain to everyone around you. You are selfish, brutish, unkind. Jealous of other people's happiness as well, determined to destroy other ways of happiness they find. I've spent fifteen years of my life trying to help you, simply trying to be kind, and my great comfort has been that I am waiting for some indication from you . . . some sign that you have valued this kindness of mine. Some love perhaps. Love. Perhaps. Insane.

> *He smiles.*

And yet . . . I really shan't ever give up, I won't surrender till you're well again. And that to me would mean your admitting one thing: that in the life you have led you have utterly failed, failed in the very, very heart of your life. Admit it. Then perhaps you might really move on.

> *Pause.*

Now I'm going to go and give our doctor a ring. I plan at last to beat you at your own kind of game. I am going to play as dirtily and as ruthlessly as you. And this time I am certainly not giving in.

> *Brock goes out. A pause.*

SUSAN: Well.

> *Pause.*

Well, goodness. What's best to do?

> *Pause.*

What's the best way to start stripping this room?

ALICE: Susan, I think you should get out of this house. I'll help you. Any way I can.

SUSAN: Well, that's very kind.

ALICE: Please . . .

SUSAN: I'll be going just as soon as this job is done.

>   *Pause.*

ALICE: Listen, if Raymond really means what he says . . .

>   *Susan turns and looks straight at Alice.*

You haven't even asked me, Susan, you see. You haven't asked me yet what I think of the idea.

>   *Susan frowns.*

SUSAN: Really, Alice, I shouldn't need to ask. It's a very sad day when one can't help the poor.

>   *Alice suddenly starts to laugh. Susan sets off across the room, resuming a completely normal social manner.*

ALICE: For God's sake, Susan, he'll put you in the bin.

SUSAN: Don't be silly, Alice, it's Easter weekend. It must have occurred to you . . . the doctor's away.

>   *Brock reappears at the open door, the address book in his hand. Susan turns to him.*

All right, Raymond? Anything I can do? I've managed to rout out some whisky over here.

>   *She sets the bottle down on the table, next to the nembutal.*

Alice was just saying she might slip out for a moment or two. Give us a chance to sort our problems out. I'm sure if we had a really serious talk . . . I could keep going till morning. Couldn't you?

>   *Susan turns to Alice.*

All right, Alice?

ALICE: Yes. Yes, of course. I'm going, I'm just on my way.

>   *She picks up her coat and heads for the door.*

All right if I get back in an hour or two? I don't like to feel I'm intruding.

>   *She smiles at Susan, then closes the door. Susan at once goes back to the table. Brock stands watching her.*

SUSAN: Now, Raymond. Good. Let's look at this thing.

>   *Susan pours out a spectacularly large scotch, filling the glass to the very rim. Then she pushes it a few inches across the table to Brock.*

Where would be the best place to begin?

Scene 11

Two months later, Susan and a man lie on a bed in a shabby hotel room in Blackpool. He traced her through her radio interview. The BBC gave him her address. He'd gone there to find she'd departed. He had met Brock. "He said there'd been trouble. He'd only just managed to get back into his house." No, the man says in response to her question, Brock did not seem to be angry. Mostly he seemed to be missing her.

Susan tells the man about her habit of losing control, of the time she shot a man (not seriously) and Brock bought her out of trouble and married her. The man offers to be similarly candid, but Susan would prefer not to know. Their business together (and the grass they smoked) finished, they think about leaving the room and going their separate ways.

The man now begins to talk about his disappointment with postwar life. He'd hoped to lead a life with an edge to it. "Some sort of feeling their death was worthwhile." He tells of the soul-shrivelling compromises.

Susan tells him she's just about to "go." "I've eaten nothing. So I just go . . ."

"I hate, I hate this life that we lead," says the man. Susan, about to drift away, asks for a kiss. He tries to embrace her, but she flops listlessly back to the bed. The man picks up his suitcase. "A fine undercover agent will move so that nobody can ever tell he was there." He has turned off the lights. In the darkness, she asks his name. "Code name," he insists. "Code name Lazar." *"Lazar opens the door of the room. At once music plays. Where you would expect a corridor you see the fields of France shining brilliantly in a fierce green square. The room scatters."*

Scene 12

The years fall away to that day in August 1944 when the war was finally over in France. On a bright, bright French hillside, Susan, age 19 and looking *"radiantly well,"* meets a French farmer. He is gloomy and seemingly not terribly moved by the news of the end of the war. He complains of what he expects to be a bad harvest this year.

FRENCHMAN: . . . . . The land is very poor. I have to work each moment of the day.
SUSAN: But you'll be glad I think. You're glad as well?
         Susan turns, so the Frenchman cannot avoid the question. He reluctantly concedes.
FRENCHMAN: I'm glad. Is something good, is true. (*He looks puzzled.*) The English . . . have no feelings, yes? Are stiff?
SUSAN: They hide them, hide them from the world.
FRENCHMAN: Is stupid.
SUSAN: Stupid, yes. It may be . . .
         Pause.
FRENCHMAN: Huh?
SUSAN: That things will quickly change. We have grown up. We will improve our world.
         The Frenchman stares at Susan.
FRENCHMAN (*gravely*): Perhaps . . . perhaps you like some soup. My wife.
SUSAN: All right.
         Susan smiles. They look at each other, about to go.
FRENCHMAN: The walk is down the hill. Comrade.
SUSAN: My friend.
         Pause.
There will be days and days like this.

FOXFIRE

A Play With Songs in Two Acts

BY SUSAN COOPER AND HUME CRONYN

MUSIC BY JONATHAN HOLTZMAN

LYRICS BY SUSAN COOPER, HUME CRONYN AND JONATHAN HOLTZMAN

Cast and credits appear on page 344

*SUSAN COOPER (co-author) was born in 1935 in Burnham in Buckinghamshire, England. She remembers beginning to write at about age 8, and at 10 she wrote three plays for the puppet theater built by the boy next door. She graduated from Somerville College, Oxford in 1956 and went on to the London Sunday Times as a reporter and feature writer (Ian Fleming was her first boss). She has become best known as a novelist (*The Dark Is Rising, Behind the Golden Curtain*), the author of children's books and of a biography of J.B. Priestley, and the winner of the Newbery Medal in the U.S., the Carnegie Honor Awards in Great Britain and other international citations.*

Ms. Cooper also wrote short pieces for the theater and TV, "intermittently," so that her collaboration with Hume Cronyn is her first full professional production and first Best Play. With Mr. Cronyn, she has also written a three-hour TV play, The Dollmaker, *commissioned by Jane Fonda. Ms. Cooper is married to an American; they have two children and live in Cambridge, Mass.*

HUME CRONYN (co-author) was born in London, Ontario July 18, 1911 and received his education at Ridley College, McGill University and the American Academy of Dramatic Arts, from which he graduated in 1934. His first appearance as an actor in the professional theater had already taken place with the National Theater Stock Company in Washington, D.C. in 1931. His first appearance on the New York stage took place in Hipper's Holiday *in 1934, and there has followed an internationally distinguished acting career on stage, screen and television, sometimes co-starring with his equally renowned wife, Jessica Tandy (as in* The Fourposter, The Gin Game *and* Foxfire*), honored by Tony, Obie and many other awards, with a list of credits far too long to be detailed here.*

Cronyn has also served as director and producer in all dramatic media, and he is the author of the screen versions of Rope *(1947) and* Under Capricorn *(1948), as well as of short stories and articles. With* Foxfire, *in collaboration with Susan Cooper, he now has entered the field of professional playwriting with a Best Play the first time out.* Foxfire *was produced at the Stratford, Ontario Festival in 1980 and the Guthrie Theater in Minneapolis in 1981 before appearing on Broadway Nov. 11, 1982.*

Cronyn helped with the founding of the Guthrie Theater and the Phoenix Theater. He has served the American Academy of Dramatic Arts and the Actors Lab, Los Angeles as a lecturer and the Stratford, Ontario Festival as a member of its board of governors. The professional organizations of which he is a member include AFTRA, the Screen Actors and Writers Guilds, Actors' Equity, the Society of Stage Directors and Choreographers and the Dramatists Guild. The Cronyns have three children and live in New York State.

JONATHAN HOLTZMAN (composer and co-lyricist) was born in Neptune, N.J. in 1953 and was writing music for his Brielle School band at age 10. At 18 he was faced with a choice between acting and composing, chose music and received his BA in music from New York University. The author of many pop/rock and rhythm and blues recordings, he was selected in auditions in 1979 by the authors of Foxfire *to write their show's songs, of which "My Feet Took t' Walkin' " is the principal number.*

Mr. Holtzman is special projects director of the American Guild of Authors and Composers (the songwriters' guild), where he conducts classes in the art, and he is the originator of the New York Songwriters Contest. He lives in New York City and is married, with one child.

Time: Now—and before that

Place: Rabun County, Georgia

ACT I

SYNOPSIS: The dooryard of the mountain farm "Stony Lonesome" is backed by a vista of the Blue Ridge Mountains (*"The land falls off steeply upstage.*

Jessica Tandy as Annie Nations in *Foxfire*

Nothing can be seen between set and distant mountains except perhaps the tops of tall trees or a tumbledown shed roof"). The view is framed by the porch of the farm cabin at left and a shed at right, with a path leading down the mountain at right and access to the orchard and other parts of the farm at left. The porch is furnished with a sturdy table and a rocker, and scattered around is the paraphernalia of life in a mountain home.

The occupants of Stony Lonesome become visible as the lights come up: Annie Nations (*"a mountain woman of 79, wearing an apron over a long dark dress"*) sitting in her rocker wearing steel-rimmed spectacles and sewing a quilt; and Hector Nations (*"77, dressed in the worn and patched workclothes of a mountain farmer"*) leaning against a porch pillar enjoying the view, while the voice of their son Dillard is heard offstage, in their imagination, singing of how he left the homeplace because "My feet took t' walkin'."

Hector accuses Annie of worrying about Dillard, who has written to say that he is giving a concert this weekend at Hiawassee Fairground, 30 miles from here, and will stop by to see his mother.

HECTOR: What's chewin' on y'?

ANNIE: Don't rightly know. Wish he'd told more 'bout the children. I ain't heared from Cheryl since last Christmas.

HECTOR: I never wrote a letter in m' life, 'cept t' President Hoover—an' he never answered that.

ANNIE: It ain't hardly the same.

HECTOR: Well, he says everythin's fine.

ANNIE: No, he says, "Don't worry, everythin's fine." Makes me uneasy.

HECTOR: Dillard always done that.

ANNIE: He's a good boy.

HECTOR: He's a grown man! Traipsin' round the country with a guitar—what kinda work's that?

ANNIE: Now, Hector.

HECTOR: Well, this land woulda took care a' him.

ANNIE: He weren't cut out.

Dillard's wife Cheryl gave him two beautiful children (though Hector hardly knows them because he usually makes himself scarce when his son's family visits the farm) and seems to be making Dillard happy, though she never did like these mountains. Annie goes inside to the kitchen where she is preparing to make souse meat from a hog's head, but Hector goes on talking just as though she were there, telling how his father brought his mother up here and they raised nine children.

Annie brings the pot out onto the porch where it's cooler, but Hector hears someone coming up the hill and drifts off left to the orchard. Prince Carpenter (*"in his mid-40s: an amiable, successful, hard-working real estate man with a ready sense of humor . . . . . a shrewd but not unprincipled operator"*) appears and introduces himself. He is a local boy who met Hector when he was up here handling a project for the Scouts. Now he represents the Mountain Development Corporation, which wants to buy this farm.

Annie startles Prince by placing a bloody hog's head before him and going to work with a knife, extracting the eye. Annie isn't quite strong enough to do the job properly and asks Prince to help her. Prince cuts squeamishly into the eye socket and splatters himself as he does so.

Prince asks Annie about her family. She has two boys and a girl—and five grandchildren—all living away.

PRINCE: Then you're all alone up here. You and Mr. Nations, that is.

ANNIE: Most times. Course, we got good neighbors.

PRINCE: Sure. Not too many of them left, though. The Harts gone, the Angels, the Burrells, the Bookers.

ANNIE: You knew all them folk?

PRINCE: You betcha. Dealt with every one a' them.
   He hands Annie back the knife.

ANNIE: Y' done it! Thank y'.
   She continues to cut and trim, dropping scraps in the bucket and waving away flies.

PRINCE: About *your* land. I made Mr. Nations an offer for it, that summer, but he wasn't of a mind to sell.

ANNIE: Oh, I knowed that.

PRINCE: Well, ma'am, we're now prepared to double that offer. One hundred thousand dollars cash down, on delivery of a free and clear title.

Prince has plans for this place: "Vacation homes—beautiful! Caddies, Continentals—none of y'r camper people, nothin' like that." Annie agrees to talk it over with Hector who, she tells Prince, is "Up in th' orchard." Prince suggests that he have a word with Hector himself. Annie observes, "You could try."

Prince, rinsing the traces of the hog's head from his hands, informs Annie that another car is on its way up the road and warns her against "Florida sharpies" who might take advantage of her. She promises to take no action without consulting Prince. He goes off to find Hector, just as Hector appears around the corner of the house, announcing, "He ain't gonna find me."

Hector advises Annie, "All y' got t' do is say no," and he decries city folk who go around picking what they want from stores instead of making or growing it and live like rolling stones, like Dillard. He indicates their wagon, long unused: "Remember this? *That's* when y' had t' know how t' make a livin'. First thing I built. Used t' fill her up with corn, sorghum, cabbage, take the stuff t' market —bring it right back home agin an' feed it t' the hogs! Ol Hoover's time. If it hadn't been f'r corn liquor an' smart tradin' we'd a had an empty table round here."

Hector hears someone else approaching up the hill and departs as Holly Burrell (*"about 25; attractive, bright and slightly offbeat; an engaging mixture of eagerness and vulnerability"*) enters. She is a local girl who has a successful teaching career in the high school and loves the mountains. She calls Mrs. Nations "Aunt Annie." She has brought Annie a poster advertising Dillard's concert and offers to take Annie to it—today is Saturday, August 30, Annie learns, and the concert is tonight.

Annie goes indoors to wash up, taking the hog's head with her, as Dillard

Nations appears. ("*He wears time-weathered boots, jeans, shirt and denim jacket: a man in his early 40s with an attractive, lived-in face. He is carrying a mesh bag of oranges.*") Holly greets Dillard and asks after his wife Cheryl (not accompanying him here) and his children ("They got their mother's looks and their daddy's talent"). Holly goes inside to tell Annie that Dillard has arrived, then comes back out.

HOLLY: It's good to see you again.

DILLARD: Hey, will you do something for me?

HOLLY: I'll try.

DILLARD: It ain't hard—jus' tell me who the hell you are?

HOLLY: You don't remember?

DILLARD: Guess not.

HOLLY: Right here on this porch. Your pa was in the rocking chair, and—oh God!—I asked him if he'd ever shot anybody. And you sang a hymn—right over there.

DILLARD: I'll be damned—you're that kid with the tape recorder . . . Holly—?

HOLLY: Burrell.

DILLARD: Holly Burrell. You still live around here?

HOLLY: I teach at the high school.

Annie comes out in a clean apron, excited.

ANNIE: Where is he?

DILLARD: Hello, Ma.

He goes to her and kisses her; she returns it a trifle perfunctorily.

ANNIE: I weren't expectin' you.

DILLARD: Didn't you get my letter?

ANNIE: I got mixed up. You playin' tonight?

DILLARD: Yes ma'am.

ANNIE: But y' can stay over.

DILLARD: 'Fraid not, Ma—I gotta get back to the kids. I told you it'd have to be a real short visit.

ANNIE: Well, I ain't gonna cry about it. I got y' now.

HOLLY: I'm taking her to the concert.

ANNIE: Oh, I'd dearly love that, Holly, I dearly would, but it's a far piece for old bones like me. An' I don't believe Hector'd go. Let me jus' turn down that damper—I'll think about it.

She goes hastily into the kitchen.

DILLARD: She won't come. She don't go nowhere. Jus' makes it down to the store an' the post office when she has to. She's glued up here.

There's a pause.

HOLLY: Dillard—she said "Hector."

DILLARD: Yup.

HOLLY: Your pa.

DILLARD: That's right.

HOLLY: But he's dead.

DILLARD: Not for her he ain't. (*He sighs.*) Go in the bedroom there, his clothes are still hangin' up, his tools under the bed. I moved 'em once, an' she put 'em right back. When Pa was alive, she used t' wash an' get into her nightgown behind a curtain in the corner. Curtain's still there.

HOLLY: Is she all right?

DILLARD: In the head, you mean? She's clearer'n I am.

Annie comes back with blackberry drinks for all. Holly and Dillard press Annie to come to the concert (she hasn't heard him at a concert since he won a medal at the State Fair at age 17). Dillard promises to sing something special for his mother, and Holly offers to bring her straight home afterwards, assuring Annie that she doesn't need anything special to wear. Annie finally accepts: "I guess maybe it'll be all right. Just this once."

As Holly leaves, she notices a man in the orchard—"Jus' some man pickin' apples," Annie informs them. Alone with his mother, Dillard reports that his wife and family are O.K., and that one of his children is learning the guitar. Dillard will play an engagement in Tampa this winter in order to be near his family, and he wants his mother to join them down in Florida.

DILLARD: . . . . . You don't have t' sell the house—jus' come where I can keep an eye on you.

ANNIE: Now Dillard honey, don't start that agin.

DILLARD: It'd mean a lot t' the kids.

ANNIE: I belong here.

DILLARD: Come for the winter, then.

ANNIE: Who'd feed the chickens?

DILLARD: Ma—y'can buy eggs. (*Pause.*) It's Pa, ain't it?

Annie doesn't answer. After a moment Dillard gets up and moves to her. He kneels in front of her and takes her two hands in his.

Now I ain't gonna say no prayers—I jus' want you t' listen t' me. Ma—you ain't s' young no more. You're up here all on y'r own. An' winter's comin'—y' c'd trip on them steps an' jus' lie there an' freeze. Now you let Pa rest, an' come live with us.

ANNIE: I ain't seen y' look s' serious since y' used t' talk about y'r music.

DILLARD: I ain't talkin' about music now. Please, Ma.

ANNIE: No, you let me go on. You're talkin' about y'r pa restin'—an' he is. Right here. Up in the old orchard, with *his* ma and pa, an' y'r little brother an' sister. An' when my time comes I'm gonna lay right down there beside him. Nothin's ever gonna change that—not you, nor Florida, nor nothin' . . . . .

Annie is determined to continue sleeping in the same bed she's slept in since she was married, and Dillard means to continue to try to convince her to move. Dillard notices that the smokehouse has caved in and its door is broken open—it seems Annie was caught in there for a whole night after the door stuck and was released the next morning only because a neighbor came to cut some wood and heard her cries for help. That is just the sort of accident Dillard fears might happen to his mother. She escapes into the house while he expostulates, "You could break y'r neck up here and nobody'd know!—an' all 'cause a' Pa!"

Prince Carpenter comes around the corner of the house with a basket of apples he's picked. He sees the oranges Dillard has brought for his mother, guesses that he's from Florida and assumes he's a rival real estate developer. Prince informs Dillard that it's no sale because Hector Nations "won't budge . . . . . ain't *never* goin' to sell." Prince pretends he's just talked to Hector, until Dillard reveals that he's the son and that his father has been dead for five years. Undaunted, Prince informs Dillard that he has doubled his original offer and hopes that Annie will decide to move on, like Prince's own mother, to some nice little place with all the conveniences in a town like Greenville, where someone can keep an eye on her.

DILLARD: Ma's got good neighbors.

PRINCE: Had, Dillard, had. You're outa touch. Must get mighty lonely up here —guess that's why she brought back y'r pa, huh?

DILLARD: You knew about that?

PRINCE: Hell, Dillard, this is my territory.

DILLARD: You didn't call her on it.

PRINCE: What do you take me for? I wasn't about to spoil anythin' for a fine old lady. I like these people, an' everybody likes ol' Prince.

DILLARD: This place ain't for sale.

PRINCE: You won't get a better offer. We can't use all the land anyway. There's about six acres of swamp—plus your old burial ground up there. Law won't let us touch that. Don't just piss on it, Dillard—think it over.

DILLARD: You're wasting y'r breath, Mr. Carpenter. It ain't my land—it ain't my life.

PRINCE: It's *your* mother. Face it, Dillard—everythin's changed since you an' me grew up in these mountains. The kids with any get up an' go have got up an' went—jus' like you did. The old ones are jus' hangin' on like foxfire on rotten wood.

Prince departs as Annie returns to the porch and discusses with Dillard the disposition of the farm. Hector would have told Prince flatly no sale, and Annie has no mind to sell but would give it to Dillard and his children (who will inherit it anyway) if they wanted it. Dillard declines: "I do love this place, but I can't live here." Annie remarks sadly, "No. You never could, once you was growed."

Dillard advises Annie not to talk to the real estate man if he should return. It's time for Dillard to leave, and Hector enters and watches as Annie tells Dillard to give her love to the children and promises to give his to Hector.

DILLARD: . . . . . I won't try t' see you after the show—I gotta get back t'Atlanta an' catch that plane. Hope y' like it.

ANNIE: I'll clap real loud.

DILLARD: Sorry it was s' short. (*He is finding it very hard to leave.*) I'll write when I get back. Don't you go closin' no more doors on y'rself.

     He's gone. Annie stands still, looking after him. we hear the treefrogs.

ANNIE: He sent you his love.

HECTOR: I heared.

ANNIE: Somethin's wrong, Hector.

HECTOR: He on at you t' go live with him agin'? (*Annie doesn't answer.*) That's it, ain't it? Come t' Florida. Well, *I* ain't goin'.

ANNIE: He ain't asked y'.

HECTOR: You gonna leave me? You're way too old f'r that now.

ANNIE: What I'm too old for I'll decide. Dillard's goin' through rough waters.

HECTOR: Well, we went through 'em too.

ANNIE: Times is different.

HECTOR: They ain't harder. Like the Bible says, man is born unto trouble—not just t' pickin' a banjo.

ANNIE: Hector honey, the Lord forgive me, but I sometimes get a little tired a' what the Bible says. An' he weren't born t' trouble—he made a good start. April 7th, 1945. You were right there beside me.

Annie goes indoors, as the lighting changes to a flashback. The doctor (*"in his 60s, a weary, kindly man"*) comes up the hill. Hector assures him that Annie is O.K. and is surprised to learn that the doctor will want $5 cash—just about all Hector has—for delivering the baby, unlike the midwife of 13 years before, who took her fee in liquor and tobacco.

The doctor lays out his instruments, as Annie appears—42 and very pregnant —bringing clean rags, a quilt and a sheet. Hector continues badgering the doctor about the midwifery of bygone days.

HECTOR: Them old grannies had a whole heap of experience. Seems t' me there ain't nothin' t' beat self-experience.

DOCTOR: And she took the baby upside down, so its liver wouldn't grow to its sides.

HECTOR: What d' you do?

DOCTOR: I don't give it catnip tea either.

HECTOR: Cures the hives.

DOCTOR: Newborn babies don't have the hives.

He turns to Annie, takes the sheet from her pile, indicates the table. You scrubbed this like I told you?

ANNIE: It's clean.

The doctor is spreading the sheet on the table. Aunt Bessie always took care a' me in the bed.

DOCTOR: I'm sure she did.

HECTOR: Built that bed m'self. Aunt Bessie liked it fine.

DOCTOR: Too soft, too low—and I've got a bad back.

The doctor instructs Hector to wash his hands in whiskey. Annie is seized with pain, and together the men get her onto the table. Hector insists on bringing catnip tea, but the doctor waves it away and tests Annie's blood pressure. At Annie's request, Hector covers her with the quilt while the doctor washes his hands and Hector tells how they lost two previous children: one strangled on the umbilical cord at birth and one carried off at age 5 by the flu.

Hector fetches an axe to put under the table to cut the pain—and now he must wash his hands again. Annie asks Hector to sing something. Hector obliges with

"Young lady take a warnin'/Take a warnin' from me/Don't waste your affection-/On a young man so free." He breaks off, startled, when he sees the doctor handle a pair of forceps, but he takes up the song again as the lights fade and then come up on Dillard dressed in white for his concert and singing a lilting version of the same song: "They'll hug you, they'll kiss you/They'll tell you more lies/Than the crossties on the railroad/Or the stars in the skies."

Dillard speaks in a mountain vernacular exaggerated for the stage performance, introducing a number about his father's trading skill, presented in song and instrumentally by Dillard and his "Stony Lonesome Boys":

> Oh he'd study an' he'd scratch an' he'd grow what he was able
> But he could not grow the money to put meat upon the table;
> So he'd swap a little somethin' and he'd always get back more
> An' when he got through tradin' there was cash for the store:
> He was a sweet talker
> Pa was a tradin' man;
> Sweet talker
> Best count y'r fingers if y' shake his hand:
> A sweet talker . . . . .
> Ain't nothin' like a tradin' fool:
> He was a sweet talker,
> He could swap a bent nail for a blue-eyed mule!

Dillard announces a song to be sung especially for his mother, who is in the audience. It is the song which was heard offstage in the opening scene:

> Sure I remember the homeplace,
> Sure I remember it clear,
> Because the day that I left her
> Was just this time of year;
> I could see her smile, almost every mile,
> But my feet took to walkin',
> My feet took to walkin' . . .

Lights fade on Dillard's concert and come up on Annie and Holly returning to Stony Lonesome later that evening, in the moonlight. Annie was impressed by the applause. While Holly goes inside to make tea, Annie sits and is soon joined by Hector, who reproaches her for going off and forgetting to feed the chickens. Annie tells Hector about the song celebrating his trading skill.

To Annie and Holly's astonishment, Dillard appears coming up the hill—he's decided to stay over until the next day. Dillard wants to know how they liked his performance. "Real nice" is Annie's comment, though she noticed what hot work it was and promises to wash Dillard's shirt tomorrow. "Y'r pa woulda bin proud a' you, boy," Annie tells her son before she goes inside to bed after the tiring day.

Dillard presses Holly to tell him what she thought of his performance.

HOLLY: Well, loud and . . . joky. Oh Dillard, I'm no critic.
DILLARD: What didn't you like?

HOLLY (*hesitates*): Well, I tell y'—us'uns down here in good ol' Rabun County ain't all hillbillies.

DILLARD: I am. Up there I am. That's just what they want. I do what I have t' do for the customers.

HOLLY: D'you have to dress up like an ice-cream soda?

DILLARD: All part a' the image.

HOLLY: It's not you.

DILLARD: Now what d' you know about me?

HOLLY: I know we both come from the same place, and we don't talk like Li'l Abner. Turning your daddy into a joke—you're a singer. You sounded like a salesman.

DILLARD: I'm sweet-talkin', honey—jus' like m' pa. He used t' say, y' make a nickel any way y' can.

HOLLY: He made it by plain hard work! I remember your daddy. He wasn't all sweet talk.

Holly carries a bucket off to get water while Dillard, remembering the past of 30 years ago, evokes a memory of his father making the rocker which is now on the porch. While working on the chair, Hector tells how he once eked out a living: "First job I had after I married y'r ma paid ten cents an hour. Farmin'. Couldn't make it—no way. So I started diggin' wells. Dug 'em eighty, a hundred foot deep. Dollar a foot. That's good quick money—but mean work. Y're down in that hole, y' look up and the sky ain't no bigger'n a nickel. Sometimes y'hit gas. Comes spewin' outa the bank—sounds like bees swarmin'. They don't pull you out quick, y're a goner. I had a moustache in those days, sandy-colored. Gas turned it blacker'n a crow." One day a jokester threw a live cat into the hole with Hector, and Hector managed to kill it with a shovel before it tore him to pieces. After that, Annie wouldn't let him dig wells any more.

Back in the present, Holly returns and carries water into the house, while Dillard takes from his guitar case a pair of life-sized paper cutouts of a boy of 8 and a girl of 5—images made by Dillard's children, a present for their grandmother. He pins them on the wall so they'll be the first thing Annie sees when she wakes up.

Holly apologizes to Dillard for criticizing his performance (she likes the way he used to sing and play the guitar solo). She asks after Cheryl, whom Dillard describes as "fastest credit-card in the South"—a city girl.

Dillard mentions Prince Carpenter's offer to buy this place. Holly warns him against it; her family place went that route, and now "my daddy's boxed up in a little house in town, staring at the walls." She hints that Dillard and Cheryl might have an ulterior motive in asking Annie to move near them, so Grandmother could take care of the children sometimes. On the contrary, Dillard declares, it's Annie they would want to look after and keep safe. Holly replies that Annie isn't afraid to live alone up here, and her visions of Hector mean more to her than the conveniences of civilization. "Don't push too hard, Dillard. Just think about it—is leaving here what she wants—or what you want?" Commenting that she still likes the way Dillard *used* to sing, Holly departs.

After Holly is gone, Dillard picks up the song "My feet took t' walkin" in his simple, non-concert style, and Annie appears in the doorway in her nightdress, listening. Hector also comes in.

DILLARD (*sings*):
    The wild rose hung by the roadside
    With the honeysuckle above
    An' the breeze was gently singin',
    As sweet as the mournin' dove;
    An' I've never found such a heartbreak sound
    Till my feet took t' walkin',
    My feet took t' walkin',
    No sense in talkin' it out—
        He breaks off suddenly, striking a discord on the guitar, and sits brooding. We hold for a moment on Annie watching him and Hector watching her. Then the lights go down. Curtain.

ACT II

Early the next morning, Hector is gazing at the mountains while Annie, having washed Dillard's shirt, enters with a pot of coffee. Dillard enters in undershirt and jeans. He has found the guitar he played in childhood and starts tuning it.

Annie questions Dillard about his family and finds that the children are staying with friends—Cheryl is away. Annie serves Dillard the coffee, while Hector comments that there's something Dillard isn't telling, but it's bound to come out.

DILLARD: Ma? When you talk t' Pa—d'y' see him?
ANNIE: Clear as clear.
DILLARD. But is he *there?*
HECTOR: I'm here.
ANNIE: Sometimes.
DILLARD: Can y' touch him?
ANNIE: Y'r pa weren't much f'r touchin'.
DILLARD: Y' had five kids, f'r God's sake!
ANNIE (*reprovingly*): That's right. F'r the Lord's sake—an' mine and y'r pa's —an' for this place.
DILLARD: Why this place?
ANNIE: What else is there? Fam'ly's gotta have a place.
    Pause.
DILLARD: Y' remember the time I brought Cheryl an' the kids up here jus' before Pa died? Pa planted a tree. I remember it real well. You was holdin' young Heckie by the hand while he tromped down the dirt, an' Pa said, "That's *your* tree, boy. Now y' got somethin' here belongs t' you."
HECTOR: I didn't say that. Said, "Now y' got roots here, boy."

Dillard wants to know whether his mother always loved his father. Not at first, Annie admits (and Hector disappears, not wanting to hear this). She was a bit

Hume Cronyn, Keith Carradine and Jessica Tandy in *Foxfire*

scared of him at first. She remembers a day of corn-shucking, with the fiddles playing and the men competing to find a jug of whiskey hidden in the pile of corn —and the first one to find a red ear got to kiss the prettiest girl.

Annie goes back 62 years in memory to the sound of the fiddles, and the square dancing, and Hector triumphantly waving the red ear, then awkwardly kissing Annie; then confessing to her that he didn't really find a red ear, he had one hidden in his pocket. He wanted to create this opportunity of asking her to marry him and raise a family together on the homeplace. Annie protests that she's still in school, and besides, she's scared of him. She likes him, but, "You're too— hasty." Hector promises to change, and to take care of her, as the lights indicate a change back to the present, where Annie tells Dillard she made Hector wait two years for her hand. Dillard wishes he and Cheryl had waited, too.

DILLARD (*not looking at her*): She's gone, Ma.
ANNIE: Gone?
DILLARD: Took off. Left.
ANNIE: Why?
DILLARD: Lots a' reasons.
ANNIE: You strike her?
DILLARD: No!—Mebbe I should've.
ANNIE: Another man?
DILLARD: Yup.
ANNIE: Did she take the children?
DILLARD: They didn't have room in the trunk. She wants a divorce. Got herself a lawyer.
ANNIE: What you gonna do about it?
DILLARD: I ain't gonna let her have my kids.
ANNIE: Her kids too.
DILLARD: She quit. I didn't.
ANNIE: How you gonna look after two younguns—you travellin' all the time?
DILLARD: I'll work somethin' out. They're all I got. And godammit, I'm their pa.
ANNIE (*wearily*): Yeah, you're their pa, but y' got no wife an' no real home.
DILLARD: I'm way ahead a' you, Ma. I cain't come back here.
        Pause.
ANNIE (*slowly*): You want—I should go there?
DILLARD (*passionately*): No! Yes, of course I do! I been tryin' f'r years—but not jus' t' bail me out. No way! I don't want that—an' I don't wanta wait for that phone call tells me t' come carry you out feet first. It's not *me,* it's *you.* Y' cain't make it alone, an' Pa's dead! (*Wildly.*) How do I get through t' you on that? He's dead—dead!

Annie stares Dillard down, then asks him gently if he doesn't sometimes hear his father's voice too. Yes, always telling him things he'd rather not hear, Dillard admits. As the lights indicate a flashback to a time when Dillard was 16, Dillard continues strumming while his father returns from working in the fields and is annoyed to learn that Dillard hasn't yet checked the planting calendar, as he was told to do. While Hector goes inside to change his clothes, Dillard reveals to his mother that he earned $5 playing at a dance and offers to buy eggs—the chickens aren't laying well. Annie is grateful for Dillard's offer, but her immediate reaction is, "Don't you tell y'r pa."

Hector comes in with the planting calendar. Dillard assures him he's done all his other chores: "Brought in the wood, filled the buckets, watered the stock, mucked out the stall, cleaned the trough, collected the eggs—there was only three." Tomorrow, then, Hector decides, they'll plant potatoes.

DILLARD: I though y' wanted me t' paint the barn.
HECTOR: Not tomorrow.
DILLARD: But it's gonna be fine. We got all next week t' plant taters.
HECTOR: No we ain't. It's new moon Wednesday.
DILLARD: We shoulda done it today, then.
HECTOR: Signs was in the feet today.
DILLARD: Oh Pa. What's the difference?
ANNIE: (*warning*): Dillard . . .
DILLARD: Well . . . it's old-timey talk, Ma.
HECTOR: An' what's wrong with that?
DILLARD: Nothin', I guess.
HECTOR: You get it straight about taters now. Y' always plant 'em in the last quarter. Y' plant 'em in the light a' the moon, they make all vine and no tater. Any fool knows that.
DILLARD: Yes, Pa.
ANNIE: People's been goin' by the signs for a long time, boy.
DILLARD (*sighs*): I know.
ANNIE: We don't never kill a hog on the new a' the moon, y' know that. Y'r cracklin's'll come out all soft an' puffy if y' do.

Dillard quotes the County Agent, Wilson, who teaches a course in tenth grade (and who also plays the guitar), that there's no scientific basis for the so-called Signs. Hector, irritated, defies the learned scientist to stand an egg on end as he proceeds to do—by putting it down hard enough to crack and flatten the shell at the base. He then quotes Genesis: "Let there be light in the firmament t' divide night from day, an' let them be f'r *signs.*"

Dillard cites a nearby family who ignored their grandfather's advice about the Signs, did just the opposite and harvested a fine crop of corn. (Hector declares, "Foolishness. If they'd planted it in the right Sign, they'd a got *twice* as fine a crop.") And Wilson consistently gets a good crop.

HECTOR: I'm gettin' a mite tired a' that feller's name.
DILLARD: He plants by the weather an' the seasons.
HECTOR (*with his last ounce of patience*): An' I plant by what controls the weather an' the seasons.
DILLARD: Oh Pa.
HECTOR (*erupting*): Don't you *Oh Pa* me. You get that know-all outa your voice, boy.

DILLARD: But y' can't prove it, Pa.

HECTOR: Don't you tell me I ain't proved it!

ANNIE (*hurriedly*): Mr. Wilson jus' don't understand the way we do things. Now you fetch me a cup and I'll save that yolk.

>*Dillard rises, starts to cross.*

HECTOR: It ain't just his Mr. Wilson. Now you listen t' me, boy. You been gettin' way above y'rself lately. Always makin' out like we don't know nothin'. Well, we know a goddam sight more than some a' these big-talkin' friends a' yours!

>*Dillard ducks into the kitchen.*

ANNIE: There's no need t' cuss in front a' the boy, Hector.

HECTOR: There's no need f'you an' me t' spat in front a' him neither, but this is *my* house, an' if I have t' cuss t' get through t' him, I'll cuss. I bin workin' this land thirty-five years, an m'daddy thirty years before that. He taught me, an' I got it all uphill tryin' t' teach *him*. There's no guitar-playin' teacher c'n tell y' —y'learn it by doin' it!

>*Dillard has returned with the cup. Annie retrieves the leaking egg.*

If you want t' study farmin', y' c'd keep y'r eyes open right here. Seems like every time I turn round y'r pickin' at that thing! That ain't no fit occupation f'r a man!

DILLARD (*stung*): I made five dollars pickin' at this thing!

HECTOR: How'd y' do that?

ANNIE (*hastily*): Hector, y'ought t' look t' Beauty real quick.

HECTOR: Why?

ANNIE: Seems like she's got the heaves.

HECTOR (*back to Dillard*): How'd you make five dollars?

ANNIE: Her sides is goin' in and out like the bellows!

HECTOR: How'd y' make it?

DILLARD (*subdued, lost*): Playin' at the dance.

HECTOR: Sat'day night?

DILLARD: Yes sir.

>*Pause.*

HECTOR: You tol' me you was goin' coon-huntin'.

DILLARD: Yes sir.

HECTOR: You tol' me you never even *seen* a coon.

DILLARD: That was true, Pa.

But the rest of it was a lie. Hector hands Dillard his jackknife and orders him to go cut a switch about the thickness of a finger. Annie pleads for Dillard, but Hector is adamant. He feels that Annie has always been too soft in handling their sons (another one, Jed, left and hasn't been back in eight years).

Dillard returns with the switch, and Hector takes him into the house to punish him for the lie. When Annie hears the blows begin to fall, she tries to distract herself by seizing a broom and sweeping the porch, but she feels each of them herself.

Hector comes back outside, breaks the switch, throws it away and goes to see about the mare, Beauty. Annie tells Hector she lied about Beauty, but Hector stalks off anyway, with Annie calling after him, "I'm right sorry for y', Hector!"

The time changes to the present, where Dillard is telling his mother that the whipping didn't hurt because he had put the planting calendar into his britches. He doesn't remember pain, he remembers only anger. He also remembers that his brother, Jed, was almost murderously furious at Hector when he left home (and they also have a sister, Millie, whose oldest boy is studying for the priesthood).

Dillard has to leave now, but he promises to bring the children back for Thanksgiving. Meanwhile, Annie won't feel lonely, as she has both the Lord and Hector looking after her. As Dillard goes into the house to get his things, Hector comes to watch him leave. Annie tells Hector she always wished to have her family around her and is tired of watching her children disappear down the hill one by one. When Dillard reappears, Annie kisses him and waves him away, then sits cradling his old guitar in her lap.

HECTOR: He'll be back.

ANNIE: No—he's got the family now.

HECTOR: An' you got this place.

ANNIE: Place 'r family. That the choice?

HECTOR: Well, mebbee we was lucky. No choices. Y' married, an' y' stayed married. I'm still here.

ANNIE (*looks at him for a long moment*): No, Hector. You're up in th'old orchard.

    Pause.

HECTOR: Was *you* brung me down. You wanta change that?

ANNIE (*anguished*): Please, Hector. Things change whether we want 'em to or not . . . . .

There are two grandchildren to be considered, Annie insists, and Hector must let her figure out for herself what she ought to do in the circumstances. Annie thinks back to the time five years ago when Hector left her. The scene changes to that past time, "*and when Hector turns he is a frail, querulous, deaf old man.*" Dillard appears with Hector's jacket and helps his father into the rocker. Holly comes in with recorder and camera, snapping pictures for her school magazine.

Hector has just come out of the hospital and didn't like being down there in the town. He declares, "So I been poorly—but I don't aim t' slack off none. When the Lord made a man he made him good. He made him tough. An' this ol' body is really put together, buddy. Y' cain't hardly tear it apart, it's so well put together. An' I'm gonna live jus' as long as I see anybody else a-livin'! Now ain't nobody need say nothin' about that!"

Holly brings up the subject of children leaving their mountain home and families selling out. Holly herself loves this area and means to stay here and teach after she finishes school. Holly assumes that this farm is the most important thing in Hector's life, but Hector sets her straight, nodding at Annie and declaring, "She is"—thus sending Annie inside in a fluster of embarrassment.

Most people she knows mean to stay here, Holly says, but some like her grandmother would like to have a trailer and a TV set. Hector expounds the evils of TV—"all sex and guns. Betcha half those fellers never handled a gun in their life." Did Hector ever shoot anybody? Holly asks. If so, he isn't about to tell her. But when Holly comments, "My daddy said a revenuer got shot right over in the next holler," Hector freezes and there is an awkward silence among them all, including Annie, who has come back outside.

Hector takes his pill, as they recall the primitive medical and dental treatments of the old days. Hector admits that some of today's improvements—a tractor, for example, to work the farm in place of horses—are desirable, but he insists that some of the old ways were better—the neighborliness, the closeness to the land. The bell down in the valley would toll the years of a deceased person, and everyone would gather to help with the burial and maybe sing a song or two. Dillard remembers one called "Dear Lord" and sings it while the rest of the stage goes dark:

> Now the stars is restin', settin' on the hill,
> An' nothin' is a-soundin' but a whippoorwill;
> Down in our holler there the foxfire glows,
> Dear Lord, give all your creatures their repose:
>
> The day is done, dear Lord,
> Tomorrow's sun, dear Lord,
> Is sure to come . . .

A distant bell tolls, and the lights come up on Annie laying out Hector's dead body on the table, his arms folded on his chest. She must tie his necktie and put coins on his eyelids. Neighbors are taking care of the cows and making a coffin. As the bell sounds its 77th and last ring for Hector, Annie is telling Dillard that his father boasted to the doctor about the medal Dillard once won, second place in a statewide guitar competition. Annie is not going to weep for Hector, because he didn't like tears, she recalls; Annie once caught Hector crying when Dillard's sister died, but then he hated himself for it. Annie also remembers: "I caught him one other time too—but he weren't cryin'. I never *ever* told anyone 'bout that, but I guess it don't matter now. It was at a dance over t' Highlands. I was carryin' you, so I was jus' watchin'. But my back began t'ache, so I went out t' the wagon, and y'r pa had his arm round the Bryson girl. She was a pretty little thing. Had long black hair down t' her waist, an' she'd shake her head like a filly troubled by the flies. They was both laughin'. I jus' went back in an' sat down agin. It was hurtful—an' every time after that, when he travelled over that way, I wondered some. Needn't have, I guess."

Annie has lost one of the quarters she was to put on Hector's eyelids, so Dillard takes out his wallet and gives his mother the medal he won at the guitar contest. She puts the coin and the medal on Hector's eyelids, strokes his hair and then goes inside while Dillard sings a second verse of "Dear Lord."

When Annie comes out again, Hector is standing, leaning against the table, and time has moved forward again from Hector's death five years ago to the present. Annie hums the tune Dillard was singing, then crosses toward Hector.

HECTOR: They built me a good enough box, but they was poor hands at carpenterin'. Grady shoulda stuck t' milkin' an' Gudger t' playin' his fiddle.

Spaces a quarter-inch wide between them planks. Lucky it wasn't rainin' that day.

ANNIE: It weren't rainin'. Ground was real hard.

> *She turns, leaving him—for good—and goes back to the house. When she reaches the cut-out figures on the wall she touches them, then goes into the kitchen.*

HECTOR: They dug that hole up in th'old orchard, an' they laid my box in the dirt. (*He looks at the audience.*) That sound messy t'you? Well, I'm real proud of it. (*He rubs his hand on the ground.*) This is it. Dirt. Dirt cheap, as the sayin' goes. Dirt cheap yet y' can't put a price on it, no more'n y' can on a man's life. Now that's peculiar, ain't it? This here's mine. My dirt. My land. (*He looks out at the surrounding hills for a moment; then grins and gets up.*) Course, it ain't mine exclusive. It's where we all come from, and where we'll all end up one way 'r another. The very best grade fertilize. I respeck that . . . . . Nothin' wasted. The year after they put me down I had that ol' apple tree bloomin' like the finest spring.

Annie comes out wearing her coat and carrying a handbag. She proceeds to take down the cut-out figures as Dillard comes out of the house with a roped box. The rocker and the other things will be sent along soon, Dillard assures her—and he promises to take good care of her.

Hector tries to speak to Annie, but she can no longer hear him. Prince Carpenter appears with his surveyor's measuring tape, promising, "Gonna be some fine homes up here." Dillard reminds him, "Always was."

Annie is assured that they can come back if they've forgotten anything.

ANNIE: Oh, I'm comin' back. You sure he's got that in the paper now?

PRINCE: Y' don't have t' worry about that. Private burial ground's protected by law—we can't touch it. You got a hammer somewhere, Aunt Annie?

ANNIE: Under the bed. Put it back.

> *Prince withdraws.*

DILLARD: You leavin' Pa's tools?

ANNIE: You wanta move 'em? You best lend me y'r arm down the hill. Light's goin' fast.

DILLARD: Don't you want t' look around?

ANNIE: Honey, there ain't a rock 'r a tree 'r a blade a' grass here I don't know better'n my own hand. So let's jus' get along. I don't have t' wave.

> *They go off down the hill. Hector crosses to watch them go. There is a pause filled only by the sound of the treefrogs. Then Prince comes out of the house, carrying a placard and a hammer. He has a nail in his mouth. Coming down the steps, he nails the placard to the porch upright beside them. Then he goes back up and seats himself in Annie's rocker, looking out in satisfaction at the view. As he sits rocking, hammer on knee, Hector comes close and reads the placard aloud.*

HECTOR: SOLD. Title to this property, Block 19, Section 27, Rabun County Tax Roll 1982, resides with the Mountain Development Corporation, Greenville, South Carolina. TRESPASSERS WILL BE PROSECUTED. (*He turns.*) Y' know, all m' life, all m' daddy's life, there wasn't one single "trespasser" come up that hill we didn't say howdy to, an' offer 'em a little something. Includin' this son-of-a-bitch that's got my hammer.

> *Right on cue, Prince drops the hammer. He looks at it in surprise, picks it up and takes it back into the house.*

Well, like I said, times change. An' the law's the law, I guess, even if I did tickle it now an' then. "Trespassers." I guess that's me. (*He laughs.*) Well, they got a big job a' diggin' t' do t' get rid a' me. (*He looks down the hill again.*) She'll be back.

> *The light begins to fade, the treefrogs shirr, the whippoorwill calls far-off once more as Hector stands there looking down the hill. His figure, outlined against the sweep of the mountains, is the last thing we see as the lights go to black. Curtain.*

EXTREMITIES

A Play in Two Acts

BY WILLIAM MASTROSIMONE

Cast and credits appear on page 401

*WILLIAM MASTROSIMONE was born in 1947 in Trenton, N.J., where he still resides. He studied at Tulane for three and a half years, working toward a biology major but with increasing doubts that he was on the right track. Agreeing with Nietzche that "a man should find in his work the joy he found as a child in play," Mastrosimone began taking stock of himself and had to admit that he was procrastinating from his studies by dipping into Sophocles and Shakespeare. Furthermore, he remembered that as a child his greatest fun had been to make up dramatic stories and act them out, sometimes in costume. Mastrosimone finally left Tulane and set out to write plays. He got his B.A. at Rider College in New Jersey in 1974 and went on to study for his M.F.A. at Rutgers's Mason Gross School of the Arts. Prior to his first professional production, he wrote, he guesses, about 15 scripts, one of which—*Devil Take the Hindmost—*was staged at Rutgers and won the David Library Award at the 1977 American College Theater Festival.*

Mastrosimone's first professional production was the two-character The Woolgatherer *off Broadway at Circle Repertory Company June 5, 1980 for 92 performances (it had previously been staged at Rutgers). That same season his* Extremities *was produced at Actors' Theater of Louisville and was cited as one of the year's outstanding new plays in the American Theater Critics Association review published in* The Best Plays of 1980–81. *In off-Broadway production Dec. 22, 1982, Extremities is now cited as Mastrosimone's first Best Play.*

Other Mastrosimone play titles include Shivaree, A Tantalizing *and* The Understanding, *and he has been working recently on an as yet unreleased motion picture. When* Extremities *appeared in Louisville, it was attended and very favorably received by the Norwegian critic Erik Pierstorff, which led to productions of that play in Scandinavia. For his newest play,* Sciamachies *(per Webster Two, "fights with a shadow"), Mastrosimone did his research in Afghanistan disguised as a freedom fighter. Its premiere took place in Bergen, Norway, in March 1983.*

The following synopsis of Extremities *was prepared by Sally Dixon Wiener.*

Time: The present, September

Place: Between Trenton and Princeton, New Jersey, where the cornfield meets the highway.

ACT I

SYNOPSIS: The set is the living room of a dilapidated farmhouse with furniture that perhaps was collected at a rummage sale. There is a good-sized fireplace upstage center, and a locked bicycle is against the wall. A dining table and three chairs are at stage left, and upstage left stairs lead to other rooms in the house. A wicker sofa and another table are also in the room, and at stage right there is a large window with many hanging plants and a door leading to the outside. Upstage right a door leads to a kitchen, partly in view.

Sunlight is coming through the window as Marjorie enters with a cup and saucer. A healthy-looking, attractive woman, probably in her late 20s, she is wearing no makeup and has a short bathrobe on over an abbreviated cotton knit shift and panties. She is barefoot. She dials the phone and hangs up when no one answers, waters a wilted plant, then takes it outside. As she hits at a wasp that is attacking her, the potted plant drops, and the pot breaks. And the wasp has stung her.

As Marjorie takes an aerosol can of insecticide and proceeds to attack and kill the wasp, Raul enters. He is a stockily-built man, probably in his early 30s, with close-cropped dark hair. He says he is looking for someone named Joe. Marjorie belts her robe and tells him that there is no Joe here. At first it seems that Raul will leave, but he keeps harping on the subject of Joe (he's forgotten Joe's last name, but "he said he had a room here"). Marjorie tells him to go.

Raul notices the bicycle, strokes the seat, and Marjorie grows more tense as she again tries to get him to leave. Raul tells her Joe owes him money, and again she tells him there is no Joe and that her husband is upstairs asleep, and that he's a cop. Raul goes on insisting that he left Joe off here last week: "He's about six two. Rides a Triumph. Red beard. Wears cowboy boots. Short guy."

Marjorie calls out for Tony.

RAUL: Tony! Tony! What's amatter wit him? Maybe he ain't here. Maybe you're tellin' me a little lie, eh, pretty momma? Maybe you think I scare easy.

Susan Sarandon as Marjorie (wielding shovel), James Russo as Raul
(in fireplace) and Deborah Hedwall as Patricia *(left)* in *Extremities*

Go 'head. Go for the door. Let's see who's faster. So where's the other two chicks
that live here?

MARJORIE: Kitchen.

RAUL: House full of people, and when you holler, nobody comes.

> *She bolts for the door; he cuts her off.*

MARJORIE: Get out!

RAUL: You got a lousy bunch of friends.

MARJORIE: Get out right now!

RAUL: Take it easy, lovely. I saw the other two chicks leave this morning. The
one wit the ratty car should get here about five-thirty. The one wit specs, 'bout
six. Today's gonna be a triple header.

MARJORIE: Get out or I'll call the police.

> *Long pause. Raul goes to door, looks at Marjorie, laughs, goes to phone,*
> *rips the wire out.*

RAUL: Your move.

MARJORIE: I'm expecting people any time now. Any time.

RAUL: No kidding? Dressed like that? Mind if I stick around for the fun? Your
move.

MARJORIE: Don't touch me!

RAUL: Don't fight me. I don't want to hurt you. You're too sweet to hurt. You smell pretty. Is that your smell or the perfume?

> *She swipes at him. He catches her hand and kisses it sweetly. She burns him with the cigarette and tries to escape. He latches onto her hair, brings her down, mounts her, forces a pillow to her face. We hear her muffled screams.*

You gonna be nice?

MARJORIE (*muffled*): Yes!

RAUL: You sure?

MARJORIE (*muffled*): Yes!

RAUL (*removing pillow slightly*): Please don't wreck it. You made me hurt you, and I don't want to hurt you, but if you kick and scream and scratch, what else can I do, eh, babe?

Raul continues to subdue Marjorie with the pillow as she tries to escape again. She begs him not to kill her. When he smothers her again and she goes limp he discovers she has freckles. He wants to kiss them all, "give 'em names and kiss 'em all goodnight." He wants her to kiss him nicely and insists she act out a role, inviting him in and telling him she loves him, and warns her not to make him do something ugly. He tells her to touch him "down there." Marjorie offers him jewelry or anything he wants, which only infuriates him further. He wants her to say that she wants to make love.

RAUL: . . . . . Say you're my puta.

MARJORIE: Puta?

RAUL: Puta, puta, whore, my whore, my puta! Say it!

MARJORIE: I'm your puta.

RAUL: Say it and smile!

MARJORIE: I'm your puta.

RAUL: You like to tease me, eh, puta?

MARJORIE: No. Yes. Yes.

RAUL: You like to tease everybody.

MARJORIE: No.

RAUL: Know what you need, puta? You need acouple slashes here and here and here, stripes t'make you a zebra-face t'scare the shit outta anybody you go teasin', puta, 'cause you're mine, all mine. Say it!

MARJORIE: Yours!

RAUL: Undo the belt.

MARJORIE: Please! God!

RAUL: Undo it! This is gonna be beautiful, so you keep telling me, puta, and don't stop . . .

MARJORIE: I love you, I love you . . . . .

She notices that the aerosol can is almost close enough to reach, and she continues to tell him she loves him, embracing him to be able to get closer to the can. She tells him, yes, she put the perfume on just for him, as she takes the can and sprays him on the face and in the eyes. He is screaming with pain as she attempts to get to the door, but he manages to grab her leg. Still trying to escape, she pulls an extension cord out of its socket, puts it around his neck and tugs it tight. As he screams, there is a blackout. We hear the sound of a wasp, or wasps, which covers the blackout.

As the lights go up, Raul is on the floor, trussed up with an arrangement of extension cords, clothesline, belts, etc. He is also blindfolded and fighting his restraints. Marjorie goes to the kitchen sink, splashes her face and the wasp sting with water and puts the kettle on the stove.

RAUL: You there? My eyes burn! I need a doctor! You there? I'm hurt bad! Help me! You there?
Marjorie dials the phone.
Call the cops, pussy! You can't prove a fuckin' thing!
Realizing the phone is dead, Marjorie drops it and watches Raul buck.
Why don't you fuckin' answer me! You bitch! I'll kill ya! Get the cops! They gotta let me go!
Marjorie runs upstairs.
Your Honor, I goes out lookin' for work 'cause I got laid off the car wash, and I sees this farmhouse and goes t'ask if there was any work 'cause I got three babies t'feed, and this crazy lady goes and sprays me with this stuff, Your Honor.

Raul taunts Marjorie, pointing out the absence of physical evidence—no bruises, no telltale biological signs of rape. He calls her by name, bringing her up short.

MARJORIE: How do you know my name?
RAUL: I demand my rights! I want medical attention! I wanna call my attorney! Palmieri! The fuckin' best!
MARJORIE: How do you know my name?
RAUL: And when you're alone in the room wit the pigs and tell 'em what happened, and they say, You sure, sweetheart? They don't believe no pricktease, Marjorie.
MARJORIE: Don't say my name.
RAUL: And little Margie gets a little write-up in the paper, and wit Daddy's heart condition that could be real sweet if the old fucker croaks. . . . .

They have no case against him—they'll read him his rights and then let him go, Raul insists. And then he'll come back and knife her when he catches her alone. *"Marjorie snaps"*—she takes the steaming kettle and dumps boiling water on him. They both scream, as the lights go to black.

Again the wasp sound covers the blackout, and when the lights go up again we see Raul caged in the fireplace, still bound, still blindfolded, still with a restraining cord around his neck. Marjorie has tied and chained the upright part of an old metal bedstead across the opening of the fireplace to imprison Raul in the aperture.

By pulling at the noose around his neck, she gets him to reveal that he knows her name because he has been reading her mail. He took some letters from the mailbox. Again he uses Joe as an excuse: "Joe asked me come pick up his mail." Raul has seen letters from Marjorie's father, her brother and someone called Tony who wants Marjorie to come live with him in New York.

Marjorie wants to know "Why me?" Raul says, "I saw you around." He won't say where, so she pokes him with a fireplace tool. He says Joe told him if he walked in and asked for Joe she would know what he meant.

Raul wants to know where he is. Marjorie tells him he's in the fireplace and that she has some gas and some matches. She shakes a plastic bottle of ammonia and a box of wooden matches to convince him, still trying to get at the truth. He gives her another story—he's a narco. She shakes ammonia on him.

RAUL: Hey! What the hell! Hey! I got a wife and three kids!
    She strikes a match very near.
MARJORIE: Maybe you'll tell the truth when you're on fire!
    Raul coughs uncontrollably. He fights for breath in the chemicalized air. Marjorie strikes a match, holds it close to his face.
RAUL: All right! This is it! The honest-to-god truth. I don't know why I didn't tell you this from the beginning because this is it.
    Pause.
I used to work on the pothole crew. For the County. We went around patchin' up potholes. That's why they called us the pothole crew. One day we went around patchin' up potholes on the highway. In front of your driveway. Bitchin' day. In the nineties. Working with hot tar. Sweatin'. Thirsty. Gettin' dizzy. Foreman bustin' balls. Somebody says, look at this. And you come ridin' down the highway on your bike in your little white shorts, and every time you pedal you could see what was tan and what wasn't and your blouse tied in a knot and the sun shinin' off your hair, beautiful. And that's it.
MARJORIE: So you did it because I looked beautiful?
RAUL: I don't know what to fuckin' say.
MARJORIE: You're going to burn.
    She strikes a match.
RAUL: That's the truth. It was hot. You had on your little white shorts, and I wanted to feel beautiful again!
MARJORIE: So what if I was naked!
RAUL: Please! We had a deal! On the milk of Mary! You rode by in your shorts! I said, "How ya doin'?" You didn't say nothin'. Looked at me like I was a dead dog. You pissed me off, so I came here to fuck you!
    Marjorie stops flicking matches. Raul whimpers and slumps down. Marjorie sits. Long pause.

Raul asks what she's going to do with him and she tells him "nothing". He wonders if this means she's going to let him go, but she says not. Marjorie tells him she can't wait to hear what he'll say after two days without food and water, lying in his own filth unable to scream. He urges her to call the police, but she repeats his statement that they would let him go because she has no proof. It's too late to call in the police. She will bury his body in the graveyard near the woods where she buries animals killed on the highway. This time she'll "dig deeper".

Raul pleads that he wants to go straight; he will, Marjorie assures him, "straight into a hole." When her housemates come home (Raul insists) they'll stop her from killing him. Marjorie assures him that one will help her dig and the other help drag his body out. She goes for her shovel and then pretends to leave the room, slamming the door. Raul believes she's gone to dig the hole and prays to the Virgin for his release, then sings a little song: "Found a peanut/It was rotten/Ate it anyway just now/Then I died/Went to heaven. . . . ." He thrashes around, gags, then falls and lies still. When Marjorie goes to see if he is all right and loosens the noose a bit, Raul bites her hand. In retaliation, she pours Clorox over him.

Raul hears a car and prays that it's the police, but Marjorie warns him not to speak again. It is Terry, one of the two young women with whom Marjorie shares the house, perhaps a bit younger than Marjorie and slighter in appearance. She begins to tell Marjorie that she can't help scrape and paint tonight, that she has a dinner-date. Terry is asking Marjorie if she can borrow a dress when she discovers Raul. Marjorie tells her of the attempted rape, and that Raul knows everything about them because he's been watching them. Raul asks for help, but Marjorie warns him against talking and hits him again. He screams. Terry tries to calm Marjorie by telling her the police will lock Raul up. Marjorie asks her, "On what charge?" and Terry says rape—but there was no rape, and attempted rape is virtually impossible to prove.

MARJORIE: So they let him go and he said he'd come back to get me. So it's him or me. Him or me. Choose. Him or me.

TERRY: You, you, of course. But I'd rather call the police.

MARJORIE: Do it.

TERRY: It would make me feel safe.

MARJORIE: Then do it.

TERRY: What should I say?

MARJORIE: Whatever makes you feel safe.

TERRY: Phone's dead.

MARJORIE: Animal ripped it out of the wall. I got lucky. If I didn't you would've come home and found my body . . .

TERRY: Don't talk like that.

MARJORIE: You try and run. He catches you by the hair. Smothers you off and on till you're too weak to move.

TERRY: All right!

MARJORIE: And then he toys with you. Makes you beg for a breath. Makes you undo his belt.

TERRY: Stop it!

MARJORIE: Makes you touch him. All over. His mouth. His neck. Between his legs . . .

TERRY: Why are you doing this to me!

MARJORIE: So it won't happen to you!—Terry, if it happened to you, I'd say, Terry, tell me what to do.

TERRY: Tell me what to do.

MARJORIE: Be with me.

TERRY: I am with you.

    Pause.

What can I do?

MARJORIE: Help me make him disappear.

Terry says they should wait for Patricia, the other housemate, but Marjorie says they don't need her, they only need the shovel to dig a hole, and that's the end of it. Terry is horrified, but Marjorie says it's him or us—and if Terry says so she will let him go, but then if he gets Terry, Terry shouldn't blame her. Terry decides us. Marjorie instructs her to watch Raul and not leave the room. Then Marjorie goes off to dig the hole.

Once assured Marjorie is gone, Raul begins a desperate campaign to elicit help from Terry, despite her repeatedly telling him not to talk. He tells her his eyes are killing him, that his Good Humor truck broke down on the highway and he had just asked to use the phone. He tells her it's called complicity "when you sit there like an asshole and watch somebody do a crime." And if she's not interested in what he has to say, would she be interested in what his attorney has to say if she were in court as a witness? He mentions the name Palmieri, and it is obvious Terry knows of the attorney's reputation. She doesn't say anything, but pours herself a glass of wine. He recognizes the sounds and asks for a drink. Again she tells him to be quiet, and he says he understands. She's doing this for "good friend Marjorie."

RAUL: . . . Friends to the ends, eh? You borrow her dress, she borrows your boyfriend.

    Pause.

Tony.

TERRY: What?

RAUL: Forget it.

TERRY: No. What did you say?

RAUL: Oh, you want something from me, but when I ask you for a little drink, you gimme a cup o dust? Get lost, you and your drink.

TERRY: You're a goddam liar.

RAUL: Am I?

TERRY: What'd she say?

RAUL: Don't believe me. I'm a liar. Go believe your good friend out there diggin' a hole. She's nice. She buries people.

TERRY: What'd she tell you?

RAUL: Look, nobody likes to be the one to bring the bad news.

    Pause.

She's fuckin' him.

TERRY: You liar. He doesn't even live around here any more.

RAUL: New York.

    Pause.

Photographer.

> *Pause.*

She goes to see him every Wednesday. You drop her off the train station.

TERRY: How do you know that?

RAUL: Now she's gonna take you for a ride. Think what you're doin', Terry. —She get raped?—She got broken bones?—I pinched her ass, she took a freak and mangled me.—Think, sweetheart, think.—Ever get your ass pinched?— Course you did.—Did you mangle the guy?—Course not, 'cause you know these things happen between a man and a woman.—Save yourself. Run. Get the cops. Think, honey, think.

Marjorie comes back; she has cut her foot and needs her shoes. It's shale underneath where she was digging, and now she's going to dig by the creek. Terry tells her she is leaving. Marjorie wants to know what Raul said to her and reminds her that she said she'd help her. Terry lashes out at her: Marjorie didn't get raped, but Terry got raped once, and it was all her own fault. She was all dressed up at a Halloween party, had too much beer and some grass and hitchhiked home. She almost got away, but "a nice guy with glasses" pulled her back by her ballerina skirt. When she got home her mother cried and her father called her a whore. They wouldn't let her talk. She made believe it was a bad dream. "You know what they'd say—I asked for it," she tells Marjorie. "At least we didn't get hurt. At least we're alive."

There is the sound of a car again, and Patricia, the third housemate, a substantial young woman with a briefcase and a box from a bakery, comes in. When she becomes aware that there is a man in the fireplace, she laughs and asks what the joke is. Terry explains that he tried to rape Marjorie. Marjorie assures Patricia that she's okay, at least she thinks so, and admits it was she alone who got Raul tied up and into the fireplace.

Patricia wonders where the police are. Didn't Marjorie call them?

MARJORIE: No.

PATRICIA: Why not?

MARJORIE: I'm going to fix him.

PATRICIA: Fix?

MARJORIE: Fix.

RAUL: Don't let her torture me no more!

MARJORIE: Shut the fuck up!

PATRICIA: What are you doing?

MARJORIE: I want him to hurt like me!

RAUL: Please help me.

PATRICIA: Stop it!

MARJORIE: I want him to hurt like me!

PATRICIA: Looks like you've done that. Now we have to put him away.

MARJORIE: I have no proof! They'll let him go! He'll come back and slash up my face!

Patricia tries to persuade Marjorie that his being on the premises should be enough to put him away. She is trying very hard to keep everything under control and wants Terry to go get the police, to tell them to come quickly and take Raul away. Terry points out that if the police see Raul like that, Marjorie is in trouble. Terry thinks they'd better get a lawyer for Marjorie's protection before the police are called in, and Patricia tells her to look in the phone book for Palmieri.

Terry suggests they make up a story, she could say she was with Marjorie, but Patricia says that's perjury and they will tell the truth. Terry's sure Raul's lawyer will file countercharges. Again Terry suggests making up a story.

MARJORIE: Police. Charges. Arraignment. Lawyers. Money. Time. Judge. Jury. Proof. His word against mine. Defendant's attorney—a three-piece button down summa cum laude fresh from Harvard fuck-off: Did my client rape you? No. Assualt you? Yes. How? With a pillow. Did you resist? Yes. Evidence? None. Witnesses? None. Did you tie him up? beat him? lock him in a fireplace? Six months for me, that animal goes free. And if I survive being locked up, then what do I do? Come home and lock myself up. Chainlock, boltlock, deadlock. And wait for him. Hear him in every creak of wood, every mouse in the wall, every twig tapping on the window. Start from sleep, 4 a.m., see something in the dark at the foot of my bed. Eyes black holes. Skin speckled gray like a slug. Hit the lights. He's not there. This time. So then what do I do? Wait for him? Or move three thousand miles, change my name, unlist my phone, get a dog. I don't want to taste my vomit every time the doorbell rings. I don't want to flinch when a man touches me. I won't wear a goddam whistle. I want to live my life. He's never leaving this house.

    A pause.
PATRICIA: Marjorie, I think you're in shock and don't know what you're saying. I'm going to a phone booth and call the police, and everything's going to be all right.

MARJORIE: I'm not in shock, and more than ever I know exactly what I'm saying, and you're not going anywhere.

Marjorie picks up Patricia's car keys and refuses to give them to her. Patricia says they'll walk, but Marjorie warns her that if they leave, Raul will die. Patricia doesn't believe she means it, but Raul says she does, and to please not leave him.

From now on she's making her own law, Marjorie says. She locks the door, and Patricia and Terry sit down. "Mother of God," Raul says, and the lights fade. *Curtain.*

ACT II

It is a moment later, and the lights go up quickly. Marjorie is still barricading the door. Patricia, trying to calm everybody down, suggests they have a drink and some food and talk. She goes to the kitchen to get some wine and opens a window. Marjorie tells her to close and lock it, and Marjorie locks the other windows.

Terry wants to go to her room but Marjorie demands she stay. Patricia continues to be solicitous and seems to calm Marjorie briefly. Then Marjorie begins to wonder about Terry's date, if he knows where she lives. He does, Terry admits, but she thinks he would probably call first, rather than come to the house, to see

Deborah Hedwall and Susan Sarandon in a scene from *Extremities*

why she was standing him up. With the phone broken, Marjorie isn't sure what he'd hear. Terry thinks a busy signal; Patricia thinks he'd hear nothing. Patricia adds that she'll call the phone company from work tomorrow, and Marjorie says they both will have to take tomorrow off from work. They object. It's Patricia's staff meeting day, and Terry has used up her sick days. She'd be fired. "Then I could be like you and polish my nails and read glamour magazines all day," she tells Marjorie.

Marjorie warns Terry that she wants her in the kitchen if her date shows up, until she can get rid of him. Terry brings food to the table. As they begin to eat she asks Marjorie what she did in the city yesterday. Marjorie doesn't answer, and Patricia intervenes, suggesting that for now they just eat. But Raul in his fireplace prison cell keeps complaining about Marjorie's cruelty to him, arousing Patricia's sympathy. She tries to bring Raul something to eat, but Marjorie forbids even "talking to the animal," defying Patricia to come up with an excuse for him: "So, what's your analysis? Is it his childhood? His environment? His Greek traumas? Let's hear the dime store psychiatrist explain this sick creep animal fuck." Marjorie herself is behaving like an animal, Patricia suggests, declaring "Nobody dies in my house."

Patricia and Terry sit down, and when Terry drops a fork, they all jump. When Raul asks if he can talk to Patricia, Marjorie tells him to be quiet and to not use anyone's name "as if you knew us." Patricia wants to know what Raul wants, and what his name is, but Marjorie forbids Raul to say his name. What he wants is a drink of water; he feels sick: "Bad sick. Dizzy. Headache. My eyes burn bad. She sprayed that stuff in my mouth," he tells Patricia. Patricia reads the aerosol can with its warnings. She wants to go get some antidote, atrophine, at a drug store. Marjorie says no. Patricia warns her it could be fatal, but Marjorie still says no.

Marjorie rails at Patricia. She is not one of her social worker cases and will not tolerate her "superior bullshit." Patricia tells her the reality is that a man is hurt and she doesn't have a case. Marjorie explains that's why she has a hammer. Marjorie wants a confession from Raul, in front of both Patricia and Terry, to protect her from the law.

RAUL: I didn't do nothin'.
PATRICIA: This is your chance to save yourself.
RAUL: I didn't do nothin', Patti.
PATRICIA: She's giving you a chance.
RAUL: Chance for what? Go the wall for a bit I didn't pull? Thanks.
MARJORIE: You tell them what you did to me.
RAUL: Look at her and look at me. Who did what to who?
MARJORIE: Tell them. Please?
RAUL: I wanna call my attorney. I want my rights. This country's got a fuckin' constitution!
MARJORIE: Tell them how you smothered me.
RAUL: This land got laws, jack, and nobody's above the law!
MARJORIE: You made me touch you!
TERRY: Pat! Do something!
MARJORIE: Tell them. Please. Let's end it.
RAUL: No innocent person's got nothin' to fear in this country. I demand my fuckin' rights!
    Marjorie bangs Raul's hand with the hammer. He screams.
MARJORIE: If you knew what it was like under the pillow, sucking for breath that wasn't there—further from life than you've ever been . . .
PATRICIA: Tell me—talk about the pillow.
MARJORIE: Talk, hell, let me show you.
    Marjorie forces a pillow to Patricia's face.
PATRICIA: Get the hell away from me with that thing!
MARJORIE: This is not a thing! This is a pillow! Let's define our terms!
PATRICIA: It'll all come out in court!
MARJORIE: Before they believe a woman in court, she has to be dead on arrival!
PATRICIA: You are not the law! You are not God! You have to bring it to court!

The three woman continue arguing among themselves, but Marjorie insists that this matter must be settled between Raul and herself without interference from anyone else. Patricia fears Marjorie is beginning to resemble her attacker. Marjorie agrees emphatically, yes, she'd like to be a survivor. "Don't I count?" Marjorie asks her. Patricia apologizes and assures Marjorie that they will take the day off tomorrow and will do the best thing for Marjorie, but Terry says it has nothing to do with *her,* she is not taking tomorrow off.

Recognizing Terry's alienation, Patricia wants to get back to the facts. "We got a man here. He's tied up. He's injured." She defines the problem as a question of what laws are violated. She asks Marjorie if she has any bruises. The fact that Raul bit her ("I bit her because she was chokin' me with a wire!") is good evidence for a court, Patricia says, because it shows. There was an attempted rape, but Marjorie can't prove it. Then there was torture, which *can* be proved and could get Marjorie into a great deal of trouble with the law. That's the crux of the problem and, Patricia observes, "I do know your lives are joined now. If he goes under, so do you. If he's kept well, so are you."

The one thing Patricia is sure of is that, at the moment, Marjorie has a choice. She can use the hammer or not, but if Raul dies, she has no choice. A powerful witness of Marjorie's humanity would be giving Raul some bread "to absorb the poison," and she convinces Marjorie to allow this, to help herself. Raul asks that Patricia feed the bread to him; he says his hand is broken, and Patricia also, after further argument, gets Marjorie to unlock Raul and to allow her to loosen the noose. When he gags on the bread, Patricia quickly gets a glass of the wine. Raul drinks it all, and, thanking her, asks for some of the meat. Marjorie sarcastically asks him if he wants mustard, and when he asks if there's any mayo she becomes enraged with him again.

While feeding Raul, Patricia checks his face under the blindfold.

PATRICIA: Oh my God. His face.

RAUL: What?

PATRICIA: Bubbled up. Blood's running out his nose. The ammonia burned his nose linings.

RAUL: You three are gonna get a snapshot, front and profile, down at the cop shop, jack.

PATRICIA: I'm going to the drug store. For the atropine.

MARJORIE: For my good, right?

PATRICIA: Why don't you look under the blindfold? Or is that why you covered it? You can't stand to see the damage you caused? I want that atrophine.

MARJORIE: I'll let Terry go.

TERRY: Where should I go?

MARJORIE: Drug store at the mall.

TERRY: I'm broke.

PATRICIA: I blew my last few bucks on the cheescake. Do you have any money?

MARJORIE: You want me to pay for the animal's medicine?

PATRICIA: Can I borrow it?

MARJORIE: I should've crushed his skull in the first two seconds, had it all cleaned up by the time you got home and never said a word. But I let myself talk, and in talk I squandered it. Talk, talk, talk, talk, talk. No phone calls.

TERRY: Alright.

MARJORIE: Say it.

TERRY: No phone calls.

MARJORIE: If you bring the police, I'll do it, Terry, and it'll be just like you did it. When I see 'em pull up, one hit, he's out, two, he's dead. Two seconds. That's all it takes. And I'll be watching every second.

Handing her keys and money.

It should take seven minutes to get there, five in the store, seven to get back, even if you catch the light both ways. I give you one extra minute for the unaccountable. Seven, plus five, plus seven, plus one . . . Twenty minutes.

PATRICIA: Don't speed. You might get stopped. Get atropine and something for burns.

As Terry is about to leave, Raul says "Complicity." Marjorie locks the door after Terry is gone, notes the time, seats herself to wait.

RAUL: Excuse me. Can I say something?

Silence, which he takes as consent.

I want to thank you very much for the bread. And for putting up that money for my medicine. I think that was very kind of you. Most people wouldn't go that far. But you went all-out, and I'm all choked up and want to thank you from the bottom of my heart because it was generous and it was kind and it was nice. So nice of you. You wouldn't have an extra cigarette, would you? Or maybe one that was smoked halfway?

MARJORIE: Menthol filter all right?

RAUL: Thank you very much.

MARJORIE: Reach your hand out and I'll give it to you.

RAUL: No thank you. Bad for the lungs.

Lights fade.

It is fifteen minutes later when the lights go up. Patricia asks Marjorie if her wasp stings hurt. Marjorie shakes her head no. Marjorie has her mind on the time: it's been seventeen minutes now since Terry left. Patricia asks Marjorie if she pulled the stinger out, and again she shakes her head no. Patricia exits to get tweezers.

RAUL: Ain't no stinger in there.

MARJORIE: Says who?

RAUL: Wasps don't leave no stinger. A bee leaves a stinger and croaks. But a wasp keeps on stingin'.

MARJORIE: How do you know that?

RAUL: I know what I know. A wasp don't sing, a bird don't sting. They're gonna call you Hammer. And one night them hefty lesbies are gonna test your mojo, jump you in your roachy piss-smellin' six by ten, bust your nose, make it flat, spit your teeth in a toilet bowl, and when bull says get down in the bush, Hammer jumps in the weeds smokin' dry beaver, cause you're like me, you do what ya gotta do to keep alive. And don't holler 'cause them hacks get a sudden case of deaf cause they don't get involved in petty in-house business. So keep your ass close to the wall or some cannibal puts a dull screwdriver in your back and nobody hears nothin' when them showers are splashin' and them radios are blastin' them funky tunes and your blood washin' down the drain reminds you of once upon a time in a cozy little house, me and you, to have and to hold, forever.

Patricia returns with the tweezers, and Marjorie tells her that wasps don't leave a stinger. Raul suggests rubbing the stings with alcohol. "I mean if we can't help each other out, what the hell are we on this earth for?" he remarks.

It seems that Marjorie is a stewardess and is supposed to fly tomorrow—Paris, Rome, Munich, London and return. She doesn't want Patricia to call her in sick because she needs the money. It's twenty minutes now since Terry left, and Marjorie believes she has been betrayed. Raul opines that Terry's car needs a valve job and bets the car broke down. Marjorie prepares to make good her threat. *"Patricia grabs the hammer. They struggle. Patricia is hurt,"* but Raul is spared.

Terry enters with the bag from the drugstore and Marjorie berates her for being late. Terry, thinking Marjorie has killed Raul, says she's going to tell the police everything and that Marjorie will go to "the goddam wall." After she realizes that Marjorie hasn't carried out her threat, she informs Patricia that you can't buy atropine over the counter. She did not ask them for a substitute antidote because Patricia hadn't said to do that. She was delayed because she ran into someone called Sally in the parking lot who wanted to talk about her divorce and wouldn't let go of her arm. The medicine she has brought is for cuts, not for burns, Patricia complains, but Patricia will apply it, and she's going to take off the noose to do so. "First bread. Then medicine. Now the noose. Why don't you just fuck him. Maybe that'll make him feel better," Marjorie rages at Patricia.

When his blindfold is removed, the bloody sight makes Terry gasp. Marjorie drops her hammer. Raul asks if he is ugly. He can't see and says to give him "a crown of thorns and finish me off." Patricia hands Marjorie the hammer and asks her why she doesn't finish what she started. Raul tells Patricia she's a traitor and says they're all going to burn. In answer to a question from Patricia, he tells her his name is Mike, Mike Mentiras. Marjorie asks him how many women he's raped and murdered. She wants him to tell them why he came here. Raul says he came in to use the phone, and she slaps his raw face, then apologizes. Raul insists that he came in here to make a phone call and was aroused by the sight of Marjorie walking around with her robe open and wearing nothing underneath. Raul challenges Marjorie to tell Patricia about the grave.

PATRICIA: What grave?

RAUL: Oh! I don't hear Marjorie talkin' now!—Terry comes home, and they decide to dig a grave in the garden and bury me!

PATRICIA: Is that true?

RAUL: Between the tomatoes and the flowers! with the possums and the dogs! A fuckin' grave!

PATRICIA: That can't be true!

RAUL: Don't believe me. Let the grave talk!

PATRICIA: Is there a grave out there?

TERRY: Ask her.

PATRICIA: I'm asking you! The one who wanted to make up a story!
TERRY: I didn't dig it!
RAUL: See! See! Bury me alive, Patti! Alive! Whacko and Terry!
TERRY: All's I did was watch him! Marjorie said she would drag him out, throw him in and cover it herself!
PATRICIA: Did you get enough justice today? Two eyes enough? Burn a man alive? Is that savage enough?
MARJORIE: Not as savage as a human roach forcing your legs apart!

Raul asks her why he would do that, that he has sex at home, Marjorie says she thought his wife was dead. Raul says, "My first wife." Marjorie tells the other women Raul has stolen their mail.

PATRICIA: Leave the man alone! Can't you see he's in pain?
RAUL: Don't say one bad thing about Marjorie. We're all human. We're weak. We do things we don't mean, and I forgive her everything. All I wanted was a kind word, a little closeness, to forget my troubles; all she wanted was to forget about some guy in New York. Tony.
MARJORIE: Tony wrote to me and animal took one of the letters.
TERRY: He wrote you?
MARJORIE: I never answered.
TERRY: Why didn't you tell me?
MARJORIE: I didn't want to hurt you.
TERRY: Is that why he came here when he knew I was at work?
MARJORIE: Terry, please believe me.
TERRY: Is that why you changed from jeans to bathrobe when I brought him here?
MARJORIE: I must've been ready for bed.
TERRY: You're always ready for bed!

Patricia backs her up and accuses Marjorie of parading around the house like "it was a centerfold," unhappy until she has every man in the room begging for it—and when one did, she wants to get him. She says Marjorie goes through men "like most women go through kleenex" and then complains after being provocative.

Patricia opens Raul's jacket. There is a hunting knife, sheathed, hanging from a leather thong. Marjorie takes it and lays it flat on Raul's shoulder. He explains that he uses it for work, for cutting boxes open in a warehouse. Marjorie comments that it's very sharp, "The kind of knife they use to gut a deer," and she puts the knife under his chin, asking him where he would like her to touch him. Then she says, finally, that she remembers.

MARJORIE: Down there!
        Putting the blade in Raul's crotch and lifting him off the chair an eighth of an inch. Pause.
Tell me you love it. Say it!
RAUL: I love it.

MARJORIE: Say it nice.

RAUL: I love it.

MARJORIE: Say it sweet.

RAUL: I love it . . .

MARJORIE: Sweeter!

RAUL: I love it.

MARJORIE: You say that beautiful. Again.

RAUL: I love it.

MARJORIE: Now tell me cut 'em off.

RAUL: I can't say that!

MARJORIE: This is your last chance.

RAUL: You can't make me say that!

MARJORIE: Say it!

RAUL: Mother of God! I stole letters! Watched the house! Came here to fuck yous all!

MARJORIE: Who!

RAUL: You and Terry and Patti, like Paula Wyshneski and Linda Martinex, Debbie Parks and some I forget. They screamed. I begged 'em not to scream. I hate when they scream.

> *Marjorie runs a stiff hand across Raul's throat. Thinking himself slashed, he writhes on the floor.*

Mother of God!

> *Realizing he's not slashed.*

Thank you.

> *Pause.*

Every time I do it, it's in the papers, and I gets up in the morning, and my wife and her mother they're talkin' about it, and I says, what happened? And they says, the raper got another girl last night, and they show me the paper and a picture of the dude somebody saw runnin' away, but it don't look nothin' like me. And my wife says, fix the back door, Raul, cause I don't want no raper comin' in here, and I says, don't worry, he don't want you, and she bitches, and I fix the door real good so the raper can't get in.

> *Pause.*

Tell 'em lock me in a room. Not with locks. I know about locks. I can pick 'em. A room with nobody else. And maybe if I could have a little radio so's I could listen the ball game so it won't be so quiet, because I hate the quiet, because the dark, I don't care, but the quiet, please don't let it be quiet.

Patricia now agrees that she should go out and find somebody to help them cope with Raul. Marjorie suggests Terry keep her company. Terry asks Marjorie if she won't be afraid, and Marjorie says no. Patricia wonders what they should say, and Marjorie says to tell them a man is hurt, a man needs help. Raul asks if he can say Marjorie's name. She says yes, and he asks a favor—no red lights and no siren. When Patricia and Terry exit, Raul hears the door close.

RAUL: You there?

MARJORIE: Yes.

RAUL: Thank you. Don't leave me alone?
MARJORIE: I'm right here.
RAUL: Thank you. They comin'?
MARJORIE: Yes.
RAUL: Don't let 'em beat me?
MARJORIE: No.
RAUL: Thank you very much. You there?
MARJORIE: Yes.
RAUL: Marjorie?
MARJORIE: Yes?
RAUL: Can I wait in the fireplace?
MARJORIE: If you want.
RAUL: Thank you.
> *Getting to his knees.*

Show me.

> *Marjorie puts the knife down, directs him to the mouth of the fireplace.*
> *He crouches inside. . . . .Lights fade slowly.*

Thank you. Thank you very much.

> *He rocks slightly. Almost imperceptibly he sings slowly, Marjorie weeps.*

Found a peanut
Found a peanut
Found a peanut just now
Just now I found a peanut
Found a peanut just now

Cracked it open
Cracked it open
Cracked it open just now . . .

> *Lights fade to darkness. Curtain.*

QUARTERMAINE'S TERMS

A Play in Two Acts

BY SIMON GRAY

Cast and credits appear on page 403

SIMON GRAY was born on Hayling Island, Hampshire, in 1936 and was educated at Portsmouth Grammar and Westminster Schools and at universities in Canada and France before going to Cambridge, where he majored in English. His produced plays include Wise Child, *done in London in 1967 starring Alec Guinness and on Broadway in 1972 starring Donald Pleasence;* Dutch Uncle *(London, 1969); an adaptation of* The Idiot *for the National Theater (1971);* Spoiled *(London, 1971);* Butley *starring Alan Bates (London, 1971, Broadway 1972, a Best Play);* Otherwise Engaged *(London 1975, Broadway 1977, a Best Play and the Critics Award winner);* Dog Days *(Oxford Playhouse, 1976);* Molly *(London 1977, off off Broadway 1978);* The Rear Column *(London 1978, off Broadway 1978);* Close of Play *(National Theater 1979, off Broadway 1981); and* Stage Struck *(London 1979).*

Gray's third Best Play, Quartermaine's Terms, *was first produced in London in 1981. It arrived off Broadway on Feb. 24 in the Long Wharf Theater production after playing at that New Haven, Conn. establishment in December and January. Gray is also the author of a number of novels and TV plays including* Death of a Teddy Bear, *for which he won the Writers' Guild Award. He is married and now lectures in English literature at Queen Mary College in London.*

Simon Gray's *Quartermaine's Terms* (the script of which will not be synopsized here) is a worthy successor to its author's other two Best Plays, *Butley* and *Otherwise Engaged.* Also like them, it puts forward a central character whose most conspicuous trait is his failure (as in *Butley*), or refusal (as in *Otherwise Engaged*), or inability (as in *Quartermaine's Terms*) to maintain connections with the world around him. As expressed in an understated style of contemporary playwriting also practised with great success by Harold Pinter, this mysterious detachment produces an emotional tension within the most mundane events in all three plays.

229

Remak Ramsay as St. John Quartermaine and John Cunningham as Henry Windscape in *Quartermaine's Terms*

In *Butley,* as we reported ten years ago in *The Best Plays of 1972–73,* the title role (played by Alan Bates in that season's best performance by an actor) is that of a college professor whose will has been eaten away by sexual dissatisfaction and academic disillusionment long before the play begins. What we see onstage is the day the whole structure of his life collapses. The younger man who has been sharing his office, his apartment and his life goes off with another, more solid companion; his ex-wife has decided to marry a rival professor whom he considers a clown and a clod; he cannot seem to relate to his students or perform his duties. He is unable to cope with reality even physically—he cannot pick up an object from his desk without dropping it, and he has even cut himself shaving. Finally he has nothing left except the intellectual prop of quoting nursery rhymes as though they contained the wisdom and poetry of the ages (which perhaps they do, but they are of little help to Butley). In the hollowed-out, helpless state in which we find him, the simplest procedure, such as a routine conference with a student, becomes a disaster of the spirit for Butley.

In Gray's *Otherwise Engaged,* the 1976–77 New York Drama Critics Circle best-of-bests winner, the other-worldly protagonist is called Simon Hench. Hench's detachment is more of a defense against life than a drowning in it—but by the time the play begins, Hench has reached the point, willingly or no, where he could no longer come back into the world even if he wanted to. As we noted in the 1976–77 *Best Plays* volume, he shines with a high intellectual gloss while underneath he is either an empty but impenetrable shell or an immovably solid object (and a close look at the play didn't necessarily determine which). Hench (played by Tom Courtenay in a production which, like *Butley,* was directed by Harold Pinter) is at the center of a gathering storm of relationships with friends and family—the calm center, where he can blot out the cries of human pain by putting another record on his player. He insists on maintaining a cool, rational detachment when others expect heated involvement, and therefore he is "otherwise engaged," increasingly incapable or unwilling to share in others' lives or to permit others a share in his. Certainly Hench's wound is arrogantly self-inflicted, where Butley's has festered from a personality weakness—but it is the same wound, crippling both with alienation.

St. John Quartermaine of *Quartermaine's Terms* is the opposite of arrogant and suffers from no evident trauma but is equally detachable from the circumstances in which the author places him. We first see Quartermaine taking his ease in the faculty room of the school which he has served from its beginning, apparently a comfortable member of a well-defined, close-knit group—and then we watch him being slowly torn from this environment and discarded like an irrelevant page in a notebook. If the connections Butley was able to maintain destroyed him; if Hench did everything possible to avoid connections, Quartermaine (played in various keys of apology by Remak Ramsay) does everything he can to keep physical and emotional contact with the only outside world he knows. His efforts are obvious, unceasing, pathetic, courteous—and failing, as his colleagues put him at further and further distance, like a herd of animals shrinking from a dying member. Quartermaine is going to suffer the same wound as Butley and Hench, and in his case it will be as near mortal as makes no difference.

Quartermaine's "terms" are school terms in the Cull-Loomis School of English for Foreigners in Cambridge, England. Early on a Monday morning at the beginning of a spring term in the 1960s, the staff room is furnished with arm-chairs, a table and a row of lockers and is accessible by a door to the school's hallway and French windows to the outdoors. Quartermaine too seems to be a fixed part of the room (in due course we learn that he is a bachelor and an ex-Cantabridgian, raised in the home of an aunt). Anita Manchip, a fellow teacher, joins Quartermaine and apologizes for cancelling a dinner party the previous night because her husband had a business meeting. "Oh Lord," Quartermaine exclaims, he doesn't mind (he will repeat this same bland exclamation to punctuate every occurrence, major and minor). And even when Anita inadvertently lets out that they gave the dinner party after putting him off, he still doesn't mind. He spent the evening happily baby-sitting for another colleague. He was obligingly available, just as he is obligingly unresentful at having been left out. At this point, his inveterate willingness might possibly be mistaken for simple good fellowship.

Other colleagues who drift in and out of the faculty room are Mark Sackling, who is preoccupied with writing a novel and whose wife has just left him, taking both their son and their automobile; Eddie Loomis, the co-principal, questioning Quartermaine about a former student whom Quartermaine should but does not clearly remember and reminding Quartermaine that a new part-time teacher is expected imminently; the latter, Derek Meadle, who arrives in torn trousers following a minor bicycle collision; Henry Windscape, with whose children Quartermaine was sitting; and Melanie Garth, whose mother, a once illustrious Cambridge professor, is recovering from a stroke.

After welcoming Meadle, who remains acutely embarrassed by the tear in his trousers, Loomis tells the others of the school's growing reputation and enrollment. While he is reminding them all that this may call for increased effort and commitment, Sackling, who has spent a sleepless weekend, keels over in a faint. "Oh Lord! Oh Lord!" exclaims Quartermaine, making moves to cover Sackling with his jacket and phone for an ambulance—both of which actions are quickly accomplished by others before Quartermaine is able to carry them out, almost as though Quartermaine were not really present.

Some weeks later, just before 5 o'clock on a sunny Friday afternoon, Quartermaine is looking forward to a weekend visit to the theater (a Strindberg or an Ibsen, he can't remember which). He confesses to Loomis that he let his class out early from a special lecture with slides (a program especially favored by the other co-principal, Thomas Cull, who never appears onstage) because he couldn't manage the new projector—and his class wasn't well attended, anyway. It's almost as though Quartermaine were beginning to lose contact with his pupils: either he is withdrawing from them, or they from him, or both.

All the others (including Anita, who's in distress just now because her husband is having an affair) beg off from Quartermaine's invitation to accompany him to the theater. Sackling makes good his escape before Quartermaine can pin him down to a weekend luncheon date. Windscape's croquet group out on the lawn are just finishing their game and don't intend to start another. Having let out his class early, and unable to join any of his colleagues in activity or conversation or weekend plans, Quartermaine departs. Finally, when everyone has left the staff

Remak Ramsay, Caroline Lagerfelt and Roy Poole in *Quartermaine's Terms*

room, Quartermaine returns and stands alone. At this point—the end of Act I —it is obvious that his alienation from the people and purposes of the Cull-Loomis school is well advanced. But Quartermaine has nowhere else to go.

A year later on a Monday morning at the beginning of summer, the gap is widening as the members of the faculty drift in and out discussing their adventures during the holiday week they've all just enjoyed (Quartermaine of course stayed home). Their careers seem to be steadily progressing. Sackling is pleased with the way his novel is going. Meadle is ready to ask to be made a full-fledged member of the staff instead of just a part-timer (but when he does, he is actually cut back, as the school is now economizing after a drop in enrollment).

Quartermaine, on the other hand, has been finding it more and more difficult to manage his pupils. He can hardly distinguish their individual faces or names, and he has been known to sit for the entire class hour without speaking. His response to his friends' emotional and/or professional problems is now expressed exclusively in the form of bland cliches, and in exchange his friends now give only the minimum polite notice of his presence or his part in any conversation. He watches while Loomis enters the staff room and harangues the faculty on the subject of increasing efficiency in order to reduce costs, but when the bell rings for class he finds himself trying to figure out which subject he's supposed to be teaching now. We know in what direction Quartermaine is headed, and we are witnessing acceleration in the rate of his decline.

Months later on a Friday evening, ironically, Quartermaine is invited to two dinner parties (by Sackling and Meadle) on the same evening but has previously accepted Melanie's invitation to attend a revivalist meeting, and he goes off with her. Loomis informs the others that Quartermaine didn't bother to show up for his last class this afternoon. He has obviously become an administrative problem for the school, but they can't just chuck him out to fend for himself.

A year and a half later, around Christmas, the faculty are all present when Loomis comes to tell them that the expected death of co-principal Thomas Cull has just taken place. Loomis has no desire to stay on without his friend, but the school is to continue with Windscape as principal.

Windscape asks Quartermaine (who is dressed in a dinner jacket, not because he is going anywhere, but because he was trying it on when he was summoned) to remain behind after the others leave. Carefully but firmly, Windscape tells Quartermaine that there will no longer be any place for him here at the school under the new circumstances. Quartermaine admits that he hasn't been fulfilling his duties, and his manner is apologetic as he asks Windscape's permission to stay here in this room for a few minutes to collect his thoughts. Windscape leaves. Quartermaine sits in his accustomed chair, as the play ends.

And so ends Quartermaine's world—not with a bang or a whimper, but with another mechanical "Oh Lord!" His alienation from his only possible association is now complete. It had begun long before the play's events, during which Quartermaine may usually have been conscious of the relationships and stresses experienced by those around him, but nothing in them really affected or touched him—not Anita's troubled marriage, Sackling's novel, Loomis's attachment to the invisible Thomas, Meadle's strivings, Windscape's measured observations or Melanie's distressed and distressing mother.

The roots of Quartermaine's detachment from reality were never exposed by the author of *Quartermaine's Terms,* any more than he made them explicit in either *Butley* or *Otherwise Engaged.* Despite Quartermaine's frequent lapses of concentration, it wasn't creeping senility that slowly strangled his personality. Perhaps the author meant to imply an early-implanted fear of commitment, disguised as overreaction to every kind of personal contact and overeagerness to please in small ways. Here's how some of the leading reviewers figured Quartermaine and his plight in their published reviews:

"The central character, St. John Quartermaine. . . . .is not merely absent-minded, he is absent. He is almost saintly in his simplicity and in his desire to be of service. Naturally, he is as expendable as a sacrificial lamb"—Mel Gussow, WQXR.

"With his tall posture, cheery disposition and unfailing good manners, he epitomizes the well-bred English gentleman. But Quartermaine is all manners and no substance: he is an anachronism carried through life by sheer inertia"—Frank Rich, New York *Times.*

"He is a poignant victim of a life he never really lived. . . . .His despair is absolutely bewitching. You watch his very reticence as if it was heroic—which, in a sense I suppose it is. Playwright, director and actor combine here to let the character be tonguetied into eloquence"—Clive Barnes, New York *Post.*

"What of his gift for reinterpreting slights, slaps and catastrophes. . . . .as footling stumbling-stones to be serenely risen above—if not, indeed, blessings in disguise? By lifting myopic meliorism to the level of quixotic magnanimity, Quartermaine, though no Cambridge Don, becomes a sort of greater, Cervantian, Don"—John Simon, *New York* Magazine.

"He is losing *himself,* shrinking into a stupor of nonexistence that's both hilarious and terrifying. Quartermaine and his colleagues are Gray's metaphor for a Britain atrophying into spiritual noodledom"—Jack Kroll, *Newsweek.*

"St. John Quartermaine is not so much obtuse as simply too good-hearted to suspect the infidelities, rivalries and submerged relationships that swirl around him. . . . .Quartermaine's astigmatic observation prevents him from knowing of the comparable sorrows of others"—Allan Wallach, *Newsday.*

"In so many of Simon Gray's other plays we have watched men fall apart, many times through controllable self-destruction. Quartermaine's final fall is such a quiet one, so very touchingly sad, that true tragedy . . . as well as incredible wit . . . is with us"—William A. Raidy, Newark *Star-Ledger.*

" 'Alienated' is too weak a word to describe British playwright Simon Gray's latest hero. St. John Quartermaine is downright disconnected"—Jacques le Sourd in the Gannett Newspapers.

In any case, as portrayed with unwavering skill by Remak Ramsay in this season's off-Broadway production, Quartermaine is a pitiable shred of humanity, much less forbidding and therefore much more likeable than either Butley or Hench, but sharing a similar fate in a third Best Play from Simon Gray.

Jeffrey De Munn as Taylor (on rope, *above*) climbs the spectacular ice wall designed by
Ming Cho Lee, with Jay Patterson as Harold looking on, in a scene from *K2*

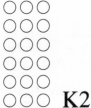

K2

A Play in One Act

BY PATRICK MEYERS

Cast and credits appear on page 355

PATRICK MEYERS was born in Phoenix, Ariz. in July 1947, the son of a professional gambler. He was educated at Colorado State University and Merritt College in Oakland, Calif., receiving an arts degree in 1972. He became an actor, and in 1973 "just for the fun of it" he wrote a play, Feedlot, then put it in a drawer. A few years later, an actor friend happened to see it, asked to read it and insisted on letting others see it. It was produced at the Berkeley, Calif. Stage Company, and then off Broadway in October 1977 for 49 performances by Circle Repertory Company. His second play, An Actor Repairs, was first done at Laney College in Oakland in 1977. His third, Glorious Morning, was produced in October 1978 for 29 performances by Circle Rep. His fourth, K2, named after a Himalayan peak, was first produced in 1982 at Theater by the Sea, Portsmouth, N.H., with productions immediately afterward at Arena Stage in Washington, D.C. and Syracuse, N.Y. Stage, followed by its Broadway debut March 30, 1983 and its author's first Best Play citation.

Meyers has been a recipient of a Spingold Foundation grant and has been a playwright-in-residence at Circle Rep since 1978. He is married and lives in Oakland.

Place: A ledge at 27,000 feet, 1,250 feet below the summit of K2, the world's second highest mountain

SYNOPSIS: The house lights dim as though a sudden gust of wind (which we hear) was blowing them out, while the haunting sound of a Japanese flute is heard.

There in blue moonlight is a huge ice wall soaring past the very top of the proscenium and obviously plunging for thousands of feet below a ledge which cuts across it a few feet above stage level. After a distant rumble is heard, snow drifts down the face of the ice onto the ledge.

"Slowly, in a rainbow of colors, the dawn breaks on the icy crystal face. Finally, bright yellow rays cut across the ledge, spreading slowly over the entire wall. There is a beat of complete stillness, and then slowly the mound of snow on the ledge begins to move and break up. A man's head, then torso rises from the mound."

It is Taylor, laughing to see the sun, then digging into the mound next to him to uncover his teammate, Harold. Taylor shouts at Harold and shakes him out of his torpor. Almost gleefully, Taylor digs their equipment from the snow, while reminding Harold that their place in mountain-climbing history—second place among climbers after having conquered the 27,000 feet of K2—is now secure.

Taylor finds their oxygen cylinder, reviving Harold by making him breathe some of it, taking a few restorative whiffs himself while estimating that they have about three hours before it is likely to start snowing again. And the other members of their team must know they are in trouble now (Harold has injured his leg) and will come partway up to help them.

> *Taylor delicately peels back the heavy woolen sock from Harold's leg and pulls the leg of the suit open. We can see that the leg is badly broken.*
>
> TAYLOR: . . . Holy shit . . . we gotta get off this fuckin' mountain.
>
> HAROLD: Stupid.
>
> *Taylor puts the sock back on, then the overboot, and zips the pant leg up again, talking rapidly while he works.*
>
> TAYLOR: Can't do anything for it now. Have to get you off fast as possible. They might be able to save it. The quicker we get to base, better chance you've got. So just hang in there . . . Harold . . . just hang in there . . . all right?
>
> HAROLD: I'm O.K. It's just stupid. I should have known you were still on the rope.
>
> TAYLOR: What the hell's it matter now? Right now we got to get off this mountain. Right?
>
> HAROLD: Right.

Taylor takes stock of their equipment. They have water and sun screen. In Harold's pack Taylor finds 120 feet of rope, one ice hammer (Taylor threw his away), nylon tubing for a sling, two meat bars. Checking out his own pack, Taylor finds ice screws, then utters a great cry as he finds that he has forgotten to include his backup rope. The discovery of this omission nearly throws him (he requires a whiff of oxygen to recover), but Harold calms him down, reminding him to put on sun screen and check the rest of the pack. It seems they have enough "beaners" to lower Harold in a sling, but "Unfortunately we don't have half the rope we need to run through the little buggers." Harold thinks maybe he could make it straight down on the single strand of rope, but Taylor knows he couldn't.

In spite of the fact that Taylor has a sore shoulder because Harold landed on it with his crampons in the accident, Taylor knows that he must climb back up the mountain to retrieve the rope they left there, if Harold is to be lowered in a sling (and there's no other way he can get down and survive). Harold protests that Taylor can't make it, they're both half frozen, but Taylor roars at him that there's no other way.

TAYLOR: . . . . . We've got one one-hundred-and-twenty-foot rope. The wall we are on is six hundred feet if it is a fucking inch! WE are maybe half way down it . . . if we are lucky. We couldn't have fallen more than twenty, twenty-five feet to this ledge. We'd've bounced right off the motherfucker if it'd been any farther than that. That's three hundred feet to go—one more ledge if we're lucky! The rope will be doubled, using a beaner as a pulley for the sling . . . one one-hundred-and-twenty-foot rope will become just sixty feet long. One ledge, Harold, if that . . . We need two ropes to be in striking distance of that ledge. God help us if it's not there. Do you understand now, Harold? Do you understand?

We hear the wind. Taylor looks up, then down at the ledge they are on.

HAROLD: I thought you had a ledge. I thought you were off the rope. I couldn't see you in the snow. There wasn't any tension!

TAYLOR: I had a crack. I was takin' a little breather. You should've called down to me.

HAROLD: . . . I know.

TAYLOR: Wait a minute . . . Harold . . . what would you say the odds are of two climbers on a six-hundred-foot, ninety degree ice wall coming off their rope . . . and then surviving the night with a temperature somewhere between forty and fifty degrees below zero in nothing but Emergency High Altitude suits, overboots and a couple of fucking ponchos . . . what would you say the odds are of that happening?

HAROLD: No odds—too improbable.

TAYLOR: No odds . . . no odds. I'm goin' up there and get the rope. With the luck we've had so far, I may dance up the son of a bitch.

Taylor is going to climb until he can grasp the discarded rope and pull it free. He tests the ice wall, finds a likely area to make a traverse and starts up, asking Harold to talk to him while he does so. Harold makes up a tale about a cyclops with a glass eye, starting them both laughing. Then at Taylor's request he explains (as Taylor is crossing the face of the ice) how he first got interested in physics in the seventh grade. The American educational system of cramming facts and hoping for the best was doing little for him until he came across a textbook explaining Albert Einstein's Unified Field Theory. With it, Harold found "A believable God. A fluid, flexible, mutable, ever changing, always constant God. God, as a subatomic intelligence that pervades, is the very core of the physical universe. A God forever exploring all the possibilities of existence . . . A God with the balls to hoist the mainsail and head for infinity!"

But later, in college, Einstein's theory failed Harold in confrontation with quantum mechanics—"a branch of physics that deals with physical phenomena that do not adhere to the main law of physical science." In his disillusionment, Harold became a bum and a drug user (he tells Taylor, as Taylor disappears above him but remains a physical presence because Harold is holding and paying out the end of the safety rope which Taylor is passing through the fasteners as he climbs the mountain). But then Harold discovered blind faith—"blind faith was the plain wrapper that carried the supreme intelligence, the cosmic glue"—that put him back on the right track. He went back to college and earned his Ph.D.

Suddenly Taylor's cry "I got it!" comes from above. He has reached the discarded rope and is trying to pull it loose, but finds he can't.

TAYLOR: COME ON YOU BASTARD!!! COME ON!!!
> *A few chunks of ice fall past Harold.*
Oh my God . . . oh my God . . . TENSION!
> *Harold quickly tightens the rope.*
Just relax . . . it's okay . . . it doesn't matter.
HAROLD: Are you all right?
TAYLOR: Yes . . . I'm just fine . . . I'm just fine . . . and I'm coming down slowly . . . I'm coming slowly down . . . slowly down . . . slowly. A journey of a thousand miles begins with one step . . . one small step for mankind . . . a giant step for man . . .
> *We can see Taylor again. He is moving carefully down. He has snapped the rope through a carabiner at his highest point, and Harold is paying out rope, slowly lowering him as he climbs back down the wall. He stops at the ice screw and unsnaps the rope from it.*
A horrible thing . . . a temper . . . a horrible thing. Only thing it's good for is P.D.s and scum . . . Hell hath no fury like an assistant D.A. . . . Maybe it's my Italian blood . . . all that tomato sauce. Yeah, it's gotta be the tomato sauce. You know how most families have orange juice for breakfast? We had tomato sauce . . . nice big glass of tomato sauce in the morning . . . you ever take a good look at a tomato? Nasty little fruit . . . yeah, it's gotta be the tomato sauce . . . funny the things you talk about when you're about to die. . . . .
> *He reaches the ledge and drops the carabiner and ice screw next to Harold, who places them on the ledge. Taylor vomits.*
Oh God . . . she's a bitch . . . a nut bustin' bitch.

Harold has a suggestion: Taylor could make a descent alone on the rope they've got, secured at this ledge; then when Taylor reaches the end of it, Harold could let this end of the rope go, so that Taylor could reach the bottom of the ice wall and go for help. Taylor rejects this course of action as impossible. They only have a couple of hours until the snow flies again, and Taylor couldn't do it in that time, even if he were sure that the others were coming up to meet him. Instead, Taylor informs him, "We wait a little longer—say another half an hour, and let the sun work on the ice—and then I go back up and try the rope again."

Harold doesn't think this will work. Angrily, Taylor declares that Harold will die if he has to spend another night up here. Harold replies in anger, but Taylor refuses to give up.

TAYLOR: . . . . .I haven't lost faith—you know, that crap you were goin' on about while I was on the wall—I still have faith in my ability to face this challenge and win . . . and winning means getting me and what I care about off this wall . . . I was just making a little joke when I referred to dying. It was a joke. I didn't realize you were so sensitive about the subject. I apologize.

HAROLD: I'm not so sensitive . . . I think about it quite often, as a matter of fact. More than you do, I think.

TAYLOR: I doubt that, Harold. Death is my job, it's what I'm paid for. (*Pause.*) Every day I go into court and put at least a couple of lousy scum on ice. I salt their tails for two, five, ten, twenty years at a whack, Harold. You have any idea the kind of dent twenty years of prison puts in a man's life? Usually I don't get to kill 'em all at once, but I take chunks out of the fuckin' scum, I take as big a chunk as I can get . . . and I think about it all the time.

HAROLD: I never realized you were so . . . possessed.

TAYLOR: Possessed? Yeah. Well . . . I try to keep it to myself. I know I wouldn't get much sympathy from our hip young friends. . . . .Listen, Harold, you don't know what's goin' on down there all around you every day, every night—while you sleep, make love with Cindy, eat Chinese food, play with atoms at Lawrence Radiation Center. All around you all the time, you don't know, buddy. Sure you read about some of it in the papers, selected atrocities for your viewing pleasure . . . . .all a ya, sittin' around bitchin' about crime in the neighborhood and social injustice all in the same breath. Christ, if you guys had any idea of what's really goin' on out there under your fuckin' noses, you'd be so damn scared you'd shit and die . . . there's a war goin' on down there—and the barbarians are winning! They're kickin' our civilized asses all over the streets. . . . .

Taylor claims that 90 per cent of the crimes he prosecutes are committed by members of minorities; Harold attributes this to racism in society. Taylor argues that liberal humanitarianism has produced "a black male, average age thirteen to twenty-five, average weight one hundred and thirty to two hundred and twenty pounds, who has the reflexes of a rattler, the strength of a rhino and the compassion of a pit bull. He can rip off you and your grandma before you can count to one. . . . .That's what you get when you take away somebody's dignity and try to make it up to 'em by givin' 'em a free bag of groceries and a place to sleep." It's Taylor's job—which he does extremely well—to serve Harold by sending these criminals to jail, to "clean up after all you Pollyanna jerks."

No, it's not for the benefit of the likes of Harold (Harold argues forcefully), it's to protect the world of the gizmo, the "zillion different little gadgets to keep your mind off the fact that it's all getting tooo big tooo fast," manufactured and distributed around the whole world. And man has finally developed a bomb— the neutron bomb—that will blow away all the people without damaging any of the gizmos. Harold tells Taylor, "Listen big boy, we can drop you in your tracks without so much as altering the flesh tones on your Sony Trinitron . . . THAT'S REAL . . . the culmination of Gizmo Madness."

Compared to the gizmo problem, Taylor's efforts hardly matter. Harold calls Taylor "a romantic. . . . .the Clint Eastwood of mountain climbing" for believing he can pull loose a rope attached to two screws set in solid ice, while clinging precariously to the cliff face. Taylor is determined to try, however, and he accepts

Jeffrey De Munn (*left* in both photos) and Jay Patterson,
philosophical *(above)* and panicking *(below)* in scenes from *K2*

Harold's suggestion that he take the nylon tubing with him, attach it to the rope and let it down so the two of them can pull together.

Taylor returns to the ice face and climbs, with Harold helping by hauling on the rope from his supine position, while continuing his monologue where he left off at "blind faith." He proceeded to fall in love with Cindy, who soon bore him a son, Eric, though mother and child nearly perished in the process. Harold admits that he finally resorted to prayer to pull them through. God answered Harold by giving him a sense of eternal spiritual union with his wife and son: "I was in my wife and in my son and I would never leave them ever ever ever."

Meanwhile, Taylor has reached the discarded rope, tied the nylon tubing to it and returned to the ledge. The two men take in some oxygen and eat the meat bars to gain strength, while Taylor confesses he couldn't establish a loving relationship with a woman—his affairs are more like battles. Of course he's lonely, he puts up with that. "Love costs too much. It's way overpriced," Taylor declares, settling instead for a sort of mutually agreed-upon rape.

The two men adjust their protective gear, then take hold of the nylon tubing and pull with all their strength and weight. The rope above them comes loose and falls past them, tied firmly to the nylon—success! But *a rumbling of splitting ice and tearing snow can be heard faintly. . . . .Suddenly the whole face of the wall is engulfed in falling white. It is a massive avalanche. Harold and Taylor disappear beneath a thundering waterfall of ice. When they reappear, the rope they were holding is gone, as is the piece of ledge on which their equipment was placed.*"

Taylor curses as he sees that the only remaining rope is that which he fastened to the ice wall. Harold has been struck on the head by a piece of falling ice, wounded but not seriously. Taylor binds Harold's new injury with a piece of poncho, then searches the snow. He finds the hammer, one pack, a canteen, a poncho, then asks Harold for his ice axe.

TAYLOR (*with increasing intensity, finally approaching dementia*): Your ice axe, Harold! I'm asking you about your crummy fucking ice axe. It's next to you in the snow there, isn't it? Just say yes. Say yes, you stupid fucking jerk. Say it before I throw you off this ledge, you fucking crippled clown!
> *Harold just stares woozily at Taylor. Suddenly Taylor grabs him by the collar and begins shaking him violently.*
SAY IT! SAY IT! SAY IT! SAY IT! SAY IT! SAY IT!
HAROLD: . . . help . . . Taylor . . . help me . . . help . . . please . . .
TAYLOR (*stops shaking Harold*): . . . Oh God . . . of my God . . . (*Moves away from Harold.*) . . . oh no . . . no, no, no, oh God . . . I'm sorry, Harold . . . I'm sorry.
HAROLD: . . . You can make it. You can still make it, but you gotta go now . . . now.
> *Harold searches in the snow around him.*
Here. It's here.
> *Harold pulls the ice axe out of the snow.*
I got it, Taylor. Look, you got a chance. You could get down before the snow. You could . . . if you're lucky.
TAYLOR: No . . . no, no, no . . .

HAROLD: You could. Do it like I said before . . . you could make it.
TAYLOR: It's no good. We're dead. We're dead.
HAROLD: Secure the rope here and . . .
TAYLOR: The screws! They're gone, Harold . . . It's all gone.
HAROLD: What about the wall? (*Looks up at the rope.*) There must be some left on the wall.
TAYLOR: No.
HAROLD: Look.
TAYLOR: No.

Taylor curses the ice wall for trying to make him lose his temper, then yields to hysteria, chopping at the ice as though he could disable or kill the mountain with his axe, screaming obscenities at the looming peak until, exhausted, he lies down. Harold tries to calm him: "Mountains are metaphors, buddy, in case you forgot—the purest, simplest metaphors on this whole crazy planet. The higher you go, the deeper you get. It's that God damn simple . . . and when you can't run away from where the hell you are . . . then guess what? You have to be there."

The discovery of quarks (Harold tells Taylor) vindicated Einstein and confirmed the laws of cause and effect, which had been brought into question by previous quantum research. "There is method," he declares as the final conclusion, "There is method all around us. We found God's house, buddy, and we called it—Quarks."

Harold induces Taylor to look at the wall to see how many ice screws they have left—three, it seems, so they might just as well assume that there are only three more ledges between here and the base of the wall. Taylor doesn't believe he can go onto the wall again to get the screws, but Harold persuades him to do so while Harold diverts him with further philosophical conclusions.

HAROLD: . . . . . I am one of the discoverers of the quark. I was the answer man . . . I was the answer man. I never grew up . . . it's so clear up here. It doesn't need me to explain it. I mean it all goes on. Understanding has no meaning . . . holding on, holding on . . . just holding on . . . that has meaning.
TAYLOR: I got one, Harold! I got one!
HAROLD: Great . . . (*The wind.*) Listen, I want you to give a message to Eric when he gets older . . . I want you to tell him that life's about holding on. Tell him . . . Will you do that for me, Taylor?
TAYLOR: Oh my God!
HAROLD: Taylor?
TAILOR: HAROLD! FAAAAALLLLLLIIINNNNGGGG!!!!
Taylor falls from above and then is dangling on the rope.

Taylor is hanging over the edge of the precipice, virtually paralyzed from the shock of his fall. Harold gets him to swing himself in pendulum motion until he can grab a loop on the other end of the rope and pull himself in to safety, having retrieved one ice screw.

Harold gives Taylor the rest of the water to drink. Taylor resents Harold's suggestion that he try to save himself with what little equipment they have left, telling him, "I don't have a Cindy, Harold, and I never wanted one. I only ever wanted one God damn real friend . . . Harold, you're my friend . . . my friend. I AM NOT gonna spend the endless seconds of the rest of my days with the fact that I left you to die on some stinking mountain while I scurried back to life! I'm not gonna wake up and brush my teeth with that. I'm not gonna drive to work with that. I'm not."

The wind is howling as they pause for a moment to think the situation over, then Harold tells Taylor that life is too great a gift to be demeaned by clinging to it in panic. He would like Cindy to know that he made a graceful exit, and "I want to hold her and tell her I love her and I'm thinking of her . . . that I'm caring till the last second . . . And I want her to know that I know . . . I messed up . . . I took it for granted . . . livin' on the outside of our happiness." Harold also would like to have his son Eric realize how sorry his father is that he can't be there while Eric is growing up: "I want to hug him one more time . . . hello and goodbye . . . that's what I want . . . and I can have it all . . . I can have it . . . if you go back . . . if you live with what you'll have to live with . . . I can have it all Taylor . . . if you go back . . . if you just go back. I want it . . . I want it bad . . . I want it bad."

After a moment of studied silence, Taylor finally agrees—he will try to make it down the ice wall with one rope and one ice screw.

HAROLD: Okay . . . situation assessment . . . take your time . . . try to find a crack within twenty feet of the end of the rope. Drive the screw and give the rope a couple healthy snaps . . . I'll let it go . . . by the end of your second rappell you'll be about forty feet from the base of the wall. Here, run this through your gizmo.
    Harold hands Taylor the rope and he runs it through his figure eight descender.
Crampons tight? (*Taylor nods affirmative.*) You've got the axe . . . it'll be enough . . . you'll make it . . . try not to get lost, Taylor. I don't want you droppin' into China.
TAYLOR: I'll be all right.
HAROLD: Ready?
    Taylor nods. They sit staring at each other for a moment.
Thank you. (*Taylor nods.*) Take care of yourself, Taylor.
TAYLOR: . . . you too.
HAROLD: Go.
TAYLOR: Right . . . I love you . . .
HAROLD: I love you too . . . Go.
    Taylor slips over the ledge in one motion and is gone. Harold sits for a long moment looking down the cliff after him. Harold is breathing more and more spasmodically, his chest rising and falling rapidly. He leans back and closes his eyes and eventually his breathing slows, calms.

Harold has his hand on the rope to feel the tension. He talks aloud as though telling his beloved Cindy a story about Japanese glacier foxes, some of which are albinos inevitably blinded by the glare of the sun on the glacier. Their fellow creatures care for them for awhile, bringing them food in the burrow, but eventually some instinct forces them to come down the mountain onto the beach and sit there facing the rolling sea, motionless, waiting for the waves to rise around them until they disappear under the water.

HAROLD: . . . . .The Japanese fishermen see one sometimes—once in a great while . . . at dawn . . . sitting . . . waiting . . . on the beach.

The rope snaps sharply twice.

Taylor found a crack. Taylor's got a crack, baby . . . I love you.

Harold unties the rope and holds it closely to him.

Taylor's goin' home . . . Taylor's gonna see your pretty smile. Taylor's gonna be warm again.

Harold's breathing starts to become violent again. He closes his eyes. It calms.

Hold on . . . hold on . . . I have to hold on. Help me hold on, honey. I want to stay with you now. I want to be calm like the little fox . . . and stay with you . . . I love you forever . . . forever.

The rope snaps sharply in Harold's hands.

. . . You know what I know? I know why the little fox sits so still . . . My one . . . It's because he knows he'll be back . . . and he'll have eyes next time.

Harold throws the rope into space, and it disappears.

. . . He knows he'll have eyes next time.

We hear Harold softly, very softly, as the lights dim out in blues.

. . . hold on . . . hold on . . . hold on . . . hold on . . .

Curtain.

'NIGHT, MOTHER

A Play in One Act

BY MARSHA NORMAN

Cast and credits appear on page 355

MARSHA NORMAN was born Marsha Williams (Norman being a married name) in Louisville, Ky. in 1947, the daughter of a realtor. She went to school in Louisville and received her B.A. from Agnes Scott College in Decatur in 1969. After gradua- tion she married Michael Norman, a teacher (they were divorced in 1974). She worked with emotionally disturbed children at Central State Hospital in Louisville while getting her M.A. at the University of Louisville, receiving it in 1971. She served as a filmmaker in schools under the aegis of the Kentucky Arts Commission, which sent her to the Center for Understanding Media in New York City for postgraduate study during two summers. She pursued her interest in writing through free-lance book reviews and features, and in putting out a newspaper for children, The Jelly Bean Journal, *under the masthead of the Louisville* Times.

In 1976 Ms. Norman began writing full time. Seeking "more sustained involve- ment" with a piece of work, she decided to go ahead with a play, her first, commis- sioned by Jon Jory, producing director of the Actors Theater of Louisville. She enjoyed the playwriting experience because "nothing else was ever this hard." The play was Getting Out *(and its author then billed herself with her middle initial, Marsha W. Norman), produced by Actors Theater in November 1977 and at the Mark Taper Forum in Los Angeles in February 1978. It was cited by the American Theater Critics Association as an outstanding new play of the cross-country season and was therefore represented in our 1977–78 Best Plays volume in a synopsis in our section on The Season Around the United States.* Getting Out *became a Best*

Kathy Bates *(foreground)* as Jessie Cates and Anne Pito-niak as Thelma Cates in a scene from *'night, Mother*

Play when it came to New York in the off-Broadway Phoenix Theater production for 22 performances beginning Oct. 19, 1978, then moving to the Theater De Lys May 15, 1979 for an extended run of 237 more performances.

Subsequent plays by Ms. Norman have included Laundromat *(off off Broadway, 1979) and* Third and Oak *and* Circus Valentine *at Actors Theater of Louisville, where she served as playwright-in-residence during the 1978–79 season. Her* 'night, Mother *was presented off off Broadway in November 1981 as a Circle Repertory project-in-progress and in December 1982 at American Repertory Theater in Cambridge, Mass. (on the basis of which production it was awarded the Pulitzer Prize) before opening on Broadway March 31 and winning its author's second Best Play designation.*

A new Norman playscript, The Holdup, *was presented this season at American Conservatory Theater in San Francisco following its project-in-progress appearance at Circle Rep. Ms. Norman is also the author of screen and TV plays and is now working on a musical,* The Shakers, *with Norman L. Berman. She has been the recipient of grants from the National Endowment and the Rockefeller Foundation. She has remarried (her new husband is Dann Byck, who produced his wife's play on Broadway) and lives in New York City.*

Time: *The present, about 9 p.m.*

Place: *A relatively new house built way out on a country road*

SYNOPSIS: The living room area at right is cluttered with magazines, needle-work, candy dishes and an assortment of unremarkable furniture and decoration. The kitchen area, about one-third of the floor space, is at left. A door upstage leads into the hall, on the far side of which a bedroom door is visible, and there is a door to the porch at left. A clock on the wall shows that it is about 9 p.m., and it will run through the continuous action which follows.

Thelma Cates is in the kitchen getting herself a tidbit from the shelf of her candies and cookies. She is in her late 50s or early 60s, and *"her sturdiness is quite obvious, although she has begun to feel her age. . . . .she speaks quickly and enjoys talking."* As she moves to the living room area, her daughter Jessie enters carrying a stack of newspapers which she deposits by the porch door. Jessie Cates is in her late 30s or early 40s, *"pale and vaguely unsteady, physically. It is not possible to tell why she distrusts her body, but she does. . . . .She wears pants and a long black sweater with deep pockets. . . . .There is a familiarity between these two women that comes from having lived together for a long time."*

Jessie is looking for old towels and pillows. Her mother reminds her that it's Saturday night, so Jessie is due to give her her weekly manicure. Jessie has this on her schedule for this evening, but right now she wants to find her father's pistol —it's probably in a shoe box in the attic.

After she tends her mother's immediate needs, cleaning her eyeglasses and measuring her knitting, Jessie pulls down the attic ladder from the hall ceiling. Thelma warns her that the attic floor is unsafe. Jessie knows it: "They didn't mean this house to last two minutes. Built it just to sell it, didn't they?" But she disappears into the attic while Thelma decries the idea of their needing firearms. There are no criminals around, they are too far out in the country, and "We don't have anything anybody'd want, Jessie. I mean, I don't even want what we got, Jessie."

Jessie finds the pistol and comes down the ladder, as Thelma comments that she wouldn't want Jessie's son Ricky to know they have a gun in the house. "Don't worry. It's not for him, it's for me," Jessie tells her mother and then goes on, ". . . . .don't talk to me any more about Ricky. Those two rings he took were the last valuable things I had, so now he's started in on other people, door to door. Like he's going down a list of the world, taking everybody's things. I hope they put him away some time. I'd turn him in if I knew where he was."

Jessie intructs Thelma to wash her hands for the manicure, then sets about cleaning the pistol. Thelma scoffs again at the idea of thieves coming here, and Jessie insists again that the gun isn't for them, it's for her.

MAMA: Well, you can have it if you want. You can mind your manners and ask first, and you can have anything in the house, Jessie. When I die, you'll get it all anyway.

JESSIE: I'm going to kill myself, Mama.

MAMA: You are not, don't even say such a thing, Jessie.

JESSIE: How would you know if I didn't say it? You want it to be a surprise? You're lying there in your bed or maybe you're just brushing your teeth and you hear this . . . noise down the hall?

MAMA: Kill yourself.

JESSIE: Shoot myself. In a couple of hours. (*Holds the gun to her head.*) Like so.

MAMA: It must be time for your medicine.

JESSIE: Took it already.

MAMA: What's the matter with you?

JESSIE: Not a thing. Feel fine.

MAMA: You feel fine. You're just going to kill yourself.

JESSIE: Waited until I felt good enough, in fact. Feel fine.

MAMA: Don't make jokes, Jessie. I'm too old for jokes. It's not a bit funny.

JESSIE: It's not a joke, Mama.

Thelma suggests that the gun may not work, or the ammunition may be too old, but Jessie tries the action and shows her mother bullets she bought only last week. Mama threatens to call Jessie's brother, Dawson; but if she does, Jessie will simply shoot herself before Dawson can get here: "Go ahead, call him. Then call the police. Then call the funeral home. Then call Loretta and see if *she'll* do your nails."

Thelma tries to use the phone, but Jessie stops her, insisting that this is to be a private matter between just the two of them. Thelma warns her she may miss

(Jessie doesn't think so), challenges Jessie about being afraid to die. Jessie denies this—death is what she longs for, dark and quiet and safe, dead quiet. Thelma threatens her with hell, to no effect (and Jessie rather believes that Jesus himself was a suicide).

Jessie goes toward the bedroom carrying the box with the pistol, which she has loaded with bullets. Grasping at straws, Thelma forbids Jessie to kill herself in this house, which like the gun itself belongs to Thelma.

JESSIE: I have to go in the bedroom and lock the door behind me so they won't arrest you for killing me. They'll probably test your hands for gunpowder anyway, but you'll pass.

MAMA: Not in my house!

JESSIE: If I'd known you were going to act like this, I wouldn't have told you.

MAMA: How am I supposed to act? Tell you to go ahead? O.K. by me, sugar? Makes real good sense. What took you so long? Might try it myself. Hold your hand?

JESSIE: There's just no point in fighting me over it, that's all. Want some coffee?

MAMA: Your birthday's coming up, Jessie. Don't you want to know what we got you?

JESSIE: You got me dusting powder, Loretta got me a new housecoat, pink probably, and Dawson got me new slippers, too small, but they go with the robe, he'll say.

Mama cannot speak.

Right.

Jessie pats her on the shoulder.

Be back in a minute.

While Jessie takes the gun, the towels and the plastic bags into the bedroom, Thelma picks up the phone, then thinks better of using it. Jessie comes back and sets about refilling all the candy jars, telling her mother, "I'm going to do what I can before I go. We're not just going to sit around tonight. I made a list of things." Thelma has to be told, for example, exactly how to work the washing machine, where the soap is kept and how to get repairs done.

Thelma offers to keep Dawson and his wife Loretta away from this house, because clearly they get on Jessie's nerves—as members of the family, they have too easy access to the private recesses of Thelma's and Jessie's lives—but Jessie wouldn't kill herself simply out of annoyance with Dawson and Loretta. She merely leaves the room when they come over.

Jessie's son Ricky has caused her considerable pain—nobody would be surprised if Ricky killed somebody some day—and Thelma offers suggestions as to how the Ricky problem might be solved. Jessie ignores the subject of Ricky, explaining various household procedures of ordering candy, food and medicine which her mother will need to know. Thelma suggests that Jessie is sick, and Jessie denies it.

MAMA: Epilepsy is sick, Jessie.

JESSIE: It won't kill me. (*Pause.*) If it would, I wouldn't have to.

MAMA: You don't *have* to!

JESSIE: No, I don't. That's what I like about it.

MAMA: Jessie!

JESSIE: I want to hang a big sign around my neck, like Daddy's on the barn. Gone Fishing.

MAMA: Well, I won't let you!

JESSIE: It's not up to you.

MAMA: You don't like it here.

JESSIE (*smiles*): Exactly.

MAMA: I meant here in my house.

JESSIE: I know you did.

MAMA: You never should have moved back in here with me. If you'd kept your little house or found another place when Cecil left you, you'd have made some new friends at least. Had a life to lead. Had your own things around you. Give Ricky a place to come see you. You never should've come here.

JESSIE: Maybe.

MAMA: But I didn't force you, did I?

JESSIE: I didn't have any better ideas. And you wanted me.

MAMA: You didn't have any business being by yourself right then, but I can see how you might want a place of your own. A grown woman should . . .

JESSIE: If it was a mistake, we made it together. You took me in. I appreciate that.

MAMA: It's not too late to move out. You could be as close or as far away as you wanted.

JESSIE: Mama . . . I'm just not having a very good time and I don't have any reason to think it'll get anything but worse. I'm tired. I'm hurt. I'm sad. I feel used.

MAMA: Tired of what?

JESSIE: It all.

MAMA: What does that mean?

JESSIE: I can't say it any better.

MAMA: Well, you'll have to say it better because I'm not letting you alone till you do. What were those other things? Hurt . . . (*Before Jessie can answer.*) You had this all ready to say to me, didn't you? Did you write this down? How long have you been thinking about this?

JESSIE: Off and on, ten years. On all the time, since Christmas.

MAMA: What happened at Christmas?

JESSIE: Nothing.

MAMA: So why Christmas?

JESSIE: That's it. On the nose.

> A pause. Mama knows exactly what Jessie means. She was there too, after all.

(*Putting the candy sacks away.*) See where all this is? Red hots up front, sour balls and horehound mixed together in this one sack. New packages of toffee and licorice right in back there.

MAMA: Go back to your list. You're hurt by what?

JESSIE (*as if Mama knows perfectly well*): Mama . . .

MAMA: O.K. Sad about what? There's nothing real sad going on right now. If it was after your divorce or something, that would make sense.

JESSIE (*straightening the drawer as she talks*): Now, this drawer has everything in it that there's no better place for. Extension cords, batteries for the radio, extra lighters, sand paper, masking tape, Elmer's Glue, thumbtacks, that kind of stuff. The mousetraps are under the sink, but you call Dawson if you've got one and let him do it.

MAMA: Sad about what?

JESSIE: The way things are.

MAMA: Not good enough. What things?

JESSIE: Oh, everything from you and me to Red China.

Jessie is being facetious, but at heart she's convinced that things aren't going any better out there in the wide world than they are right here in this room. Thelma offers to give up TV (kicking the set in demonstration) if the TV news is depressing her daughter. She even offers to get Jessie a dog, but Jessie continues her evasion in a series of instructions about household chores. "You don't have to take care of me, Jessie," Thelma says, declaring herself fit to take over most of the duties if that's what's upsetting her daughter. Jessie is aware that Thelma has been letting her do most of the housework simply to give Jessie something to occupy herself with. She tries to explain to her mother: "Mama, I know you used to ride the bus. Riding the bus and it's hot and bumpy and crowded and too noisy and more than anything in the world you want to get off and the only reason in the world you don't get off is it's still fifty blocks from where you're going? Well, I can get off right now if I want to, because even if I ride fifty more years and get off then, it's the same place when I step down to it. Whenever I feel like it, I can get off. As soon as I've had enough, it's my stop. I've had enough."

You have to work at learning to have a good time in life, Thelma insists. She suggests that Jessie stop acting like a brat and pull herself together—rearrange the furniture, or get a job. Jessie has tried the latter, working in a hospital gift shop, but she made the customers feel uncomfortable in the way she smiled at them. She once kept her father's books but did an inadequate job of that too.

Jessie can have an epileptic seizure at any time, which has alienated her from other people, at least in her own mind. Her life is all Jessie has that truly belongs to her; as far as she can see, she can't improve it, but she can shut it down.

Jessie suggests they enjoy their last evening together by making cocoa and caramel apples. Jessie sits for the first time this evening, while her mother stirs herself to buy time by brewing up the cocoa.

Jessie asks about Thelma's friend Agnes, and Thelma reveals that Agnes, as a child, made a practise of burning down each house she lived in—but no one was ever hurt in the fires or came around afterward to ask questions. Thelma thinks Agnes might do it again some day.

Thelma makes Jessie laugh talking about Agnes's pet birds. But Jessie knows that Agnes won't come here to visit Thelma, and that it has something to do with her. Thelma insists that her friend Agnes is crazy but admits that Agnes won't

Kathy Bates and Anne Pitoniak in *'night, Mother*

come here because she has an irrational fear of Jessie. Thelma offers to force Agnes to come over, but Jessie doesn't want that, she just wanted to know.

They try the cocoa and decide they don't like it after all; meanwhile, Jessie inquires about whether her parents loved each other, and Thelma tells her about her father, whom she had known all her life: "He felt sorry for me. He wanted a plain country woman, and that's what he married, and then he held it against me the rest of my life like I was supposed to change and surprise him somehow . . . . ." There was very little communication between them.

Jessie remembers that "I liked him better than you did, but I didn't know him any better." He used to make playthings for her occasionally, though a lot of the time he would just sit quietly in his chair. Jessie enjoyed talking to her father about mundane, everyday things, and Thelma was a bit jealous of that. Jessie misses him. She thought Thelma's life would improve, she'd get around more, after he died—but it didn't.

Thelma suggests Jessie might not be wanting to kill herself if her father were still alive, but she denies this. Thelma sums up her marriage: "It didn't matter whether I loved him. It didn't matter to me, and it didn't matter to him. And it didn't mean we didn't get along. It wasn't important. We didn't talk about it."

Thelma starts gathering kitchen equipment to throw out, declaring that from now on she'll live on tuna fish and candy. She orders Jessie to throw out all the pots and pans—she'll cook no more—but Jessie refuses, suggesting that maybe

Agnes could move in here so that Thelma wouldn't be alone. But Thelma wouldn't have her. Agnes is just a long-established habit with Thelma, who takes no real pleasure in her company.

Thelma and Jessie argue over the contents of the refrigerator, Jessie insisting that her mother ought to drink more milk. Jessie will clean out the refrigerator now, otherwise Thelma will merely let the contents spoil.

MAMA: Nothing I ever did was good enough for you, and I want to know why.

JESSIE: That's not true.

MAMA: And I want to know why you've lived here this long feeling the way you do.

JESSIE: You have no earthly idea how I feel.

MAMA: Well how could I? You're real far back there, Jessie.

JESSIE: Back where?

MAMA: What's it like over there, where you are? Do people always say the right thing or get whatever they want, or what?

JESSIE: What are you talking about?

MAMA: Why do you read the newspaper? Why don't you wear that sweater I made for you? Do you remember how I used to look, or am I just any old woman now? When you have a fit do you see stars, or what? How did you fall off the horse, really? Why did Cecil leave you? Where did you put my old glasses?

JESSIE: They're in the bottom drawer of your dresser in an old Milk of Magnesia box. Cecil left me because he made me choose between him and smoking.

MAMA: Jessie, I know he wasn't that dumb.

JESSIE: I never understood why he hated it so much when it's so good. Smoking is the only thing I know that's always just what you think it's going to be. Just like it was the last time and right there when you want it and real quiet.

MAMA: Your fits made him sick, and you know it.

JESSIE: Say seizures, not fits. Seizures.

MAMA: It's the same thing. A seizure in the hospital is a fit at home.

JESSIE: They didn't bother him at all. Except he did feel responsible for it. It *was* his idea to go horseback riding that day. It was his idea I could do *anything* if I just made up my mind to. I fell off the horse because I didn't know how to hold on. Cecil left for pretty much the same reason.

MAMA: He had a girl, Jessie. I walked right in on them in the tool shed.

JESSIE (*after a moment*): O.K. That's fair. (*Lights another cigarette.*) Was she very pretty?

MAMA: She was Agnes's girl, Carlene. Judge for yourself.

Thelma pretends she never thought Cecil was good enough for Jessie, but in fact she spotted him and hired him to build a porch, bringing him around so that Jessie could meet him. Jessie thinks it might have been better if her mother had let well enough alone, even if it meant Jessie remaining unmarried. But Jessie admits she loved Cecil and tried to be the woman he wanted—thinner, more alert —but perhaps she tried too hard or too obviously. As for their son Ricky, he is "as much like me as it's possible for any human to be. . . . . I see it on his face. I hear it when he talks. We look out at the world and we see the same thing. Not

Fair. And the only difference between us is, Ricky's out there trying to get even. And he knows not to trust anybody, and he got it straight from me . . . . . ." He's going from bad to what Jessie knows is sure to be worse.

Thelma suggests that Jessie get ahold of Cecil and try again, but she already tried hard enough, begging Cecil to take her with him even if it meant leaving Ricky behind. She has now reconciled herself to Cecil's absence, she tells Thelma as she takes the garbage outside (Thelma mentions the caramel apple, but Jessie has now decided she doesn't want one). Once again Thelma goes toward the phone and again decides against using it. When Jessie comes back inside, Thelma mentions that perhaps Jessie's father's silences were a form of fit, but Jessie doesn't believe it.

Thelma doesn't seem interested in the proposed manicure, so instead Jessie proceeds to replace the recently-laundered slipcovers on the sofa, with her mother helping. They are discussing Jessie's seizures—she doesn't see stars and most of the time has no warning and doesn't know she's having one. Thelma has noticed that Jessie's eyes seem to enlarge just before one of the seizures, which arrive in various forms. Sometimes Thelma can't bear to watch. Afterwards, Thelma cleans Jessie up before calling Dawson to come over and help her lift Jessie into bed. With the medicine she's now taking, Jessie hasn't had a recurrence in a whole year and might never have another. She feels good, and her memory has improved. She doesn't need to make so many lists to remind herself what she should be doing.

Thelma suggests that possibly Jessie inherited her illness from her father, but Jessie is sure it was caused by the fall from the horse. Thelma then reveals that the seizure following the fall from the horse wasn't the first one, as Jessie had supposed. The seizures started at age 5, but the truth was kept from Jessie and everyone else by Thelma, until one day after the horse incident Cecil was watching and told Jessie. Even Jessie's father didn't realize what was wrong.

Jessie reflects angrily that she should have been told much sooner—if she'd known she was an epileptic, she might have sought treatment earlier, and she wouldn't have gone horseback riding.

Jessie suggests that Thelma bring the manicure tray, but Thelma throws the tray onto the floor.

MAMA (*beginning to break down*): Maybe I fed you the wrong thing. Maybe you had a fever some time, and I didn't know it soon enough. Maybe it was a punishment.

JESSIE: For what?

MAMA: I don't know. Because of how I felt about your father. Because I didn't want any more children. Because I smoked too much or didn't eat right when I was carrying you. It has to be something I did.

JESSIE: It does not. It's just a sickness, not a curse. Epilepsy doesn't mean anything. It just is.

MAMA: I'm not talking about the fits here, Jessie! I'm talking about this killing yourself. It has to be me that's the matter here. You wouldn't be doing this if it wasn't. I didn't tell you things, or I married you off to the wrong man, or I took you in and let your life get away from you, or all of it put together. I don't know what I did, but I did it, I know. This is all my fault, Jessie, but I don't know what to do about it, now!

JESSIE (*exasperated at having to say this again*): It doesn't have anything to do with you!

MAMA: Everything you do has something to do with me, Jessie. You can't do *anything*, wash your face or cut your finger, without doing it to me. That's right! You might as well kill me as you, Jessie, it's the same thing. This has to do with me, Jessie.

JESSIE: Then what if it does! What if it has everything to do with you! What if you are all I have and you're not enough? What if I could take all the rest of it if only I didn't have you here? What if the only way I can get away from you for good is to kill myself? What if it *is*? I can *still* do it!

MAMA (*in desperate tears*): Don't leave me Jessie!

Jessie goes into the bedroom, but only to bring out a box of mementos she wants distributed to various people after her death. Thelma picks up the bottles from the manicure tray. When Jessie returns, Thelma pleads with her not to leave her alone to cope with all the problematical details of living and also with the remorseful feeling that she could have done something to help Jessie: "Stay with me a little longer. Just a few more years. I don't have that many more to go, Jessie. And as soon as I'm dead, you can do whatever you want. And maybe with me gone, it'll be quiet enough here in the house that you won't have to . . . do this." And maybe some day Ricky will straighten out and bring grandchildren here to visit.

Jessie sees what she is putting her mother through and regrets it along with all the other ill-fated events of a life which she so despises. Thelma challenges her to try it a little while longer, something unexpectedly good might turn up.

MAMA: . . . . . Try it for two more weeks. We could have more talks like tonight. I'll pay more attention to you. Listen more. Act better. Not feel so sorry for myself. Tell the truth when you ask me. Let you have your say.

JESSIE: We wouldn't have more nights like tonight because it's this next part that's made this last part so good, Mama. And you've already been as sweet to me as you had any right to be. This is all I can really do that will make me feel like I was worth anything at all. Like I knew who I was, anyway, and I knew what I wanted to do about it. This *is* how I have my say, Mama. This is how I say what I thought about it *all* and I say No. To Dawson and Loretta and the Red Chinese and epilepsy and Ricky and Cecil and you. And me. And hope. I say No. Just let me go easy, Mama.

MAMA: How can I let you go, Jessie?

JESSIE: You can because you have to. It's what you've always done.

MAMA: You are my child!

JESSIE: I am what became of your child.

Mama cannot answer.

I found an old baby picture of me. And it was somebody else, not me. It was somebody pink and fat who never heard of sick or lonely, somebody who cried and got fed, and reached up and got held, and kicked but didn't hurt anybody, and slept whenever she wanted to, just by closing her eyes . . . . . That's who I started out, and this is who is left. (*There is no self-pity here.*) That's what this is about. It's somebody I lost, all right. Only it's not anybody out there, Cecil or Daddy, it's my own self. Who I never was. Or who I tried to be and never got there. Somebody I waited for who never came. And never will. So, see, it doesn't much matter what else happens in the world or in this house, even. I'm what was worth waiting for, and I didn't make it. Me . . . who might have made a difference to me . . . I'm not going to show up, so there's . . . no reason to stay, except to keep you company, and that's . . . not reason enough because I'm not . . . very good company.

     A pause.

Am I?

    MAMA (*desperate pained truth*): No. Not in the way you mean. No. And neither am I.

If there was something—anything, like rice pudding—Jessie really liked, she might stay, but there isn't. Thelma resents Jessie's casual rejection of the life she clings to so tenaciously, but then she realizes that mentally, at least, Jessie has already gone. If Jessie thinks she will attract sympathy from others with her suicide, she is making a mistake—it's Thelma they'll all feel sorry for, they'll just be ashamed of Jessie, Thelma tells her vehemently. Outbursts like this make Jessie almost wish she'd just left her mother a note instead of telling her what she was going to do.

Jessie gives Thelma instructions about how to handle the modest funeral and the guests afterwards. Thelma finds herself receiving these instructions as though she were accepting Jessie's death as an accomplished fact. Jessie instructs her further: "Now, somebody's bound to ask you why I did it, and you just say you don't know. That you loved me and you know I loved you and we just sat around tonight like every other night of our lives and then I came over and kissed you and said, " 'night, Mother," and you heard me close my bedroom door, and the next thing you heard was the shot. And whatever reasons I had, well, you guess I just took them with me. You guess it was something personal. And let them think whatever they want." Thelma is not to try to explain further even to Dawson and Loretta, because this evening is a private matter between mother and daughter only.

Jessie warns Thelma not to try to enter the bedroom after she hears the shot, but to phone Dawson, then the police, then occupy herself by washing the chocolate pan, several times if necessary, until the doorbell rings. Thelma should ask Dawson to bring his extra set of keys so the police won't have to break down the bedroom door. Thelma is to stay in the living room with Dawson and Loretta while the police do their work and then go stay with them if she wants to or have Agnes come to stay here (Thelma doesn't want that).

Jessie gives instructions for the box of mementos, which includes a letter to Dawson about Thelma, telling him where all the important documents are kept and advising him what to give Thelma for Christmas and birthdays. Jessie wants Thelma to phone Cecil, mainly for Cecil to inform Ricky what has happened. Jessie has saved her watch to give to Ricky: "I appreciate him not stealing it already, so I'm just letting him know that, and saving him the trouble, and maybe he'll have something other than chili for supper for once. I'd like to buy him a good meal."

Most of the box's contents are gift-wrapped and are for Thelma—"not bought presents, just things I thought you might like to look at, pictures or things you think you've lost"—whenever Thelma feels the need of a present. Thelma thinks maybe she'd like to have that manicure now, but it's too late, as Jessie informs her: "It's time for me to go, Mama."

MAMA: It's not too late!

JESSIE: I don't want you to wake Dawson and Loretta when you call. I want them to still be up and dressed so they can get right over.

As Jessie backs up, Mama moves in on her, but carefully.

MAMA: They wake up fast, Jessie, if they have to. They don't matter here, Jessie. You do. I do. We're not through yet. We've got a lot of things to take care of here. *(Trying to get close enough to grab her.)* I don't know where my prescriptions are, and you didn't tell me what to tell Doctor Davis when he calls or how much you want me to tell Ricky or who I call to rake the leaves or . . .

JESSIE: Don't try and stop me, Mama, you can't do it.

MAMA *(grabbing her again, this time hard):* I can too! I'm a lot stronger than you are and you know it! And I'll stand in front of this hall and you can't get past me, I've got forty pounds on you at least!

They struggle.

You'll have to knock me down to get away from me, Jessie, or I'll knock you out cold before I'll . . .

Mama reaches for the phone book or some other implement to hit Jessie with, and as she does, Jessie gets away from her.

JESSIE *(almost a whisper):* 'night, Mother.

She vanishes into her bedroom, and we hear the door lock just as Mama gets to it.

MAMA *(screams):* Jessie!

Thelma pounds on the unyielding door and shouts at her daughter that none of her orders will be obeyed unless she comes out and sees to them herself. There is no answer, and Thelma cries out to Jessie to give herself another chance: "Jessie! Please!" The shot is heard—"*it sounds like an answer, it sounds like 'No.'*"

Thelma, in tears and in shock, leaves the door, goes to the sink and picks up the hot chocolate pan. Then she goes to the phone and dials. Loretta answers, and Thelma asks for Dawson. "*She looks down at the pan, holding it tight like her life depended on it. Curtain.*"

Tommy Tune as Capt. Billy Buck Chandler and Charles "Honi"
Coles as Mr. Magix in a tap dance number in *My One and Only*

MY ONE AND ONLY

A Musical Comedy in Two Acts

BOOK BY PETER STONE AND
TIMOTHY S. MAYER

MUSIC BY GEORGE GERSHWIN

LYRICS BY IRA GERSHWIN

Cast and credits appear on page 360

PETER STONE (co-author of book) was born Feb. 27, 1930 in Los Angeles, the son of the late John Stone, movie producer and writer. He took his B.A. degree at Bard (which also granted him a D. Litt. in 1971) and his M.F.A. at Yale Drama School in 1953. He began his writing career in France, where he contributed to all media. His first work for the Broadway theater was the book for a musical version of Jean-Paul Sartre's Kean *(1961), and there followed the librettos of* Skyscraper *(1965),* 1776 *(1969, a Best Play and the winner of the Critics and Tony Awards for best musical),* Two by Two *(1970),* Sugar *(1972),* Woman of the Year *(1981) and now* My One and Only, *the musical with the Gershwin score which reached Broadway May 1, 1983 and became its co-author's second Best Play.*

Stone also adapted Erich Maria Remarque's Full Circle *as a straight play for Broadway in 1973 and contributed to American Place's program of sketches* Straws in the Wind: A Theatrical Look Ahead *in 1975. The long list of his screen plays began with* Charade *in 1963 and has included* Father Goose *(1964, for which he won an Oscar) and* Sweet Charity *(1969). He is also the author of many TV scripts and was awarded an Emmy in 1963 for his work on* The Defenders *series. He has also been the recipient of the Mystery Writers (1964), Drama Desk (1969) and Christopher (1973) Awards.*

Stone is now serving his second term as president of the Dramatists Guild, the craft organization of playwrights, composers, librettists and lyricists. He is married and lives in New York City.

TIMOTHY S. MAYER (co-author of book) was born in Binghamton, N.Y. June 9, 1944, the son of an industrialist. He was educated at the Taft School, Watertown, Conn., graduating in 1962, and at Harvard in the class of 1966, where he wrote shows for the student organization Hasty Pudding, founded the Agassiz Theater Company with fellow-student and fellow-dramatist Thomas Babe, won the Phyllis Anderson Award for his first full-length play, Prince Erie *(about the New York boss Jim Fiske, produced in the year after his graduation) and to which he has returned from time to time as artist-in-residence and guest lecturer.*

Included among Mayer's subsequent playscripts were Red Eye *(produced in 1979 in New York),* Aladdin in Three Acts *(produced as part of his residency program at Harvard in 1981) and* Jesus: A Passion Play, *a musical which ran for several years as a Good Friday TV special. He has also been an active designer and director for imaginative reinterpretations of classics in Minneapolis, Cambridge, New York, Lenox, Mass. and other centers of theater activity. From 1973 to 1979 he was drawn into industry but managed to win free, creating a story and characters upon which the multi-collaborative* My One and Only *took off into the upper reaches of the 1983 Best Plays list.*

Mayer is now free-lancing, concentrating on the writing of verse and rock 'n' roll songs. He has been a Rockefeller Fellow and a Levine Senior Fellow at Yale. He is single and lives in the Cape-and-Islands area of Massachusetts.

GEORGE and IRA GERSHWIN (music and lyrics) are, literally, marquee names in the Broadway theater—the Uris Theater, home of the Theater Hall of Fame, at 1633 Broadway was renamed the Gershwin Theater in their honor at this year's Tony Award ceremonies. Their operatic masterpiece Porgy and Bess *was staged at Radio City Music Hall this season, and their record of accomplishment is so long and has been so meticulously set forth in many a study and biographical work that it would be redundant to attempt to outline it here.*

Instead—thanks to the book Songs of the American Theater *compiled by Richard Lewine and Alfred Simon—we will set down here the sources for the musical numbers in their "new" Best Play* My One and Only. *This score is a collection of Gershwin numbers, from previous Broadway shows unless otherwise noted, as follows in the order of their appearance in the 1983 show:*

"I Can't Be Bothered Now" *from* A Damsel in Distress *(film, 1937)*
"Blah, Blah, Blah" *from* Delicious *(film, 1931)*
"Boy Wanted" *from* Primrose *(English show, 1924)*
"Soon" *from* Strike Up the Band *(1930)*
"High Hat" *from* Funny Face *(1927)*
"Sweet and Low-Down" *from* Tip-Toes *(1925)*
"Just Another Rhumba" *from* Goldwyn Follies *(film, 1938; cut)*
"He Loves and She Loves" *from* Funny Face *(1927)*

" '*S Wonderful*" *from* Funny Face *(1927)*
"*Strike Up the Band!*" *from* Strike Up the Band *(1930)*
"*In the Swim*" *from* Funny Face *(1927)*
"*What Are We Here For?*" *from* Treasure Girl *(1928)*
"*Nice Work If You Can Get It*" *from* A Damsel in Distress *(film, 1937)*
"*My One and Only*" *from* Funny Face *(1927)*
"*Funny Face*" *from* Funny Face *(1927)*
"*Kickin' the Clouds Away*" *from* Tell Me More *(1925)*
"*How Long Has This Been Going On?*" *from* Rosalie *(1928)*

ACT I

Scene 1: Limbo and Pennsylvania Station, May 1, 1927

SYNOPSIS: A trio appears, singing "I Can't Be Bothered Now," as Captain Billy Buck Chandler—a tall, gangling, Lindbergh-like aviator—appears above, hanging from the straps of a parachute. As he descends to earth he joins the song and disappears from view as a railroad station and the last car of a train appear on the set.

Prince Nikki descends from the car with six girls dressed in bathing suits. They are his "Fish," his Aquacade girls, as he explains: "Are being lovely, yes? And now—piece of resistance!—star of Aquacade—third woman to swim English channel but first attractive one—presently making spectaular, heartstopping high dive into extremely shallow pool—*Miss Edythe Herbert!*"

With this introduction, Edythe—a beautiful young woman coiffed and dressed in 1920s flapper style—appears and poses for the photographers. At the same time, Billy enters to get a package from the train porter, who wonders what this long, thin shape can be. "It's a new kind of propellor," Billy explains, "and it's gonna get me to Paris, France."

Billy turns, sees Edythe and is immediately smitten, using the song "Blah, Blah, Blah" to express his feelings. Then he exits, as Edythe and her chorus of Aquacade beauties echo "I Can't Be Bothered Now."

Scene 2: Billy's Hangar

Billy is at the controls of the Lone Star, his monoplane, with propellor spinning. His female mechanic, Mickey, guides the plane into the hangar.

MICKEY: Captain! what the hell were you doing putting the Lone Star through all those double barrel-rolls and inside-out loop-the-loops? What're you trying to do, kill yourself?

BILLY: Stop worryin', Mickey, she handled like a dream. There ain't another plane in the sky that can touch her.

MICKEY: Did you pick up that new aluminum propellor?

BILLY *(retrieving it; it is now unwrapped)*: Sure did. Have you seen the newspaper? I bet my announcement that I'm flyin' non-stop to Paris is all over the front page.

MICKEY: It sure is, Captain— *(Pulls a paper from her pocket.)* Listen to this: "19th Flyer Enters Race."

BILLY *(waits for more; there isn't any):* You mean that's all? They didn't even mention my name!

Billy takes the paper to check the story and sees an interview with Edythe. His interest in the Channel swimmer makes Mickey nervous: "Maybe you've forgotten why I joined up with you in the first place. I coulda gone with anyone—they was all after me, all the great flyers—even Commander Byrd—and you know why? Cuz I'm the best! I can make a goddamn double-decker *bus* fly! But I went with you, Captain—a dumbass Texas farmer with cowflop on his shoes—'cuz you didn't give diddlysquat about anything else in the whole world except flyin' non-stop to Paris, France. So I said to myself, 'Mick? That dumbass Texas farmer's gonna get there first!' "

Billy agrees he shouldn't be sidetracked, especially since he'd like to become famous so that Edythe will then notice him.

Edythe, in another section of the stage, answering reporters' questions about what she's looking for, sings "Boy Wanted," emphasizing her loneliness in the limelight. In his stage area, Billy sings "Soon."

In further consultation with Mickey, Billy decides he's not stylish enough to be noticed by Edythe. But he already has some notoriety because of his flying circus exploits. The Rt. Rev. J.D. Montgomery, bishop of the Uptown Apostolic Mission and proprietor of the Club Havana on the same premises, comes into the hangar and requests Billy's presence at one of his Friday night parties, attended by such celebrities as Babe Ruth and Edythe Herbert the Channel swimmer. Billy accepts instantly. Montgomery, "minister to the distressed spirit by day, minister of the *distilled* spirit by night" in these days of Prohibition, senses Billy's longing to improve himself and his appearance. He offers to escort Billy uptown to Mr. Magix's Tonsorial and Sartorial Emporial, which specializes in such matters.

Scene 3: Mr. Magix's Emporial

Mr. Magix, "an elegantly dressed older gentleman," is seated in an ornate barber chair, surrounded by various assistants. Billy tells his tale: he's about to meet this girl who, according to the newspaper stories, is looking for someone more sophisticated than "some tongue-tied aviator in grease-stained old overalls." Mr. Magix can help Billy learn to dress and behave in a style more beguiling to the ladies. Mr. Magix's instruction takes the form of the song numbers "High Hat" and "Sweet and Low-Down," with Mr. Magix and Billy acting out the advice in the form of a tap dance.

Scene 4: Club Havana

Billy arrives at Montgomery's establishment dressed in evening clothes and ready to meet Edythe, but it's a little too early for the celebrities, who don't usually begin arriving until after 11 P.M. Finally Edythe enters on Nikki's arm and is shown to a table. Montgomery reminds Billy to "high hat" the object of his affections, as Mr. Magix taught him.

Meanwhile, Edythe has spotted Billy and is instantly smitten by him as he was by her, as she declares in a reprise of "Blah, Blah, Blah." Billy plucks up his courage and asks Edythe to dance. Nikki doesn't permit Edythe to answer for herself but turns Billy away. Edythe is angry, but Nikki is firm.

NIKKI: Little fish must be protected.
EDYTHE: From what, having a little fun?
NIKKI: Fun is being first step to romance.
EDYTHE: Yeah, well, I could use a little romance in my life.
NIKKI: Romance you want? Go to movies.
EDYTHE: I do nothing but go to the movies. I *live* in the movies.
NIKKI: Is better so.
EDYTHE (a beat as she regards him): I think it's time you and me parted company.
NIKKI: Yes? How amusing.
EDYTHE: I mean it, Nikki. I want out.
NIKKI: Fish is forgetting—Nikki has old photographs, photographs you let Nikki take.
EDYTHE: I was seventeen—
NIKKI: Very grown-up seventeen.
EDYTHE: You wouldn't never show them snaps to no one, would you Nikki?
NIKKI: Of course not. (A beat.) Unless absolutely necessary.
EDYTHE: You bastard. I'll run away—I'll leave the country—
NIKKI: Fish is again forgetting—Prince Nikki is holding passport. Without passport, you can go nowhere.
EDYTHE: You really are a prince, Nikki.

Montgomery announces the finals of the club's beauty pageant, with all the contestants dressed as products of Cuba, the musical background being "Just Another Rhumba." At the climax of the pageant there is a raid by the police—but by the time the police enter, the Rt. Rev. Montgomery and his assistants are dressed as bishop and nuns, and the patrons have vanished.

Scene 5: Cinema

At a movie house, Edythe enters and finds a seat. On a large screen facing the audience, a romantic silent film (represented by a series of still photographs flashed on the screen, with titles) is in progress, set in the casbah of "Fayoum, Sin City of the Nile." The actor and actress playing the love scenes on the screen are Edythe ("the fair Circassian dancing girl,") Billy ("Achille de Carcassonne, an intellectual") and Nikki ("Murad Bey, great lord of all the Mamelukes. He is cruel, lewd and disgusting"). As the movie begins to unfold, Billy enters carrying a number of bags and boxes, finds Edythe, sits near her and pretends that this is a chance meeting. He tempts her with everything from fudge to hot soup (while other patrons command them to be quiet), and gradually Edythe accepts his presence, at least for the duration of the movie. Billy sings "He Loves and She Loves" and gradually gets Edythe to sing it too.

The last titles flash on the screen: "I must remain what I have become—White Baggage of the Casbah" and then "The End." The lights come up and Edythe quickly prepares to leave.

BILLY: Where are you going? When am I going to see you again?
EDYTHE: Never!
BILLY: Miss Herbert—*Edythe*—wait!—
    He follows her. As they come downstage, the movie house disappears and they are outside.
Miss Herbert, why don't we go somewhere and have dinner?
    EDYTHE (*turning back*): We just *had* dinner. Now be a good fellow and buzz off.
BILLY: But I've got plans—plans that include you—
    EDYTHE: Look, do I have to spell it out? Okay, here it is: I'm not available! Did you catch that? I belong to somebody else! There's no place for you in my life! So if you don't stop annoying me I'm going to call a—
    Suddenly, impulsively, he stops her mouth with a kiss.

The kiss becomes a dance to the reprised music of "He Loves and She Loves," after which they exit arm in arm, while a quartet sings the same lyrics to four girls in an open touring car.

Scene 6: Central Park

Edythe, parked with Billy in a roadster in Central Park, confesses that she hated swimming the Channel but loves her Aquacade high-diving, at least the part where she soars through the air. "You're a flyer! Just like me," Billy declares. He tells Edythe of his ambition to become the first to fly non-stop to Paris.

EDYTHE (*a thought occurs*): Do you—need a passport to do that?
BILLY: I ain't never been asked for one yet.
EDYTHE (*a beat*): Can I come with you?
BILLY: To Paris? We'd be too heavy.
EDYTHE: I don't weigh very much—
BILLY: The plane'd never make it.
EDYTHE: Oh. (*Thinking.*) Do you ever go anywhere else?
BILLY: Sure. I'm flying to Margate in the morning—to pick up an extra gas tank.
EDYTHE: Margate! Really?! I come from there!
BILLY: Margate, New Jersey.
EDYTHE: Oh. That's no good. Don't you ever fly out of the country? How about Havana? I'd *love* to see Havana! Would you take me there?
BILLY: Sure, I guess we could go there some time—
EDYTHE: You're really awfully nice—
    They kiss.

But Nikki, hiding in the bushes, has overheard this conversation, as Billy promises Edythe to change his plans and fly her to Havana tomorrow instead of New Jersey.

Scene 7: Billy's Hangar

The tail of the Lone Star is visible at left. Nikki enters, contemplating sabotaging the plane in order to rid himself of Billy (and at the same time he would fulfill some unexplained secret mission). Mickey enters, sees that Nikki is smoking near the fuel tanks and orders him out of the hangar. Nikki manages to overpower Mickey, run water into the gasoline and drag her away before Billy and Edythe enter, bound for Havana. They disappear behind the plane. Soon there is the sound of an engine and the Lone Star moves off. The engine roars as the plane takes off (and Mickey runs in, too late to warn them); then the engine is heard sputtering and faltering and finally failing, as the trio reprises "I Can't Be Bothered Now."

Scene 8: A Deserted Beach

A newscaster announces that Capt. Billy Buck Chandler's plane is missing and probably lost, as the lights come up on Billy and Edythe lying on a deserted beach, tattered but obviously happy, expressing their mood and feelings for each other with the song " 'S Wonderful" and a dance duet performed in the shallow water at the edge of the sand. Then they begin to consider their plight.

BILLY: Edythe—we could be stranded here for years—someone's gonna beat me to Paris.

EDYTHE: Does it really matter that much?

BILLY: Of course it does!

EDYTHE: What's the difference if you're first or not?

BILLY: Don't you realize what it's gonna be like for the first one who actually does it? He'll be rich and famous, with parades and brass bands playing and his picture on the cover of *Time* Magazine—isn't that what everybody wants?

EDYTHE: Not me, kid. Not me.

BILLY: Then why'd you swim the Channel?

EDYTHE: Someone told me to.

BILLY: You didn't want to be famous?

EDYTHE: What for? It isn't what other people think of you, Billy—it's what *you* think. All the others really don't care about you. They just want to stare at you—and touch you—and make money off you. They don't give a damn if you're *happy* or not. You're the only one who cares about that. You and one other person, if you're lucky. Just the two of you.

BILLY (*staring at her, moved*): I love you, kid.

EDYTHE: Oh, yeah?

BILLY: Uh huh. I do. I surely do love you, kid. Do you love me?

EDYTHE: It sure looks that way—(*As they kiss.*) It sure *feels* that way. (*Kiss again.*)

A ship appears and draws closer; then Mickey and Nikki disembark from it. After seeing that Billy is safe and sound, Mickey's first thought is for the plane, which may be repairable.

Seeing that Edythe is all right, Nikki orders her to return with him. Edythe protests that Nikki no longer has any hold on her, as she has escaped to foreign soil. She is informed that they didn't get far in the plane—this island is Staten Island, so she still has her passport problem. Besides, Nikki probably has brought along those embarrassing photos to show Billy. Edythe turns to Billy with the plea, "Say it doesn't matter and I'll stay—" But Billy's reply is, "This guy doesn't know what he's talking about. He doesn't know you," as though he took her innocence for granted and could not imagine any alternative. This is not enough for Edythe, who coolly bids him goodbye and departs with Nikki.

Mickey enters with good news: the Lone Star can be easily and quickly repaired.

MICKEY: . . . . . A couple of days in the hangar and then it's Paris, France here you come—you're going to make it, Captain. You're going to see more goddam parades, confetti and brass bands than General John Blackjack Pershing put together!

BILLY: Then what are you doing standing around here for, Mickey? We've got work to do!

MICKEY: Aye, aye, Captain.
She runs off.

Billy faces the audience and sings "Strike Up the Band" solo, quietly, pensively. *Curtain.*

ACT II

Scene 1: Aquacade

Nikki and his six Aquacade girls are rehearsing an elaborately-costumed starfish number to the music of "In the Swim" and "What Are We Here For?". After the number is over and the girls have departed, Edythe shows up, having missed rehearsal. Nikki tries to sweet-talk her, but she has had enough of him and brushes him off. Before leaving, Nikki can't help reminding Edythe that she wasn't so hostile when he was making her a star. After he exits, Edythe sings "Nice Work if You Can Get It" and departs, pointedly, in the opposite direction.

Scene 2: Mr. Magix's Emporial

Billy comes to Mr. Magix with a new problem: should he keep on giving Edythe the "high hat" treatment because she seems to have had a somewhat checkered past, even though Billy loves her? No, no, Mr. Magix advises him, "We're all through using our heads—now it's strictly up to the heart." Billy and Edythe are way past such approaches as "Soon," " 'S Wonderful" or "Blah, Blah, Blah." It's truth-telling time, time for "My One and Only," as Mr. Magix demonstrates and prompts Billy to follow him in a tap dance duet.

In compensation for Mr. Magix's valuable advice, Billy agrees to take him for an airplane ride some day. Billy goes in search of Edythe but finds the Aquacade company has checked out of their boarding house.

Scene 3: Pennsylvania Station

At the railroad station, Billy learns from the Aquacade girls that Edythe has vanished and Nikki has disbanded the show. Edythe told one of the girls that because of a movie she saw, "White Baggage of the Casbah," she decided to stow away on a steamer headed for Morocco.

Scene 4: Billy's Hangar

Mickey is working on the Lone Star, at left, when Nikki enters brandishing a pistol, demanding to be told Edythe's whereabouts. Nikki is momentarily distracted by Billy's entrance, and Mickey manages to draw her own pistol and wing Nikki, who crumples to the floor.

BILLY: Mickey! You just shot the Prince!
MICKEY: He isn't a prince, he isn't even a Georgian really, although his father was. His name is Joseph Tchatchavilli. In 1910 he was a petty thief and gym instructor working resort towns along the Baltic. Soon afterwards, he joined up with some Menshevik adventurers acting as a sort of bouncer at many of their rallies. Arrested for arson by the Stalinist police, he was turned into a spy and sent to England as a swimming teacher, and finally to the U.S. of A. where he was ordered to make sure no American flew to Paris, France first. Oh we've been looking for him, I can tell you that.
BILLY: What are you *saying,* Mickey? How do you know all that stuff?
MICKEY (*showing her badge*): I'm a Fed, Captain—Agent Lucy Ann Fergusson, at your service. There's been one of us assigned to protect every plane that's in the running. It's been a top government priority, Captain—we've been after this bozo for some time.
BILLY: Gosh, I'd really like to hear more about this, Mickey, I mean, Lucy Ann, but I'm in too much of a hurry right now. I've just gotta find Edythe and tell her she's my one and only.
NIKKI (*from the floor*): Wanting to see one and only? Miss Edythe Herbert—
    Produces photographs from his pocket and offers them to Billy.
See how you like these old photographs—
    Billy takes them and studies them for a moment.
BILLY (*finally*): I like 'em.

Billy goes to get into his plane; the motor is heard as it disappears and takes off.
Mickey checks her prisoner's wound and finds it not serious. She has been on his case so long and knows so much about him that she is almost sorry she has to take him downtown to book him; and Nikki is kind of glad that it's Mickey who caught him. They express themselves to each other by singing "Funny Face."

Scene 5: Club Oasis

At the edge of the Sahara, Legionnaires and their women are carousing. Billy enters leading a camel and telling the club owner, Achmed, that he is looking for

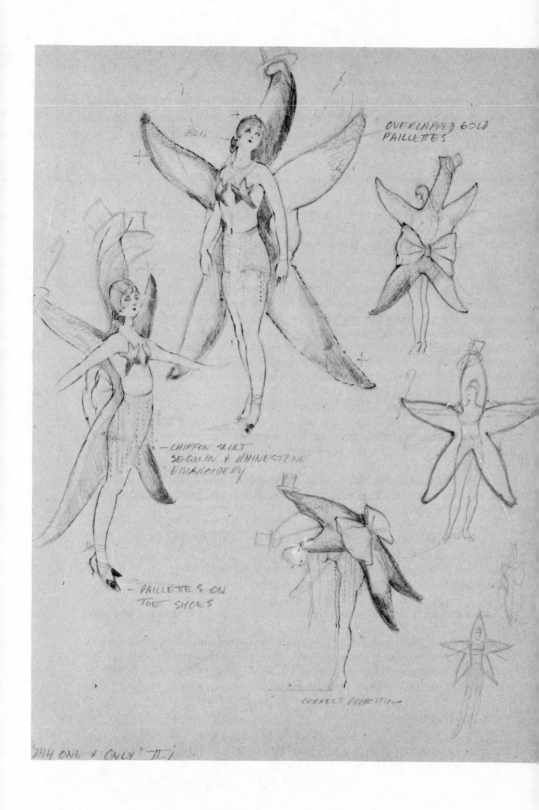

OVERLAPPED GOLD
PAILLETTES

BOW

CHIFFON SKIRT
SEQUIN & RHINESTONE
EMBROIDERY

PAILLETTES ON
TOE SHOES

CORRECT PROPORTION

"MY ONE & ONLY" II-1

Examples of Rita Ryack's costume designs for *My One and Only* are pictured here. On opposite page are the designer's sketches for the chorus's starfish costumes in the "In the Swim" number. On this page are sketches of Tommy Tune's elegant evening clothes in the musical's finale

a certain girl and has tracked her here. Achmed lines up the girls, who are all veiled, so that Billy can't see whether one of them is Edythe. So he sings "My One and Only" to the whole group. He is interrupted by a Legionnaire, who calls their attention to a radio announcement. It is the voice of Lowell Thomas telling the world that Lindbergh made it to Paris. Amid the cheers from everyone, Edythe steps out of the line of girls, takes off her veil and approaches Billy.

BILLY (*smiles*): Are you all right?
EDYTHE: Sure. Are you all right?
BILLY: I am now.

EDYTHE: I'm sorry about Lindbergh. I know how much it meant to you. You must feel awful.

BILLY: You mean because of him beatin' me across the Atlantic?

EDYTHE: Yes.

BILLY: He didn't.

EDYTHE: What do you mean?

BILLY: I got here three days ago. Non-stop from New York to Morocco in twenty-nine hours and fourteen minutes.

EDYTHE: Go on.

BILLY: I flew right over Paris, France—I coulda touched down but my heart just wasn't in it. I was in too big a hurry to find you.

EDYTHE: So you really were the first—

BILLY: Just like I promised.

EDYTHE: But nobody knows it.

BILLY: Except me. *I* know it. Isn't that what you said, Edythe? I'm the only one who really cares—me and one other person if I'm lucky? Am I lucky, Edythe? *(She turns away)* Come back with me—

EDYTHE *(very quietly)*: No, my place is here. I must remain what I have become —White Baggage of the Casbah.

BILLY: Edythe—I *forgive* you.

EDYTHE *(wheeling)*: But I don't forgive you! You let me go! We were *happy*, Captain—don't you know how little of that there is?

BILLY: I do now. *(He moves to her.)* I had twenty-nine hours and fourteen minutes to think things over. What right did I have anyway, expecting anyone as wonderful as you—a gift to this earth—to be sittin' around all those years just waitin' for me? We can't be judgin' one another—we live the only way we can. Shoot, just gettin' from one day to the next deserves brass bands and confetti. And the past doesn't mean a thing once you've got a present. You're *my* present, Edythe. A gift to this earth. Marry me. Please.

Billy drops to one knee and emphasizes his request with a verse of "My One and Only." It is obvious what Edythe's reply is going to be.

Scene 6: The Uptown Chapel

The Rt. Rev. Mongomery appears with his deacons swinging their censers and joined by the Aquacade girls for a song and dance, "Kickin' the Clouds Away." Billy and Edythe appear dressed as bride and groom, and Montgomery performs his unique version of the wedding ceremony. Finally, Billy and Edythe are left alone to sing "How Long Has This Been Going On?" to each other. Edythe remembers to throw her bridal bouquet to the audience, and Billy carries her upstage as the curtain falls.

As an encore, taking their bows, the entire cast lines up on the stage for a song and dance number, "Strike Up the Band!"

A GRAPHIC GLANCE

Tommy Tune in *My One and Only*

Charles "Honi" Coles in *My One and Only*

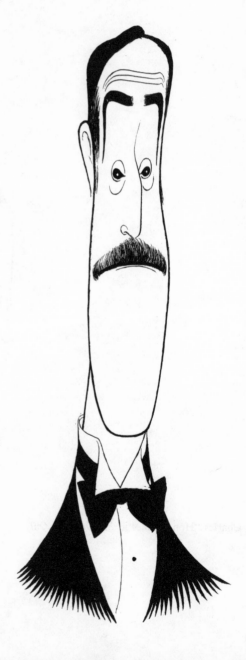

Dana Ivey (above) and Remak Ramsay
in *Quartermaine's Terms*

Stephen Hanan in *Cats*

James Russo and Farrah Fawcett in *Extremities*

Jeffrey De Munn in *K2*

Doug Henning, Chita Rivera, Rebecca Wright and Nathan Lane in *Merlin*

Lara Teeter and Natalia Makarova in the revival of *On Your Toes*

Dina Merrill in the revival
of *On Your Toes*

Al Green in *Your Arms Too Short to Box With God*

Fritz Weaver (left) and Barnard Hughes in *Angels Fall*

(Clockwise from bottom left) Reed Jones, Anna McNeely, Timothy Scott, Kenneth Ard, Terrence V. Mann, Stephen Hanan, Christine Langner, Rene Clemente and Ken Page in *Cats*

HIRSCHFELD 5

Christine Lahti in the revival of *Present Laughter*

George C. Scott in the revival of *Present Laughter*

David Rounds in *Herringbone*

Lynn Milgrim in *Talking With*

Polly Pen in *Charlotte Sweet*

John Neville, Kevin Spacey and Liv Ullmann in the revival of *Ghosts*

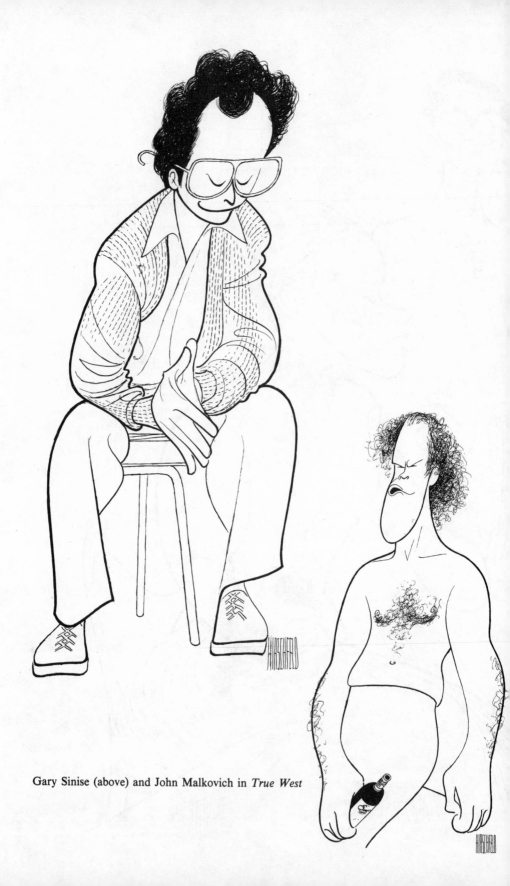

Gary Sinise (above) and John Malkovich in *True West*

Liz Robertson, George Rose and Len Cariou in *Dance a Little Closer*

Elizabeth Taylor and Richard Burton in the revival of *Private Lives*

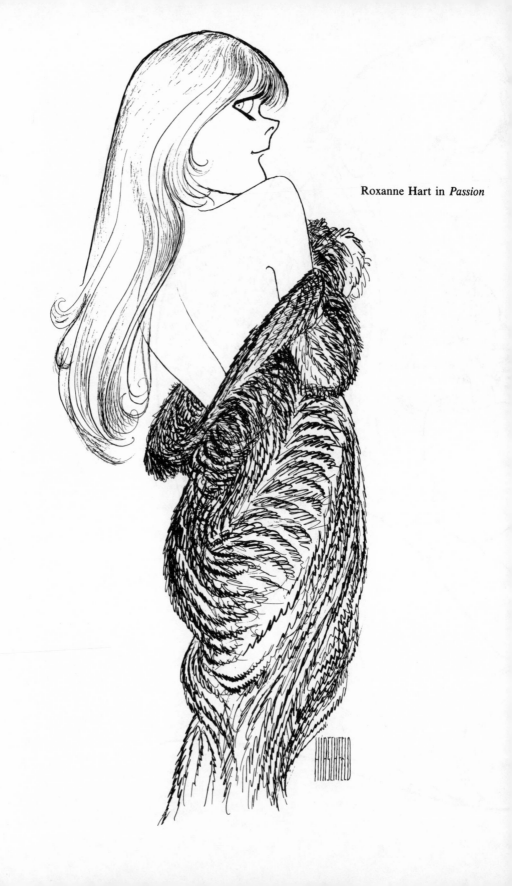

Roxanne Hart in *Passion*

Trey Wilson in *Foxfire*

(Clockwise from bottom left) Mandy Ingber, Joyce Van Patten, Elizabeth Franz, Matthew Broderick (center), Jodi Thelen, Peter Michael Goetz and Zeljko Ivanek in *Brighton Beach Memoirs*

Mary Beth Hurt in *The Misanthrope*

Thuli Dumakude in *Poppie Nongena*

Kevin Bacon in *Slab Boys*

(Left to right) Lonette McKee, Avril Gentles, Bruce Hubbard, Donald O'Connor (center), Karla Burns, Sheryl Woods and Ron Raines in the revival of *Showboat*

George Martin in *Plenty*

HIRSCHFELD

Edward Herrmann in *Plenty*

HIRSCHFELD WASHINGTON. D.C. 5

James Coco in the revival of
You Can't Take It With You

Nancy Marchand in *Sister Mary Ignatius
Explains It All for You*

Debbie Reynolds in *Woman of the Year*

HIRSCHFELD

Raquel Welch in *Woman of the Year*

Mark Linn-Baker, Robert Joy, Bob Gunton and John Vickery in *The Death of Von Richtofen as Witnessed From Earth*

Ellen Greene in *Little Shop of Horrors*

Joseph Maher in *84 Charing Cross Road*

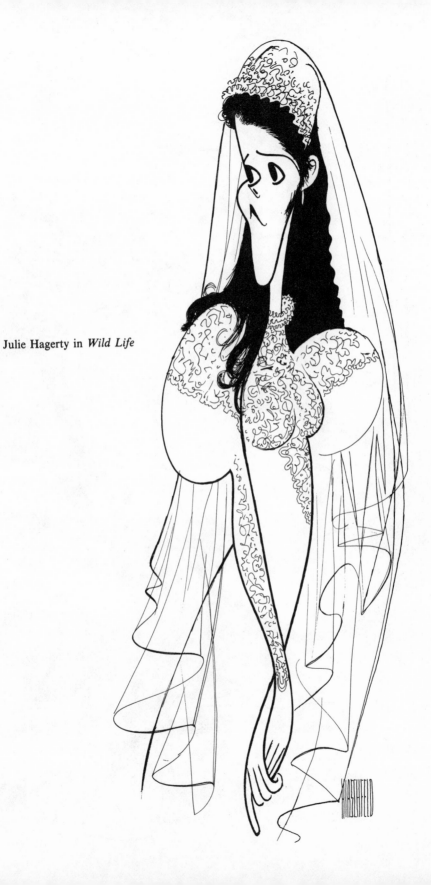

Julie Hagerty in *Wild Life*

Hume Cronyn, Keith Carradine and
Jessica Tandy in *Foxfire*

Eli Wallach and Anne Jackson
in *Twice Around the Park*

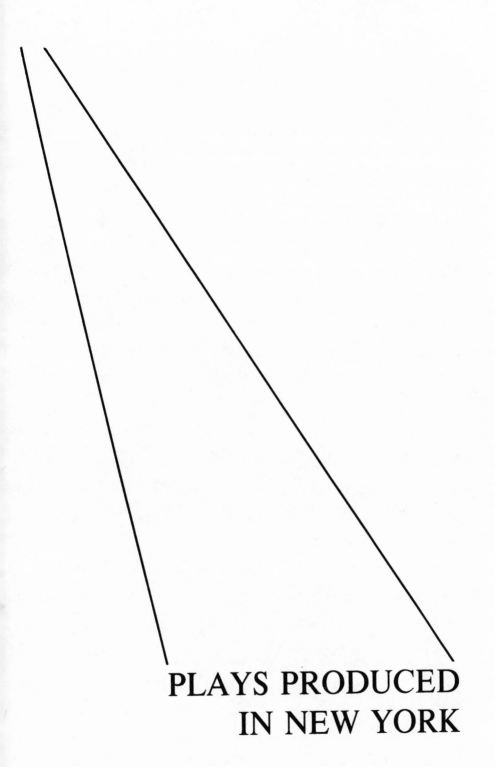

PLAYS PRODUCED
IN NEW YORK

PLAYS PRODUCED ON BROADWAY

Figures in parentheses following a play's title give number of performances. These figures are acquired directly from the production offices and do not include previews or extra non-profit performances. In the case of a transfer, the off-Broadway run is noted but not added to the figure in parentheses.

Plays marked with an asterisk (*) were still running on June 1, 1983. Their number of performances is figured through May 31, 1983.

In a listing of a show's numbers—dances, sketches, musical scenes, etc.—the titles of songs are identified wherever possible by their appearance in quotation marks (").

HOLDOVERS FROM PREVIOUS SEASONS

Plays which were running on June 1, 1982 are listed below. More detailed information about them appears in previous *Best Plays* volumes of appropriate years. Important cast changes since opening night are recorded in the Cast Replacements section of this volume.

*A Chorus Line (3,249). Musical conceived by Michael Bennett; book by James Kirkwood and Nicholas Dante; music by Marvin Hamlisch; lyrics by Edward Kleban. Opened April 15, 1975 off Broadway where it played 101 performances through July 13, 1975; transferred to Broadway July 25, 1975.

*Oh! Calcutta! (2,840). Revival of the musical devised by Kenneth Tynan; with contributions (in this version) by Jules Feiffer, Dan Greenberg, Lenore Kandel, John Lennon, Jacques Levy, Leonard Melfi, David Newman and Robert Benton, Sam Shepard, Clovis Trouille, Kenneth Tynan and Sherman Yellen; music and lyrics (in this version) by Robert Dennis, Peter Schickele and Stanley Walden; additional music by Stanley Walden and Jacques Levy. Opened September 24, 1976 in alternating performances with *Me and Bessie* through December 7, 1976, continuing alone thereafter.

Annie (2,377). Musical based on the Harold Gray comic strip *Little Orphan Annie;* book by Thomas Meehan; music by Charles Strouse; lyrics by Martin Charnin. Opened April 21, 1977. (Closed January 2, 1983.)

Deathtrap (1,793). By Ira Levin. Opened February 26, 1978. (Closed June 13, 1982).

Dancin' (1,774). Musical with music and lyrics by Johann Sebastian Bach, Ralph Burns, George M. Cohan, Neil Diamond, Bob Haggart, Ray Bauduc, Gil Rodin and Bob Crosby, Jerry Leiber and Mike Stoller, Johnny Mercer and Harry Warren, Louis Prima, John Philip Sousa, Carole Bayer Sager and Melissa Manchester, Barry Mann and Cynthia Weil, Felix Powell and George Asaf, Cat Stevens, Edgar Varèse and Jerry Jeff Walker. Opened March 27, 1978. (Closed June 27, 1982.)

The Best Little Whorehouse in Texas (1,639). Musical with book by Larry L. King and Peter Masterson; music and lyrics by Carol Hall. Opened April 17, 1978 off Broadway where it played 64 performances through June 11, 1978; transferred to Broadway June 19, 1978. (Closed March 27, 1982 after 1,576 performances) Reopened May 31, 1982. (Closed July 24, 1982 after 63 additional performances)

*Evita (1,535). Musical with book by Andrew Lloyd Webber; lyrics by Tim Rice. Opened September 25, 1979.

Sugar Babies (1,208). Burlesque musical conceived by Ralph G. Allen and Harry Rigby; sketches by Ralph G. Allen based on traditional material. Opened October 8, 1979. (Closed August 28, 1982)

*42nd Street (1,154). Musical based on the novel by Bradford Ropes; book by Michael Stewart and Mark Bramble; music and lyrics by Harry Warren and Al Dubin; other lyrics by Johnny Mercer and Mort Dixon. Opened August 25, 1980.

*Amadeus (1,022). By Peter Shaffer. Opened December 17, 1980.

The Pirates of Penzance (772). Revival of the operetta with book and lyrics by W. S. Gilbert; music by Arthur Sullivan. Opened July 15, 1980 off Broadway (Delacorte Theater) where it played 42 performances; transferred to Broadway January 8, 1981. (Closed November 28, 1982)

Sophisticated Ladies (767). Musical revue conceived by Donald McKayle, based on the music of Duke Ellington. Opened March 1, 1981. (Closed January 2, 1983)

Woman of the Year (770). Musical based on the M-G-M film by Ring Lardner Jr. and Michael Kanin; book by Peter Stone; music by John Kander; lyrics by Fred Ebb. Opened March 29, 1981. (Closed March 13, 1983)

Lena Horne: The Lady and Her Music (333). Musical revue designed as a concert by Lena Horne. Opened May 12, 1981. (Closed June 30, 1982)

Crimes of the Heart (535). By Beth Henley. Opened November 4, 1981. (Closed February 13, 1983)

*Dreamgirls (601). Musical with book and lyrics by Tom Eyen; music by Henry Krieger. Opened December 20, 1981.

*Joseph and the Amazing Technicolor Dreamcoat (638). Revival of the musical based on the Old Testament story; music by Andrew Lloyd Webber; lyrics by Tim Rice. Opened November 18, 1981 off Broadway where it played 77 performances; transferred to Broadway January 27, 1982.

*Pump Boys and Dinettes (553). Musical with music and lyrics by Jim Wann, John Foley, Mark Hardwick, Debra Monk, Cass Morgan and John Schimmel. Opened October 1, 1981 off Broadway where it played 112 performances; transferred to Broadway February 4, 1982.

Encore (288). Radio City Music Hall Golden Jubilee Spectacular. Opened March 26, 1982. (Closed September 6, 1982)

*Agnes of God (486). By John Pielmeier. Opened March 30, 1982.

Medea (65). Revival of the play by Euripides; adapted by Robinson Jeffers. Opened May 2, 1982. (Closed June 27, 1982)

"MASTER HAROLD" . . . and the boys (344). By Athol Fugard. Opened May 4, 1982. (Closed February 26, 1983)

*Nine (441). Musical with book by Arthur Kopit; music and lyrics by Maury Yeston; adaptation from the Italian by Mario Fratti. Opened May 9, 1982.

Beyond Therapy (11). Revised version of the play by Christopher Durang. Opened May 26, 1982. (Closed June 12, 1982)

PLAYS PRODUCED JUNE 1, 1982-MAY 31, 1983

Blues in the Night (53). Musical conceived by Sheldon Epps; music and lyrics by various composers and lyricists. Produced by Mitchell Maxwell, Alan J. Schuster, Fred H. Krones and M2 Entertainment, Inc. at the Rialto Theater. Opened June 2, 1982. (Closed July 18, 1982)

Woman #1	Leslie Uggams	Woman #3	Jean Du Shon
Woman #2	Debbie Shapiro	Saloon Singer	Charles Coleman

Standbys: Women—Ann Duquesnay; Mr. Coleman—David Brunetti.

Directed by Sheldon Epps; musical direction, supervision and vocal arrangements, Chapman Roberts; co-musical direction, arrangements and orchestrations, Sy Johnson; scenery, John Falabella; costumes, David Murin; lighting, Ken Billington; associate producers, Joshua Silver, Elaine Brownstein; production stage manager, Zoya Wyeth; stage manager, William D. Buxton Jr.; press, Judy Jacksina, Glenna Freedman, Diane Tomlinson, Susan Chicoine, Lorin Klaris.

Time: 1938. Place: A hotel in Chicago. The play was presented in two parts.

Concert-style show, with three women telling their troubles in the form of 24 song numbers, most of them blues, in a run-down Chicago hotel in the 1930s.

MUSICAL NUMBERS, ACT I: "Blues Blues" (by Bessie Smith)—Company; "Four Walls (and One Dirty Window) Blues" (by Willard Robison)—Charles Coleman; "I've Got a Date With a Dream" (by Mack Gordon and Harry Revel)—Leslie Uggams, Debbie Shapiro; "These Foolish Things Remind Me of You" (by Harry Link, Jack Strachey and Holt Marvell)—Uggams; "New Orleans Hop Scop Blues" (by George W. Thomas)—Jean Du Shon; "It Makes My Love Come Down" (by Bessie Smith)—Uggams, Shapiro, Du Shon; "Copenhagen" (by Walter Melrose and Charlie Davis)—Shapiro.

Also "Wild Women Don't Have the Blues" (by Ida Cox)—Coleman; "Lover Man" (by Jimmy Davis, Roger Ramirez and Jimmy Sherman)—Uggams; "Take Me for a Buggy Ride" (by Leola and Wesley Wilson)—Du Shon; "Willow Weep for Me" (by Ann Ronell)—Shapiro; "Kitchen Man" (by Andy Razaf and Alex Bellenda)—Du Shon; "Low" (by Vernon Duke, Milton Drake and Ben Oakland)—Uggams; "Take It Right Back" (by H. Grey)—Uggams, Shapiro, Du Shon.

ACT II: "Wild Women Don't Have the Blues" (Reprise)—The Band; "Blues in the Night" (by Johnny Mercer and Harold Arlen)—Uggams, Shapiro; "Dirty No Gooder Blues" (by Bessie Smith) —Du Shon; "When a Woman Loves a Man" (by Johnny Mercer, Bernard Hanighen and Gordon Jenkins)—Coleman; "Am I Blue" (by Grant Drake and Harry Akst)—Uggams, Shapiro, Du Shon; "Rough and Ready Man" (by Alberta Hunter)—Uggams.

Also "Reckless Blues" (by Bessie Smith)—Shapiro; "Wasted Life Blues" (by Bessie Smith)—Du Shon; "Baby Doll" (by Bessie Smith)—Coleman; "Nobody Knows You When You're Down and Out" (by Jimmy Cox, vocal arrangement by Sy Johnson)—Uggams, Shapiro, Du Shon; "I Gotta Right to Sing the Blues" (by Ted Koehler and Harold Arlen)—Uggams, Shapiro, Du Shon; "Blues Blues/Blues in the Night" (Reprise)—Uggams, Shapiro, Du Shon.

*Torch Song Trilogy (408). Transfer from off Broadway of the play by Harvey Fierstein. Produced by Kenneth Waissman, Martin Markinson, John Glines and Lawrence Lane with BetMar and Donald Tick in the Glines production at the Little Theater. Opened June 10, 1982.

Lady Blues................	Susan Edwards	Alan	Paul Joynt
Arnold Beckoff	Harvey Fierstein	David	Fisher Stevens
Ed........................	Court Miller	Mrs. Beckoff	Estelle Getty
Laurel....................	Diane Tarleton		

Standbys: Mr. Fierstein—Richard DeFabees; Mr. Miller—Peter Ratray. Understudies: Miss Tarleton—Susan Edwards; Miss Edwards—Diane Tarleton; Messrs. Joynt, Stevens—Christopher Stryker; Miss Getty—Sylvia Kauders; keyboard understudy—Scott Oakley.

Directed by Peter Pope; scenery, Bill Stabile; costumes, Mardi Philips; lighting, Scott Pinkney; musical direction and arrangements for *The International Stud,* Ned Levy; original music for *Fugue in a Nursery,* Ada Janik; associate producer, Howard Perloff; production stage manager, Herb Vogler; press, Betty Lee Hunt, Maria Cristina Pucci, James Sapp.

Part I: *The International Stud*—1. January. Arnold backstage at nightclub. 2. February. Ed in the "International Stud" bar. 3. June. Ed and Arnold in their respective apartments. 4. September. Arnold in the "International Stud" bar. 5. November. Ed and Arnold backstage.

Part II: *Fugue in a Nursery*— Time, one year later. Place, Arnold's apartment and various rooms of Ed's farmhouse.

Part III: *Widows and Children First!*— Time, five years later. 1. Arnold's apartment, 7 A.M. on a Thursday in June. 2. Same, 5 P.M. that day. 3. A bench in the park below, immediately following. 4. The apartment, 6 A.M. the next morning.

Three related one-acters about the emotional adventures of a drag queen in a four-and-one-half-hour context. Previously produced off Broadway 1/15/82 where it played 117 performances through 5/30/82 and was named a Best Play of its season.

Barbara Barrie replaced Estelle Getty 1/31/83–2/12/83.

Cleavage (1). Musical with book by Buddy and David Sheffield; music and lyrics by Buddy Sheffield. Produced by Up Front Productions at the Playhouse Theater. Opened and closed at the evening performance June 23, 1982.

Daniel David	Jay Rogers
Tom Elias	Sharon Scruggs
Mark Fite	Dick Sheffield
Terese Gargiulo	Pattie Tierce
Marsha Trigg Miller	

Directed by Rita Baker; musical numbers staged by Alton Geno; arrangements, Keith Thompson; scenery, Morris Taylor; costumes, James M. Miller; lighting and scenic and costume supervision, Michael Hotopp and Paul de Pass; production stage manager, Gary Ware; stage manager, Arlene Grayson; press, Susan L. Schulman.

Orchestra: Keith Thompson conductor, keyboards; Philip Fortenberry piano, synthesizer; Jeff Myers bass; Howard Joines drums.

The pursuit of love by various couples, young and old.

MUSICAL NUMBERS, ACT I: "Cleavage"—Ensemble; "Puberty"—Mark Fite, Ensemble; "Only Love"—Sharon Scruggs, Daniel David; "Surprise Me"—Terese Gargiulo; "Reprise Me"— Gargiulo, Fite; "Boys Will Be Girls"—Jay Rogers, Dancers; "Give Me an And"—Marsha Trigg Miller, Dancers; "Just Another Song"—Fite; "Believe in Me, or I'll Be Leavin' You"—Pattie Tierce, Dick Sheffield.

ACT II: "The Thrill of the Chase"—Tom Elias, Fite, David; "Lead 'Em Around by the Nose" —Miller, Tierce, Gargiulo; "Only Love" (Reprise)—Gargiulo; "Bringing Up Badger"—David, Ensemble; "Voices of the Children"—Ensemble; "All the Lovely Ladies"—Elias; "Living in Sin"— Elias, Tierce, Ensemble; Finale—Ensemble.

Play Me a Country Song (1). Musical with book by Jay Broad; music and lyrics by John R. Briggs and Harry Manfredini. Produced by Frederick R. Selch at the Virginia Theater. Opened and closed at the evening performance, June 27, 1982.

Norm	Reed Jones	Frances	Karen Mason
Ellen	Mary Gordon Murray	Penny	Mary Jo Catlett
Tony	Stephen Crain	Buster	Kenneth Ames
Fred	Jay Huguely	Meg	Candace Tovar
Howard	Ronn Carroll	Jerome	Rene Clemente
Lizzie	Louisa Flaningam	Hank	Rick Thomas

Directed by Jerry Adler; choreography, Margo Sappington; musical direction and vocal arrangements, Phil Hall; scenery, David Chapman; costumes, Carol Oditz; lighting, Marc B. Weiss; sound, Robert Kerzman; associate producer, Cheryl Raab; stage managers, Alisa Adler, Jonathan Weiss; press, Alpert/LeVine, Mark Goldstaub.

A bundle of country songs packaged as an all-night party in a favorite truck-stop saloon that is about to close.

MUSICAL NUMBERS, ACT I: "Sail Away," "Rodeo Dreams," "Why Does a Woman Leave Her Man?", "Eighteen-Wheelin' Baby," "Waitin' Tables," "Playing for Position," "Just Thought I'd Call," "Sing-a-Long," "If You Don't Mind," "Play Me a Country Song."

ACT II: "Coffee, Beer and Whiskey," "Only a Fool," "You Can't Get Ahead," "You Have to Get It Out to Get Away," "Big City," "My Sweet Woman," "All of My Dreams," "Rodeo Rider."

Seven Brides for Seven Brothers (5). Musical based on the M-G-M film and *The Sobbin' Women* by Stephen Vincent Benet; book by Lawrence Kasha and David Landay; music by Gene de Paul; lyrics by Johnny Mercer; new songs by Al Kasha and Joel Hirschhorn. Produced by Kaslan Productions, Inc. at the Alvin Theater. Opened July 8, 1982. (Closed July 11, 1982)

Adam	David-James Carroll	Martha	Laurel van der Linde
Benjamin	D. Scot Davidge	Sarah	Linda Hoxit
Ephraim	Jeffrey Reynolds	Liza	Jan Mussetter
Caleb	Lara Teeter	Alice	Nancy Fox
Daniel	Jeff Calhoun	Dorcas	Manette LaChance
Frank	Michael Ragan	Jeb	Russell Giesenschlag
Gideon	Craig Peralta	Zeke	Kevin McCready
Mr. Bixby	Fred Curt	Carl	Don Steffy
Mrs. Bixby	Jeanne Bates	Matt	Gary Moss
Preacher	Jack Ritschel	Luke	James Horvath
Mr. Perkins	Gino Gaudio	Joel	Clark Sterling
Indian	Conley Schnaterbeck	Dorcas's Sister	Marylou Hume
Milly	Debby Boone	Mrs. Perkins	Marykatherine Somers
Ruth	Sha Newman	Townsboy	David Pavlosky

Lumbermen: James Horvath, Russell Giesenschlag, Don Steffy, Gary Moss, Clark Sterling, Kevin McCready.

Townspeople: Jeanne Bates, Cheryl Crandall, Fred Curt, Gino Gaudio, Russell Giesenschlag, James Horvath, Marylou Hume, Kevin McCready, Gary Moss, David Pavlosky, Jack Ritschel, Conley Schnaterbeck, Sam Singhaus, Marykatherine Somers, Don Steffy. Clark Sterling, Stephanie Stromer.

Understudies: Miss Boone—Cheryl Crandall; Messrs. Carroll, Ritschel—Gino Gaudio; Mr. Peralta—Russell Giesenschlag; Mr. Calhoun—Gary Moss; Mr. Davidge—Don Steffy; Mr. Ragan—Kevin McCready; Mr. Reynolds—Clark Sterling; Mr. Teeter—James Horvath; Misses Fox, Hoxit—Marylou Hume; Misses LaChance, Newman, Bates—Marykatherine Somers; Misses Mussetter, van der Linde—Stephanie Stromer; Messrs. Horvath, McCready—David Pavlosky; Messrs. Steffy, Moss —Conley Schnaterbeck; Messrs. Giesenschlag, Sterling—Sam Singhaus; Messrs. Curt, Gaudio—Jack Ritschel; Miss Somers—Jeanne Bates; Alternates—Stephanie Stromer, Sam Singhaus; Orchestra Personnel—Earl Shendel.

Directed by Lawrence Kasha; choreography and musical staging, Jerry Jackson; musical direction, Richard Parrinello; scenery, Robert Randolph; costumes, Robert Fletcher; lighting, Thomas Skelton; sound, Abe Jacob; orchestrations, Irwin Kostal; dance arrangements, Robert Webb; associate producers, Martin Gould, Bernard Hodes; production stage manager, Larry Dean; stage manager, Polly Wood; press, David A. Powers, Barbara Carroll.

Time: The 1850s. Place: The Pacific Northwest.

Stage version of the 1954 movie musical choreographed by Michael Kidd, about a frontier family of brothers gradually tamed by women.

ACT I

On the road
"Bless Your Beautiful Hide"...Adam
The town square
The restaurant
"Wonderful, Wonderful Day"..Milly, Brides
The Pontipee house
*"One Man"...Milly
The Pontipee house, later the same evening
The Pontipee house, the next morning
"Goin' Courting"...Milly, Brothers
Churchyard
"Social Dance".....................Milly, Adam, Bride, Brothers Suitors, Townspeople
The road home
The Pontipee House
*"Love Never Goes Away".................................Adam, Milly, Gideon
The barn
"Sobbin' Women"..Adam, Brothers

ACT II

The town
Echo Pass
*"The Townsfolk's Lament"..................................Suitors, Townspeople
The Pontipee yard
*"A Woman Ought to Know Her Place".................................Adam
The barn
*"We Gotta Make It Through the Winter"..............................Brothers
*"You Gotta Make It Through the Winter" (Reprise).....................Milly, Brides
The Pontipee yard
*"Spring Dance"...Brides, Brothers
The trapping cabin
*"A Woman Ought to Know Her Place" (Reprise)......................Adam, Gideon
The Pontipee house
*"Glad That You Were Born"..............................Milly, Brides, Brothers
The woods
Churchyard
"Wedding Dance".....................Milly, Adam, Brides, Brothers, Townspeople
*Asterisks signify new songs written for this production

*Circle in the Square. Schedule of four revivals. **Present Laughter** (180). By Noel Coward. Opened July 15, 1982. (Closed January 2, 1983) **The Queen and the Rebels** (45). By Ugo Betti; translated by Henry Reed. Opened September 30, 1982. (Closed November 7, 1982) **The Misanthrope** (69). By Molière; English verse translation by Richard Wilbur. Opened January 27, 1983. (Closed March 27, 1983) ***The Caine Mutiny Court-Martial** (30). By Herman Wouk. Co-produced by Kennedy Center in the Hartman Theater production. Opened May 5, 1983. Produced by Circle in the Square, Theodore Mann artistic director, Paul Libin managing director, at Circle in the Square Theater (*The Queen and the Rebels* at the Plymouth Theater).

THE CAINE MUTINY COURT-MARTIAL—Michael Moriarty as Queeg in Circle in the Square's revival of the play by Herman Wouk

PRESENT LAUGHTER

Daphne Stillington	Kate Burton	Roland Maule	Nathan Lane
Miss Erikson	Bette Henritze	Henry Lyppiatt	Richard Woods
Fred	Jim Piddock	Morris Dixon	Edward Conery
Monica Reed	Dana Ivey	Joanna Lyppiatt	Christine Lahti
Garry Essendine	George C. Scott	Lady Saltburn	Georgine Hall
Liz Essendine	Elizabeth Hubbard		

Standby: Mr. Scott—Mart Hulswit. Understudies: Misses Burton, Hentritze—Linda Noble; Messrs. Piddock, Lane—Jerry Mettner; Misses Lahti, Hubbard, Ivey, Hall—Elizabeth Perry.

Directed by George C. Scott; scenery, Marjorie Bradley Kellogg; costumes, Ann Roth; lighting, Richard Nelson; production stage manager, Michael F. Ritchie; stage manager, Duncan Scott; press, Merle Debuskey, David Roggensack.

Time: Sometime before World War II. Place: London. Act I: Garry Essendine's studio about 10:30 A.M. Act II, Scene 1: Midnight, three days later. Scene 2: The next morning, about 10:30 A.M. Act III: a week later, 10 P.M.

Present Laughter was first produced on Broadway 10/29/46 for 158 performances. Its only previous revival was on Broadway 1/31/58 for 6 performances.

THE QUEEN AND THE REBELS

Porter	Sean Griffin	Gen. Biante	Clarence Felder
Traveller	Peter Michael Goetz	Maupa	Anthony DeFonte
Engineer	Donald Gantry	Elizabetta	Betty Miller
Raim	Scott Hylands	Boy	Christopher Garvin
Argia	Colleen Dewhurst		

Travellers: Jeffrey Holt Gardner, Jack R. Marks, Etain O'Malley, Fiddle Viracola. Soldiers: Marek Johnson, Campbell Scott, Stanley Tucci.

Directed by Waris Hussein; scenery, David Jenkins; costumes, Jane Greenwood; lighting, John McLain; produced by special arrangement with Ken Marsolais and Lita Starr; production stage manager, Ken Marsolais; stage manager, Buzz Cohen.

Time: The present. Place: A large hall in the main public building of a hillside village. The play was presented in two parts.

This translation of *The Queen and the Rebels* was previously produced in London and in Purchase, N.Y. The last New York production of this play was off Broadway 2/25/65 for 22 performances.

THE MISANTHROPE

Philinte	Stephen D. Newman	Clitandre	Munson Hicks
Alceste	Brian Bedford	Acaste	George Pentecost
Oronte	David Schramm	Guard	Steve Hendrickson
Celimene	Mary Beth Hurt	Arsinoe	Carole Shelley
Basque	Duffy Hudson	Dubois	Stanley Tucci
Eliante	Mary Layne		

Understudies: Messrs Newman, Schramm, Hicks, Hudson—Steve Hendrickson; Mr. Tucci—Duffy Hudson; Messrs. Bedford, Pentecost—Stanley Tucci; Mr. Hendrickson—A. Robert Scott. Standby: Misses Shelley, Hurt, Layne—Pamela Lewis.

Directed by Stephen Porter; scenery, Marjorie Bradley Kellogg; costumes, Ann Roth; lighting, Richard Nelson; wigs, Peg Schierholz; production stage manager, Michael F. Ritchie; stage manager, A. Robert Scott.

Place: Celimene's house in Paris. The play was presented in two parts.

The last major New York revival of *The Misanthrope* took place off Broadway in the Comédie Française production in French 5/1/79 for 10 performances. Its last major New York production in English was a musical adaptation of Richard Wilbur's version off Broadway 10/5/77 for 63 performances.

Stephen McHattie replaced Brian Bedford 3/8/83.

THE CAINE MUTINY COURT-MARTIAL

Lt. Greenwald	John Rubinstein	Lt. Keefer	J. Kenneth Campbell
Lt. Maryk	Jay O. Sanders	Signalman 3d Class Urban	Jace Alexander
Stenographer	Tom Paliferro	Lt. J.G. Keith	Jonathan Hogan
Orderly	Richard Arbolino	Capt. Southard	Brad Sullivan
Lt. Cmdr. Challee	William Atherton	Dr. Lundeen	Leon B. Stevens
Capt. Blakely	Stephen Joyce	Dr. Bird	Geoffrey Horne
Lt. Cmdr. Queeg	Michael Moriarty		

Six Members of the Court: Clinton Allmon, Warren Ball, Chad Burton, Sam Coppola, Daniel Davin, Oliver Dixon. Officers of the Caine: Clinton Allmon, Chad Burton, Sam Coppola.

Understudies: Messrs. Sullivan, Stevens—Sam Coppola; Mr. Horne—Tom Paliferro; Mr. Moriarty—Geoffrey Horne; Mr. Rubinstein—Michael Moriarty; Mr. Joyce—Chad Burton; Messrs. Campbell, Hogan—Clinton Allmon; Messrs. Atherton, Alexander, Paliferro—Richard Arbolino.

Directed by Arthur Sherman; scenery, John Falabella; costumes, David Murin; lighting, Richard Nelson; production stage manager, Michael F. Ritchie; stage manager, Jace Alexander.

Time: February 1945. Place: The General Court-Martial Room of the Twelfth Naval District, San Francisco, and a banquet room in the Fairmont Hotel, San Francisco. Act I: The prosecution. Act II, Scene 1: The defense. Scene 2: The Fairmont Hotel.

GHOSTS—John Neville and Liv Ullmann in the Ibsen revival

The Caine Mutiny Court-Martial was first produced on Broadway 1/20/54 for 415 performances and was named a Best Play of its season. This is its first major New York revival.

Ghosts (40). Revival of the play by Henrik Ibsen; adapted by Arthur Kopit. Produced by the John F. Kennedy Center, CBS Broadcast Group and James M. Nederlander at the Brooks Atkinson Theater. Opened August 30, 1982. (Closed October 2, 1982)

Regina Engstrand . . . . Jane Murray
Jacob Engstrand . . . . Edward Binns
Pastor Manders . . . . John Neville
Mrs. Helen Alving . . . . Liv Ullmann
Oswald Alving . . . . Kevin Spacey

Standbys: Messrs. Neville, Binns—Tom Klunis; Miss Murray—Madeleine Potter; Mr. Spacey—John Bellucci.

Directed by John Neville; scenery, Kevin Rupnik; costumes, Theoni V. Aldredge; lighting, Martin Aronstein; produced for the Kennedy Center by Roger L. Stevens and Ralph Allen; production stage manager, Mitchell Erickson; stage manager, John Hand; press, John Springer Associates, Meg Gordean.

Place: Mrs. Alving's country house beside one of the large fjords in western Norway. The play was presented in two parts.

The last major New York revival of *Ghosts* took place off Broadway in the Shaliko Company guest production at New York Shakespeare Festival Public Theater 3/6/75 for 37 performances. This production originated at the Eisenhower Theater, Washington, D.C.

Your Arms Too Short to Box With God (70). Return engagement of the musical conceived from the Book of St. Matthew by Vinnette Carroll; music and lyrics by Alex Bradford and Micki Grant. Produced by Barry and Fran Weissler in association with Anita MacShane and the Urban Arts Theater at the Alvin Theater. Opened September 9, 1982. (Closed November 7, 1982)

Julius Richard Brown	Elmore James
Nora Cole	Linda James
Jamil K. Garland	Tommi Johnson
Elijah Gill	Patti LaBelle
L. Michael Gray	Janice Nunn Nelson
Al Green	Dwayne Phelps
Ralf Paul Haze	Quincella
Cynthia Henry	Kiki Shepard
Bobby Hill	Leslie Hardesty Sisson
Rufus E. Jackson	Marilynn Winbush

Directed by Vinnette Carroll; choreography, Talley Beatty; musical direction and arrangements, Michael Powell; scenery and costumes, William Schroder; lighting, Richard Winkler; sound, R. Shepard, J. Esher; orchestrations and dance music, H.B. Barnum; choreography restaged by Ralf Paul Haze; associate producer, Jerry R. Moore; stage manager, Jonathan Weiss; press, Burnham-Callaghan Associates, Owen Levy.

Your Arms Too Short to Box With God was produced on Broadway 12/22/76 for 429 performances and 6/2/80 for 149 performances. Its list of musical numbers (including authorship of individual song numbers) appears on page 299 of *The Best Plays of 1976–77.*

A Doll's Life (5). Musical with book and lyrics by Betty Comden and Adolph Green; music by Larry Grossman. Produced by James M. Nederlander, Sidney L. Shlenker, Warner Theater Productions, Joseph Harris, Mary Lea Johnson, Martin Richards and Robert Fryer, in association with Harold Prince, at the Mark Hellinger Theater. Opened September 23, 1982. (Closed September 26, 1982)

Nora	Betsy Joslyn
Actor; Torvald; Johan	George Hearn
Otto	Peter Gallagher
Eric	Edmund Lyndeck
Astrid	Barbara Lang
Audition Singer; Selma; Jacqueline	Penny Orloff
Conductor; Gustafson; Escamillo; Audition Singer; Loki; Mr. Zetterling	Norman A. Large
Stagehand; Dr. Berg; Audition Singer; Ambassador	David Vosburgh
Stage Manager; Hamsun; Petersen; Warden Nilson	Michael Vita
Dowager	Diane Armistead
Musician; Mr. Kloster	Gordon Bovinet
Camilla Forrester	Willi Burke
Asst. Stage Manager; Helga	Patti Cohenour
Prison Guards	John Corsaut, David Cale Johnson
Helmer's Maid; Waitress	Carol Lurie
Musician; Waiter	Larry Small
Waiter; Audition Singer; Muller	Paul Straney
Maid; Widow	Olga Talyn
Ivar	Jim Wagg
Emmy	Kimberly Stern
Bob	David Seaman
Woman in White	Lisa Peters
Woman in Red	Teri Gill

Woman in Black... Patricia Parker
Man in Black .... David Evans

Understudies: Miss Joslyn—Patti Conhenour; Messrs. Hearn, Lyndeck—Norman A. Large; Mr. Gallagher—Larry Small; Miss Lang—Willi Burke; Miss Orloff—Olga Talyn, Sisu Raiken; Messrs. Large, Vosburgh, Vita, Evans—Kevin Marcum; Miss Burke—Patricia Parker; Miss Gill—Lisa Peters; Messrs. Wagg, Seaman, Miss Stern—Katie Ertmann; Swings—Sisu Raiken, Kevin Marcum.

Directed by Harold Prince; choreography, Larry Fuller; musical direction, Paul Gemignani; scenery, Timothy O'Brien, Tazeena Firth; costumes, Florence Klotz; lighting, Ken Billington; orchestrations, Bill Byers; sound, Jack Mann; production stage manager, Beverley Randolph; stage manager, Richard Evans; press, Mary Bryant, Becky Flora.

Sequel to Ibsen's *A Doll's House,* imagining what happened to Nora after she slammed the door on her home and went out alone into the world of the 19th century. Previously produced in Los Angeles.

ACT I

Scene 1: A rehearsal of Ibsen's *A Doll's House,* 1982
Prologue... Nora, Company
Scene 2: The train
"A Woman Alone" .... Nora, Otto, Conductor, Company
Scene 3: The Cafe Europa
"Letter to the Children" .... Nora
"New Year's Eve" .... Eric, Johan, Dr. Berg, Mr. Gustafson
Scene 4: Street outside the Cafe Europa
Scene 5: Otto's room
"Stay With Me, Nora"... Otto, Nora
Scene 6: Backstage at the opera
Scene 7: An opera reading—the opera audition
"Arrival".. Astrid, Company
"Loki and Baldur".. Otto, Singers
"You Interest Me"... Johan
"Departure" .... Astrid, Company
Scene 8: Otto's Room
"Letter From Klemnacht"....................................... Astrid
"Learn To Be Lonely"... Nora
Scene 9: Cannery
"Rats and Mice and Fish" .... Women
Scene 10: Prison
"Jailer, Jailer"/"Letter to the Children" (Reprise)........................ Nora, Women
Scene 11: The opera house
"Excerpts from Loki and Baldur" .... Company
"Rare Wines" .... Eric, Nora

ACT II

Scene 1: Eric's bedroom
"No More Mornings" .... Nora
Scene 2: Billiard room
"There She Is" .... Johan, Eric, Otto
"Power"... Nora
Scene 3: Billiard Room, the next morning
"Letter to the Children" (Reprise)... Nora
"At Last" .... Johan
Scene 4: The Grand Cafe (spring, fall winter)
"The Grand Cafe" .... Company
Scene 5: The living room
Finale.. Company

*Cats (270). Musical based on *Old Possum's Book of Practical Cats* by T.S. Eliot; music by Andrew Lloyd Webber. Produced by Cameron Mackintosh, The Really Useful Company, Ltd., David Geffen and The Shubert Organization at the Winter Garden. Opened October 7, 1982.

Alonzo . . . . Hector Jaime Mercado	Mistoffolees . . . . Timothy Scott
Bustopher Jones; Asparagus;	Munkustrap . . . . Harry Groener
Growltiger . . . . Stephen Hanan	Old Deuteronomy . . . . Ken Page
Bombalurina . . . . Donna King	Plato; Macavity; Rumpus Cat . . Kenneth Ard
Carbucketty . . . . Steven Gelfer	Pouncival . . . . Herman W. Sebek
Cassandra . . . . Rene Ceballos	Rum Tum Tugger . . . . Terrence V. Mann
Coricopat; Mungojerrie . . . . Rene Clemente	Sillabub . . . . Whitney Kershaw
Demeter . . . . Wendy Edmead	Skimbleshanks . . . . Reed Jones
Etcetera; Rumpleteazer . . . . Christine Langner	Tantomile . . . . Janet L. Hubert
Grizabella . . . . Betty Buckley	Tumblebrutus . . . . Robert Hoshour
Jellylorum; Griddlebone . . . . Bonnie Simmons	Victoria . . . . Cynthia Onrubia
Jennyanydots . . . . Anna McNeely	

The Cats Chorus: Walter Charles, Susan Powers, Carol Richards, Joel Robertson.

Standbys/Understudies: Mr. Ard—Hector Jaime Mercado; Miss Buckley—Janet L. Hubert; Miss Ceballos—Marlène Danielle, Diane Fratantoni; Mr. Clemente—Steven Hack, Herman W. Sebek; Miss Edmead—Janet L. Hubert, Marlène Danielle; Mr. Gelfer—Steven Hack; Mr. Groener—Bob Morrisey; Mr. Hanan—Steven Gelfer; Mr. Hoshour—Steven Hack; Miss Hubert—Marlène Danielle, Whitney Kershaw; Mr. Jones—Bob Morrisey; Miss Kershaw—Diane Fratantoni; Miss King—René Ceballos, Marlène Danielle; Miss Langner—Diane Fratantoni; Mr. Mann—Bob Morrisey; Miss McNeeley—Susan Powers; Mr. Mercado—Bob Morrisey, Herman W. Sebek; Miss Onrubia—Whitney Kershaw, Christine Langner; Mr. Page—Walter Charles; Mr. Scott—Rene Clemente; Mr. Sebek—Steven Hack; Miss Simmons—Diane Fratantoni.

Directed by Trevor Nunn; associate director and choreographer, Gillian Lynne; production musical director, Stanley Lebowsky; musical director, Rene Wiegert; scenery and costumes, John Napier; lighting, David Hersey; sound, Martin Levan; orchestrations, David Cullen, Andrew Lloyd Webber; executive producers, R. Tyler Gatchell Jr., Peter Neufeld; production stage manager, David Taylor; stage manager, Lani Sundsten; press, Fred Nathan & Associates, Eileen McMahon, Anne S. Abrams.

Eliot's words (with exceptions noted) set to music in a series of comic character sketches of cats in a dump setting. "The Marching Songs of the Pollicle Dogs" and the story of Grizabella are taken from unpublished Eliot writings, as were lines in the prologue and "Pollicle Dogs and Jellicle Cats." Growltiger's aria is taken from an Italian translation of *Practical Cats*. A foreign play previously produced in London.

A Best Play; see page 138.

PART I: *When Cats Are Maddened by the Midnight Dance*

"Jellicle Songs for Jellicle Cats" . . . . Company
     (additional lyric material by Trevor Nunn and Richard Stilgoe)
"The Invitation to the Jellicle Ball" . . . . Victoria, Mistoffolees
"The Old Gumbie Cat" . . . . Jennyanydots, Cassandra, Bombalurina, Jellylorum
"The Rum Tum Tugger" . . . . Rum Tum Tugger
"Grizabella, the Glamour Cat" . . . . Grizabella, Demeter, Bombalurina
"Bustopher Jones" . . . . Bustopher, Jennyanydots, Jellylorum, Bombalurina
"Mungojerrie and Rumpleteazer" . . . . Mistoffolees, Mungojerrie, Rumpleteazer
"Old Deuteronomy" . . . . Munkustrap, Rum Tum Tugger, Old Deuteronomy
"The Awefull Battle of the Pekes and Pollicles" together with
     "The Marching Songs of the Pollicle Dogs" . . . . Munkustrap, Rumpus Cat
"The Jellicle Ball" . . . . Company
"Memory" . . . . Grizabella
     (lyric by Trevor Nunn, based on *Rhapsody on a Windy Night* and other Eliot poems of the *Prufrock* period)

PART II: *Why Will the Summer Day Delay—When Will Time Flow Away*

"The Moments of Happiness"............................. Old Deuteronomy, Tantomile
"Gus: The Theater Cat" .... Jellylorum, Asparagus
"Growltiger's Last Stand".................................... Growltiger, Griddlebone
    The Crew—Harry Groener, Reed Jones, Terrence V. Mann, Hector Jaime Mercado, Timothy
    Scott; Genghis—Steven Gelfer
"Skimbleshanks"... Skimbleshanks
"Macavity" .... Demeter, Bombalurina, Alonzo, Macavity, Munkustrap
"Mr. Mistoffolees" .... Mistoffolees, Rum Tum Tugger
"Memory" (Reprise) .... Victoria, Grizabella
"The Journey to the Heaviside Layer" .... Company
"The Ad-dressing of Cats" .... Old Deuteronomy

Good (125). Play with music by C.P. Taylor. Produced by David Geffen, Warner Theater Productions, Inc., Elizabeth I. McCann and Nelle Nugent and The Shubert Organization in the Royal Shakespeare Company production at the Booth Theater. Opened October 13, 1982. (Closed January 30, 1983)

Halder	Alan Howard	Helen	Meg Wynn-Owen
Sister Elizabeth	Kate Spiro	Bouller; Eichmann	Nicholas Woodeson
Mother	Marjorie Yates	Anne	Felicity Dean
Doctor; Despatch Rider	Timothy Walker	Freddie	Pip Miller
Maurice	Gary Waldhorn	Hitler; Bok	David Howey

Musicians: Michael Dansicker piano, accordion; Beryl Diamond violin; Edward Salkin clarinet, alto sax; John Sutton banjo, guitar; Larry Etkin trumpet; Bill Grossman standby pianist.

Understudies: Misses Yates, Wynn-Owen—Irene Hamilton; Mr. Howard—David Howey; Miss Spiro—Catherine Riding; Miss Dean—Kate Spiro; Messrs. Walker, Woodeson, Howey—Paul Teague; Mr. Miller—Timothy Walker; Mr. Waldhorn—Nicholas Woodeson.

Directed by Howard Davies; musical direction, Michael Dansicker; scenery and costumes, Ultz; lighting, Beverly Emmons; music arranged by George Fenton; American production designed in association with John Kasarda (scenery) and Linda Fisher (costumes); produced by arrangement with the Royal Shakespeare Theater and Michael White; production stage manager, Janet Beroza; stage manager, Brian Meister; press, Solters/Roskin/Friedman, Inc., Joshua Ellis, David LeShay.

From 1933 onward, the gradual making of a Nazi out of the unlikely material of a university professor, with familiar music interpolated to point up the ironies. The play was presented in two parts. A foreign play previously produced in London.

A Best Play; see page 123.

The Wake of Jamey Foster (12). By Beth Henley. Produced by FDM Productions (Francois De Menil, Harris Maslansky), Elliot Martin, Ulu Grosbard, Nan Pearlman and Warner Theater Productions, Inc. at the Eugene O'Neill Theater. Opened October 14, 1982. (Closed October 23, 1982)

Marshael Foster	Susan Kingsley	Collard Darnell	Patricia Richardson
Leon Darnell	Stephen Tobolowsky	Pixrose Wilson	Holly Hunter
Katty Foster	Belita Moreno	Brocker Slade	Brad Sullivan
Wayne Foster	Anthony Heald		

Standby: Misses Kingsley, Moreno, Richardson—Annalee Jefferies. Understudies: Messrs. Heald, Tobolowsky—Gregory Grove; Mr. Sullivan—Bing Russell; Miss Hunter—Mary Anne Dorward.

Directed by Ulu Grosbard; scenery, Santo Loquasto; costumes, Jennifer Von Mayrhauser; lighting, Jennifer Tipton; sound, David Rapkin; associate producer, Arla Sorkin Manson; production stage manager, Franklin Keysar; stage manager, Wendy Chapin; press, Jeffrey Richards Associates, C. George Willard.

Place: Throughout Marshael Foster's house and yard in Canton, Miss. Act I, Scene 1: Morning.

Scene 2: Supper time. Act II, Scene 1: Late that night. Scene 2: Throughout the night. Scene 3: The following morning.

Members of a small town family, some of them eccentrics, gather for a wake. Previously produced at the Hartford, Conn. Stage Company.

Rock 'n Roll! The First 5,000 Years (9). Musical revue conceived by Bob Gill and Robert Rabinowitz. Produced by Jules Fisher and Annie Fargue in association with Dick Clark, Inc. and Fred Disipio at the St. James Theater. Opened October 24, 1982. (Closed October 31, 1982)

Bob Barnes	Bob Miller
Joyce Leigh Bowden	Michael Pace
Ka-ron Brown	Raymond Patterson
Sandy Dillon	Marion Ramsey
Andrew Dorfman	Jim Riddle
Rich Hebert	Shaun Solomon
Lon Hoyt	Tom Teeley
William Gregg Hunter	Russell Velazquez
Bill Jones	Barbara Walsh
Jenifer Lewis	Patrick Weathers
Dave MacDonald	Carl E. Weaver
Wenndy Leigh MacKenzie	Lillias White
Karen Mankes	

Directed and choreographed by Joe Layton; musical continuity and supervision, John Simon; musical direction, Andrew Dorfman; special consultant, Dick Clark; scenery, Mark Ravitz; costumes, Franne Lee; lighting, Jules Fisher; sound, Bran Ferren; co-choreographer, Jerry Grimes; orchestrations, dance and vocal arrangements, John Simon; media, Gill & Rabinowitz; producers' associate, Robin Ullman; associate producers, Charles Koppelman, Martin Bandier; production stage manager, Peter Lawrence; stage manager, Jim Woolley; press, The Merlin Group, Ltd., Cheryl Sue Dolby, Joel W. Dein, Merle Frimark, Dennis Decker.

The origins and growth of rock 'n roll music from 1955 to 1982, set forth in more than 60 musical numbers in this genre.

MUSICAL NUMBERS, ACT I: "Love Is a Many Splendored Thing" (by Sammy Fain and Paul Francis Webster)—Frank Sinatra recording; "Tutti Frutti"—Carl E. Weaver, Company; "Rock Around the Clock" (by Max Friedman and Jimmy DeKnight)—Jim Riddle, Company; "Blueberry Hill" (by Al Lewis, Larry Stock and Vincent Rose)—William Gregg Hunter, Company; "Wake Up Little Susie" (by Boudleaux and Felice Bryant)—Russell Velazquez, Tom Teeley, Company; "Great Balls of Fire" (by Otis Blackwell and Jack Hammer)—Teeley, Company.

Also "Johnny B. Goode" (by Chuck Berry)—Weaver, Company; "Heartbreak Hotel" (by Max Boren Axton, Tommy Durden and Elvis Presley)—Patrick Weathers, Company; "Hound Dog" (by Jerry Leiber and Mike Stoller)—Weathers, Company; "Love Me Tender" (by Vera Matson and Elvis Presley)—Weathers, Company; "Why Do Fools Fall in Love" (by F. Lymon and M. Levy)—Weaver, Bob Barnes, Shaun Solomon, Hunter, Raymond Patterson, Company; "Sh-Boom" ("Life Could Be a Dream") by James Edwards, Carl Feaster, James Keyes and Floyd F. McRae)—Dave MacDonald, Company.

Also "Will You Still Love Me Tomorrow" (by Jerry Goffin and Carole King)—Marion Ramsey, Company; "Da Doo Ron Ron" (by Jeff Barry, Ellie Greenwich and Phil Spector)—Wenndy Leigh MacKenzie, Company; "The Twist" (by Hank Ballard)—Patterson, Ka-ron Brown, Company; "Land of a Thousand Dances" (by Chris Kenner and Antoine Domino)—Hunter, Brown, Company; "I'll Be There" (by Hal Davis, Berry Gordy, Bob West and Willie Hutch)—Bob Barnes, Company; "You Keep Me Hanging On" (by Eddie Holland, Lamont Dozier and Bryant Holland)—Jenifer Lewis, Lillias White, Ramsey, Company.

Also "Proud Mary" (by John C. Fogerty)—Ramsey, Company; "A Hard Day's Night"—Riddle, Velazquez, Teeley, Bob Miller, Company; "I Got You Babe" (by Sonny Bono)—Karen Mankes, Michael Pace, Company; "Good Vibrations" (by Brian Wilson and Mike Love)—Rich Hebert,

Weaver, Riddle, Company; "Here Comes the Sun"—Teeley, Company; "The Sunshine of Your Love" (by Jack Bruce, Eric Clapton and Peter Brown)—Teeley, Velazquez, Company; "Blowin' in the Wind" (by Bob Dylan)—Weathers, Company.

Also "Like a Rolling Stone" (by Bob Dylan)—Weathers, Company; "Whiter Shade of Pale" (by Keith Reid and Gary Brooker)—MacDonald, Brown, Company; "Mrs. Robinson" (by Paul Simon) —Velazquez, Teeley, Brown, Company; "White Rabbit" (by Grace Slick)—Barbara Walsh, Mankes, MacKenzie, Company; "Respect" (by Otis Redding)—White, Company; "The Night They Drove Old Dixie Down" (by J. Robbie Robertson)—Weathers, Company.

Also "People Got To Be Free" (by Edward Brigate and Felix Cavaliere)—Velazquez, Company; "Cry Baby" (by Burt Russell and Norman Meade)—Sandy Dillon, Company; "Forever Young" (by Bob Dylan)—Walsh, Company; "Everybody's Talking" (by Fred Neil)—Pace, Company; "Joy to the World" (by Hoyt Axton)—Velazquez, Company; "Both Sides Now" (by Joni Mitchell)—MacKenzie, Company; "Higher and Higher" (by Renard Miner, Gary Jackson and Carl Smith)—Patterson, Company.

ACT II: "Tubular Bells" (by Mike Oldfield)—Miller, Company (instrumental); "I Feel the Earth Move" (by Carole King)—Joyce Leigh Bowden, Company; "Satisfaction" (by Mick Jagger and Keith Richards)—MacDonald, Company; "When Will I Be Loved" (by Phil Everly)—Bowden, Company; "My Generation" (by Peter Townshend)—Riddle, Company; "You've Got a Friend" (by Carole King)—Pace, Company.

Also "Nothing From Nothing" (by Billy Preston and Bruce Fisher)—Hunter, Brown, Company; "Say It Loud I'm Black and Proud" (by James Brown)—Barnes, Company; "Summer in the City" (by John Sebastian, Steve Boone and Mark Sebastian)—Riddle, Brown, Company; "Whole Lotta Love" (by John Baldwin, John Bonham, and James Patrick Page)—Velazquez, Riddle, Company; "Star Spangled Banner" (arranged by Jimi Hendrix)—Teeley (instrumental); "Boogie Woogie Bugle Boy" (by Don Raye and Hughie Prince)—Bowden, Company.

Also "I Feel Like I'm Gonna Die Rag" (by Joe McDonald)—MacDonald, Company; "American Pie" (by Don McLean)—Hebert, Company; "Imagine"—Teeley, Company; "School's Out" (by Alice Cooper and Michael Bruce)—MacDonald, Company; "Rock & Roll All Night" (by Paul Stanley and Gene Simmons)—Riddle, Company; "Benny and the Jets" (by Elton John and Bernie Taupin)—Lon Hoyt, Company.

Also "Space Oddity" (by David Bowie)—Pace, Velazquez, Company; "Take a Walk on the Wild Side" (by Lou Reed)—Weathers, Company; "Everybody Is a Star" (by Sylvester Stewart)—Weaver, White, Patterson, Hunter, Brown, Company; "Stayin' Alive" (by Barry Gibb, Robin Gibb and Maurice Gibb)—Hoyt, Pace, Herbert, Company; "Love to Love You Baby" (by Pete Bellote, Giorgio Morder and Donna Summer)—Lewis, Company; "I Will Survive" (by Dino Fekaris and Frederick J. Perren)—White, Company.

Also "On the Run" (by Roger Waters, David Gilmour and Rick Wright)—Andrew Dorfman, Velazquez (instrumental); "Jocko Homo" (by Mark Mothersbaugh)—MacDonald, Company; "Message in a Bottle" (by Sting Summer)—Hoyt, Company; "Our Lips Are Sealed" (by Jane Weidlin and Terry Hall)—Mankes, Company; "Concrete Shoes" (by Rod Swenson and Chosei Funahara Power) —Dillon, Solomon, Company; "Rock and Roll Music" (by Chuck Berry)—Company.

Twice Around the Park (124). Program of two one-act comedies by Murray Schisgal: *A Need for Brussels Sprouts* and *A Need for Less Expertise*. Produced by Peter Witt, Margo Korda and Warner Theater Productions in association with the John F. Kennedy Center for the Performing Arts at the Cort Theater. Opened November 4, 1982. (Closed February 20, 1983)

A Need for Brussels Sprouts		*A Need for Less Expertise*	
Leon Rose	Eli Wallach	Edie Frazier	Anne Jackson
Margaret Heinz	Anne Jackson	Gus Frazier	Eli Wallach
Time: The present. Place: An apartment on Manhattan's West Side.		Dr. Oliovsky's Voice	Paulson Mathews
		Time: The present. Place: A co-op on Manhattan's East Side.	

Standbys: Mr. Wallach—Ben Kapen; Miss Jackson—Donna Dundon.
Directed by Arthur Storch; scenery, James Tilton; costumes, Ruth Morley; lighting, Judy Ras-

muson; sound, David S. Schnirman; stage manager, John Vivian; press, Joe Wolhandler Associates, Kathryn Kempf.

Two New York City couples—in *A Need for Brussels Sprouts* an out-of-work actor and a woman policeman and in *A Need for Less Expertise* an affluent married pair—the former trying to get together and the latter, with the help of a marriage counselor, trying to stay together.

Foxfire (213). Play with songs by Susan Cooper and Hume Cronyn; music by Jonathan Holtzman; based on materials from the *Foxfire* books. Produced by Robert Lussier, Warner Theater Productions (Claire Nichtern), Mary Lea Johnson and Sam Crothers at the Ethel Barrymore Theater. Opened November 11, 1982. (Closed May 15, 1983)

Annie Nations	Jessica Tandy	Holly Burrell	Katherine Cortez
Hector Nations	Hume Cronyn	Dillard Nations	Keith Carradine
Prince Carpenter	Trey Wilson	Doctor	James Greene

Musicians: Marc Horowitz banjo, Ken Kosek fiddle, Roger Mason bass.

Understudies: Miss Cortez—Bess Gatewood; Messrs. Greene, Wilson, Carradine—Terrance O'-Quinn; Mr. Cronyn—James Greene.

Directed by David Trainer; musical direction, Jonathan Holtzman; scenery, David Mitchell; costumes, Linda Fisher; lighting, Ken Billington; sound, Louis Shapiro; production stage manager, Martha Knight; stage manager, James M. Arnemann; press, David Powers, Leo Stern.

Time: Now—and before that. Place: Rabun County, Ga. The play was presented in two parts.

Based on the books of Appalachian Mountain folklore edited by Eliot Wigginton and his students, the life and times of a 20th century mountain family including an indomitable mother, a bull-headed father and a son who runs off to become a pop singer. Previously produced at Stratford, Ont. and the Guthrie Theater, Minneapolis.

A Best Play; see page 191.

84 Charing Cross Road (96). By Helene Hanff; adapted by James Roose-Evans. Produced by Alexander H. Cohen, Hildy Parks and Cynthia Wood at the Nederlander Theater. Opened December 7, 1982. (Closed February 27, 1983)

Helene Hanff	Ellen Burstyn	George Martin	William Francis
Frank Doel	Joseph Maher	William Humphries	Mark Chamberlin
Cecily Farr	Ellen Newman	Joan Todd	Etain O'Malley
Megan Wells; Maxine Stuart	Jo Henderson	Matthew	Thomas Nahrwold

Standbys: Miss Burstyn—Elizabeth Perry; Mr. Maher—Miller Lide; Misses Henderson, Newman—Etain O'Malley. Understudy: Mr. Chamberlain—Thomas Nahrwold.

Directed by James Roose-Evans; scenery, Oliver Smith; costumes, Pearl Somner; lighting, Marc B. Weiss; co-producer, Roy A. Somlyo; production stage manager, Robert L. Borod; stage manager, Christopher A. Cohen; press, Merle Debuskey, David Roggensack.

Time: 1949–1971. Place: The New York apartments of Helene Hanff and in Marx & Co., booksellers, 84 Charing Cross Road, London. The play was presented in two parts.

The friendship of an American author and a London bookseller (who never meet) expressed in their correspondence, previously published as a novel in 1970. Previously produced in London.

Herman van Veen: All of Him (6). One-man musical performance conceived by Herman van Veen and Michel LaFaille; English adaptation and lyrics by Christopher Adler; with Herman van Veen. Produced by Joost Taverne, Michael Frazier and Ron van Eeden in association with the Harlekyn U.S.A. Company at the Ambassador Theater. Opened December 8, 1982. (Closed December 12, 1982)

Musicians: Erik van der Wurff keyboards; Nard Reijnders saxophone; Cees van der Laarse bass, electric bass guitar.

Directed by Michel LaFaille; musical direction, Erik van der Wurff; scenery, Gerard Jongerius, Ed de Boer; costumes, Ellen van der Horst; lighting, Rob Munnik; sound, Hans van der

Linden; English translations and associate producer, Patricia Braun; production stage manager, Luc Hemeleers; press, Solters/Roskin/Friedman, Inc., Joshua Ellis, Jan Greenberg.

Dutch stage star in his U.S. debut in a one-man performance in English combining singing, mime, comedy and commentary. The show was presented in two parts.

MUSICAL NUMBERS: "A Girl" (music by Herman van Veen and Erik van der Wurff), "A Loose Woman" (music by Herman van Veen, original lyrics by Willem Wilmink, English lyrics by Christopher Adler), "Cranes" (traditional music adapted by Herman van Veen, original lyrics by Willem Wilmink, English lyrics by Christopher Adler), "Do You Remember" (original lyrics by Hans Lodeizen, English lyrics by Christopher Adler), "Hello" (music by Herman van Veen and Erik van der Wurff), "Heroes" (music by Chris Pilgrim, original lyrics by Rob Chrispijn, English lyrics by Christopher Adler), "Hole-in-One" (music by Erik van der Wurff and Herman van Veen).

Also "I Don't Want Any Help" (music by Erik van der Wurff and Herman van Veen, original lyrics by Herman van Veen, English lyrics by Christopher Adler), "I Won't Let That Happen to Him" (music by Georges Delerue), "Jacob Is Dead" (music by Herman van Veen), "Kitchen Sink" (music by Erik van der Wurff and Herman van Veen, original lyrics by Herman van Veen, English lyrics by Christopher Adler), "Ode to Suicide" (music by Joop Stokkermans, original lyrics by Guus Vleugel, English lyrics by Christopher Adler), "Parade of Clowns" (music by Erik van der Wurff and Herman van Veen, original lyrics by Rob Chrispijn, English lyrics by Christopher Adler), "Sarabande" (music by J.B. Senaille, Herman van Veen and Erik van der Wurff).

Also "Station" (music by Erik van der Wurff and Herman van Veen), "Tell Me Who I Was" (music by Philippe-Gerard, original French lyrics by Gébé, Dutch lyrics by Willem Wilmink, adapted from the Dutch by Christopher Adler), "The Back of Life" (music by Herman van Veen, original lyrics by Willem Wilmink, English lyrics by Christopher Adler); "The Fence" (music by Erik van der Wurff), "The Interview" (music by Erik van der Wurff and Herman van Veen), "The Rules of the Asylum" (music by Herman van Veen, original lyrics by Rob Chrispijn), "Time Passed Her By" (original music and lyrics by Jean Ferrat, adapted from the Dutch by Christopher Adler), "What a Day" (music by Erik van der Wurff).

Steaming (65). By Nell Dunn. Produced by Ronald S. Lee, Robert S. Fishko, Gene Wolsk, Sheila Tronn Cooper and Carol Cogan by arrangement with Eddie Kulukundis, John Wallbank and Christopher Malcolm at the Brooks Atkinson Theater. Opened December 12, 1982. (Closed February 5, 1983)

Violet	Pauline Flanagan	Dawn	Lisa Jane Persky
Bill	John Messenger	Josie	Judith Ivey
Nancy	Linda Thorson	Jane	Margaret Whitton
Mrs. Meadow	Polly Rowles		

Directed by Roger Smith; scenery, Marjorie Bradley Kellogg; costumes, Jennifer Von Mayrhauser; lighting, Pat Collins; sound, David Rapkin; production stage manager, Steve Zweigbaum; stage manager, Scott Glenn; press, Seymour Krawitz, Patricia Krawitz.

Time: The late 1970s. Place: In a Turkish bath, London. Act I, Scene 1: November. Scene 2: A week later. Scene 3: A week later. Scene 4: A week later. Act II, Scene 1: January. Scene 2: Two days later. Scene 3: Later that evening.

Woman-talk, a lot of it about sex, in a group of a half dozen regular and sometimes nude customers of a Turkish bath. A foreign play previously produced in London.

Monday After the Miracle (7). By William Gibson. Produced by Raymond Katz, Sandy Gallin and the John F. Kennedy Center at the Eugene O'Neill Theater. Opened December 14, 1982. (Closed December 18, 1982)

Annie	Jane Alexander	Pete	Matt McKenzie
Helen	Karen Allen	Ed	Joseph Warren
John	William Converse-Roberts		

Understudies: Miss Alexander—Geraldine Baron; Miss Allen—Denise Lute; Messrs. Converse-Roberts, McKenzie—Francois De La Giroday; Mr. Warren—Paul Haggard.

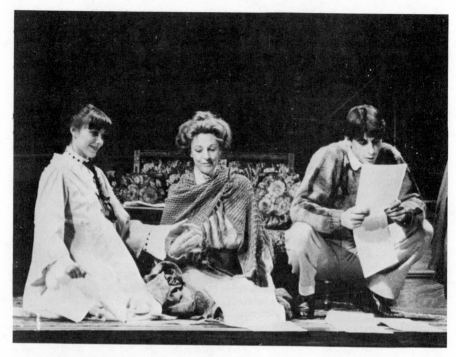

MONDAY AFTER THE MIRACLE—Karen Allen as Helen Keller, Jane Alexander as Annie Sullivan and William Converse-Roberts as John Macy in a scene from the play by William Gibson

Directed by Arthur Penn; scenery, John Lee Beatty; costumes, Carol Oditz; lighting, F. Mitchell Dana; incidental music, Claude Kerry-White; production stage manager, Susie Cordon; stage manager, Laura deBuys; press, Solters/Roskin/Friedman, Inc., Joshua Ellis, David LeShay.

Time: In the early part of this century. Place: Boston environs—first Cambridge, then Wrentham. The play was presented in three parts.

Helen Keller and her mentor Annie Sullivan 20 years after the events in Gibson's 1959 play *The Miracle Worker*. Previously produced in Pretoria and Johannesburg, South Africa, and Charleston, S.C.

A Little Family Business (13). By Jay Presson Allen; adapted from a play by Pierre Barillet and Jean-Pierre Gredy. Produced by Harry Saltzman, Arthur Cantor and Warner Theater Productions, Inc. at the Martin Beck Theater. Opened December 15, 1982. (Closed December 26, 1982)

Lillian	Angela Lansbury	
Ben	John McMartin	
Nadine	Sally Stark	
Scott	Anthony Shaw	
Connie	Tracy Brooks Swope	
Sal	Theodore Sorel	

Works Committee:

Marco	Tony Cummings
Sophia	Hallie Foote
Vinnie	Gordon Rigsby
Joe	Donald E. Fischer

Recorded roles: Aerobic Dance Instructor—B.J. Ward; TV News Commentator—Tony Cummings.

Understudies: Messrs. McMartin, Sorel—Gordon Rigsby; Misses Stark, Swope—Hallie Foote; Mr. Shaw—Tony Cummings; Mr. Cummings—Donald E. Fischer.

Directed by Martin Charnin; scenery, David Gropman; costumes, Theoni V. Aldredge; lighting,

Richard Nelson; sound, Chuck London; production associate, Harvey Elliott; produced in association with Center Theater Group/Ahmanson Theater; production stage manager, Frank Hartenstein; stage manager, Edward R. Fitzgerald; press, Arthur Cantor Associates, Harvey Elliott.

Place: The Ridley home in Cobbsville, Mass. Act I, Scene 1: A May morning. Scene 2: The following morning. Scene 3: A few hours later. Act II, Scene 1: Three months later. Scene 2: Two weeks later.

Comedy, wife takes over the management of a corporation from her ailing husband. Previously produced in Los Angeles; the original was produced in Paris as *Potiche*.

Almost an Eagle (5). By Michael Kimberley. Produced by Frederick M. Zollo, Susan R. Rose, Gail Berman, William P. Suter, Nicholas Paleologos, Melvyn J. Estrin and Sidney Shlenker at the Longacre Theater. Opened December 16, 1982. (Closed December 19, 1982)

Billy Spencer .... Jeffrey Marcus	Shawn Haley .... Neil Barry
Terry Matthews.............. Scott Simon	Colonel................. James Whitmore
Mark Lillard .... John P. Navin Jr.	

Directed by Jacques Levy; scenery and costumes, Karl Eigsti; lighting, Roger Morgan; associate producers, Paul D'Addario, Barbara Livitz; production stage manager, Steve Beckler; press, Judy Jacksina, Glenna Freedman.

Comedy, a Boy Scout troupe in Table Rock, Iowa. The play was presented in two parts.

Alice in Wonderland (21). Revival of the play adapted by Eva Le Gallienne and Florida Friebus from Lewis Carroll (illustrated by John Tenniel); music by Richard Addinsell. Produced by Sabra Jones and Anthony D. Marshall in the Eva Le Gallienne production at the Virginia Theater. Opened December 23, 1982. (Closed January 16, 1983)

CAST: Singers—Nancy Killmer, Marti Morris; Alice—Kate Burton; Small White Rabbit, Four of Hearts—Mary Stuart Masterson; Mouse, Three of Hearts, Tweedledee—John Remme; Lory, Seven of Hearts—John Miglietta; Duck, Dormouse, Train Guard—Nicholas Martin; Dodo, Mock Turtle —James Valentine; Eaglet, Two of Hearts—Rebecca Armen; White Rabbit, White Knight—Curt Dawson; Caterpillar, Ten of Hearts, Sheep—John Heffernan; Fish Footman, Voice of Cheshire Cat, Ace of Hearts, Man in White Paper—Geddeth Smith; Frog Footman, Five of Hearts, Goat— Claude-Albert Saucier; Duchess—Edward Zang; Cook, Nine of Hearts—Richard Sterne.

Also March Hare, Front of Horse—Josh Clark; Mad Hatter—MacIntyre Dixon; Two of Spades —Geoff Garland; Five of Spades, Tweedledum—Robert Ott Boyle; Seven of Spades, Voice of Leg of Mutton—Steve Massa; Three of Clubs—Skip Harris; Seven of Clubs, Back of Horse—Cliff Rakerd; Six of Hearts—Marti Morris; Eight of Hearts—Nancy Killmer; Knave of Hearts—John Seidman; Queen of Hearts—Brian Reddy; King of Hearts, Voice of Humpty Dumpty—Richard Woods; Gryphon, Old Frog—Edward Hibbert; Red Queen—Mary Louise Wilson; White Queen— Eva Le Gallienne (Joan White, alternate).

Understudies: Miss Burton—Mary Stuart Masterson; Miss Armen, Mr. Sterne—Nancy Killmer; Mr. Boyle—Skip Harris, John Seidman; Messrs. Clark, Reddy, Smith—Cliff Rakerd; Mr. Dixon—Robert Ott Boyle; Messrs. Garland, Rakerd—Skip Harris; Mr. Heffernan—Geddeth Smith; Mr. Martin—Steve Massa; Mr. Massa—John Remme; Miss Masterson—Marti Morris; Messrs. Miglietta, Valentine—Richard Sterne; Mr. Remme—MacIntyre Dixon; Messrs. Saucier, Seidman—John Miglietta; Miss Wilson—Rebecca Armen; Mr. Woods—Nicholas Martin, Richard Sterne; Mr. Zang—Claude-Albert Saucier.

Conceived and directed by Eva Le Gallienne; co-director, John Strasberg; scenery, John Lee Beatty; costumes, Patricia Zipprodt; lighting, Jennifer Tipton; puppets, The Puppet People; music adaptation and supervision, Jonathan Tunick; movements, Bambi Linn; sound, Jack Mann; conductor, Les Scott; special effects, Chic Silber; produced in association with WNET/Thirteen; production stage manager, Alan Hall; stage manager, Ruth E. Rinklin; press, Solters/Roskin/Friedman, Inc., Joshua Ellis, David LeShay.

Act I: Alice at Home, The Looking-Glass House, Pool of Tears, Caucus Race, Caterpillar, Duchess, Cheshire Cat, Mad Tea Party, Queen's Croquet Ground, By the Sea, The Trial. Act II: Red Chess

Queen, Railway Carriage, Tweedledum and Tweedledee, White Chess Queen, The Sheep Shop, Humpty Dumpty, White Knight, Alice With the Two Queens, Alice's Door, The Banquet, Alice at Home Again.

This stage version of the Alice stories was first produced on Broadway by Civic Repertory Theater 12/12/32 for 127 performances. It was revived by the American Repertory Theater 4/5/47 for 100 performances.

Whodunnit (157). By Anthony Shaffer. Produced by Douglas Urbanski, Robert A. Buckley and E. Gregg Wallace Jr. at the Biltmore Theater. Opened December 30, 1982. (Closed May 15, 1983)

Archibald Perkins . . . . Gordon Chater	Lavinia Hargreaves . . . . Lauren Thompson
Andreas Capodistriou . . . . George Hearn	Roger Dashwell . . . . John Glover
Silas Bazeby . . . . Jerome Dempsey	Dame Edith Runcible . . . . Hermione Baddeley
Rear-Admiral Knatchbull	Inspector Bowden . . . . Fred Gwynne
Folliatt . . . . Ronald Drake	Sergeant . . . . Jeffrey Alan Chandler
Lady Tremurrain . . . . Barbara Baxley	

Standbys: Messrs. Dempsey, Drake, Gwynne—John Hallow; Misses Baxley, Baddeley—Patricia Gage; Messrs. Glover, Chandler—Robert Nadir; Miss Thompson—Johanna Leister.

Directed by Michael Kahn; scenery, Andrew Jackness; costumes, Patricia Zipprodt; lighting, Martin Aronstein; hair and makeup, Patrik D. Moreton; sound, Richard Fitzgerald; production stage manager, Frank Marino; stage manager, Judith Binus; press, Marilynn LeVine, Michael Alpert.

Place: The library of Orcas Champflower Manor. Act I: An evening in the 1930s. Act II: Some time later.

Comedy thriller, a takeoff on the British country-house murder mystery novel. A foreign play previously produced in London under the title *The Case of the Oily Levantine*.

Robert Nadir replaced John Glover 3/22/83–4/5/83. Frank Gorshin replaced George Hearn 4/12/83.

Plenty (92). Transfer from off Broadway of the play by David Hare. Produced by Joseph Papp in the New York Shakespeare Festival production at the Plymouth Theater. Opened January 6, 1983. (Closed March 27, 1983)

Alice Park . . . . Ellen Parker	Louise . . . . Johann Carlo
Susan Traherne . . . . Kate Nelligan	M. Aung . . . . Conrad Yama
Raymond Brock . . . . Edward Herrmann	Mme. Aung . . . . Ginny Yang
Codename Lazar . . . . Ben Masters	Dorcas Frey . . . . Madeleine Potter
Frenchman #1 . . . . Ken Meseroll	John Begley . . . . Jeff Allin
Leonard Darwin . . . . George N. Martin	Sir Andrew Charleson . . . . Bill Moor
Mick . . . . Daniel Gerroll	Frenchman #2 . . . . Pierre Epstein

Standby: Miss Nelligan—Randy Danson. Understudies: Messrs. Masters, Gerroll—Jeff Allin; Mr. Yama—Victor Wong; Miss Yang—Kiya Ann Joyce; Misses Parker, Carlo, Potter—Elizabeth Norment; Messrs. Martin, Moor, Epstein—Tom Klunis; Messrs. Allin, Meseroll—Robert Curtis-Brown.

Directed by David Hare; scenery, John Gunter; costumes, Jane Greenwood; lighting, Arden Fingerhut; incidental music, Nick Bicat; production supervisor, Jason Steven Cohen; production stage manager, Michael Chambers; stage manager, Anne King; press, Merle Debuskey, Richard Kornberg.

Act I, Scene 1: Knightsbridge, Easter 1962. Scene 2: St. Benoit, November 1943. Scene 3: Brussels, June 1947. Scene 4: Pimlico, September 1947. Scene 5: Festival of Britain, May 1951. Scene 6: Pimlico, December 1952. Scene 7: Knightsbridge, October 1956. Act II: Scene 8: Knightsbridge, July 1961. Scene 9: Whitehall, January 1962. Scene 10: Knightsbridge, the day before Easter 1962. Scene 11: Blackpool, June 1962. Scene 12: St. Benoit, August 1944.

From World War II to the 1960s, an Englishwoman's disillusionment and emotional decline is seen as a metaphor of the values and moods of her country. A foreign play previously produced at the

National Theater, London; in Chicago; and in this production at New York Shakespeare Festival Public Theater for 45 performances 10/21/82–11/28/82 (see its entry in the Plays Produced Off Broadway section of this volume).

Jenny Wright replaced Madeleine Potter 2/83.

A Best Play; see page 173.

Angels Fall (64). Transfer from off Broadway of the play by Lanford Wilson. Produced by Elliot Martin, Circle Repertory Company, Lucille Lortel, The Shubert Organization and Kennedy Center in the Circle Repertory Company production at the Longacre Theater. Opened January 22, 1983. (Closed March 13, 1983)

Niles Harris	Fritz Weaver	Marion Clay	Tanya Berezin
Vita Harris	Nancy Snyder	Salvatore (Zappy) Zappala	Brian Tarantina
Don Tabaha	Danton Stone	Father William Doherty	Barnard Hughes

Understudies: Messrs. Hughes, Weaver—Matthew Lewis; Misses Snyder, Berezin—Trish Hawkins; Messrs. Stone, Tarantina—Daniel Hutchison.

Directed by Marshall W. Mason; scenery, John Lee Beatty; costumes, Jennifer Von Mayrhauser; lighting, Dennis Parichy; sound, Chuck London Media/Stewart Werner; original music, Norman L. Berman; production stage manager, Fred Reinglas; stage manager, Ginny Martino; press, Jeffrey Richards Associates, C. George Willard.

Time: A late Saturday afternoon in June. Place: A mission in northwest New Mexico. The play was presented in two parts.

Character studies of six individuals confined in a group by a nearby nuclear accident. Previously produced off Broadway by Circle Repertory Company 10/17/82 for 65 performances through 11/28/82; see its entry in the Plays Produced Off Broadway section of this volume.

A Best Play; see page 153.

*A View From the Bridge (135). Revival of the play by Arthur Miller. Produced by Zev Bufman and Sidney Shlenker in the Long Wharf Theater production at the Ambassador Theater. Opened February 3, 1983.

Louis	Stephen Mendillo	Rodolpho	James Hayden
Mike	John Shepard	1st Immigration Officer	Ramón Ramos
Alfieri	Robert Prosky	2d Immigration Officer	James Vitale
Eddie	Tony Lo Bianco	Mr. Lipari	Mitchell Jason
Catherine	Saundra Santiago	Mrs. Lipari	Rose Arrick
Beatrice	Rose Gregorio	1st "Submarine"	Tom Nardini
Marco	Alan Feinstein	2d "Submarine"	Joseph Adams
Tony	Paul Perri		

Standbys: Mr. Lo Bianco—Michael Baseleon; Mr. Prosky—Mitchell Jason; Miss Gregorio—Rose Arrick; Miss Santiago—Yolanda Lloyd; Mr. Hayden—Joseph Adams; Mr. Feinstein—Stephen Mendillo.

Directed by Arvin Brown; scenery, Hugh Landwehr; costumes, Bill Walker; lighting, Ronald Wallace; fights, B.H. Barry; associate producer, Barbara Livitz; production stage manager, James Harker; press, Fred Nathan & Associates, Eileen McMahon, Anne S. Abrams, John Howlett, John Traub.

Time: the 1950s. Place: In the apartment and environment of Eddie Carbone, all in Red Hook, on the bay seaward from Brooklyn Bridge. The play was presented in two parts.

A View From the Bridge was first produced on Broadway in a one-act version 9/29/55 for 149 performances and was named a Best Play of its season. The present full-length version was first produced off Broadway 1/28/65 for 780 performances. This revival was previously produced at the Long Wharf Theater and elsewhere.

*Merlin (121). Musical based on an original concept by Doug Henning and Barbara De Angelis; book by Richard Levinson and William Link; songs and incidental music by

MERLIN—Doug Henning *(top, center)* and company in a scene from the musical

Elmer Bernstein; lyrics by Don Black; magic illusions created by Doug Henning. Produced by Ivan Reitman, Columbia Pictures Stage Productions, Inc., Marvin A. Krauss and James M. Nederlander at the Mark Hellinger Theater. Opened February 13, 1983; see note.

Old Merlin; Old Soldier . George Lee Andrews	Prince Fergus. . . . . Nathan Lane
Young Merlin; Arthur . . . . . . Christian Slater	Merlin's Vision; Water . . . . . . Debby Henning
Wizard . . . . Edmund Lyndeck	Ariadne. . . . . Michelle Nicastro
Merlin. . . . . Doug Henning	Acolyte; Manservant. . . . . Alan Brasington
Philomena . . . . Rebecca Wright	Earth. . . . . Peggy Parten
Queen . . . . Chita Rivera	Air . . . . Robyn Lee
Queen's Companion . . . . Gregory Mitchell	Fire. . . . . Spence Ford

Creatures of the Glade: Robin Cleaver, Ramon Galindo, Todd Lester, Claudia Shell, Robert Tanna. Ladies of the Court: Pat Gorman, Leslie Hicks, Robyn Lee, Peggy Parten, Iris Revson.

Ladies of the Ensemble: Robin Cleaver, Spence Ford, Pat Gorman, Andrea Handler, Debby Henning, Leslie Hicks, Sandy Laufer, Robyn Lee, Peggy Parten, Iris Revson, Claudia Shell.

Men of the Ensemble: David Asher, Ramon Galindo, Todd Lester, Joe Locarro, Fred C. Mann III, Gregory Mitchell, Andrew Hill Newman, Eric Roach, Robert Tanna, Robert Warners.

Understudies: Mr. Henning—Andrew Hill Newman; Miss Rivera—Sandy Laufer; Mr. Lane—Robert Warners; Mr. Lyndeck—David Asher, Alan Brasington; Miss Wright—Claudia Shell; Miss Nicastro—Leslie Hicks; Mr. Andrews—Alan Brasington; Mr. Brasington—David Asher; Mr. Slater—Ron Meier.

Directed by Ivan Reitman; choreography, Christopher Chadman, Billy Wilson; musical direction and vocal arrangements, David Spear; scenery, Robin Wagner; costumes, Theoni V. Aldredge; lighting, Tharon Musser; sound, Abe Jacob; orchestrations, Larry Wilcox; dance arrangements, Mark Hummel; magic consultant, Charles Reynolds; associate producer, Joe Medjuck; produced by Ivan Reitman and Marvin A. Krauss; production supervisor, Jeff Hamlin; production stage manager, Jeff Lee; stage manager, Bonnie Panson; press, The Merlin Group, Ltd., Cheryl Sue Dolby, Merle Frimark.

Time: The time of sorcery.

Pre-Arthurian fantasy as a vehicle for a performance by magician Doug Henning.

Note: The official opening date of *Merlin* was 2/13/83, though some publications of record reviewed it as a finished show before that date, in the midst of its long series of preview performances.

ACT I

Scene 1: Merlin's glade
   "It's About Magic" .... Old Merlin, Young Merlin, Merlin, Philomena, Ensemble
Scene 2: The palace of the Queen
   "I Can Make It Happen" .... Queen
Scene 3: The glade
   "Beyond My Wildest Dreams" .... Ariadne
   "Something More" .... Merlin, Ariadne
Scene 4: A crystal grove
   "The Elements" .... Merlin, Wizard, Ensemble
Scene 5: A river
   "Fergus's Dilemma" .... Fergus, Ladies of the Court
Scene 6: The hall of the angels
   "Nobody Will Remember Him" .... Queen, Wizard

ACT II

Scene 1: A far away village
   "Put a Little Magic in Your Life" .... Old Merlin, Merlin, Philomena, Ensemble
   "He Who Knows the Way" .... Wizard
Scene 2: The palace
   "I Can Make It Happen" (Reprise) .... Queen
Scene 3: A marsh
   "He Who Knows the Way" (Reprise) .... Wizard
Scene 4: The palace ramparts
   "We Haven't Fought a Battle in Years" .... Fergus, Soldiers
Scene 5: The Queen's dungeon
   "Satan Rules" .... Queen
   "Nobody Will Remember Him" (Reprise) .... Queen
Scene 6: On the Way to London
   "He Who Knows the Way" (Reprise) .... Merlin, Wizard, Arthur

Moose Murders (1). By Arthur Bicknell. Produced by Force Ten Productions, Inc. at the Eugene O'Neill Theater. Opened and closed at the evening performance, February 22, 1983.

Snooks Keene	June Gable	Stinky Holloway	Scott Evans
Howie Keene	Don Potter	Gay Holloway	Mara Hobel
Joe Buffalo Dance	Jack Dabdoub	Lauraine Holloway Fay	Lillie Robertson
Nurse Dagmar	Lisa McMillan	Nelson Fay	Nicholas Hormann
Hedda Holloway	Holland Taylor	Sidney Holloway	Dennis Florzak

Directed by John Roach; scenery, Marjorie Bradley Kellogg; costumes, John Carver Sullivan; lighting, Pat Collins; sound, Chuck London Media/Stewart Warner; dance coordinator, Mary Jane Houdina; stage violence, Kent Shelton; associate producer, Ricka Kanter Fisher; production stage manager, Jerry Bihm; stage manager, Clifford Schwartz; press, Betty Lee Hunt, Maria Cristina Pucci, James Sapp, Maurice Turet.

Time: The present. Place: The Wild Moose Lodge. Act I: Evening, early fall. Act II: Several hours later.

Comedy melodrama, a satire on the mystery genre.

*On Your Toes (98). Revival of the musical with book by Richard Rodgers, Lorenz Hart and George Abbott; music by Richard Rodgers; lyrics by Lorenz Hart. Produced by Alfred de Liagre Jr., Roger L. Stevens, John Mauceri, Donald R. Seawell and André Pastoria in the ANTA-Kennedy Center production at the Virginia Theater. Opened March 6, 1983.

Phil Dolan II; Oscar..... Eugene J. Anthony	"Princess Zenobia" Ballet:
Lil Dolan; Reporter .... Betty Ann Grove	Princess Zenobia........ Natalia Makarova
Phil Dolan III (Junior)... Philip Arthur Ross	Beggar .... George de la Peña
Stage Manager.............. Dirk Lumbard	Kringa Khan.............. George Kmeck
Lola .... Mary C. Robare	Ali Shar.............. Eugene J. Anthony
Junior (15 yrs. later)........... Lara Teeter	Ahmud Ben B'Du .... David Gold
Sidney Cohn................. Peter Slutsker	Hank Jay Smith .... Michael Vita
Frankie Frayne .... Christine Andreas	"On Your Toes" Ballet:
Joe McCall.................. Jerry Mitchell	Ballet Leaders.......... Alexander Filipov,
Vera Baronova.......... Natalia Makarova	Starr Danias
Vera Baranova (Sat. matinees)... Starr Danias	Tap Leaders .. Dirk Lumbard, Dana Moore
Anushka................... Tamara Mark	Cop .... Michael Vita
Peggy Porterfield............. Dina Merrill	Messenger Boy .... Dean Badolato
Sergei Alexandrovitch...... George S. Irving	"Slaughter on Tenth Avenue" Ballet:
Konstantine Morrosine.... George de la Peña	Hoofer..................... Lara Teeter
Stage Doorman .... David Gold	Strip Tease Girl .... Natalia Makarova
Dimitri................... Chris Peterson	Big Boss .... Michael Vita
Ivan .... Don Steffy	Cop .... Jerry Mitchell
Louie .... George Kmeck	

Ensemble: Melody A. Dye, Michaela K. Hughes, Tamara Mark, Dana Moore, Mary C. Robare, Marcia Lynn Watkins, Leslie Woodies, Sandra Zigars, Dean Badolato, Alexander Filipov, Wade Laboissonniere, Dirk Lumbard, Robert Meadows, Jerry Mitchell, Chris Peterson, Don Steffy, Kirby Tepper, David Gold, George Kmeck.

Understudies: Miss Grove—Dana Moore; Mr. Teeter—Dana Lumbard; Miss Andreas—Marcia Lynn Watkins; Mr. Slutsker—Kirby Tepper; Miss Makarova—Starr Danias; Miss Merrill—Michaela K. Hughes; Mr. Irving—David Gold; Mr. de la Peña—Alexander Filipov; Mr. Kmeck—Jerry Mitchell; Mr. Anthony—Dirk Lumbard; Mr. Ross—Steven Ross.

Directed by George Abbott; original choreography, George Balanchine; musical numbers choreographed by Donald Saddler; additional ballet choreography, Peter Martins; musical direction, John Mauceri; scenery and costumes, Zack Brown; lighting, John McLain; original orchestrations, Hans Spialek; coordinating producer, Charlene Harrington; production stage manager, William Dodds; stage manager, Sarah Whitham; press, Jeffrey Richards Associates, C. George Willard.

On Your Toes was first produced on Broadway 4/11/36 for 315 performances. It was revived on Broadway 10/11/54 for 64 performances. This production was previously presented at Kennedy Center, Washington, D.C. and Seattle, Wash.

ACT I

Scene 1: A vaudeville stage, about 1920
"Two a Day for Keith"....................... Phil Dolan II, Lil Dolan, Phil Dolan III
Scene 2: The vaudeville dressing room
Scene 3: A classroom at Knickerbocker University—WPA Extension
"Questions and Answers (The Three B's)" .... Junior, Students
"It's Got To Be Love"..................................... Frankie, Junior, Students

Scene 4: Vera's apartment, the next morning
"Too Good for the Average Man".................................... Sergei, Peggy
"The Seduction"... Vera, Junior
Scene 5: The schoolroom
"There's a Small Hotel" .... Frankie, Junior
Scene 6: The bare stage, Cosmopolitan Opera House, the next morning
Scene 7: Cosmopolitan Opera House
"Princess Zenobia" Ballet

ACT II

Scene 1: The bare stage, Cosmopolitan Opera House
"The Heart Is Quicker Than the Eye".................................. Peggy, Junior
"Glad To Be Unhappy"... Frankie
Scene 2: The classroom
"Quiet Night"... Hank Jay Smith, Students
"On Your Toes".. Frankie, Students
Scene 3: The bare stage, Cosmopolitan Opera House
Scene 4: The stage door, Cosmopolitan Opera House
"Quiet Night" (Reprise)... Sergei
Scene 5: Stage of the Cosmopolitan Opera House
"Slaughter on Tenth Avenue" Ballet

Slab Boys (48). By John Byrne. Produced by Paramount Theater Productions in the Laura Shapiro Kramer and Roberta Weissman production at the Playhouse Theater. Opened March 7, 1983. (Closed April 17, 1983)

George "Spanky" Farrell .... Sean Penn	Jack Hogg .... Brian Benben
Hector McKenzie .... Jackie Earle Haley	Alan Downie.................. Val Kilmer
Phil McCann................. Kevin Bacon	Sadie...................... Beverly May
Willie Curry............ Merwin Goldsmith	Lucille Bentley........... Madeleine Potter

Understudies: Messrs. Penn, Haley, Bacon, Benben, Kilmer—Ron Fassler; Mr. Goldsmith—Joel Kramer; Misses May, Potter—Barrie Moss.
Directed by Robert Allan Ackerman; scenery, Ray Recht, after designs by John Byrne; costumes, Robert Wojewodski, after designs by John Byrne; lighting, Arden Fingerhut; production stage manager, Thomas Kelly; stage manager, Barrie Moss; press, Judy Jacksina, Glenna Freedman, Stephanie Hughley, Susan Chicoine, Marcy Granata, Mari Thompson.
Time: The winter of 1957. Place: The Slab Room, a small, paint-bespattered hole adjacent to the Design Studio at A.F. Stobo & Co., Carpet Manufacturers of Elderslie, near Paisley, Scotland. Act I: The morning of a Friday. Act II: That afternoon.
The pranks and ordeals of slab boys (who knead ground pigments into smooth paints for the designers) and those just above then in the pecking order at a carpet factory. A foreign play (first part of a trilogy entitled *Paisley Patterns*) previously produced in Edinburgh, London, Frankfort, Cape Town and Actors Theater of Louisville and the Hudson Guild Theater.

Marcel Marceau on Broadway (47). One-man program of pantomime by Marcel Marceau. Produced by Ken Myers and The Shubert Organization, Peter C. Wiese and Ronald A. Wilford associate producers, at the Belasco Theater. Opened March 9, 1983. (Closed April 17, 1983)

With Jonathan Lambert, Jean-Jerome Raclot. Stage manager, Antoine Casanova; press, Fred Nathan, John Howlett, Anne S. Abrams.
Repertory includes eight new numbers by the noted French mime, whose last New York appearance took place on Broadway 3/25/75 for 24 performances. Individual programs were selected from the following:
Style Pantomimes—Walking, Walking Against the Wind, The Staircase, The Tight Rope Walker, The Public Garden, The Bill Poster, The Kite, The Sculptor, The Painter, The Cage, The Bureaucrats,

The Hands, Remembrances, The Side Show, The Pickpocket's Nightmare, The Amusement Park, Contrasts, The Maskmaker, The Seven Deadly Sins; Youth, Maturity, Old Age and Death; The Tango Dancer, The Small Cafe, The Dice Players, The Four Seasons, The Dream, The Creation of the World, The Trial, The Angel, The Dress, The Tree.

Bip Pantomimes: Bip in the Subway, Bip Travels by Train, Bip as a Skater, Bip Hunts Butterflies, Bip Plays David and Goliath, Bip at a Ballroom, Bip Commits Suicide, Bip as a Soldier, Bip at a Society Party, Bip as a Street Musician, Bip as a China Salesman, Bip as a Fireman, Bip as a Great Artist, Bip Has a Date, Bip Remembers, Bip as a Baby Sitter, Bip as a Professor of Botany, Bip as a Lion Tamer; Bip, the Illusionist; Bip Looks for a Job, Bip in the Modern and Future Life, Bip as a Tailor in Love, Bip Dreams He Is Don Juan, Bip and the Dating Service; Bip, Great Star of a Travelling Circus.

Aznavour (14). Concert performance by Charles Aznavour. Produced by Ron Delsener and Levon Sayan at the Lunt-Fontanne Theater. Opened March 14, 1983. (Closed March 26, 1983)

Background Vocals: Diana Green, Ednah Holt, Carol Steele.

Musicians: Aldo Frank conductor, piano, contractor; Bob Cranshaw bass; Miohisa Takada, Tom Suarez, Noel Dacosta, Masako Yanagrita, Susan Winterbottom, Karen Eley, Nina Simon violins; Marin Alsop, Bernard Zeller, Judy Geost violas; Akua Turre, Barbara Bogatin cellos; Akita Tana percussion; Grady Tate drums; Ken Hatfield guitar. Cheryl Hardwick fender rhodes, synthesizer.

Musical direction, Aldo Frank; lighting, Maurice Giraud; sound, Robert Kerzman; press, Solters/Roskin/Friedman, Inc., Milly Schoenbaum, Warren Knowlton.

Concert performance, in two parts, by the French singing star and song writer.

MUSICAL NUMBERS (music and lyrics by Charles Aznavour unless otherwise noted): "Le Temps" (music, Davis), "In Your Room," "I Didn't See the Time Go By," "Etre" (music, Garaventz), "Happy Anniversary," "In Times To Be" (lyrics, Plante), "L'Amour, Bon Dieu, L'Amour," "I Act as If" (lyrics, Plante), "To Be a Soldier," "Nous n'Avons Pas d'Enfant" (music, Garaventz), "I'll Be There" (music, Garaventz).

Also "Les Comediens" (lyrics, Plante), "She" (lyrics, Kretzmer), "Take Me Along," "The Happy Days," "Mon Ami—Mon Judas," "And I in My Chair," "Isabelle," "You've Let Yourself Go," "Mon Emouvant Amour," "Ave Maria" (music, Garaventz), "What Makes a Man," "La Boheme" (lyrics, Plante), "The Old Fashioned Way" (music, Garaventz), "Yesterday When I Was Young," "You've Got to Learn," "La Mama" (lyrics, Gail).

Also "Mourir d'Aimer," "De t'Avoir Aimee, "Qui," "Que C'est Triste Venise (music, Dorin), "Non Je N'ai Rien Oublie" (music, Garaventz), "Ils Sont Tombes," "The First Dance."

*Brighton Beach Memoirs (75). By Neil Simon. Produced by Emanuel Azenberg, Wayne M. Rogers and Radio City Music Hall Productions in association with Center Theater Group/Ahmanson at the Alvin Theater. Opened March 27, 1983.

Eugene	Matthew Broderick	Nora	Jodi Thelen
Blanche	Joyce Van Patten	Stanley	Zeljko Ivanek
Kate	Elizabeth Franz	Jack	Peter Michael Goetz
Laurie	Mandy Ingber		

Standbys: Misses Franz, Van Patten—Donna Haley; Miss Thelen—Robin Morse; Messrs. Broderick, Ivanek—Timothy Busfield; Miss Ingber—Pamela Segall; Mr. Goetz—Stefan Gierasch; Mr. Ivanek—J. Patrick Breen.

Directed by Gene Saks; scenery, David Mitchell; costumes, Patricia Zipprodt; lighting, Tharon Musser; stage managers, Martin Herzer, Barbara-Mae Phillips; press, Bill Evans, Sandra Manley.

Time: September, 1937. Place: Brighton Beach, Brooklyn. Act I: 6:30 p.m. Act II: Wednesday, a week later, about 6:45 in the evening.

Adolescence in Brooklyn in the 1930s, with two families sharing a house and just barely making ends meet. Previously produced in Los Angeles and San Francisco.

*K2 (71). By Patrick Meyers. Produced by Mary K. Frank and Cynthia Wood by arrangement with Saint-Subber at the Brooks Atkinson Theater. Opened March 30, 1983.

Taylor .... Jeffrey De Munn
Harold .... Jay Patterson

Standby: Mr. De Munn—Michael Tolaydo.
Directed by Terry Schreiber; scenery, Ming Cho Lee; costumes, Noel Borden; lighting, Allen Lee Hughes; audio composition, Herman Chessid; sound, David Schnirman; assistant director, William S. Morris; associate producers, Shaun Beary, Charles H. Duggan; production stage manager, Arlene Grayson; stage manager, Diane Ward; press, Joe Wolhandler Associates, Kathryn Kempf, Julianne Davidow.
Place: A ledge at 27,000 feet, 1,250 feet below the summit of K2, the world's second highest mountain. The play was presented without intermission.
A pair of mountain climbers in peril during their descent from the summit. Previously produced by Arena Stage, Washington, D.C., Theater by the Sea, Portsmouth, N.H. and Syracuse, N.Y. Stage.
A Best Play; see page 237.

*'night, Mother (70). By Marsha Norman. Produced by Dann Byck, Wendell Cherry, The Shubert Organization and Frederick M. Zollo at the John Golden Theater. Opened March 31, 1983.

Thelma Cates .... Anne Pitoniak
Jessie Cates .... Kathy Bates

Standbys: Miss Pitoniak—Helen Harrelson; Miss Bates—Phyllis Somerville.
Directed by Tom Moore; scenery and costumes, Heidi Landesman; lighting, James F. Ingalls; associate producer, William P. Suter; production stage manager, Steven Beckler; press, Betty Lee Hunt, Maria Cristina Pucci, James Sapp.
Place: A relatively new house built way out on a country road. The play was presented without intermission.
Daughter informs mother she means to commit suicide and proceeds to get her mother's life organized before she goes. Previously produced at American Repertory Theater, Cambridge, Mass.
A Best Play; see page 247.

*You Can't Take It With You (65). Revival of the play by Moss Hart and George S. Kaufman. Produced by Ken Marsolais, Karl Allison and Bryan Bantry at the Plymouth Theater. Opened April 4, 1983.

Penelope Sycamore .... Elizabeth Wilson		Alice .... Maureen Anderman
Essie .... Carol Androsky		Henderson .... Orrin Reiley
Rheba .... Rosetta LeNoire		Tony Kirby .... Nicolas Surovy
Paul Sycamore................ Jack Dodson		Boris Kolenkhov .... James Coco
Mr. DePinna .... Bill McCutcheon		Gay Wellington .... Alice Drummond
Ed..................... Christopher Foster		Mr. Kirby .... Richard Woods
Donald .... Arthur French		Mrs. Kirby.................. Meg Mundy
Martin Vanderhof .... Jason Robards		Olga .... Colleen Dewhurst

G-Men: Page Johnson, Wayne Elbert, William Castleman.
Understudies: Messrs. Robards, Woods, Dodson—William Cain; Messrs. Johnson, Elbert—William Castleman; Mr. French—Wayne Elbert; Messrs. Coco, Reiley, McCutcheon—Page Johnson; Messrs. Foster, Surovy—Orrin Reiley; Misses Wilson, Drummond, Mundy, Dewhurst—Frances Helm; Misses Anderman, Androsky—Rosemary Loar; Miss LeNoire—Alyce Webb.
Directed by Ellis Rabb; scenery and lighting, James Tilton; costumes, Nancy Potts; musical staging, Reed Jones; production stage manager, Mitchell Erickson; stage managers, John Handy, William Castleman; press, Henry Luhrman, Terry M. Lilly, Kevin P. McAnarney, Keith Sherman.

YOU CAN'T TAKE IT WITH YOU—Jason Robards and
Elizabeth Wilson in a scene from the Kaufman-Hart revival

Place: The home of Martin Vanderhof, New York. Act I: A Wednesday evening. Act II: A week later. Act III: The next day.

You Can't Take It With You was first produced on Broadway 12/14/36 for 837 performances and was named a Best Play of its season and won the Pulitzer Prize. It was revived on Broadway 3/26/45 for 17 performances; and in the APA production under Ellis Rabb's direction 11/23/65 for 255 performances and returning 2/10/67 for 16 performances.

The Man Who Had Three Arms (16). By Edward Albee. Produced by Allen Klein at the Lyceum Theater. Opened April 5, 1983. (Closed April 17, 1983)

The Man . . . . William Prince   Himself . . . . Robert Drivas
The Woman . . . . Patricia Kilgarriff

Standbys: Mr. Drivas—Stephen Markle; Mr. Prince—Wyman Pendleton.
Directed by Edward Albee; scenery, John Jensen; costumes, John Falabella; lighting, Jeff

Davis; executive producer, Iris W. Keitel; associate producer, Kenneth Salinsky; production stage manager, James Bernardi; stage manager, Laura deBuys; press, Solters/Roskin/Friedman, Inc., Joshua Ellis, David LeShay.

Diatribe by a central character (Himself) about the onset of fame after he grows a third arm and its disappearance after the arm withers and vanishes. The play was presented in two parts. Previously produced by the Miami, Fla. New World Festival and the Goodman Theater, Chicago.

Porgy and Bess (45). Revival of the musical based on the play *Porgy* by Dorothy and DuBose Heyward; book by DuBose Heyward; music by George Gershwin; lyrics by DuBose Heyward and Ira Gershwin. Produced by Radio City Music Hall, Bernard Gersten executive producer, and Sherwin M. Goldman Productions at Radio City Music Hall (see note). Opened April 7, 1983. (Closed May 15, 1983)

Jasbo Brown .... Edward Strauss	(Crown) .... Gregg Baker,
(Clara) .. Priscilla Baskerville, Luvenia Garner	George Robert Merritt
Mingo.................... Timothy Allen	(Bess) .... Priscilla Baskerville,
(Jake) .... Alexander Smalls, James Tyeska	Henrietta Elizabeth Davis, Naomi Moody,
Sportin' Life................ Larry Marshall	Daisy Newman
Robbins .... Tyrone Jolivet	Detective .... Larry Storch
(Serena) .. Shirley Baines, Regina McConnell,	Policeman.................. William Moize
Wilma A. Shakesnider, Veronica Tyler	Undertaker.............. Joseph S. Eubanks
Jim .... Donald Walter Kase	Annie .... Lou Ann Pickett
Peter................ Mervin Bertel Wallace	Frazier .... Raymond H. Bazemore
Lily................. Y. Yvonne Matthews	Strawberry Woman.......... Denice Woods
(Maria)................ Loretta Holkmann,	Crab Man................ Thomas J. Young
Gwendolyn Shepherd	Nelson .... Everett McCorvey
Scipio .... Akili Prince	Coroner .... Richert Easley
(Porgy)....... Robert Mosley Jr., Michael V.	(Parentheses indicate roles in which the perform-
Smartt, Jonathan Sprague, James Tyeska	ers alternated)

Ensemble: Loretta Abbott, Timothy Allen, Earl L. Baker, Emerson Battles, Raymond H. Bazemore, Shirley Black-Brown, Roslyn Burrough, Vertrelle Cameron, Seraiah Carol, Duane Clenton Carter, Dabriah Chapman, Louise Coleman, Janice D. Dixon, Diallobe Dorsey, Cisco Xavier Drayton, Alberta M. Driver, Joseph S. Eubanks, Karen E. Eubanks, Lori Eubanks, Beno Foster, Jerry Godfrey, Earl Grandison, Milton B. Grayson Jr., Elvira Green, Lawrence Hamilton, Gurcell Henry, Angela Holcomb, Lisa D. Holkmann, Janice T. Hutson, David-Michael Johnson, Leavata Johnson, Tyrone Jolivet, Dorothy L. Jones, Donald Walter Kase, Robert Kryser.

Also Roberta Alexandra Laws, Eugene Little, Jason Little, Ann Marie Mackey, Barbara Mahajan, Amelia Marshall, Richard Mason, Y. Yvonne Matthews, Everett McCorvey, John McDaniels, William Moize, Byron Onque, H. William Penn, Marenda Perry, Lou Ann Pickett, Herbert Lee Rawlings Jr., Roumel Reaux, Noelle Richards, David Robertson, Lattilia Ronrico, Renee L. Rose, Myles Gregory Savage, Sheryl Shell, Kiki Shepard, Kevin L. Stroman, Charee Adia Thorpes, Pamela Warrick-Smith, Mervin Bertel Wallace, Cornelius White, Rodney Wing, Tarik Winston, Denice Woods, Thomas J. Young.

Understudies: Porgy, Crown—Duane Clenton Carter; Clara—Gurcell Henry; Maria—Elvira Green; Jake—Donald Walter Kase, Rodney Wing; Sportin' Life—Herbert Lee Rawlings Jr.; Mingo —David-Michael Johnson; Robbins—John McDaniels; Peter—Beno Foster; Annie—Leavata Johnson; Frazier—Earl Grandison; Lily—Sheryl Shell; Strawberry Woman—Y. Yvonne Matthews; Jim—Byron Onque; Crab Man—Myles Gregory Savage; Detective—Richert Easley; Nelson —William Moize.

Directed by Jack O'Brien; choreography, George Faison; musical director, C. William Harwood; scenery, Douglas W. Schmidt; costumes, Nancy Potts; lighting, Gilbert V. Hemsley Jr.; associate conductor, John Miner; assistant conductor, Edward Strauss; musical preparation, George Darden; associate producer, Virginia Hymes; assistant director and production supervisor, Helaine Head; production stage manager, John Actman; press, Gifford/Wallace, Inc., Bob Burrichter.

Time: The early 1930s. Place: Charleston, S.C. Act I, Scene 1: Catfish Row, a summer evening. Scene 2: Serena's room, the following night. Scene 3: Catfish Row, a month later. Scene 4: Kittiwah

Island, late afternoon. Act II, Scene 1: Catfish Row, before dawn a week later. Scene 2: Serena's room, the dawn of the following day. Scene 3: Catfish Row, the next night. Scene 4: Catfish Row, the next afternoon. Scene 5: Catfish Row, a week later.

Porgy and Bess was first produced on Broadway 10/10/35 for 124 performances. It has been revived on Broadway 1/22/42 for 286 performances; 9/13/43 for 24 performances and returning 2/7/44 for 48 performances; 3/10/53 for 305 performances; 5/17/61 for 16 performances; 5/6/64 for 15 performances and 9/26/76 for 122 performances. This 1983 production is the uncut version.

ACT I

"Brown Blues" .... Piano
"Summertime" .... Clara
"A Woman Is a Sometime Thing" .... Jake, Men
"Here Come de Honey Man" .... Peter
"They Pass By Singin' " .... Porgy
"Oh Little Stars" .... Porgy
"Gone, Gone, Gone" .... Ensemble
"Overflow" .... Ensemble
"My Man's Gone Now" .... Serena
"Leavin' for the Promise' Lan' " .... Bess, Ensemble
"It Takes a Long Pull to Get There" .... Jake, Men
"I Got Plenty o' Nuttin' " .... Porgy, Ensemble
"Struttin' Style" .... Maria
"Buzzard Song" .... Porgy, Ensemble
"Bess, You Is My Woman Now" .... Porgy, Bess
"Oh, I Can't Sit Down" .... Ensemble
"I Ain't Got No Shame" .... Ensemble
"It Ain't Necessarily So" .... Sportin' Life, Ensemble
"What You Want Wid Bess" .... Bess, Crown

ACT II

"Oh, Doctor Jesus" .... Serena, Maria, Peter, Lily, Porgy
"I Loves You, Porgy" .... Porgy, Bess
"Oh, He'venly Father" .... Ensemble
"Oh, de Lawd Shake de Heavens" .... Ensemble
"Oh, Dere's Somebody Knockin' at de Do' " .... Ensemble
"A Red Headed Woman" .... Crown, Ensemble
"Clara, Clara" .... Ensemble
"There's a Boat That's Leavin' Soon for New York" .... Sportin' Life, Bess
"Good Mornin', Sistuh!" .... Ensemble
"Oh, Bess, Oh Where's My Bess" .... Porgy, Serena, Maria
"Oh Lawd, I'm on My Way" .... Porgy, Ensemble

Note: Radio City Music Hall also presented a return engagement of *The Magnificent Christmas Spectacular* for 92 performances 11/19/82–1/6/83 at Radio City Music Hall, produced and directed by Robert F. Jani; scenery, Charles Lisanby; costumes, Frank Spencer; lighting, Ken Billington; principal staging, Frank Wagner; staging and choreography, Violet Holmes, Linda Lemac, Frank Wagner; choral arrangements, Tom Bahler, Don Pippin; orchestrations, Elman Anderson, Robert M. Freedman, Michael Gibson, Arthur Harris; with a cast of Chet Carlin, Edward Prostak, Kimberly Moke, Amy Dolan, Michael Polloway, Rickie Cramer, Patricia Ward, Joan Cooper-Miraella, David Roman, Jeff Johnson, Thuri Ravenscroft, The Rockettes and The New Yorkers.

All's Well That Ends Well (38). Revival of the play by William Shakespeare. Produced by The Shubert Organization, Elizabeth I. McCann and Nelle Nugent, ABC Video Enterprises, Inc., Roger S. Berlind, Rhoda R. Herrick, Jujamcyn Theaters (Richard G. Wolff), MGM/UA Home Entertainment Group, Inc. and Mutual Benefit Productions (Karen Crane) in the Royal Shakespeare Company production at the Martin Beck Theater. Opened April 13, 1983. (Closed May 15, 1983)

Rossillion:
Countess of Rossillion .... Margaret Tyzack
Bertram .... Philip Franks
Helena .... Harriet Walter
Capt. Parolles .... Stephen Moore
Rynaldo .... David Lloyd Meredith
Lavache .... Geoffrey Hutchings
Bertram's Servant .... John McAndrew
Maids: Vivienne Argent, Noelyn George, Elizabeth Rider, Susan Jane Tanner, June Watts.
Paris:
King of France ..... John Franklyn-Robbins
Lord Lafeu .... Robert Eddison
Gentleman .... George Raistrick
Capt. Dumaine, elder .... Peter Land
Capt. Dumaine,
    younger .... Simon Templeman

Gentlemen and Suitors: Tom Hunsinger, Christopher Hurst, John McAndrew, Gary Sharkey, Graham Turner. Ladies: Vivienne Argent, Noelyn George, Elizabeth Rider, Susan Jane Tanner, June Watts.
Florence:
Duke of Florence .... John Rogan
Widow Capilet .... Gillian Webb
Diana .... Deirdra Morris
Violenta .... Susan Jane Tanner
Mariana .... Elizabeth Rider
Morgan .... Roger Allam
Soldiers: Tom Hunsinger, Christopher Hurst, John McAndrew, Gary Sharkey, Graham Turner. Waitresses: Vivienne Argent, Noelyn George, June Watts.

Musicians: Donald Johnson music director, piano, accordion; David Weiss flute, piccolo; Jeremy Szabo oboe, English horn; Matthew Goodman clarinet; Ethan Bauch bassoon; William Hamilton, French horn; Richard Henley trumpet; Grant Keast trumpet; Dennis Elliot trombone, tuba; Dean Plank trombone; Michael Epstein drums; Mark Belair percussion; Batia Lieberman cello.

Understudies: Miss Walter—Deirdra Morris; Misses Morris, Tanner—Elizabeth Rider; Misses Webb, Rider—Susan Jane Tanner; Miss Tyzack—Gillian Webb, Mr. Moore—Roger Allam; Messrs. Franks, Templeton—Christopher Hurst; Mr. Meredith—Tom Hunsinger; Messrs. Allam, Rogan—John McAndrew; Mr. Franklyn-Robbins—George Raistrick; Mr. Eddison—John Rogan; Messrs. Raistrick, Land—Gary Sharkey; Messrs. Hutchings, McAndrew—Graham Turner.

Directed by Trevor Nunn; scenery, John Gunter, American scenery in association with John Kasarda; costumes, Linda Fisher after original designs by Lindy Hemming; lighting, Beverly Emmons after original designs by Robert Bryan; music composed and arranged by Guy Woolfenden; dances, Geraldine Stephenson; sound, T. Richard Fitzgerald; musical director, Donald Johnston; production stage manager, Janet Beroza; company stage manager, Jane Tamlyn; press, Solters/Roskin/Friedman, Inc., Joshua Ellis, Irene Gandy, David LeShay.

This 1981 (in Stratford) and 1982 (in London) production by the Royal Shakespeare Company, with the play's period transposed to the Edwardian era, was presented in two parts. The last major New York revivals of *All's Well That Ends Well* were by New York Shakespeare Festival at the Delacorte Theater 6/15/66 for 16 performances and 6/29/78 for 28 performances.

Teaneck Tanzi: The Venus Flytrap (2). By Claire Luckham. Produced by Charlene and James Nederlander, Richard Vos, Stewart F. Lane and Kenneth-Mark Productions at the Nederlander Theater. Opened April 20, 1983 matinee. (Closed April 20, 1983 evening)

Tanzi .... Caitlin Clarke, Deborah Harry
Dean Rebel .... Scott Renderer,
                            Thomas G. Waites
Tanzi's Mom .... Zora Rasmussen

Tanzi's Dad .... Clarence Felder
Platinum Sue .... Dana Vance
The Ref .... Andy Kaufman

Directed by Chris Bond; scenery and costumes, Lawrence Miller; lighting, Arden Fingerhut; composer, Chris Monks; wrestling, Brian Maxine; sound, Richard Fitzgerald; musical arrangements and supervision, Martin Silvestri, Jeremy Stone; stage managers, Kate Pollock, Paul Schneeberger; press, Judy Jacksina, Glenna Freedman.

Comedy about the war between the sexes, waged in the form of a wrestling match. A foreign play previously produced in Liverpool, London and Paris. The play was presented in two parts.

*Show Boat (43). Musical revival based on the novel by Edna Ferber; book and lyrics by Oscar Hammerstein II; music by Jerome Kern. Produced by James M. Nederlander, John F. Kennedy Center and Denver Center in the Houston Grand Opera production at the Uris Theater. Opened April 24, 1983.

Windy......................	Richard Dix	La Belle Fatima.............	Lynda Karen
Steve.....................	Wayne Turnage	Old Sport;	
Pete......................	Glenn Martin	Young Man With Guitar.....	Larry Hansen
Queenie...................	Karla Burns	Landlady; Old Lady on Levee...	Mary Rocco
Parthy Ann Hawkes.........	Avril Gentles	Jim; Vallon.............	Jacob Mark Hopkin
Cap'n Andy............	Donald O'Connor	Magnolia	Sheryl Woods
Ellie	Paige O'Hara	Charlie	P.L. Brown
Frank	Paul Keith	Mother Superior	Linda Milani
Mahoney; Barker; Jake......	Randy Hansen	Young Kim	Tracy Paul
Julie	Lonette McKee	Lottie	Gloria Parker
Gaylord Ravenal..............	Ron Raines	Dolly......................	Dale Kristien
Joe.......................	Bruce Hubbard	Older Kim	Karen Culliver
Backwoodsman; Barker	Lewis White	Radio Announcer's Voice.......	Hal Douglas
Jeb; Barker..................	James Gedge		

Chorus: Women—Vanessa Ayers, Joanna Beck, Karen Culliver, Olivia Detante, Kim Fairchild, Cheryl Freeman, Lynda Karen, Dale Kristien, Linda Milani, Gloria Parker, Veronica Rhodes, Mary Rocco, Molly Wassermann, Carrie Wilder; Swings—Jeane July, Suzanne Ishee.

Chorus: Men—P.L. Brown, Michael-Pierre Dean, Merwin Foard, Joe Garcia, James Gedge, Michael Gray, Larry Hansen, Randy Hansen, Jacob Mark Hopkin, Glenn Martin, Randy Morgan, Dennis Perren, Leonard Piggee, Alton Spencer, Robert Vincent, Lewis White, Wardell Woodard; Swings—Tom Garrett, Ed Battle.

Understudies: Mr. O'Connor—Richard Dix; Miss McKee—Gloria Parker; Mr. Raines—Wayne Turnage; Miss Woods—Dale Kristien; Miss Burns—Vanessa Ayers; Messrs. Keith, Randy Hansen—Larry Hansen; Miss O'Hara—Carrie Wilder; Mr. Hubbard—P.L. Brown; Messrs. Dix, Hopkin—Lewis White; Messrs. Turnage, Martin—Robert Vincent; Mr. White—James Gedge; Miss Rocco—Linda Milani; Mr. Brown—Dennis Perren; Miss Milani—Kim Fairchild; Messrs. Gedge, Larry Hansen—Tom Garrett; Misses Parker, Culliver—Suzanne Ishee; Miss Kristien—Joanna Beck; Miss Karen—Jeane July; Miss Paul—Karen Culliver. Standby: Miss Gentles—Lizabeth Pritchett.

Directed by Michael Kahn; choreography, Dorothy Danner; music director, John DeMain; scenery, Herbert Senn, Helen Pond; costumes, Molly Maginnis; lighting, Thomas Skelton; sound, Richard Fitzgerald; conductor, Jack Everly; executive producers, Robert A. Buckley, Douglas Urbanski; production stage manager, Warren Crane; stage manager, Amy Pell; press, Marilynn LeVine.

The last major New York production of *Show Boat* was by Music Theater of Lincoln Center 7/19/66 for 63 performances.

The list of musical numbers in *Show Boat* appears on page 353 of *The Best Plays of 1966–67*.

Total Abandon (1). By Larry Atlas. Produced by Elizabeth I. McCann, Nelle Nugent, Ray Larsen, William J. Meloche, Patrick S. Brigham and John Roach at the Booth Theater. Opened and closed at the evening performance, April 28, 1983.

Lenny Keller	Richard Dreyfuss	Walter Bellmon..........	George N. Martin
Henry Hirsch.................	John Heard	Ben Hammerstein	Clifton James

Directed by Jack Hofsiss; scenery, David Jenkins; costumes, Julie Weiss; lighting, Beverly Emmons; associate producers, Marc E. Platt, Sander Jacobs, Tommy DeMaio; press, Solters/Roskin/Friedman Inc. Joshua Ellis, David LeShay.

Place: The antechamber of a midwestern courtroom. The play was presented in two parts.

Father's emotional upset in a failed marriage causes him violently to abuse his two-year-old son.

*My One and Only (33). Musical with book by Peter Stone and Timothy S. Mayer; music by George Gershwin from *Funny Face* and other shows; lyrics by Ira Gershwin. Produced by Paramount Theater Productions, Francine Lefrak and Kenneth-Mark Productions at the St. James Theater. Opened May 1, 1983.

New Rhythm Boys .... David Jackson,
Ken Leigh Rogers, Ronald Dennis
Capt. Billy Buck Chandler..... Tommy Tune
Mickey .... Denny Dillon
Prince Nicolai Erraclyovitch
Tchatchavadze; Achmed ..... Bruce McGill
Fish:
Flounder .... Nana Visitor
Sturgeon .... Susan Hartley
Minnow................. Stephanie Eley
Prawn .... Jill Cook

Kipper..................... Niki Harris
Anchovie............. Karen Tamburrelli
Edith Herbert .... Twiggy
Rt. Rev. J.D.
Montgomery .... Roscoe Lee Browne
Mr. Magix .... Charles "Honi" Coles
Policeman;
Stage Doorman....... Paul David Richards
Mrs. O'Malley........... Ken Leigh Rogers
Conductor .... Adrian Bailey

Ritz Quartette: Casper Roos, Paul David Richards, Carl Nicholas, Will Blankenship. Dancing
Gentlemen: Adrian Bailey, Bar Dell Conner, Ronald Dennis, David Jackson, Alde Lewis Jr., Bernard
Manners, Ken Leigh Rogers.

Standbys: Messrs. Tune, McGill—Ronald Young; Miss Twiggy—Nana Visitor; Mr. Browne—
Leon Morenzie; Miss Dillon—Jill Cook; Mr. Coles—David Jackson. Swings: Merilee Magnuson,
Melvin Washington.

Directed and choreographed by Thommie Walsh and Tommy Tune; musical and vocal direction,
Jack Lee; scenery, Adrianne Lobel; costumes, Rita Ryack; lighting, Marcia Madeira; sound, Otts
Munderloh; musical concept and dance arrangements, Wally Harper; orchestrations, Michael
Gibson; dance arrangements, Peter Larson; associate choreographer, Baayork Lee; associate director,
Phillip Oesterman; associate producer, Jonathan Farkas; musical consultant, Michael Feinstein; a
King Street production, Bernard Carragher, Obie Bailey and Bernard Bailey, produced by Lewis
Allen; production stage manager, Peter Von Mayrhauser; stage manager, Robert Kellogg; press, Judy
Jacksina, Glenna Freedman, Marcy Granata, Susan Chicoine, Mari H. Thompson, John Howl-
ett.

A 1920s aviator might have beaten Lindbergh to Paris if he had not been distracted by falling in
love with a Channel swimmer (originally mounted as a revival version of the musical *Funny
Face* with music by George Gershwin, lyrics by Ira Gershwin and book by Fred Thompson and Paul
Gerard Smith but converted into a new work with Gershwin songs from *Funny Face* and other
shows).

A Best Play; see page 261.

ACT I

Pennsylvania Station, May 1, 1927
"I Can't Be Bothered Now" .... New Rhythm Boys, Billy, Edith, Prince Nikki,
Mickey, Ensemble
"Blah, Blah, Blah" .... Billy
Billy's hangar
"Boy Wanted" .... Edith, Reporter
"Soon".. Billy
Mr. Magix's Emporial
"High Hat"/"Sweet and Low Down" .... Magix, Billy, New Rhythm Boys Ensemble
Club Havana
"Blah, Blah, Blah" (Reprise)....................................... Edith
"Just Another Rhumba" .... Montgomery, Ensemble
Cinema
"He Loves and She Loves".. Billy, Edith
"He Loves and She Loves" (Reprise)................................. Ritz Quartette
Central Park
The hangar
"I Can't Be Bothered Now" (Reprise)............................. New Rhythm Boys
A deserted beach
" 'S Wonderful" .... Billy, Edith
" 'S Wonderful" (Reprise) .... Ritz Quartette
"Strike Up the Band" .... Billy

ACT II

Aquacade
"In the Swim"/"What Are We Here For?" .... Fish, Nikki
"Nice Work If You Can Get It" .... Edith
Mr. Magix's Emporial
"My One and Only" .... Magix, Billy
Pennsylvania Station
The hangar
"Funny Face" .... Mickey, Nikki
Club Oasis
"My One and Only" (Reprise) .... Billy
The Uptown Chapel
"Kickin' the Clouds Away" .... Montgomery, Ensemble
(lyrics by B.G. DeSylva and Ira Gershwin; dance arrangements by Peter Howard)
"How Long Has This Been Goin' On?" .... Edith, Billy
Bows
Finale
"Strike Up the Band" (Reprise) .... Company

The Ritz (1). Revival of the play by Terrence McNally. Produced by Bavar/Culver
Productions in association with James R. Cunningham at Henry Miller's Theater. Opened
and closed at the evening performance May 2, 1983.

Abe	Joey Faye	Carmine Vespucci	Danny Dennis
Claude	Don Potter	Vivian Proclo	Dolores Wilson
Gaetano Proclo	Taylor Reed	Crisco	Peer Radon
Chris	Michael Greer	Sheldon Farenthold	Paige Edwards
Googie Gomez	Holly Woodlawn	Patron in Chaps	George Sardi
Maurine	Jan Meredith	Patron From Sheridan Sq.	Tom Terwilliger
Michael Brick	Casey Donovan	ChaCha	Jon Koons
Tiger	Pi Douglass	Butch	John Burke
Duff	Roland Rodriguez		

Directed by Michael Bavar; scenery, Gordon Micunis; costumes, George Potts; lighting, Todd
Lichtenstein; choreography, Robert Speller; sound, David Schnirman; music, Man Parrish; produc-
tion stage manager, T.L. Boston; press, Shirley Herz, Peter Cromarty.
The Ritz was first produced on Broadway 1/20/75 for 400 performances and was named a Best
Play of its season.

*Private Lives (26). Revival of the play by Noel Coward. Produced by The Elizabeth
Theater Group (Zev Bufman and Elizabeth Taylor) at the Lunt-Fontanne Theater.
Opened May 8, 1983.

Sibyl Chase	Kathryn Walker	Amanda Prynne	Elizabeth Taylor
Elyot Chase	Richard Burton	Louise	Helena Carroll
Victor Prynne	John Cullum		

Standbys: Miss Taylor—Kathryn Walker; Mr. Burton—John Cullum; Misses Walker, Carroll—
Judith McGilligan; Mr. Cullum—Larry Pine.
Directed by Milton Katselas; scenery, David Mitchell; costumes, Theoni V. Aldredge; lighting,
Tharon Musser; additional music, Stanley Silverman; sound, Jack Mann; production stage manager,
Patrick Horrigan; stage manager, Brian Meister; press, Fred Nathan and Associates, Eileen
McMahon, Leo Stern, Anne S. Abrams.
Time: 1930. Act I: The terrace of a hotel in Deauville on the coast of France, a summer evening.
Act II: Amanda's flat in Paris, a few days later, evening. Act III: The same, next morning.
The last major New York revival of Private Lives was a touring London production 2/6/75 for
92 performances.

THE FLYING KARAMAZOV BROTHERS—They aren't flyers, Karamazovs or brothers, but they do juggle as part of their comedy act

*The Flying Karamazov Brothers (25). Variety revue devised by the performers. Produced by Mace Neufeld and Viacom International, Inc. at the Ritz Theater. Opened May 10, 1983.

Dmitri.	Paul David Magid	Smerdyakov	Sam Williams
Alyosha	Randy Nelson	Ivan	Howard Jay Patterson
Fyodor	Timothy Daniel Furst		

Musicians: Douglas Wieselman soprano and tenor saxophone, clarinet, electric guitar, bass clarinet, mandolin, percussion; Mike Van Liew trumpet, cornet, flute, orchestra bells, percussion; Gina Leishman piccolo, ukelele, flute, bass clarinet, accordion, cello, percussion, mandolin; Bud Chase tuba, string bass, electric bass, percussion, mandolin; Alec Willows drums, percussion, soprano saxophone.

Scenery and costumes, Robert Fletcher; lighting, Marc B. Weiss; associate producers, Harold Thau, Robert Courson; stage managers, Phil Friedman, Amy Richards; press, Henry Luhrman Associates, Terry M. Lilly, Kevin P. McAnarney.

A show composed of juggling, comedy and music, presented in two parts.

Dance a Little Closer (1). Musical based on *Idiot's Delight* by Robert E. Sherwood; book and lyrics by Alan Jay Lerner; music by Charles Strouse. Produced by Frederick Brisson, Jerome Minskoff, James M. Nederlander and Kennedy Center at the Minskoff Theater. Opened and closed at the evening performance, May 11, 1983.

Roger Butterfield	Don Chastain	Contessa Carla Pirianno	Elizabeth Hubbard
Harry Aikens	Len Cariou	Capt. Mueller	Noel Craig
Johannes Hartog	David Sabin	Charles Castleton	Brent Barrett

"The Delights":

Shirley	Diane Pennington	Hester Boyle	Joyce Worsley
Bebe	Cheryl Howard	Heinrich Walter	Joseph Kolinski
Elaine	Alyson Reed	Cynthia Brookfield-Bailey	Liz Robertson
Edward Dunlop	Jeff Keller	Dr. Josef Winkler	George Rose
Bellboy	Philip Mollet	Cynthia's Double	Robin Stephens
Waiter; Harry's Double	Brian Sutherland	Rink Attendant; Violinist	James Fatta
Rev. Oliver Boyle	I.M. Hobson	Ice Skater	Colleen Ashton

Harry, Harry, Harry, Harry: Peter Wandel, Philip Mollet, Brian Sutherland, James Fatta.

Hotel Guests: Colleen Ashton, Candy Cook, Mary Dale, James Fatta, Philip Mollet, Linda Poser, Robin Stephens, Brian Sutherland, Peter Wandel.

Standby: George Rose—David Sabin. Understudies: Mr. Cariou—Don Chastain; Miss Robertson —Elizabeth Hubbard; Messrs. Kolinski, Barrett, Keller—Brian Sutherland; Misses Hubbard, Worsley—Linda Poser; Mr. Craig—Philip Mollet; Miss Reed—Colleen Ashton; Miss Pennington—Candy Cook; Mr. Sabin—Reuben Singer; Miss Howard—Joanne Genelle; Mr. Sutherland—Peter Wandel; Swings—Joanne Genelle, Mark Lamanna.

Directed by Alan Jay Lerner; musical staging and choreography, Billy Wilson; musical direction, Peter Howard; scenery, David Mitchell; costumes, Donald Brooks; lighting, Thomas Skelton; orchestrations, Jonathan Tunick; dance music, Gene Kelly; sound, John McClure; associate producer, Paul N. Temple; production supervisor, Stone Widney; assistant to the producer, Dwight Frye; production stage manager, Alan Hall; stage manager, Steven Adler; press, Jeffrey Richards Associates, C. George Willard.

Time: The avoidable future. Place: The Barclay-Palace Hotel on a hillside in the Austrian Alps.

World War III looms over an American cabaret artist and a collection of guests of various nationalities at an elegant Austrian resort hotel, in an update of Sherwood's 1936 Best Play and Pulitzer Prizewinner.

ACT I

Scene 1: The night club of the Barclay-Palace Hotel on New Year's Eve, shortly before midnight
"It Never Would Have Worked" . . . . Harry, Delights
"Happy, Happy New Year" . . . . Harry, Delights, Guests
Scene 2: The main entrance lounge of the hotel, 2 a.m. that night
"No Man Is Worth It" . . . . Cynthia
"What Are You Going to Do About It?" . . . . Harry, Walter
Scene 3: The Winkler suite, later that night
"A Woman Who Thinks I'm Wonderful" . . . . Winkler
Scene 3A: Harry's memory
Pas de deux . . . . Harry's Double, Cynthia's Double
Scene 4: A bedroom in a mid-western hotel ten years earlier
"There's Never Been Anything Like Us" . . . . Harry
"Another Life" . . . . Cynthia
Scene 5: The skating rink at the hotel, New Year's Day morning
"Why Can't the World Go and Leave Us Alone?" . . . . Charles, Edward
"He Always Comes Home to Me" . . . . Cynthia, Harry
Scene 6: The night club of the hotel, that evening
"I Got a New Girl" . . . . Harry, Delights
"Dance a Little Closer" . . . . Harry, Cynthia, Guests
"There's Always One You Can't Forget" . . . . Harry

ACT II

Scene 1: The main entrance lounge of the hotel, the following morning
"Homesick" . . . . Shirley, Bebe, Elaine
"Mad" . . . . Harry, Delights
"I Don't Know" . . . . Harry, Boyle, Contessa, Delights, Charles, Edward, Cynthia
"Auf Wiedersehen" . . . . Winkler
"I Never Want to See You Again" . . . . Harry

Scene 2: Cynthia's memory
"On Top of the World"... Cynthia, Men
Scene 3: The main entrance lounge of the hotel, immediately following
"I Got a New Girl" (Reprise).. Harry, Cynthia
"Dance a Little Closer" (Reprise) .... Harry, Cynthia

*Passion (18). By Peter Nichols. Produced by Richmond Crinkley and Eve Skina, Tina Chen, BMP Productions, Martin Markinson, Mike Merrick and John Roach at the Longacre Theater. Opened May 15, 1983.

Kate	Roxanne Hart	Agnes	Stephanie Gordon
James	Bob Gunton	Jim	Frank Langella
Eleanor..................	Cathryn Damon	Nell....................	E. Katherine Kerr

Others: Louis Beachner, Jonathan Bolt, Lisa Emery, Charles Harper, William Snovell, C.B. Toombes.
Understudies: Messrs. Langella, Gunton—Jonathan Bolt; Miss Hart—Lisa Emery; Company—Valerie Karasek, Ken Kliban. Standby: Misses Damon, Gordon, Kerr—Catherine Byers.
Directed by Marshall W. Mason; scenery, John Lee Beatty; costumes, Jennifer Von Mayrhauser; lighting, Ron Wallace; sound, Chuck London Media/Stewart Werner; associate producer, Robert Pesola; produced by arrangement with the Royal Shakespeare Theater; production stage manager, Franklin Keysar; stage manager, Jody Boese; press, Betty Lee Hunt, Maria Cristina Pucci, James Sapp, Robert W. Larkin.
Time: Autumn. Place: London. The play was presented in two parts.
The loves of a married couple with others and each other, with husband and wife each portrayed by two performers representing different aspects of their nature. A foreign play previously produced in London.

*Breakfast With Les and Bess (14). By Lee Kalcheim. Produced by Howard J. Burnett, David E. Jones and Steven K. Goldberg in the Hudson Guild Theater (David Kerry Heefner producing director) production at the Lambs Theater. Opened May 19, 1983.

Bess Christian Dischinger.....	Holland Taylor	Roger Everson............	Jeff McCracken
Les Dischinger..............	Keith Charles	David Dischinger	John Leonard
Shelby Dischinger	Kelle Kipp	Nate Moody; Announcer	Daniel Ziskie

Directed by Barnet Kellman; scenery, Dean Tschetter; costumes, Timothy Dunleavy; lighting, Ian Calderon; sound, Michael Jay; production stage manager, Andrea Naier; press, Henry Luhrman Accociates, Keith Sherman, Terry M. Lilly, Kevin P. McAnarney.
Time: 1961. Place: The living room of Les and Bess Dischinger, Central Park South. Act I: 7:30 a.m. Act II, Scene 1: The next morning. Scene 2: The following morning.
A husband-and-wife radio talk-show team in professional and family crisis. Previously produced off off Broadway at Hudson Guild Theater.

PLAYS WHICH CLOSED
PRIOR TO BROADWAY OPENING

Productions which were organized by New York producers for Broadway presentation but which closed during their production and tryout period are listed below.

Outrage. By Henry Denker. Produced by the John F. Kennedy Center for the Performing Arts, Roger L. Stevens chairman, Marta Istomin artistic director, at the Eisenhower

OUTRAGE—Ralph Bell, Alan Hewitt and Peter Evans in the Washington, D.C. production of Henry Denker's courtroom drama

Theater in a pre-Broadway engagement. Opened December 15, 1982. (Closed January 8, 1983)

Lester Crewe .... Kene Holliday
Benjamin Franklyn Gordon ..... Peter Evans
Dennis Riordan .... Michael Higgins
Attendant .... Walter Flanagan
Stenographer .... Rony Clanton
Judge Aaron Klein .... Ralph Bell

William Simmons .... Michael Medeiros
Wilbert Ward.................. Jim Moody
Lt. Salvatore Marchi......... Lou Criscuolo
Dr. Allan Frost................. Mel Cobb
Victor Coles........ Humbert Allen Astredo
Judge Michael Lengel......... Alan Hewitt

Directed by Edwin Sherin; scenery, John Falabella; costumes, David Murin; lighting, Marcia Madeira; production stage manager, Amy Pell.

Time: Now. Place: A courtroom in Supreme Court, New York County, Criminal Part. The play was presented in two parts.

Courtroom drama, the trial of a man who has killed his daughter's murderer.

Make and Break. By Michael Frayn. Produced by Kennedy Center, Elliot Martin, Arnold Bernhard and Michael Codron in a pre-Broadway tryout. Opened at the Wilmington, Del. Playhouse March 28, 1983. (Closed at the Eisenhower Theater, Washington, D.C. May 7, 1983)

Tom Olley .... Biff McGuire
Frank Prosser .... Stephen D. Newman
Colin Hewlett .... Jim Piddock
Mrs. Rogers............... Cynthia Harris

Verhaeren..................... Drew Eliot
Shariq................... Alexander Spencer
Japanese Customer .... Ron Faber
Ted Shaw.................... Roy Cooper

Anni . . . . Linda Kozlowski	Peter David . . . . Douglas Stender
John Garrard . . . . Peter Falk	Doctor . . . . Don Howard
Dr. Horvath . . . . David Hurst	

Directed by Michael Blakemore; scenery and costumes, Michael Annals; lighting, Martin Aronstein; press, Jeffrey Richards, C. George Willard.

Comedy, members of a building trades firm at a trade fair in Frankfurt, Germany. The play was presented in two parts. A foreign play previously produced in London.

PLAYS PRODUCED
OFF BROADWAY

Some distinctions between off-Broadway and Broadway productions at one end of the scale and off-off-Broadway productions at the other were blurred in the New York theater of the 1970s and 1980s. For the purposes of this *Best Plays* listing, the term "off Broadway" is used to distinguish a professional from a showcase (off-off-Broadway) production and signifies a show which opened for general audiences in a mid-Manhattan theater seating 499 or fewer and 1) employed an Equity cast, 2) planned a regular schedule of 7 or 8 performances a week and 3) offered itself to public comment by critics at a designated opening performance.

Occasional exceptions of inclusion (never of exclusion) are made to take in visiting troupes, borderline cases and a few nonqualifying productions which readers might expect to find in this list because they appear under an off-Broadway heading in other major sources of record.

Figures in parentheses following a play's title give number of performances. These figures do not include previews or extra non-profit performances.

Plays marked with an asterisk (*) were still running on June 1, 1983. Their number of performances is figured from opening night through May 31, 1983.

Certain programs of off-Broadway companies are exceptions to our rule of counting the number of performances from the date of the press coverage. When the official opening takes place late in the run of a play's regularly-priced public or subscription performances (after previews) we count the first performance of record, not the press date, as opening night—and in each such case in the listing we note the variance and give the press date.

In a listing of a show's numbers—dances, sketches, musical scenes, etc.—the titles of songs are identified wherever possible by their appearance in quotation marks (").

Most entries of off-Broadway productions which ran fewer than 20 performances or scheduled fewer than 8 performances a week are somewhat abbreviated, as are entries on running repertory programs repeated from previous years.

HOLDOVERS FROM PREVIOUS SEASONS

Plays which were running on June 1, 1982 are listed below. More detailed information about them appears in previous *Best Plays* volumes of appropriate date. Important cast changes since opening night are recorded in a section of this volume.

*The Fantasticks (9,600; longest continuous run of record in the American theater). Musical suggested by the play *Les Romantiques* by Edmond Rostand; book and lyrics by Tom Jones; music by Harvey Schmidt. Opened May 30, 1960.

One Mo' Time (1,372). Vaudeville show conceived by Vernel Bagneris. Opened October 22, 1979. (Closed February 6, 1983)

*Cloud 9 (847). By Caryl Churchill. Opened May 18, 1981.

American Buffalo (262). Revival of the play by David Mamet. Opened June 3, 1981. (Suspended performances October 31, 1981) Reopened February 25, 1982. (Closed July 11, 1982)

*Playwrights Horizons. *Sister Mary Ignatius Explains It All for You and *The Actor's Nightmare (669). Program of two one-act plays by Christopher Durang. Opened October 21, 1981. *The Dining Room (552). By A.R. Gurney Jr. Opened February 24, 1982. Geniuses (344). By Jonathan Reynolds. Opened May 13, 1982. (Closed March 13, 1983)

The Negro Ensemble Company. A Soldier's Play. (468). By Charles Fuller. Opened November 20, 1981. (Closed January 2, 1983)

Roundabout Theater Company. The Browning Version by Terence Rattigan and The Twelve-Pound Look by J.M. Barrie (200). Opened March 23, 1982. (Closed September 12, 1982) The Chalk Garden by Enid Bagnold (96). Opened March 30, 1982. (Closed June 20, 1982)

New York Shakespeare Festival Public Theater. Antigone (109). Revival of the play by Sophocles; translated by John Chioles. Opened April 27, 1982. (Closed June 6, 1982)

Cast of Characters (55). One-woman show adapted by Patrizia Norcia, David Kaplan and William Bixby Jr.; based on *The Art of Ruth Draper* by Morton Dauwen Zabel. Opened May 5, 1982. (Closed June 20, 1982)

Livingstone and Sechele (152). By David Pownall. Opened May 11, 1982. (Closed September 20, 1982)

The Six O'Clock Boys (159). By Sidney Morris. Opened May 12, 1982. (Closed September 26, 1982)

The American Place Theater. The Regard of Flight and The Clown Bagatelles (83). Comedy entertainment written by Bill Irwin; original music by Doug Skinner. Opened May 23, 1982. (Closed August 22, 1982)

The Freak (22). By Granville Wyche Burgess. Opened May 27, 1982. (Closed June 13, 1982)

PLAYS PRODUCED JUNE 1, 1982-MAY 31, 1983

*Forbidden Broadway (441). Cabaret revue with concept and lyrics by Gerard Alessandrini. Produced by Playkill Productions, Inc. at Palsson's Supper Club. Opened May 4, 1982 (see note).

Gerard Alessandrini
Fred Barton
Bill Carmichael

Nora Mae Lyng
Chloé Webb

Directed by Jeff Martin (originally produced and directed by Michael Chapman, original night club act mounted by Gerard Alessandrini, Pete Blue and Nora Mae Lyng); executive producer, Sella Palsson; production stage manager, Steven Adler; press, Becky Flora.

Send-up of some of the past and present hits and misses among the shows on Broadway, with music to match, and with the program changing to reflect the changing New York theater scene.

Understudies: Miss Lyng, Webb—Karen "La" Wilder; Messrs. Alessandrini, Carmichael—Jeffrey Etjen.

Note: *Forbidden Broadway* opened in this same space 1/15/82 as an off-off-Broadway production and was listed in the Plays Produced Off Off Broadway section of *The Best Plays of 1981–82.* Just before the beginning of the 1982–83 season its production status was raised to full off-Broadway, and the show has continued as such.

Harold Clurman Theater. Schedule of two programs (see note). **With Love and Laughter** (23). An evening of theater by various authors. Opened June 2, 1982. (Closed June 20, 1982) **Hannah** (15). By Israel Eliraz; music by Mark Kopytman. Opened February 16, 1983. (Closed February 27, 1983) And *What Where, Catastrophe* and *Ohio Impromptu,* program of one-act plays by Samuel Beckett, scheduled to open 6/15/83. Produced by the Harold Clurman Theater, Jack Garfein artistic director, at the Harold Clurman Theater.

WITH LOVE AND LAUGHTER

The Woman................. Celeste Holm   The Other Man............ Gordon Connell
The Man .... Wesley Addy

Directed by Peter Bennett; scenery, Harry Feiner; lighting, Todd Elmer; production coordinator, Suzanne Soboloff; stage manager, Anthone Petito; press, Burnham-Callaghan Associates.

Presented in two parts, the play explores the question "Has the basic relationship between men and women changed?" in excerpts from the works of de la Rochefoucauld, Sigmund Freud, William Shakespeare, Celius Dougherty, Phyllis McGinley, Jean Anouilh, Roberta White, Max Shulman, Harry Revel, Mack Gordon, William Saroyan, George Bernard Shaw, Alfred Sutro, Richard Wilbur, Howard Lindsay, Russel Crouse, Margaret Mead, Richard Rodgers, Oscar Hammerstein II, John Adams, James Thurber, Gretchen Cryer, Abigail Adams, Francis Hopkinson and anonymous authors.

HANNAH

Hannah................... Blanche Baker   Brother..................... Steve Pesola
Mother...................... Lois Smith   Soldiers........ David Sharpe, Joel Kaufman
Interrogator .... Stephen Lang

Kibbutz Members, Hungarian Citizens, Soldiers, Guests, Prisoners: Amanda Kercher, Leah Kreutzer, Andrew Krichels, Jim May, Lorry May, Stuart Smith, Brian Taylor, Susan Thomasson.

Understudies: Miss Baker—Debra Griboff; Miss Smith—Lorry May; Messrs. Pesola, Lang—Stuart Smith; Swing Dancer—Lorry May; Dance Captain—Leah Kreutzer.

Directed and choreographed by Anna Sokolow; produced by arrangement with Jack Lawrence; scenery, Wolfgang Roth; costumes, Ruth Morley; lighting, Edward Effron; production stage manager, Tom W. Picard; press, Shirley Herz Associates, Sam Rudy, Peter Cromarty.

Time: 1937–1944. The play was performed without intermission.

Dramatization, with music and dances, of the actual feats of a heroic Jewish woman who fought against the Nazis in World War II and was captured and killed by the Hungarian Gestapo at age 23.

Note: The Harold Clurman Theater also produced off-off-Broadway programs this season; see their entries in the Plays Produced Off Off Broadway section of this volume.

Booth (12). By Robert A. Morse. Produced by Kevin C. Donahue and John Hart Associates, Inc. in association with the South Street Theater, Inc. at the South Street Theater. Opened June 10, 1982. (Closed June 20, 1982)

Directed by Christopher Catt; scenery, David Chapman; costumes, Lindsay Davis; lighting, Frances Aronson; musical sequences, David Spangler; combat choreography, A.C. Weary; sound, Lewis Mead; artistic advisor, Tim Lovejoy; press, Howard Atlee. With Michael Nouri, Michael Connolly, Steve Bassett, Jane Cronin, Howard Korder, Peter Boyden, John Glover.

The Booth brothers—Edwin, Junius and John Wilkes—and the assassination of President Lincoln.

Looking-Glass (1). By Michael Sutton and Cynthia Mandelberg. Produced by Dan Fauci, Joseph Scalzo and the Actors Institute in association with Frances T. Hillin, Allen Schoer and Entermedia, Inc. at the Entermedia Theater. Opened and closed at the evening performance June 14, 1982.

Directed by David H. Bell; scenery, John Arnone; costumes, Jeanne Button; lighting, Frances Aronson; music by David Spangler and Marc Elliot; production stage manager, Douglas F. Goodman; press, Merle Frimark, Cheryl Sue Dolby. With John Vickery, Richard Clarke, Robert Machray, Nicholas Hormann, Richard Peterson, Mitchell Steven Tebo, Tara Kennedy, Tudi Wiggins, Innes-Fergus McDade, Melanie Hague.

The Oxford University life and times of the author of *Alice in Wonderland* and the persons on whom he based some of his characters. The play was presented in two parts.

Manhattan Theater Club. 1981–82 schedule ended with **The Singular Life of Albert Nobbs** (27). By Simone Benmussa, from a short story by George Moore; translated by Barbara Wright. Produced by the Manhattan Theater Club, Lynne Meadow artistic director, Barry Grove managing director, at Manhattan Theater Club Downstage. Opened June 16, 1982. (Closed July 10, 1982)

Hubert Page	Lucinda Childs	Helen Dawes	Pippa Pearthree
Albert Nobbs	Glenn Close	1st Chambermaid	Keliher Walsh
2d Chambermaid	Lynn Johnson	George Moore's Voice	David Warrilow
Kitty Maccan	Anna Levine	Alec's Voice	D. King Rodger
Mrs. Baker	Patricia O'Connell	Joe Macklin's Voice	Jamey Sheridan

Directed by Simone Benmussa; design, Simone Benmussa; scenery supervisor, Ron Placzek; lighting supervisor, Mal Sturchio; production stage manager, Amy Schecter; press, Patricia Cox, Bob Burrichter.

Impoverished girl maintains a disguise as a man in order to hold a job as a waiter in a Dublin hotel. The play was presented without intermission. A foreign play previously produced in Paris and London.

Divine Hysteria (19). By Anthony P. Curry. Produced by William Ellis at the Nat Horne Musical Theater. Opened June 18, 1982. (Closed July 4, 1982)

Directed by William Ellis; scenery, Don Clay; costumes, Nina Roth; lighting, William Stallings; sound, Sam Agar; stage manager, Arlene Roseman; press, Francine L. Trevens. With Brenda Thomas, Jay Aubrey Jones, Betty Lester, Barbara Nadel, Phil Di Pietro, Michael Varna, Kathleen Monteleone, Jeffrey Howard Kaufman, James Bartz, Althea Lewis.

Comedy, New Yorkers confront doomsday. The play was presented in two parts.

A Drifter, the Grifter & Heather McBride (9). Musical with book and lyrics by John Gallagher; music by Bruce Petsche. Produced by Popcorn Productions at the 47th Street Theater. Opened June 20, 1982. (Closed June 27, 1982)

Directed by Dick Sasso; musical direction and arrangements, Jeremy Harris; musical staging and choreography, George Bunt; scenery and costumes, Michael Sharp; lighting, Richard Winkler; production stage manager, Perry Cline; press, Cheryl Sue Dolby, Merle Frimark. With Ronald Young, Elizabeth Austin, William Francis, Dennis Bailey, Chuck Karel, Mary Ellen Ashley.

An ad agency dropout, a ne'er-do-well and a Hoosier maid in a romantic triangle in a folksy setting.

Jane Avril (40). By Jane Marla Robbins. Produced by Jenny Maybrook Besch at the Provincetown Playhouse. Opened June 22, 1982. (Closed July 25, 1982)

Jane Avril.	Jane Marla Robbins	Jean-Pierre Dufferin	Richard Council
Henri de Toulouse-Lautrec.	Kevin O'Connor	Musician.	William Schimmel

Directed by Albert Takazauckas; scenery, Peter Harvey; costumes, David Murin; lighting, Mal Sturchio; music, William Schimmel; dances, Ron Dabney; press, Jeffrey Richards, C. George Willard.

The famous painter and his dancer-model.

The Negro Ensemble Company. 1981–82 schedule ended with **Abercrombie Apocalypse** (32). By Paul Carter Harrison. Produced by The Negro Ensemble Company, Douglas Turner Ward artistic director, Leon B. Denmark managing director, at the Westside Arts Theater. Opened June 22, 1982. (Closed July 18, 1982)

Culpepper.	Graham Brown	Bethesda.	Barbara Montgomery
Jude	Timothy B. Lynch		

Directed by Clinton Turner Davis; scenery, Wynn Thomas; costumes, Myrna Colley-Lee; lighting, Shirley Prendergast; sound, Gary Harris; production stage manager, Femi Sarah Heggie; press, Howard Atlee, Ellen Levene.

Subtitled "An American Tragedy," drama of confrontation between a warped young man and the caretaker of his family's mansion. The play was presented in two parts.

Roundabout Theater Company. 1981–82 schedule ended with **The Learned Ladies** (48). Revival of the play by Molière; English verse translation by Richard Wilbur. Opened June 22, 1982; see note. (Closed August 1, 1982). **The Fox** (85). By Allan Miller; based on the novella by D.H. Lawrence. Opened July 8, 1982; see note (Closed September 19, 1982). Produced by Roundabout Theater Company, Gene Feist and Michael Fried producing directors, *The Learned Ladies* at the Haft Theater, *The Fox* at Roundabout Stage One.

BOTH PLAYS: Scenery, Roger Mooney; sound, Philip Campanella; press, Susan Bloch & Co., Adrian Bryan-Brown, Ellen Zeisler.

THE LEARNED LADIES

Chrysale.	Philip Bosco	Clitandre	Randle Mell
Philaminte	Rosemary Murphy	Trissotin.	Richard Kavanaugh
Armande	Jennifer Harmon	Vadius.	Gordon Chater
Henriette	Cynthia Dozier	Martine.	Ann MacMillan
Belise	Carol Teitel	Lepine.	Thomas Delaney
Ariste	Robert Stattel	Julien	George Holmes

Servants: Bonita Beach, Paul Booth, Marcia Cross.

Directed by Norman Ayrton; costumes, John David Ridge; lighting, David F. Segal; production stage manager, Howard Kolins.

Time: 1672. Place: Chrysale's house in Paris. The play was presented in two parts.

Both 20th century New York productions of record of *The Learned Ladies* (*Les Femmes Savantes*) have been in the French language, by Le Tréteau de Paris 2/6/67 for 9 performances and the Comédie Française 2/13/70 for 5 performances.

THE FOX

Nellie March	Jenny O'Hara	Henry Grenfel	Anthony Heald
Jill Banford	Mary Layne		

THE LEARNED LADIES—Rosemary Murphy, Randle Mell, Cynthia Dozier and Philip Bosco in the Roundabout's Molière revival

Directed by Allan Miller; scenery, Roger Mooney; costumes, A. Christina Giannini; lighting, Ronald Wallace; sound, Philip Campanella; production stage manager, M.R. Jacobs.

Time: November, 1918. Place: The old Bailey farm in England. The play was presented in two parts.

Young soldier enters the life of two women living in a secluded farmhouse. The play was presented in two parts.

Note: Press date for *The Learned Ladies* was 7/14/82, for *The Fox* was 8/19/82.

Life Is Not a Doris Day Movie (37). Musical with book and lyrics by Boyd Graham; music by Stephen Graziano. Produced by Reid-Dolph, Inc., Stephen O. Reid producer, at the Top of the Gate. Opened June 25, 1982. (Closed July 25, 1982)

Lingerie Salesman . . . . Boyd Graham   Waitress . . . . Neva Small
Singing Telegram Lady. . . . . Mary Testa

Understudy: Misses Testa, Small—Olga Merediz.

Directed by Norman René; musical direction, Jim Cantin; choreography, Marcia Milgrom Dodge; scenery, Mike Boak; costumes, Walter Hicklin; lighting, Debra J. Kletter; arrangements, Elliot Weiss; production stage manager, Susi Mara; press, Betty Lee Hunt, Maria Cristina Pucci, James Sapp.

Time: Dawn. Place: A bus stop at the tip of Manhattan.

Show business aspirants wish someone would give them a chance and show (in Act II) what they could do if someone did.

MUSICAL NUMBERS, ACT I: "Waiting for the Bus of Life," "Don't Cry for Me," "Lament," "Oh, William Morris," "The Fashion Show," "The Last Thing That I Want to Do Is Fall in Love," "You'll Be Sorry," "Tribute," "Little Girl-Big Voice," "I'm So Fat," "The Uh Oh Could It Be That I'm an Oh No Tango," "The Right Image/The Last Chance Revue."

ACT II: "It's a Doris Day Morning," "Influenza," "Last Chance Series," "Super Wasp," "Report on Status," "A Man Who Isn't," "Geographically Undesirable," "Whoa Boy," "Junk Food Boogie," "Public Service Message," "Singer Who Moves Well," "Not Mister Right," "Pause for Prayer," "Cavalcade of Curtain Calls," "Think of Me."

New York Shakespeare Festival. Summer schedule of two outdoor revivals. **Don Juan** (26). By Molière; translated by Donald M. Frame. Opened June 25, 1982; see note. (Closed July 24, 1982) **A Midsummer Night's Dream** (29). By William Shakespeare. Opened August 3, 1982; see note. (Closed September 5, 1982) Produced by New York Shakespeare Festival, Joseph Papp producer, at the Delacorte Theater in Central Park.

DON JUAN

Sganarelle	Roy Brocksmith	Poor Man	Christopher McCann
Gusman	Burke Pearson	Don Carlos	Frank Maraden
Don Juan	John Seitz	Don Alonse	Andreas Katsulas
Dona Elvire	Pamela Payton-Wright	Statue	George McGrath
Charlotte	Margaret Whitton	La Violette	Marcell Rosenblatt
Pierrot	Clarence Felder	M. Dimanche	William Hickey
Mathurine	Deborah Offner	Ragotin; Spectre	Wanda Bimson
La Ramee	William Duff-Griffin	Don Louis	James Cahill

French Ladies and Gentlemen: Jere Burns, Frank Dahill, Kate Falk, Cynthia Gillette, Katherine Gowan, Yolanda Hawkins, Timothy Jeffryes, Ric Lavin, Melissa Leo, Kelly McGillis, Christine Morris, Thomas Q. Morris, Susan Murray; Laurence Overmire, Alex Paul, Ken Scherer, Jack Stehlin, Darrell Stern.

Understudies: Mr. Seitz—Christopher McCann; Mr. Brocksmith—Burke Pearson; Miss Payton-Wright—Kelly McGillis; Mr. Maraden—Jere Burns; Messrs. Katsulas, McGrath—Frank Dahill; Mr. Cahill—Ric Lavin; Messrs. Felder, Hickey—Thomas Q. Morris; Miss Offner—Melissa Leo; Miss Whitton—Christine Morris; Mr. Duff-Griffin—Alex Paul; Mr. McCann—Jack Stehlin; Miss Rosenblatt—Penelope Smith; Miss Bimson—Katherine Gowan; Mr. Pearson—William Duff-Griffin.

Directed by Richard Foreman; scenery, Richard Foreman; associate set designer, Nancy Winters; costumes, Patricia Zipprodt; lighting, Spencer Mosse; sound, Daniel M. Schreier; production supervisor, Jason Steven Cohen; production stage manager, Michael Chambers; stage manager, Susan Green; press, Merle Debuskey, John Howlett, Richard Kornberg, Bruce Campbell.

Molière's *Don Juan* was last produced off Broadway in Classic Stage Company repertory 1/20/80. The play was presented in two parts.

A MIDSUMMER NIGHT'S DREAM

Philostrate	Ricky Jay	Bottom	Jeffrey De Munn
Hippolyta	Diane Venora	Flute	Paul Bates
Theseus	James Hurdle	Starveling	J. Patrick O'Brien
Egeus	Ralph Drischell	Snout	Andreas Katsulas
Hermia	Deborah Rush	Snug	Peter Crook
Demetrius	Rick Lieberman	Puck	Marcell Rosenblatt
Lysander	Kevin Conroy	Oberon	William Hurt
Helena	Christine Baranski	Titania	Michele Shay
Quince	Steve Vinovich		

Prologue: Tina Paul, Tim Flavin, Paul Kreshka, Cheryl McFadden. Fairies: Tessa Capodice, Tim Flavin, Leah Carla Gordone, Roshi Handwerger, Paul Kreshka, Emmanuel Lewis, Cheryl McFadden, Nicky Paraiso, Tina Paul, Angela Pietropinto, Rosemary Richert. Attendants to the Duke: Caroline McGee, David Logan-Morrow, Marcie Shaw.

Musicians: Katherine Muellor conductor, alto flute, piccolo; Deborah Gilwood piano, celeste; William Uttley percussion; John Gustafson oboe, English horn; Michael A. Ellert bassoon, bass clarinet, flutes; Paul Friedman violin, viola; Mary Rowell violin; Stephen Ametrano trumpet, flugelhorn, piccolo trumpet; Matthew Zory double bass; Marcie Shaw vocalist.

Understudies: Messrs. Lieberman, Conroy—Peter Crook; Miss Shay—Caroline McGee; Misses Venora, Baranski—Cheryl McFadden; Messrs. De Munn, Vinovich, Bates, Katsulas—Paul Kreshka; Messrs. Crook, O'Brien—Nicky Paraiso; Messrs. Hurdle, Drischell, Jay—David Logan-Morrow; Misses Rosenblatt, Rush—Angela Pietropinto.

Directed by James Lapine; choreography, Graciele Daniele; music Allen Shawn; scenery, Heidi Landesman; costumes, Randy Barcelo; lighting, Frances Aronson; magic effects, Ricky Jay; production stage manager, D.W. Koehler; stage manager, Johnna Murray.

Place: Athens, and a wood not far from it. The play was presented in two parts.

A Midsummer Night's Dream was last produced off Broadway by the Acting Company 4/25/81 for 2 performances.

Note: Press date for *Don Juan* was 7/1/82, for *A Midsummer Night's Dream* 8/15/82.

Circle Repertory Company. 1981–82 schedule ended with **A Think Piece** (19). By Jules Feiffer. Opened June 26, 1982. (Closed July 11, 1982) **Johnny Got His Gun** (27). By Bradley Rand Smith; adapted from the novel by Dalton Trumbo. Opened August 10, 1982. (Closed September 2, 1982) Produced by Circle Repertory Company, Marshall W. Mason artistic director, Richard Frankel managing director, at the Circle Theater.

A THINK PIECE

Betty	Debra Mooney	Ginny	Tenney Walsh
Pam	Katherine Cortez	Lulu	Samantha Atkins
Gordon	Andrew Duncan	Zero	Patches
Mandy	Ann Sachs		

Directed by Caymichael Patten; scenery, Kert Lundell; costumes, Denise Romano; lighting, Dennis Parichy; sound, Chuck London Media/Stewart Werner; production stage manager, Ginny Martino; press, Reva Cooper.

The humdrum conventions of family life conceal below the surface of its individuals an emotional turbulence revealed in the course of the play. The play was presented in two parts.

JOHNNY GOT HIS GUN

Joe Bonham . . . . Jeff Daniels

Directed by Elinor Renfield; scenery, Kert Lundell; costumes, Miriam Nieves; lighting, Mal Sturchio; musical consultant, Carman Moore; sound, Chuck London Media; production stage manager, Ann Bridgers.

Thoughts of a World War I quadriplegic casualty. The play was presented without intermission.

Playwrights Horizons. 1981–82 schedule ended with **Herringbone** (46). Play with songs based on an original play by Tom Cone; book by Tom Cone; music by Skip Kennon; lyrics by Ellen Fitzhugh. Opened June 30, 1982. (Closed August 27, 1982) Produced by Playwrights Horizons, Andre Bishop artistic director, Paul Daniels managing director, at Playwrights Horizons Mainstage.

Thumbs DuBois	Skip Kennon
Herringbone	David Rounds

Directed by Ben Levit; musical numbers staged by Theodore Pappas; scenery, Christopher Nowak; costumes, Karen Matthews; lighting, Frances Aronson; production stage manager, Pam Marsden; press, Bob Ullman, Louise Ment.

Southern-born youth is possessed by an evil spirit and driven to a career as a performer. The ten roles, old and young, male and female, were all played by David Rounds, with Skip Kennon at the piano. The play was presented in two parts. Previously produced at the St. Nicholas Theater, Chicago.

Note: During the 1982-83 season, Playwrights Horizons also co-produced with American Place Theater *Buck* by Ronald Ribman at American Place Theater (see its entry elsewhere in this section of this volume). The Playwrights Horizons production of the musical *America Kicks Up Its Heels*, book and lyrics by Charles Rubin, music by William Finn, directed by Mary Kyte and Ben Levit, choreography by Mary Kyte, musical direction and orchestrations by Michael Starobin, scenery and costumes by Santo Loquasto, lighting by Frances Aronson, with Robin Boudreau, Robert Dorfman, Peggy Hewett, I.M. Hobson, Rodney Hudson, Alexandra Korey, Dick Latessa, Patti LuPone and Lenora Nemetz, was presented in previews 3/3/83–3/27/83 but its opening was cancelled.

Playwrights Horizons also presented programs off off Broadway this season; see their entries in the Plays Produced Off Off Broadway section of this volume.

Broken Toys (29). Musical with book, music and lyrics by Keith Berger. Produced by Dani Ruska and Marina Spinola at the Actors' Playhouse. Opened July 16, 1982. (Closed August 8, 1982)

Melissa	Debra Greenfield	Randy	Lonnie Lichtenberg
Rooty Kazooty	Keith Berger	Golly	Daud Svitzer
Kanga	Nerida Normal	Pretty Polly	Lucille
Big Dolly	Oona Lind	3-D Jesus	Johnny Zeitz
Kandy	Cheryl Lee Stockton		

Directed by Carl Haber; scenery, Lisa Beck; costumes, Mara Lonner, Karen Dusenbury; lighting, Kevin Jones; musical arrangements, Lou Forestieri; production stage manager, Alan Preston; press, Shirley Herz Associates, Sam Rudy, Peter Cromarty.

Place: The bedroom and attic of a suburban house.

Young girl falls in love with a toy soldier who comes to life, life-sized.

MUSICAL NUMBERS, ACT I: "This Life's the Right One for Me," "We're on a Shelf in Your Attic," "Play With Me," "Broken & Bent," "Let's Play Let's Say," "I Don't Play With Humans," "Prayer Song," "Johnny Space," "Choo Choo Rap, "Lady Ride With Me," "Not of Her World," "Kangaroo Court," "I Don't Think I Like This Game."

ACT II: "The Temperance Song," "So Ya Wanna Be a Toy," "I Got That Other Lady's With My Baby Feeling," "Ain't Worth a Dime," "Rag Doll Rag," "Funny Wind-Up Toy," "Left Alone To Be," "Weird Fun," "Wind-Up in New York City."

*Little Shop of Horrors (356). Musical based on the film by Roger Corman; book and lyrics by Howard Ashman; music by Alan Menken. Produced by the WPA Theater, Kyle Renick producing director, David Geffen, Cameron Mackintosh and The Shubert Organization at the Orpheum Theater. Opened July 27, 1982.

Chiffon	Leilani Jones	Derelict	Martin P. Robinson
Crystal	Jennifer Leigh Warren	Orin; Bernstein; Snip;	
Ronnette	Sheila Kay Davis	Luce; Everyone Else	Franc Luz
Mushnik	Hy Anzell	Audrey II	
Audrey	Ellen Greene	(Manipulation)	Martin P. Robinson
Seymour	Lee Wilkof	Audrey II (Voice)	Ron Taylor

Musicians: Robert Billig piano, Robby Merkin electronic keyboards, Steve Gelfand bass guitar, Steve Ferrera percussion.

Standbys: Miss Greene—Katherine Meloche; Mr. Anzell—Fyvush Finkel; Misses Jones, Warren, Davis—Deborah Lynn Sharpe; Messrs. Wilkof, Luz, Taylor—Brad Moranz; Mr. Robinson—Anthony Asbury.

Directed by Howard Ashman; musical staging, Edie Cowan; musical direction, supervision and vocal arrangements, Robert Billig; scenery, Edward T. Gianfrancesco; costumes, Sally Lesser; lighting, Craig Evans; sound, Otts Munderloh; puppets, Martin P. Robinson; orchestrations, Robby Merkin; production stage manager, Paul Mills Holmes; press, Milly Schoenbaum, Solters/Roskin/Friedman, Inc., Warren Knowlton, Kevin Patterson.

Comic fantasy about a carnivorous plant growing out of control. Previously produced off off Broadway by the WPA Theater.

Fyvush Finkel replaced Hy Anzell, Faith Prince replaced Ellen Greene, Brad Moranz replaced Lee Wilkof, Anthony B. Asbury replaced Martin P. Robinson, Robert Frisch replaced Franc Luz 3/18/83.

ACT I

Prologue ("Little Shop of Horrors") .... Chiffon, Crystal, Ronnette
"Skid Row (Downtown)" .... Company
"Grow for Me".. Seymour
"Don't It Go to Show Ya Never Know" .... Mushnik, Chiffon, Crystal, Ronnette, Seymour
"Somewhere That's Green"... Audrey
"Closed for Renovations" .... Seymour, Audrey, Mushnik
"Dentist!" .... Orin, Chiffon, Crystal, Ronnette
"Mushnik and Son"... Mushnik, Seymour
"Git It!" .... Seymour, Audrey II
"Now (It's Just the Gas)".. Seymour, Orin

ACT II

"Call Back in the Morning" .... Seymour, Audrey
"Suddenly, Seymour"... Seymour, Audrey
"Suppertime" .... Audrey II
"The Meek Shall Inherit" .... Company
Finale ("Don't Feed the Plants") .... Company

New York Shakespeare Festival. 1981–82 schedule ended with **The Death of Von Richtofen as Witnessed From Earth** (45). Musical written and composed by Des McAnuff. Opened July 29, 1982. (Closed September 5, 1982) Produced by New York Shakespeare Festival, Joseph Papp producer, at the Estelle R. Newman Theater.

R. Raymond-Barker	Robert Westenberg	Karl Bodenschatz	Jeffrey Jones
N.C.O. Secull..............	Marek Norman	Violinist	Sigrid Wurschmidt
Robert Buie	Robert Joy	Lutanist	Susan Berman
William Evans	Mark Linn-Baker	Flautist....................	Peggy Harmon
Wolfram Von Richtofen	Brent Barrett	German Lance Corporal.......	Mark Petrakis
Manfred Von Richtofen	John Vickery	Hermann Goering............	Bob Gunton

The Flying Circus: Michael Brian, Eric Elice, Davis Gaines, Karl Heist, Tad Ingram, Ken Land, Martha Wingate.

Musicians: Michael S. Roth conductor, piano; Joe Barone bass, percussion; Paul Litteral trumpet, flugelhorn, piccolo trumpet; Phil Marsh electric-acoustic guitars; James McElwaine clarinet, synthesizer, alto-soprano saxophones; Don Mikkelsen trombone, tuba; Glenn Rhian drums, timpani, vibes; James Tunnell electric-acoustic guitars.

Understudies: Mr. Joy—Karl Heist; Messrs. Gunton, Petrakis—Tad Ingram; Mr. Barrett—Eric Elice; Mr. Linn-Baker—Michael Brian; Mr. Jones—Ken Land; Mr. Westenberg—Davis Gaines; Mr. Vickery—Robert Westenberg; Misses Wurschmidt, Berman, Harmon—Martha Wingate; Swing—David Jordan.

Directed by Des McAnuff; choreography, Jennifer Muller; musical direction, Michael S. Roth; scenery, Douglas W. Schmidt; costumes, Patricia McGourty; lighting, Richard Nelson; sound effects,

James Lebrecht; orchestrations, Michael Starobin; vocal arrangements, Michael Starobin, Michael S. Roth, Des McAnuff; production supervisor, Jason Steven Cohen; production stage manager, Fredric H. Orner; stage manager, Loretta Robertson; press, Merle Debuskey, Richard Kornberg, John Howlett, Bruce Campbell.

Time: 1918, the afternoon and evening of April 20 and the morning of April 21. Place: France, the West, No Man's Land, the East

Self-described as "a play with flying and songs," about the death of Baron Manfred Von Richtofen and Germany's hunger for a larger than life-sized, Hitlerian idol.

ACT I

"All I Wanted Was a Cup of Tea" .... Raymond-Barker, Secull
"Our Red Knight".. Wolfram, Flying Circus
"Good Luck" .... Flying Circus
"Speed"... Manfred
"Sweet Eternity"...................................... Raymond-Barker, Secull
"Take What You Can" .... Three Women (Violinist, Lutanist, Flautist)
"If I Have the Will" .... Lance Corporal
"I've Got a Girl".................................. Buie, Evans, Secull, Three Women
"England—The U.K." .... Raymond-Barker, Secull, Flying Circus
"Save the Last Dance" .... Three Women, Goering, Bodenschatz
"If I Have the Will" (Reprise) .... Lance Corporal, Three Women
"Here We Are" .... Manfred, Buie, Evans, Secull, Flying Circus
"Congratulations"........................... Bodenscatz, Goering, Three Women
"Stand Up the Fatherland"............. Bodenschatz, Goering, Wolfram, Buie, Evans, Secull,
Three Women, Flying Circus

ACT II

"Sitting in the Garden.................. Secull, Raymond-Barker, Buie, Evans, Flying Circus
"It's All Right God/Four
   White Horses" .... Buie, Evans, Raymond-Barker, Secull, Manfred, Flying Circus
"1918".. Raymond-Barker, Secull, Buie, Evans
"Dear Icarus"... Three Women
"Sarah".. Manfred
"I Don't Ask About Tomorrow"...................................... Lance Corporal
"April Twenty-One" .... Buie, Evans, Raymond-Barker, Secull, Flying Circus
"The Skies Have Gone Dry" .... Bodenschatz, Goering, Wolfram
"Sarah" (Reprise).. Three Women

Charlotte Sweet (102). Musical with libretto by Michael Colby; music by Gerald Jay Markoe. Produced by Power Productions and Stan Raiff at the Westside Arts Center. Opened August 12, 1982. (Closed November 7, 1982)

Harry Host............	Michael McCormick	Katinka Bugaboo...........	Sandra Wheeler
Cecily MacIntosh	Merle Louise	Barnaby Bugaboo	Alan Brasington
Skitzy Scofield	Polly Pen	Charlotte Sweet..........	Mara Beckerman
Bob Sweet	Nicholas Wyman	Ludlow Ladd Grimble	Christopher Seppe

Standbys: Misses Beckerman, Louise, Pen, Wheeler—Tricia Witham; Messrs. McCormick, Wyman, Brasington, Seppe—Michael Dantuano.

Directed by Edward Stone; choreography, Dennis Dennehy; musical direction, Jan Rosenberg; scenery, Holmes Easley; costumes, Michele Reisch; lighting, Jason Kantrowitz; orchestrations, John McKinney; production stage manager, Peter Weicker; press, Jeffrey Richards Associates, C. George Willard.

Time: The turn of the century. Place: England.

All-music musical with a Victorian-style melodramatic plot. previously produced off off Broadway.

Jeffrey Keller replaced Alan Brasington, Timothy Landfield replaced Nicholas Wyman and Lynn Eldredge replaced Sandra Wheeler during the show's run.

ACT I

"At the Music Hall" .... Harry, Ensemble
"Charlotte Sweet". .... Bob, Charlotte, Ensemble
"A Daughter of Valentine's Day" .... Charlotte, Ensemble
"Forever" .... Ludlow, Charlotte
"Liverpool Sunset". .... Ensemble
"Layers of Underwear". .... Bob, Katinka, Barnaby, Charlotte
"Quartet Agonistes". .... Katinka, Barnaby, Charlotte, Bob
"The Circus of Voices" .... Barnaby, Katinka, Skitzy, Cecily, Harry, Charlotte
"Keep It Low". .... Katinka, Men's Chorus
"Bubbles in Me Bonnet" .... Cecily
"Vegetable Reggie". .... Harry
"My Baby and Me". .... Skitzy
"A-Weaving". .... Charlotte, Women's Chorus
"Your High Note!" .... Charlotte, Barnaby, Katinka
"Katinka/The Darkness" .... Barnaby

ACT II

"On It Goes" .... Ensemble
"You See in Me a Bobby". .... "Patrick," Barnaby, Katinka
"A Christmas Buche" .... Charlotte, Cecily, Skitzy, Harry
"The Letter" (Me Charlotte Dear). .... Ludlow
"Dover". .... Skitzy
"Good Things Come" .... Cecily
"It Could Only Happen in the Theater" .... Harry, "Patrick," Skitzy, Cecily
"Lonely Canary" .... Charlotte
"Queenly Comments" .... "The Queen," Barnaby, Katinka, "Patrick," Charlotte
"Surprise! Surprise!". .... Ensemble
"The Reckoning" .... Ensemble
"Farewell to Auld Lang Syne". .... Ensemble

R.S.V.P. (127). Revue with sketches, music and lyrics by Rick Crom. Produced by Pierrot Productions at Theater East. Opened August 24, 1982. (Closed December 26, 1983)

Christopher Durham   Julie Sheppard
John Fucillo   John Wyatt
Lianne Johnson

Directed by Word Baker and Rod Rogers; musical director, Glen Kelly; scenery, Carleton Varney; costumes, Jerry Hart; lighting, Dan Fabrici; stage manager, Louise Miller; press, Free Lance Talents, Inc., Francine L. Trevens.

Topical revue, the problems of living in New York City. The show was presented in two parts.

Jeri Winbarg replaced Julie Sheppard 9/21/82; Christopher Tracy replaced Christopher Durham 9/29/82.

Inserts (14). By John Byrum. Produced by D.E. Betts, Ned Davis and Michael Saltz at the Actors & Directors Theater. Opened September 8, 1982. (Closed September 19, 1982)

Directed by Larry Loonin; scenery, Norm Dodge; costumes, Andrew Marley; press, Burnham-Callaghan Associates, Owen Levy. With Kevin O'Connor, Patrick Hurley, Edward Setrakian, Wendell Meldrum, Hope Stansbury.

Adaptation of 1975 movie about a Hollywood director reduced to making blue movies.

Manhattan Theater Club. Schedule of eight programs; see note. **Talking With** (56). By Jane Martin; the Actors Theater of Louisville production. Opened September 21, 1982; see note. (Closed November 7, 1982) **Standing on My Knees** (40). By John Olive. Opened

ELBA—Audra Lindley and Barbara Sohmers in the Manhattan Theater Club production of a play by Vaughn McBride

October 12, 1982; see note. (Closed November 14, 1982) **Three Sisters** (48). Revival of the play by Anton Chekhov; new English version by Jean-Claude van Itallie. Opened November 30, 1982; see note. (Closed January 9, 1983) **Skirmishes** (72). By Catherine Hayes. Opened December 21, 1982; see note. (Closed February 20, 1983) **Summer** (48). By Edward Bond. Opened January 25, 1983; see note. (Closed March 6, 1983).

Also **Triple Feature** (40). Program of one-act plays: *Slacks and Tops* by Harry Kondoleon, *Half a Lifetime* by Stephen Metcalfe and *The Groves of Academe* by Mark Stein. Opened March 8, 1983; see note. (Closed April 10, 1983) **Elba** (25). By Vaughn McBride. Opened March 22, 1983; see note. (Closed May 1, 1983) **Early Warnings** (40). Program of one-act plays by Jean-Claude van Itallie: *Bag Lady*, *Sunset Freeway* and *Final Orders*. Opened April 26, 1983; see note. (Closed May 29, 1983) Produced by Manhattan Theater Club, Lynne Meadow artistic director, Barry Grove managing director, at Manhattan Theater Club.

ALL PLAYS: Associate artistic director, Douglas Hughes; literary manager, Jonathan Alper; production manager, Peter Glazer; press, Patricia Cox, Eliza Gaynor.

TALKING WITH

ACT I: *Fifteen Minutes*—Laura Hicks; *Scraps*—Penelope Allen; *Clear Glass Marbles*—Sally Faye Reit; *Audition*—Ellen Tobie; *Rodeo*—Margo Martindale; *Twirler*—Lisa Goodman.
ACT II: *Lamps*—Anne Pitoniak; *Handler*—Susan Cash; *Dragons*—Lee Anne Fahey; *French Fries*—Theresa Merritt; *Marks*—Lynn Milgrim.

Directed by Jon Jory; scenery, Tony Straiges; costumes, Jess Goldstein; lighting, Pat Collins; production stage manager, Elizabeth Ives; stage manager, David K. Rodger.
Program of 11 monologues by widely varied women characters, previously produced at Actors Theater of Louisville and named an outstanding new play of last season in regional theater by the American Theater Critics Association (see *The Best Plays of 1981–82*).

STANDING ON MY KNEES

Catherine	Pamela Reed	Alice	Jean DeBaer
Joanne	Tresa Hughes	Robert	Robert Neches

Directed by Robert Falls; scenery, David Emmons; costumes, Nan Cibula; lighting, William Mintzer; production stage manager, Johnna Murray; stage manager, Alice Jankowiak.

A poet's schizophrenia has an impact upon her work and her friends. The play was presented in two parts. Previously produced at the Wisdom Bridge, Chicago.

THREE SISTERS

Olga	Lisa Banes	Nicolai Lvovich Tuzenbach	Bob Balaban
Masha	Dianne Wiest	Vasily Vasilevich Solyony	Stephen McHattie
Irina	Mia Dillon	Ivan Romanich Chebutykin	Jack Gilford
Andrei Sergeevich Prozorov	Jeff Daniels	Alexei Fedotik	Brian Hargrove
Natasha	Christine Ebersole	Vladimir Rode	Gene O'Neill
Fyodor Ilych Kulygin	Baxter Harris	Ferapont	Jerome Collamore
Alexander Ignatevich		Anfisa	Margaret Barker
Vershinin	Sam Waterston	Maid	Rosemary Quinn

Standbys: Messrs. McHattie, Hargrove, O'Neill—George Bamford; Messrs Harris, Waterston—James Burge; Misses Barker, Quinn—Sheila Coonan; Mr. Balaban—Brian Hargrove; Mr. Daniels—Gene O'Neill; Misses Banes, Wiest—Rosemary Quinn; Misses Dillon, Ebersole—Denise Stephenson; Messrs. Gilford, Collamore—John Straub.

Directed by Lynne Meadow; scenery, Santo Loquasto; costumes, Dunya Ramicova; lighting, Pat Collins; music, Jonathan Sheffer; sound, Chuck London Media/Stewart Werner; associate artistic director, Douglas Hughes; production stage manager, Wendy Chapin; stage manager, Alice Dewey.

Place: A provincial Russian town. Act I: The Prozorovs' house, lunchtime. Act II: The same, a year and a half later, 8 o'clock in the evening. Act III: Olga's and Irina's room, a year later, 3 o'clock in the morning. Act IV: The garden, eight months later, noon. The play was presented in three parts with intermissions following Acts II and III.

Three Sisters was last produced off Broadway by the BAM Theater Company 4/26/77 for 24 performances.

SKIRMISHES

Jean	Suzanne Bertish	Mother	Hope Cameron
Rita	Fran Brill		

Directed by Sharon Ott; scenery, Kate Edmunds; costumes, Susan Hilferty; lighting, Dennis Parichy; production stage manager, Barbara Abel.

Time: The present. Place: England. The play was presented without intermission.

Tale of two sisters, one having remained at home to take care of mother, one having left for marriage. A foreign play previously produced in Liverpool and London.

SUMMER

David	David Pierce	Marthe	Betty Miller
Xenia	Frances Sternhagen	Heinrich Hemmel	Tom Brennan
Ann	Caitlin Clarke		

Standbys: Mr. Brennan—John Clarkson; Misses Sternhagen, Miller—Jean Matthiessen; Miss Clarke—Denise Stephenson.

Directed by Douglas Hughes; scenery, Tony Straiges; costumes, Linda Fisher; lighting, Pat Collins; music, Paul Sullivan; sound, Chuck London Media/Stewart Werner; associate artistic director, Douglas Hughes; production stage manager, John Beven; stage manager, Susi Mara.

Time: The present. Place: Eastern Europe, the terrace of a cliff house facing the sea. Scene 1: The terrace, late Friday night. Scene 2: The terrace, Saturday morning. Scene 3: The terrace, Saturday afternoon. Scene 4: The island, Sunday afternoon. Scene 5: The terrace, Sunday night. Scene 6: The terrace, early Monday morning. Scene 7: (The Agreement) The terrace, late Monday morning. The play was presented in three parts.

Two women in confrontation over past events which included the Nazi occupation of their area. A foreign play previously produced in London.

TRIPLE FEATURE

The Groves of Academe
Bill Groves. . . . . Terrance O'Quinn
Paul Morris . . . . Neal Jones
   Directed by Steven Schachter.
   Time: The present. Place: Groves's office. Personal and professional relationships of a student and teacher.

Half a Lifetime
Tobias. . . . . James Rebhorn
Spalding . . . . Peter Zapp
Winninger . . . . John Goodman
Winter . . . . J.T. Walsh
   Directed by Dann Florek.

   Time: The present. Place: A basement family room. High school students in crisis.

Slacks and Tops
Wanda . . . . Sasha von Scherler
Connie . . . . Amy Wright
Todd . . . . Dan B. Sedgwick
Edwin . . . . Eddie Jones
Ginger . . . . Jessica René Carroll
   Directed by Douglas Hughes.
   Time: The present. Place: A motel room near J.F.K. Airport. An American family in flight to Africa to escape their problems.

Scenery, Pat Woodbridge; costumes, Jess Goldstein; lighting, Ann Wrightson; production stage manager, David K. Rodger.

ELBA

Don. . . . . James Whitmore
Flo . . . . Audra Lindley
Young Roy Eames . . . . Frank Hamilton

Harley. . . . . Ann Wedgeworth
Lete. Barbara Sohmers

Standbys: Miss Lindley—Helen Jean Arthur; Messrs. Whitmore, Hamilton—Nesbitt Blaisdell.
Directed by Tom Bullard; scenery, Kate Edmunds; costumes, Patricia McGourty; lighting, Dennis Parichy; sound, Chuck London Media/Stewart Werner; production stage manager, Susie Cordon; stage manager, James Dawson.
Time: Summer, early 1960s. Place: The main room of a small ranch house in Elba, Idaho. The play was presented in two parts.
Elderly couple runs away from a nursing home and returns to the old homestead.

EARLY WARNINGS

Bag Lady
Clara. . . . . Shami Chaikin
   Hallucinations of a street derelict, previously produced off off Broadway at Theater for the New City.

Sunset Freeway
Judy . . . . Rosemary Quinn

   Actress on her way to a casting couch audition.

Final Orders
Angus McGrath . . . . Colin Stinton
Mike Patterson . . . . Evan Handler
   Two doomed astronauts on an outer-space mission.

Recorded voices: Joyce Aaron, Roger Babb, Shami Chaikin, Patrick D'Antonio, Rosemary Quinn, Colin Stinton, Vladimir Velasco.
Directed by Steven Kent; scenery, David Potts; costumes, Gwen Fabricant; lighting, Dennis Parichy; sound, Bill Dreisbach, Don Preston; TV entertainment time sequences from Laurel and Hardy's *Their First Mistake*; production stage manager, Ruth Kreshka; stage manager, Patrick D'Antonio.
Note: The Manhattan Theater Club's Upstage programs (*Standing on My Knees*, *Skirmishes*, *Triple Feature* and *Early Warnings*), formerly listed in our Plays Produced Off Off Broadway section, were

upgraded this season to full off-Broadway status along with the group's Downstage programs (*Talking With*, *Three Sisters*, *Summer* and *Elba*). Press date for *Talking With* was 10/3/82, for *Standing on My Knees* was 10/24/82, for *Three Sisters* was 12/21/82, for *Skirmishes* was 12/30/82, for *Summer* was 2/10/83, for *Triple Feature* was 3/29/83, for *Elba* was 4/10/83, for *Early Warnings* was 5/8/83.

*Roundabout Theater Company. Schedule of four revival programs. **The Holly and the Ivy** (199). By Wynyard Browne. Opened September 21, 1982; see note. (Closed March 13, 1983) **The Entertainer** (96). By John Osborne. Opened December 21, 1982; see note. (Closed March 12, 1983) ***Duet for One** (38). By Tom Kempinski. Opened March 15, 1983; see note. ***Winners** by Brian Friel and ***How He Lied to Her Husband** by George Bernard Shaw (46). Opened March 22, 1983; see note. Produced by the Roundabout Theater Company, Gene Feist producing director, Todd Haimes managing director, at the Roundabout Theater, *The Entertainer* and *Duet for One* at Stage One, *The Holly and the Ivy* and *Winners* at the Susan Bloch Theater (formerly Stage Two).

THE HOLLY AND THE IVY

Rev. Martin Gregory	Gwyllum Evans	Aunt Lydia	Betty Low
Jenny	Jennifer Harmon	Aunt Bridget	Helen Lloyd Breed
Margaret	Pamela Brook	Richard Wyndham	Thomas Ruisinger
Mick	Frank Grimes	David Paterson	Gerald Walker

Directed by Lindsay Anderson; scenery, Roger Mooney; costumes, A. Christina Giannini; lighting, Ronald Wallace; sound, Philip Campanella; production stage manager, Kurt Wagemann; press, Susan Bloch & Co., Adrian Bryan-Brown, Ron Jewell, Ellen Zeisler.

Time: 1949. Place: The living room of a vicarage in Norfolk, England. Act I: Christmas Eve. Act II: After dinner, the same evening. Act III: Christmas morning.

The vicar's children come home for Christmas, each bringing a severe personal problem. American premiere of 1948 British play, previously produced in London and on the screen in 1952.

THE ENTERTAINER

Billy Rice	Humphrey Davis	William Rice	Richard M. Davidson
Jean Rice	Ellen Tobie	Graham Dodd	John Curless
Archie Rice	Nicol Williamson	Conductor	David Brunetti
Phoebe Rice	Frances Cuka	Gorgeous Gladys	Elizabeth Owens
Frank Rice	Keith Reddin		

Understudies: Mr. Williamson—Richard M. Davidson; Misses Cuka, Tobie—Elizabeth Owens; Messrs. Reddin, Curless—David Brunetti; Mr. Davidson—John Curless.

Directed by William Gaskill; scenery, Michael Sharp; costumes, A. Christina Giannini; lighting, Barry Arnold; music, John Addison; choreography, David Vaughan; production stage manager, Patrick J. O'Leary.

Time: 1956. Scene 1: Billy and Jean. Scene 2: Archie Rice—"Don't take him seriously!" Scene 3: Billy, Jean and Phoebe. Scene 4: Archie Rice—"In trouble again." Scene 5: Billy, Jean, Phoebe and Archie. Scene 6. Billy, Phoebe, Jean, Archie and Frank. Scene 7: Archie Rice—"Interrupts the program." Scene 8: Billy, Phoebe Jean, Archie and Frank. Scene 9: Billy, Phoebe, Jean, Archie and Frank. Scene 10: The good old days again. Scene 11: Jean and Graham—Archie and Bill. Scene 12: Archie Rice—The one and only.

The Entertainer was first produced on Broadway 2/12/58 for 97 performances and was named a Best Play of its season. This is its first major New York revival of record.

DUET FOR ONE

Stephanie Abrahams	Eva Marie Saint
Dr. Alfred Feldmann	Milton Selzer

Directed by Jeffrey Hayden; scenery, Michael Sharp; costumes, Jessica Hahn; lighting, Judy Rasmuson; sound, Philip Campanella; associate producer, Yale R. Wexler; production stage manager, Robert Townsend.

Time: The present. Place: Dr. Feldmann's consulting room. The play was presented in two parts.

This play about a psychiatrist and his patient, a cellist whose career has been disrupted by a crippling disease, was first produced in New York last season on Broadway 12/17/81 for 20 performances.

HOW HE LIED TO HER HUSBAND

He	....	Michael Butler
She	....	Jeanne Ruskin
Her Husband	....	Bernie McInerney

Time: The 1880s. Place: Ballymore House, Ire-land. This Shaw one-acter has been often revived in modern times off off Broadway, the last occasion having been by Counterpoint Theater Company 5/6/77.

WINNERS

Man	....	Bernie McInerney
Mag	....	Kate Burton
Woman	....	Jeanne Ruskin
Joe	....	Michael Butler

Time: 1966. Place: Northern Ireland. *Win-ners* was produced by Lincoln Center on Broadway in a program of two one-act plays entitled *Lovers* 7/25/68 for 148 performances and was named a Best Play of its season. This is its first major New York revival.

Directed by Nye Heron; scenery, Roger Mooney; costumes, Richard Hieronymous; lighting, Pat Kelly; sound, Philip Campanella; production stage manager, Kurt Wagemann.

Note: Press date for *The Holly and the Ivy* was 11/18/82, for *The Entertainer* was 1/20/83, for *Duet for One* was 4/28/83, for *Winners* and *How He Lied to Her Husband* was 4/21/83.

a/k/a Tennessee (1). Devised by Maxim Mazumdar; words by Tennessee Williams. Produced by June Hunt Mayer at the South Street Theater. Opened and closed at the evening performance, September 26, 1982.

Directed by Albert Takazauckas; design, Peter Harvey; lighting, Mal Sturchio; production stage manager, William Hare; press, Warren Knowlton. With Maxim Mazumdar, Carrie Nye, J.T. Walsh.

Self-described as "facts and fictions of Thomas Lanier Williams," a compilation of excerpts from his writings. Previously produced off off Broadway at Manhattan Theater Club.

The Price of Genius (22). By Betty Neustat. Produced by Bruce Levy in association with Leslie Steinweiss (Levy/Steinweiss Productions) at the Lambs Theater. Opened September 28, 1982. (Closed October 17, 1982)

Juana Ines de la Cruz	.... Patrizia Norcia	Jose	.... Timothy Wahrer
Carlos; Prof. Martinez;		Manuel	.... Sterling Swann
Cardinal Minelli	.... Fred Velde	Father Nunez	.... Jeremy Brooks
Viceroy de Mancera	.... Alfred Karl	Bishop	.... Bob Cooper
Dona Leonor de Mancera	.... Rae Kraus	Anita	.... Jody Catlin
Eduardo	.... Fred Rivers	Abbess	.... Patricia Mertens

Understudies: Miss Norcia—Jody Catlin; Mr. Swann—Timothy Wahrer; Mr. Velde—Fred Rivers; Mr. Karl—Bob Cooper; Miss Kraus—Patricia Mertens; Mr. Brooks—Fred Velde; Miss Mertens—Rae Kraus.

Directed by Sande Shurin; scenery, David Potts; costumes, Patricia Adshead; lighting, Richard Nelson; incidental music, Leslie Steinweiss; production stage manager, Rick Ralston; press, Shirley Herz Associates, Sam Rudy, Peter Cromarty, Sandra Manley.

Time: 1666 to 1695. Place: Mexico City. The play was presented in two parts.

The life of Sister de la Cruz, 17th century Mexican poet and playwright. Previously produced off off Broadway at the Interart.

Baseball Wives (45). By Grubb Graebner. Produced by Tom E. Greene III at the Harold Clurman Theater. Opened September 29, 1982. (Closed November 7, 1982)

Janelle.................. Marcella Lowery   Becky .... Lynn Goodwin
Doris...................... Carol Teitel

Understudy: Miss Goodwin—Gigi Benson-Smith.
Directed by Gloria Maddox; scenery and costumes, John Falabella; lighting, Jeff Davis; sound, Gordon Kupperstein; associate producer, Jessie B. Greene; production stage manager, David Rubinstein; press, Shirley Herz, Sam Rudy, Peter Cromarty.
Three women of varying ages and temperaments cope with their marriages to baseball superstars, from the season opener through the World Series. The play was presented in two parts. Previously produced off off Broadway.

Lennon (25). By Bob Eaton. Produced by Sid Bernstein and Stanley Bernstein in association with Abe Margolies and Dennis Paget in the Liverpool Everyman Theater production at the Entermedia Theater. Opened October 5, 1982. (Closed October 26, 1982)

CAST: Julia, Yoko Ono—Gusti Bogok (tambourine, banjo); Mimi, Cynthia—Katherine Borowitz (piano, electric keyboard, synthesizer); Jeff Mohammed, George Harrison, Gerry Marsden, Tony Palma—Lee Grayson (guitar, drums); Paul McCartney, Tony Tyler, Bertrand Russell—Vincent Irizarry (guitar, bass, piano, drums); Arthur Ballard, Herr Koschmider, George Martin, Dick Gregory, Elton John, Bob Wooler—John Jellison (piano, guitar, electric keyboard, synthesizer, drums, bass, banjo).
Also Younger John, Pierre Trudeau, Night Club Manager—David Patrick Kelly (guitar, bass, harmonica, piano); Older John, Stuart Sutcliffe, Les Chadwick, Brian Epstein—Robert LuPone (guitar, sax, bass, recorder); Pete Best, Ringo Starr, Harry Nilsson, Tony Barrow, Tim Leary—Greg Martyn (drums, electric keyboard, tea chest bass); Pete Shotton, Alan Williams, Victor Spinetti, Arthur Janov, Andy Peebles—Bill Sadler (guitar, drums, piano, washboard).
Standbys: Elizabeth Bayer, Joseph Pecorino, Stuart Warmflash, Mitch Weissman.
Directed by Bob Eaton; musical supervision, Mitch Weissman; scenery, Peter David Gould; costumes, Deborah Shaw; lighting, Dennis Parichy; sound, Tom Morse; Liverpool set design, Sue Mayes; Liverpool music design, Chris Monks; production stage manager, Peter B. Mumford; stage manager, Gary M. Zabinski; press, Judy Jacksina, Glenna Freedman, Diane Tomlinson, Susan Chicoine, Leslie Anderson.
Play with music about the life and times of John Lennon, the late member of the Beatles. The play was presented in two parts. A foreign play previously presented in Liverpool and Sheffield, England.

Anthem for Doomed Youth (6). One-man show written and performed by Michael Adler. Produced by the Anthem Company in association with Sari Weisman at the Actors' Playhouse. Opened October 6, 1982. (Closed October 10, 1982)

Directed by Patricia Turner; scenery, Don Gardiner, Lee Mills; lighting, Seth Orbach; production stage manager, Janet Friedman; press, Bob Ullman.
Characterization of the poet Wilfrid Owen (killed in World War I) based on his poems and letters. The play was presented without intermission.

*Circle Repertory Company. Schedule of six programs. **Angels Fall** (65). By Lanford Wilson. Opened October 17, 1982. (Closed November 28, 1982 and transferred to Broadway; see its entry in the Plays Produced on Broadway section of this volume) **Black Angel** (25). By Michael Cristofer. Opened December 19, 1982. (Closed January 9, 1983) **What I Did Last Summer** (37). By A.R. Gurney Jr. Opened February 6, 1983. (Closed February 20, 1983) **Domestic Issues**. (25). By Corinne Jacker. Opened March 13, 1983. (Closed April 3, 1983) **Young Playwrights Festival** (24). Program of four one-act plays: *A New Approach to Human Sacrifice* by Peter Getty, *I'm Tired and I Want to Go to*

Bed by David Torbett, *Third Street* by Richard Colman and *The Birthday Present* by Charlie Schulman. Opened April 13, 1983; co-produced by the Foundation of the Dramatists Guild. (Closed May 1, 1983). ***Fool for Love** (7). By Sam Shepard, in the Magic Theater of San Francisco production. Opened May 26, 1983. Produced by Circle Repertory, Marshall W. Mason artistic director, Richard Frankel managing director, B. Rodney Marriott acting artistic director, at the Circle Theater.

ANGELS FALL

Niles Harris................. Fritz Weaver	Marion Clay................ Tanya Berezin
Vita Harris................. Nancy Snyder	Salvatore (Zappy) Zappala... Brian Tarantina
Don Tabaha................. Danton Stone	Father William Doherty..... Barnard Hughes

Directed by Marshall W. Mason; scenery, John Lee Beatty; costumes, Jennifer Von Mayrhauser; lighting, Dennis Parichy; original music, Norman L. Berman; sound, Chuck London Media/Stewart Werner; production stage manager, Fred Reinglas; press, Richard Frankel, Reva Cooper.

Time: A late Saturday afternoon in June. Place: A mission in northwest New Mexico. The play was presented in two parts.

Character studies of six individuals confined in a group by a nearby nuclear accident. Previously produced in Miami, Westport and Saratoga.

A Best Play; see page 153.

BLACK ANGEL

Martin Engel................ Josef Sommer	Jimmie Ray Weeks; Bob Hawkins, M.P., 3d
Simone Engel............. Mary McDonnell	Hooded Man—Robert LuPone; M.P., 2d
Claude .... Burke Pearson	Hooded Man—Lou Liberatore; Hooded Men—
Louis Puget .... Tom Aldredge	Evan A. Georges, William Snovell, Randell
August Moreault............. Jonathan Bolt	Spence.
Also Andy Raines, M.P., 1st Hooded Man—	

Directed by Gordon Davidson; scenery and costumes, Sally Jacobs; lighting, John Gleason; sound, Chuck London Media/Stewart Werner; production stage manager, Jody Boese.

Study of degrees of guilt, as a Nazi war criminal returns to the scene of his crimes. The play was presented in two parts. Previously produced at the Mark Taper Forum, Los Angeles.

WHAT I DID LAST SUMMER

Elsie .... Christine Estabrook	Grace .... Debra Mooney
Charlie .... Ben Siegler	Bonny.................. Ann McDonough
Ted .... Robert Joy	Anna Trumbull.............. Julie Bovasso

Directed by Joan Micklin Silver; scenery, John Lee Beatty; costumes, Jennifer Von Mayrhauser; lighting Craig Miller; sound, Chuck London Media/Stewart Werner; production stage manager, Suzanne Fry.

Time: Summer 1945. Place: A summer "colony" on the Canadian shore of Lake Erie, near Buffalo, N.Y. The play was presented in two parts.

Talented 14-year-old boy trying to outgrow his spiritually confining WASP blackground.

Bruce McCarty replaced Robert Joy 2/15/83.

DOMESTIC ISSUES

Susan Porter .... Joyce Reehling Christopher	Nancy Graham .... Glynnis O'Connor
Larry Porter................ Robert Stattel	George Allison............ James Pickens Jr.
Stephen Porter............... Michael Ayr	Ellen Porter............... Caroline Kava

Directed by Eve Merriam; scenery, David Potts; costumes, Joan E. Weiss; lighting, Dennis Parichy; sound, Chuck London Media/Stewart Werner; production stage manager, Jody Boese.

Time: September, this year. Place; Larry Porter's house in a Chicago suburb. Act I: Early Friday evening. Act II: Several hours later.

1960s radical in the mainstream of today. Previously produced at Yale Repertory Theater.

YOUNG PLAYWRIGHTS FESTIVAL

A New Approach to Human Sacrifice
by Peter Getty, age 17

Mrs. Wall	Deborah Rush
Michael	Christopher Durang
Mr. Wall	Edward Power
Susan	Blanche Baker
Alvin	Greg Germann
Bobby	Brendan Murphy

Directed by Garland Wright; dramaturg, Wendy Wasserstein. Place, the Wall household. A suburban family behaving in the manner of a TV household, with some distinctly unsavory practises.

The Birthday Present
by Charlie Schulman, age 17

Wallace	Christopher Durang
Mary	Jean DeBaer
Sheila	Deborah Rush
Henry	Bill Moor
Hopp	Burke Pearson
Lucy	Kim Beaty
Newscaster	Novella Nelson
Joe Flanagan	Edward Power
TV Host	Brian Tarantina

Directed by John Ferraro; dramaturg, A.R. Gurney Jr. Act I: The Coopers' living room, the present. Act II: Wallace's apartment, 20 years later. Farce, the world's last fertile male must save the human race.

I'm Tired and I Want to Go to Bed
by David Torbett, age 18

Narrator	Novella Nelson
Jerome	Greg Germann
Mother	Jean DeBaer
Father	Edward Power

Directed by Gerald Chapman; dramaturg, Michael Weller. Place: Jerome Williams's house. Problem adolescent fails in school but succeeds in fantasy, dabbling in devil-worship.

Third Street
by Richard Colman, age 17

Ren	Keith Gordon
John	Robert Alan Morrow
Frank	Brian Tarantina

Directed by Michael Bennett; dramaturg, Michael Weller. Place: a graveyard in Brooklyn. Three high school friends destined to be separated by their needs and ambitions, cope with the impending breakup of their long and cherished friendship.

ALL PLAYS: Scenery, John Arnone; costumes, Patricia McGourty; lighting, Mal Sturchio; sound, Chuck London Media/Stewart Werner; original music for *The Birthday Present*, Richard Weinstock; Festival artistic director, Gerald Chapman; Festival managing director, Peggy Hansen; production supervisor, B. Rodney Marriott; production stage manager, Kate Stewart; stage manager, Suzanne Fry.

These four plays by young people (ages given above at the time of submission of scripts) were selected from hundreds of entries in the Foundation of the Dramatist Guild's Second Annual Young Playwrights Festival for this off-Broadway production under the aegis of Circle Repertory Company. In addition to these full productions, the Festival included staged readings of *Scraps* by Tagore Joseph McIntyre (age 10), *Teens Today* by Arthur W. French III (age 17) and *Weltschmerz* by Michael Aschner (age 18).

FOOL FOR LOVE

May	Kathy Baker	Martin	Dennis Ludlow
Eddie	Ed Harris	Old Man	Will Marchetti

Directed by Sam Shepard; scenery, Andy Stacklin; costumes, Ardyss L. Golden; lighting, Kurt Landisman, supervised by Mal Sturchio; sound, J.A. Deane; associate director, Julie Hebert; production stage manager, Suzanne Fry.

Battle of the sexes in a Mojave Desert motel room. The play was presented without intermission.

*True West (258). Revival of the play by Sam Shepard. Produced by Harold Thau and Wayne Adams in association with Robert Courson, Jay J. Miller and Richard Sturgis at the Cherry Lane Theater. Opened October 17, 1982.

Lee	John Malkovich	Saul Kimmer	Sam Schacht
Austin	Gary Sinise	Mom	Margaret Thomson

Understudies: Miss Thomson—Joan Kendall; Messrs. Malkovich, Sinise, Schacht—Bruce Lyons.
Directed by Gary Sinise; scenery, Kevin Rigdon, Deb Gohr; lighting, Kevin Rigdon; production stage manager, Larry Bussard; press, Judy Jacksina, Glenna Freedman, Diane Tomlinson, Susan Chicoine, Leslie Anderson.

Time: The present. Place: A Southern California suburb. The play was presented in two parts.

Love-hate relationship between two brothers, one a screen writer and one a drifter. Previously produced off Broadway by New York Shakespeare Festival Public Theater 12/23/80 for 24 performances, in a production which was repudiated by its author (who acknowledges this new version of the same script).

Dan Butler replaced Gary Sinise, Wayne Adams replaced Sam Schacht and Mary Copple replaced Margaret Thomson 4/17/83; Bruce Lyons replaced John Malkovich 4/26/83.

*Greater Tuna (273). By Jaston Williams, Joe Sears and Ed Howard. Produced by Karl Allison in association with Bryan Bantry at the Circle in the Square Downtown. Opened October 21, 1982.

CAST: Joe Sears, Jaston Williams. Understudy—Trip Plymale.

Directed by Ed Howard; scenery, Kevin Rupnik; costumes, Linda Fisher; lighting, Judy Rasmuson; associate producer, Salisbury Productions, Ltd.; production stage manager, Marjorie Horne; press, Henry Luhrman, Terry M. Lilly, Kevin P. McAnarney.

Time: One late-summer day. Place: Tuna, Texas's third-smallest town. Act I, Scene 1: Morning news, Radio Station OKKK. Scene 2: Breakfast. Scene 3: The interview. Scene 4: Pet-of-the-week. Scene 5: Leonard on the line. Scene 6: The bitter pill. Act II, Scene 1: The funeral parlor. Scene 2: The midday report. Scene 3: The smut snatchers of the new order. Scene 4: The interrogation. Scene 5: Evening prayers. Scene 6: Sign off.

Life in a small Texas town among 20 characters played by two actors, as follows: Thurston Wheelis, Bertha Bumiller, Leonard Childers, Elmer Watkins, Aunt Pearl Burras, R.R. Snavely, Rev. Spikes, Sheriff Givens, Hank Bumiller, Yippy—Joe Sears; Arles Struvie, Harold Dean Lattimer, Petey Fisk, Little Jody Bumiller, Stanley Bumiller, Charlene Bumiller, Chad Hartford, Phinas Blye, Vera Carp, Didi Snavely—Jaston Williams. Previously produced in Texas at Houston, Austin and San Antonio and in Atlanta and Hartford, Conn.

*New York Shakespeare Festival. Schedule of six programs; see note. **Plenty** (45). By David Hare. Opened October 21, 1982. (Closed November 28, 1982 and transferred to Broadway; see its entry in the Plays Produced on Broadway section of this volume) **Hamlet** (37). Revival of the play by William Shakespeare. Opened December 2, 1982. (Closed January 16, 1983) **Top Girls** (129). By Caryl Churchill. Opened December 29, 1982. (Closed January 30, 1983 after 40 performances) Reopened March 15, 1983; see note. (Closed May 29, 1983) **Buried Inside Extra** (31). By Thomas Babe. Opened May 4, 1983. (Closed May 29, 1983) ***Fen** (9). By Caryl Churchill. Opened May 24, 1983. ***Egyptology: My Head Was a Sledgehammer** (17). Text and scoring by Richard Foreman. Opened May 17, 1983. Produced by New York Shakespeare Festival (*Top Girls* in the Royal Court Theater production, *Fen* in the Joint Stock Theater Group production), Joseph Papp producer, at the Public Theater.

ALL PLAYS: Production supervisor, Jason Steven Cohen; press, Merle Debuskey, John Howlett, Richard Kornberg, Bruce Campbell.

PLENTY

Alice Park	Ellen Parker	Codename Lazar	Kelsey Grammer
Susan Traherne	Kate Nelligan	Frenchman #1	Ken Meseroll
Raymond Brock	Edward Herrmann	Leonard Darwin	George Martin

AT NEW YORK SHAKESPEARE FESTIVAL PUBLIC THEATER—*Above, in fore-ground,* Kathryn Grody, Lise Hilboldt and Linda Hunt and, *in background,* Freda Foh Shen and Sara Botsford in the American cast of Caryl Churchill's *Top Girls; below,* Sandy Dennis, Hal Holbrook, William Converse-Roberts, Dixie Carter and Vincent Gardenia in a scene from Thomas Babe's *Buried Inside Extra*

Mick	Daniel Gerroll	Dorcas Frey	Madeleine Potter
Louise	Johann Carlo	John Begley	Stephen Mellor
M. Aung	Conrad Yama	Sir Andrew Charleson	Bill Moor
Mme. Aung	Ginny Yang	Frenchman #2	Dominic Chianese

Understudies: Messrs. Grammer, Gerroll—Stephen Mellor; Mr. Yama—Victor Wong; Miss Yang—Freda Foh Shen; Miss Nelligan—Randy Dawson; Misses Parker, Carlo, Potter—Elizabeth Norment; Messrs. Martin, Moor, Chianese—Tom Klunis.

Directed by David Hare; scenery, John Gunter; costumes, Jane Greenwood; lighting, Arden Fingerhut; incidental music, Nick Bicat; production stage manager, Michael Chambers; stage manager, Anne King.

Act I, Scene 1: Knightsbridge, Easter 1962. Scene 2: St. Benoit, November 1943. Scene 3: Brussels, June 1947. Scene 4: Pimlico, September 1947. Scene 5: Festival of Britain, May 1951. Scene 6: Pimlico, December 1952. Scene 7: Knightsbridge, October 1956.

Act II, Scene 8: Knightsbridge, July 1961. Scene 9: Whitehall, January 1962. Scene 10: Knightsbridge, the day before Easter 1962. Scene 11: Blackpool, June 1962. Scene 12: St. Benoit, August 1944.

From World War II to the 1960s, an Englishwoman's disillusionment and emotional decline is a metaphor of the values and moods of her country. A foreign play previously produced at the National Theater, London, and in Chicago.

A Best Play; see page 173.

HAMLET

Bernardo; Fortinbras	Jamey Sheridan	Hamlet	Diane Venora
Francisco; Cornelius	Stephen McNaughton	Ophelia	Pippa Pearthree
Marcellus; Hecuba Speech; Luciano;		Reynaldo; Player Queen;	
English Ambassador	J.T. Walsh	Apprentice Gravedigger	Raphael Sbarge
Horatio	James Cromwell	Rosencrantz	Rick Lieberman
Ghost; Player King	George Hamlin	Guildenstern	Ralph Byers
Claudius	Bob Gunton	Norwegian Captain	Brett Porter
Gertrude	Kathleen Widdoes	Switzer;	
Voltemand; Priest	Ric Lavin	Messenger	Jimmy Smits, Brian Delate
Laertes	Robert Westenberg	Osric	Rocco Sisto
Polonius; Old Gravedigger	George Hall	Lady in Waiting; Player	Annette Heide

Directed by Joseph Papp; scenery, Robert Yodice; costumes, Theoni V. Aldredge; lighting, Ralph K. Holmes; music, Allen Shawn; fight sequences, B.H. Barry; stage managers, Fredric Orner, Jane Hubbard.

A virtually uncut *Hamlet* with an actress in the title role. The play was presented in two parts. *Hamlet* was last produced off Broadway by Circle Repertory 12/12/79 for 37 performances.

TOP GIRLS

Marlene	Gwen Taylor	Dull Gret; Angie	Carole Hayman
Waitress; Kit; Shona	Lou Wakefield	Pope Joan; Louise	Selina Cadell
Isabelle Bird; Joyce;		Patient Griselda; Nell;	
Mrs. Kidd	Deborah Findlay	Jeanine	Lesley Manville
Lady Nijo; Win	Lindsay Duncan		

Directed by Max Stafford-Clark; scenery, Peter Hartwell; costumes, Pam Tait; lighting, Robin Myerscough-Walker; production stage manager, Julie Davies; stage manager, Susan Green.

Act I, Scene 1: A restaurant. Scene 2: Top Girls Employment Agency, London. Scene 3: Joyce's back yard in Suffolk. Act II, Scene 1: Top Girls Employment Agency. Scene 2: A year earlier, Joyce's Kitchen.

In scrambled time sequence, a businesswoman's rise to the top, plus her metaphorical relationship with prominent women of the historical past. A foreign play previously produced in London.

Note: The above-listed British cast ended a limited 40-performance engagement 1/30/83, after which the following American cast prepared to resume performances (with a few of the character names changed), reopening 3/15/83 for 89 additional performances:

Marlene .... Lise Hilboldt   Dull Gret; Angie........... Kathryn Grody
Waitress; Jeanine; Win .... Donna Bullock   Pope Joan; Louise.............. Linda Hunt
Isabella Bird; Joyce; Nell ..... Sara Botsford   Patient Griselda; Kit;
Lady Nijo; Mrs. Kidd....... Freda Foh Shen   Shona................. Valerie Mahaffey

Understudies: Misses Grody, Hunt—Elaine Hausman; Misses Mahaffey, Bullock—Sherie Berk;
Misses Hilboldt, Shen—Fredi Olster; Miss Botsford—Dale Hodges.
Polly Draper replaced Lise Hilboldt 4/26/83.

BURIED INSIDE EXTRA

Jake L. Bowsky.............. Hal Holbrook   Don Kane .... William Converse-Roberts
Liz Conlon.................. Dixie Carter   Sophia Bowsky .... Sandy Dennis
Wild Bob Culhane......... Vincent Gardenia

Understudies: Misses Carter, Dennis—Linda Selman; Messrs. Holbrook, Gardenia—William H.
Andrews.
Directed by Joseph Papp; scenery, Mike Boak; costumes, Theoni V. Aldredge; lighting, Ralph K.
Holmes; stage managers, Susan Green, Stephen McCorkle.
Comedy, a bomb threat adds to the problems of a group of graveyard-shift employees of a dying
newspaper. The play was presented in two parts and was transferred to London's Royal Court
Theater 6/13/83 for six weeks in exchange for their production of *Top Girls*.

FEN

CAST: Boy Scaring Crows, Angela, Deb, Mrs. Finch—Amelda Brown; Japanese Businessman,
Nell, May, Mavis—Cecily Hobbs; Wilson, Frank, Mr. Tewson, Geoffrey—Bernard Strother; Shirley,
Shona, Miss Cade, Margaret—Linda Bassett; Val, Woman Working in the Fields—Jennie
Stoller; Mrs. Hassett, Becky, Alice, Ivy—Tricia Kelly.

Directed by Les Waters; design, Annie Smart; lighting, Tom Donellan; original music, Ilona
Sekacz; stage manager, Ginny Martino.
Rural folk as socioeconomic underdogs in Fen country of England. A foreign play previously
produced in London in this production by the Joint Stock Theater Group. The play was presented
without intermission.

EGYPTOLOGY: MY HEAD WAS A SLEDGEHAMMER

CAST: Seth Allen, Raymond Barry, Gretel Cummings, William Duff-Griffin, Cynthia Gillette,
Kate Manheim, Frank Maraden, George McGrath, Christine Morris, Lola Pashalinski.

Directed by Richard Foreman; scenery, Richard Foreman, Nancy Winters; lighting, Spencer
Mosse; costumes, Patricia McGourty; sound, Daniel M. Schreier; production stage manager, Michael
Chambers; stage manager, Anne Marie Hobson.
Another of the Foreman Ontological-Hysteric Theater productions, a series of nightmarishly
comic, melodramatic and musical impressions with overtones of social comment on various interna-
tional cultures. The play was presented without intermission.
Note: In Joseph Papp's Public Theater there are many auditoria. *Plenty*, *Top Girls* played the
Estelle R. Newman Theater, *Hamlet* played the Anspacher Theater, *Buried Inside Extra* played
Martinson Hall, *Fen* played LuEsther Hall, *Egyptology* played The Other Stage.
Note: New York Shakespeare Festival also produced a number of off-off-Broadway programs this
season; see their entries in the Plays Produced Off Off Broadway section of this volume.

American Place Theater. Schedule of two programs. **Do Lord Remember Me** (127). By
James DeJongh. Opened October 24, 1982. (Closed February 26, 1983; see note)
Buck (5). By Ronald Ribman. Co-produced by Playwrights Horizons, Andre Bishop
artistic director, Paul Daniels managing director. Opened March 10, 1983. (Closed March

13, 1983) Produced by The American Place Theater, Wynn Handman director, Julia Miles associate director, at the American Place Theater.

DO LORD REMEMBER ME

CAST: Frances Foster, Ebony Jo-Ann, Lou Myers, Charles H. Patterson, Glynn Turman.

Directed by Regge Life; scenery, Julie Taymor; costumes, Judy Dearing; lighting, Sandra L. Ross; production stage manager, Nancy Harrington; stage manager, Dwight R.B. Cook; press, Jeffrey Richards Associates, Robert Ganshaw.

Firsthand memories of slavery recorded in the 1930s, previously presented as a Federal Theater project in 1936 and a New Federal Theater production off off Broadway in 1978, and revised for this production, presented without intermission.

Note: *Do Lord Remember Me* closed 1/23/83 at American Place after 97 performances and reopened 1/29/83 at Town Hall, where it played 30 additional performances.

BUCK

Buck Halloran . . . . Alan Rosenberg	Joy . . . . Priscilla Lopez
Charlie Corvanni . . . . Robert Silver	Salesman. . . . . Michael Lipton
Mr. Lollipop;	Mr. Heegan . . . . Richard Leighton
Milton Berman . . . . Bernie Passeltiner	Vendor; Vincente. . . . . Jimmy Smits
Mr. Hawaiian Shirt; Mr. Goglas . . . . . Ted Sod	Woman With Hat;
Prof. Pipe in the Mouth . . . . . . Jack Davidson	Mme. Madeleine. . . . . . . Madeleine Le Roux
Fred Milly . . . . Morgan Freeman	Mr. Nathan . . . . Joseph Leon

Stagehands: Mitchell Gossett, Nick Iacovino, Charles Kindl, Michael Linden, Kenneth Lodge, Richard Mandel, Michael O'Boyll, Jason O'Malley, David Sennett.

Directed by Elinor Renfield; scenery, John Arnone; costumes, David C. Woolard; lighting, Frances Aronson; sound, Paul Garrity; fight, Robert Aberdeen; production stage manager, Jay Adler; press, Jeffrey Richards Associates, Robert Ganshaw.

Cable TV seen as an exploiter of brutality and other sensationalism. The play was presented in two parts.

Edmond (77). By David Mamet. Produced by the Goodman Theater, the Provincetown Playhouse, David Jiranek, I. Michael Kasser, Marjorie Oberlander, J.P. Pavanelli, Ltd. and David Weil at the Provincetown Playhouse. Opened October 27, 1982. (Closed January 2, 1983)

CAST: Mission Preacher, Prisoner—Paul Butler; Manager, Leafleteer, Customer, Policeman, Guard—Rick Cluchey; B-Girl, Whore—Joyce Hazard; Peep Show Girl, Glenna—Laura Innes; Man in a Bar, Hotel Clerk, Man in Back, Chaplain—Bruce Jarchow; Edmond's Wife—Linda Kimbrough.

Also Fortuneteller, Manager, Woman in the Subway—Marge Kotlisky; Cardsharp, Guard—José Santana; Shill, Pimp—Lionel Mark Smith; Edmond—Colin Stinton; Bartender, Bystander, Pawnshop Owner, Interrogator—Jack Wallace.

Directed by Gregory Mosher; scenery, Bill Bartelt; costumes, Marsha Kowal; lighting, Kevin Rigdon; fight choreographer David Woolley; associate producer, Margot Harley; stage manager, Ken Porter; press, Shirley Herz Associates, Sam Rudy, Peter Cromarty, Sandra Manley.

Place: New York City. The play was presented without intermission.

Middle class New Yorker explores the under side of the the city. Previously produced at the Goodman Theater, Chicago.

Patti LuPone replaced Linda Kimbrough 11/12/82.

Some Men Need Help (53). By John Ford Noonan. Produced by Frank Gero, Mark Gero and Chris Gero in association with Jane Holzer at the 47th Street Theater. Opened October 28, 1982. (Closed December 12, 1982)

Hudley T. Singleton III . . . . Treat Williams
Gaetano Altobelli . . . . Philip Bosco

Directed by John Ferraro; scenery, Eugene Lee; costumes, Shay Cunliffe; lighting, Gregory C. MacPherson; original music, Richard Weinstock; fights, B.H. Barry; production stage manager, Louis D. Pietig; press, Shirley Herz Associates, Sam Rudy, Peter Cromarty.

Place: 77 Huckleberry Drive, Roman Hills, Fairfield County, Conn. Act I, Scene 1: Late September, Monday morning just after 9 A.M. Scene 2: Tuesday, 9 A.M. Scene 3: Wednesday, 10:30 A.M. Act II. Scene 1: Almost three months later, the week between Christmas and New Year's, Thursday, 2 P.M. Scene 2: Friday, just before 9 A.M. Scene 3: Early afternoon a few days later, just after the first of the year.

The friendship of two men in their fight against alcoholism.

*Upstairs at O'Neals' (286). Cabaret revue conceived by Martin Charnin. Produced by Martin Charnin, Michael O'Neal, Patrick O'Neal and Ture Tufvesson at O'Neals'. Opened October 29, 1982.

Douglas Bernstein	Michon Peacock
Randall Edwards	Richard Ryder
Bebe Neuwirth	Sarah Weeks

Pianos: David Krane, Paul Ford.
Understudies: Kathryn McAteer, Neal Klein.
Directed by Martin Charnin; choreographer, Ed Love; musical direction and arrangements, David Krane; scenery and lighting, Ray Recht; costumes, Zoran; production stage manager, Edward R. Isser; stage manager, Neal Klein; press, Patt Dale Associates, Jim Baldassare.
Mixed bag of subjects exposed to musical satire, presented without intermission.

MUSICAL NUMBERS: Overture; "Upstairs at O'Neals' " (music and lyrics by Martin Charnin) —Ensemble; "Stools" (music and lyrics by Martin Charnin)—Douglas Bernstein, Richard Ryder; "Cancun" (music and lyrics by Michael Leeds and John Forster)—Ryder; "Something" (music and lyrics by Douglas Bernstein and Denis Markell)—Bernstein; "I Furnished My One Room Apartment" (music by Stephen Hoffman, lyrics by Michael Mooney)—Sarah Weeks; "Little H and Little G" (music and lyrics by Ronald Melrose)—Ensemble; "The Ballad of Cy and Beatrice" (music by Paul Trueblood, lyrics by Jim Morgan)—Randall Edwards; "Signed, Peeled, Delivered" (music and lyrics by Ronald Melrose)—Ensemble, Ryder.

Also "The Feet" (music by Seth Friedman, lyrics by David L. Crane, Seth Friedman and Marta Kauffman)—Ensemble; "The Soldier and the Washerworker" (music and lyrics by Ronald Melrose) —Bebe Neuwirth; Table D'Hote (by Archie T. Tridmorten)—Bernstein, Ryder, Edwards; "Soap Operetta" (music by Seth Friedman, words by David L. Crane, Seth Friedman and Marta Kauffman) —Ensemble; "Talkin' Morosco Blues" (lyrics by Murray Horwitz, guitar accompaniment by Willie Nininger)—Ryder; "Mommas' Turn" (music and lyrics by Douglas Bernstein and Denis Markell) —Ladies; We'll Be Back Right After This Message (by Douglas Bernstein and Denis Markell)— Neuwirth, Edwards, Bernstein; "All I Can Do Is Cry" (music and lyrics by Sarah Weeks and Michael Abbott)—Weeks; "Cover Girls" (music by Seth Friedman, lyrics by David L. Crane, Seth Friedman and Marta Kauffman)—Michon Peacock, Neuwirth, Edwards, Bernstein; "Boy, Do We Need It Now" (music and lyrics by Charles Strouse)—Peacock, Ensemble; "Finale"—Company.
Carole Schweid replaced Michon Peacock 12/27/82.

Classic Stage Company (CSC). Repertory of five programs (also see note). (214) **Faust Part One** and **Faust Part Two**. By Johann Wolfgang von Goethe; adapted from the translation by Philip Wayne. Opened October 31, 1982 (*Part One* at the matinee, *Part Two* at the evening performance). **Wild Oats**. Revival of the play by John O'Keeffe. Opened January 9, 1983. **Balloon**. By Karen Sunde. Opened February 13, 1983. **Danton's Death**. By George Buechner; English version by Christopher Martin. Opened March 27, 1983. Produced by Classic Stage Company, Christopher Martin artistic director, Dan J. Martin managing director, at CSC Repertory. (Repertory closed May 8, 1983)

ALL PLAYS: Directed by Christopher Martin (*Ghost Sonata* and *Balloon* co-directed by Karen Sunde); scenery, Christopher Martin; costumes, Miriam Nieves; lighting, Rick Butler; dramaturg, Karen Sunde; stage manager, Christine Michael; press, Krista M. Altok, Will M. Weiss.

FAUST PART ONE

Prologue
Director.............. Christopher Martin
Poet...................... Gary Sloan
Actor................. Tom Spackman
Mephisto.............. Noble Shropshire
The Lord.............. Walter Williamson
1. Night
Faust................ Christopher Martin
Mephisto.............. Noble Shropshire
Earth Spirit.............. Tom Spackman
Wagner.................... Tom Spiller
Old Man................. Thomas Lenz
Girl...................... Ginger Grace
Student.............. Barry Mulholland
    Peasants: Brenda Lynn Bynum, Dennis La Valle, Christy Lowery, Bill Nickerson, Diane Rieck, Van Santvoord, Rivka Szatmary, Pam Welch.
2. Beer Hall
Faust................ Christopher Martin
Mephisto.............. Noble Shropshire
Frosch.................... Thomas Lenz
Brander............. Walter Williamson
Altmayer.................... Tom Spiller
Siebel.................. Howard Lucas
3. Witch's Kitchen
Faust................ Christopher Martin
Mephisto.............. Noble Shropshire
He-Ape................. Tom Spackman
She-Ape.................. Amy Warner
Witch............ Mary Eileen O'Donnell
Faust...................... Gary Sloan
    Apes: Bill Nickerson, Van Santvoord, Rivka Szatmary.
4. Gretchen

Faust...................... Gary Sloan
Mephisto.............. Noble Shropshire
Gretchen................... Ginger Grace
Martha......... Mary Eileen O'Donnell
Lizabeth.................. Amy Warner
Valentine.............. Barry Mulholland
Soldiers..... Bill Nickerson, Van Santvoord
    Citizens: Dennis La Valle, Thomas Lenz, Christy Lowery, Howard Lucas, Tom Spiller, Rivka Szatmary, Pam Welch, Walter Williamson.
5. Walpurgisnacht
Faust...................... Gary Sloan
Mephisto................. Noble Shropshire
Will-o-Wisp.............. Tom Spackman
General...................... Tom Spiller
Minister.............. Barry Mulholland
Author................... Howard Lucas
Huckster Witch............ Thomas Lenz
Lilith..................... Amy Warner
Old Witch........ Mary Eileen O'Donnell
Critic................. Walter Williamson
    Witches: Brenda Lynn Bynum, Christy Lowery, Diane Rieck, Rivka Szatmary, Pam Welch. Warlocks: Dennis La Valle, Bill Nickerson, Van Santvoord.
6: Dungeon
Faust...................... Gary Sloan
Mephisto.............. Noble Shropshire
Gretchen................... Ginger Grace
Epilogue
Faust...................... Gary Sloan
Ariel.................... Tom Spackman
    The play was presented in two parts with the intermission following Scene 3.

FAUST PART TWO

Prologue
Faust.................... Tom Spackman
Ariel....................... Gary Sloan
1. Masquerade
Faust; Plutus............. Tom Spackman
Mephisto; Greed......... Noble Shropshire
Emperor.................. Howard Lucas
Archbishop............. Walter Williamson
Commander................. Tom Spiller
Treasurer............. Barry Mulholland
Chamberlain............... Thomas Lenz
Poetry.................... Gary Sloan
1st Woman................ Ginger Grace
2d Woman.......... Brenda Lynn Bynum

3d Woman........ Mary Eileen O'Donnell
Paris.................... Dennis La Valle
Helen..................... Amy Warner
    Workmen: Dennis La Valle, Bill Nickerson, Van Santvoord.
2: Classical Walpurgisnacht
Faust.................... Tom Spackman
Mephisto............... Noble Shropshire
1st Pedant.............. Thomas Lenz
2d Pedant............... Van Santvoord
3d Pedant............... Bill Nickerson
Student; Chiron........ Barry Mulholland
Wagner; Thales............. Tom Spiller
Homunculus................ Gary Sloan

Erichto; Empusa.... Mary Eileen O'Donnell
Sphinx .... Amy Warner
Manto .... Ginger Grace
Nereus .... Howard Lucas
Proteus .. Walter Williamson, Thomas Lenz
Lamiae: Christy Lowery, Rivka Szatmary,
Pam Welch. Porkyads: Mary Eileen O'Donnell, Ginger Grace, Thomas Lenz.

3. Helen
Helen..................... Amy Warner
Chorus Leader ..... Mary Eileen O'Donnell
Porkyas .... Noble Shropshire
Faust .... Tom Spackman
Watchman................... Tom Spiller
Knights ..... Bill Nickerson, Van Santvoord
Euphorion .... Gary Sloan
Chorus: Brenda Lynn Bynum, Ginger
Grace, Christy Lowery, Diane Rieck, Rivka
Szatmary, Pam Welch.

4. War Games
Faust .... Tom Spackman
Mephisto .... Noble Shropshire
Emperor .... Howard Lucas
Commander.................. Tom Spiller
1st Aide............... Barry Mulholland
2d Aide................. Thomas Lenz
Archbishop .... Walter Williamson

Maneuvers: Dennis La Valle, Bill Nickerson, Van Santvoord.
5. Under the Lindens
Wanderer.............. Christopher Martin
Baucis .... Ginger Grace
Philemon.................... Gary Sloan
6. Utopia
Faust .... Christopher Martin
Mephisto .... Noble Shropshire
Watchman................... Tom Spiller
Want .... Thomas Lenz
Guilt .... Howard Lucas
Need .... Mary Eileen O'Donnell
Care...................... Amy Warner
Lemures: Thomas Lenz, Barry Mulholland, Tom Spiller.
Epilogue
Mephisto .... Noble Shropshire
Gretchen .... Ginger Grace
The Lord.............. Walter Williamson
Faust: Tom Spackman, Gary Sloan, Christopher Martin. Angels: Dennis La Valle, Howard Lucas, Bill Nickerson, Van Santvoord. Penitents: Christy Lowery, Mary Eileen O'Donnell, Rivka Szatmary, Amy Warner, Pam Welch.
The play was presented in two parts with the intermission following Scene 2.

BOTH PLAYS: Wedekind lieder sung by Helmut Lohner; associate director, Karen Sunde; songs, Frank Wedekind.

WILD OATS

John Dory .... Tom Spiller
Sir George Thunder ...... Barry Mulholland
Ephraim Smooth .... Noble Shropshire
Lady Amaranth.............. Amy Warner
Muz; 1st Ruffian .... Van Santvoord
Harry Thunder .... Tom Spackman
Jack Rover.................... Gary Sloan
Farmer Gammon........ Walter Williamson

Sim .... Thomas Lenz
Jane....................... Ginger Grace
Banks .... Howard Lucas
Twitch .... Bill Nickerson
Landlord; 3d Ruffian......... Robert Quinn
Lamp .... Donn Youngstrom
Trap; 2d Ruffian .... Dennis La Valle
Amelia .... Mary Eileen O'Donnell

Brats: Brenda Lynn Bynum, Christy Lowery, Diane Rieck, Rivka Szatmary, Pam Welch. Locals: Dennis La Valle, Bill Nickerson, Robert Quinn, Van Santvoord, Donn Youngstrom.
Stage manager, Christine Michael.
The play was presented in two parts. *Wild Oats* was last produced off Broadway in CSC repertory 1/7/79.

BALLOON

Helvetius .... Mary Eileen O'Donnell
Morellet .... Barry Mulholland
Roche.................... Howard Lucas

Turgot .... Walter Williamson
Cabanis...................... Gary Sloan
Franklin .... Christopher Martin

Pantomime Roles: Polly Stevenson, Miss Howe—Helvetius; Admiral Howe, Beaumarchais—Morellet; Montaudoin—Roche; Wedderburn, Chaumont—Turgot; William Franklin, Louis XVI—Cabanis.
Original music, Noble Shropshire, Robert Burns; stage manager, Thomas Lenz.
Time: About 1783. Place: The salon of Madame Helvetius.

A Paris salon the evening Benjamin Franklin decides to return to the U.S. (with flashbacks to some of the important events in his life).

DANTON'S DEATH

Georges Danton . . . . Tom Spiller	3d Citizen; Young Gentleman;
Camille Desmoulins . . . . Tom Spackman	LaFlotte. . . . . Dennis La Valle
Lacroix. . . . . Barry Mulholland	Robespierre . . . . Noble Shropshire
Herault-Sechelles. . . . . Gary Sloan	St. Just . . . . Howard Lucas
Julie Danton . . . . Diane Riek	Collot . . . . Walter Williamson
Lucile Desmoulins. . . . . Ginger Grace	Couthon; Man From Lyons;
Legendre; Fouquier-Tinville;	Executioner. . . . . Donn Youngstrom
Beggar; Executioner. . . . . Thomas Lenz	Marion . . . . Amy Warner
Simon . . . . Van Santvoord	Rosalie . . . . Pam Welch
Simon's Wife;	Adelaide. . . . . Rivka Szatmary
Ballad Singer. . . . . . . Mary Eileen O'Donnell	Card Lady; Mother. . . . . Brenda Lynn Bynum
1st Citizen; Soldier;	Card Lady; Young Lady . . . . Patricia Fletcher
Chaumette. . . . . Robert Quinn	Paine. . . . . Christopher Martin
2d Citizen; Gen. Dillon . . . . . . Bill Nickerson	

Original music, Noble Shropshire.

Danton's Death, a 19th century German play, was produced on Broadway by the Mercury Theater 11/2/38 for 21 performances and by the Repertory Theater of Lincoln Center 10/21/65 for 46 performances.

Note: The Classic Stage Company season also included the running repertory production of *Ghost Sonata*, revival of the play by August Strindberg, English version by Christopher Martin, entering the repertory 11/12/82, with a cast consisting of Noble Shropshire, Tom Spackman, Amy Warner, Mary Eileen O'Donnell, Walter Williamson, Ginger Grace, Barry Mulholland, Howard Lucas, Tom Spiller, Brenda Lynn Bynum and Donn Youngstrom (see its entry in the Plays Produced Off Broadway section of *The Best Plays of 1981–82*).

Two Fish in the Sky (16). By Michael Hastings. Produced by The Phoenix Theater, T. Edward Hambleton managing director, Steven Robman artistic director, Harold Sogard general manager at the Theater at Saint Peter's Church. Opened October 31, 1982; see note. (Closed November 14, 1982)

Raymond Borrall. . . . . Gavin Reed	Irene Connor . . . . Laura Esterman
Meadowlark Rachel Warner . . . Cleavon Little	Edna Walter. . . . . Lorraine Toussaint
Gerald Radinski . . . . Christopher Murney	Elliott Brucknell . . . . Michael Tucker

Directed by Steven Robman; scenery, Wynn P. Thomas; costumes, Robert Wojewodski; lighting, Arden Fingerhut; sound, David Rapkin; dialect consultant, Timothy Monich; production stage manager, Loretta Robertson; press, Susan L. Schulman, Keith Sherman.

Time: The present. Place: The Brixton section of London and Gatwick Airport. The play was presented in two parts.

A resourceful Jamaican vs. the British immigration authorities. A foreign play previously produced in London.

Note: Press date for *Two Fish in the Sky* was 11/7/82.

The Light Opera of Manhattan (LOOM). Repertory of three new revival productions and 12 running operetta revivals. **H.M.S. Pinafore** (36, following 14 performances of former production) Book by W.S. Gilbert; music by Arthur Sullivan. Opened November 3, 1982. (Closed January 16, 1983) **The Gondoliers** (14). Book by W.S. Gilbert; music by Arthur Sullivan. Opened February 9, 1983. (Closed February 20, 1983) **Rose Marie** (28). Book and lyrics by Otto Harbach and Oscar Hammerstein II; music by Rudolf Friml and Herbert Stothart. Opened May 4, 1983 (Closed May 29, 1983) Produced by The Light

IN REPERTORY—Raymond Allen as Ko-Ko in *The Mikado (left)*
and Sir Joseph in *H.M.S. Pinafore* at Light Opera of Manhattan

Opera of Manhattan, William Mount-Burke producer-director, at the Eastside Playhouse
(Repertory closed May 29, 1983)

ALL PLAYS: Directed by William Mount-Burke; musical director, William Mount-Burke; assistant musical director and pianist, Brian Molloy; assistant conductor and organist, Stanley German; choreography, Jerry Gotham; stage manager, Jerry Gotham; press, Mary Jane Gibbons.

H.M.S. PINAFORE

Sir Joseph................ Raymond Allen	Carpenter.............. Kenneth McMullen
Capt. Corcoran............. Robert Barker	Josephine........ Sylvia Lanka/Joyce Bolton
Ralph Rackstraw........... Anthony Emeric	Hebe....................... Irma Rogers
Dick Deadeye .... Ryan Allen	Buttercup............... Ethelmae Mason
Boatswain.................. Francis Rella	

Ensemble: Janette Leslie Jones, Karen Sussman, Christopher McFadden, Cole Mobley, Lorie Mayorga, Joanne Jamieson, Kenneth McMullen, Bob Cuccioli, Bruce Biggins, John Palmore, Anthony Mellor, Barbara Rouse, Donna Campion, Karly Rothenberg, Krisztina Laurio, Diana Blankman, Francis Rella, Douglas Dally, Roger Kirby, Michael Winther, Mary Martello, Lisa Smith.

Ellen Greiss percussionist; Nancy McFarland violinist.

Scenery, Daniel Aronson; costumes, Bradford Wood; lighting, Mary Edith Jamison.

Place: The quarterdeck of H.M.S. Pinafore, off Portsmouth. Act I: Noon. Act II: Night.

This new revival production of the operetta (which was first produced in London 5/25/1878) replaced the former LOOM production which played for 14 performances in June, August and September this season.

THE GONDOLIERS

Duke of Plaza-Toro .... Raymond Allen
Luiz .... Robert Barker
Don Alhambra .... Vashek Pazdera
Marco Palmieri .... Anthony Emeric
Giuseppe Palmieri.......... Stephen Rosario
Antonio .... Bob Cuccioli
Francesco .... John Palmore/Roger Kirby
Giorio.................... Anthony Mellor
Annibale................. Michael Winther

Duchess of Plaza-Toro .... Elizabeth
                                 Burgess-Harr
Casilda .... Georgia McEver
Gianetta .... Joyce Bolton
Tessa..................... Harriet Couch
Fiametta.................. Donna Campion
Vittoria.................. Lorie Mayorga
Giulia .... Barbara Rouse
Inez.................. Janette Leslie Jones
Page .... Gregory Mobley

Ellen Greiss percussionist; David Thorpe string.

Scenic artist, Ellen Kurrelmeyer; costumes, Melody Schneider; lighting, Mary Edith Jamison.

Time: About 1750. Act I: The Piazzetta, Venice. Act II: Pavilion in the Palace of Barataria, three months later.

This new revival production of the operetta (which was first produced in London 12/7/1889) replaced the former LOOM production.

ROSE MARIE

Sgt. Malone .... Anthony Emeric
Lady Jane................. Millie Petroski
Black Eagle .... Anthony Mellor
Edward Hawley........... Robert Barker/
                          Bruce McKillip
Emile La Flamme............. Bob Cuccioli

Wanda .... Joyce Bolton
Hard-Boiled Herman .... Raymond Allen
Jim Kenyon............... Stephen Rosario
Rose Marie La Flamme .... Sylvia Lanka
Ethel Brander .... Ann Kirschner

Scenery, Ellen Kurrelmeyer; costumes, George Stinson; lighting, Mary Edith Jamison; music consultant, Alfred Simon; script consultant, Alice Hammerstein Mathias; script preparation, Karen Schlotter; musical arrangements, Brian Molloy; special musical arrangements and orchestrations, Stanley German

Rose Marie (*Rose-Marie*) was first produced on Broadway in the season of 1924–25, and its last major New York revival of record took place in the 1926–27 season.

ACT I

Scene 1: Lady Jane's Totem Pole Saloon
  "Vive la Canadienne"... Ensemble
  "Totem Tom-Tom" .... Wanda, Ensemble
  "Hard-Boiled Herman" .... Herman, Jane, Ladies
  "Rose Marie" .... Jim
  "Rose Marie (Reprise)........................... Malone, Hawley, Emile, Gentlemen
  "Like Jim" .... Rose Marie
  "Indian Love Call"... Rose Marie, Jim
Scene 2: Sgt. Malone's Campfire in the Northern Canadian Woods
  "Song of the Mounties"....................................... Malone, Gentlemen
Scene 3: Black Eagle's cabin
Scene 4: At Kootenay Pass
  "Indian Love Call" (Reprise) .... Rose Marie, Jim
  "Why Shouldn't We"... Jane, Herman
  "Pretty Things" .... Ethel, Hawley, Ensemble
  "Indian Love Call" (Reprise) .... Rose Marie, Jim
  Finale..................... Rose Marie, Jane, Ethel, Malone, Hawley, Emile, Ensemble

ACT II

Entr'acte
Scene 1: Ballroom of the Chateau Fortenac, Quebec, three weeks later
  "Minuet of the Minute"....................................... Ethel, Emile, Ensemble

"All I Ask Is That I May Forget You" .... Rose Marie, Wanda, Ethel, Jim, Hawley, Emile
"Door of My Dreams" .... Rose Marie, Ladies
Finaletto .... Rose Marie, Wanda, Ethel, Hawley, Malone, Emile, Ensemble
Scene 2: The cellar of 24 River Front
"Why Shouldn't We" (Reprise) .... Jane, Herman
Scene 3: Path to Rose Marie's castle
"Indian Love Call" (Reprise) .... Rose Marie, Jim

LOOM'S 1982–83 repertory included 12 running productions mounted in previous seasons and presented on the following schedule (operettas have book and lyrics by W.S. Gilbert and music by Arthur Sullivan unless otherwise noted): *The Mikado* (56), opened June 2, October 20, February 23 and April 6; *H.M.S. Pinafore* (14; old production), opened June 16 and August 25; *The Merry Widow* (28), based on the book by Victor Leon and Leo Stein, music by Franz Lehar, English lyrics by Alice Hammerstein Mathias, opened June 30 and April 20; *The Pirates of Penzance* (28), opened July 14 and March 23; *Ruddigore* (14), opened July 28; *A Night in Venice* (14), book by William Mount-Burke and Alice Hammerstein Mathias, based freely on an idea by Zell & Genée, music by Johann Strauss, lyrics by Alice Hammerstein Mathias, opened August 11.

Also *The Red Mill* (21), book and lyrics by Henry Blossom, music by Victor Herbert, opened September 8; *Mlle. Modiste* (21), book and lyrics by Henry Blossom, music by Victor Herbert, opened September 29; *Iolanthe* (14), opened November 17; *Babes in Toyland* (28), book by William Mount-Burke and Alice Hammerstein Mathias, lyrics by Alice Hammerstein Mathias, music by Victor Herbert, opened December 8; *The Desert Song* (21), book and lyrics by Otto Harbach, Oscar Hammerstein II and Frank Mandel, music by Sigmund Romberg, opened January 19; *Patience* (14), opened March 9.

Performers in LOOM running repertory during the 1982–83 season included Raymond Allen, Ryan Allen, Robert Barker, Joyce Bolton, Rob Bersworth, John J. Bonk, Elizabeth Burgess-Harr, Cathy Cosgrove, Donna Campion, Harriet Couch, Bob Cuccioli, Rebecca Darnauer, Anthony Emeric, Antonio Garza, Billy Hester, Lloyd Harris, Karen Hartman.

Also Janette Leslie Jones, Roger Kirby, Ann J. Kirschner, Renee Kramer, Jacqueline Kroschell, Sylvia Lanka, Catherine Lankford, Lief Lorenz, Georgia McEver, Anthony Mellor, Anthony Michalik, Ethelmae Mason, Kenneth McMullen, Lorie Mayorga, Christopher McFadden, Raul Melo, Cole Mobley, Bruce McKillip, Dick O'Mara, Claudia O'Neill, Stephen O'Mara, Jennifer O'Rourke, Susanna Organek, Gary Pitts, Vashek Pazdera, Maria Politano, Millie Petroski, John Palmore.

Also Stephen Rosario, Francis Rella, Irma Rogers, Barbara Rouse, Gary Ridley, Karly Rothenberg, Cheryl Savitt, Karen Sussman, Peter Sham, John Sacco, Samuel Silvers, Kevin Usher, Michael Winther.

Nurse Jane Goes to Hawaii (20). By Allan Stratton. Produced by Theater in the Park, Sue Lawless artistic director, Sharon Rupert managing director, at the New York State Pavilion, Flushing Meadows. Opened November 4, 1982. (Closed November 21, 1982)

Doris Chisholm	Jennifer Bassey	Peggy Scant	Julie Osburn
Vivien Bliss	Georgia Engel	Peter Prior	Jeffrey Dreisbach
Edgar Chisholm	Brandon Maggart	Betty Scant	Liz Otto
Bill Scant	Ronn Carroll		

Directed by Sue Lawless; scenery, Kevin Wiley; costumes, Mary-Anne Aston; lighting, Mark Hendren; production stage manager, Joe Watson; press, Shirley Herz Associates, Peter Cromarty.

Place: The living room of Edgar and Doris Chisholm, 16 The Bridle Path, Toronto, Canada. Act I: A Friday in October, late afternoon. Act II: The same day, early evening.

The farcical adventures of a woman writer of romantic novels. A foreign play previously produced in Toronto and Allentown, Pa.

Penelope (1). By J. Radloff. Produced by Vince Rhomberg in association with Patrick Campbell, David Larkin and P.D. Mazza at the Perry Street Theater. Opened and closed at the evening performance, November 23, 1982.

Directed by Vince Rhomberg; scenery, Cecilia Gilchrest; costumes, Karen Matthews; lighting, Vivien Leone; stage manager, Beth Prevor; press, Burnham-Callaghan Associates. With Joy Franz, David Snizek, Mike Champagne, Robert Walsh, Paul O'Connor.

Comedy, a temperamental stage star of the 1930s. The play was presented in three parts.

A Christmas Carol (34). Adapted by Orson Bean from the novel by Charles Dickens. Produced by Thomas C. Anderson Jr. and Triskaidek Productions at the Perry Street Theater. Opened December 9, 1982. (Closed January 1, 1983)

CAST: Scrooge—Orson Bean; Bob Cratchit, Dick Williams—Michael Champagne; 1st Businessman, 1st Gravedigger, Ghost of the Past, Poulterer, Christmas Shopper—Mitchell Greenberg; Fan, Belinda, Daughter of Man—Debbie Hines; Tiny Tim—Knowl Johnson; Marley, Ghost of Present, Debtor—Sherman Lloyd; Peter, Son of Man, Turkey Boy—Albie Polinsky; Charity Collector, Gravedigger, Fop—Jay E. Raphael; Mrs. Cratchit, Mrs. Fezziwig—Mary Stout.

Directed by Christopher Catt; scenery, Johnienne Papandreas; costumes, Lindsay W. Davis; lighting, Curt Ostermann; choreographer, Mary Corsaro; sound and special effects, Peter Kallish; musical direction, Bonita LaBossiere; production stage manager, J. Barry Lewis; press, Judy Jacksina, Glenna Freedman.

Accent on comedy in a version of the Christmas classic.

Snoopy (152). Musical based on the Charles M. Schulz comic strip *Peanuts*; book by Charles M. Schulz Creative Associates, Warren Lockhart, Arthur Whitelaw and Michael L. Grace; music by Larry Grossman; lyrics by Hal Hackady. Produced by Gene Persson in association with Paul D. Hughes, Martin Markinson, Donald Tick and United Media Productions (Robert Roy Metz president) at the Lambs Theater. Opened December 20, 1982. (Closed May 1, 1983)

Charlie Brown	Terry Kirwin	Peppermint Patty	Vicki Lewis
Linus	Stephen Fenning	Snoopy	David Garrison
Sally Brown	Deborah Graham	Woodstock	Cathy Cahn
Lucy	Kay Cole		

Orchestra: Ronald Melrose piano, conductor; Robert Fisher piano; Michael Epstein drums.

Standbys: Jason Grace, Nina Hennessey.

Directed by Arthur Whitelaw; choreography, Marc Breaux; musical direction and additional orchestrations, Ronald Melrose; scenery and costumes, David Graden; lighting, Ken Billington; associate producer, Miranda Smith; production stage manager, Melissa Davis; press, Jeffrey Richards Associates, C. George Willard, Richard Humleker.

The dog Snoopy and his bird friend Woodstock at the center of the *Peanuts* children's activities, as in *You're a Good Man Charlie Brown* (but written by a different team and not a direct sequel to that 1967 musical Best Play). Previously produced in San Francisco.

Jason Graae replaced David Garrison and Lorna Luft replaced Vicki Lewis (and a new song "Hurry Up, Face" was added for her) 2/21/83.

ACT I

Overture	Orchestra
"The World According to Snoopy"	Ensemble
"Snoopy's Song"	Snoopy, Ensemble
Woodstock's Theme	Orchestra
"Edgar Allan Poe"	Peppermint Patty, Lucy, Sally, Linus, Charlie Brown
"Mother's Day"	Snoopy
"I Know Now"	Lucy, Sally, Peppermint Patty
"Vigil"	Linus
"Clouds"	Ensemble
"Where Did That Little Dog Go?"	Charlie Brown
"Dime a Dozen"	Lucy, Peppermint Patty, Sally, Snoopy
"Daisy Hill"	Snoopy

SNOOPY—Terry Kirwin as Charlie Brown and David Garrison as Snoopy in musical based on Charles M. Schulz's "Peanuts"

ACT II

Entr'acte . . . . Orchestra
"Bunnies" . . . . Snoopy
"The Great Writer" . . . . Snoopy
"Poor Sweet Baby" . . . . Peppermint Patty
"Don't Be Anything Less Than
    Everything You Can Be" . . . . Charlie Brown, Linus, Sally, Peppermint Patty
"The Big Bow-Wow" . . . . Snoopy
"Just One Person" . . . . Ensemble
"Bows" . . . . Ensemble

*Extremities (182). By William Mastrosimone. Produced by Frank Gero, Mark Gero, Chris Gero, Jason Gero and Della Koenig at the Cheryl Crawford Theater. Opened December 22, 1982.

Marjorie	Susan Sarandon	Terry	Ellen Barkin
Raul	James Russo	Patricia	Deborah Hedwall

Directed by Robert Allan Ackerman; scenery, Marjorie Bradley Kellogg; costumes, Robert Wojewodski; lighting, Arden Fingerhut; action sequences, B.H. Barry; sound, Scott Lehrer; production stage manager, Louis D. Pietig; stage manager, Jonathan Gero; press, Solters/Roskin/Friedman, Inc., Milly Schoenbaum, Warren Knowlton, Kevin Patterson.

Place: Between Trenton and Princeton, N.J., where the cornfield meets the highway. Act I: The present, September. Act II: A moment later.

Emotions and tensions in the aftermath of an attempted rape. Previously produced by Rutgers Theater Company, New Brunswick, N.J. and Actors Theater of Louisville.

Karen Allen replaced Susan Sarandon 3/29/83. Glenne Headley replaced Ellen Barkin. Priscilla Lopez replaced Glenne Headley 4/7/83. Farrah Fawcett replaced Karen Allen 5/24/83.

A Best Play; see page 211.

Poppie Nongena (131). By Sandra Kotze and Elsa Joubert; based on the novel by Elsa Joubert. Produced by Edward Miller at St. Clement's. Opened January 12, 1983. (Closed May 8, 1983)

Poppie	Thuli Dumakude	Uncle; Suitor; Husband	Selaelo Maredi
Grandmother; Mother	Sophie Mgcina	Preacher	Fana Kekana
Brothers		Mmes. Constantia, Retief, Swanepoel;	
Mosie	Seth Sibanda	Narrator	Maggie Soboil
Plank	Tsepo Mokone	Policeman; Pass Official;	
Jakkie	Fana Kekana	Mr. Green	Alex Wipf

Understudies: Miss Dumakude—Cheryl Bruce; Messrs. Sibanda, Mokone, Kekana, Maredi—Lowell Williams; Miss Soboil—Sara Gromley Plass; Mr. Wipf—Norman Marshall.

Directed by Hilary Blecher; scenery, John Ringbom; lighting, William Armstrong; costumes, Shura Cohen; consultants to the producer, Barney Simon, Hilary Blecher; "Wedding Song," Travelling Song," "Second Hymn" by Sophie Mgcina; traditional songs arranged by Sophie Mgcina; stage manager, Meyer Baron; press, Monina Von Opel, Jeffrey Richards Associates.

Time: 1949–1972. Place: South Africa. The play was presented in two parts.

True story (with the names changed) of the travails of a black woman working as a maid in South Africa. A foreign play previously produced off off Broadway at the Cubiculo and by the Music-Theater Group/Lenox Arts Center.

*The Negro Ensemble Company. Schedule of three programs. **Sons and Fathers of Sons** (29). By Ray Aranha. Opened January 28, 1983. (Closed February 20, 1983) **About Heaven and Earth** (24). Program of three one-act plays: *The Redeemer* by Douglas Turner Ward, *Nightline* by Julie Jensen and *Tigus* by Ali Wadad. Opened April 12, 1983. (Closed May 1, 1983) ***Manhattan Made Me** (17). By Gus Edwards. Opened May 17, 1983. Produced by The Negro Ensemble Company, Douglas Turner Ward artistic director, Leon B. Denmark managing director, at Theater Four.

SONS AND FATHERS OF SONS

Sister 2	Olivia Virgil Harper	Clyde; Reuben Johnson	Eugene Lee
Sister 1	Sarallen	Bubba; Bruce Mitchell	Robert Gossett
Sister 3	Ethel Ayler	Emmitt	Howard Baines
Vickie; Melanie	Phylicia Ayers-Allen	Fred T. Blachley; Johnny	Graham Brown

Directed by Walter Dallas; scenery, Wynn Thomas; costumes, Vicki Jones; lighting, William H. Grant III; sound, Gary Harris; costumes supervisor, Judy Dearing; production stage manager, Horacena J. Taylor; stage managers, Janice C. Lane, Edward De Shae; press, Howard Atlee, Barbara Atlee.

Time and Place: Around 1943 in a rural Southern town in Mississippi; around 1953 in the same rural town; around 1960 in an all-black university in Tallahassee, Fla. The play was presented in two parts.

A student, a professor and a sharecropper's son in three time frames.

ABOUT HEAVEN AND EARTH

The Redeemer		Feminist	Kathleen Forbes
Black Woman	L. Scott Caldwell	Black Man	Eugene Lee
White Revolutionary	David Davies	Old Lady	Naomi Riseman

Rabbi .... Curt Williams
Comedy, a motley group awaits the Second
Coming on Judgment Day. Previously produced
at Actors Theater of Louisville.

Nightline
Raimy................... L. Scott Caldwell
Ogilvy...................... Eugene Lee
Sarah................... Naomi Riseman

Driver..................... Curt Williams
Passengers journey through the night on a
Greyhound bus.

Tigus
Tigus............... Douglas Turner Ward
A man's monologue about his women and his
barroom friends.

BOTH PLAYS: Directed by Douglas Turner Ward; production stage manager, Femi Sarah
Heggie.

MANHATTAN MADE ME

Barry Anderson............... Eugene Lee
Claire McKenzie.......... Kathleen Forbes

Duncan................... Robert Gossett
Alan McKenzie.............. David Davies

Directed by Douglas Turner Ward; scenery and costumes, Felix E. Cochren; lighting, Sylvester N.
Weaver Jr.; sound, Bernard Hall; stage managers, Ed De Shae, Jessie Wooden Jr.
Blacks and whites living together in the Big Apple while looking for employment as actors.

*Quartermaine's Terms (111). By Simon Gray. Produced by John A. McQuiggan and
Ethel Watt in association with Brent Peek Productions in the Long Wharf Theater
production at Playhouse 91. Opened February 24, 1983.

St. John Quartermaine ...... Remak Ramsay
Anita Manchip .... Caroline Lagerfelt
Mark Sackling........... Kelsey Grammer
Eddie Loomis................. Roy Poole

Derek Meadle .... Anthony Heald
Henry Windscape .... John Cunningham
Melanie Garth................. Dana Ivey

Directed by Kenneth Frankel; scenery, David Jenkins; costumes, Bill Walker; lighting, Pat
Collins; stage manager, George Darveris; press, Betty Lee Hunt, Maria Cristina Pucci, James
Sapp, Maurice Turet.
Time: A period of three years during the early 1960s. Place: the staff room of the Cull-Loomis
School of English for Foreigners, Cambridge, England. Act I, Scene 1: Springtime, Monday, 9:30 in
the morning. Scene 2: Some weeks later, Friday afternoon, a few minutes before 5. Act II, Scene 1:
The following year, towards summer; Monday morning, about 9:30. Scene 2: A Friday evening, some
months later. Scene 3: Eighteen months later, around Christmas, evening.
The increasing loneliness and isolation of one individual within a close-knit faculty group. A foreign
play previously produced in London and at the Long Wharf Theater, New Haven, Conn.
A Best Play; see page 229.

Goodnight, Grandpa (6). By Walter Landau. Produced by Walin Productions in association with Arthur Albert at the Entermedia Theater. Opened March 2, 1983. (Closed
March 6, 1983)

Directed by Jay Broad; scenery, David Potts; costumes, Robert Wojewodski; lighting, Todd Elmer;
associate producer, Paul B. Berkowsky; production stage manager, William Hare; press, Jeffrey
Richards Associates, C. George Willard. With Lorry Goldman, Laurie Heineman, Milton Berle, Lee
Wallace, Maxine Taylor-Morris, Martin Haber, Jean Barker, Estelle Kemler, P. Jay Sidney.
A centenarian (portrayed by Milton Berle) and his memories. Previously produced at PAF Play-
house, Huntington, L.I. and Syracuse, N.Y., Stage.

A Bundle of Nerves (33). Musical revue with music by Brian Lasser; lyrics by Geoff
Leon and Edward Dunn. Produced by Leonard Finger, Howard J. Burnett and Terry
Spiegel at the Top of the Gate. Opened March 13, 1983. (Closed April 10, 1983)

Gary Beach	Vicki Lewis
Carolyn Casanave	Karen Mason
Ray Gill	

Directed by Arthur Faria; choreography, Arthur Faria; musical director, Clay Fullum; scenery and lighting, Barry Arnold; costumes, David Toser; sound, Tom Morse; vocal arrangements and orchestrations, Steven Margoshes; stage manager, Joseph De Pauw; press, Henry Luhrman, Terry Lilly, Kevin P. McAnarney, Keith Sherman.

Satire on major neuroses of our time.

MUSICAL NUMBERS, ACT I: "A Bundle of Nerves"—Company; "The News"—Company; "I Eat"—Karen Mason; "She Smiled at Me"—Ray Gill; "Boogey Man"—Carolyn Casanave, Mason, Vicki Lewis; "Flying"—Gary Beach; "Old Enough to Know Better"—Casanave, Lewis; "Studs"—Beach, Gill; "What's That?"—Casanave; "I Don't Know How to Have Sex"—Company.

ACT II: "The Fatality Hop"—Company; "Waiting"—Company; "After Dinner Drinks"—Casanave, Beach; "Slice of Life"—Lewis, Gill; "What Do You Do"—Karen; "Connie"—Gill, Casanave, Mason, Lewis; "I'm Afraid"—Company; "That Sound"—Company; "A Bundle of Nerves" (Reprise) —Company.

*The Middle Ages (78). By A.R. Gurney Jr. Produced by Alison Clarkson, Stephen Graham, Joan Stein and The Shubert Organization at the Theater at St. Peter's Church. Opened March 23, 1983.

Barney	Jack Gilpin	Charles	Andre Gregory
Eleanor	Ann McDonough	Myra	Jo Henderson

Standby: Miss McDonough—Connie Coit.

Directed by David Trainer; scenery, John Lee Beatty; costumes, David Murin; lighting, Frances Aronson; sound, Paul Garrity; production stage manager, M.A. Howard; press, David Powers.

Time: The mid-1940s to the late 1970s. Place: The trophy room of a men's club in a large city. Comedy, the emotional and social crises within a WASP family over a span of four decades.

It's Better With a Band (47). Musical revue with music by Wally Harper, Doug Katsaros, Rob LaRocco, Alan Menken, Jimmy Roberts, Jonathan Sheffer, Bryon Sommers and Pamala Stanley; lyrics by David Zippel. Presented by The Better Company, Roger Alan Gindi executive producer, at The Club Room at Sardi's. Opened March 28, 1983. (Closed April 30, 1983)

Scott Bakula	Nancy LaMott
Catherine Cox	Jenifer Lewis

Directed by Joseph Leonardo; musical direction, Rob LaRocco; scenery, Michael J. Hotopp, Paul de Pass; costumes, Cinthia Waas; lighting, John Hastings; associate producer, Joseph Hartney; production stage manager, Perry Cline; stage manager, Trey Hunt; press, Francine L. Trevens, Penny M. Landau, Amy Carr, Elaine Campbell.

Topical revue presented at the famous theatrical restaurant on West 44th Street. The show was presented without intermission.

MUSICAL NUMBERS: "It's Better With a Band" (music by Wally Harper)—Company; "The Camel Song" (music by Doug Katsaros)—Jenifer Lewis; "You'll Never See Me Run" (music by Alan Menken)—Scott Bakula; "Loud Is Good" (music by Jonathan Sheffer)—Nancy LaMott; "The Ingenue" (music by Wally Harper)—Catherine Cox; "What I Like Is You" (music by Pamala Stanley) —Cox, LaMott; "God's Gift" (music by Rob LaRocco)—Bakula; "Why Don't We Run Away" (music by Bryon Sommers)—LaMott; "Make Me a Star/Movie Queen" (music by Bryon Summers and Pamala Stanley)—Lewis, Company.

Also "Lullaby" (music by Doug Katsaros from *Just So*)—Bakula; "I Can't Remember Living Without Loving You" (music by Wally Harper)—Cox; "Horsin' Around" (music by Jimmy Roberts) —LaMott; "Forget It" (music by Ron LaRocco)—Cox, LaMott; "I Reach for a Star" (music by

Jonathan Sheffer from *Going Hollywood*)—Bakula; "Time on Our Side" (music by Bryon Sommers) —Lewis; "Life's Ambition" (music by Wally Harper)—Cox; "Another Mr. Right" (music by Jonathan Sheffer from *Going Hollywood*)—LaMott; "A Song for Myself" (music by Pamala Stanley)— Company

The Other Side of the Swamp (62). By Royce Ryton. Produced by William Alan at the Actors' Playhouse. Opened March 31, 1983. (Closed May 22, 1983)

Terence Jenkins . . . . Alexander Wilson
Leslie Brown . . . . David Schmitt

Directed by Lawrence Hardy; scenery, Jan S. Utstein; costumes, George Potts; lighting, Bruce Kahle; production stage manager, Charles Y. Doyle; press, Francine L. Trevens, T. David Dobris.

Place: The sitting room of Terry's flat in Kensington, London. Act I, Scene 1: Evening, Winter, 1977. Scene 2: Afternoon, the same year. Scene 3: Evening, a few days later. Scene 4: Morning, two years later. Scene 5: Afternoon, a few weeks later. Act II, Scene 1: Mid-morning, a few days later. Scene 2: Early morning, several weeks later. Scene 3: Mid-morning, two years later. Scene 4: Midnight, a few weeks later.

Love affair between homosexuals. A foreign play previously produced in London.

The Acting Company. Repertory of three revivals. **Pericles, Prince of Tyre** (8). By William Shakespeare. Opened April 19, 1983. (Closed April 24, 1983) **Tartuffe** (4). By Molière; English verse translation by Richard Wilbur. Opened April 26, 1983. (Closed April 28, 1983) **Play and Other Plays** (4). Program of one-act plays by Samuel Beckett: *Play*, *Krapp's Last Tape* and *Come and Go*. Opened April 29, 1983. (Closed May 1, 1983) Produced by The Acting Company, John Houseman producing artistic director, Margot Harley executive producer, Muriel Kahn and Alan Schneider artistic directors, at the American Place Theater.

ALL PLAYS: Production stage manager, Giles F. Colahan; stage manager, Michael S. Mantel; press, Fred Nathan and Associates, Anne S. Abrams, Eileen McMahon, Leo Stern, Bert Fink.

PERICLES, PRINCE OF TYRE

Gower . . . . J. Andrew McGrath
Antiochus; Bawd . . . . David Manis
Pericles . . . . Tom Hewitt
Thaliard; Leonine . . . . Michael Manuelian
Helicanus; Lychorida; Diana . . Libby Colahan
Cleon . . . . John Stehlin
Dionyza; Boult . . . . Margaret Reed

1st Fisherman; Pandar . . . . Jack Kenny
2d Fisherman; Lysimachus . . David O. Harum
3d Fisherman; Philemon;
  Philoten . . . . Ray Virta
Simonides . . . . Richard S. Iglewski
Thaisa; Marina . . . . Ronna Kress
Cerimon . . . . Philip Goodwin

Lords, Knights, Gentlemen, Messengers, Sailors, Whores: Libby Colahan, Philip Goodwin, J. Andrew McGrath, Jack Kenny, Ray Virta, David Manis, Michael Manuelian, John Stehlin, Richard S. Iglewski, Margaret Reed, David O. Harum.

Understudies: Mr. Hewitt—David Manis; Mr. McGrath—Michael Manuelian; Mr. Manis—Philip Goodwin; Messrs. Stehlin, Iglewski—Ray Virta; Messrs. Goodwin, Kenny—Morton Milder; Misses Kress, Reed, Colahan—Lynn Chausow, Libby Colahan.

Directed by Toby Robertson; scenery, Franco Colavecchia; costumes, Judith Dolan; lighting, Dennis Parichy; musical direction, Jim Cummings; music composition, Carl Davis, Jim Cummings; choreography, Devorah Fong; associate director, Morton Milder.

Time: The present. Place: The Mediterranean seaboard. The play was presented in two parts.

Pericles as theater of the absurd, set in a modern madhouse. Its last major New York production was by New York Shakespeare Festival in Central Park 6/20/74 for 24 performances.

TARTUFFE

Mme. Pernell	Libby Colahan	Tartuffe	Philip Goodwin
Orgon	Richard S. Iglewski	Dorine	Lynn Chausow
Elmire	Megan Gallagher	M. Loyal	Jack Kenny
Damis	John Stehlin	Police Officer	Michael Manuelian
Mariane	Margaret Reed	Flipote	Ronna Kress
Valere	Ray Virta	Laurent	David O. Harum
Cleante	J. Andrew McGrath	Servant	David Manis

Understudies: Misses Reed, Colahan—Ronna Kress; Messrs. Iglewski, Virta—David O. Harum; Miss Gallagher—Margaret Reed; Miss Chausow—Libby Colahan; Messrs. Stehlin, Kenny, Manuelian—Tom Hewitt; Mr. McGrath—David Manis; Mr. Goodwin—J. Andrew McGrath; Mr. Manis—Morton Milder.

Directed by Brian Murray; scenery, Michael Yeargan; costumes, Jane Greenwood; lighting, Gregory C. McPherson; composer and musical director, Catherine MacDonald.

The last major New York revival of *Tartuffe* was by Circle in the Square on Broadway in this translation 9/6/77 for 88 performances.

PLAY AND OTHER PLAYS

Play

W1	Libby Colahan
M	Jack Kenny
W2	Megan Gallagher

Understudies: Miss Colahan—Ronna Kress; Mr. Kenny—Morton Milder; Miss Gallagher—Margaret Reed.

The last major New York revival of *Play* took place on a program also entitled *Play and Other Plays*, also under Alan Schneider's direction, at Manhattan Theater Club 12/14/77 for 35 performances.

Krapp's Last Tape

Krapp . . . . Richard S. Iglewski
    Understudy: Mr. Iglewski—Philip Goodwin.

Time: A late evening in the future. Place: Krapp's den

The last major New York revival of *Krapp's Last Tape* took place off Broadway 11/22/72 for 15 performances.

Come and Go

Flo	Margaret Reed
Vi	Libby Colahan
Ru	Megan Gallagher

Understudy: Misses Reed, Colahan, Gallagher—Ronna Kress.

Come and Go—written in English in 1965 and first presented in 1966 in German in Berlin at the Schiller Theater—was last revived off off Broadway in November 1976.

Directed by Alan Schneider; scenery, Mark Fitzgibbons; costumes, John David Ridge; lighting, Dennis Parichy.

Note: The Acting Company also produced a revival of *The Cradle Will Rock* this season, with a cast composed of Acting Company alumni. It is separately listed in this section of this volume.

*Win/Lose/Draw (42). Program of three one-act plays: *Little Miss Fresno* by Ara Watson and Mary Gallagher, *Final Placement* by Ara Watson and *Chocolate Cake* by Mary Gallagher. Produced by Rosita Sarnoff, Anne Wilder, Joseph L. Butt and Doug Cole at the Provincetown Playhouse. Opened April 24, 1983.

Little Miss Fresno

Ginger Khabacki	Christine Estabrook
Doris Nettles	Lynn Milgrim

Place: A fairground, Fresno, Calif. Two mothers compare their daughters during a beauty contest.

Final Placement

Mary Hanson	Lynn Milgrim
Luellen James	Christine Estabrook

Place: A child welfare office, Tulsa, Okla. A

social worker's handling of a child-abuse case. Commissioned and first produced by Actors Theater of Louisville.

Chocolate Cake

Annmarie Fitzer	Christine Estabrook
Delia Baron	Lynn Milgrim

Place: A motel room, Western Mass. A pair of dieters trying to resist temptation. Commissioned and first produced by Actors Theater of Louisville.

WIN/LOSE/DRAW—Christine Estabrook and Lynn Milgrim
in the *Little Miss Fresno* segment of the one-acter program

Understudies: Jeanne Michaels, Jeanne Cullen.
Directed by Amy Saltz; scenery, Louis Nelson; costumes, Ruth Morley; lighting, David F. Segal; sound, Bob Kerzman; associate producers, Joseph K. Fisher, Betsy Rosenfield; stage manager, Peter Weicker; press, Shirley Herz, Peter Cromarty.

*Wild Life (33). Program of one-act plays by Shel Silverstein: *I'm Good to My Doggies*, *Chicken Suit Optional* and *The Lady or the Tiger Show*. Produced by Stevie Phillips in association with Universal Pictures at the Vandam Theater. Opened May 2, 1983.

I'm Good to My Doggies
Louis Benjamin Hinkle... Henderson Forsythe
Arthur Pitler .... W.H. Macy
  Place: A bad street in a bad neighborhood. A blind man searches for a Seeing Eye dog.

Chicken Suit Optional
Martin .... James Cahill
Thomas.................. Moultrie Patten
  Place: The bathroom of the Yale Club. Two men obsessed with conformity.

The Lady or the Tiger Show
Elliot Cushman .... Christopher Murney

Tucker Pym.............. Howard Sherman
Kenny Crane.............. Conard Fowkes
Bishop Cooley .... Henderson Forsythe
Lavinia Tremaine .... Jody Gelb
Florence Haskins............. Julie Hagerty
Lamar Darfield .... Raynor Scheine
  Understudy: Miss Hagerty—Jody Gelb.
  Time: The present. Place: Elliot Cushman's office underneath the Houston Astrodome. The Lady-Tiger drama played as a modern spectacle complete with TV coverage. Previously produced off off Broadway by Ensemble Studio Theater.

Directed by Art Wolff; scenery, Marjorie Bradley Kellogg; costumes, Franne Lee; lighting, Arden Fingerhut; sound, Bruce Ellman; associate producer, Bonnie Champion; production stage manager, David S. Felder; press, Jeffrey Richards Associates, C. George Willard, Ben Morse.

*My Astonishing Self (33). Revival of the one-man performance devised by Michael Voysey from the writings of George Bernard Shaw. Produced by Howard J. Burnett and Morton Wolkowitz at the Players Theater. Opened May 3, 1983.

George Bernard Shaw .... Donal Donnelly

Scenery and lighting, Victor Capecce; lighting associate, Andrea Wilson; production stage manager, Larry Bussard; press, Henry Luhrman Associates, Terry M. Lilly, Kevin McAnarney, Keith Sherman.
  Portrait of Shaw assembled from his own writings. The play was presented in two parts. Originally produced off Broadway 1/18/78 for 48 performances.

The Cradle Will Rock (24). Revival of the musical by Marc Blitzstein. Produced by the Acting Company at the American Place Theater. Opened May 9, 1983. (Closed May 29, 1983)

Moll; Sister Mister .... Patti LuPone
Gent; Editor Daily .... Tom Robbins
Dick; Junior Mister........... Henry Stram
Cop; Gus Polock.............. Casey Biggs
Rev. Salvation; Prof. Trixie .... James Harper
Yasha .... Gerald Gutierrez
Dauber; Larry Foreman....... Randle Mell
Pres. Prexy................. Paul Walker
Prof. Mamie; Harry Druggist ... Brian Reddy

Dr. Specialist; Bugs... Charles Shaw-Robinson
Clerk.................... Michael Barrett
Mrs. Mister .... Mary Lou Rosato
Mr. Mister .... David Schramm
Steve; Prof. Scoot;
  Reporter #1............. Daniel Corcoran
Sadie Polock; Reporter #3 ..... Laura Hicks
Ella Hammer....... Michele-Denise Woods
Reporter #2 .... Susan Rosenstock

Musicians: Jayne Hill trumpet, Susan Owens piccolo, Larry Spivack percussion.
Understudies: Miss LuPone—Michele-Denise Woods, Laura Hicks; Mr. Robbins—Gerald Gutierrez; Mr. Stram—Randle Mell; Mr. Harper—Tom Robbins, Casey Biggs; Messrs. Schramm,

Gutierrez, Corcoran—Paul Walker; Mr. Walker—Charles Shaw-Robinson; Mr. Reddy—Henry Stram; Mr. Shaw-Robinson—Brian Reddy; Mr. Barrett—Charles Berigan; Misses Rosato, Woods—Susan Rosenstock; Mr. Stram—Daniel Corcoran; Mr. Mell—James Harper.

Directed by John Houseman; musical direction, Michael Barrett; produced by Margot Harley; scenery, Mark Fitzgibbons; costumes, Judith Dolan; lighting, Dennis Parichy; stage managers, Don Judge, Kathleen B. Boyette; press, Fred Nathan Associates, Anne S. Abrams.

Time: The night of a union drive. Place: Steeltown, U.S.A. Scene 1: Streetcorner. Scene 2. Night court. Scene 3: Mission. Scene 4: Lawn of Mr. Mister's home. Scene 5: Drugstore. Scene 6: Hotel lobby. Scene 7: Night court. Scene 8: Faculty room. Scene 9: Dr. Specialist's office. Scene 10: Night court. The play was presented in two parts, with the intermission following Scene 6.

This production, produced by the Acting Company, was cast with its alumni in a limited engagement (the company's current repertory is listed elsewhere in this section of this volume). *The Cradle Will Rock* was originally produced by the Mercury Theater 1/3/38 for 108 performances and has been revived several times, the most recent one having taken place off Broadway 11/8/64 for 82 performances.

*Out of the Night (24). Adapted by Eric Krebs from a book by Jan Valtin. Produced by George Street Playhouse at the Douglas Fairbanks Theater. Opened May 11, 1983.

CAST: Robertson Carricart, Gary Armagnac, Luke Sickle, Giulia Pagano, Douglas Werner.

Directed by Eric Krebs; costumes, Linda Reynolds; lighting, Daniel Stratman; sound, Peter Kalish; stage manager, Maureen Heffernan; press, Jeffrey Richards Associates.

A German-born Communist breaks with the party in the 1930s; based on his autobiography. The play was presented in two parts.

*Jacques Brel Is Alive and Well and Living in Paris (18). Revival of the musical conceived by Eric Blau and Mort Shuman; music by Jacques Brel, Francois Rauber, Gerard Jouannest and Jean Corti; English lyrics and additional material by Eric Blau and Mort Shuman; based on Jacques Brel's lyrics and commentary. Produced by Pat Productions in the Eric Blau production at the First City Theater. Opened May 15, 1983.

Leon Bibb	Joseph Neal
Margery Cohen	Jacqueline Reilly
J.T. Cromwell	Betty Rhodes

Directed by Eric Blau; scenery and costumes, Don Jensen; lighting and sound, Steve Helliker; director of production of First City, Art D'Lugoff; press, M.J. Boyer.

The 15th anniversary production of this revue, first produced off Broadway 1/22/68 for 1,847 performances and last revived on Broadway 2/19/81 for 21 performances.

The list of musical numbers in *Jacques Brel, etc.* appears on page 366 of *The Best Plays of 1980–81.*

*Jeeves Takes Charge (15). One-man show conceived, adapted and performed by Edward Duke; based on works of P.G. Wodehouse. Produced by Lawrence N. Dykun, Michael J. Needham and Robert L. Sachter at the Space at City Center. Opened May 17, 1983.

Directed by Gillian Lynne; scenery, Carl Toms; costumes, Una-Mary Parker; lighting Craig Miller; choreography, Susan Holderness; press, Judy Jacksina, Glenna Freedman.

Prologue: The Drones Club, 1925. Act I (*Jeeves Takes Charge;* place, Berkeley Mansions, London W.1.), Scene 1: *Jeeves Takes Charge* told by Bertie Wooster. Scene 2: *Bertie Changes His Mind* told by Jeeves. Act II (*Wooster in Wonderland*), Scene 1: Bertie's bedroom. Scene 2: A village tent.

Bertie Wooster, his gentleman's gentleman Jeeves and ten other Wodehouse characters, all portrayed by Edward Duke. A foreign play previously produced in London. The play was presented in two parts.

Welcome Home Jacko (16). By Mustapha Matura. Produced by Black Theater Cooperative at the Quaigh Theater. Opened May 17, 1983. (Closed May 29, 1983)

Fret........................ Gary Beadle   Sandy .... Maggie Shevlin
Dole .... Chris Tummings   Gail.................... Shope Shodeinde
Zippy .... Brian Bovell   Jacko................. Malcolm Frederick
Marcus .... Victor Romero Evans

Directed by Charlie Hanson; costumes, Gemma Jackson; stage managers, Melvyn Jones, Dennis Lieberson; press, Max Eisen.

Time: 1980. Place: A youth club in London.

Doings among Rastafarian members of a black youth club. A foreign play previously produced in London and in this production, brought to New York for a limited engagement, at Theater Royal, Stratford East.

PLAYS PRODUCED OFF OFF BROADWAY

AND ADDITIONAL PRODUCTIONS

Here is a comprehensive sampling of off-off-Broadway and other experimental or peripheral 1982–83 productions in New York, compiled by Camille Croce. There is no definitive "off-off-Broadway" area or qualification. To try to define or regiment it would be untrue to its fluid, exploratory purpose. The listing below of hundreds of works produced by more than 75 OOB groups and others is as inclusive as reliable sources will allow, however, and takes in all leading Manhattan-based, new-play-producing, English-language organizations.

The more active and established producing groups are identified in **bold face type,** in alphabetical order, with artistic policies and the name of the managing director(s) given whenever these are a matter of record. Each group's 1982–83 schedule is listed with play titles in CAPITAL LETTERS. Often these are works-in-progress with changing scripts, casts and directors, sometimes without an engagement of record (but an opening or early performance date is included when available).

Many of these off-off-Broadway groups have long since outgrown a merely experimental status and are offering programs which are the equal in professionalism and quality (and in some cases the superior) of anything in the New York theater, with special contractual arrangements like the showcase code, letters of agreement (allowing for longer runs and higher admission prices than usual) and, closer to the edge of the commercial theater, a so-called "mini-contract." In the list below, all available data on opening dates, performance numbers (with a plus sign + in the case of a show still running) and major production and acting credits (almost all of them Equity members) is included in the entries of these special-arrangement offerings.

A large selection of lesser-known groups and other shows that made appearances off off Broadway during the season appears under the "Miscellaneous" heading at the end of this listing.

Amas Repertory Theater. Dedicated to bringing all people regardless of race, creed, color or economic background, together through the creative arts. Rosetta LeNoire, founder and artistic director.

16 performances each

LOUISIANA SUMMER. Book, Robert and Bradley Wexler; music, Rocky Stone; lyrics, Robert Wexler. October 28, 1982. Director, Robert Stark; choreographer, Keith Rozie; musical director, Lea Richardson; scenery, Tom Barnes; lighting, Ronald L. McIntyre; costumes, Eiko Yamaguchi. With Garrick Lavon, Raymond Zipf, Steve Fickinger, Wendy Kimball, Lani Marrell, Tracy Heffernan, Kimberly Mucci, Sonia Bailey, Ann Talman.

MISS WATERS, TO YOU. Book, Loften Mitchell, based on a concept by Rosetta LeNoire; music from Miss Waters's repertoire. February 24, 1983. Director, Billie Allen; choreographer, Keith Rozie; musical director, Luther Henderson; scenery, Tom Barnes; lighting, Gregg Marriner;

411

AMERICAN PLACE THEATER—Caroline Kava as Susan B. Anthony
and Linda Hunt as Joan of Arc in Lavonne Mueller's *Little Victories*

costumes, Jeff Mazor. With Mary Louise, Jeff Bates, Denise Morgan, Keith David, Leon Summers, Jr., Stanley Ramsey, Yolanda Graves, Melodee Savage.

OPENING NIGHT. Book, music, and lyrics, Corliss Taylor-Dunn and Sandra Reaves-Phillips. April 21, 1983. Director, William Michael Maher; choreographer, Mabel Robinson; musical director, Grenoldo; scenery, Larry Fulton; lighting, Gregg Marriner; costumes, Judy Dearing. With Adjora F. McMillan, Avery Sommers, Dan Strayhorn, Bob McAndrew, Becky Woodley, Leslie Dockery, Adam Hart.

American Place Theater. In addition to the regular off-Broadway subscription season, cabaret and other special projects are presented. Wynn Handman, director, Julia Miles, associate director.

American Humorists Series

THE STAGE THAT WALKS (24). With Bruce D. Schwartz. September 21, 1982. Lighting, Christine Wopat.

SPEAKEASY: AN EVENING OUT WITH DOROTHY PARKER (28). Adapted and directed by Michael Feingold. December 28, 1982. Scenery and costumes, Brian Martin; lighting, Edward M. Greenberg. With Kit Flanagan, W.H. Macy.

The Women's Project

LITTLE VICTORIES (18). By Lavonne Mueller. January 26, 1983. Director, Bryna Wortman; scenery, William M. Barclay; lighting, Phil Monat; costumes, Mimi Maxmen; music, Clay Fullum. With Caroline Kava, Linda Hunt, Terrence Markovich, Bill Cwikowski, Jimmy Smits, John Griesemer, Randy Spence.

Circle Repertory Projects in Progress. Developmental programs for new plays. Marshall W. Mason, artistic director.

ROCK COUNTY by Bill Elverman. October 4, 1982. Directed by Bryna Wortman; with Peter Bergman, Patricia Wettig, Toni James, Helen Stenborg, John Dossett, William Severs, Michael Ayr.

THE PAPER BOY by Jonathan Feldman. October 25, 1982. Directed by Joan Micklin Silver; with John Dossett, Laura Hughes, Barbara Baxley, Jonathan Bolt, Stephanie Gordon, Jack Davidson, Jonathan Hogan.

OUT OF ORDER by Janet Neipris. November 15, 1982. Directed by Eve Merriam; with Jack Davidson, Willie Reale, Stephanie Gordon, Richard Seff.

IN PLACE by Corinne Jacker. January 17, 1983. Directed by John Henry Davis; with Mary Alice, Ken Kliban, Stephanie Gordon.

LEVITATION by Timothy Mason. February 7, 1983. Directed by B. Rodney Marriott; with Michael Higgins, Robert Joy, Bobo Lewis, Eric Schiff, Willie Reale, Stephanie Gordon, Helen Stenborg, Ed Seamon.

I WON'T BE HERE FOREVER by Milan Stitt. February 28, 1983. Directed by Austin Pendleton; with Helen Stenborg, Lisa Emery, Jo Henderson, Roger Chapman, Richard Seff, Brendan Murphy.

THE CHERRY ORCHARD PART II by Anthony Holland and William M. Hoffman. March 14, 1983. Directed by David Fitelson; with Kitty Muldoon, Terrence Markovich, Richard Seff, Trish Hawkins, Nancy Donohue, Jonathan Hogan, Ken Kliban, Jack Davidson, Ben Siegler, Stephanie Gordon.

FADED GLORY by Timothy Burns. May 21, 1983. Directed by Marshall W. Mason.

Ensemble Studio Theater. Nucleus of playwrights-in-residence dedicated to supporting individual theater artists and developing new works for the stage. Almost 300 projects each season, initiated by E.S.T. members. Curt Dempster, artistic director.

WELCOME TO THE MOON (13). By John Patrick Shanley. November 22, 1982. Director, Douglas Aibel; scenery, Evelyn Sakash; lighting, Mal Sturchio; costumes, Deborah Shaw; musical director, Barry Koron. With Robert Joy, John Henry Kurtz, Michael Albert Mantel, Anne O'Sullivan, James Ryan, June Stein.

THE MODERN LADIES OF GUANABACOA (30). By Eduardo Machado. January 19, 1983. Director, James Hammerstein; scenery and lighting, Bennet Averyt; costumes, Deborah Shaw; music, Rick Vartorella. With Tresa Hughes, Larry Bryggman, Ellen Barber, John Rothman, Stefano Loverso, Robert Hallak, Julie Garfield, Susan Merson, Jose Santana.

THE HOUSE OF RAMON IGLESIA (25). Jose Rivera. March 16, 1983. Director, Jack Gelber; scenery, Brian Martin; lighting, Cheryl Thacker; costumes, Deborah Shaw. With Robert Badillo, Norman Briski, Giancarlo Esposito, Ramon Franco, Lisa Maurer, Carla Pinza.

MARATHON 1983 (one-act play festival): TOUCH BLACK by Bill Bozzone, directed by Risa Bramon; THE DOLPHIN POSITION by Percy Granger, directed by Jack Gelber; THE SURVIVALIST by Robert Schenkkan, directed by Steven D. Abrezzi; POISONER OF THE

WELLS by Brother Jonathan, directed by James A. Simpson; POSTCARDS by Carol K. Mack, directed by Joan Micklin Silver; FIVE UNRELATED PIECES by David Mamet, directed by Curt Dempster; PASTORAL, OR RECOLLECTIONS OF COUNTRY LIFE by Peter Maloney, directed by John Schwab; EULOGY by James G. Richardson, directed by Heidi Helen Davis; CASH by Stuart Spencer, directed by Charles I. Karchmer; TENDER OFFER by Wendy Wasserstein, directed by Jerry Zaks; I LOVE YOU, I LOVE YOU NOT by Wendy Kesselman, directed by Julianne Boyd; DELUSIONS OF A GOVERNMENT WITNESS by Louis Lippa, directed by Pamela Berlin; FAST WOMEN by Willie Reale, directed by W.H. Macy; TWO HOT DOGS WITH EVERYTHING by William Wise, directed by Richard Russell Ramos. May 4–June 20, 1983.

Equity Library Theater. Actors' Equity sponsors a series of revivals each season as showcases for the work of actor-members and an "informal series" of original, unproduced material. George Wojtasik, managing director.

NOT NOW, DARLING by Ray Cooney and John Chapman. September 23, 1982. Directed by William Koch; with Robert Lydiard, Richard Portnow, Frederick Walters, Jane Culley, Rusty Riegelman, Marilyn Alex, Harry Bennett.

NEW FACES OF '52 (revue). October 28, 1982. Directed by Joseph Patton; with Randy Brenner, Suzanne Dawson, Jack Doyle, Michael Ehlers, Lillian Graff, Anna Marie Gutierrez, Philip Wm. McKinley, Roxann Parker, Michele Pigliavento, Alan Safier, Denise Schafer, Staci Swedeen, Michael Waldron.

WHO'LL SAVE THE PLOWBOY? by Frank D. Gilroy. December 2, 1982. Directed by Stephen Jarrett; with Hardy Rawls, Suzanne Toren, Michael Rothhaar, Emmett O'Sullivan-Moore, Martha Miller, Jon Mindell, Kirk Caliendo.

THE ROBBER BRIDEGROOM (musical) book and lyrics by Alfred Uhry, music by Robert Waldman; based on the novella by Eudora Welty. January 6, 1983. Directed by Richard Casper; with Stephen Crain, Libby Garten, Carolyn Marlow, Michael McCarty, Patrick Richwood.

HAPPY BIRTHDAY, WANDA JUNE by Kurt Vonnegut Jr. February 10, 1983. Directed by Elowyn Castle; with Joyce Cohen, Mark Ballou, Dale Place, James Mathers, David Adamson, Ward Asquith, Richard Voigts, Marcia Savella, Victoria Gabrielle Platt.

WHERE'S CHARLEY? (musical) book by George Abbott, music and lyrics by Frank Loesser; based on Brandon Thomas's *Charley's Aunt*. March 10, 1983. Directed by Dennis Grimaldi; with Charles Abbott, Austin Colyer, Virginia Seidel, Marin Mazzie, Don Moran, William McClary, Clayton Davis, Byron Conner.

THE CHANGELING by Thomas Middleton and William Rowley. April 14, 1983. Directed by Thomas Edward West; with Ken Costigan, Alan Brooks, Christopher Stafford Nelson, Lisa Bansavage, Myra Morris, Kim Ivan Motter, Jesse Caldwell.

PROMISES, PROMISES (musical) book by Neil Simon, music by Burt Bacharach, lyrics by Hal David; based on the screenplay *The Apartment* by Billy Wilder and I.A.L. Diamond. May 12, 1983. Directed by Alan Fox; with Gordon Lockwood, Lew Resseguie, Beth Leavel, C.J. Critt, Lorena Palacios, Larry Hirschhorn.

Informal Series: 3 performances each

TAKING IN THE GRAVE OUTDOORS: THE KESTREL, THE BIRDS and THE BEES (one-act plays) by Ted Enik. September 20, 1982. Directed by Kip Rosser; with Jeffrey Bingham, Terrence Markovich, Brian Rosnik, Jill Tomarken, Susan Blommaert.

MY EARLY YEARS by Charles Leipart. October 18, 1982. Directed by Pat McCorkle; with Alice Elliott, Tom Toner.

NOBODY'S PERFECT (musical) book by Ron Sproat, music by Earl Rose, lyrics by Frank Evans. November 22, 1982. Directed by J. Barry Lewis; with Doug McQueen, Peggy Stamper, Marilyn Pasekoff, James Harder, Joe S. Wyatt.

DREAMBOATS by Irene Wagner. December 13, 1982. Directed by Lise Liepmann; with Ken Rubenfeld, Avery Hart, Doug Popper, Paul Mantell, Dale Place, Davis Hall, Edwin Gur, David Carson.

LEAD US NOT INTO PENN STATION by Maura Swanson. January 17, 1983. Directed by Darlene Kaplan; with Alice Elizabeth Pearl, Jo Deodato Clark, Warren Keith.

LOOSE JOINTS (musical revue) by Jim Morgan. February 14, 1983. Directed by Bill Gile; with Sara Kreiger, Barbara Marineau, Diana Szlosberg, William Thomas Jr., Eric Weitz.

SHARING by James Van Maanen. March 14, 1983. Directed by Stuart Ross; with John Patrick Hurley, Gene Lindsey, Tom Gerard, David Wirth.

INDEPENDENT STUDY by Don Rifkin. April 25, 1983. Directed by Duane Sidden; with Brian Keeler, Neil Alexander, Elf Fairservis, Julia Murray.

MEDUSA IN THE SUBURBS by David Steven Rappoport and LE PETIT MORT by Stephen Essex (one-act plays). May 9, 1983. Directed by Julie Cesari; with Richard M. Tanner, Frances Ford, Anne Chapin, Lou Bonacki.

Gene Frankel Theater Workshop. Development of new works and revivals for the theater. Gene Frankel, artistic director.

UNEASY LIES (16). By Andrew Glaze. March 4, 1983. Director, Susann Brinkley; lighting, Bernadette Englert; costumes, Jeff Wolz. With Adriana Keathley, Lois Meredith.

Hudson Guild Theater. Presents plays in their New York, American, or world premieres. David Kerry Heefner, producing director, Daniel Swee, general manager.

HOOTERS by Ted Tally. October 13, 1982. Directed by David Kerry Heefner; with Griffin Dunne, Paul McCrane, Susan Greenhill, Polly Draper.

28 performances each

BREAKFAST WITH LES AND BESS. By Lee Kalcheim. November 23, 1982. Director, Barnet Kellman; scenery, Dean Tschetter; lighting, Ian Calderon; costumes, Timothy Dunleavy. With Holland Taylor, Keith Charles, Amy Wright, Tom Nolan, John Leonard, Daniel Ziskie.

BLOOD RELATIONS. By Sharon Pollock. February 2, 1983. Director, David Kerry Heefner; scenery, Ron Placzek; lighting, Paul Wonsek; costumes, Mariann Verheyen. With Kathleen Chalfant, Maurice Copeland, Marti Maraden, Gerald Quimby, Sloane Shelton, Adrian Sparks, Jennifer Sternberg.

SUS. By Barrie Keeffe. April 6, 1983. Director, Geoffrey Sherman; scenery and lighting, Paul Wonsek; costumes, Barbara Hladsky. With Terry Alexander, John Curless, David Leary.

INTAR. Innovative culture center for the Hispanic American community of New York City, focusing on the art of theater. Max Ferra, artistic director, Dennis Ferguson-Acosta, managing director.

EXILES (16). Musical by Ana Maria Simo; music, Elliot Sokolov, Louis Milgrom. December 9, 1982. Director, Maria Irene Fornes; scenery, Carlos Almada and Paulette Crowther; lighting, Edward M. Greenberg; costumes, Gabriel Berry. With Nicole Baptiste, Jose Febus, Maria Garcia, Anita Keal, Karen Ludwig, Jose Antonio Maldonado, Rebecca Schull.

UNION CITY THANKSGIVING (35). By Manuel Martin Jr. March 9, 1983. Director, Andre Ernotte; scenery, Michael Sharp; lighting, Rachel Budin; costumes, Karen Matthews. With Marge Aviles, Miriam Cruz, Emilio Del Pozo, Caren More, Diva Osorio, Marcelino Rivera, Nestor Serrano, Regina Suarez.

THE SENORITA FROM TACNA (40). By Mario Vargas Llosa. May 25, 1983. Director, Michael Kahn; scenery, Loren Sherman; lighting, Rachel Budin; costumes, Deborah Shaw. With Norman Briski, Emilio Del Pozo, Anthony Ferrer, Olga Merediz, Ruben Pla, Jaime Sanchez, Christina SanJuan, Susan Stevens, Maria Tucci.

Interart Theater. A professional environment primarily for women playwrights, directors, designers, and performers to participate in theatrical activity. Margot Lewitin, artistic director, Colette Brooks, associate artistic director.

LAMAMA ETC—Thomas Ikeda, Harris Yulin and Du Yee Chang in a scene from *Barnum's Last Life* by Richard Ploetz

MERCENARIES (50). By James Yoshimura. June 9, 1982. Director, Margot Lewitin; dramaturg, Colette Brooks; scenery, Kate Edmunds; lighting, Ann Wrightson; costumes, Kate Edmunds, Tom McAlister. With Reg E. Cathey, Andrew Davis, Kenneth Ryan, William Winkler, Roger Brown, Anna Deavere Smith, L.B. Williams, Jeffrey Joseph.

GROWING UP GOTHIC (12). By Claire Coss. January 6, 1983. Director, Margot Lewitin; scenery and costumes, Christina Weppner; lighting, Rachel Budin. With Joyce Aaron, George Bartenieff, Crystal Field, Chris Tanner.

FISH RIDING BIKES (60). By Claire Luckham. May 6, 1983. Director, Denise A. Gordon; dramaturg, Colette Brooks; scenery and costumes, Christina Weppner; lighting, David N. Weiss; music, Skip LaPlante. With Melissa Smith, Anita Keal, Rebecca Nelson, Anneke Gough, Anne Barclay, JoAnne Jacobson, Mary Van Dyke, Caris Corfman.

LaMama Experimental Theater Club (ETC). A busy workshop for experimental theater of all kinds. Ellen Stewart, founder, Wesley Jensby, artistic director.

Schedule included:

RED SNOW. Written and directed by Du Yee Chang. June 1, 1982.

OLYMPIC MAN MOVEMENT. By Els Joglars (Catalan Theater Group). June 15, 1982. Director, Albert Boadella; scenery, J.M. Ibanez; lighting, sound and electronic systems, Jordi Costa, J.M. Ibanez and Ramon de la Torre; costumes, J.M. Turrell; music, J.M. Avrizabalaga. With Jesus Agelet, Anna Barder, Jordi Cano, Alicia Escurriola, Jaume Sorribas, Jordi Martinez, Ingrid Riera.

MONEY: A JAZZ OPERA (fragments). By George Gruntz and Amiri Baraka; music, George Gruntz. July 2, 1982. Director, George Ferencz.

SPIEGELS. Created by Bart Stuyf Movement Group of the Netherlands. July 13, 1982.
THE LIBERATION OF SKOPJE. By Dusan Jovanovic. September 16, 1982. Director, Ljubisa Ristic; scenery, Dinka Jericevic; lighting, Damir Kruhak; costumes, Visnja Postic; music, Bread and Salt. With the Zagreb Theater Company (co-production with and performed outdoors at Cathedral of St. John the Divine).
ANNA INTO NIGHTLIGHT. Created and directed by Ping Chong. October 1, 1982. Scenery, Ping Chong, Deborah Cohen; lighting, Blu; costumes, Kim Druce; narrators, Roger Babb, Kay Hines; cinematographer and editor, David Gearey. With L. Smith, Wendelien Haveman, Betty Chong, John Fleming, Tobey Sanford, David Wolpe, Colette Berge.
THE THREE TRAVELS OF ALADDIN WITH THE MAGIC LAMP (chamber opera). Conceived, directed and designed by Francoise Grund; music, Elizabeth Swados. October 13, 1982. Scenery, Jun Maeda, Donald Eastman; lighting, Ann Militello; costumes, Aline Landais; special designs, Jun Maeda, Yoshihico Tanaka. With Larry Marshall, Michael Edward-Stevens, Endo Suanda, Youn Cho Park.
NAROPA. By Jean-Claude van Itallie. October 27, 1982. Directors, Ching Yeh, Michael Brody; music, Steve Gorn. With Zignal 1 Theater.
SEANCE. Written and directed by Cecile Guidote-Alvarez. November 6, 1982. Music, Lutgardo Labad. With PETAL (Philippine Educational Theater Arts League).
ANDREA'S GOT TWO BOYFRIENDS. Written and directed by David Willinger. November 24, 1982.
COME DOG, COME NIGHT. By Bernard-Marie Koltes, translated by Matthew Ward. December 7, 1982. Director, Francoise Kourilsky; scenery, Roberto Moscoso; lighting, Beverly Emmons. With Louis Zorich, Afemo, Barbara Eda-Young, Ron Frazier (co-production with Ubu Repertory Theater).
A PETICION DEL PUBLICO. By Franz Xaver Kroetz. December 26, 1982. Director, Elia Schneider; music, Juan Carlos Nunez. With Teatro Dramma.
AN EVENING, AN AFTERNOON. Book and lyrics, Tad Truesdale; music, J. Hamilton Grandison. January 1, 1983. Directed by and with Tad Truesdale.
THE TIBETAN BOOK OF THE DEAD, OR HOW NOT TO DO IT AGAIN. By Jean-Claude van Itallie. January 11, 1983. Director, Assurbanipal Babilla; music, Steve Gorn; scenery, Jun Maeda; lighting, Blu; costumes, Gabriel Berry. With Cristobal Carambo, Kevin O'Meara, Hooshang Touzie, Ching Valdes, Robinson Youngblood, Du Yee Chang, Susan Deihim.
FANTASIES OF PUSHKIN written and directed by Edward Staroselsky. January 19, 1983.
RESIDENT ALIEN. By Marianne Marcellin. January 27, 1983. Director, Katherine Adamov; scenery, Charlie Mangel; music, Guy Klucevsek. With Marianne Marcellin, Guy Klucevsek.
THE AMERICAN MYSTERIES. Written and directed by Matthew Maguire. February 3, 1983. Music, Glenn Branca, Vito Ricci, Clodagh Simonds; landscape designer, Elizabeth Diller.
LET'S START A MAGAZINE. Based on poems of e.e. cummings. February 16, 1983. With A Hard Werken Netherlands Association.
BURNING HEART. Written and directed by Roger Babb. March 3, 1983. Music, Neal Kirkwood. With the Otrabanda Company.
LIES AND SECRETS (collaborative chamber theater piece). By and with the Other Theater; music, Peter Golub. March 10, 1983. Director, Joseph Chaikin.
BARNUM'S LAST LIFE. By Richard Ploetz. April 1, 1983. Director, Paul Lazarus; scenery, Keith Gonzales; lighting, Rick Butler; costumes, Karen Hummel. With Harris Yulin, Brent Collins, Sharita Hunt, Daniel Leventritt, Paul LaGreca, Don Plumley, Thomas Ikeda, Du-Yee Chang.
HOT LUNCH APOSTLES. By Sidney Goldfarb. April 1, 1983. Director, Paul Zimet; music, Sybille Hayn, Ellen Maddow, Harry Mann. With The Talking Band.
PLAGUES FOR OUR TIME. Book and lyrics, Eve Merriam; music and directed by Tom O'Horgan. April 1, 1983. Scenery, Bill Stabile; costumes, Gabriel Berry.
I DIED YESTERDAY. By Nick Markovich. April 21, 1983. Director, Robert Speller.
GOODBYE GOODBYE. By Rina Yerushalmi, in collaboration with Jonathan Paul Brasuell, Amy Brentano, Stephen Grafenstine, Terry Knickerbocker, Kevin Kuhlke, Jessica Litwak, Wendy vanden Heuvel, and Jo L. Wadsworth. April 28, 1983. Music, Gerald Bushy; scenery, Hank Stevens; lighting, Manny Cavaco; costumes, Marie Ann Chiment. With Jonathan Paul

Brasuell, Amy Brentano, Stephen Grafenstine, Terry Knickerbocker, Kevin Kuhlke, Jessica Litwak, Wendy vanden Heuvel, Jo L. Wadsworth.

EMOTION (one-man show). By and with Min Tanaka. May 13, 1983.

TANGO GLACIALE. Conceived and directed by Mario Martone. May 17, 1983. Scenery, Mario Martone; design, Lino Fiorito; costumes, Ravelle; cartoons, Daniele Bigliardo. With Tomas Arana, Licia Maglietta, Andrea Renzi.

JADE. Written and directed by Mel Wong; music, Skip LaPlante. May 20, 1983.

CONJUR WOMAN. By Beatrice Manley-Blau. May 25, 1983. Director, George Ferencz.

IN THE BEGINNING . . . LUCIFER . . . THE BIBLE written and directed by Esteban Fernandez Sanchez. May 25, 1983.

Lion Theater Company. Actors' company with an eclectic repertory. Gene Nye, artistic director, David Craven, managing director.

MACBETH by William Shakespeare. April 22, 1983; in repertory with EDWARD II by Bertolt Brecht, English version by Eric Bentley. May 6, 1983. Directed by Gene Nye; with Maria Cellario, Giancarlo Esposito, Michael Golding, Robyn Hatcher, Robert Hock, Charles Johnson, Alice King, Casey Korda, James Lieb, Barry Malawer, Gene Nye, Albert Owens, Steve Pudenz, Chip Richman, Ennis Smith, Daniel Whitner, Ronald Willoughby, Nan Wray.

Manhattan Punch Line. Comedy theater. Steve Kaplan, Mitch McGuire, Jerry Heymann, Richard Erickson, producing directors.

20 performances each

IT'S ONLY A PLAY. By Terrence McNally. November 18, 1982. Director, Paul Benedict; scenery, Bob Phillips; lighting, Ruth Roberts; costumes, Judianna Makovsky. With Reg E. Cathey, Frances Cuka, Paul Guilfoyle, Ken Kliban, Jill Larson, Richard Leighton, Harriet Rogers, Michael Sacks.

WITHOUT WILLIE. By Barrie Cockburn. February 3, 1983. Director, Jerry Heymann; scenery, John Wright Stevens; lighting, Gregory MacPherson; costumes, Oleksa. With Lamis Beasley Faris, Joan Lorring, Loris Sallahian, John Milligan, David Khouri.

THE BUTTER AND EGG MAN by George S. Kaufman. December 16, 1982. Directed by Steve Kaplan; with Tom Costello, Mitch McGuire, Mary Boucher, Valerie Mahaffey, Louise Shaffer, Terry Layman, Neal Alan Lerner, James Hawthorne, Doug Baldwin, Therese Hanly, Kathryn King Segal, Kelly Connell, Robert McFarland.

COMEDIANS by Trevor Griffiths. April 14, 1983. Directed by Munson Hicks; with Tim Choate, Tom Costello, Joseph Daly, Arthur Erickson, Gladys Fleischman, Sam McMurray, Tony Noll, Alan North, Stefan Weyte.

Manhattan Theater Club. A producing organization with stages for fully-mounted off-Broadway productions, readings, workshop activities and cabaret. Lynne Meadow, artistic director, Barry Grove, managing director.

Special Event

DON'T START ME TALKIN' OR I'LL TELL EVERYTHING I KNOW (sayings from the life and writings of Junebug Jabbo Jones). By John O'Neal with Ron Castine and Glenda Lindsay. November 9, 1982. Director, Steven Kent. With John O'Neal.

MTC After Hours series (cabaret)

ABOUT FACE (10). Conceived, written and performed by Stephanie Cotsirilos. February 25, 1983. Musical director, Cheryl Hardwick.

A VAUDEVILLE (6). By Camille Saviola and Peter Dallas. March 10, 1983. Director, Peter Dallas; musical director, Marc Shaiman. With Camille Saviola.

NEW TUNES (6). Lyrics, Alan Mark Poul; music, Jonathan Sheffer. March 25, 1983. Director, Alan Mark Poul. With David-James Carroll, Terri Klausner.

New Dramatists. An organization devoted to playwrights; member writers may use the facilities for anything from private cold readings of their material to public script-in-hand readings. Casey Childs, program director.

Staged readings

ONLY CONNECT by Eric Anderson. October 4, 1982. Directed by Scott Rubsam; with James Strafford, Steven Keyes.

SIGNS OF LIFE by Joan Schenkar. November 3, 1982. Directed by Susan Gregg; with Barton Heyman, John Wylie, Ian Thomson, Deidre O'Connell, Gale Garnett, Sara Botsford.

MAGGIE MAGALITA by Wendy Kesselman. November 10, 1982. Directed by Carole Rothman; with Trini Alvarado, Alma Cuervo, Teresa Yenque, Bernie Telsey.

APRIL SNOW by Romulus Linney. December 1, 1982. Directed by M. Elizabeth Osborn; with Leon Russom, Kent Broadhurst, Nancy Franklin, Kent Thompson, Kari Jenson.

THE FULL CIRCLE OF THE TRAVELLING SQUIRREL by Robert Lord. December 8, 1982. Directed by Jack Hofsiss; with Mark Blum, Priscilla Lopez, Richard Cox, Kevin Bacon, Dorothy Lyman, Tom Cashin.

THE EDUCATION OF PAUL BUNYAN by Barbara Field. December 13, 1982. Directed by Robert Moss; with Keith McDermott, Chuck Allen, Michael Morin, Quincy Long, Christopher Wells, Greg Bostwick.

HIS MASTER'S VOICE by Dick D. Zigun. December 15, 1982. Directed by Susan Gregg; with Todd Stockman, Deidre O'Connell, William Preston, Michael Harres, Mary Ellinger.

EINSTEIN IN IXTLAN by Scott Christopher Wren. January 10, 1983. Directed by Scott Rubsam; with Kensyn Crouch, Natalie Strauss, Jean Barker, Ken Grantham, Bill McNulty, Eleanor Garth, Helen Jean Arthur, Dick D. Zigun.

CIVILIZATION & ITS MALCONTENTS and ARISTOTLE SAID (one-act plays) by Stanley Taikeff. January 19, 1983. Directed by Thomas Gruenewald; with Linda Selman, Nicholas Kepros, Socorro Santiago, Colgate Salsbury.

THE BATHERS by Victor Steinbach. February 2, 1983. Directed by Steven Robman; with Yusef Bulos, Paul Sparer, Fred Coffin, Philip Bosco.

KID PURPLE by Donald Wollner. February 16, 1983. Directed by Dallas Murphy Jr; with Royce Rich, Linda Selman, Loren Brown, Elaine Rinehart, Willie Carpenter, John McCurry.

CARRIE AND NELL by Tom Dunn. February 20, 1983. Directed by Susan Gregg; with Helen Jean Arthur, Joseph Warren, Anna Minot.

GYM RATS by Farrell J. Foreman. February 21, 1983. Directed by Gus Edwards; with Jim Doerr, Leonard Jackson, Charles Michael Brown, Ken Kliban, Alvin Alexis, Nick Smith.

WELCOME TO SODOM AND GOMORRAH by Daniel Du Plantis. February 22, 1983. Directed by Steve Carter; with Michael Morin, Graham Brown.

NO MORE SUMMERS by Brenda Faye Collie. February 23, 1983. Directed by Alma Becker; with Carl Gordon, Frances Foster, Mac Randall.

HIDDEN PARTS by Lynne Alvarez. March 2, 1983. Directed by Harvey Seifter; with Tom McDermott, Mary Alan Hokanson, Pamela Pascoe, Jerry Finnegan.

GYM RATS by Farrell J. Foreman. March 5, 1983. Directed by Casey Childs; with Jim Doerr, Bill Cobbs, Brent Jennings, Ken Kliban, Alvin Alexis, Nick Smith, Kent Gash.

PARTIAL OBJECTS by Sherry Kramer. March 16, 1983. Directed by Jim Milton; with Michael Morin, John Getz, Robin Karfo, Carlisle Stockton, Gretchen Van Ryper.

HOSS DRAWIN' and BILLY CHOPS BRICK by Leon Martell. March 21, 1983. Directed by Alma Becker; with Elizabeth Ruscio, Chuck Allen, Jack R. Marks, Preston Keith Smith, Leon Martell.

THE MUSEUM OF OLDE TYME LIFE by Warren Kliewer. March 24, 1983. Directed by Gideon Schein; with Lyn Tyrrell, Bob Horan, J. Smith Cameron.

TENEMENT by Gus Edwards. March 30, 1983. Directed by Bob Engels; with Robyn Hatcher, Rony Clanton, Dennis Tate, Marilyn Berry, Willie Carpenter, Thelma Louise Carter, Sharon Shambourger, Jason Fitz-Gerald.

OHIO TIP-OFF by James Yoshimura. April 13, 1983. Directed by Charles Edward Shain; with Tony Todd, Richard Brooks, Robert Frederick, Sturgis Warner, Allen Taylor, Joseph Wigfall, Daniel Barton, Peter Waldron.

CHOPIN IN SPACE by Philip Bosakowski. April 19, 1983. Directed by Robert Hall; with

Kenneth Kurtenbach, Stephanie Musnik, Michael Morin, Dolores Kenan, John P. Connolly, Corrine Mandell.

INFERNO by John Patrick Shanley. April 27, 1983. Directed by Susan Gregg.

FLIES IN THE BUTTERMILK by Steven Levi. May 11, 1983. Directed by Thomas Gruenewald.

BEYOND HERE ARE MONSTERS by James Nicholson. May 18, 1983. Directed by Gideon Schein.

JACINTA by Peter Dee. May 25, 1983. Directed by Susan Gregg.

New Federal Theater. The Henry Street Settlement's training and showcase unit for playwrights, mostly black and Puerto Rican. Woodie King Jr., producer.

LOVE (poems of Carolyn M. Rodgers) (12). Conceived and directed by Shauneille Perry. June 3, 1982. Scenery, Robert Edmonds; lighting, Sandra Ross; costumes, Judy Dearing. With Yvette Hawkins, Andrew Robinson Jr., Leone Thomas, Judy Dearing.

SHANGO DIASPORA by Angela Jackson, music by Eli Hoenai. July 9, 1982. Directed by Abena Joan Brown; with Leslie A. Benoit, Linda Bright, Soyini Dyson, Runako Jahi, Gwen Lester.

JAZZ SET (12). By Ron Milner. July 15, 1982. Director, Norman Riley; music, Max Roach; scenery, Robert Edmonds; lighting, Shirley Prendergast; costumes, Judy Dearing. With S. Epatha Merkerson, William Kennedy, E.L. James, Rony Clanton, Mansoor Najee-Ullah, Nick Smith.

PORTRAIT OF JENNIE (7). Adapted by Enid Futterman and Dennis Rosa from Robert Nathan's novel; music, Howard Marren; lyrics, Enid Futterman. December 10, 1982. Director and choreographer, Dennis Rosa; musical director, Uel Wade; scenery, Michael H. Yeargan; lighting, Jeff Davis; costumes, Charles Schoonmaker. With Donna Bullock, Stratton Walling, Brent Barrett, Paul Milikin, Maggie O'Connell, Karyn Lynn Dale, David Wohl, Brian Phipps, John Bedford-Lloyd.

THE UPPER DEPTHS (9). By David Steven Rappoport. December 3, 1982. Director, Robert Kalfin; scenery, Bob Edmonds; lighting, John Tomlinson; costumes, Judy Dearing. With Rikke Borge, Marilyn Chris, Meg Guttman, Elizabeth Longo, Bill Mooney, Steven Gary Simon. (Co-produced by Chelsea Theater Center.)

ADAM (12). Book, June Tansey; music and lyrics, Richard Ahlert. January 20, 1983. Director, Don Evans; choreography and musical staging, Dianne McIntyre; scenery, Llewellyn Harrison; lighting, Shirley Prendergast; costumes, Judy Dearing. With Reuben Green, Jackee Harry, Frederick Beals, Hugh Harrell III, Raymond Stough, Jim Keels, Bill Boss, Randy Flood, Rosetta Jefferson, S. Epatha Merkerson.

CHAMPEEN! (23). Book, music, lyrics, and director, Melvin Van Peebles. March 18, 1983. Choreographer, Louis Johnson; musical director, Bob Carten; scenery, Chris Thomas, Bob Edmonds; lighting, Shirley Prendergast; costumes, Quay Truitt. With Sandra Reaves-Phillips, Ruth Brown, David Connell, Lawrence Vincent, Ted Ross.

LIBERTY CALL (12). By Buriel Clay. March 31, 1983. Director, Samm-Art Williams; scenery and lighting, Llewellyn Harrison; costumes, Karen Perry. With Samm-Art Williams, Nick Smith, Michael Jameson, Dale Shields, Danyl Smith, Lilah Kan, Machiko Izawa, Constance Boardman, Khin-Kyaw Maung.

TRIO (program of three one-act plays) (12). By Bill Harris. April 28, 1983. Director, Nathan George; scenery, Llewellyn Harrison; lighting, Dewarren Moses; costumes, Vicki Jones. With Otis Young-Smith, Minnie Gentry, LeeRoy Giles, Myra Anderson, Ellis Williams, Barbara Smith, Obaka Adedunyo, S. Epatha Merkerson, Adetobi Akinloye.

THE WILDERNESS OF SHUR (12). By Nicholas Biel. May 5, 1983. Director Gordon Edelstein; scenery and lighting, Dale Jordan; costumes, Penny Howell; projections, Nora Jacobson. With Ron Foster, Reuben Schafer, Jon Krupp, Kelly Monaghan, Judy Tate, Rosemary Foley, Evan Thompson, David James Forsyth, William Walsh, Phillip Lindsay, Hubert B. Kelly Jr., Reg E. Cathey.

New York Shakespeare Festival Public Theater. Schedule of workshop productions and guest residencies, in addition to its regular productions. Joseph Papp, producer.

RUMBA (work-in-progress) by Leopoldo Fleming. June 28, 1982. Directed by Poli Rogers; with Elaine Beener, Lady Helena Walquer, Raul Ramos, Dean Badarou, Willie Barnes.

MEN INSIDE and VOICES OF AMERICA (solo pieces) (4). By and with Eric Bogosian. July 8, 1982. Lighting and sound, John Gibson. (Reopened September 9, 1982 for 9 performances.)

In Repertory:

WHAT EVERYWOMAN KNOWS (21). By Tulis McCall, in collaboration with Nancy-Elizabeth Kammer. August 10, 1982. Scenery, Jesse Rosenthal; lighting, Allen Lee Hughes; costumes, Elena Pellicciaro. With Tulis McCall.

UNCLE VANYA by Anton Chekhov, translated by Ann Dunnigan. Directed by Peter Von Berg; with Louise Campbell, Colin Garrey, James Maxon, Charles Duval, Nancy-Elizabeth Kammer, Joe Parisi, Anna Galiena, Muriel Mason, Michael Sullivan.

NECESSARY ENDS (20). By Marvin Cohen. December 12, 1982. Director, James Milton; scenery, Jim Clayburgh; lighting, John Gisondi; costumes, Amanda J. Klein; music, Robert Dennis. With Alma Cuervo, Larry Pine, Gretchen Van Ryper, Bill Sadler.

Mabou Mines Productions:

COMPANY (20). By Samuel Beckett. January 7, 1983. Directors, Honora Fergusson, Frederick Neumann; scenery, Gerald Marks; lighting, Craig Miller; music, Philip Glass. With Honora Fergusson, Frederick Neumann.

COLD HARBOR (63). Conceived and directed by Bill Raymond and Dale Worsley, text by Dale Worsley with excerpts from the memoirs of Ulysses S. Grant and Julia Dent Grant. February 22, 1983. Scenery, Linda Hartinian; lighting, B-St. John Schofield; costumes, Greg Mehrten; music, Philip Glass; projections, Stephanie Rudolph. With Bill Raymond, Greg Mehrten, B-St. John Schofield, Ellen McElduff, Terry O'Reilly.

HAJJ (22) (performance poem). Conceived in collaboration by Ruth Maleczech, performer; poem and direction, Lee Breuer; design, Julie Archer; music, Chris Abajian; video, Craig Jones. April 29, 1983.

GOODNIGHT LADIES! (21). By the Hesitate and Demonstrate Company. June 3, 1983. Lighting, Tom Donnellan; sound, John Darling. With Lizza Aiken, Alex Mavro, Andrzej Borkowski, Rick Fisher.

No Smoking Playhouse. Emphasis on new plays and adaptation of classics, stressing the comedic. Norman Thomas Marshall, artistic director.

DICK DETERRED (19). Books and lyrics, David Edgar; music, William Schimmel. January 13, 1983. Director, George Wolf Reily; choreographer, Mary Pat Henry; scenery, Ted Reinert and Beate Kessler; lighting, Leslie Ann Kilian; costumes, Marla Kaye. With Steve Pudenz, Malcolm Gray, Ted Reinert, Richard Litt, Mary Kay Dean, Carl Williams, Sylvester Rich, Elf Fairservis, Rhonda Rose.

JULIUS CAESAR by William Shakespeare. April 24, 1983. Directed by George Wolf Reily; with Adam Redfield, Darryl Croxton, Marc Krone, Ted Reinert, Caroline Meade, Mary Kay Dean, Sylvester Rich.

SHAKESPEARE MARATHON (fully-staged readings of 37 of William Shakespeare's plays). May 19–23, 1983.

The Open Space Theater Experiment. Emphasis on experimental works. Lynn Michaels, Harry Baum, directors.

THE TWO-CHARACTER PLAY by Tennessee Williams. October 16, 1982. Directed by Tom Brennan; with Austin Pendleton, Barbara Eda-Young.

IN THE COUNTRY (20). By Griselda Gambaro, adapted and translated by Francoise Kourilsky and Susana Meyer. April 6, 1983. Director, Francoise Kourilsky; scenery, Beth Kuhn;

OPEN SPACE THEATER EXPERIMENT—Douglass Watson, Leslie Lyles and Ken Chapin in *Upside Down on the Handlebars* by Leslie Weiner

lighting, Gregory MacPherson; costumes, Deborah Van Wetering; music, Michael Sirotta. With Colette Berge, James Eckhouse, Adam Le Fevre, Daniel Ziskie, Emmanuel Dom, Eric Hall, Tom Radigan.

UPSIDE DOWN ON THE HANDLEBARS (16). By Leslie Weiner. May 18, 1983. Director, Salem Ludwig; scenery, Bob Phillips; lighting, Richard Dorfman; costumes, Barbara Weiss. With Douglass Watson, Tom Amick, Ken Chapin, Robert Heller, Jacqueline Knapp, Leslie Lyles, Rick Weatherwax.

The Garret of the Open Space

THE CREATION OF THE WORLD AND ITS TRUE MEANING and PLAYING WITH FIRE (16). By August Strindberg, translated by Harry G. Carlson. November 18, 1982. Director, Susan Einhorn; scenery, Johnienne Papandreas; lighting, Ann Wrightson; costumes, Muriel Stockdale. With Bonnie Brewster, William Carden, Bernie Passeltiner, Lucille Patton, John Gould-Rubin, Keliher Walsh.

MIRANDOLINA by Carlo Goldoni. February 10, 1983. Adapted and directed by Jonathan Amacker; with Tom Vazzana, Patrick Skelton, Jonathan Epstein, Denise Assante, Jonathan Amacker.

THE RUFFIAN ON THE STAIR by Joe Orton. May 12, 1983. Directed by Rosemary Hay; with Rudi Caporaso, Laura Copland, Leon Russom.

Pan Asian Repertory Theater. Aims to present professional productions which employ Asian American theater artists, to encourage new plays which explore Asian American themes, and to combine traditional elements of Far Eastern theater with Western theatrical techniques. Tisa Chang, artistic director.

YELLOW FEVER (58). By R.A. Shiomi, story co-conceived by Marc Hayashi. December 1, 1982. Director, Raul Aranas; scenery, Christopher Stapleton; lighting, Dawn Chiang; costumes, Lillian Pan. With Donald Li, Carol A. Honda, James Jenner, Henry Yuk, Freda Foh Shen, Jeffrey Spolan, Ernest Abuba.

TEAHOUSE (22). By Lao She, translated by Ying Rocheng and John Howard-Gibbon. March 17, 1983. Director, Tisa Chang; scenery, Atsushi Moriyasu; lighting, Victor En Yu Tan; costumes, Eiko Yamaguchi. With Henry Yuk, Ernest Abuba, Tom Matsusaka, Alvin Lum, Michael G. Chin, Donald Li, Mel D. Gionson, Natsuko Ohama, Lynette Chun, Ron Nakahara, Toshi Toda, William Hao.

A MIDSUMMER NIGHT'S DREAM by William Shakespeare, Chinese translation by Liang Shi Chiu. April 15, 1983. Directed by Tisa Chang; with Jodi Long, Lu Yu, Yung Yung Tsuai, Ron Nakahara, Tina Chen, Elizabeth Sung.

Playwrights Horizons. Dedicated to the development of American playwrights, composers and lyricists through the production of their work in readings, workshops and full-scale productions. Andre Bishop, artistic director.

THE RISE AND RISE OF DANIEL ROCKET (32). By Peter Parnell. November 17, 1982. Director, Gerald Gutierrez; scenery, Andrew Jackness; lighting, James F. Ingalls; costumes, Ann Emonts; incidental music, Robert Waldman. With Thomas Hulce, Jack Gilpin, Ann McDonough, James Eckhouse, Shelley Rogers, Tom Robbins, Scott Waara, Kathryn C. Sparer, Jane Jones, Jane Connell.

THE TRANSFIGURATION OF BENNO BLIMPIE written and directed by Albert Innaurato. March 9, 1983. With Peter Evans, Clement Fowler, Natalija Nogulich, Jane Hickey, Jay Thomas.

Puerto Rican Travelling Theater. Professional company presenting bilingual productions primarily of Puerto Rican and Hispanic playwrights, emphasizing subjects of relevance today. Miriam Colón Edgar, founder and producer.

THE STORY OF DON CRISTOBAL and THE LOVE OF DON PERLIMPLIN AND BELISA IN THE GARDEN by Federico Garcia Lorca. August 6, 1982. Directed by Victoria Espinosa; with Brenda Feliciano, Tony Diaz, Carlos Augusto Cestero, Norberto Kerner, Ricardo Matamoros, Ilka Tanya Payan, Iraida Polanco, Noemi Figueroa, Wilson Florenciani.

INQUISITION (12 +). By Fernando Arrabal, translated by Gregory Rabassa. January 26, 1983. Director, Fernando Arrabal; scenery, Reagan Cook; lighting, John Tissot; costumes, Nancy Thun. With Ilka Tanya Payan, Hugo Halbrich, George Bass.

THE GREAT CONFESSION (12 +). By Sergio De Cecco and Armando Chulak, translated by Pilar Zalamea. March 9, 1983. Director, Max Ferrá; scenery, Loren Sherman; lighting, Gary D. Cooper; costumes, Deborah Shaw. With Lillian Hurst, Jose Maldonado, Carlos Cestero, Norberto Kerner, Michael Lazarus.

THE OXCART (LA CARRETA) (18 +). By René Marqués, translated by Dr. Charles Pilditch. April 20, 1983. Director, Roberto Rodríguez Suárez; scenery, Reagan Cook; lighting, Jeffrey Schissler; costumes, Maria Contessa. With Nina Polan, Carmen Maya, Laura Figueroa, George Bass, Freddy Valle, Margarita Morales, Iraida Polanco, Maria Garcia, Victor Gil de Lamadrid, Aixa Clemente, R. Sebastian Russ.

Quaigh Theater. Primarily a playwrights' theater, devoted to the new playwright, the established contemporary playwright and the modern (post-1920) playwright. Will Lieberson, artistic director.

BIRDBATH (7). Opera by Kenneth Lieberson, based on Leonard Melfi's play. August 1, 1982. Director, John Margulis. With Marthe Ihde, Michael Kutner.

THE CLOSED DOOR (20). By Graham Reid. October 23, 1982. Director, Dennis Lieberson; scenery and lighting, Linda Tate. With Michael O'Sullivan, Sarah Venable, Noel Lawlor, Ron Berliner, Tom Sminkey, James Pyduck, Sally Parrish, Jack Poggi, Naomi Riseman.

THE VENTRILOQUIST (18). Book, Steven Otfinoski; music and lyrics, Eddie Garson. April 19, 1983. Director, Will Lieberson; choreography, Dan Walsh; musical director, Rick Lewis; scenery, Bob Phillips; lighting, John C. Merriman; costumes, Mary Ellen Bosché. With Barbara Nicoll, Barbara Mappus, Herbert Rubens, Michele Franks, Russell Ochocki, Eric Kornfeld, Annie Heller, Frank Anderson, Scott Bylund, Eddie Garson.

DRAMATHON '82 (one-act plays in marathon). Schedule included: ST. MARK'S PLACE (musical) book by Ira Rosenstein, music and lyrics by Hilary Schmidt, directed by Kathy Popper; ESCOFFIER: KING OF CHEFS written and performed by Owen S. Rackleff, directed by Laurence Carr; THE GOOD LIFE by Jack McCleland, directed by Tony DeNonno; SEPTEMBER SONG by Nicky Silver, directed by Ezra Litwok; STRATAGEM adapted and directed by Don Durant from the Belvue Ensemble's Pawns; ELEANOR by John Cameron, directed by Joe Rettura; REGENCY ROMANCE by Geralyn Horton, directed by Leslie Hoban Blake; HAVE YOU SEEN SEAN? by Kit Jones, directed by Eleanor Johnson; UNVEILINGS by P.J. Gibson, directed by Bette Howard; STEVE AND STEVE by Charles LaTourette, directed by J.B. Nader; LIFE BENEATH THE ROSES by Gene Franklin Smith, directed by Richard Beck-Meyer; PORPOISE by Sharyn Cooper and Rene Savitt, directed by Rene Savitt; HADES FOR SOME IS THE RED DOG SALOON by Jane F. Bonin, directed by Will Lieberson; LUNACY by Gayle Marriner, directed by Wick O'Brien; OLD GRAND-DAD by Christine Child, directed by Robyn Lyn Smith; GREAT MOMENTS FROM THE GOOD BOOK by Steven Otfinoski, directed by Chuck Noell; THE ONION AND THE STRAWBERRY SEED by Edna Schappert, directed by Alice Kellman; A LADY NEEDS PROTECTION by Edward Eriksson, directed by Terence Cartwright; AUTOEROTIC MISADVENTURE by F.J. Hartland, directed by Peter Gordon; THE HOOKER AND THE JOHN by Richard Vetere, directed by Joe Rettura; THE FEEBLE HUSBAND by Clayton J. Delery, directed by Bill Condee; APRES MIDI by Donald Kvares, directed by Ted Mormel; DIN DIN WITH FRAN & TED by Olga Humphries, directed by Lester Malizia; THE MAN FROM PORLOCK by Jack A. Kaplan, directed by Cecelia Critchley; DAY OF THE RACES by Julie Jensen, directed by Diane Busch; THE SEVENTH DAY by Lucille Hauser, directed by Liz Diamond; DAY GAME by Scott Caming, directed by James Paradise; THE GHOST OF GLOOMY MANOR (musical) book and lyrics by Steven Otfinoski; music by Karl Blumenkrantz, directed by Mallie Boman; THE BIRDFEEDER by Steven Otfinoski, directed by Benita Gold; THE BOOKWORM by Steven Otfinoski, directed by Marion Brasch; BREAKING IN by James T. Cartin, directed by Chris Jones; P.W.B. by Kathryn Capofari, directed by David Weiss; OUR LIFE (musical) book by Virginia Masterman Smith, music and lyrics by Barbara DeAngelis, directed by Barbara DeAngelis; TITANIA BARYTONOS by Douglas Glenn Clark, directed by Richard Harden; GREEN APPLES written and directed by Peter Josyph; THE KEY AND THE WALL by Ralph Falco, directed by Norman Rhodes; GROSSBECKS by Stuart Stelly, directed by Iris Posner; BERLIN BLUES (musical) book and lyrics by Ilsa Gilbert, music by Katrina Cameron, directed by Barbara Sandek; GHOST WRITER by Maureen A. Martin, directed by Ken Lowstetter; SLEEPOVER written and directed by Ronnie Paris. December 31, 1982–January 2, 1983.

Lunchtime Series

LOUISIANA CURRENT by Stuart Stelly. November 22, 1982. Directed by Rita Tiplitz; with Philip Soltanoff, Frank P. Ryan, George McGrath, Art Kempf.

ELBOW TO ELBOW by Glauco Disalle, adapted by Mario Fratti. December 5, 1982. Directed by Bill Cosgriff; with Timothy Lewis, David Carlyon, Martitia Palmer.

DAY GAME by Scott Caming. January 10, 1983. Directed by Jim Paradise; with Christopher Boyd, Anne Gartlan, David Gideon, Bob Heck, Richard Patrick-Warner, Andy Stahl, Earl Vedder.

THE BOOKWORM by Steven Otfinoski. January 24, 1983. Directed by Marion Brasch; with R. Bruce Ross, Peter Levine, Juanita Walsh.

ELEANOR by John Cameron, directed by Joseph Rettura and STEVE AND STEVE by Charles LaTourette, directed by J.B. Nader. February 7, 1983.

THE KEY AND THE WALL by Ralph Falco, directed by Norman Rhodes; AUTOEROTIC MISADVENTURE by F.J. Hartland, directed by Peter Gordon. February 21, 1983. With Gaetano Provenzano, Robin Nolan, Paul Mantell, Susan Burkheimer, Jon Wool, Paul Zappala.

AFTER MAIGRET by Julia Hoban. March 8, 1983. Directed by Janet Sarno; with Lezlie Dalton, Vernon Hinkle, Julia Hoban.

CRAWLING ARNOLD by Jules Feiffer. March 22, 1983. Directed by Lauire Eliscu; with Warner Schreiner, Stuart Zagnit, Dru-Ann Chuckran.

A LADY NEEDS PROTECTION by Edward Eriksson. April 4, 1983. Directed by Terence Cartwright; with Artie Gerunda, Laurie Oudin, Remo Portelli.

GROSSBECKS by Stuart Stelly. April 18, 1983. Directed by Iris Posner; with George Cron, Billie Jackson, Michael Juzwak.

GARBAGE CAN MAN by and with Tom Coble. May 2, 1983. Directed by Joe Nikola.

LOUISIANA PLAYWRIGHTS' FESTIVAL: GUN CITY written and directed by Bruce Bradley; PSUICIDE by Michael Lackey, directed by Kim Aldridge; HAPPY FATHER'S DAY written and directed by Sonny Hyles. May 16–20, 1983.

A VISIT WITH THE MUSE by Lewis Gardner. May 23, 1983. Directed by James Struthers.

FRIENDS by Kevin O'Connor. May 30, 1983. Directed by Mary Tierney; with Pat McNamara, Jarlath Conroy.

The Ridiculous Theatrical Company. Charles Ludlam's camp-oriented group devoted to productions of his original scripts and broad adaptations of classics. Charles Ludlam, aristic director and director of all productions.

EXQUISITE TORTURE. By Charles Ludlam. October 6, 1982. Scenery, Jack Kelly; costumes, Everett Quinton; lighting, Lawrence Eichler; music composed by Peter Golub. With Edward McGowan, Everett Quinton, Charles Ludlam, Eureka, Deborah Petti, Black-Eyed Susan, Steven Samuels.

LE BOURGEOIS AVANT-GARDE. By Charles Ludlam. April 12, 1983. Scenery, Charles Ludlam; costumes, Everett Quinton; lighting, Lawrence Eichler; music composed by Peter Golub. With Bill Vehr, Michael Belanger, Edward McGowan, Charles Ludlam, Zelda Patterson, Everett Quinton, John Heys, Deborah Petti, Larry Maxwell, Black-Eyed Susan.

The Second Stage. Committed to producing plays of the last ten years believed to deserve another chance, as well as new works. Robyn Goodman, Carole Rothman, artistic directors.

PAINTING CHURCHES (30). By Tina Howe. February 8, 1983. Director, Carole Rothman; scenery, Heidi Landesman; lighting, Frances Aronson; costumes, Nan Cibula. With Marian Seldes, Donald Moffat, Frances Conroy.

WINTERPLAY (18). By Adele Edling Shank. May 22, 1983. Director, Harris Yulin; scenery, Douglas Stein; lighting, William Armstrong; costumes, Ann Emonts. With James Olson, Carlin Glynn, Geoffrey Sharp, Ann Talman, Judith Roberts, Reed Birney, Robert Dorfman, Cristine Rose.

SOMETHING DIFFERENT by Carl Reiner. March 15, 1983. Directed by Michael Kahn; with Andrew Duncan, Robyn Goodman, Norman Parker, Wendy Wolfe, Audree Rae, Ellen March, Theresa Merritt.

Shelter West. Aims to offer an atmosphere of trust and a place for unhurried and constructive work. Judith Joseph, artistic director.

16 performances each

GENUINE RHINESTONES. By Vincent Gaeta. January 13, 1983. Director, Judith Joseph; scenery, Rudy Kocevar; lighting, Pat Dignan; costumes, MaryAnn D. Smith. With Robin Thomas, Kathy Lichter, Cheryl Henderson, Stephen Marshall, Joseph Noah, Lou Mantis.

THEATER AT ST. CLEMENT'S—Eddie Jones and Jenny Wright in Roma Greth's *The Greatest Day of the Century*

FOUR LANES TO JERSEY. By Roma Greth. April 14, 1983. Director, Jude Schanzer; scenery, Loy Arcenas; lighting, Pat Dignan; costumes, MaryAnn D. Smith. With James Farkas, Roma Friedman, K.C. Kelly, Helen Zelon.

Soho Rep. Infrequently or never-before-performed plays by the world's greatest authors, with emphasis on language and theatricality. Marlene Swartz, Jerry Engelbach, artistic directors.

THE SILVER TASSIE by Sean O'Casey. October 21, 1983. Directed by Carey Perloff; with Victor Talmadge, Ralph Drischell, Jonathan Chappell, Dustin Evans.

FANSHEN (27). By David Hare. January 27, 1983. Director, Michael Bloom; scenery, Raymond Kluga; lighting, David Noling; costumes, Steven Birnbaum. With Robertson Dean, Shelly Desai, Dustin Evans, Ryn Hodes, Sharita Hunt, Fredric Mao, Patrizia Norcia, Tom Sminkey, Time Winters.

KID TWIST (20). By Len Jenkin. March 10, 1983. Director, Tony Barsha; scenery, Dorian Vernacchio; lighting, Chaim Gitter; costumes, Elene Pelliciaro. With Richard Bright, Mark Margolis, Richard Council, Michael Brody, Ray Xifo, Anthony Risoli, Judson Camp, Andrew Clark, Brian Delate, Kathryn Beckwith, Diane Cypkin.

RAPE UPON RAPE (20). By Henry Fielding (first New York production of record of this 1730 London play). April 29, 1983. Director, Anthony Bowles; scenery, Raymond Kluga; lighting, David Noling; costumes, Gene Lakin. With Ward Asquith, Andrew Barnicle, Victor Caroli, Suzanne Ford, Richard Behren, Jim Denton, Ann MacMillan, George Maguire, Marilyn Redfield, Steve Sterner, Alan Zampese.

South Street Theater Company. Presents dramatizations of American literature and translations of new European plays in their American premieres. Jean Sullivan, Michael Fischetti, co-artistic directors, Leslie Erich Comens, project director.

A MOSCOW HAMLET and A CASUAL AFFAIR (short stories) by Anton Chekhov, adapted, directed and performed by Jean Sullivan and Michael Fischetti. June 14, 1982.

THE WORLD OF RUTH DRAPER (25). Adapted by Alan Levy from Morton Dauwen Zabel's *The Art of Ruth Draper*. December 4, 1982. Director, Franz Schafranek; musical director, James Logan Cramer; scenery and costumes, Tamare; narration, Eugene Hartzell. With Ruth Brinkmann.

Theater at St. Clement's. Primarily new American plays presented in New York premieres. Anita Khanzadian, artistic director, Stephen Berwind, producing director.

THE LEGAL MACHINE (16). By Alfonso Vallejo, translated by Susan Meredith. June 2, 1982. Director, Jordan Deitcher; scenery, David Potts; lighting, Victor En Yu Tan; costumes, Margo LaZaro. With Neil Vipond, Jack Hollander, Howard Lee Sherman, Nada Rowand, Cora Hook, Socorro Santiago, Raynor Scheine.

THE GREATEST DAY OF THE CENTURY (18). By Roma Greth. April 22, 1983. Director, Anita Khanzadian; scenery and lighting, Gary Jennings; costumes, Margo LaZaro. With Eddie Jones, Jenny Wright, Jeb Ellis-Brown, Adrienne Wallace.

Theater for the New City. Developmental theater, incorporating live music and dance into new American experimental works. George Bartenieff, Crystal Field, artistic directors.

BEFORE SHE IS EVEN BORN (10). By Leah K. Friedman. September 19, 1982. Director, Susan Einhorn; scenery, Audrey Hemenway; lighting, Victor En Yu Tan; costumes, Muriel Stockdale; music and sound, Skip La Plante. With Karen Ludwig, Dayne Lee, Rebecca Schull, Leslie Ayvazian.

24 INCHES (15). Book and lyrics, Robert Patrick; music, David Tice. October 7, 1982. Scenery and lighting, John Jewell. With Sandy Bigtree, Stephen Cross, Barry Greenberg, Kevin Hurley, Terry Talley, J.R. Wells, Stacia Goad, Nancy Crumpler, Jeff Lucchese.

DIAGONAL MAN (THEORY AND PRACTICE) (20). By and with Bread and Puppet Theater. November 30, 1982.

FRED BREAKS BREAD WITH THE DEAD: FRAGMENTS OF A LOST REPERTOIRE. Conceived, directed and performed by Fred Curchack. December 23, 1982.

GROWING UP GOTHIC (co-production with Interart Theater; see Interart Theater for full entry).

THE DANUBE (16). Written and directed by Maria Irene Fornes. February 17, 1983. Scenery, Monica Lorca; lighting, Joe Ray; costumes, Gabriel Berry; puppets, Esteban Fernandez. With Michael Sean Edwards, Arthur Williams, Margaret Harrington, Martin Treat.

STARBURN (16). Book and lyrics, Rosalyn Drexler; music, Michael Meadows. February 24, 1983. Director, John Vaccaro; musical director, Bruce Coyle; scenery, Elwin Charles Terrel III; lighting, Anne Militello; costumes, Bernard Roth. With Kristi Rose, John Albano, John Barilla, Alicia Brandt, John D. Brockmeyer, Alison Gordy, Gloria Harper, Dori Hartley, Lola Pashalinski, Joe Pichette, Tony Zanetta.

ROSETTI'S APOLOGETICS (16). By Leonard Melfi; music, Mark Hardwick. April 7, 1983. Director, Crystal Field; musical director, David Caldwell; scenery, Ron Kajawara; lighting, John P. Dodd; costumes, Edmund Felix. With George Bartenieff, Alex Bartenieff, Crystal Field, Kenneth La Ron Johnson, Beness Mardenn, Leonard Melfi, Carmen Mathis, Alex Mustelier, Jill Wissoff.

THE DEPARTMENT (20). By Barbara Garson. April 21, 1983. Director, Chris Kraus; scenery, L.B. Dallas; lighting, Harry Darrow. With Victoria Abrash, Jessica Bloom, Cynthia Jordan,

Daniel Daily, Catherine Hoeg, Sharon Shambourger, Vi Torbett, Susana Tubert, Michael Twain, Scott Wakefield.

Theater of the Open Eye. Total theater involving actors, dancers, musicians and designers working together, each bringing his own talents into a single project. Jean Erdman, producing artistic director, Amie Brockway, associate artistic director.

THE DITCH (18). Adapted and directed by Ann Scofield from Jakov Lind's radio play, *Anna Laub*. June 2, 1982. Scenery and lighting, Clayton Campbell; costumes, Esther Smith; music, David Simons. With Mary Alice, Dain Chandler, Alexis Genya, Elaine May Morrison, Mario Arrambide, Marc Murray, Andrew Traines.

BEHIND A MASK (20). Adapted by Karen L. Lewis from Madeleine Stern's *Behind a Mask, the Unknown Thrillers of Louisa May Alcott*. February 3, 1983. Director, Amie Brockway; scenery, lighting and costumes, Adrienne J. Brockway. With Constance Bahr, Sally Chamberlin, Helen Eleasari, Edward D. Griffith, Ryan Hilliard, Annalee Jefferies, Mark Johannes, Meg Van Zyl.

PHANTOM LIMBS (25). By Charles Borkhuis. March 31, 1983. Director, Gitta Honegger; scenery, Powers Boothe; lighting, Scott Breindel; costumes, Jane Clark. With Joyce Aaron, Andrew Davis, Kenneth Ryan, Henry Stram.

LA BELLE AU BOIS (24). By Jules Supervielle, translated by Irma Brandeis. May 26, 1983. Directors, Jean Erdman, Amie Brockway; choreographer, Jean Erdman; music, Elliot Sokolov; scenery and lighting, Clayton Campbell; costumes, Adrienne J. Brockway. With Nora Chester, Marylou DiFilippo, Ronnie Newman, Tony Pasqualini, Calvin Remsberg, Amy Stoller, John Wallace Wilson, Deidre Stafford, Jeanne Stafford.

Theater Off Park. Provides Murray Hill-Turtle Bay residents with a professional theater, showcasing the talents of new actors, playwrights, designers and directors. Patricia Flynn Peate, executive director.

16 performances each

THE WILDE SPIRIT. Conceived and performed by Kerry Ashton. June 2, 1982. Scenery, Mina Albergo; lighting, Dawn Chiang; costumes, Ken Brown.

SWEET PRINCE. By A.E. Hotchner. September 21, 1982. Director, Susie Fuller; scenery and costumes, Don Jensen; lighting, Richard Nelson; fencing choreography, Peter Moore. With Keir Dullea, Ian Abercrombie.

DETAILS WITHOUT A MAP. By Barbara Schneider. October 26, 1982. Director, James Milton; scenery, Bob Phillips; lighting, John Gisondi; costumes, Amanda J. Klein. With Jo Henderson, Stephen Joyce, Margaret Baker, Cordis Heard, Marc Riffon, Michael Ornstein, Lionel Chute.

THE BANANA DANCER. Conceived, written, and directed by Len Calder and Robin Courbet. February 22, 1983. Scenery, Joseph A. Varga; lighting, Robin Courbet and James R. Gibby; costumes, George Vallo. With Angela Logan.

BALZAMINOV'S WEDDING. By Alexander Ostrovsky, translated by Edythe Haber. April 6, 1983. Director, Timor Djordjadze; choreographer, Dorothy Massalski; music directed and compiled by Deena Kaye; scenery, Lynda Wormell; lighting, William J. Plachy; costumes, Muriel Stockdale. With Sally Deering, Jan Jalenak, Penelope Safranek, Marc Raymond, Rebecca Schull, Melissa Weber, Mimi Rogers Weddell.

MIRAGE. By Malcolm Stewart. May 18, 1983. Directed by Granville Burgess; scenery, Jane Clark; lighting, Betsy Adams; costumes, Ginnie Weidmann. With Fran Barnes, Gregory Chase, Michael Coerver, David Hunt, Amy Lemon, Meg Myles, Emmett O'Sullivan-Moore.

THE WATER HEN by Stanislaw Witkiewicz, translated by Daniel Gerould and C.S. Durer. January 5, 1983. Directed by Bradford Mays; with Betty LaRoe, Tobias Haller, James Curran, Nat Warren-White, Stanley Keyes, Linda Chambers, James Fleming, Lee Taylor-Allan.

WPA Theater. Produces neglected American classics and new American plays in the realistic idiom. Kyle Renick, artistic director, Wendy Bustard, managing director, Edward T. Gianfrancesco, resident designer/technical director.

25 performances each

BACK TO BACK. By Al Brown. October 28, 1982. Director, Douglas Johnson; scenery, Edward T. Gianfrancesco; lighting, Craig Evans; costumes, Don Newcomb. With Eugene Lee, Keith Gordon.

A DIFFERENT MOON. By Ara Watson. January 27, 1983. Director, Sam Blackwell; scenery, Jim Steere; lighting, Craig Evans; costumes, Don Newcomb. With Christopher Cooper, Zina Jasper, Betsy Aidem, Linda Lee Johnson.

VIEUX CARRÉ. By Tennessee Williams. March 26, 1983. Director, Stephen Zuckerman; scenery, James Fenhagen; lighting, Charles Cosler; costumes, Mimi Maxmen. With Jacqueline Brooks, Louise Stubbs, Mark Soper, Anne Twomey, Tom Klunis, Alex Stuhl, Elaine Swann, Anna Minot, John Bedford-Lloyd, Jeff Garrett, Brian Hargrove.

ASIAN SHADE. By Larry Ketron. May 12, 1983. Director, Dann Florek; scenery, Ross A. Wilmeth; lighting, Phil Monat; costumes, Don Newcomb. With Mark Benninghofen, Lenny Von Dohlen, Tom Brennan, Marissa Chibas, Dianne Neil, J. Smith-Cameron.

The York Players. Each season, productions of classics and contemporary plays are mounted with professional casts, providing neighborhood residents with professional theater. Janet Hayes Walker, artistic director.

THE WISTERIA TREES by Joshua Logan. November 20, 1982. Directed by Peter Phillips; with Carrie Nye, Diane Kirksey, Susan Pellegrino, David Little, Hubert Kelly Jr., Avon Long, Louis Edmonds, J.R. Horne.

THE BOY'S OWN STORY (14). By Peter Flannery. January 13, 1983. Director, Richard Seyd; scenery, James Morgan; lighting, Mary Jo Dondlinger. With Jim Piddock.

COLETTE COLLAGE (17). Book and lyrics, Tom Jones; music, Harvey Schmidt. March 31, 1983. Director, Fran Soeder; choreographer, Janet Watson; musical director, Eric Stern; scenery, James Morgan; lighting, Mary Jo Dondlinger; costumes, Sigrid Insull. With Steven F. Hall, George Hall, Joanne Beretta, Timothy Jerome, Jana Robbins, Howard Pinhasik, Susan J. Baum, Dan Shaheen, Suzanne Bedford, Terry Baughan, Tim Ewing.

A MIDSUMMER NIGHT'S DREAM by William Shakespeare. May 10, 1983. Directed by Janet Hayes Walker; with Lisa Barnes, Laurie Klatscher, Scott Ellis, Thomas Narhwold, Scott Rhyne, Julie Ramaker, Viveca Parker, Kurt Johnson, Frederick Walters, John Newton.

Miscellaneous

In the additional listing of 1982–83 off-off-Broadway productions below, the names of the producing groups or theaters appear in CAPITAL LETTERS and the titles of the works in *italics*. This list consists largely of new or reconstituted works and excludes most revivals, especially of classics. It includes a few productions staged by groups which rented space from the more established organizations listed previously.

ACTORS REPERTORY THEATER. *After You've Gone* by Marjorie Kellogg. June, 1982. Directed by Jason Buzas; with Sylvia Short, Lily Lodge, Barry Ford. *The Men's Room* by Jess Gregg. November 19, 1982. Directed by Warren Robertson; with Burt Young, Lewis VanBergen, Frankie Faison, Jim Lynch, James Gara.

AMERICAN JEWISH THEATER. *The Tenth Man* by Paddy Chayefsky. October 23, 1982. Directed by Dan Held; with Lydia Leeds, Art Burns, Sol Frieder, Norman Golden, Milton

YORK PLAYERS—Jana Robbins as Colette in *Colette Collage*

Lansky, Victor Jacoby, Albert S. Bennett. *David and Paula* by Howard Fast. November 7, 1982. Directed by Stanley Brechner; with Veronica Castang, David Margulies. *The Man in the Glass Booth* by Robert Shaw. January 8, 1983. Directed by Dan Held; with Albert Sinkys, Art Burns. *The Rise of David Levinsky* (musical) book and lyrics by Isaiah Sheffer, based on Abraham Cahan's novel, music by Bobby Paul. March 12, 1983. Directed by Sue Lawless; with Avi Hoffman, Larry Keith, Marilyn Sokol.

ARK THEATER. *Lumiere* by Donald Marcus. February 13, 1983. Directed by Irene Lewis; with J.T. Walsh, William Converse-Roberts, Concetta Tomei, Kate Wilkinson, Denise DeLong.

ASIA SOCIETY. *Kutiyattam* (Sanskrit drama). August 24, 1982.

BROOKLYN ACADEMY OF MUSIC. *The Flying Karamazov Brothers.* October, 1982. With Howard Jay Patterson, Paul David Magid, Samuel Ross Williams, Timothy Daniel Furst.

COOPER-HEWITT MUSEUM. *Tiffany, Mackaye and Edison* (one-act play) by Howard Pflanzer. April 28, 1983. Directed by Susan Miller London; with Lucy McMichael, Arnold Willens, Eric Himes, Robin Strange.

DANCE THEATER WORKSHOP/ECONOMY TIRES THEATER. *Grupo Contadores de Estorias* (The Story Tellers) written, directed and performed by Rachel Ribas and Marcos Caetano Ribas, music by Helena Pinheiro. August, 1982 (Brazilian puppets). *Inclined to Agree* conceived and performed by Daniel Stein, created and directed by Daniel Stein and Christopher Gibson. May 19, 1983.

THE GLINES. *If This Isn't Love* by Sidney Morris. June, 1982. Directed by Leslie Irons.

GREEK THEATER OF NEW YORK. *Alexandriad: the Early Years* written and directed by Yannis Simonides. November 2, 1982. With Louis J. Chambers, Russ Fast, Felicia Faulkner, William Hanauer, Tony Simotes, Ahvi Spindell, Alex Bellas. *The Birds* by Aristophanes, translated by Walter Kerr; songs composed and arranged by Evangelos Pampas, lyrics by John-Neil Harris. May 16, 1983. Directed by Russ Fast; with Yannis Simonides, Alexis Mylonas, Russ Fast, Julia Kiley, Demetra Karras.

GREENWICH HOUSE THEATER. *Ceremony in Bohemia* by Jon Forester. November, 1982. Directed by Kenna Hunt; with Ludmila Shikhverg, Jiri Fisher, Zdenka Fisher, Gerard D'Antonio.

HAROLD CLURMAN THEATER. *From Brooks With Love* (musical) book and lyrics by Wayne Sheridan, music by George Koch and Russ Taylor. March 30, 1983. Directed by William Michael Maher; with Ralph Anthony, Gillian Walke, Gwen Arment, Fred Bishop, Richard Sabellico, Geraldine Hanning, Peter Blaxill.

INTAR (rental). *American Princess* (musical) book by Leonard Orr, Jed Feuer and David Hurwitz, music and directed by Jed Feuer, lyrics by Leonard Orr. October, 1982. With Mark Yetter, Mary Testa, Jack Sevier, Florence Levitt. *Night Fishing in Beverly Hills* by Louis C. Adelman. November 10, 1982. Directed by Cash Baxter; with John Arch-Carter, Brett Somers, Michael Beckett, James Pritchett, Jake Turner, William Swan, Ann Gentry. *Knights Errant* by John Hunt with Martin Kaplan. December 1, 1982. Directed by Geoffrey Shlaes; with Harry Spillman, Frances Barnes, J.D. Clarke, Richard M. Davidson, Eddie Jones, James DeMarse, Tudi Wiggins.

JAPAN HOUSE. *Bunraku Puppet Theater of Japan*. March 12, 1983.

JEAN COCTEAU REPERORY. *The Condemned of Altona* by Jean-Paul Sartre. September 16, 1982. Directed by Eve Adamson. *Swanwhite* by August Strindberg. October 7, 1982. Directed by Susan Flakes. *Saint Joan* by George Bernard Shaw. December 7, 1982. Directed by Eve Adamson. *The School for Scandal* by Richard Brinsley Sheridan. February 10, 1983. Directed by Robert Moss. *Don Carlos* by Friedrich von Schiller. March 24, 1983. Directed by Eve Adamson. *Philoctetes* by Sophocles, new English version and directed by Karen Sunde. April 11, 1983.

JEWISH REPERTORY THEATER. *Friends Too Numerous to Mention* by Neil Cohen and Joel Cohen. November 27, 1982. Directed by Allen Coulter; with Barbara Speigel, William Wise, Salem Ludwig, Robin Karfo, Jack Kehler, Thomas Kopache, Grace Roberts. *Taking Steam* by Kenneth Klonsky and Brian Shein. April 2, 1983. Directed by Edward M. Cohen; with Herb Duncan, Jack Aaron, Maurice Sterman, Felix Fibich, Herman O. Arbeit, Harvey Pierce, Frank Nastasi. *My Heart Is in the East* (musical) book by Linda Kline, music by Raphael Crystal, lyrics by Richard Engquist. May 28, 1983. Directed by Ran Avni; with Dave DeChristopher, Adam Heller, Nancy Mayans, Susan Victor.

JONES BEACH THEATER. *Grease* (musical) book, music and lyrics by Jim Jacobs and Warren Casey. July 13, 1982. Directed by Frank Wagner; with Mark Martino, Laurie Stephenson, Pamela Blasetti. *West Side Story* (musical) book by Arthur Laurents, music by Leonard Bernstein, lyrics by Stephen Sondheim. August 3, 1982. Directed by Leslie B. Cutler; with Jack Magradey, Barry Williams, Christine Andreas, Michael Rivera, Rob Marshall, Loida Santos.

LABOR THEATER. *Bottom Line* (musical) by C.R. Portz, music by Martin Burman. December 7, 1982. With Martin Burman, Gussie Harris, Marcia McIntosh, David Ossian, Guy Sherman.

LION THEATER (rental). *Soap* (musical) book, lyrics and direction by David Man, music by Aaron Egigian. September 10, 1982. With Cindy Benson, Suzanne Blakeslee, Karen Bruhn, Mark Goetzinger, Joseph Kelly, James Leach, Todd Robinson, Aileen Savage, Catherine Schultz, Gwen Strong, Porcina LeSeur. *Sunday Afternoon* by Marshall Borden. January 8, 1983. Directed by Michael Hardstark; with Gina Batiste, Willie Carpenter, Ed Easton, Lawrence Guardino, Fred Keeler, Kathleen McKiernan, George J. Peters.

MARYMOUNT MANHATTAN THEATER. *In Agony* by Miroslav Krleza, translated by John Stark and Mihajlo Starcevic, adapted by Tom Grainger. October, 1982. Directed by John Stark; with Margret Warnke, Marshall Borden, Roy Steinberg, Aurelia De Felice.

MEAT AND POTATOES COMPANY. *A Place on the Magdalena Flats* by Preston Jones. October, 1982. Directed by Jon Teta; with Jennifer Sullivan, Bill Fears, Jeanne Morrissey, Scott Renderer.

MOONLIGHT PRODUCTIONS. *Tales From the Vermont Woods* by Sharon Linnea. February 10, 1983. Directed by Robert Owens Scott; with Chel Chenier, Paul Duke, Charles Dinstuhl, Elizabeth Lage, Jayne Heller, Jack Schmidt.

MUSIC-THEATER GROUP/LENOX ARTS CENTER. *The Mother of Us All* (opera) text by Gertrude Stein, music by Virgil Thomson. March 15, 1983. Directed by Stanley Silverman; with Richard Frisch, Ruth Jacobson, Carmen Pelton, Linn Maxwell, John Vining, Harris Poor, Paula Siebel, Avery J. Tracht, Kate Hurney. *The Juniper Tree, a Tragic Household Tale* (musical) written and composed by Wendy Kesselman. April 19, 1983. Directed by Michael Montel; with Anthony Crivello, Deborah Offner, Wendy Kesselman. *The Day, the Night* conceived, composed and directed by Welcome Msomi. May 18, 1983. With Robert Jason, Deborah Malone, Terrance T. Ellis, Stephanie R. Berry, Vanessa Shaw, Ghanniyya Green.

NEW YORK GILBERT AND SULLIVAN PLAYERS. *Iolanthe* libretto by W. S. Gilbert, music by Arthur Sullivan. December 31, 1982. Directed by Albert Bergeret; with Cheryl Fenner, Claire Bennett, Louis Dal'Ava, Del-Bouree Bach, Keith Jurosko, Richard Holmes. *The Gondoliers* libretto by William S. Gilbert, music by Arthur Sullivan. April 7, 1983. Directed by Albert Bergeret.

NEW YORK THEATER STUDIO. *Our Lord of Lynchville* by Snoo Wilson. January 30, 1983. Directed by Richard V. Romagnoli; with Leon Russom, Gisele Richardson.

O'NEALS' 43d. *Broadway Scandals of 1982* (revue) music by Jeffrey Silverman, lyrics, scenario, and directed by Walter Willison. July, 1982. With Jessica James, Shelley Bruce, Jo Anna Lehmann, Kenny D'Aquila, Gwen Hiller Lowe, Rose Scudder, Steve Jerro, Bill Johnson.

THE OTHER END. *Slap Happy* (comedy revue) written by and with Jeff Ernstoff, Allan Jacobs, Jan Kirschner, Brian O'Connor. January, 1983. Directed by Munson Hicks.

PALSSON'S. *Corkscrews!* (musical revue) by Tony Lang and Arthur Siegel. April, 1983. Directed by Miriam Fond; with Tony Lang, Arthur Siegel, Miriam Fond.

PARK ROYAL THEATER. *Red Rover, Red Rover* by Oliver Hailey. March 19, 1983. Directed by Tony Napoli; with Helen Gallagher, Phyllis Newman.

THE PERFORMING GARAGE. *The Confessions of a Dope Fiend* by Jeffrey M. Jones. September 9, 1982. Directed by Matthew Maguire; with Michael Harris, Ron Vawter. *Voodoo Automatic* written and directed by Alan Finneran; *Red Rain* written and directed by Bean Finneran, music by Bob Davis. March 1, 1983. With Soon 3.

PERRY STREET THEATER. *All of the Above* (musical revue) by Michael Eisenberg. July 14, 1982. Directed by Tony Berk; with Linda Gelman, Ann Morrison, Michelan Sisti, Ed Ellner. *The Provoked Wife* by Sir John Vanbrugh. May, 1983. Directed by John Retallack; with Russell Enoch, Valerie Braddell, Chris Barnes, Christine Bishop, Raymond Sawyer, Susan Colverd.

PRODUCTION COMPANY. *Blood Moon* by Nicholas Kazan. January 5, 1983. Directed by Allen R. Belknap; with Dana Delany, David Canary, Nicholas Saunders. *The Gilded Cage* (musical) conceived and directed by James Milton. January 9, 1983. With Marianne Tatum, Tom McKinney, Robert Stillman, Paula Sweeney, Susan Blommaert, Marilyn Firment. *Jazz Poets at the Grotto* conceived and directed by Greg McCaslin. March 9, 1983. With Randy Danson, John Pankow, John Korkes, Michael Butler, Judith Ivey, Ruthe Staples, John Shearin.

QUAIGH THEATER (rental). *Going Steady and Other Fables of the Heart* by E. Eugene Baldwin. November 5, 1982. Directed by William E. Hunt.

RIVERSIDE SHAKESPEARE COMPANY. *Richard III* by William Shakespeare. November 19, 1982. Directed by John Clingerman; with J. Kenneth Campbell, Richard Hoyt-Miller, Mary McTigue, Elton Beckett.

PRODUCTION COMPANY—Dana Delany and David
Canary in a scene from *Blood Moon* by Nicholas Kazan

SAN FRANCISCO MIME TROUPE. *Americans, or Last Tango in Huahuatenango* by Joan
Holden. November, 1982. Directed by Daniel Chumley; with Sahron Lockwood, Gus Johnson,
Audrey Smith, Ruben Garfias, Arthur Holden.

S.N.A.F.U. *Etiquette* (musical revue) by William M. Hoffman and John Braden. January, 1983.
Directed by John Vaccaro; with Cindy Benson, Marcia McClain, Jerry Cunliffe, Molly Regan.

SOUNDSCAPE. La Troupe Makandal (staged voodoo rituals). May, 1983.

SOUTH STREET THEATER (rentals). *The Music Keeper* by Elliot Tiber and Andre Ernotte. July
14, 1982. Directed by Andre Ernotte; with Jan Miner, Dennis Bacigalupi. *The Workroom*
(L'Atelier) by Jean-Claude Grumberg, American version by Daniel A. Stein and Sara O'Connor.
October 22, 1982. Directed by Aaron Levin; with Rita Gardner, Margaret Dulaney, June
Squibb, Robin Leary, Elaine Grollman, Carrie Zivetz, Eugene Troobnick.

T.R.G. REPERTORY COMPANY. *The Gospel According to Al* (musical revue of Al Carmines's
songs) by Al Carmines. October 15, 1982. Directed by William Hopkins; with Cathleen Axelrod,
Georgia Creighton, Paul Farin, Kate Ingram, Tad Ingram.

THEATER FOR ACTORS AND PLAYWRIGHTS. *Victims of Duty* by Eugene Ionesco, translated by Donald Watson. July, 1982. Directed by Herman Babad; with John Marolakos, Beege Barkett, David Edelman, Val Bisoglio.

TROUPE THEATER. *The Actors* by Ward Morehouse III. November, 1982. Directed by Andy Milligan; with Lester J. Schaffner, Lon Freeman, Che Moody, Jane Harvey.

VINEYARD THEATER. *Living Quarters* by Brian Friel. February 21, 1983. Directed by Susan Einhorn; with John Braden, Ralph Williams, Robin Bartlett, Anne O'Sullivan, Keliher Walsh, Laura Gardner.

VITAL ARTS THEATER. *Victims: a Triangle* by Amirh Bahati. November 26, 1982. Directed by Nathan George.

WESTSIDE MAINSTAGE. *Journey to Gdansk*, *Tea with Milk* and *A Walk Before Dawn* by Janusz Glowacki. August 10, 1982. Directed by Kent Paul; with Allan Carlsen, Cara Duff-MacCormick, John Miglietta, Jennifer Grey. *Saigon Rose* by David Edgar. November 26, 1982. Directed by Ted Davis; with Linda Cook, Celia Lee, Allan Wasserman.

CAST REPLACEMENTS AND TOURING COMPANIES

Compiled by Stanley Green

The following is a list of the more important cast replacements in productions which opened in previous years, but were still playing in New York during a substantial part of the 1982–83 season; or were still on a first-class tour in 1982–83, or opened in New York in 1982–83 and went on tour during the season (casts of first-class touring companies of previous seasons which were no longer playing in 1982–83 appear in previous *Best Plays* volumes of appropriate years).

The name of each major role is listed in *italics* beneath the title of the play in the first column. In the second column directly opposite appears the name of the actor who created the role in the original New York production (whose opening date appears in *italics* at the top of the column). Indented immediately beneath the original actor's name are the names of subsequent New York replacements, together with the date of replacement when available.

The third column gives information about first-class touring companies, including London companies (produced under the auspices of their original New York managements). When there is more than one roadshow company, #1, #2, etc., appear before the name of the performer who created the role in each company (and the city and date of each company's first performance appears in *italics* at the top of the column). Their subsequent replacements are also listed beneath their names, with dates when available.

AGNES OF GOD

	New York 3/30/82
Dr. Martha Livingstone	Elizabeth Ashley
	Diahann Carroll 9/27/82
	Elizabeth Ashley 10/11/82
	Diahann Carroll 5/2/83
Mother Miriam Ruth	Geraldine Page
Agnes	Amanda Plummer
	Mia Dillon 9/7/82
	Amanda Plummer 9/14/82
	Carrie Fisher 1/3/83
	Maryann Plunkett 4/12/83

AMADEUS

	New York 12/17/80	*Los Angeles 12/8/82*
Antonio Salieri	Ian McKellen	John Wood
	John Wood 10/13/81	
	Frank Langella 4/13/82	
	David Dukes 11/16/82	
	David Birney 5/24/83	

Wolfgang Amadeus Mozart	Tim Curry	Mark Hamill
	Peter Firth 7/7/81	John Pankow 4/28/83
	John Pankow 3/10/82	
	Dennis Boutsikeris 4/13/82	
	John Pankow 11/16/82	
	John Thomas Waite 4/19/83	
	Mark Hamill 4/28/83	
Constanze Weber	Jane Seymour	Michele Seyler
	Caris Corfman 5/26/81	
	Amy Irving 7/7/81	
	Caris Corfman 2/16/82	
	Michele Farr 3/23/82	
	Suzanne Lederer 4/13/82	
	Maureen Moore 5/24/83	

ANNIE

	New York 4/21/77	*West Point 9/11/81*
Oliver Warbucks	Reid Shelton	Ron Holgate
	Keene Curtis 2/6/78	Gary Holcombe 9/12/82
	Reid Shelton 2/27/78	
	John Schuck 12/25/79	
	Harve Presnell 12/17/80	
	John Schuck 1/7/81	
	Rhodes Reason 6/23/81	
	Harve Presnell 9/1/81	
Annie	Andrea McArdle	Mollie Hall
	Shelley Bruce 3/6/78	Kathleen Sisk 8/31/82
	Sarah Jessica Parker 3/6/79	
	Allison Smith 1/29/80	
	Alyson Kirk 9/8/82	
Miss Hannigan	Dorothy Loudon	Ruth Williamson
	Alice Ghostley 8/15/78	
	Dolores Wilson 8/21/79	
	Alice Ghostley 1/29/80	
	Betty Hutton 9/17/80	
	Alice Ghostley 10/8/80	
	Marcia Lewis 4/29/81	
	Ruth Kobart 2/24/82	
	Marcia Lewis 3/10/82	
	June Havoc 10/6/82	
Grace Farrell	Sandy Faison	Lynne Wintersteller
	Lynn Kearney 1/22/79	Donna Thomason 9/12/82
	Mary Bracken Phillips 8/79	
	Kathryn Boulé 7/29/80	
	Ann Kerry 4/29/81	
	Lauren Mitchell 1/13/82	
Rooster Hannigan	Robert Fitch	Guy Stroman
	Gary Beach 1/29/80	William McClary 4/6/82
	Richard Sabellico 4/29/81	Dick Decareau 9/26/82
	Bob Morrisey 8/4/82	
	Michael Calkins 9/19/82	
Lily	Barbara Erwin	Ann Casey
	Annie McGreevey 9/78	

Barbara Erwin 5/29/79
Rita Rudner 1/29/80
Dorothy Stanley 2/11/81

FDR   Raymond Thorne   William Metzo
Tom Hatten 8/18/82
Raymond Thorne 8/31/82

Note: Casts, including replacements, of the first touring company and the London company of *Annie* appear on pages 446–447 of *The Best Plays of 1980–1981.*

CAMELOT

	New York 11/15/81	*London 11/23/82*
Arthur	Richard Harris	Richard Harris
Guenevere	Meg Bussert	Fiona Fullerton
Lancelot du Lac	Richard Muenz	Robert Meadmore
King Pellinore	Barrie Ingham	Robin Bailey
Mordred	Richard Backus	Michael Howe

Note: Previous casts of this *Camelot* company, both in New York and on tour, appear on page 418 of *The Best Plays of 1981–1982.*

A CHORUS LINE

	N.Y. Off Bway 4/15/75 *N.Y. Bway 7/25/75*

Kristine	Renee Baughman
	  Cookie Vazquez 4/26/76
	  Deborah Geffner 10/76
	  P.J. Mann 9/78
	  Deborah Geffner 1/79
	  Christine Barker 3/79
	  Kerry Casserly 8/81
	  Christine Barker 10/81

Sheila	Carole Bishop (name changed to Kelly Bishop 3/76)
	  Kathrynann Wright 8/76
	  Bebe Neuwirth 6/80
	  Susan Danielle 3/81
	  Jan Leigh Herndon 9/82
	  Jane Summerhays 9/82

Val	Pamela Blair
	  Barbara Monte-Britton 4/26/76
	  Karen Jablons 10/76
	  Mitzi Hamilton 3/1/77
	  Karen Jablons 12/77
	  Mitzi Hamilton 3/78
	  Lois Englund 7/78
	  Deborah Henry 10/79
	  Mitzi Hamilton 10/80
	  Joanna Zercher 6/81
	  Mitzi Hamilton 7/81

Mike	Wayne Cilento Jim Litten 6/77

Jeff Hyslop 1/79
Don Correia 6/79
Buddy Balou' 6/80
Cary Scott Lowenstein 7/81
Scott Wise 7/82
Danny Herman 4/83

Larry   Clive Clerk
Jeff Weinberg 10/76
Clive Clerk 1/77
Adam Grammis 2/77
Paul Charles 12/77
R.J. Peters 3/79
T. Michael Reed 11/79
Michael-Day Pitts 3/80
Donn Simione 4/81
J. Richard Hart 7/81
Scott Plank 9/82
Brad Jeffries 11/82

Maggie   Kay Cole
Lauree Berger 4/26/76
Donna Drake 2/77
Christina Saffran 7/78
Betty Lynd 6/5/79
Marcia Lynn Watkins 8/79
Pam Klinger 9/81

Richie   Ronald Dennis
Winston DeWitt Hemsley 4/26/76
Edward Love 6/77
A. William Perkins 12/77
(name changed to Wellington Perkins 6/78)
Larry G. Bailey 1/79
Carleton T. Jones 3/80
Ralph Glenmore 6/80
Kevin Chinn 1/81

Judy   Patricia Garland
Sandahl Bergman 4/26/76
Murphy Cross 12/77
Victoria Tabaka 11/78
Joanna Zercher 7/79
Angelique Ilo 8/79
Jannet Horsley 9/80
(name changed to Jannet Moranz 2/81)
Melissa Randel 12/81

Don   Ron Kuhlman
David Thomé 4/26/76
Dennis Edenfield 3/80
Michal Weir 8/81
Michael Danek 10/81
Randy Clements 11/82
Michael Danek 12/82

Bebe   Nancy Lane
Gillian Scalaci 4/26/76
Rene Ceballos 9/77
Karen Meister 1/78

Rene Ceballos 3/81
Pamela Ann Wilson 1/82

Connie

Baayork Lee
Lauren Kayahara 4/26/76
Janet Wong 2/77
Cynthia Carrillo Onrubia 11/79
Janet Wong 2/77
Lauren Tom 10/80
Lily-Lee Wong 10/81

Diana

Priscilla Lopez
Barbara Luna 4/26/76
Carole Schweid 5/7/76
Rebecca York 8/76
Loida Iglesias 12/76
Chris Bocchino 10/78
Diane Fratantoni 9/79
Chris Bocchino 12/79
Gay Marshall 7/80
Chris Bocchino 8/80
Dorothy Tancredi 3/82
Diane Fratantoni 6/82
Kay Cole 8/82
Roxann Caballero 10/82
Gay Marshall 11/82
Roxann Caballero 1/83
Loida Santos (prev. known as Loida Iglesias) 3/83

Zach

Robert LuPone
Joe Bennett 4/26/76
Eivind Harum 10/76
Robert LuPone 1/31/77
Kurt Johnson 5/77
Clive Clerk 7/77
Kurt Johnson 8/77
Anthony Inneo 8/78
Eivind Harum 10/78
Scott Pearson 8/79
Tim Millett 3/81
Steven Boockvor 8/23/82

Mark

Cameron Mason
Paul Charles 10/76
Timothy Scott 12/77
R.J. Peters 4/78
Timothy Wahrer 3/79
Dennis Daniels 5/80
Timothy Wahrer 6/80
Gregory Brock 8/80
Danny Herman 5/81
Fraser Ellis 11/82
Danny Herman 12/82
Chris Marshall 4/83

Cassie

Donna McKechnie
Ann Reinking 4/26/76
Donna McKechnie 9/27/76
Ann Reinking 11/29/76
Vicki Fredericks 2/9/77

Pamela Sousa 11/14/77
Candace Tovar 1/78
Pamela Sousa 3/78
Cheryl Clark 12/78
Deborah Henry 10/80
Pamela Sousa 11/81

Al

Don Percassi
Bill Nabel 4/26/76
John Mineo 2/77
Ben Lokey 4/77
Don Percassi 7/77
Jim Corti 1/79
Donn Simione 9/79
James Warren 5/80 (name changed to James Young 9/80)
Jerry Colker 5/81
Scott Plank 11/82
Buddy Balou' 3/83

Greg

Michel Stuart
Justin Ross 4/26/76
Danny Weathers 6/78
Ronald A. NaVarre 9/83

Bobby

Thomas J. Walsh
Christopher Chadman 6/77
Ron Kurowski 1/78
Tim Cassidy 11/78
Ronald Stafford 3/79
Michael Gorman 8/80
Matt West 9/80

Paul

Sammy Williams
George Pesaturo 4/26/76
René Clemente 2/78
Timothy Wahrer 9/81
René Clemente 10/81
Tommy Aguilar 5/82

Note: Original casts of the three touring companies of *A Chorus Line* appear on pages 472–3 of *The Best Plays of 1978–1979.*

CLOUD 9

New York 5/18/81

Ellen; Mrs. Saunders; Betty

E. Katherine Kerr
Kate MacGregor Stewart 3/2/82
Cynthia Harris 6/29/82
Judith Barcroft 11/2/82
Cheryl McFadden 3/26/83

Edward; Victoria

Concetta Tomei
Caroline Lagerfelt 7/10/82
Sherry Steiner 10/19/82
Elaine Bromka 5/3/83

Betty; Gerry

Zeljko Ivanek
Michael Jeter 4/13/82
John Pankow 6/29/82
Lenny Von Dohlen 10/26/82
Bill Sadler 4/26/83

Clive; Edward   Jeffrey Jones
                                        Ivar Brogger 6/26/82
                                        Stephen Stout 12/28/82

Joshua; Cathy   Don Amendolia
                                        Michael Jeter 6/29/82
                                        Ian Trigger 10/22/82
                                        James Lecesne 11/23/82

Maud; Lin   Veronica Castang
                                        Caroline Kava 7/13/82
                                        Veronica Castang 1/25/83
                                        Elizabeth Norment 4/5/83

Harry Bagley; Martin   Nicolas Surovy
                                        Barry Cullison 9/21/82

CRIMES OF THE HEART

	N.Y. Off Bway 12/9/80 *N.Y. Bway 11/4/81*	*Los Angeles 4/17/83*

Meg MaGrath	Mary Beth Hurt
	   Holly Hunter 6/8/82
	   Kathy Danzer 9/7/82
		Mary Beth Hurt

Babe Botrelle	Mia Dillon J. Smith-Cameron 8/3/82	Mia Dillon
Lenny MaGrath	Lizbeth Mackay Caryn West 9/7/82	Lizbeth Mackay
Barnette Lloyd	Peter MacNicol Tim Choate 8/3/82	Peter MacNicol

THE DINING ROOM

	New York 2/24/82	*Washington, D.C. 6/5/82*

	Remak Ramsay
	   Charles Kimbrough 6/22/82
	   Rex Robbins 1/83
		Barry Nelson

	John Shea
	   John Getz 6/15/82
	   Nicholas Hormann 4/83	

	Lois de Banzie Debra Mooney 8/10/82	Frances Sternhagen

	Pippa Pearthree
	   Patricia Wettig 5/29/82
	   Cara Duff-MacCormick 4/83	

DREAMGIRLS

	New York 12/20/81	*Los Angeles 3/20/83*
Effie Melody White	Jennifer Holliday Vanessa Townsell 12/6/82	Jennifer Holliday
Lorrell Robinson	Loretta Devine	Arnetia Walker
C. C. White	Obba Babatunde	Lawrence Clayton

James Thunder Early	Cleavant Derricks	Clinton Derricks-Carroll
Curtis Taylor Jr.	Ben Harney	Larry Riley
Deena Jones	Sheryl Lee Ralph	Linda Leilani Brown
Michelle Morris	Deborah Burrell Terry Burrell 3/83	Deborah Burrell
Marty	Vondie Curtis-Hall	Weyman Thompson

EVITA

New York 9/25/79

Eva Peron Patti LuPone (eves.)
Terri Klausner (mats.)
  Nancy Opel (mats.) 10/80
  Derin Altay (eves.) 1/12/81
  Loni Ackerman (eves.) 4/5/82
  Pamela Blake (mats.) 5/25/83
  Florence Lacey (eves.) 5/30/83

Juan Peron Bob Gunton
David Cryer 10/20/80

Che Mandy Patinkin
James Stein 10/20/80
Anthony Crivello 4/5/82
Scott Holmes 4/5/83

Note: Touring company casts, including replacements, of *Evita* appear on page 423 of *The Best Plays of 1981–1982.*

THE FANTASTICKS

New York 5/3/60

El Gallo Jerry Orbach
Gene Rupert
Bert Convy
John Cunningham
Don Stewart 1/63
David Cryer
Keith Charles 10/63
John Boni 1/13/65
Jack Metter 9/14/65
George Ogee
Keith Charles
Tom Urich 8/30/66
John Boni 10/5/66
Jack Crowder 6/13/67
Nils Hedrick 9/19/67
Keith Charles 10/9/67
Robert Goss 11/7/67
Joe Bellomo 3/11/68
Michael Tartel 7/8/69
Donald Billett 6/70
Joe Bellomo 2/15/72
David Rexroad 6/73
David Snell 12/73

Hal Robinson 4/2/74
Chapman Roberts 7/30/74
David Brummel 2/18/75
David Rexroad 8/31/75
Roger Brown 9/30/75
David Rexroad 9/1/76
Joseph Galiano 10/14/76
Douglas Clark 5/2/78
Joseph Galiano 5/23/78
Richard Muenz 10/78
Joseph Galiano 2/20/79
George Lee Andrews 11/27/79
Sal Provenza 5/13/80
Lance Brodie 9/8/81
Roger Neil 5/17/83

Luisa

Rita Gardner
Carla Huston
Liza Stuart 12/61
Eileen Fulton
Alice Cannon 9/62
Royce Lennelle
B. J. Ward 12/1/64
Leta Anderson 7/13/65
Carole Demas 11/22/66
Anne Kaye 5/28/68
Carolyn Mignini 7/29/69
Virginia Gregory 7/27/70
Leta Anderson
Marti Morris 3/7/72
Sharon Werner 12/73
Sarah Rice 6/24/74
Cheryl Horne 7/1/75
Sarah Rice 7/29/75
Betsy Joslyn 3/23/76
Kathy Vestuto 7/18/78
Betsy Joslyn 8/8/78
Kathryn Morath 11/28/78
Debbie McLeod 4/17/79
Joan Wiest 10/9/79
Marti Morris 11/6/79
Carol Ann Scott 5/20/80
Beverly Lambert 9/2/80
Judith Blazer 12/1/80
Elizabeth Bruzzese 8/15/81
Virginia Gregory 12/7/82

Matt

Kenneth Nelson
Gino Conforti
Jack Blackton 10/63
Paul Giovanni
Ty McConnell
Richard Rothbard
Gary Krawford
Bob Spencer 9/5/64
Erik Howell 6/28/66
Gary Krawford 12/12/67
Steve Skiles 2/6/68

Craig Carnelia 1/69
Samuel D. Ratcliffe 8/5/69
Michael Glenn-Smith 5/26/70
Jimmy Dodge 9/20/70
Geoffrey Taylor 8/31/71
Erik Howell 3/14/72
Phil Killian 7/4/72
Richard Lincoln 9/72
Bruce Cryer 7/24/73
Phil Killian 9/11/73
Michael Glenn-Smith 6/17/74
Ralph Bruneau 10/29/74
Bruce Cryer 9/30/75
Jeff Knight 7/19/77
Michael Glenn-Smith 1/9/79
Christopher Seppe 3/6/79
Howard Lawrence 12/29/81

Note: As of May 31, 1983, 30 actors had played the role of El Gallo, 26 actresses had played Luisa, and 22 actors had played Matt.

FORBIDDEN BROADWAY

	New York 5/4/82	*Los Angeles 4/26/83*
	Gerard Alessandrini	Gerard Alessandrini
	Jason Alexander 4/5/83	
	Fred Barton	Fred Barton
	Jeff Etjen 4/5/83	
	Bill Carmichael	Bill Carmichael
	Brad Garside 4/5/83	
	Nora Mae Lyng	Dee Hoty
	Ann Morrison 4/5/83	
	Chloé Webb	Chloé Webb
	Marilyn Pasekoff 4/5/83	

42nd STREET

	New York 8/25/80	*Chicago 1/1/83*
Julian Marsh	Jerry Orbach	Ron Holgate
Dorothy Brock	Tammy Grimes	Elizabeth Allen
	Milicent Martin 10/28/81	Milicent Martin 4/26/83
	Elizabeth Allen 4/26/83	
Peggy Sawyer	Wanda Richert	Nancy Sinclair
	Nancy Sinclair 10/15/80	
	Karen Prunczik 10/20/80	
	Wanda Richert 10/25/80	
	Lisa Brown 7/26/82	
Billy Lawlor	Lee Roy Reams	Jim Walton
Maggie Jones	Carole Cook	Bibi Osterwald
	Peggy Cass 9/81	
	Jessica James 10/4/82	
Bert Barry	Joseph Bova	William Linton

FORBIDDEN BROADWAY—Members of the Los Angeles company (Bill Carmichael, Chloé Webb, Gerard Alessandrini and Dee Hoty) in a scene from the long-running off-Broadway revue

GENIUSES

New York 5/13/82

Sky Bullene   Joanne Camp
                       Christine Ebersole 7/6/82
                       Morgan Fairchild 12/28/82
                       Joanne Camp 3/1/83

Jocko Pyle   Michael Gross
                       Peter Evans 5/24/82

JOSEPH AND THE AMAZING TECHNICOLOR DREAMCOAT

N.Y. Off B'way 11/18/81
N.Y. B'way 1/27/82   *New Orleans 3/2/82*

Joseph   Bill Hutton   Michael Croach
               Allen Fawcett 6/24/82   Bill Hutton 6/24/82

	Andy Gibb 12/1/82 Doug Voet 1/13/83 David Cassidy 3/6/83	Andy Gibb
Narrator	Laurie Beechman Sharon Brown 12/1/82	Sharon Brown

LITTLE SHOP OF HORRORS

	New York 7/27/82	Los Angeles 4/27/83
Mushnik	Hy Anzell Fyvush Finkel 3/83	Hy Anzell
Audrey	Ellen Greene Faith Prince 3/83	Ellen Greene
Seymour	Lee Wilkof Brad Moranz 3/83	Lee Wilkof
Audrey II	Martin P. Robinson Anthony B. Asbury 3/83	Martin P. Robinson

MASS APPEAL

	N.Y. Off B'way 4/22/80 N.Y. B'way 11/12/81	Chicago 7/21/82
Father Tim Farley	Milo O'Shea Milo O'Shea	Milo O'Shea
Mark Dolson	Eric Roberts Michael O'Keefe	Adam Redfield

"MASTER HAROLD" . . . AND THE BOYS

	New York 5/4/82	Boston 3/15/83
Sam	Zakes Mokae James Earl Jones 11/12/82	James Earl Jones
Willie	Danny Glover Delroy Lindo 2/3/83	Delroy Lindo
Hally	Lonny Price	Charles Michael Wright

NINE

	New York 5/9/82
Guido Contini	Raul Julia Bert Convy 1/10/83 Raul Julia 1/24/83 Sergio Franchi 5/9/83
Luisa Contini	Karen Akers Maureen McGovern 12/6/82
Liliane La Fleur	Liliane Montevecchi Priscilla Lopez 11/8/82 Liliane Montevecchi 11/22/82

Carla	Anita Morris Beth McVey 5/2/83 Anita Morris 5/16/83
Claudia	Shelly Burch Kim Criswell 1/31/83

THE PIRATES OF PENZANCE

New York 1/8/81

Pirate King	Kevin Kline Treat Williams 8/25/81 Walter Niehenke 1/12/82 Treat Williams 1/26/82 Gary Sandy 3/25/82 James Belushi 7/27/82 Wally Kurth 9/14/82
Ruth	Estelle Parsons Kaye Ballard 9/15/81 Marsha Bagwell 9/28/82
Mabel Stanley	Linda Ronstadt Karla DaVito 6/2/81 Maureen McGovern 9/8/81 Kathryn Morath 2/16/82 Maureen McGovern 3/2/82 Pam Dawber 6/29/82 Maureen McGovern 7/20/82
Major-General Stanley	George Rose George S. Irving 12/8/81 Joseph Pichette 3/9/82 George Rose 3/16/82
Frederic	Rex Smith Robby Benson 8/11/81 Patrick Cassidy 1/5/82 Rex Smith 4/13/82 Patrick Cassidy 4/27/82 Peter Noone 7/27/82
Sergeant	Tony Azito David Garrison 12/8/81 Tony Azito 3/16/82

Note: Casts of touring company and London company of *The Pirates of Penzance* appear on pages 427 and 428 of *The Best Plays of 1981–82.*

PUMP BOYS AND DINETTES

New York 2/4/82

Jim	Jim Wann Loudon Wainwright III 8/25/82 Tom Chapin 1/5/83
Rhetta Cupp	Cass Morgan Ronee Blakley 9/29/82 Cass Morgan 1/3/83 Margaret LaMee 2/9/83

SISTER MARY IGNATIUS EXPLAINS IT ALL FOR YOU

New York 10/21/81

Sister Mary Ignatius	Elizabeth Franz Nancy Marchand 9/28/82 Mary Louise Wilson 3/15/83
Aloysius Benheim	Jeff Brooks Christopher Durang 7/13/82 Jeff Brooks 7/27/82 Christopher Durang 12/24/82 Jeff Brooks 12/28/82 Brian Keeler
Dame Ellen Terry	Mary Catherine Wright Deborah Rush 5/24/82 Alice Playten 7/13/82
Meg	Polly Draper Carolyn Mignini 5/24/82

A SOLDIER'S PLAY

		#1 Los Angeles 8/19/82
	New York 11/20/81	#2 Chicago 6/3/83
Tech. Sgt. Vernon Waters	Adolph Caesar Arthur French 8/17/82 Adolph Caesar 10/5/82 Arthur French	#1 Adolph Caesar #2 Adolph Caesar
Capt. Richard Davenport	Charles Brown	#1 Robert Hooks #2 Charles Brown
Pvt. C.J. Memphis	Larry Riley David Allen Grier 8/17/82 Larry Riley 10/5/82	#1 Larry Riley #2 Ben Epp

SOPHISTICATED LADIES

		#1 Las Vegas 12/28/82
	New York 3/1/81	#2 Pittsburgh 5/24/83
	Gregory Hines Maurice Hines 1/5/82	#1 Harold Nicholas #2 Gregg Burge Ira Hawkins
	Judith Jamison	#1 Paula Kelly #2 Janet Hubert
	Phyllis Hyman	#1 Freda Payne #2 Dee Dee Bridgewater
	Priscilla Baskerville	#1 Freda Payne #2 Dee Dee Bridgewater
	Hinton Battle Gary Chapman 1/5/82 T.A. Stephens 10/82	#1 Eugene Fleming #2 Bruce Anthony Davis
	P.J. Benjamin Don Correia 3/29/82	#1 George Ratliff #2 Jamie Rocco

Terri Klausner	#1 Beth Bowles
Donna Drake 1/5/82	#2 Christina Saffran
Gregg Burge	#1 Garry Q. Lewis
Michael Scott Gregory 1/5/82	#2 Gregg Burge

Note: Cast of the first touring company of *Sophisticated Ladies* appears on page 428 of *The Best Plays of 1981–1982*. Note, too, that Mr. Hines's assignments in New York have been taken over in Tour #2 by a dancer (Mr. Burge) and a singer (Mr. Hawkins), and that the songs sung by both Miss Hyman and Miss Baskerville in New York have been assumed by Miss Payne in Tour #1 and by Miss Bridgewater in Tour #2.

SUGAR BABIES

New York 10/8/79	*Chicago 11/8/82*
Ann Miller	Ann Miller
Helen Gallagher 9/21/81	Toni Kaye 2/10/83
Ann Miller 10/12/81	Carol Lawrence 3/14/83
	Ann Miller 4/27/83
Mickey Rooney	Mickey Rooney
Joey Bishop 2/2/81	
Mickey Rooney 3/2/81	
Rip Taylor 6/29/81	
Mickey Rooney 7/8/81	
Rip Taylor 12/17/81	
Mickey Rooney 12/26/81	
Eddie Bracken 5/31/82	
Mickey Rooney 6/14/82	

Note: Cast of first touring company of *Sugar Babies* appears on page 428–429 of *The Best Plays of 1981–1982*.

TORCH SONG TRILOGY

	N.Y. Off B'way 1/15/82 *N.Y. B'way 6/10/82*
Arnold Beckoff	Harvey Fierstein
	Harvey Fierstein
	Donald Corren (mats.) 4/83
Mrs. Beckoff	Estelle Getty
	Estelle Getty
	Barbara Barrie 1/31/83
	Estelle Getty 2/14/83
David	Matthew Broderick
	Fisher Stevens 3/21/82
	Fisher Stevens
Ed	Joel Crothers
	Court Miller
	Court Miller

WOMAN OF THE YEAR

	New York 3/29/81
Tess Harding	Lauren Bacall
	Raquel Welch 12/1/81
	Lauren Bacall 12/15/81

Raquel Welch 6/29/82
Debbie Reynolds 2/11/83
Louise Troy 3/5/83
Debbie Reynolds 3/8/83

Sam Craig   Harry Guardino
Jamie Ross 12/1/81
Harry Guardino 12/15/81
Jamie Ross 6/29/82

Jan Donovan   Marilyn Cooper
Carol Arthur 10/13/81
Marilyn Cooper 10/20/81

Note: Performances of *Woman of the Year* were suspended between 1/2/83 and 2/11/83.

FACTS AND
FIGURES

LONG RUNS ON BROADWAY

The following shows have run 500 or more continuous performances in a single production, usually the first, not including previews or extra non-profit performances, allowing for vacation layoffs and special one-booking engagements, but not including return engagements after a show has gone on tour. In all cases the numbers were obtained directly from the shows' production offices. Where there are title similarities, the production is identified as follows: (p) straight play version, (m) musical version, (r) revival.

THROUGH MAY 31, 1983

(PLAYS MARKED WITH ASTERISK WERE STILL PLAYING JUNE 1, 1983)

Plays	Number Performances	Plays	Number Performances
Grease	3,388	How To Succeed in Business	
*A Chorus Line	3,249	Without Really Trying	1,417
Fiddler on the Roof	3,242	Hellzapoppin	1,404
Life With Father	3,224	The Music Man	1,375
Tobacco Road	3,182	Funny Girl	1,348
Hello, Dolly	2,844	Mummenschanz	1,326
*Oh! Calcutta! (r)	2,840	Oh! Calcutta!	1,314
My Fair Lady	2,717	Angel Street	1,295
Annie	2,377	Lightnin'	1,291
Man of La Mancha	2,328	Promises, Promises	1,281
Abie's Irish Rose	2,327	The King and I	1,246
Oklahoma!	2,212	Cactus Flower	1,234
Pippin	1,944	Sleuth	1,222
South Pacific	1,925	1776	1,217
The Magic Show	1,920	Equus	1,209
Deathtrap	1,793	Sugar Babies	1,208
Gemini	1,788	Guys and Dolls	1,200
Harvey	1,775	Cabaret	1,165
Dancin'	1,774	Mister Roberts	1,157
Hair	1,750	*42nd Street	1,154
The Wiz	1,672	Annie Get Your Gun	1,147
Born Yesterday	1,642	The Seven Year Itch	1,141
The Best Little Whorehouse in		Butterflies Are Free	1,128
Texas	1,639	Pins and Needles	1,108
Ain't Misbehavin'	1,604	Plaza Suite	1,097
Mary, Mary	1,572	They're Playing Our Song	1,082
The Voice of the Turtle	1,557	Kiss Me, Kate	1,070
*Evita	1,535	Don't Bother Me, I Can't Cope	1,065
Barefoot in the Park	1,530	The Pajama Game	1,063
Mame (m)	1,508	Shenandoah	1,050
Same Time, Next Year	1,453	The Teahouse of the August	
Arsenic and Old Lace	1,444	Moon	1,027
The Sound of Music	1,443	*Amadeus	1,022

Plays	Number Performances	Plays	Number Performances
Damn Yankees	1,019	Sophisticated Ladies	767
Never Too Late	1,007	Bubbling Brown Sugar	766
Any Wednesday	982	State of the Union	765
A Funny Thing Happened on		The First Year	760
the Way to the Forum	964	You Know I Can't Hear You	
The Odd Couple	964	When the Water's Running	755
Anna Lucasta	957	Two for the Seesaw	750
Kiss and Tell	956	Death of a Salesman	742
Dracula (r)	925	For Colored Girls, etc.	742
Bells Are Ringing	924	Sons o' Fun	742
The Moon Is Blue	924	Candide (mr)	740
Beatlemania	920	Gentlemen Prefer Blondes	740
The Elephant Man	916	The Man Who Came to Dinner	739
Luv	901	Call Me Mister	734
Chicago	898	West Side Story	732
Applause	896	High Button Shoes	727
Can-Can	892	Finian's Rainbow	725
Carousel	890	Claudia	722
Hats Off to Ice	889	The Gold Diggers	720
Fanny	888	Jesus Christ Superstar	720
Children of a Lesser God	887	Carnival	719
Follow the Girls	882	The Diary of Anne Frank	717
Camelot	873	I Remember Mama	714
I Love My Wife	872	Tea and Sympathy	712
The Bat	867	Junior Miss	710
My Sister Eileen	864	Last of the Red Hot Lovers	706
No, No, Nanette (r)	861	Company	705
Song of Norway	860	Seventh Heaven	704
Chapter Two	857	Gypsy (m)	702
A Streetcar Named Desire	855	The Miracle Worker	700
Barnum	854	Da	697
Comedy in Music	849	The King and I (r)	696
Raisin	847	Cat on a Hot Tin Roof	694
That Championship Season	844	Li'l Abner	693
You Can't Take It With You	837	Peg o' My Heart	692
La Plume de Ma Tante	835	The Children's Hour	691
Three Men on a Horse	835	Purlie	688
The Subject Was Roses	832	Dead End	687
Inherit the Wind	806	The Lion and the Mouse	686
No Time for Sergeants	796	White Cargo	686
Fiorello!	795	Dear Ruth	683
Where's Charley?	792	East Is West	680
The Ladder	789	Come Blow Your Horn	677
Forty Carats	780	The Most Happy Fella	676
The Prisoner of Second Avenue	780	The Doughgirls	671
Oliver	774	The Impossible Years	670
The Pirates of Penzance (1980 r)	772	Irene	670
Woman of the Year	770	Boy Meets Girl	669

Plays	Number Performances	Plays	Number Performances
Beyond the Fringe............	667	No Strings	580
Who's Afraid of Virginia Woolf?	664	Brother Rat	577
Blithe Spirit	657	Show Boat	572
A Trip to Chinatown	657	The Show-Off................	571
The Women	657	Sally	570
Bloomer Girl	654	Golden Boy (m).............	568
The Fifth Season	654	One Touch of Venus.........	567
Rain	648	Happy Birthday.............	564
Witness for the Prosecution	645	Look Homeward, Angel.......	564
Call Me Madam..............	644	Morning's at Seven (r)	564
Janie	642	The Glass Menagerie.........	561
The Green Pastures..........	640	I Do! I Do!.................	560
Auntie Mame (p).............	639	Wonderful Town	559
*Joseph and the Amazing		Rose Marie..................	557
Technicolor Dreamcoat (r) ..	638	Strictly Dishonorable..........	557
A Man for All Seasons........	637	Sweeney Todd, the Demon	
The Fourposter	632	Barber of Fleet Street.......	557
Two Gentlemen of Verona (m) .	627	A Majority of One............	556
The Tenth Man	623	The Great White Hope........	556
Is Zat So?..................	618	Toys in the Attic.............	556
Anniversary Waltz............	615	Sunrise at Campobello.........	556
The Happy Time (p).........	614	Jamaica.....................	555
Separate Rooms..............	613	Stop the World—I Want to Get	
Affairs of State...............	610	Off	555
Star and Garter	609	Florodora	553
The Student Prince	608	*Pump Boys and Dinettes	553
Sweet Charity................	608	Ziegfeld Follies (1943).........	553
Bye Bye Birdie..............	607	Dial "M" for Murder	552
Irene (r)	604	Good News	551
Broadway	603	Peter Pan (r)	551
Adonis.....................	603	Let's Face It.................	547
*Dreamgirls	601	Milk and Honey..............	543
Street Scene (p)	601	Within the Law	541
Kiki.......................	600	The Music Master...........	540
Flower Drum Song	600	Pal Joey (r)..................	540
A Little Night Music	600	What Makes Sammy Run?.....	540
Don't Drink the Water........	598	The Sunshine Boys	538
Wish You Were Here	598	What a Life	538
A Society Circus	596	Crimes of the Heart	535
Absurd Person Singular	592	The Unsinkable Molly Brown ..	532
Blossom Time................	592	The Red Mill (r)	531
A Day in Hollywood/A Night		A Raisin in the Sun...........	530
in the Ukraine.............	588	Godspell	527
The Me Nobody Knows.......	586	The Solid Gold Cadillac.......	526
The Two Mrs. Carrolls........	585	Irma La Douce	524
Kismet	583	The Boomerang	522
Detective Story..............	581	Follies	521
Brigadoon..................	581	Rosalinda	521

Plays	Number Performances	Plays	Number Performances
The Best Man	520	Sugar	505
Chauve-Souris	520	Shuffle Along	504
Blackbirds of 1928	518	Up in Central Park	504
The Gin Game	517	Carmen Jones	503
Sunny	517	The Member of the Wedding	501
Victoria Regina	517	Panama Hattie	501
Fifth of July	511	Personal Appearance	501
Half a Sixpence	511	Bird in Hand	500
The Vagabond King	511	Room Service	500
The New Moon	509	Sailor, Beware!	500
The World of Suzie Wong	508	Tomorrow the World	500
The Rothschilds	507		

LONG RUNS OFF BROADWAY

Plays	Number Performances	Plays	Number Performances
*The Fantasticks	9,600	The Connection	722
The Threepenny Opera	2,611	The Passion of Dracula	714
Godspell	2,124	Adaptation & Next	707
Jacques Brel	1,847	Oh! Calcutta!	704
Vanities	1,785	Scuba Duba	692
You're a Good Man Charlie		The Knack	685
Brown	1,547	The Club	674
The Blacks	1,408	The Balcony	672
One Mo' Time	1,372	*Sister Mary Ignatius Explains	
Let My People Come	1,327	It All for You & The Actor's	
The Hot l Baltimore	1,166	Nightmare	669
I'm Getting My Act Together		America Hurrah	634
and Taking It on the Road	1,165	Hogan's Goat	607
Little Mary Sunshine	1,143	The Trojan Women (r)	600
El Grande de Coca-Cola	1,114	Krapp's Last Tape & The Zoo	
One Flew Over the Cuckoo's		Story	582
Nest (r)	1,025	The Dumbwaiter & The	
The Boys in the Band	1,000	Collection	578
Your Own Thing	933	Dames at Sea	575
Curley McDimple	931	The Crucible (r)	571
Leave It to Jane (r)	928	The Iceman Cometh (r)	565
The Mad Show	871	*The Dining Room	552
*Cloud 9	847	The Hostage (r)	545
Scrambled Feet	831	Six Characters in Search of an	
The Effect of Gamma Rays on		Author (r)	529
Man-in-the-Moon		The Dirtiest Show in Town	509
Marigolds	819	Happy Ending & Day of	
A View From the Bridge (r)	780	Absence	504
The Boy Friend (r)	763	The Boys From Syracuse (r)	500
The Pocket Watch	725		

NEW YORK CRITICS AWARDS, 1935–36 to 1982–83

Listed below are the New York Drama Critics Circle Awards from 1935–36 through 1982–83 classified as follows: (1) Best American Play, (2) Best Foreign Play, (3) Best Musical, (4) Best, regardless of category (this category was established by new voting rules in 1962–63 and did not exist prior to that year).

1935–36—(1) Winterset
1936–37—(1) High Tor
1937–38—(1) Of Mice and Men, (2) Shadow and Substance
1938–39—(1) No award, (2) The White Steed
1939–40—(1) The Time of Your Life
1940–41—(1) Watch on the Rhine, (2) The Corn Is Green
1941–42—(1) No award, (2) Blithe Spirit
1942–43—(1) The Patriots
1943–44—(2) Jacobowsky and the Colonel
1944–45—(1) The Glass Menagerie
1945–46—(3) Carousel
1946–47—(1) All My Sons, (2) No Exit, (3) Brigadoon
1947–48—(1) A Streetcar Named Desire, (2) The Winslow Boy
1948–49—(1) Death of a Salesman, (2) The Madwoman of Chaillot, (3) South Pacific
1949–50—(1) The Member of the Wedding (2) The Cocktail Party, (3) The Consul
1950–51—(1) Darkness at Noon, (2) The Lady's Not for Burning, (3) Guys and Dolls
1951–52—(1) I Am a Camera, (2) Venus Observed, (3) Pal Joey (Special citation to Don Juan in Hell)
1952–53—(1) Picnic, (2) The Love of Four Colonels, (3) Wonderful Town
1953–54—(1) Teahouse of the August Moon, (2) Ondine, (3) The Golden Apple
1954–55—(1) Cat on a Hot Tin Roof, (2) Witness for the Prosecution, (3) The Saint of Bleecker Street
1955–56—(1) The Diary of Anne Frank, (2) Tiger at the Gates, (3) My Fair Lady
1956–57—(1) Long Day's Journey Into Night, (2) The Waltz of the Toreadors, (3) The Most Happy Fella
1957–58—(1) Look Homeward, Angel, (2) Look Back in Anger, (3) The Music Man
1958–59—(1) A Raisin in the Sun, (2) The Visit, (3) La Plume de Ma Tante
1959–60—(1) Toys in the Attic, (2) Five Finger Exercise, (3) Fiorello!
1960–61—(1) All the Way Home, (2) A Taste of Honey, (3) Carnival
1961–62—(1) The Night of the Iguana, (2) A Man for All Seasons, (3) How to Succeed in Business Without Really Trying
1962–63—(4) Who's Afraid of Virginia Woolf? (Special citation to Beyond the Fringe)
1963–64—(4) Luther, (3) Hello, Dolly! (Special citation to The Trojan Women)
1964–65—(4) The Subject Was Roses, (3) Fiddler on the Roof
1965–66—(4) The Persecution and Assassination of Marat as Performed by the Inmates of the Asylum of Charenton Under the Direction of the Marquis de Sade, (3) Man of La Mancha
1966–67—(4) The Homecoming, (3) Cabaret
1967–68—(4) Rosencrantz and Guildenstern Are Dead, (3) Your Own Thing
1968–69—(4) The Great White Hope, (3) 1776
1969–70—(4) Borstal Boy, (1) The Effect of Gamma Rays on Man-in-the-Moon Marigolds, (3) Company
1970–71—(4) Home, (1) The House of Blue Leaves, (3) Follies
1971–72—(4) That Championship Season, (2) The Screens, (3) Two Gentlemen of Verona (Special citations to Sticks and Bones and Old Times)
1972–73—(4) The Changing Room, (1) The Hot l Baltimore, (3) A Little Night Music
1973–74—(4) The Contractor, (1) Short Eyes, (3) Candide
1974–75—(4) Equus, (1) The Taking of Miss Janie, (3) A Chorus Line
1975–76—(4) Travesties, (1) Streamers, (3) Pacific Overtures
1976–77—(4) Otherwise Engaged, (1) American Buffalo, (3) Annie
1977–78—(4) Da, (3) Ain't Misbehavin'
1978–79—(4) The Elephant Man, (3) Sweeney Todd, the Demon Barber of Fleet Street
1979–80—(4) Talley's Folly, (2) Betrayal, (3) Evita (Special citation to Peter Brook's Le Centre International de Créations Théâtrales for its repertory)
1980–81—(4) A Lesson From Aloes, (1) Crimes of the Heart (Special citations to Lena

Horne: The Lady and Her Music and the New York Shakespeare Festival production of The Pirates of Penzance)
1981–82—(4) The Life & Adventures of Nicho-

las Nickleby, (1) A Soldier's Play
1982–83—(4) Brighton Beach Memoirs, (2) Plenty, (3) Little Shop of Horrors (Special citation to Young Playwrights Festival)

NEW YORK DRAMA CRITICS CIRCLE VOTING, 1982–83

The New York Drama Critics Circle voted Neil Simon's *Brighton Beach Memoirs* the best play of the season on a fourth multiple-choice ballot, after no play received a majority of first choices on the first ballot. With 3 points given for a critic's first choice, 2 for second and 1 for third, in order to win on this ballot under the Circle's voting rules a play must receive a point total of three times the number of members present and voting (16 without the proxies), divided by two, plus one, i.e. 25 points. *Brighton Beach Memoirs* led on every ballot including the first, on which only the critics' first choices were named as follows, including 3 proxies: *Brighton Beach Memoirs* 6 (Clive Barnes, John Beaufort, Richard Hummler, Hobe Morrison, Marilyn Stasio, Edwin Wilson), *'night, Mother* 3 (Mel Gussow, Don Nelsen, John Simon), *Plenty* 3 (Howard Kissel, William Raidy, Frank Rich), *Painting Churches* 2, (Glenne Currie, Edith Oliver), *Passion* 1 (Ted Kalem), *Top Girls* 1 (Julius Novick), *Quartermaine's Terms* 1 (Allan Wallach), *Angels Fall* 1 (Douglas Watt), *Edmond* 1 (Michael Feingold).

In the shifting weight of proportional scoring, with a couple of critics expressing as much rooting interest as esthetic judgment in the way they voted, *Brighton Beach Memoirs* gained ground through two ballots and finally attracted the necessary number of points to win, 25, in competition with *'night, Mother* (23), *Plenty* (11), *Quartermaine's Terms* (11), *Top Girls* (8), *Angels Fall* (4), *Moose Murders* (4), *Passion* (3), *Painting Churches* (3), *Edmond* (2), *Skirmishes* (1), *Private Lives* (1, an ineligible selection).

Having named an American play its best of bests, the Circle proceeded to vote on a best foreign play. David Hare's *Plenty* was the front-runner on the first-choice ballot with 8 (Barnes, Feingold, Gussow, Kissel, Nelsen, Raidy, Rich, Stasio) in competition with *Quartermaine's Terms* 5 (Hummler, Morrison, Oliver, Simon, Wallach), *Top Girls* 4 (Beaufort, Currie, Novick, Wilson) and *Passion* 1 (Kalem). Though it did not have the necessary majority of first-place votes on this ballot, *Plenty* won handily on the second, point-weighted ballot with 28 points in competition with *Top Girls* (23), *Quartermaine's Terms* (22), *Passion* (13), *Slab Boys* (2), *Skirmishes* (2), *Good* (2), *Teahouse* (2), *Rape Upon Rape* (1, a Henry Fielding play which had never before been produced in New York).

Little Shop of Horrors by Alan Menken and Howard Ashman won the Circle's citation as best musical on the first ballot with the necessary majority of 10 (Barnes, Currie, Feingold, Gussow, Hummler, Nelsen, Novick, Oliver, Rich, Stasio) of 18 voting critics, in competition with *Cats* 4 (Beaufort, Kalem, Raidy, Wallach) and 4 abstentions.

Before adjourning their 1983 voting meeting, the Circle voted a special citation to the Young Playwrights Festival co-sponsored by The Foundation of the Dramatists Guild and Circle Repertory Company.

Hobe Morrison *(Variety)*, William Raidy (Newhouse Papers) and Douglas Watt *(Daily News)* were absent but voted by proxy on first ballots (Morrison for play only). Walter Kerr *(Times)* and Jack Kroll *(Newsweek)* were absent and not voting.

FOURTH BALLOT FOR BEST PLAY

Critic	1st Choice (3 pts.)	2d Choice (2 pts.)	3d Choice (1 pt.)
Clive Barnes *Post*	Brighton Beach Memoirs	Moose Murders	Passion
John Beaufort *Monitor*	Brighton Beach	Angels Fall	Quartermaine's Terms
Glenne Currie *UPI*	Brighton Beach	Top Girls	Painting Churches
Michael Feingold *Village Voice*	'night, Mother	Edmond	Plenty
Mel Gussow *Times*	'night, Mother	Plenty	Angels Fall
Richard Hummler *Variety*	Brighton Beach	Quartermaine	Skirmishes
Ted Kalem *Time*	Brighton Beach	Moose Murders	Private Lives
Howard Kissel *Women's Wear*	Plenty	Quartermaine	'night, Mother
Don Nelsen *Daily News*	'night, Mother	Plenty	Brighton Beach
Julius Novick *Village Voice*	'night, Mother	Top Girls	Passion
Edith Oliver *New Yorker*	Brighton Beach	Painting Churches	Top Girls
Frank Rich *Times*	'night, Mother	Plenty	Passion
John Simon *New York*	'night, Mother	Quartermaine	Angels Fall
Marilyn Stasio *Post*	Brighton Beach	Quartermaine	Top Girls
Allan Wallach *Newsday*	'night, Mother	Quartermaine	Plenty
Edwin Wilson *Wall St. Journal*	Brighton Beach	Top Girls	'night, Mother

SECOND BALLOT FOR BEST FOREIGN PLAY

Critic	1st Choice (3 pts.)	2d Choice (2 pts.)	3d Choice (1 pt.)
Barnes	Plenty	Passion	Top Girls
Beaufort	Top Girls	Quartermaine's Terms	Plenty
Currie	Top Girls	Slab Boys	Plenty
Feingold	Plenty	Teahouse	Rape Upon Rape
Gussow	Plenty	Passion	Quartermaine
Hummler	Quartermaine	Skirmishes	Plenty

Kalem	Passion	Quartermaine	Plenty
Kissel	Plenty	Quartermaine	Top Girls
Nelsen	Plenty	Top Girls	Passion
Novick	Top Girls	Passion	Good
Oliver	Top Girls	Quartermaine	Good
Rich	Plenty	Passion	Quartermaine
Simon*		Quartermaine	Top Girls
Stasio	Plenty	Quartermaine	Top Girls
Wallach	Quartermaine	Plenty	Passion
Wilson	Top Girls	Quartermaine	Plenty

*Voted for only two plays, so that by the Circle's rules his choices counted for only 2 pts. and 1 pt.

CHOICES OF SOME OTHER CRITICS

Critic	Best Play	Best Musical
Casper Citron Modern Satellite	Angels Fall	Cats
Judith Crist WOR-TV, *TV Guide, Saturday Review*	Torch Song Trilogy	My One and Only
John Gambling WOR Radio	Plenty	Cats
Alvin Klein WNYC Radio, New York *Times*	Torch Song Trilogy	Little Shop of Horrors
James McLaughlin WCBS-TV	Plenty	Cats
Joel Siegel ABC-TV	Torch Song Trilogy	Little Shop of Horrors
Leida Snow WINS, ABC Radio	Torch Song Trilogy	My One and Only
Richard Scholem Radio Long Island	Passion & Brighton Beach Memoirs	Show Boat
Seymour Steinhardt WVNY and Channel 60-68	Torch Song Trilogy	Cats

PULITZER PRIZE WINNERS, 1916–17 to 1982–83

1916–17—No award

1917–18—Why Marry?, by Jesse Lynch Williams

1918–19—No award

1919–20—Beyond the Horizon, by Eugene O'Neill

1920–21—Miss Lulu Bett, by Zona Gale

1921–22—Anna Christie, by Eugene O'Neill

1922–23—Icebound, by Owen Davis

1923–24—Hell-Bent fer Heaven, by Hatcher Hughes

1924–25—They Knew What They Wanted, by Sidney Howard

1925–26—Craig's Wife, by George Kelly

1926–27—In Abraham's Bosom, by Paul Green

1927–28—Strange Interlude, by Eugene O'Neill

1928–29—Street Scene, by Elmer Rice

1929–30—The Green Pastures, by Marc Connelly

1930–31—Alison's House, by Susan Glaspell

1931–32—Of Thee I Sing, by George S. Kaufman, Morrie Ryskind, Ira and George Gershwin

1932–33—Both Your Houses, by Maxwell Anderson

1933–34—Men in White, by Sidney Kingsley

1934–35—The Old Maid, by Zoë Akins

1935–36—Idiot's Delight, by Robert E. Sherwood

1936–37—You Can't Take It With You, by Moss Hart and George S. Kaufman

1937–38—Our Town, by Thornton Wilder

1938–39—Abe Lincoln in Illinois, by Robert E. Sherwood

1939–40—The Time of Your Life, by William Saroyan

1940–41—There Shall Be No Night, by Robert E. Sherwood

1941–42—No award

1942–43—The Skin of Our Teeth, by Thornton Wilder

1943–44—No award

1944–45—Harvey, by Mary Chase

1945–46—State of the Union, by Howard Lindsay and Russel Crouse

1946–47—No award

1947–48—A Streetcar Named Desire, by Tennessee Williams

1948–49—Death of a Salesman, by Arthur Miller

1949–50—South Pacific, by Richard Rodgers, Oscar Hammerstein II and Joshua Logan

1950–51—No award

1951–52—The Shrike, by Joseph Kramm

1952–53—Picnic, by William Inge

1953–54—The Teahouse of the August Moon, by John Patrick

1954–55—Cat on a Hot Tin Roof, by Tennessee Williams

1955–56—The Diary of Anne Frank, by Frances Goodrich and Albert Hackett

1956–57—Long Day's Journey Into Night, by Eugene O'Neill

1957–58—Look Homeward, Angel, by Ketti Frings

1958–59—J.B., by Archibald MacLeish

1959–60—Fiorello!, by Jerome Weidman, George Abbott, Sheldon Harnick and Jerry Bock

1960–61—All the Way Home, by Tad Mosel

1961–62—How to Succeed in Business Without Really Trying, by Abe Burrows, Willie Gilbert, Jack Weinstock and Frank Loesser

1962–63—No award

1963–64—No award

1964–65—The Subject Was Roses, by Frank D. Gilroy

1965–66—No award

1966–67—A Delicate Balance, by Edward Albee

1967–68—No award

1968–69—The Great White Hope, by Howard Sackler

1969–70—No Place To Be Somebody, by Charles Gordone

1970–71—The Effect of Gamma Rays on Man-in-the-Moon Marigolds, by Paul Zindel

1971–72—No award

1972–73—That Championship Season, by Jason Miller

1973–74—No award

1974–75—Seascape, by Edward Albee

1975–76—A Chorus Line, by Michael Bennett, James Kirkwood, Nicholas Dante, Marvin Hamlisch and Edward Kleban

1976–77—The Shadow Box, by Michael Cristofer

1977–78—The Gin Game, by D.L. Coburn

1978–79—Buried Child, by Sam Shepard

1979–80—Talley's Folly, by Lanford Wilson

1980–81—Crimes of the Heart, by Beth Henley

1981–82—A Soldier's Play, by Charles Fuller

1982–83—'night, Mother, by Marsha Norman

THE TONY AWARDS, 1982–83

The Antoinette Perry (Tony) Awards are voted by members of the League of New York Theaters and Producers, the governing bodies of the Dramatists Guild, Actors' Equity, the American Theater Wing, the Society of Stage Directors and Choreographers, the United Scenic Artists Union and members of the first-night and second-night press, from a list of four nominees in each category.

The four nominations in each category (Broadway shows only; off Broadway excluded) are made by a committee of critics whose personnel changes annually at the invitation of the abovementioned League, which administers the Tony Awards under an agreement with the American Theater Wing. The 1982–83 Nominating Committee was composed of Clive Barnes of the New York *Post*,

Jay P. Carr of the Detroit *News,* Richard L. Coe, drama critic emeritus of the Washington *Post,* Brendan Gill of *The New Yorker,* William Glover, former drama critic for the Associated Press, Henry Hewes of the American Theater Critics Association, Mary C. Henderson, curator of the theater collection of the Museum of the City of New York, Norris Houghton, former president of the National Theater Conference, Kevin Kelly of the Boston *Globe,* Elliot Norton, former drama critic of the Boston *Herald American,* Seymour Peck of the New York *Times,* Frank Rich of the New York *Times,* Jay Sharbutt of the Associated Press and Douglas Watt of the New York *Daily News.*

The list of 1982–83 nominees follows, with winners in each category listed in **bold face type.**

BEST PLAY (award goes to both producer and author). *Angels Fall* by Lanford Wilson, produced by Elliot Martin, Circle Repertory Company, Lucille Lortel, The Shubert Organization and Kennedy Center; '*night, Mother* by Marsha Norman, produced by Dann Byck, Wendell Cherry, The Shubert Organization and Frederick M. Zollo; *Plenty* by David Hare, produced by Joseph Papp; **Torch Song Trilogy** by **Harvey Fierstein,** produced by **Kenneth Waissman, Martin Markinson, Lawrence Lane, John Glines, BetMar** and **Donald Tick.**

BEST MUSICAL (award to producers). *Blues in the Night* produced by Mitchell Maxwell, Alan J. Schuster, Fred H. Krones and M2 Entertainment, Inc.; **Cats** produced by **Cameron Mackintosh, The Really Useful Company, Ltd., David Geffen** and **The Shubert Organization;** *Merlin* produced by Ivan Reitman, Columbia Pictures Stage Productions, Inc., Marvin A. Krauss and James M. Nederlander; *My One and Only* produced by Paramount Theater Productions, Francine LeFrak and Kenneth-Mark Productions.

BEST BOOK OF A MUSICAL. *A Doll's Life* by Betty Comden and Adolph Green; *Cats* by **T.S. Eliot;** *Merlin* by Richard Levinson and William Link; *My One and Only* by Peter Stone and Timothy S. Mayer.

BEST SCORE OF A MUSICAL. *A Doll's Life,* music by Larry Grossman, lyrics by Betty Comden and Adolph Green; *Cats,* music by **Andrew Lloyd Webber,** lyrics by **T.S. Eliot;** *Merlin,* music by Elmer Bernstein, lyrics by Don Black; *Seven Brides for Seven Brothers,* music by Gene de Paul, Al Kasha and Joel Hirschhorn, lyrics by Johnny Mercer, Al Kasha and Joel Hirschhorn.

OUTSTANDING ACTOR IN A PLAY. Jeffrey De Munn in *K2,* **Harvey Fierstein** in *Torch Song*

Trilogy, Edward Herrmann in *Plenty,* Tony Lo Bianco in *A View from the Bridge.*

OUTSTANDING ACTRESS IN A PLAY. Kathy Bates in '*night, Mother,* Kate Nelligan in *Plenty,* Anne Pitoniak in '*night, Mother,* **Jessica Tandy** in *Foxfire.*

OUTSTANDING ACTOR IN A MUSICAL. Al Green in *Your Arms Too Short to Box With God,* George Hearn in *A Doll's Life,* Michael V. Smartt in *Porgy and Bess,* **Tommy Tune** in *My One and Only.*

OUTSTANDING ACTRESS IN A MUSICAL. **Natalia Makarova** in *On Your Toes,* Lonette McKee in *Show Boat,* Chita Rivera in *Merlin,* Twiggy in *My One and Only.*

OUTSTANDING FEATURED ACTOR IN A PLAY. **Matthew Broderick** in *Brighton Beach Memoirs,* Zeljko Ivanek in *Brighton Beach Memoirs,* George N. Martin in *Plenty,* Stephen Moore in *All's Well That Ends Well.*

OUTSTANDING FEATURED ACTRESS IN A PLAY. Elizabeth Franz in *Brighton Beach Memoirs,* Roxanne Hart in *Passion,* **Judith Ivey** in *Steaming,* Margaret Tyzack in *All's Well That Ends Well.*

OUTSTANDING FEATURED ACTOR IN A MUSICAL. **Charles "Honi" Coles** in *My One and Only,* Harry Groener in *Cats,* Stephen Hanan in *Cats,* Lara Teeter in *On Your Toes.*

OUTSTANDING FEATURED ACTRESS IN A MUSICAL. Christine Andreas in *On Your Toes,* **Betty Buckley** in *Cats,* Karla Burns in *Show Boat,* Denny Dillon in *My One and Only.*

OUTSTANDING DIRECTION OF A PLAY. Marshall W. Mason for *Angels Fall,* Tom

Tony nominees Zeljko Ivanek *(left)* and Matthew Broderick as brothers in Neil Simon's Critics Award-winning *Brighton Beach Memoirs*

Moore for *'night, Mother,* Trevor Nunn for *All's Well That Ends Well,* **Gene Saks** for *Brighton Beach Memoirs.*

OUTSTANDING DIRECTION OF A MUSICAL. Michael Kahn for *Show Boat,* **Trevor Nunn** for *Cats,* Ivan Reitman for *Merlin,* Tommy Tune and Thommie Walsh for *My One and Only.*

OUTSTANDING SCENIC DESIGN. John Gunter for *All's Well That Ends Well,* **Ming Cho Lee** for *K2,* David Mitchell for *Foxfire,* John Napier for *Cats.*

OUTSTANDING COSTUME DESIGN. Lindy Hemming for *All's Well That Ends Well,* **John Napier** for *Cats,* Rita Ryack for *My One and Only,* Patricia Zipprodt for *Alice in Wonderland.*

OUTSTANDING LIGHTING DESIGN. Ken Billington for *Foxfire,* Robert Bryan and Beverly Emmons for *All's Well That Ends Well,* **David Hersey** for *Cats,* Allen Lee Hughes for *K2.*

OUTSTANDING CHOREOGRAPHY. George Faison for *Porgy and Bess,* Gillian Lynne for *Cats,* Donald Saddler for *On Your Toes,* **Thommie Walsh** and **Tommy Tune** for *My One and Only.*

OUTSTANDING REPRODUCTION OF A PLAY OR MUSICAL. *All's Well That Ends Well* produced by The Shubert Organization, Elizabeth I. McCann, Nelle Nugent, ABC Video Enterprises, Inc., Roger S. Berlind, Rhoda R. Herrick, Jujamcyn Theatres/Richard G. Wolff, MGM/UA Home Entertainment Group, Inc., Mutual Benefit Productions/Karen Crane; *A View from the Bridge* produced by Zev Bufman and Sidney Shlenker; *The Caine Mutiny Court-Martial* produced by Circle in the Square and Kennedy Center; **On Your Toes** produced by **Alfred de Liagre Jr., Roger L. Stevens, John Mauceri, Donald R. Seawell** and **Andre Pastoria.**

SPECIAL TONY AWARDS. **Oregon Shakespearean Festival Association,** Ashland, Ore.; Theater Award '83 to **The Theater Collection, Museum of the City of New York.**

TONY AWARD WINNERS, 1947–1983

Listed below are the Antoinette Perry (Tony) Award winners in the categories of Best Play and Best Musical from the time these awards were established (1947) until the present.

1947—No play or musical award
1948—Mister Roberts; no musical award
1949—Death of a Salesman; Kiss Me, Kate
1950—The Cocktail Party; South Pacific
1951—The Rose Tattoo; Guys and Dolls
1952—The Fourposter; The King and I
1953—The Crucible; Wonderful Town
1954—The Teahouse of the August Moon; Kismet
1955—The Desperate Hours; The Pajama Game
1956—The Diary of Anne Frank; Damn Yankees
1957—Long Day's Journey Into Night; My Fair Lady
1958—Sunrise at Campobello; The Music Man
1959—J.B.; Redhead
1960—The Miracle Worker; Fiorello! and The Sound of Music (tie)
1961—Becket; Bye Bye Birdie
1962—A Man for All Seasons; How to Succeed in Business Without Really Trying
1963—Who's Afraid of Virginia Woolf?; A Funny Thing Happened on the Way to the Forum
1964—Luther; Hello, Dolly!
1965—The Subject Was Roses; Fiddler on the Roof

1966—The Persecution and Assassination of Marat as Performed by the Inmates of the Asylum of Charenton Under the Direction of the Marquis de Sade; Man of La Mancha
1967—The Homecoming; Cabaret
1968—Rosencrantz and Guildenstern Are Dead; Hallelujah, Baby!
1969—The Great White Hope; 1776
1970—Borstal Boy; Applause
1971—Sleuth; Company
1972—Sticks and Bones; Two Gentlemen of Verona
1973—That Championship Season; A Little Night Music
1974—The River Niger; Raisin
1975—Equus; The Wiz
1976—Travesties; A Chorus Line
1977—The Shadow Box; Annie
1978—Da; Ain't Misbehavin'
1979—The Elephant Man; Sweeney Todd, the Demon Barber of Fleet Street
1980—Children of a Lesser God; Evita
1981—Amadeus; 42nd Street
1982—The Life & Adventures of Nicholas Nickleby; Nine
1983—Torch Song Trilogy; Cats

THE OBIE AWARDS, 1982–83

The *Village Voice* Off-Broadway (Obie) Awards are given each year for excellence in various categories of off-Broadway—and frequently off-off-Broadway—shows, as close distinctions between these two areas are ignored in Obie Award-giving. The Obies are voted by a committee of *Village Voice* critics and others, which this year was made up of Eileen Blumenthal, Michael Feingold, Robert Massa, Erika Munk, Julius Novick and Ross Wetzsteon, with Maria Irene Fornes and John Guare as guest judges.

PERFORMANCE. **Ernest Abuba** in *Yellow Fever*, **Christine Baranski** in *A Midsummer Night's Dream*, **Glenn Close** in *The Singular Life of Albert Nobbs*, **Jeff Daniels** in *Johnny Got His Gun*, **Ruth Maleczech** in *Hajj*, **John Malkovich** in *True West*, **Donald Moffat** in *Painting Churches*, **Ray Wise** in *The Tooth of Crime*.

ENSEMBLE PERFORMANCE. Director **Kenneth Frankel** and the cast of *Quartermaine's Terms*, director **Max Stafford-Clark** and the Royal Court cast of *Top Girls*, the New York Shakespeare Festival cast of *Top Girls*.

PLAYWRITING. **Caryl Churchill** for *Top Girls*, **Tina Howe** for distinguished playwriting,

Harry Kondoleon as most promising young playwright, **David Mamet** for *Edmond* (latter three share the $1,000 prize for best new American play).

DIRECTION. **Gregory Mosher** for *Edmond*, **Gary Sinise** for *True West*.

DESIGN. **Heidi Landesman** for *A Midsummer Night's Dream* and *Painting Churches*.

SPECIAL CITATIONS. **The Big Apple Circus**; **Ethyl Eichelberger** for *Lucrezia Borgia*; **Michael Moschen, Fred Garbo** and **Bob Berky** for *Foolsfire*; **The Zagreb Theater Company** for *The Liberation of Skopje*; **The musical production** of *The Mother of Us All*; **The musical performance** of *Poppie Nongena*; **Dramatists Play Service** for its commitment to new work; **Performing Arts Journal** publications; **Theater Development Fund** for its off-off-Broadway voucher program.

SUSTAINED ACHIEVEMENT. **Lanford Wilson, Marshall W. Mason** and **Circle Repertory Company**.

ADDITIONAL PRIZES AND AWARDS, 1982–83

The following is a list of major prizes and awards for achievement in the theater this season. In all cases the names of winners appear in **bold face type.**

MARGO JONES AWARD. To the producer and producing organization whose continuing policy of producing new theater works has made an outstanding contribution to the encouragement of new playwrights. **Andre Bishop** and **Playwrights Horizons**.

JOSEPH MAHARAM FOUNDATION AWARDS. For distinguished theatrical design in original New York productions (selected by a committee comprising Henry Hewes, chairman, Tish Dace, Mel Gussow, Patricia McKay, Edward F. Kook). Scenery: **Ming Cho Lee, Leslie Taylor, Allen Lee Hughes** (lighting) and **David Schnirman** (sound) for *K2*; **Mabou Mines designers** of scenery, costumes and lighting for *Cold Harbor*, *Company* and *Hajj*. Costumes: **Patricia Zipprodt** for *Don Juan* and *Alice in Wonderland*.

Other nominations for outstanding scene design: Richard Foreman and Nancy Winters for *Egyptology: My Head Was a Sledgehammer*, John Gunter for *Plenty*, Heidi Landesman for *Painting Churches*, Christopher Martin for *Faust*, David Mitchell for *Foxfire*, Douglas W. Schmidt for *The Death of Von Richtofen as Witnessed From Earth*, Daniel and Paula Stein for *Inclined to Agree*.

Other nominations for outstanding costume design: Patricia McGourty for *The Death of Von Richtofen as Witnessed From Earth*, Everett Quinton for *The Bourgeois Avant-Garde*, Nancy Potts for *You Can't Take It With You*.

Other nominations for outstanding lighting design: Ken Billington for *Foxfire*, Rick Butler for *Faust*, Arden Fingerhut for *Plenty*, David Hersey for *Cats*, Richard Nelson for *The Death of Von Richtofen as Witnessed From Earth*, Dennis Parichy for *Angels Fall*.

39th ANNUAL THEATER WORLD AWARDS. For outstanding new talent in Broadway and off-Broadway productions in the 1982–83 season (selected by a committee comprising Clive Barnes, Douglas Watt and John Willis). **Karen Allen** in *Monday After the Miracle*, **Suzanne Bertish** in *Skirmishes*, **Matthew Broderick** in *Brighton Beach Memoirs*, **Kate Burton** in *Present Laughter, Alice in Wonderland* and *Winners*, **Joanne Camp** in *Geniuses*, **Harvey Fierstein** in *Torch Song Trilogy*, **Peter Gallagher** in *A Doll's Life*, **John Malkovich** in *True West*, **Anne Pitoniak** in *Talking With* and *'night, Mother*, **James Russo** in *Extremities*, **Brian Tarantina** in *Angels Fall*, **Linda Thorson** in *Steaming*. Special award for a star in other medium making an outstanding Broadway debut to **Natalia Markova** in *On Your Toes*.

3d ANNUAL RICHARD L. COE AWARD. For an individual who has made a significant contribution to the development of original material for the theater. **Joseph Papp**.

49th ANNUAL DRAMA LEAGUE AWARD. Delia Austrian Medal for distinguished performing. **Kate Nelligan** and **Edward Herrmann**.

CLARENCE DERWENT AWARDS. For the most promising male and female actors on the metropolitan scene during the 1982–83 season. **Dana Ivey** in *Quartermaine's Terms* and **John Malkovich** in *True West*.

OUTER CRITICS CIRCLE AWARDS. For distinguished achievement in the 1982–83 New York theater season, voted by critics of foreign and out-of-town periodicals. Broadway play: **Brighton Beach Memoirs.** Broadway musical: **Cats.** Actor: **Tony Lo Bianco** in *A View From the Bridge.* Actresses: **Anne Pitoniak** and **Kathy Bates** in *'night, Mother,* **Jessica Tandy** in *Foxfire.* Off-Broadway play: **Extremities.** Off-Broadway musical: **Little Shop of Horrors.** Direction: **Robert Allan Ackerman** for *Extremities.* Scenery and lighting: **Ming Cho Lee** and **Allen Lee Hughes** for *K2.* Debut performances: **Natalia Makarova** and **Lara Teeter** in *On Your Toes,* **Keith Carradine** in *Foxfire.* Revivals: **On Your Toes** and **You Can't Take It With You.** Score: **Alan Menken** and **Howard Ashman** for *Little Shop of Horrors.* Book: **Elsa Joubert** for *Poppie Nongena.* John Gassner Playwriting Award: **William Mastrosimone** for *Extremities.* Special awards: **Theater Development Fund** and **Classic Stage Company (CSC).**

3d ANNUAL JOHN F. WHARTON AWARD. For creative contributions to the producing of theater. **Richard Barr,** in recognition of his distinguished tenure as President of the League of New York Theaters and Producers.

GEORGE JEAN NATHAN AWARD. For drama criticism. **Julius Novick** of the *Village Voice.*

ROSAMOND GILDER AWARD for creative achievement, presented by New Drama Forum Association. **Tina Howe** and **Emily Mann.**

DRAMA DESK AWARDS. For outstanding achievement, voted by an association of New York drama reporters, editors and critics. Play: **Torch Song Trilogy.** Musical: **Little Shop of Horrors.** Director, play: **Trevor Nunn** for *All's Well That Ends Well.* Director, musical: **George Abbott** for *On Your Toes.* Actor in a play: **Harvey Fierstein** in *Torch Song Trilogy.* Actress in a play: **Jessica Tandy** in *Foxfire.* Actress in a musical: **Natalia Makarova** in *On Your Toes.* Featured actor in a play: **Alan Feinstein** in *A View From the Bridge.* Featured actress in a play: **Judith Ivey** in *Steaming.* Featured actor in a musical: **Charles "Honi" Coles** in *My One and Only.* Featured actress in a musical: **Karla Burns** in *Show Boat.* Choreography: **Thommie Walsh** and **Tommy Tune** for *My One and Only.* Music: **Andrew Lloyd Webber** for *Cats.* Lyrics: **Howard Ashman** for *Little Shop of Horrors.* Orchestrations: **Hans Spialek** for *On Your Toes* and **Michael Gibson** for *My One and*

Only (tie). Revival: **On Your Toes.** Scenic design: **Ming Cho Lee** for *K2.* Costume design: **John Napier** for *Cats.* Lighting design, **David Hersey** for *Cats.* Special effects: **Martin P. Robinson** and **Ron Taylor** as Audrey II in *Little Shop of Horrors.* Special awards: **Douglas Watt** of the *Daily News* for distinguished achievement; **Richard Wilbur** for the English translation of *The Misanthrope;* **WPA Theater** for outstanding achievement.

1982 GEORGE OPPENHEIMER/NEWSDAY AWARD. For the best new American playwright whose work is produced in New York City or on Long Island. **Harvey Fierstein** for *Torch Song Trilogy.*

COMMON WEALTH AWARD. For achievement in the dramatic arts. **Harold Prince.**

LORRAINE HANSBERRY PLAYWRITING AWARD. For a play about the black experience in America, a joint project of McDonald's Corp., the American College Theater Festival and the New Dramatists. **Gym Rats** by Farrell Foreman.

10th ANNUAL JOSEPH JEFFERSON AWARDS. For outstanding work in Chicago theater, nominated by a committee of 40 persons. Play production: **Kabuki Macbeth,** *The Tooth of Crime.* Musical production: **Little Me.** Revue: **Tintypes.** Director of a play: Stuart Gordon for *E/R,* Jim O'Connor for *The Island,* **Shozo Sato** for *Kabuki Macbeth,* Gary Sinise for *True West,* Dennis Zacek for *Clara's Play.* Director of a musical: **David H. Bell** for *Little Me.* Director of a revue: **Gary Pearle** and **Wayne Bryan** for *Tintypes.* Principal actress in a play: **Carmen Decker** in *Clara's Play,* Kit Flanagan in *Standing on My Knees,* Glenne Headley in *The House,* Mary Ann Thebus in *Sister Mary Ignatius Explains It All for You,* Peg Small in *Eve.* Principal actress in a musical: **Carol Dilley** in *Little Me,* Maria Ricossa in *They're Playing Our Song,* Alene Robertson in *Kismet.* Principal actress in a revue: **Audrie J. Neenan** in *Tintypes.* Principal actor in a play: Gary Cole and William L. Peterson in *The Tooth of Crime,* Stephen McKinley Henderson in *The Island,* Richard Lavin in *Clara's Play,* **John Malkovich** in *True West.* Principal actor in a musical: Walter Hook in *Kismet,* Lee Pelty in *Zorba,* **David Rounds** in *Herringbone,* James W. Sudik in *Little Me.* Principal actor in a revue: **Ross Lehman** in *Tintypes.* Supporting actress in a play: Pauline Brailsford in *The Entertainer,* Laurel Cronin in *The Italian Straw Hat,* Fern

Persons in *Les Belles Soeurs*, **Rondi Reed** in *Waiting for the Parade*. Supporting actor in a play: **Tom Irwin** in *The Glass Menagerie*, Michael Tezla in *Eve*, Joe Van Slyke in *The House*. Ensemble: *Waiting for the Parade*, **The House**, *Tintypes*. Scene design: Linda Buchana for *The Guardsman*, **Michael Merritt** for *Lakeboat*, Joseph Nieminski for *The Front Page*, Shozo Sato and John Murbach for *Kabuki Macbeth*. Costume design: Cookie Gluck for *Kismet*, William Ivey Long for *The Front Page*, Doug Marmee for *Little Me*, Nancy Missimi for *The Italian Straw Hat*, **Shozo Sato** for *Kabuki Macbeth*. Lighting: F. Mitchell Dana for *Lakeboat*, Gary Heitz for *Standing on My Knees*, Dawn Hollingsworth for *Clara's Play*, **Mary McAuliffe** and **Kevin Rigdon** for *The Tooth of Crime*, Robert Shook for *Kabuki Macbeth*. Choreography: **David H. Bell** for *Little Me*, Brian Lynch for *Zorba*. Original incidental music: **Fugue** (rock group) for *The Tooth of Crime*.

14th ANNUAL LOS ANGELES DRAMA CRITICS CIRCLE AWARD. For distinguished achievement in Los Angeles theater. Production: **Betrayal, Creeps, Greek**. Direction: **Steven Berkoff** for *Greek*, **Jeff Murray** for *Creeps*, **Sam Weisman** for *Betrayal*. Ensemble performance: **Ken Danziger, Gillian Eaton, Paddi Edwards, John Francis** in *Greek*. Performance in a leading role: **Matthew Broderick** in *Brighton Beach Memoirs*, **Graham Brown** in *Nevis Mountain Dew*, **Bill Erwin** in *Old Friends*, **Penny Fuller** and **Ian McShane** in *Betrayal*, **Elizabeth Huddle** in *Sister Mary Ignatius Explains It All for You*, **Laurie O'Brien** in *Mary Barnes*. Performance in a featured role: **Carmen Argenziano** in *A Prayer for My Daughter*. Scene design: **A. Clark Duncan** for *Journey's End*, **Gerry Hariton** and **Vicki Baral** for *Betrayal*. Lighting design: **Gerry Hariton** and **Vicki Baral** for *Betrayal* and *Greek*, **Russell Pyle** for *Journey's End*, **Tom Ruzika** for *Henry IV, Part 1*. Costume design: **Sam Kirkpatrick** for *The Misanthrope*, **Bob Mackie** for *Movie Star*. Sound design: **Russell Pyle** for *Journey's End*. Music and lyrics: **William Finn** for *March of the Falsettos*. Movement: **Karen Dick** for *Creeps*.

1982–1983 PUBLICATION OF RECENTLY-PRODUCED PLAYS

Agnes of God. John Pielmeier. Nelson Doubleday.
Angels Fall. Lanford Wilson. Hill and Wang (also paperback).
Balloon. Karen Sunde. Broadway Play Publishing (paperback).
Barnum. Michael Stewart, Mark Bramble, Cy Coleman. Nelson Doubleday
Battery. Daniel Therriault. Broadway Play Publishing (paperback).
Broken Promises: Four Plays. David Henry Hwang. Avon/Bard (paperback).
Can You Hear Me at the Back? Brian Clark. Amber Lane Press (paperback).
Christopher Durang Explains It All for You. Christopher Durang (four plays). Avon/Bard
Clay. Peter Whelan. Methuen (paperback).
Crimes of the Heart. Beth Henley. Viking Press (paperback, Penguin).
Deathtrap. Ira Levin. Penguin (paperback).
Dining Room, The. A.R. Gurney Jr. Nelson Doubleday.
Edmond. David Mamet. Grove Press (also paperback).
Escoffier—King of Chefs. Owen S. Rackleff. Broadway Play Publishing (also paperback).
Fox, The. Alan Miller. Nelson Doubleday.
Geniuses. Jonathan Reynolds. Nelson Doubleday.
How I Got That Story. Amlin Gray. Nelson Doubleday.
Joseph and the Amazing Technicolor Dreamcoat. Tim Rice, Andrew Lloyd Webber, Quentin Blake. Holt Rinehart Winston.
Key Exchange. Kevin Wade. Avon (paperback).
Last Summer at Bluefish Cove. Jane Chambers. JH Press (paperback).
Letters Home. Rose Leiman Goldemberg. Samuel French (paperback).
Looking-Glass. Michael Sutton, Cynthia Mandelberg. Broadway Play Publishing (paperback).
Map of the World, A. David Hare. Faber and Faber (paperback).

"Master Harold" . . . *and the Boys*. Athol Fugard. Alfred A. Knopf.
Other Places: Three Plays. Harold Pinter. Grove Press (also paperback).
Quartermaine's Terms. Simon Gray. Methuen (paperback).
Skirmishes. Catherine Hayes. Faber and Faber (paperback).
Soldier's Play, A. Charles Fuller. Hill and Wang (also paperback).
Steaming. Nell Dunn. Amber Lane (paperback).
Summer and Fables. Edward Bond. Methuen (paperback).
Table Settings. James Lapine. Performing Arts Journal Publications (paperback).
Twelve Dreams. James Lapine. Performing Arts Journal Publications (paperback).

A SELECTED LIST OF OTHER PLAYS PUBLISHED IN 1982–83

Andromache. Jean Racine. Harcourt Brace Jovanovich.
Are You Now or Have You Ever Been and Other Plays. Eric Bentley. Grove.
Best American Plays, Eighth Series (1974–1982). Clive Barnes, editor. Crown.
Best Short Plays, The. Ramon Delgado, editor. Chilton.
Drunkard's Revenge, The. Raymond Hull (paperback).
Calms of Capricorn, The. Eugene O'Neill. Ticknor & Fields.
Center Stage: An Anthology of 21 Contemporary Black-American Plays. Eileen Joyce Ostrow, editor. Sea Urchin Press.
Chris Christopherson: A Play in Three Acts. Eugene O'Neill. Random House.
Chushingura: Studies in Kabuki and the Puppet Theater. James R. Brandon, editor. University of Hawaii Press.
Collected Plays of Peter Shaffer, The. Harmony Books/Crown.
Comedies of William Congreve, The. Cambridge University.
Five Plays by Michael Weller. Plume/New American Library. (Paperback).
Four Comedies by Molière. Harcourt Brace Jovanovich.
Four Greek Plays: Andromache, Iphigenia, Phaedra, Athaliah. Jean Racine. Cambridge University Press.
Golden Age of Soviet Theater, The. Michael Glenny, editor. Penguin.
Greeks: Ten Greek Plays Given as a Trilogy, The. John Barton and Kenneth Cavander. Heinemann (paperback).
Hippolytus. Euripides. Heinemann (paperback).
Longman Anthology of American Drama, The. Lee A. Jacobus, editor. Longman (paperback).
Oresteia, The. Tony Harrison, translator of Aeschylus trilogy. Rowman & Littlefield (paperback).
Pal Joey: The Novel and the Libretto. John O'Hara. Vintage Books/Random House (paperback).
Plays by David Garrick and George Colman the Elder. E.R., editor. Cambridge University.
Plays of Heinrich von Kleist. Continuum (paperback).
Plays by Terence Rattigan: One. Grove Press (paperback).
Plays of Edward Albee: Volume Three, The. Atheneum (paperback).
Plays of Edward Albee: Volume Four, The. Atheneum (paperback).
Plays by W.S. Gilbert. Cambridge University (also paperback).
Theater of Nikolai Gogol: Plays and Selected Writings, The. University of Chicago Press.
Three Exposures. John Guare. Harcourt Brace Jovanovich.
Three Pieces. Ntozake Shangé. Penguin (paperback).
Three Theban Plays, The. Sophocles. Viking Press.
Troilus and Cressida: The Arden Shakespeare. Kenneth Palmer, editor. Methuen (paperback).
Two Plays by Bertolt Brecht: The Good Woman of Setzuan & The Caucasian Chalk Circle. Signet (paperback).
West Coast Plays 11/12. Rick Foster, editor. California Theater Council.
Word Plays 2: An Anthology of New American Drama Performing Arts Journal Publications. Bonnie Marranca and Gautam Dasgupta. Performing Arts Journal (paperback).

MUSICAL AND DRAMATIC RECORDINGS OF NEW YORK SHOWS

Title and publishing company are listed below. Each record is an original cast album unless otherwise indicated. An asterisk (*) indicates recording is also available on cassettes.

Barnum (selections played by Cy Coleman Trio). Bain.
Bring Back Birdie. Original.
Cats (Broadway production, 2 records). Geffen. (*)
Charlotte Sweet. John Hammond.
Little Shop of Horrors. Geffen. (*)
Nine. Columbia. (*)
Pump Boys and Dinettes. CBS Records.
Sophisticated Ladies (highlights from 2 LP sets). RCA. (*)

NECROLOGY

MAY 1982–MAY 1983

PERFORMERS

Adams, Eadie Ione (75)—March 13, 1983
Ahern, Will (86)—May 16, 1983
Albertson, Mabel (81)—September 28, 1982
Alexander, Brandy (38)—July 30, 1982
Alexander, John (86)—July 13, 1982
Allen, Chesney (88)—November 13, 1982
Alson, Julia (41)—Spring 1982
Ameche, Jim (68)—February 4, 1983
Anderson, Mignon (91)—February 25, 1983
Arrieu, Rene (58)—June 6, 1982
Asch, Anna Leskaya (87)—May 9, 1983
Askey, Arthur (82)—November 16, 1982
Ates, Dorothy (66)—July 6, 1982
Baker, Russell F. (66)—June 20, 1982
Baldwin, Bill (69)—November 17, 1982
Bar, Shimon (56)—April 4, 1983
Barnes, Paul J. (64)—May 16, 1983
Barton, Fred (60s)—August 13, 1982
Bayne, Beverly (87)—August 18, 1982
Beattie, William A. (52)—August 3, 1982
Bell, Myles (83)—December 17, 1982
Belt, Vernon (62)—April 7, 1983
Bennett, Marjorie (87)—June 14, 1982
Berberian, Cathy (54)—March 6, 1983
Bergman, Ingrid (67)—August 29, 1982
Berk, Dick (60)—February 25, 1983
Bilon, Michael (35)—January 27, 1983
Blake, Larry J. (68)—May 25, 1982
Blake, Marion (86)—June 26, 1982
Block, Jesse (82)—March 22, 1983
Blue, David (41)—December 2, 1982
Blumenthal, Sol (88)—May 24, 1982
Boehm, Max (66)—December 26, 1982
Bolo, Jean (62)—June 30, 1982
Borsche, Dieter (72)—August 5, 1982
Bowen, William (70)—Summer 1982
Bramley, Nellie (92)—June 10, 1982
Brauer, Julia A. (61)—July 4, 1982
Bray, Robert (65)—March 7, 1983
Breeding, Larry—September 28, 1982
Bretty, Beatrice (86)—September 4, 1982
Briarhopper, Homer (61)—May 18, 1983
Broderick, James (55)—November 1, 1982
Brown, Marie Francis (93)—October 31, 1982
Buck, Werhner (44)—July 24, 1982
Burr, Jasper (86)—December 30, 1982
Caplan, Irvin (66)—February 25, 1983

Carpenter, Karen (32)—February 4, 1983
Cassavetes, Katherine (70)—March 29, 1983
Chamarat, Georges (82)—November 21, 1982
Chapin, Victor (64)—March 4, 1983
Chatmon, Sam (84)—February 2, 1983
Chatto, Tom (60s)—August 8, 1982
Checco, Jessie (85)—April 8, 1983
Chen, Renee Shinn (6)—July 23, 1982
Christi, Frank (52)—July 9, 1982
Christian, Robert (42)—January 27, 1983
Christopher, Richard (37)—November 23, 1982
Churchill, Sarah (67)—September 24, 1982
Cianciolo, Augustine J. (61)—January 1983
Clark, Kendall (70)—January 28, 1983
Clive, Eleanor (93)—Fall 1982
Coates, Edith (74)—January 7, 1983
Cohn, Janet (92)—July 3, 1982
Connon, Robert (78)—May 2, 1983
Cook, Philip O. (58)—November 23, 1982
Coote, Robert (73)—November 26, 1982
Crabb, Bobby (34)—July 3, 1982
Crabbe, Buster (75)—April 23, 1983
Crall, Beatrice (84)—March 8, 1983
Cullen, Fred (48)—December 7, 1982
Cummins, Dorothy Louise Cassil (80)—April 19, 1983
Cunneff, Joseph P. (69)—February 11, 1983
D'Alton, Annie (78)—March 10, 1983
Darling, Gladys (84)—January 5, 1983
Darnay, Toni (61)—January 5, 1983
Davis, Gilbert (83)—Spring 1983
Davis, Herbert H. (52)—June 20, 1982
de Funes, Louis (68)—January 27, 1983
Del Monaco, Mario (67)—October 16, 1982
Del Rio, Dolores (77)—April 11, 1983
de Megyery, Sari (86)—February 5, 1983
Denison, Lewis (79)—March 13, 1983
de Noord, Jan (37)—March 6, 1983
Desmond, Mae (95)—July 13, 1982
Dewaere, Patrick (35)—July 16, 1982
Dillaway, Donald P. (78)—November 18, 1982
Donnelly, Ruth (86)—November 17, 1982
Dornfeld, Werner F. (89)—September 5, 1982
Drake, Tom (64)—August 11, 1982
Duke, E.L. (48)—September 20, 1982
Dumkow, Niko (51)—May 27, 1982
Dunn, Josephine (76)—Spring 1983

Dunne, Dominique (23)—November 4, 1982
Eaves, Margaret (77)—March 31, 1983
Ellig, Belle (50s)—October 15, 1982
Emerson, Faye (65)—March 9, 1983
Emery, Dick (65)—January 2, 1983
Enriquez, Margarita (51)—January 28, 1983
Ethridge, Ella (88)—October 3, 1982
Evan, Blanche (73)—December 24, 1982
Evans, Jessie (64)—March 2, 1983
Fair, Dick (74)—July 21, 1982
Falasca, Rossana (29)—Spring 1983
Farmer, Richard (67)—February 8, 1983
Feldman, Marty (48)—December 2, 1982
FitzGerald, Neil (90)—June 15, 1982
Fonda, Henry (77)—August 12, 1982
Forman, Joey (53)—December 9, 1982
Forster, Peter (62)—November 16, 1982
Francis, Ann—January 28, 1983
Franz, Eduard (80)—February 10, 1983
Frazer, Ron (56)—January 8, 1983
Fujikawa, Jerry (71)—April 30, 1983
Fuller, Rosalinde (90)—September 15, 1982
Fury, Billy (42)—January 28, 1983
Galli, Georges (80)—July 3, 1982
Gargan, Mary Elizabeth (76)—January 31, 1983
Garroway, Dave (69)—July 21, 1982
Gauthier, Jacqueline (62)—September 18, 1982
Gendel, Hershel (76)—May 10, 1982
George, George Val (59)—May 2, 1983
Glaze, Peter (58)—February 29, 1983
Godfrey, Arthur (79)—March 15, 1983
Golden, Eddie (71)—March 28, 1983
Gonzalez, Adalberto de Cordova—September 27, 1982
Gordon, Gavin (82)—April 7, 1983
Gorham, Kathleen (53)—April 30, 1983
Goss, Mary Ann Cromer (84)—July 19, 1982
Gray, Florence Ostfeld (70)—December 29, 1982
Greer, Bernice (89)—April 18, 1983
Guthrie, Marjorie Mazia (65)—March 13, 1983
Haida, Katsuhiko (71)—October 19, 1982
Harris, Addie (42)—June 10, 1982
Harrison, Edgar (74)—July 3, 1982
Hawkins, Hoyt (56)—October 23, 1982
Hayter, James (75)—March 27, 1983
Henson, Gladys (85)—Winter 1983
Herman, Charlotte—November 20, 1982
Herrick, Robert (87)—October 3, 1982
Hiatt, Don (70)—February 10, 1983
Hickman, Charles (78)—April 4, 1983
Hickox, Mary (71)—February 26, 1983
Higgins, Edward C. (54)—May 18, 1983
Hoerner, Ed (67)—April 5, 1983
Holland, Harve (93)—September 13, 1982

Horne, William (69)—April 19, 1983
Hough, Joe—May 26, 1982
Howell, Lottice (84)—October 24, 1982
Hoyos, Rudolfo (68)—April 15, 1983
Hubbard, Penelope (81)—February 17, 1983
Hughes, Arthur (89)—December 28, 1982
Hull, Burling (93)—November 19, 1982
Jackson, Robert—August 14, 1982
Jacobsson, Ulla (53)—August 22, 1982
Jagel, Frederick (85)—July 6, 1982
Jameson, Rex (58)—March 6, 1983
Jeritza, Maria (94)—July 10, 1982
Johnson, Franklin G. (54)—August 28, 1982
Jones, Martin B. (81)—March 23, 1983
Jurgens, Curt (60s)—June 18, 1982
Kahle, Rosemary D. (72)—July 29, 1982
Katzman, Hortense (70s)—July 8, 1982
Kay, Buddy (Irving Kaufman) (66)—May 11, 1983
Keith, Sydney (82)—November 13, 1982
Kelly, Grace (52)—September 14, 1982
Kennedy, Clair Alderdice (62)—October 18, 1982
Kibbler, Belva (69)—February 3, 1983
Kimmel, Dorothy Kingston (62)—April 4, 1983
King, Mollie (86)—December 28, 1982
Klein, Adelaide (82)—March 18, 1983
Klinger, Ruth S. (59)—July 4, 1982
Kullman, Charles (80)—February 8, 1983
Lagos, Poppy (56)—October 23, 1982
Lamas, Fernando (67)—October 8, 1982
Lamont, Syl (69)—August 7, 1982
Lane, Richard (83)—September 5, 1982
Laughery, Barbara Marie (40s)—April 30, 1983
Layde, Pat (54)—February 9, 1983
LeBouvier, Jean (62)—April 6, 1983
Lee, Mary A. (81)—December 26, 1982
Lee, My-Ca Dinh (7)—July 23, 1982
Lee, Will (74)—December 7, 1982
Leiendecker, Willem (73)—April 17, 1982
Leslie, Doris (80)—May 31, 1982
Levin, Berta—September 15, 1982
Lewis, Katharine H. (80)—July 15, 1982
Liserani, Gino (87)—December 23, 1982
Littler, Susan (33)—July 11, 1982
Lloyd, A.L. (74)—September 29, 1982
Lobato, Nelida (47)—Spring 1983
Long, Maxine A. (64)—March 27, 1983
Lorimer, Enid (94)—July 15, 1982
Lucas, Nick (84)—July 8, 1982
Lucido, Terry (48)—November 2, 1982
Lusiardo, Tito (86)—Summer 1982
Lussier, Alfred O. Sr. (75)—June 24, 1982
Macleod, Don (62)—April 15, 1983
Madden, Donald (49)—January 22, 1983

Madsen, Roy J. (68)—May 31, 1982
Magana, Angel (57)—November 13, 1982
Magee, Patrick (58)—August 14, 1982
Mahoney, Tom (50s)—July 13, 1982
Manners, Gloria (70)—October 25, 1982
Markham, Ronald (56)—October 9, 1982
Marquand, Nan—December 10, 1982
Martinelli, Jean (73)—March 13, 1983
Maskell, Dorothy M. (89)—June 25, 1982
McElrath, Ann Jones—December 14, 1982
McHugh, John (69)—January 13, 1983
McKay, Ted (75)—December 6, 1982
McMichael, Marion Rooney (77)—December 14, 1982
Merchant, Vivien (53)—October 3, 1982
Merlini, Elsa (80)—Spring 1983
Merriman, Robert (66)—February 2, 1983
Miller, Jessie M. (80)—September 24, 1982
Miller, Michael (51)—May 5, 1983
Mills, Harry (68)—June 28, 1982
Milmar, Paul (99)—January 22, 1983
Milton, Bob (54)—January 11, 1983
Mintz, Jack (87)—January 19, 1983
Miranda, Isa (77)—July 8, 1982
Mitchell, Gordon S. (71)—July 8, 1982
Monte, Mysie (90)—January 9, 1983
More, Kenneth (67)—July 12, 1982
Morris, Bobby (75)—December 26, 1982
Morrison, Meta (90)—November 28, 1982
Morrow, Vic (50)—July 23, 1982
Moulin, Velma Lyon (82)—June 19, 1982
Mujica, Alba—Winter 1982
Mullaney, Jack (51)—June 27, 1982
Murray, Stephen (70)—April 1, 1983
Nash, Gene (54)—May 18, 1983
Nesbitt, Cathleen (93)—August 2, 1982
Newman, Marion A. (72)—October 1, 1982
Nieto, Jose (80)—August 9, 1982
Nixon, Marian (78)—February 13, 1983
Norbert, Doris Beaupre (60s)—May 23, 1982
Norris, Kenneth (54)—January 23, 1983
Novello, Jay (78)—September 2, 1982
Ober, Philip (80)—September 13, 1982
O'Brien, Richard (65)—March 29, 1983
O'Brien, Sheila (80)—January 26, 1983
O'Leary, Kevin (42)—September 16, 1982
Oliver, Bette (52)—May 16, 1983
Ortiz, Humberto (46)—Fall 1982
Page, Gale (72)—January 8, 1983
Patrick, Lee (70)—November 25, 1982
Patton, Mary (66)—November 8, 1982
Paul, Queenie (87)—July 31, 1982
Pazton, Dorothy (82)—July 3, 1982
Pearl, Jack (88)—December 25, 1982
Pelish, Thelma (55)—March 6, 1983
Philbrook, James (58)—October 24, 1982
Phillips, Bernard (68)—August 17, 1982

Pickman, Kathryn (60)—November 2, 1982
Pitts, Ron (51)—March 25, 1983
Powell, Albert (82)—June 26, 1982
Quartly, Reg (71)—April 26, 1983
Quartucci, Pedro (78)—Spring 1983
Randolph, Elsie (80)—October 15, 1982
Reiner, Carlotta (84)—January 24, 1983
Richards, Digvy (43)—February 10, 1983
Richardson, James G. (37)—February 29, 1983
Richard-Willim, Pierre (87)—April 12, 1983
Riley, Ed (49)—December 25, 1982
Robart, Gene (34)—April 17, 1983
Robertson, Norah (80)—November 26, 1982
Rogers, Rod—February 23, 1983
Ronet, Maurice (55)—March 14, 1983
Ross, Bob (57)—April 17, 1983
Rotha, Wanda (60s)—August 5, 1982
Rowell, Bond (90)—Summer 1982
Royle, Selena (78)—April 23, 1983
Rugani, Dogi (84)—January 21, 1983
Rutherford, Jack (89)—August 21, 1982
Ryan, Nancy Holmes (79)—May 23, 1982
Saburi, Shin (73)—September 23, 1982
Sakata, Harold (56)—July 29, 1982
Savidge, Mary (50s)—August 20, 1982
Schaefer, Rosel (56)—July 24, 1982
Schneider, Romy (43)—May 29, 1982
Schuessler, Roy A. (71)—October 22, 1982
Scott, Lorene (74)—April 19, 1983
Sedan, Rolfe (86)—September 16, 1982
Seka, Ron (48)—July 25, 1982
Shea, Helen—January 14, 1983
Shean, Larry (80s)—December 30, 1982
Shiva, Susan Stein (46)—January 3, 1983
Simon, Francois—October 5, 1982
Sitkin, Pauline Orland (72)—November 18, 1982
Sleeper, Martha (72)—March 23, 1983
Slezak, Walter (80)—April 22, 1983
Smith, Emily (77)—April 28, 1983
Solidor, Suzy (82)—March 31, 1983
Solonitzyn, Anatoli (43)—June 1982
Space, Arthur (74)—January 13, 1983
Speegle, Paul (72)—June 6, 1982
Spencer, Tommy (81)—July 6, 1982
Stahely, Helen (52)—October 4, 1982
Stanley, Louise—December 31, 1982
Steen, Malcolm H. (55)—May 9, 1983
Strudwick, Shepperd (75)—January 15, 1983
Stuthman, Fred (60s)—July 7, 1982
Swanson, Gloria (84)—April 4, 1983
Syers, Mark (30)—May 15, 1983
Tanner, Fred (62)—October 27, 1982
Tati, Jacques (74)—November 5, 1982
Taylor, Vaugn (72)—April 26, 1983
Tex, Joe (49)—August 13, 1982
Thimig, Hermann (92)—July 7, 1982

Thoma, Michael (55)—September 3, 1982
Thorsen, Russell (mid-70s)—July 6, 1982
Tobin, Dan (72)—November 26, 1982
Tonetti, Manuel (54)—December 4, 1982
Trenier, Cliff (63)—March 2, 1983
Tucker, Bert—October 25, 1982
Valerie, Joan (68)—January 30, 1983
Vandair, Maurice (77)—December 5, 1982
Vattier, Robert (76)—December 9, 1982
Viogoreaux, Luis (54)—January 18, 1983
Vitte, Ray (33)—February 20, 1983
Wahby, Youssef (82)—Winter 1983
Wakely, Jimmy (68)—September 23, 1982
Walker, Betty (54)—July 26, 1982
Warren, Flip (69)—March 15, 1983
Wasmund, Michael (28)—March 1983
Weaver, Doodles (71)—January 15, 1983
Webb, Alan (75)—June 1982
Webb, Jack (62)—December 23, 1982
Westwell, Raymond (63)—Winter 1983
White, Alice (78)—February 19, 1983
White, Lexie (64)—May 28, 1982
Wilder, Marc (53)—April 18, 1983
Williams, John (80)—May 5, 1983
Wilson, Edwin Harold (68)—April 16, 1983
Wilson, Lois (75)—January 8, 1983
Wood, Terry (34)—June 20, 1982
Woods, Eugenia (97)—April 1, 1983
Yule, Fred (89)—December 11, 1982
Zanuck, Virginia Fox (79)—October 14, 1982

CONDUCTORS

Assaly, Edmund (62)—January 1, 1983
Bloch, Alexander (101)—March 18, 1983
Boult, Adrian Cedric (93)—February 23, 1983
Fradkin, Philip (61)—May 20, 1983
Gould, Glenn (50)—October 4, 1982
Greenfield, Alfred M. (81)—January 14, 1983
Hagen, Walter C. (63)—May 19, 1983
Hawn, Edward Rutledge (73)—June 7, 1982
Heinze, Bernard (88)—June 9, 1982
Hersenhoren, Samuel D. (73)—August 18, 1983
Jellett, Dorothea Janet (81)—March 3, 1983
Jones, J. Randolph (72)—September 17, 1982
Jusko, Ralph V. (77)—July 23, 1982
Keating, Ralph W. (77)—April 6, 1983
Larrison, Bobby (51)—July 27, 1982
Linden, Eugene (71)—January 17, 1983
Little, Irvine Francis (80)—July 6, 1982
McCune, William J. (71)—February 26, 1983
Miedel, Rainer (45)—March 25, 1983
Mueller-Lampertz, Richard (72)—September 23, 1982
Petrides, Frederique (79)—January 12, 1983

Rapp, Danny (42)—April 4, 1983
Riccio, Pat (61)—August 23, 1982
Richter, Alexander (78)—November 6, 1982
Ross, Jack (66)—December 16, 1982
Rossi, Rafael (85)—Winter 1983
Shorter, James (79)—October 10, 1982
Simmons, Calvin (32)—August 22, 1982
Strand, Joe (80)—October 2, 1982
Wallenstein, Alfred (84)—February 8, 1983
Wilson, Frank William (70)—January 29, 1983
Zeller, Robert (63)—December 5, 1982

DESIGNERS

Alexeiff, Alexander (81)—August 8, 1982
Balmain, Pierre (68)—June 29, 1982
Bell, Claire (68)—December 17, 1982
Gelpi, Germen (73)—Winter 1983
Rychtarik, Richard W. (87)—July 10, 1982
Solomon, Selma Alexander—August 28, 1982

CRITICS

Bernstein, Karl N. (89)—January 1, 1983
Clark, Kenneth (79)—May 21, 1983
Davies, Grace Golden (99)—May 30, 1982
de Schauensee, Max (83)—July 24, 1982
Dwyer, John (69)—February 6, 1983
Eigen, Jack (69)—January 23, 1983
Faber, Charles (69)—April 5, 1983
Hale, Wanda (80)—May 24, 1982
Klein, Philip (75)—August 21, 1982
Lampard, Betty (73)—August 20, 1982
Macdonald, Dwight (76)—December 19, 1982
Mattia, Ettore G. (72)—October 1982
Morrison, Don (61)—April 20, 1983
Moskowitz, Gene (61)—December 29, 1982
Palatsky, Eugene H. (49)—June 24, 1982
Pascall, Geraldine (38)—February 10, 1983
Peters, John Brod (47)—August 28, 1982
Pullen, Glenn (78)—February 25, 1983
Silvert, Conrad (34)—July 15, 1982
Somervell, Stephen (84)—July 4, 1982
Swinnerton, Frank (98)—November 6, 1982
Terry, Walter (69)—October 4, 1982

PLAYWRIGHTS

Antoine, Andre-Paul (90)—October 11, 1982
Birnkrant, Arthur (76)—February 3, 1983
Bolton, Muriel Roy (74)—March 4, 1983
Box, Sydney (76)—May 25, 1983
Brahns, Caryl (81)—December 4, 1982

Chambers, Jane (45)—February 15, 1983
Coleman, Lonnie (62)—August 13, 1982
Davidson, William F. (85)—September 11, 1982
Denham, Reginald (89)—February 4, 1983
Duncan, Ronald (68)—June 3, 1982
Francis, Charlotte (78)—February 18, 1983
Geraldy, Paul (98)—March 10, 1983
Glickman, Will (73)—March 11, 1983
Goforth, Frances (94)—September 10, 1982
Goldberg, Michael (72)—August 1982
Goodwin, Robert L. (55)—February 13, 1983
Iriarte, Victor Ruiz (70)—October 14, 1982
Johnson, Oscar E. (75)—December 5, 1982
Jovinelli, Gerardo (72)—April 29, 1983
Mason, Bruce (61)—December 31, 1982
Miller, Albert G. (76)—June 25, 1982
Neveux, Georges (82)—August 27, 1982
Remington, Fred (63)—August 11, 1982
Riley, Jean (66)—January 30, 1983
Roos, Audrey K. (70)—December 11, 1982
Sackler, Howard (52)—October 14, 1982
Tank, Herbert (60)—November 10, 1982
Terayama, Shuji (47)—May 4, 1983
Walker, Evan (49)—August 23, 1982
Ward, Theodore (80)—May 8, 1983
Williams, Lawrence (67)—January 3, 1983
Williams, Tennessee (71)—February 25, 1983
Winter, Keith (76)—February 17, 1983

COMPOSERS/LYRICISTS

Atchison, Shelby (70)—August 4, 1982
Auge, Henry J. Jr. (53)—February 8, 1983
Barlow, Samuel L.M. (90)—September 19, 1982
Barr, Ray (70)—March 13, 1983
Blake, Eubie (100)—February 12, 1983
Bowling, Roger (39)—December 25, 1982
Brown, J. Harold (79)—September 17, 1982
Brown, Steven M. (41)—May 8, 1983
Burk, Thomas H. (82)—October 28, 1982
Cole, Roberto—March 3, 1983
Cunningham, Billy (46)—December 2, 1982
Darwin, Chuck (64)—May 6, 1983
Deutsch, Max (90)—November 22, 1982
Dowling, Allan D. (79)—April 13, 1983
Ehlert, Juan (81)—September 8, 1982
Emley, Joseph F. (50)—June 13, 1982
Engel, Lehman (71)—August 29, 1982
Gordillo, Manuel (83)—August 1982
Grunewald, Jean-Jacques (71)—December 19, 1982
Hopkins, Kenyon (71)—April 7, 1983
Ito, Teiji (47)—August 16, 1982
Kaper, Bronislau (81)—April 25, 1983

King, Pete (68)—September 21, 1982
Kleinsinger, George (68)—July 28, 1982
Kohlman, Churchill (77)—May 23, 1983
Loezos, Manos (44)—September 22, 1982
Lucas, Leighton (79)—November 7, 1982
Ludwig, Carl F. (89)—June 13, 1982
Lutyens, Elizabeth (76)—April 14, 1983
Markevitch, Igor (70)—March 7, 1983
McCarty, Kenneth (74)—June 24, 1982
Meakin, Jack (76)—December 30, 1982
Morlaine, Jacques (61)—January 18, 1983
Oliver, David (40)—June 2, 1982
Peterson, Mel (75)—October 31, 1982
Rene, Leon (80)—May 30, 1982
Rinker, Al (74)—June 11, 1982
Stuchevsky, Joachin (92)—November 14, 1982
Theard, Sam (78)—December 7, 1982
Torroba, Federico Moreno-Torroba (91)—September 12, 1982
Tremblay, George (71)—July 14, 1982
Walton, William (80)—March 8, 1983
Watkins, John T. (54)—February 25, 1983
Watts, John (52)—July 2, 1982
Weigl, Valerie (88)—December 25, 1982
Wollenberger, Werner (55)—October 17, 1982

PRODUCERS, DIRECTORS CHOREOGRAPHERS

Alexander, David (68)—March 6, 1983
Angelo, Edmond—March 27, 1983
Balanchine, George (79)—April 30, 1983
Bettis, Valerie (62)—September 26, 1982
Bridge, Peter (57)—November 24, 1982
Briels, Carel (66)—March 25, 1983
Brown, Sally Stearns (68)—February 15, 1983
Carter, Peter (48)—June 5, 1982
Cinader, Robert A. (58)—November 16, 1982
Deutsch, Benoit-Leon (90)—Summer 1982
Doheny, Lawrence (57)—September 7, 1982
Emmett, Patricia (54)—January 17, 1983
Fassbinder, Rainer Werner (36)—June 10, 1982
Feigay, Paul (64)—February 26, 1983
Garcia, Victor (47)—August 28, 1982
Gaston, Den (41)—May 4, 1983
Gierow, Karl R. (78)—October 31, 1982
Gordon, Steve (44)—November 27, 1982
Hine, Donald M. (58)—December 23, 1982
Hunter, Philip (79)—December 25, 1982
Jackman, Fred H. (69)—December 9, 1982
Juaire, David (30?)—September 6, 1982
Kaesen, Robert (52)—March 5, 1983
Kipness, Joseph (71)—November 18, 1982
Konigsberg, Franklin (35)—October 16, 1982
Leavitt, Max (77)—November 7, 1982

Loring, Eugene (72)—August 30, 1982
MacDonald, Alastair Simon (43)—August 7, 1982
Mossman, Merrily (40)—May 11, 1983
Rambert, Marie (94)—June 12, 1982
Richards, Dick—Summer 1982
Richetta, Donald P. (38)—June 23, 1982
Ries, Michael (65)—April 10, 1983
Russo, James (68)—October 4, 1982
Schnitzler, Heinrich (79)—July 14, 1982
Schwezoff, Igor (78)—October 28, 1982
Streger, Paul (86)—October 4, 1982
Suggs, Charles (60?)—March 29, 1983
Walters, Charles (70)—August 13, 1982

MUSICIANS

Andreasson, Goesta (87)—June 8, 1982
Arnold, William (75)—August 26, 1982
Attwell, Winifred (69)—February 27, 1983
Austin, Johnny (72)—February 14, 1983
Baker, Arthur (79)—April 30, 1983
Barrett, Emma (85)—January 28, 1983
Baselli, Joss (56)—September 4, 1982
Bergen, Charlotte (84)—July 10, 1982
Beron, Adolfo (67)—Fall 1982
Bledsoe, George (62)—May 12, 1982
Borisoff, Alexander (74)—March 25, 1983
Brainard, Jerry (35)—September 4, 1982
Brakke, Lawrence (76)—June 22, 1982
Bresnick, Martin (53)—June 18, 1982
Brown, Frank (50)—May 13, 1983
Bushell, Donald G. (74)—July 17, 1982
Cagnolatti, Ernie J. (72)—April 7, 1983
Campbell, Harry Francis (80)—February 25, 1983
Chappell, A. Donald (78)—July 18, 1982
Chargo, Morris (75)—December 14, 1982
Cole, Frances (45)—January 24, 1983
Coltrane, John Jr. (17)—August 7, 1982
Costa, Don (57)—January 19, 1983
Curzon, Clifford (75)—September 1, 1982
Dilling, Mildred (88)—December 30, 1982
Donahue, Al (80)—February 20, 1983
Draper, Ray (42)—November 1, 1982
Eddy, Alan (78)—July 8, 1982
Estlow, Bert (89)—December 19, 1982
Evans, Lindley (87)—December 2, 1982
Fitzer, Juanita (83)—May 18, 1983
Ford, Carl (62)—July 8, 1982
Friske, Wilson B. (83)—June 6, 1982
Galbraith, Barry (63)—January 13, 1983
Gelbloom, Gerald (56)—June 2, 1982
Glantz, Harry (86)—December 18, 1982
Glenn, Carroll (64)—April 25, 1983
Goodman, Isador (73)—December 2, 1982

Graslaub, Roman (54)—July 26, 1982
Haig, Al (58)—November 16, 1982
Harms, William (75)—January 7, 1983
Hensel, Wes (65)—December 15, 1982
Hines, Earl (77)—April 22, 1983
Homes, Mabel McCabe (91)—November 16, 1982
Hotchkiss, Jess (70)—October 14, 1982
Hruby, Edward J. (86)—October 17, 1982
Jackson, Graham W. (79)—January 15, 1983
Johnson, Joseph W. (75)—July 6, 1982
Kelli, David—April 23, 1983
Kendrick, Harold (68)—November 18, 1982
Kogan, Leonid (58)—December 17, 1982
Larner, Dorothy—June 16, 1982
Larson, Dennis (58)—October 5, 1982
Lewis, Rachael (79)—February 25, 1983
Lucas, Bill (67)—December 11, 1982
Luhman, William (56)—November 4, 1982
Manone, Wingy (78)—July 9, 1982
Manusevitch, Victor (80)—March 16, 1983
Marrandino, Angelo (69)—November 15, 1982
Martinoli, Octavius (66)—April 17, 1983
McGovern, Tom (66)—October 15, 1982
Metcalfe, Norman (62)—August 2, 1982
Mundy, Jimmy (75)—April 24, 1983
North, William (75)—July 14, 1982
Nowinsky, William (64)—September 11, 1982
Olson, Edgar C. (86)—Spring 1983
Pallamary, Michael J. (61)—March 14, 1983
Pappalardi, Felix (41)—April 17, 1983
Parker, Joe (69)—November 6, 1982
Pasztory, Ditta (80)—November 21, 1982
Pepper, Art (56)—June 15, 1982
Piscitello, Charles J. (43)—May 10, 1983
Pizarro, Manuel (86)—Fall 1982
Powell, Jesse (58)—October 19, 1982
Ptashne, Theodore (72)—May 19, 1982
Puleo, Johnny (74)—May 3, 1983
Rabinowitz, Sol Roberts (62)—October 3, 1982
Rampal, Joseph (87)—January 11, 1983
Reiling, Ann C. (79)—April 1, 1983
Reilly, Betty (64)—December 22, 1982
Renzulli, Carlo (63)—June 24, 1982
Richstein, Jeanne King (44)—March 28, 1983
Rizzo, Virgil (78)—June 30, 1982
Rogers, Herbert (53)—January 29, 1983
Rogers, Merton (80)—August 18, 1982
Rosenberg, William (73)—August 29, 1982
Royal, Ernie (61)—March 17, 1983
Rubinstein, Arthur (95)—December 20, 1982
Rudman, Albert (71)—April 28, 1983
Scheurer, Karl (97)—December 20, 1982
Schnitzer, Germaine (95)—September 18, 1982
Scott, James Honeyman (25)—June 16, 1982
Shannon, Hugh (61)—October 19, 1982
Sladek, Paul (86)—July 19, 1982

Stitt, Edward (48)—July 22, 1982
Stuart, Kirk (48)—December 17, 1982
Tchaikowsky, Andre (46)—June 26, 1982
Towles, Lois (70)—March 18, 1983
Towns, Donald (53)—March 13, 1983
Trisko, Kenneth P. (73)—August 16, 1982
Ullrich, William A. (76)—July 15, 1982
Vanstone, Alan (61)—June 1, 1982
Vasey, Jane (33)—Summer 1982
Vigeland, Hans (64)—August 17, 1982
Welch, Homer (69)—July 10, 1982
Waters, Muddy (68)—April 30, 1983
Weller, Daniel Max (94)—April 27, 1983
Williams, Joe Lee (83)—December 17, 1982
Winding, Kai (60)—May 6, 1983
Zottarelle, Rocco M. (93)—January 1, 1983

OTHERS

Allen, Sheppard (92)—June 11, 1982
Impresario, Howard Theater
Antoine, Tex (59)—January 12, 1983
Weather forecaster
Arnott, James Fullerton (68)—November 23, 1982
Drama professor
Barnes, Djuna (90)—June 18, 1982
Novelist
Berg, Phil (80)—February 1, 1983
Talent agent
Bernbach, William (71)—October 2, 1982
Advertising
Bluhdorn, Charles G. (56)—February 19, 1983
Gulf & Western Industries
Bonnet, Ted (74)—January 15, 1983
Founder, Publicists Guild
Botkin, Henry (86)—March 4, 1983
Abstract painter
Burns, George (69)—May 23, 1983
Walt Disney music
Byram, Marian (78)—August 31, 1982
Publicist
Cade, Rowena (89)—March 28, 1983
Theater buff
Cappelli, Carlo Alberto (74)—Summer 1982
Shakespeare Festival, Verona
Catledge, Turner (82)—April 27, 1983
New York Times editor
Cheever, John (70)—June 18, 1982
Writer
Cort, Margretta D. (90)—June 14, 1982
Widow, Harry L. Cort
Cukor, George (83)—January 24, 1983
Film director
Davis, Loyal (86)—August 19, 1982
Adoptive father, Nancy Reagan

de Rochemont, Richard (78)—August 4, 1982
March of Time
Della Russo, Michael (67)—January 1, 1983
Revere Frolics
Delteil, Caroline (92)—July 2, 1982
Creator, Revue Negre
Desmond, Connie (73)—March 3, 1983
Voice of Brooklyn Dodgers
Downing, Sally Rush (80)—June 23, 1982
Arts patron
Dumont, Andre (74)—Fall 1982
Publicist
Edwards, Hilton (79)—November 18, 1982
Cofounder, Gate Theater
Eisler, Herbert A.—November 30, 1982
Attorney
Elise, Sister Mary (84)—July 21, 1982
Founder, Opera Ebony
Erickson, August E. (101)—August 14, 1982
Columnist
Farrell, Frank (71)—February 17, 1983
Columnist
Fell, Otto (87)—February 5, 1983
Toledo vaudeville theater
Feves, Ray M. (66)—March 9, 1983
Variety correspondent
Freedman, Alan J. (59)—December 15, 1982
Arts patron
Garafalo, Tony (67)—April 20, 1983
Mackey's Ticket Office
Garey, Norman (46)—August 17, 1982
Attorney
Gold, Aaron (45)—May 23, 1983
Columnist
Goldman, Irving (73)—May 20, 1983
Shubert executive
Goodman, Alice Hahn (70)—August 6, 1982
Arts patron
Gosden, Freeman F. (83)—December 10, 1982
Amos 'n Andy
Grossman, Milton (77)—March 23, 1983
Agent and packager
Guy, Ralph Sr. (85)—January 25, 1983
Wm. Cody circuses
Hanks, Nancy (55)—January 7, 1983
Chairman, National Endowment
Harkness, Rebekah West (67)—June 17, 1982
Arts patron
Hobbs, Rebekah (80)—December 11, 1982
Subscription manager
Hofheinz, Roy M. (70)—November 21, 1982
Ringling Bros. Circus
Holmes, Joseph R. (55)—May 27, 1983
Agent for Ronald Reagan
Howell, James (46)—October 21, 1982
Dance teacher

Jacobs, Herb (71)—September 8, 1982
Assistant to Billy Rose
Jacobson, Jim (42)—November 21, 1982
Agent
Johnson, Caroline (83)—July 19, 1982
Ice Follies
Jones, Cornelius J. (85)—October 15, 1982
Desert Inn, Las Vegas
Justis, Bill (55)—July 16, 1982
Arranger
Kilgallen, James L. (94)—December 21, 1982
Reporter
Klot, Gerald (75)—August 21, 1982
Bronx Opera Company
Koestler, Arthur (77)—March 3, 1983
Writer
Kranz, Ben (72)—January 4, 1983
Production manager
Labrum, Thomas J. (78)—June 19, 1982
Publicist
Lahinsky, Harry (74)—June 23, 1982
Royal Lipizzan Stallion Show
Levenberg, Warren F. (31)—July 21, 1982
Ringling Bros. Circus
Lockridge, Richard (83)—June 19, 1982
Writer
Lombardo, Lilliebell (82)—May 26, 1982
Widow, Guy Lombardo
MacAdams, Rhea (98)—July 30, 1982
Acted in Thomas Edison film
Makar, Edward F. (71)—February 15, 1983
Entertainment operator
Margolis, Samuel (99)—November 13, 1982
Voice teacher
Marvin, Mrs. Walter Sands (90)—August 3, 1982
Metropolitan Opera Guild
Mason, Harold T. (89)—January 11, 1983
Philadelphia Academy of Music
Mauier, Maurice (76)—September 21, 1982
Manager
Maurice, Phil (82)—Winter 1983
Canadian showman
May, Morton D. (69)—April 13, 1983
Arts patron
Mayer, Ken (63)—September 30, 1982
Columnist
Marshall, Rex (64)—March 9, 1983
Radio, TV announcer
McCall, Monica (82)—July 5, 1982
Literary agent
Moore, Joe—April 28, 1983
Publicist
Moritz, Joseph (82)—August 22, 1982
Theater owner
Myers, Robert (69)—January 19, 1983
Odeon Theaters, Canada

O'Connell, John J. (61)—September 2, 1982
Hearst Newspapers editor
O'Gallchoir, Eamonn (76)—December 27, 1982
Musical director, Abbey Theater
Okun, Henry (79)—May 23, 1982
Publicist
Oliver, H.J. (65)—July 26, 1982
Shakespeare authority
Parkinson, James (71)—February 28, 1983
Pennsylvania Opera Co.
Payne, Robert (71)—February 18, 1983
Theater biographies
Pearce, Marshall (61)—December 21, 1982
Mardi Gras Carnival
Randall, L. Kenn (72)—May 12, 1982
Manager
Rasponi, Lanfranco (69)—April 9, 1983
Publicist
Richards, Helen Stern (66)—April 9, 1983
Publicist
Rubin, Dick (71)—February 17, 1983
Agent
Schaeffer, Carl (74)—December 6, 1982
Treasurer, Actors Studio
Schmitz, Clemens Sr.—February 21, 1983
Insurance, outdoor shows
Seller, Irving I. (91)—November 20, 1982
New England restauranteur
Selvin, Herman F. (78)—November 7, 1982
Attorney
Silman, Elli (84)—November 20, 1982
Talent agent
Skolsky, Sidney (78)—May 1983
Reporter
Small, Berman (62)—February 14, 1983
Agent
Stravinsky, Vera (93)—September 17, 1982
Widow, Igor Stravinsky
Strickling, Howard (84)—July 14, 1982
Publicist
Tannenbaum, Samuel W. (92)—November 9, 1982
Attorney
Tanner, Dolores (71)—November 24, 1982
Director, Hedgerow Theater
Tillett, Emmy (85)—May 16, 1982
Concert manager
Tuck, George Jr. (58)—June 2, 1982
Lakeview Palladium
Turet, Maurice (73)—March 23, 1983
Publicist
Van Sickle, Charles L. (61)—September 4, 1982
Business manager
Vincent, J.J. (91)—March 7, 1983
Concert manager

Vondenhoff, Bruno (80)—July 7, 1982
    Frankfurt City Opera
Washer, Ben (76)—September 5, 1982
    Publicist
Webber, Bickford (51)—May 13, 1983
    Music editor
Wechsberg, Joseph (75)—April 10, 1983
    Writer
Weissberger, Arnold (59)—August 20, 1982
    Attorney

West, Rebecca (90)—March 15, 1983
    Writer
Whittemore, Jack (67)—January 21, 1983
    Agent
Williams, Percy F. (75)—July 18, 1982
    Publicist
Wishnew, Bert (72)—April 8, 1983
    Agent
Zeiger, Hal (68)—November 15, 1982
    Agent

THE BEST PLAYS, 1894–1982

Listed in alphabetical order below are all those works selected as Best Plays in previous volumes in the *Best Plays* series. Opposite each title is given the volume in which the play appears, its opening date and its total number of performances (in the case of transfers, both the Broadway and off-Broadway runs are included in the number of performances). Those plays marked with an asterisk (*) were still playing on June 1, 1983 and their number of performances was figured through May 31, 1983. Adaptors and translators are indicated by (ad) and (tr), the symbols (b), (m) and (l) stand for the author of the book, music and lyrics in the cast of musicals and (c) signifies the credit for the show's conception.

NOTE: A season-by-season listing, rather than an alphabetical one, of the 500 Best Plays in the first 50 volumes, starting with the yearbook for the season of 1919–1920, appears in *The Best Plays of 1968–69.*

PLAY	VOLUME	OPENED	PERFS
ABE LINCOLN IN ILLINOIS—Robert E. Sherwood	38–39.	.Oct. 15, 1938. .	472
ABRAHAM LINCOLN—John Drinkwater	19–20.	.Dec. 15, 1919. .	193
ACCENT ON YOUTH—Samson Raphaelson	34–35.	.Dec. 25, 1934. .	229
ADAM AND EVA—Guy Bolton, George Middleton	19–20.	.Sept. 13, 1919. .	312
ADAPTATION—Elaine May; and NEXT—Terrence McNally	68–69.	.Feb. 10, 1969. .	707
AFFAIRS OF STATE—Louis Verneuil	50–51.	.Sept. 25, 1950. .	610
AFTER THE FALL—Arthur Miller	63–64.	.Jan. 23, 1964. .	208
AFTER THE RAIN—John Bowen	67–68.	.Oct. 9, 1967. .	64
*AGNES OF GOD—John Pielmeier	81–82.	.Mar. 30, 1982. .	486
AH, WILDERNESS!—Eugene O'Neill	33–34.	.Oct. 2, 1933. .	289
AIN'T SUPPOSED TO DIE A NATURAL DEATH—(b, m, l) Melvin Van Peebles	71–72.	.Oct. 7, 1971. .	325
ALIEN CORN—Sidney Howard	32–33.	.Feb. 20, 1933. .	98
ALISON'S HOUSE—Susan Glaspell	30–31.	.Dec. 1, 1930. .	41
ALL MY SONS—Arthur Miller	46–47.	.Jan. 29, 1947. .	328
ALL OVER TOWN—Murray Schisgal	74–75.	.Dec. 12, 1974. .	233
ALL THE WAY HOME—Tad Mosel, based on James Agee's novel *A Death in the Family*	60–61.	.Nov. 30, 1960. .	333
ALLEGRO—(b,l) Oscar Hammerstein II, (m) Richard Rodgers	47–48.	.Oct. 10, 1947. .	315
*AMADEUS—Peter Shaffer	80–81.	.Dec. 17, 1980. .	1,022
AMBUSH—Arthur Richman	21–22.	.Oct. 10, 1921. .	98
AMERICA HURRAH—Jean-Claude van Itallie	66–67.	.Nov. 6, 1966. .	634
AMERICAN BUFFALO—David Mamet	76–77.	.Feb. 16, 1977. .	135
AMERICAN WAY, THE—George S. Kaufman, Moss Hart	38–39.	.Jan. 21, 1939. .	164
AMPHITRYON 38—Jean Giraudoux, (ad) S. N. Behrman	37–38.	.Nov. 1, 1937. .	153
ANDERSONVILLE TRIAL, THE—Saul Levitt	59–60.	.Dec. 29, 1959. .	179
ANDORRA—Max Frisch, (ad) George Tabori	62–63.	.Feb. 9, 1963. .	9
ANGEL STREET—Patrick Hamilton	41–42.	.Dec. 5, 1941. .	1,295
ANIMAL KINGDOM, THE—Philip Barry	31–32.	.Jan. 12, 1932. .	183
ANNA CHRISTIE—Eugene O'Neill	21–22.	.Nov. 2, 1921. .	177
ANNA LUCASTA—Philip Yordan	44–45.	.Aug. 30, 1944. .	957
ANNE OF THE THOUSAND DAYS—Maxwell Anderson	48–49.	.Dec. 8, 1948. .	286
ANNIE—(b) Thomas Meehan, (m) Charles Strouse, (l) Martin Charnin, based on Harold Gray's comic strip "Little Orphan Annie"	76–77.	.Apr. 21, 1977. .	2,377
ANOTHER LANGUAGE—Rose Franken	31–32.	.Apr. 25, 1932. .	344
ANOTHER PART OF THE FOREST—Lillian Hellman	46–47.	.Nov. 20, 1946. .	182
ANTIGONE—Jean Anouilh, (ad) Lewis Galantiere	45–46.	.Feb. 18, 1946. .	64

PLAY	VOLUME	OPENED	PERFS
LETTERS TO LUCERNE—Fritz Rotter, Allen Vincent..........	41–42.	.Dec. 23, 1941..	23
LIFE, A—Hugh Leonard................................	80–81.	.Nov. 2, 1980..	72
LIFE & ADVENTURES OF NICHOLAS NICKLEBY, THE—(ad) David Edgar, from Charles Dickens's novel	81–82.	.Oct. 4, 1981..	49
LIFE IN THE THEATER, A—David Mamet	77–78.	.Oct. 20, 1977..	288
LIFE WITH FATHER—Howard Lindsay, Russel Crouse, based on Clarence Day's book............................	39–40.	.Nov. 8, 1939..	3,224
LIFE WITH MOTHER—Howard Lindsay, Russel Crouse, based on Clarence Day's book............................	48–49.	.Oct. 20, 1948..	265
LIGHT UP THE SKY—Moss Hart	48–49.	.Nov. 18, 1948..	216
LILIOM—Ferenc Molnar, (ad) Benjamin Glazer..............	20–21.	.Apr. 20, 1921..	300
LION IN WINTER, THE—James Goldman	65–66.	.Mar. 3, 1966..	92
LITTLE ACCIDENT—Floyd Dell, Thomas Mitchell...........	28–29.	.Oct. 9, 1928..	303
LITTLE FOXES, THE—Lillian Hellman	38–39.	.Feb. 15, 1939..	410
LITTLE MINISTER, THE—James M. Barrie.................	94–99.	.Sept. 27, 1897..	300
LITTLE NIGHT MUSIC, A—(b) Hugh Wheeler, (m, l) Stephen Sondheim, suggested by Ingmar Bergman's film *Smiles of a Summer Night*..	72–73.	.Feb. 25, 1973..	600
LIVING ROOM, THE—Graham Greene	54–55.	.Nov. 17, 1954..	22
LIVING TOGETHER—Alan Ayckbourn.....................	75–76.	.Dec. 7, 1975..	76
LONG DAY'S JOURNEY INTO NIGHT—Eugene O'Neill	56–57.	.Nov. 7, 1956..	390
LOOK BACK IN ANGER—John Osborne...................	57–58.	.Oct. 1, 1957..	407
LOOK HOMEWARD, ANGEL—Ketti Frings, based on Thomas Wolfe's novel.......................................	57–58.	.Nov. 28, 1957..	564
LOOSE ENDS—Michael Weller	79–80.	.June 6, 1979..	284
LOST HORIZONS—Harry Segall, revised by John Hayden	34–35.	.Oct. 15, 1934..	56
LOST IN THE STARS—(b, l) Maxwell Anderson, based on Alan Paton's novel *Cry, the Beloved Country*, (m) Kurt Weill.....	49–50.	.Oct. 30, 1949..	273
LOVE OF FOUR COLONELS, THE—Peter Ustinov............	52–53.	.Jan. 15, 1953..	141
LOVERS—Brian Friel.................................	68–69.	.July 25, 1968..	148
LOYALTIES—John Galsworthy	22–23.	.Sept. 27, 1922..	220
LUNCH HOUR—Jean Kerr.............................	80–81.	.Nov. 12, 1980..	262
LUTE SONG—(b) Sidney Howard, Will Irwin, from the Chinese classic *Pi-Pa-Ki*, (l) Bernard Hanighen, (m) Raymond Scott..	45–46.	.Feb. 6, 1946..	385
LUTHER—John Osborne	63–64.	.Sept. 25, 1963..	211
LUV—Murray Schisgal	64–65.	.Nov. 11, 1964..	901
MACHINAL—Sophie Treadwell	28–29.	.Sept. 7, 1928..	91
MADWOMAN OF CHAILLOT, THE—Jean Giraudoux, (ad) Maurice Valency..	48–49.	.Dec. 27, 1948..	368
MAGIC AND THE LOSS, THE—Julian Funt	53–54.	.Apr. 9, 1954..	27
MAGNIFICENT YANKEE, THE—Emmet Lavery	45–46.	.Jan. 22, 1946..	160
MALE ANIMAL, THE—James Thurber, Elliott Nugent	39–40.	.Jan. 9, 1940..	243
MAMMA'S AFFAIR—Rachel Barton Butler	19–20.	.Jan. 29, 1920..	98
MAN FOR ALL SEASONS, A—Robert Bolt..................	61–62.	.Nov. 22, 1961..	637
MAN FROM HOME, THE—Booth Tarkington, Harry Leon Wilson	99–09.	.Aug. 17, 1908..	406
MAN IN THE GLASS BOOTH, THE—Robert Shaw	68–69.	.Sept. 26, 1968..	268
MAN OF LA MANCHA—(b) Dale Wasserman, suggested by the life and works of Miguel de Cervantes y Saavedra, (l) Joe Darion, (m) Mitch Leigh.............................	65–66.	.Nov. 22, 1965..	2,328
MAN WHO CAME TO DINNER, THE—George S. Kaufman, Moss Hart	39–40.	.Oct. 16, 1939..	739
MARAT/SADE (see *The Persecution and Assassination of Marat*, etc.)			
MARGIN FOR ERROR—Clare Boothe	39–40.	.Nov. 3, 1939..	264

PLAY	VOLUME	OPENED	PERFS
UNCHASTENED WOMAN, THE—Louis Kaufman Anspacher....	09–19.	.Oct. 9, 1915. .	193
UNCLE HARRY—Thomas Job	41–42.	.May 20, 1942. .	430
UNDER MILK WOOD—Dylan Thomas	57–58.	.Oct. 15, 1957. .	39
VALLEY FORGE—Maxwell Anderson	34–35.	.Dec. 10, 1934. .	58
VENUS OBSERVED—Christopher Fry	51–52.	.Feb. 13, 1952. .	86
VERY SPECIAL BABY, A—Robert Alan Aurthur	56–57.	.Nov. 14, 1956. .	5
VICTORIA REGINA—Laurence Housman	35–36.	.Dec. 26, 1935. .	517
VIEW FROM THE BRIDGE, A—Arthur Miller	55–56.	.Sept. 29, 1955. .	149
VISIT, THE—Friedrich Duerrenmatt, (ad) Maurice Valency....	57–58.	.May 5, 1958. .	189
VISIT TO A SMALL PLANET—Gore Vidal	56–57.	.Feb. 7, 1957. .	388
VIVAT! VIVAT REGINA!—Robert Bolt	71–72.	.Jan. 20, 1972. .	116
VOICE OF THE TURTLE, THE—John van Druten	43–44.	.Dec. 8, 1943. .	1,557
WAGER, THE—Mark Medoff	74–75.	.Oct. 21, 1974. .	104
WAITING FOR GODOT—Samuel Beckett	55–56.	.Apr. 19, 1956. .	59
WALTZ OF THE TOREADORS, THE—Jean Anouilh, (tr) Lucienne Hill	56–57.	.Jan. 17, 1957. .	132
WATCH ON THE RHINE—Lillian Hellman	40–41.	.Apr. 1, 1941. .	378
WE, THE PEOPLE—Elmer Rice	32–33.	.Jan. 21, 1933. .	49
WEDDING BELLS—Salisbury Field	19–20.	.Nov. 12, 1919. .	168
WEDNESDAY'S CHILD—Leopold Atlas	33–34.	.Jan. 16, 1934. .	56
WHAT A LIFE—Clifford Goldsmith	37–38.	.Apr. 13, 1938. .	538
WHAT PRICE GLORY?—Maxwell Anderson, Laurence Stallings.	24–25.	.Sept. 3, 1924. .	433
WHAT THE BUTLER SAW—Joe Orton	69–70.	.May 4, 1970. .	224
WHEN YOU COMIN' BACK, RED RYDER?—Mark Medoff	73–74.	.Dec. 6, 1974. .	302
WHERE HAS TOMMY FLOWERS GONE?—Terrence McNally...	71–72.	.Oct. 7, 1972. .	78
WHITE HOUSE MURDER CASE, THE—Jules Feiffer	69–70.	.Feb. 18, 1970. .	119
WHITE STEED, THE—Paul Vincent Carroll	38–39.	.Jan. 10, 1939. .	136
WHO'S AFRAID OF VIRGINIA WOOLF?—Edward Albee	62–63.	.Oct. 13, 1962. .	664
WHOSE LIFE IS IT ANYWAY?—Brian Clark	78–79.	.Apr. 17, 1979. .	223
WHY MARRY?—Jesse Lynch Williams	09–19.	.Dec. 25, 1917. .	120
WHY NOT?—Jesse Lynch Williams	22–23.	.Dec. 25, 1922. .	120
WITCHING HOUR, THE—Augustus Thomas	99–09.	.Nov. 18, 1907. .	212
WILD BIRDS—Dan Totheroh	24–25.	.Apr. 9, 1925. .	44
WINGED VICTORY—Moss Hart, (m) David Rose	43–44.	.Nov. 20, 1943. .	212
WINGS—Arthur L. Kopit	78–79.	.Jan. 28, 1979. .	113
WINGS OVER EUROPE—Robert Nichols, Maurice Browne	28–29.	.Dec. 10, 1928. .	90
WINSLOW BOY, THE—Terence Rattigan	47–48.	.Oct. 29, 1947. .	215
WINTERSET—Maxwell Anderson	35–36.	.Sept. 25, 1935. .	195
WINTER SOLDIERS—Daniel Lewis James	42–43.	.Nov. 29, 1942. .	25
WISDOM TOOTH, THE—Marc Connelly	25–26.	.Feb. 15, 1926. .	160
WISTERIA TREES, THE—Joshua Logan, based on Anton Chekhov's The Cherry Orchard	49–50.	.Mar. 29, 1950. .	165
WITNESS FOR THE PROSECUTION—Agatha Christie	54–55.	.Dec. 16, 1954. .	645
WOMEN, THE—Clare Boothe	36–37.	.Dec. 26, 1936. .	657
WONDERFUL TOWN—(b) Joseph Fields, Jerome Chodorov, based on their play My Sister Eileen and Ruth McKenney's stories, (l) Betty Comden, Adolph Green, (m) Leonard Bernstein	52–53.	.Feb. 25, 1953. .	559
WORLD WE MAKE, THE—Sidney Kingsley, based on Millen Brand's novel The Outward Room	39–40.	.Nov. 20, 1939. .	80
YEARS AGO—Ruth Gordon	46–47.	.Dec. 3, 1946. .	206
YES, MY DARLING DAUGHTER—Mark Reed	36–37.	.Feb. 9, 1937. .	405
YOU AND I—Philip Barry	22–23.	.Feb. 19, 1923. .	178

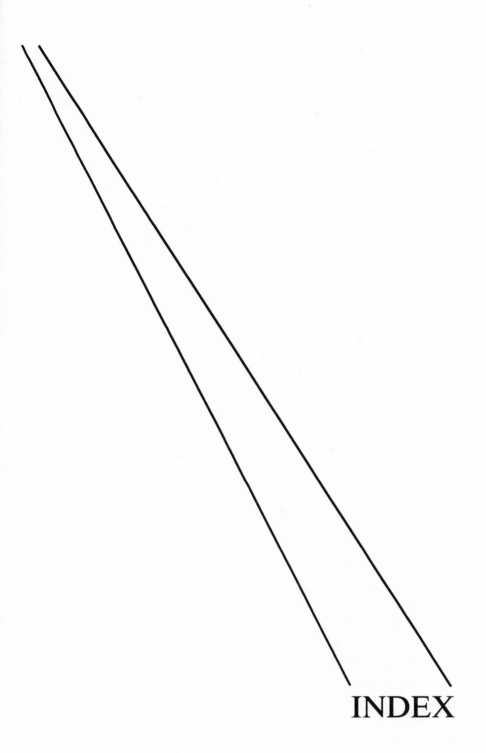

INDEX

INDEX

Play titles appear in **bold face**. ***Bold face italic*** page numbers refer to those pages where complete cast and credit listing for New York productions may be found.